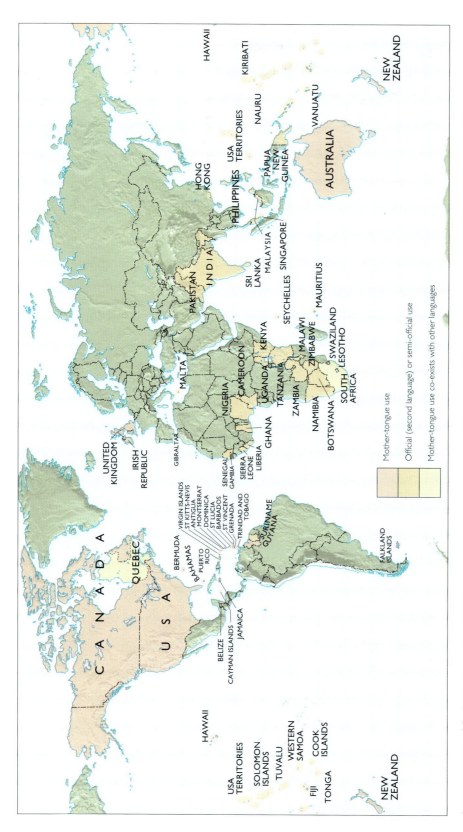

A representation of English in the world

This map distinguishes between three different types of English-speaking country: those in which English is used predominantly as a 'mother tongue'; those in which it is a second language with official or semi-official status; and those in which mother-tongue use co-exists with one or more additional languages. The map provides a useful context for discussion in the chapters that follow, but the information needs to be interpreted with caution: for instance, countries categorized as 'mother tongue' will also have speakers of additional languages. You will see from Chapter I that categorizing different groups of speakers, or different English-speaking contexts, is by no means straightforward.

(Adapted from Crystal, 1988, pp. 8–9)

Legend:

Mother-tongue use

Official (second language) or semi-official use

Mother-tongue use co-exists with other languages

English

history, diversity and change

The English Language: past, present and future *course team*

The Open University
Sally Baker (liaison librarian)
Pam Berry (compositor)
Helen Boyce (course manager)
Martin Brazier (cover designer)
Joan Carty (liaison librarian)
Christine Considine (editor)
Anne Diack (BBC producer)
Sharon Goodman (author/book co-ordinator)
David Graddol (author/book co-ordinator)
Martin Kenward (assistant project controller)
Julie Laing (BBC production assistant)
Avis Lexton (secretary)
Rob Lyon (designer)
Paul Manners (BBC producer)
Gill Marshall (editor)
Janet Maybin (author/book co-ordinator)
Barbara Mayor (author/course manager)
Neil Mercer (author/book co-ordinator)
Ray Munns (cartographer/graphic artist)
Kay Pole (developmental testing co-ordinator)
Pam Powter (course secretary)
Cathy Rosario (editor)
Lynne Slocombe (editor/editorial co-ordinator)
Gill Smith (editor)
Joan Swann (course team chair)
Nikki Tolcher (main compositor)
Iva Williams (BBC production assistant)

External assessor
Professor Peter Trudgill, University of Lausanne

Assessors for this book
Professor Jenny Cheshire, Universities of Neuchâtel and Fribourg
Professor James Milroy, University of Michigan

Developmental testers and critical readers
Kim Beckley
Nigel Blake
Susan Gander
Gilberto Giron
Anthea Fraser Gupta
Lindsay Hewitt
Diana Honeybone
Karen Hovey
Mike Hughes

The four volumes of the series form part of the second level Open University course U210 *The English Language: past, present and future.* If you wish to study this or any other Open University course, details can be obtained from the Central Enquiry Service, PO Box 200, The Open University, Milton Keynes, MK7 6YZ.

For availability of the video and audiocassette materials, contact Open University Educational Enterprises Ltd (OUEE), 12 Cofferidge Close, Stony Stratford, Milton Keynes, MK11 1BY.

English

history, diversity and change

Edited by
David Graddol, Dick Leith
and Joan Swann

The Open University

ROUTLEDGE
ROUTLEDGE
Taylor & Francis Group

LONDON AND NEW YORK

First published 1996
by Routledge
11 New Fetter Lane
London EC4P 4EE

Simultaneously published in the USA and Canada
by Routledge
a division of Routledge, Chapman and Hall, Inc.
29 West 35th Street, New York, NY 10001

Published in association with The Open University

Reprinted 1997, 2000

Routledge is an imprint of the Taylor & Francis Group

Copyright © 1996 The Open University

Edited, designed and typeset by The Open University

Printed in China through World Print Ltd

A catalogue record for this book is available from the British Library

Library of Congress Cataloguing-in-Publication Data applied for

ISBN 0 415 13118 9 (paper)
ISBN 0 415 13117 0 (hardbound)

Book editors

David Graddol is a lecturer in the Centre for Language and Communications at the Open University School of Education. He is an applied linguist with an interest in cultural and political aspects of language and discourse. He is co-author with Joan Swann of *Gender Voices* (Blackwell, 1989), and has published several papers on changing forms of textuality related to technological innovation.

Dick Leith was formerly a senior lecturer in linguistics at Birmingham Polytechnic (now University of Central England) and is now a freelance writer, currently working on a book about storytelling. He is author of *A Social History of English* (Routledge & Kegan Paul, 1983) and co-author, with George Myerson, of *The Power of Address: explorations in rhetoric* (Routledge & Kegan Paul, 1989).

Joan Swann is a lecturer in the Centre for Language and Communications at the Open University School of Education. She has a particular interest in language and gender, is co-author with David Graddol of *Gender Voices* (Blackwell, 1989), and author of *Girls, Boys and Language* (Blackwell, 1992). She is production chair of the Open University course U210 *The English Language: past, present and future.*

Other original contributors

Nikolas Coupland is Professor and Director of the Cardiff Centre for Language and Communication Research. He has written and edited many books in sociolinguistics, discourse analysis and human communication, including *Dialect in Use* (University of Wales Press, 1988) and *Language: contexts and consequences* (with Howard Giles, Open University Press, 1991).

Paul Kerswill is a lecturer in the Department of Linguistic Science at the University of Reading. He has conducted sociolinguistic surveys in both Norway and the UK. His interests are in dialect contact resulting from migration, sociolinguistic aspects of child language acquisition, and the role of children in language change. He is the author of *Dialects Converging: rural speech in urban Norway* (Oxford University Press, 1994).

Marie-Noëlle Lamy is a senior lecturer in French in the Centre for Modern Languages at the Open University, and chair of the French programme. Her main interests are in the descriptive linguistics of English and French, and theoretical and practical lexicography. She has been a major contributor to a number of bilingual and monolingual dictionaries.

Donald Mackinnon is a lecturer in the Open University School of Education. He is not a linguist, but comes to writing about language from a background in sociology, philosophy and the old-fashioned university study of English (before structuralism, let alone poststructuralism).

Jeff Siegel is Associate Professor in Linguistics at the University of New England in Australia. His main interest is in language contact. He is author of *Language Contact in a Plantation Environment: a sociolinguistic history of Fiji* (CUP, 1987) and co-author of *The Design of Language: an introduction to descriptive linguistics* (Longman Paul, 1995).

Linda Thomas is a senior lecturer in English language and linguistics at Roehampton Institute, London. She regards herself as a sociolinguist and has a particular interest in grammatical variation. She is author of *Beginning Syntax* (Blackwell, 1993).

Susan Wright is a lecturer in the history of the English language at the University of Cambridge, but will shortly be taking up a post in the English Department at Northern Arizona University, USA. She is currently working on a book about the social and linguistic histories of Englishes.

CONTENTS

INTRODUCTION

Joan Swann

This book, as the title suggests, is about history, diversity and change in English. We examine the development of English from the Old English period through to the present day, the characteristics and use of different contemporary varieties, and what the language means to its speakers in different parts of the world.

- Chapter 1 takes diversity as its main theme, and raises issues and questions that recur in later chapters. How do varieties of English differ from one another? How is the language used in different parts of the world? Is diversity increasing, and do we need an international standard English?

- Chapter 2 traces the visual history of English from early runic engravings through medieval illustrated manuscripts to contemporary texts.

- Chapter 3 provides an outline history of the English language within England up to the end of the Middle Ages. It raises some of the problems involved in writing such a history; for instance, what constitutes evidence and how this has been interpreted by different authorities.

- Chapter 4 begins with the introduction of printing in England in 1476. It examines processes of linguistic standardization as well as the cultural debates that surrounded English during its development as a 'national' language.

- Chapter 5 traces the spread of English throughout the British Isles and in various parts of the world in relation to colonialism. It explores the accounts that have been given of this spread, and the subsequent development of new varieties of English.

- Chapter 6 examines some of the grammatical characteristics of varieties of English. In what ways does English grammar vary? What are the sources of contemporary variation? Are different varieties actually as distinct as their names suggest?

- Chapter 7 asks what distinguishes one English accent from another; it looks at patterns of variation and change in English, and how these have been studied by linguists; and it considers the (often ambivalent) social meanings different accents convey.

- Chapter 8 turns to the language use of individual speakers: how speakers routinely switch between different varieties of English, or between English and other languages, to represent different aspects of their identity.

- Chapter 9 is the only chapter not written by a linguist. It examines aspects of diversity and change from a philosophical perspective. What counts as 'good' and 'bad' English? Is it reasonable to worry about 'political correctness'? Do notions of correct and incorrect English still have any validity?

Throughout the book we are concerned with processes of variation and change, and with how these have been represented by linguists in order to construct certain stories of English. We have tried to set linguistic processes and events, and their representations, within wider intellectual, social, political and cultural contexts.

The book is designed for readers who have an interest in English, but who do not necessarily have any detailed knowledge of linguistics or other forms of language study. It can be read independently but it is also the first in a series of four books (listed on the back cover) designed for an Open University under-graduate course: U210 *The English language: past, present and future*. We occasionally refer interested readers to these books, as well as *Describing Language* (Graddol et al., 1994), for further discussion of topics touched on here.

English: history, diversity and change has been prepared mostly by linguists who live and work in Britain. This inevitably affects the research traditions and ideas we draw on, in addition to our own experiences of, and familiarity with, different varieties of English. We have, however, tried to ensure that the chapters are accessible to readers from different linguistic and cultural backgrounds. We have selected examples of research and other evidence from different contexts, perspectives and experiences of English. In particular, the readings that accompany each chapter are wide-ranging. They include accounts of research, reviews of certain topics, arguments for or against certain positions; some are extracts from existing books or articles, others have been specially commissioned for this book. They are presented not as definitive statements on an issue, but as texts that are open to critical evaluation – as of course are the main chapter texts themselves.

Features of each chapter include:

- *activities*: these provide guidance on the readings or suggestions for tasks to stimulate further understanding or analysis of the material;
- *boxed text*: boxes contain illustrative material or definitions or alternative viewpoints;
- *marginal notes*: these usually refer the reader to further discussion in other parts of the book, or to other books in the series, or to *Describing Language*; where necessary, they are also added to explain conventions used in the text;
- *key terms*: key terms in each chapter are set in bold type at the point where they are explained; the terms also appear in bold in the index so that they are easy to find in the chapters.

A note on the description of English sounds

Several chapters in this book refer to the sounds that characterize English accents. We use special sets of symbols, adapted from the Roman alphabet, to represent these sounds systematically in writing:

- *Phonemic* symbols represent the distinctive sounds (or phonemes) of English accents. These are placed between slashes: for instance, /kat/ represents the three phonemes in the word *cat*.

  The term 'phoneme' is defined and explained more fully in Chapter 2. Chapter 7 compares the phoneme systems of different English accents.

- The International Phonetic Alphabet (IPA) contains a much larger set of *phonetic* symbols; these are used to provide an accurate transcription of speech sounds (from potentially any language) and they allow comparison of subtle differences in pronunciation between different accents or different speakers. IPA symbols are placed between square brackets. We use some phonetic transcription in this book, but we try to keep this to a minimum and to explain different symbols as they arise. For readers with some familiarity with the IPA but who wish to check their understanding of particular symbols we reproduce part of the IPA consonant and vowel charts on page 386. Graddol et al. (1994) provide one source of further information on phonemic and phonetic transcription.

1 ENGLISH VOICES

Joan Swann

1.1 INTRODUCTION

Since you are reading this book, the chances are that you are quite fluent in English, though it may not be the only language you speak and it may not be your first language. Different readers among you will speak, or be familiar with, different varieties of English; you will have different experiences of using English, and maybe different feelings about the language.

Such diversity is a major theme running through this chapter, and in fact through the whole of this book. Here, I look at some of the ways the English language varies and changes, at the diversity of speakers of English, and at how English is used and what it means to its speakers in different parts of the world.

Diversity and change have often been seen as problems in English as in other languages. I look also then at the debate surrounding an appeal by a prominent linguist for a single standard variety of English to be used throughout the international community.

1.2 WHAT COUNTS AS ENGLISH?

Only a few centuries ago, the English language consisted of a collection of dialects spoken mainly by monolinguals and only within the shores of a small island. Now it includes such typologically distinct varieties as pidgins and creoles, 'new' Englishes, and a range of differing standard and nonstandard varieties that are spoken on a regular basis in more than 60 different countries around the world …

(Cheshire, 1991, p. 1)

… our *Grammar* aims at … comprehensiveness and depth in treating English irrespective of frontiers: our field is no less than the grammar of educated English current in the second half of the twentieth century in the world's major English-speaking communities. Only where a feature belongs specifically to British usage or American usage, to informal conversation or to the dignity of formal writing, are 'labels' introduced in the description to show that we are no longer discussing the 'common core' of educated English.

(Quirk et al., 1972, p. v)

The language I speak
  becomes mine
Its distortions, its queernesses
  all mine, mine alone.
It is half English, half Indian
  funny perhaps, but it is honest
It is human as I am human
  Don't you see?

(Das, cited in Verma, 1982, p. 178)

If you consult a descriptive grammar of English, such as the famous grammar quoted above produced by Randolph Quirk and his colleagues, this may give the impression that English is relatively fixed, something unified and discrete. This grammar, the first in a series produced by Quirk et al., emphasizes commonality (a 'common core') and it plays down difference (the different forms that English takes, and the different ways it is used in different English-speaking countries). This is hardly surprising because such grammars provide a model that can be consulted, that will tell the reader what structures are possible in English and what are not possible. In this case, although the grammar is meant to cover 'the world's major English-speaking communities' it focuses, in practice, on 'educated' British and American usage. A later grammar in the series, *A Comprehensive Grammar of the English Language* (Quirk et al., 1985), discusses different varieties of English but it essentially deals with 'the common core that is shared by standard British English and standard American English' (p. 33). Such usage has frequently been taken as a model for teaching and learning. If you learned English in school as a foreign language, this is the kind of model you will probably have encountered.

Jenny Cheshire, on the other hand, is a sociolinguist, interested in the way language varies and changes. Her book, *English around the World* from which the first quotation is taken, contains chapters on the types of English used in several parts of the world (with one chapter on 'The UK and the USA'). The chapters are concerned with differences in the *forms* of English (pronunciation, as well as the grammar that mainly concerns Quirk et al.). There is also discussion of how English is used and what it means to its speakers in different contexts: factors that might lead speakers to *wish* to establish their own variety as distinct from others. So in this case it's not surprising that Cheshire emphasizes the diversity of English rather than seeking a 'common core'.

The meanings of English – in this case one variety of English – are also emphasized in the third quotation from the poem 'Summer in Calcutta'.

I want to look further at change and diversity below. I return to the notion of a 'common core' towards the end of the chapter.

❖   ❖   ❖   ❖   ❖

Activity 1.1   Old English   *(Allow about 5 minutes)*

Below is an extract from the glossary of an Old English reader (*Sweet's Anglo-Saxon Reader*), a collection of texts designed for students. Which words do you recognize? How many seem to be in current use, in some form or other?

fremde, fremþe   strange, foreign; foreigner

fremi(g)an   advance, benefit

(*ge*)**fremman**   do, commit, effect, bring about

fremsumness   benefit

fremu   benefit, profit, good action

frēo(h)   free

frēod   peace (poetic usage)

frēolic   noble (poetic usage)

frēols-brice   non-observance of church festivals

frēols-tīd   festival

frēond   friend, lover

frēondlēas   friendless

frēondlīce   in a friendly manner

frēondscīpe   friendship

frēorig   cold   (poetic usage)

frēo-riht   rights of freemen

frēot   freedom [the term **frēodom** is also found]

(Adapted from Whitelock, 1967, p. 329)

Comment

It may be that all of these words look rather strange! On the other hand, there is some similarity between *frēo* and *free*, *frēodom* and *freedom*; and between *frēond* and *friend*, *frēondlēas* and *friendless*, *frēondscipe* and *friendship*. The spellings have changed, but the Old English and modern words do look as though they may be related. Old English formed many compound words and some suffixes (such as *-lēas*) have survived as productive forms in modern English

In *frēo-riht, riht* also looks similar to modern *right*; in *frēols-tīd*, compare *-tīd* to the slightly old-fashioned but still recognizable *-tide* found in compounds such as *Yuletide* and *eventide* (*tīd* actually means 'time' in Old English). In *frēols-brice*, if we allow for a spelling change the similarity between *brice* and modern *breach* becomes clearer. The word *frēorig* looks unfamiliar, but compare modern *freeze*. *Fremman* is related to the modern word *frame* which can be used in a variety of senses in contemporary English.

If you know German you may be struck by the similarity between *fremde* and German *fremd*. Many other words also resemble modern German: English is termed a 'Germanic' language, related to languages such as Dutch as well as German, but the relationship looks less clear in modern English than in Old English (the changes to the language that have brought this about are discussed in Chapter 3). In fact, *fremd* (or *frem, fremt, fremmit*) still exists in some varieties of Scots.

Old English is the name normally given to the English spoken in England between the fifth and twelfth centuries. It differs from modern English in terms of its vocabulary, word meaning and spelling (it also contains letters, such as þ in *frempe*, that are not found in modern English). It also differs in other ways that are not so apparent from the reader extract – such as its pronunciation and grammar, and the ways it was used. The end result is that modern English now looks and sounds strikingly different. It is unlikely that a contemporary speaker and a speaker of Old English would be able to understand one another. This raises the question of whether Old English and modern English actually count as the same language. How different do language varieties have to become before we recognize them as distinct? David Crystal (1988) notes that the term 'Anglo-Saxon' has been used to refer to Old English, emphasizing its distinctiveness from contemporary English. And the very existence of a reader, designed for students learning the language, suggests that it has now become like a foreign language. 'Old English', by contrast, emphasizes continuity: a sense of continuing development from Old, through Middle, to modern English. You can get some sense of this development, in terms of word usage, if you look at a dictionary entry for *free* which gives examples of the use of this word at different points in its history (Figure 1.1).

Old English is sometimes felt to constitute the 'essence' of English. In *The Story of English*, for instance, McCrum et al. write:

> Anyone who speaks or writes English in the late twentieth century is using accents, words and grammar which, with several dramatic modifications,

go all the way back to the Old English of the Anglo Saxons. There is an unbroken continuity from *here* to *there* (both Old English words). When, in 1940, Winston Churchill wished to appeal to the hearts and minds of the English-speaking people it is probably no accident that he did so with the plain bareness for which Old English is noted: 'We shall fight on the beaches; we shall fight on the landing grounds, we shall fight in the fields and in the streets, we shall fight in the hills; we shall never surrender.' In this celebrated passage, only *surrender* is foreign – Norman French.

(McCrum et al., 1992, p. 58)

---

free /friː/ *a., n., & adv.* [OE *frēo* = OFris., OS, OHG *frī* (Du. *vrij*, G *frei*), Goth. *freis*, f. Gmc f. IE, repr. by Skt *priya* dear, f. base meaning 'to love'.] A *adj.* **1** Of a person: not or no longer in bondage, servitude, or subjection to another, having personal rights and social and political liberty as a member of a society or State. OE. **†2** Noble, honourable, of gentle birth and breeding. Also, (of character and conduct) noble, honourable, generous, magnanimous. OE–M17. **3** Of a State, its citizens, and institutions: enjoying national and civil liberty, not subject to foreign domination or despotic or tyrannous government. ME. b *spec.* Designating (freq. w. cap. initial) a political or racial group actively opposed to an invading, occupying, or hostile power; *esp.* denoting those who continued resistance to Germany in the war of 1939–45 after the capitulation of their respective countries. M20.
1 B. RUSSELL Sympathy not only for free Greeks, but for barbarians and slaves. *Country Life* She wanted to be an artist and a free woman, refusing to be called 'Mrs'. *fig.*: J. DENHAM Who . . free from Conscience, is a slave to Fame. **2** SHAKES. *Oth.* I would not have your free and noble nature Out of self-bounty be abus'd. MILTON Thou Goddess fair and free. **3** SHAKES. *Cymb.* Till the injurious Romans did extort This tribute from us, we were free. S. SMILES Holland . . became the chief European centre of free thought, free religion, and free industry. b C. GRAVES The scattered remnants of the Free French, Free Dutch, Free Polish, and Free Norwegian fleets.
II 4 Acting from one's own will or choice and not compelled or constrained; determining one's own action or choice without outside motivation. OE. **5** Ready to do or grant something; acting willingly or spontaneously; (of an act) done of one's own accord; (of an offer or agreement) readily given or made, made with good will. ME. b Of a horse: ready to go, willing. L15. c Ready *to do* something; eager, willing, prompt. *obs.* exc. in *free to confess* below, where the adj. is now understood as sense 16b. M17. **6** Ready to give, liberal, lavish. Foll. by *of*. ME. b (Of a gift) given out of liberality or generosity, not in return or requital for something; unrequested, unsolicited. LME. **7** (Of speech) characterized by liberty in the expression of sentiments or opinions; uttered or expressed without reserve; plain-spoken. ME. b Not observing due bounds, licentious, loose. M19. **8** Acting without restriction or limitation; allowing oneself ample scope *in* doing something. L16. b Unstinted as to supply or quantity; coming forth in profusion; administered without stint; abundant, copious. M17. **9** Frank and open in conversation or dealings; ingenuous, unreserved. Also, forward, familiar, impudent. M17.
4 E. A. FREEMAN The choice of the electors would

be perfectly free. **5c** J. CLARE Mark . . his generous mind; How free he is to push about his beer. **6** S. BUTLER For Saints themselves will sometimes be Of Gifts that cost them nothing, free. **7** H. NELSON Gave Lord Hood my free opinion that 800 troops . . would take Bastia. L. J. JENNINGS Men used rather free expressions to each other . . in the days of the Regency. b TENNYSON Earl Limours Drank till he jested with all ease, and told Free tales. **8** POPE How free the present age is in laying taxes on the next. H. BRACKEN He gives us a Caution not to be too free with such Preparations. G. BERKELEY The free use of strong fermented liquors. b S. BARING-GOULD A monthly rose that was a free bloomer. **9** DEFOE I pressed him to be free and plain with me. R. B. SHERIDAN Not so free, fellow!
III 10a Usu. foll. by *from*, *of*: released or exempt from, not liable to (a rule, penalty, or payment). OE. b Exempt from, having immunity from, not subject to (something regarded as hurtful or undesirable). ME. **11** Exempt from, or not subject to, some particular jurisdiction or lordship. Also, possessed of particular rights and privileges. ME. **12** Of real property: held without obligation on rent or service, freehold. *arch.* ME. **13** Given or provided without charge or payment, gratuitous. Also, admitted, carried, or placed without charge or payment. ME. **14** Invested with the rights or immunities of or of, admitted to the privileges of or *of* (a chartered company, corporation, city, or the like). LME. b Allowed the use or enjoyment *of* (a place etc.). L17. **15** Exempt from restrictions with regard to trade; not subject to tax, toll, or duty; allowed to trade in any market. M17.
10a LD MACAULAY Free from all the ordinary rules of morality. b J. FERRIAR Our own writers are not free from this error. N. LINDLEY The point . . appears to me . . free from any real difficulty. **13** DRYDEN Lazy Drones, without their Share of Pain, In winter Quarters free, devour the Gain. **14** J. LOCKE Is a Man under the Law of England? What made his Free of that Law? J. ENTICK The shop-keepers are obliged to be free of the city. b KEATS And I was free of haunts umbrageous.
IV 16 Not impeded, restrained, or restricted in actions, activity, or movement; unhampered, unfettered. ME. b At liberty, allowed, or permitted *to do* something. LME. c Unbiased, open-minded. Long *rare* or *obs.* M17. **17** Clear of obstruction; not blocked; open, unobstructed. ME. **18** Clear of something regarded as objectionable or an encumbrance. Foll. by *of*, *from*. ME. **19** Guiltless, innocent, acquitted. Now *rare* or *obs.* ME. **20** At liberty; able to move about or range at will; *esp.* not kept in confinement or custody; released from confinement or imprisonment; liberated. LME. **21** Of a material: yielding easily to operation; easily worked; loose and soft in structure. E16. b

Of wood: without knots. L17. **22** Not fixed, fastened, or held in one particular place. L16. **23** Released from ties, obligations, and restraints. L16. b Released or exempt from work or duty; clear of engagements; (of a room, table, etc.) not occupied or in use. E17. **24** Allowable or allowed (*to* or *for* a person *to do* something); open or permitted *to*. *arch.* L16. b *Ling.* Designating a form that can occur in isolation. E20. c *Phonet.* Of a vowel: occurring in a syllable not ended by a consonant. M20. **25** Disengaged from contact or connection with some other body or surface; relieved from the pressure of an adjacent or superincumbent body. E18. **26** Of a literary or artistic style: not observing strict laws of form. Of a translation: not adhering strictly to the original, not literal. E19. **27** *Chem.* Not combined. E19. **28** *Physics*. Of a source of power: disengaged, available to do work. E19. **29** *Naut.* Of the wind: not adverse. M19.
16 A. RADCLIFFE Her dress . . was loosened for the purpose of freer respiration. B. JOWETT The various passions are allowed to have free play. b DICKENS She was free to come and go. **17** J. NARBOROUGH They did meet with no Ice, but a free and open Sea. SIR W. SCOTT And quickly make the entrance free. **18** R. HOLME A Woman all Hairy, no part of her Face free. C. LUCAS There is hardly any mine . . free from pyrite. **20** LD MACAULAY Deer, as free as in an American forest. J. MORLEY Calvin . . set free all those souls. *Times* He wanted the accused to be allowed to go free. **21** J. SMEATON This stone was capable of being thus wrought, and was so free to the tool. **22** MILTON The tawny lion, pawing to get free His hinder parts. **23** SHAKES. *Ant. & Cl.* Free, madam! no . . He's bound unto Octavia. b G. BURNET Coleman had a whole day free to make his escape. E. WAUGH There is no table free. K. AMIS What about lunch today? Are you free? **24** J. JACKSON It was free to everyone to bastinado a Christian where he met him. **25** R. KNOX At the free surface of the mucous membrane. **29** R. H. DANA We had the wind free . . sail after sail the captain piled on her.
Phrases: **be free with**: see **make free with** below. **for free** (*colloq.*, orig. *US*), provided without payment. **free and easy** *a., adv.*, & *n. phr.* (*a*) *adj.* unconstrained, natural, unaffected; unceremonious; careless, slipshod; morally lax, permissive; *free and easiness* a state or manner of being free and easy; (*b*) *adv. phr.* (*rare*) in a free and easy manner; (*c*) *n. phr.* (*arch. siang*) a convivial gathering. **free on board**, **rail**, etc. without charge for delivery to a ship, a railway wagon, etc. **free to confess** ready and willing to make a confession. *free warren*: see WARREN *n.¹* 1b. **free, white, and over twenty-one** *colloq.* not subject to another person's control or authority, independent. **give** or **have a free hand** give or have complete liberty of action in an undertaking. **it's a free country** *colloq.* the (course of) action proposed is not illegal or forbidden. *Land of the Free*: see LAND *n.¹* **make** or **be free with** take liberties with. *set free*: see SET *v.¹* the *Wee Free Kirk*: see WEE *a.* *Wee Frees*: see WEE *a.*

Figure 1.1   Dictionary entry for 'free'

OE = Old English (–1149); LOE = late Old English (1000–1149); ME = Middle English (1150–1349, sometimes 1469); LME = late Middle English (1350–1469); otherwise numbers refer to centuries and are preceded by E, M or L which refer to periods (of years) within the century: early (0–29), mid (30–69) and late (70–99) respectively.

(Brown (ed.),1993)

The 'dramatic modifications' mentioned are important ones and you will see in later chapters how contemporary English is as much the product of its subsequent history as its Old English 'roots'. Much of the story of English is one of **contact** with other languages and resultant **borrowing** (e.g. of words such as *surrender*). It may seem odd to see a word like *surrender* described as foreign (the *Oxford English Dictionary* records its first use around six centuries ago). But attitudes towards borrowings have always varied: they may be seen as foreign or 'unEnglish', they are sometimes unwelcome, but equally they have been described as enriching the language. A later chapter in *The Story of English* refers to the 'golden age' of English from the beginning of the reign of Queen Elizabeth I in 1558, during which English achieved a 'richness of vitality of expression', men of letters 'embellished their prose with Latinate words' and Shakespeare 'filled a universe with words' (McCrum et al., pp. 90–8). One of the readings for this chapter ('*Franglais*') shows that attitudes towards borrowings from English by other languages are just as variable.

Anglo-Saxon attitudes

I don't like the word *liberation*. The word *liberation* is a foreign word, and that doesn't mean it's necessarily a bad one, but it's very inappropriate to our own context. It's associated with notions of revolutionary change, of a notion or rights being completely separate from responsibilities, which I find very unattractive. I actually believe in a good English word, and it's called *freedom*. And once upon a time Englishmen … were very proud about being free. And they were proud about being free because they had a sense of two sorts of freedom: political and judicial freedom, but also a freedom over their own, over their own property. And with their own property came a freedom over their lives, that extraordinary self-reliant independence that you see most strongly marked in those Englishmen overseas, those semi-foreign Englishmen the Americans. I would like to undo so much of what has been done in the name of liberation in the twentieth century: those awful dead blankets of collectivism, of groups, of structures that have been put upon us and have trodden us under. Too often, as we all know, liberty – crimes are committed in its name; in liberation, the name of liberation, crimes are committed too. Fewer crimes are committed in the name of that good, English thing, freedom.

(Starkey, unpublished, BBC Radio 4 *Question Time*, 10 June 1994)

So far I have talked about Old English and modern English as though these were homogeneous entities with a direct and continuing line linking the two, but in fact there were several varieties of Old English which changed, gradually and unevenly, over the years. These have given rise to a range of contemporary varieties. Even the term 'variety' is an idealization: there are not really neat dividing lines between different historical varieties of English, nor are there clear cut-off points that separate different contemporary varieties.

Activity 1.2   English(es) today   *(Allow up to 10 minutes)*

Please read through the extracts which follow. Which look to you like recognizable varieties of English? How many do you understand?

1   Bilong paitim liklik nil yu ken   Before striking a little nail you
    holim han bilong hama klostu   should hold the shaft of the
    long het bilong hama na paitim   hammer close to the head and hit
    isi.   it gently.

    (Todd, 1984, p. 177)

2   The Scots Language Society offers prizes for scrievin in the Scots
    tongue. There are three clesses: Age 18 and owre wi prizes o £20, £10
    and £5; age 12–17 wi prizes o £10, £5 and £2.50; and under 12, prizes o
    £5, £3 and £2.

    Entries maun be original and ne'er afore prentit. They may be (a)
    Poems up to 60 lines; (b) tales up to 3,000 words; (c) plays that tak
    nae mair nor 25 meenits to perform. Ilk entry maun be signed wi a
    byname, and the byname should be prentit on the outside o a sealed
    envelope, that has inside the entrant's real name and address, and, for
    them under 18, the date o birth.

    (Cited in Aitken, 1984, p. 531)

3   Syemagen kidder   Would you repeat the order waiter?
    Broonsalroond   Brown ales for my friends
                                             landlord/potman/waiter
    The tyebl's claggy   Waiter, could you bring a cloth as
                                             the table is awash with beer

    (Dobson, 1969)

4   Trust chi. Ry. Jaggu has safely landed at Gainsville. We heard that he
    landed safely at New York and had to stay there for the night as he did
    not have time to catch his flight to Orlando. Perhaps he must have
    reached his destination safely by Saturday evening (American time). He
    may join his duties as per schedule on 23/5/94 by the grace of God.
    (Unpublished)

5   Our Hindu religion so many different kinds of god. Shiva was destroy
    god and Vishnu was power and Brahma was creator. But that is only for
    totally bluff. This is not so many god. God is one.
    (Cited in Mehrotra, 1982, p. 157)

6   Having destroyed the gang's 'iron and steel and hat factories' and
    condemned its crime of savagely attacking and persecuting them, our
    cadres are displaying renewed revolutionary spirit.
    (Cited in Cheng, 1992, p. 170)

7   The ftp server on black can do automatic tar, compress and gzip.
    Appending '.tar' to the name of a directory will cause a 'get' command
    to tar the directory tree on the fly. Appending '.tar.Z' to the name of a
    directory will cause a 'get' command to tar the directory tree on the fly
    and compress the result. Appending '.Z' (respectively '.z') to a
    filename will cause a 'get' command to compress (respectively gzip)
    the file on the fly. Stripping a trailing '.Z' or '-z' (respectively '.z') from
    a filename will cause a 'get' command to uncompress (respectively
    gunzip) the file on the fly.

Comment

1   This is a brief extract from a carpenter's manual written in Tok Pisin, a
    language variety based on English that is spoken in Papua New Guinea.

Chapters 5 and 6 have more to say about the social history of English-related pidgins and creoles and about their characteristics.

Tok Pisin began life as a **pidgin**, a contact variety that develops between people who do not share a common language. Pidgins, at first, may be quite rudimentary, but they may develop as lingua francas, and eventually become the mother tongue of a group of speakers (in which case they are usually referred to as **creoles**). Tok Pisin began as a contact language in the European colonial period when people from Papua New Guinea worked as indentured labourers on European-run plantations. It is now often regarded as a creole, serving as a lingua franca within a multilingual community; it has an official orthography and a standardized variety.

Can varieties such as Tok Pisin be referred to as English? They have taken a lot of their vocabulary from English (if you look at the extract and its standard English translation you can see connections between *liklik – little, nil – nail, yu – you*, etc.), but their structure is rather different. They are sometimes referred to as 'English-related', but also sometimes as 'Englishes': Loreto Todd's book on pidgins and creoles from which I took this example is entitled *Modern Englishes*.

2   This example comes from the Scots Language Society's journal, *Lallans*. The journal is written entirely in what the Scottish linguist Jack Aitken terms 'literary Scots' or 'new Scots' (1984, pp. 530–1). This variety of Scots looks similar to English, although there are distinctive words, such as *scrievin* and *byname*, and spelling also differs (e.g. *meenit*). Spelling may be intended to reflect different pronunciations, but it also has the effect of making literary Scots look different from English on the printed page. (Some other varieties of Scots show greater differences than this extract does.)

Chapter 5 discusses the development of Scots and Scottish English.

Scots, like (English) English, developed from Anglo-Saxon or Old English. It has been regarded by some as a dialect of English, by others as a separate language. Several organizations have as their aim to preserve and develop Scots as a distinct language (the establishment of a distinct and standardized spelling system plays a part in this); it has been recognized as a language by the European Union; and it features in the curriculum in Scottish schools.

3   This is an extract from a Geordie 'phrase book', *Larn Yersel Geordie*. Geordie is a variety of British English spoken in the north-east of England. The book is aimed at people from this area – it is a humorous attempt to 'send up' this variety, playing on some of its stereotypical associations. Many of the examples depict a macho, beer-swilling culture; these examples are set against rather long-winded pompous 'translations'; and the Geordie phrases are represented in nonstandard spelling, sometimes with several words run together.

Geordie has quite a distinctive pronunciation, but in terms of vocabulary and grammar there isn't an enormous difference nowadays between the variety many people speak and standard English English. The 'phrase book' suggests, however, that Geordie is quite distinctive, almost a 'foreign language'.

4   This is an extract from a letter my friend Jayalakshmi received from her father in India. 'Jaggu' is my friend's brother, who has gone to work in the USA. The family's first language is the south Indian language Kannada; they also speak other Indian languages.

The English in the letter should seem familiar to most readers, though the phrases 'join his duties' and 'as per schedule' may seem unusual in this context to those unacquainted with Indian English. Some words and phrases also carry Indian cultural associations. 'Duties', to Jayalakshmi, has some of the connotations of the Kannada *dharma* (originally a Sanskrit term), which it is frequently used to translate. It refers here to Jaggu's new job, but also has the sense of doing a job well or to the best of one's ability. The phrase 'by the grace of God' is a translation of the Kannada expression *devru dayadinda*; the expression 'chi Ry.' stands for the Sanskrit phrase *Chiranjeevi Rajeshwari* (may he live a long and prosperous life).

Extracts 5–7 are all varieties of English intended for international communication.

5   This is another example of Indian English. It comes from a commentary given by an unofficial tourist guide in Varanasi, transcribed by Raja Ram Mehrotra. The speaker is multilingual and is likely to use English only in this restricted context. The English is simplified; Mehrotra argues that it is characterized by 'limited vocabulary, simplified structures, reduction in the number of grammatical devices, and shifts and manipulations in meaning which are often reinforced and clarified with the help of gestures' (Mehrotra, 1982, p. 159). The author is here focusing on the extent to which the text differs from a standard variety of English, but the commentary is designed for an international audience: the guide is speaking to foreign tourists, not to speakers of Indian English.

6   This comes from the English edition of the Chinese weekly *Beijing Review*. It appeared in 1978, shortly after the end of the cultural revolution. The *Beijing Review* is translated from Chinese into English by professional Chinese translators, with 'finishing touches' added by native English speakers. The intended audience for the review is the international community.

     The review claims to follow a British model of English. It does, however, contain several expressions and idioms related to cultural and social conditions in China in the 1970s. Chin-Chuan Cheng comments: '*Iron and steel and hat factories* (from the Chinese *gangtie gongchang maozi gongchang*) are where cudgels are made to beat (to criticize), and caps are fabricated to force upon someone's head (to label); hence the phrase means "wanton attack"' (Cheng, 1992, p. 170). (I feel perhaps that 'wanton attack' does not do full justice to the original!) Cheng argues that, with moves towards 'modernization' after the cultural revolution, such idioms became less common.

7   This final attempt at international communication is an extract from a message produced by my computer when I asked for help in gaining access to a file using electronic mail. I have to admit that the message was anything but helpful – I still haven't managed to get hold of the file. Although it is undoubtedly written in English I find it incomprehensible. This is mainly a question of vocabulary and word meaning: the use of unfamiliar technical terms (*tar, gzip*), and also expressions that look familiar (*compress the result*) but whose meaning in this context is not clear to an 'outsider'. This is a variety of English (sometimes known as a **register**) associated with a particular context or situation (in this case, computing) with which I've had very little experience. People recognize the existence of particularly obscure or technical registers – they are often given names ('computerese', for instance).

Technical vocabulary, and other aspects of language used in professional communication, are discussed in the second book in this series, *Using English: from conversation to canon*, (Maybin and Mercer (eds), 1996). English and 'new technology' are discussed in the fourth book, *Redesigning English: new texts, new identities* (Goodman and Graddol (eds), 1996).

These extracts are indicative of some of the complexity of English: the language is highly variable and continually changing. There is a long history of academic interest in language variation and change, which has broadened out recently with increasing attention paid to the 'new Englishes' spoken in many parts of the world.

Like other languages, English varies in several different ways. For instance, most of the examples above were produced as written texts. They might be rather different if spoken (for instance, if one speaker were telling another about the Scots literary competition, or if Jayalakshmi's father were chatting to her on the phone). Example 5 is transcribed speech, but you may still feel that it has a certain written quality: it is a rehearsed speech which has probably been delivered with some variations on countless occasions; it would be different in a spontaneous form of speech such as an impromptu conversation. Language also varies in relation to different speakers or writers, where they come from and what social groups they belong to; and it varies for the same individual in different contexts (for instance, depending on whether the speaker perceives a context as formal or informal, and depending on the purposes for speaking in that context).

The fact that I've referred to someone *speaking* in different contexts is not unusual. Linguists have tended to accord priority to speech over writing: sometimes 'language' and 'spoken language' become conflated in linguistic analyses, with language users routinely referred to as 'speakers'. Empirical studies of regional and social variation in contemporary English are often based on spoken language. But linguists' relationship with spoken and written language is rather ambivalent. Authoritative grammars of English, even those like *A Grammar of Contemporary English* that are based on spoken and written usage, tend to rely on examples with a markedly written feel to them:

> For reasons of simplicity and economic presentation … illustrative examples from our basic material are seldom given without being adapted and edited; and while informal and familiar styles of speech and writing receive due consideration in our treatment, we put the main emphasis on describing the English of serious exposition.
>
> (Quirk et al., 1972, p. 5)

Linguists concerned with different regional and social varieties of English often distinguish between **accents** (varieties that differ only in terms of pronunciation) and **dialects** (varieties that differ also in terms of grammar and vocabulary). This is a distinction we observe in this book for convenience, but we should admit that it is not clear-cut. I mentioned above that the variety of many Geordie speakers differs from the standard mainly in terms of pronunciation – but how many nonpronunciation features (particular terms or grammatical structures) does it take before an accent becomes a dialect? I have made frequent use of the term 'language variety', which is a device for letting linguists off the hook by avoiding the need to specify whether they are talking about a language, a dialect, an accent, or indeed a register associated with a certain field, such as 'computerese'.

Language varieties are not simply linguistic phenomena. They carry important social meanings. The Geordie in *Larn Yersel Geordie* is meant to be humorous (though it is rather an insider joke). The magazine *Lallans* uses Scots for serious as well as everyday purposes. But social meanings will differ in different contexts. Geordie is used by its actual speakers both routinely and more seriously; Scots may be used for humorous effect. The different social meanings attached to English resurface throughout this and later chapters.

However we describe language varieties, it's worth bearing in mind a point I made above: that these varieties themselves are idealizations. It is not possible to draw neat boundaries that delimit English. There is no obvious cut-off point beyond which we can say that variability and change *within* English have given rise

The second book in this series, *Using English: from conversation to canon* (Maybin and Mercer (eds), 1996), discusses the formal characteristics of spoken and written texts in English, and the different practices with which they are associated.

Historical studies of English necessarily rely on written sources and must use these to make inferences about how earlier varieties were pronounced. Chapter 3 discusses the evidence drawn on by those studying early varieties of English.

to new languages. In practice, even what counts as an identifiable, distinct variety of English (e.g. Geordie, Indian English), or what distinguishes English from another language (e.g. from Tok Pisin or Scots), is likely to be decided on social or political grounds rather than according to purely linguistic criteria.

Burmese Days

It was after nine now, and the room, scented with the acrid smoke of Westfield's cheroot, was stifling hot. Everyone's shirt stuck to his back with the first sweat of the day. The invisible *chokra* who pulled the punkah rope outside was falling asleep in the glare.

'Butler!' yelled Ellis, and as the butler appeared, 'go and wake that bloody *chokra* up!'

'Yes, master.'

'And butler!'

'Yes, master?'

'How much ice have we got left?'

''Bout twenty pounds, master. Will only last today, I think. I find it very difficult to keep ice cool now.'

'Don't talk like that, damn you – "I find it very difficult!" Have you swallowed a dictionary? "Please, master, can't keeping ice cool" – that's how you ought to talk. We shall have to sack this fellow if he gets to talk English too well. I can't stick servants who talk English. D'you hear, Butler?'

'Yes, master,' said the butler, and retired.

(Orwell, 1934, pp. 24–5)

1.3   WHO SPEAKS ENGLISH?

Today, English is used by at least 750 million people, and barely half of those speak it as a mother tongue. Some estimates have put that figure closer to 1 billion. Whatever the total, English at the end of the twentieth century is more widely scattered, more widely spoken and written, than any other language has ever been. It has become *the* language of the planet, the first truly global language.
(McCrum et al., 1992, pp. 9–10)

[English is] a language – *the* language – on which the sun does not set, whose users never sleep.
(Quirk, 1985, p. 1)

If the diversity of forms taken by English has provoked considerable, and increasing, academic interest, then so has the diversity of its speakers. Quirk's remark, cited above, comes from the conference 'English in the World', held to celebrate the fiftieth anniversary of the British Council, an organization which itself has done much to promote (British) English in different parts of the world. Moreover, several recent books about English have as their project (or part of their project) the emphasizing of its 'global' spread, and its role in different cultures and as an international language. This is a complex project, not least because it is difficult to detach oneself from the values with which English is associated and to present a dispassionate account of its spread and its use. The frequent focus on the large number of English speakers is interesting in itself: is

'No worries. If it can't be said in English, it ain't worth saying at all'

the implication that this makes the language more powerful, or somehow better than others? And there is more than a hint of triumphalism in Quirk's assertion of the global nature of English.

Even grappling with the sheer number of people who speak English turns out to be somewhat problematical. The figures cited in McCrum et al.'s *The Story of English* at the beginning of this section are similar to those quoted in several other sources. To that extent they are representative of current beliefs about the number of English speakers worldwide. But what is surprising about these figures is their lack of precision. How can there be such uncertainty about who does, or doesn't, speak a language?

Activity 1.3   English statistics   *(Reading A)*

Can you think of two or three reasons why there should be discrepancies between different estimates of the number of speakers of English?

Read now 'The English Language Today' by David Crystal (Reading A). Crystal is a British linguist who has written a great many books and articles on various aspects of English. Here, he discusses different types of English speakers, and why it is difficult to compile reliable statistics.

❖ ❖ ❖ ❖ ❖

Crystal draws what is a common distinction between three different types of speaker: those for whom English is a **mother tongue**; those for whom it is a **second language**; and those for whom it is a **foreign language**. Some writers make a simpler distinction between **native** (mother-tongue) and **non-native** speakers. Such distinctions have frequently been made by those concerned about teaching English to different types of learners, but distinctions may be made on different bases. In this book, Dick Leith distinguishes Englishes spoken outside the British Isles according to colonial settlement patterns (see Chapter 5).

In practice, it is difficult to draw hard and fast boundaries between 'second-language' and 'foreign-language' speakers, and even the 'native'/'non-native' distinction can be questioned in contexts such as India and Singapore, where some (notionally) non-native speakers become familiar with English from an early age and use the language routinely (Pakir, 1991). Furthermore, as I men-

Chapter 5 discusses the history of English beyond the British Isles. The third book in this series, *Learning English: development and diversity* (Mercer and Swann (eds), 1996), contains material on the learning and teaching of English in different parts of the world.

tioned in section 1.2, many non-native (at least 'second', and perhaps 'foreign') varieties of English are now recognized as 'new Englishes' in their own right. Despite these difficulties, however, there is general agreement that English continues to spread, and the spread is most extensive among non-native speakers.

The spread of English is generally seen in positive terms. Crystal comments that English gives access to 'a world of science, technology, and commerce'. Braj Kachru is equally favourable in his assessment:

> ... the acquisition of English across cultures has broad promise and is not restricted to a language specialist. It is a symbol of an urge to extend oneself and one's roles beyond the confines of one's culture and language. English continues to be accepted in this role, ever since and despite the depressing colonial experience ... The language has no claims to intrinsic superiority; rather, its pre-eminent role developed due to extralinguistic factors. The importance is in what the medium conveys about technology, science, law, and (in the case of English) literature. English has now, as a consequence of its status, been associated with universalism, liberalism, secularism, and internationalism. In this sense, then, English is a symbol of a concept that Indians have aptly expressed as *vasudhaiva kuṭumbakam* (the whole Universe is a family). True, not everyone may agree with this perception, but that there is such a positive reaction towards English cannot be denied ...
> (Kachru, 1992, pp. 10–11)

Not everyone, as Kachru concedes, would accept such a positive evaluation. P.D. Tripathi has argued that the universal importance of English is:

> an ideological production, the creation of the native and non-native élite with a material and professional interest in the language, its retention and dissemination worldwide.
> (Tripathi, 1992, p. 3)

Tripathi questions the basis of statistics on speakers of English. He argues that in many contexts they are based on impressions rather than empirical evidence (this is conceded by Crystal in Reading A). But he also suggests that they fail to take into account how the language is used: can someone who uses English for only a restricted set of activities be deemed a 'user of English'? In India, for instance, English is an associate official language; it is used for several institutional purposes and for communication between people from different states, each of which has its own state language or languages. But several Indian institutions (the education, legal and civil administration systems) have been reducing their dependence on English. And at the interstate level it is used mainly by an elite:

> To think of [English] as the language of inter-state communication (except, perhaps, at the minuscule top) is to ignore the reality of everyday life and to assume that before its advent there was no communication, and there cannot be any now without it, between one part of the country and another. The lowly worker from Bihar based in Calcutta or Bombay does not use English, which he does not know, but some local language instead, to relate with fellow workers, equally deficient in English, from other parts of the country.
> (Tripathi, 1992, p. 7)

The apparently straightforward question of who speaks English, then, raises complex issues to do with how English is used by its speakers in different contexts, and what social and cultural meanings are ascribed to it. I turn to some of these issues in the following section.

1.4 WHEN, AND WHEN NOT, TO SPEAK ENGLISH

Consider the range of items which can be used to fill the slot in the kind of question frames a social psychologist might use: 'If he speaks English, he must be ...'. Depending on where you live, so the answer might be 'British/American/an imperialist/an enemy/one of the oppressors/ well-educated/a civil servant/a foreigner/rich/trying to impress/in a bad mood ...'. There is a long list of possible clozes, and not all make pleasant reading. This conference is concerned to evaluate progress in English studies, in which case we must not forget those areas where the spread of English is bad news, and where people are antagonistic towards the language, for a variety of social, economic or political reasons.
(Crystal, 1985, p. 9)

He smiled. This, he knew, was his true self, a dichotomy of east and west that he had not quite yet managed to balance. Usually he found himself blending into the mainstream, blinded by the uniform colour of the multitude and submerging himself to becoming one of them. When in Asia, he saw himself as Chuan, his mother's son and when he in England, he saw Russell, his father's son.
    Unfortunately, it was never that cut and dry with people like him. His English relatives insisted on calling him 'Chuan' to demonstrate they are liberals, while his Singaporean relatives took great pride in being able to pronounce 'Russell'.
    In the mire of confusing personalities, he salvaged his own identity through the acceptance of others. So it was in Singapore, he spoke English with a distinctive Singlish lilt while in England, he slipped into the short clipped public school accent of the English upper class. Yet he knew he could never fool himself all the time. After a week of grilled lamb chops and peas, he hankered for a bowl of century egg porridge. Come Sunday, no matter how sumptuous the spread his Grandma Chen cooked for him, his day is not complete unless he has had roast beef and Yorkshire pudding.
(Wee Kiat, 1992, p. 196)

Precisely how, or whether, English is used, and what it means to its speakers, will vary considerably in different contexts (the quotations above give just a flavour of this – they include Crystal's comments from the British Council conference 'English in the World', and an extract from Wee Kiat's novel *Women in Men's Houses*). English may be welcomed, or resented, or rejected. It may bring considerable social and material benefits to its speakers. But its historical spread has also been at the cost of other languages (and of speakers of those languages). In many countries nowadays English is regulated: its use may be officially restricted by formal **language policies** or **language planning** in order to protect languages, cultures and speakers seen as being under threat.

    As an illustration of this I shall look now at the use of English in three different countries: patterns of language choice in Kenya, particularly the capital, Nairobi, where English is used alongside several African languages; the problematical relationship between English and French in Quebec and Ontario in Canada; and attempts by the authorities in France to limit the influence of English.

Language choice in Kenya

About 40 indigenous languages are spoken in Kenya (the major languages are shown in Figure 1.2). Swahili (also known as Kiswahili) and English are co-official languages. Speakers of English are normally bilingual, with English their second (or third, etc.) language. One estimate suggests that in Nairobi over half the population know English, but the proportion of English speakers is much lower in rural areas (Myers-Scotton, 1993b, p. 38).

Kenya is a former British colony (colonized in the late nineteenth century) that achieved independence, after a bitter struggle between African nationalists and the British, in 1963. English might be regarded as part of the colonial legacy, but in fact its current position is rather ambiguous. Mohamed Abdulaziz (1991, p. 392) points out that English is the language of most of the education system; of civil service correspondence; of the legal system (together with Swahili); of the armed forces and police; of most of the media; and 'generally of all modern sectors of socioeconomic activity, including the commercial and industrial sectors'. It is, then, a language with high status, whose use is associated with social and economic success – but Musimbi Kanyoro suggests that it is not universally welcomed:

> Kenya's capitalistic system, whose success depends on foreign investment, creates a climate for dependence on the English language. However, its pro-English policy has not been without challenge. In Kenya it is widely felt that English should not receive special attention or be promoted over any other language, but rather it should be on an equal footing with other languages in the country. It is also sometimes heard from this or that group, 'why can't Luo or Kipsigis or Kamba or Gikuyu etc. be a national language?' or 'why can't we have several Kenyan languages promoted to national status?' The argument made is that, after all, the number of speakers of any one of these languages equals or surpasses the number of English speakers in the country. The argument continues further that those unfamiliar with any of the regional languages would need to expend no more effort to learn any other local

Street signs in Nairobi, Kenya

Figure 1.2
Major languages spoken in Kenya
(Myers-Scotton, 1993b, p. 18)

language than they would to learn English. On the other hand, those who prefer English to Kiswahili or indigenous languages point out that English is neutral, with no ethnic or emotional attachments and, in addition, it provides a link to the world beyond East Africa. Opponents counter that English is a language foreign to Africa and to African thought, and carries the stigma of colonialism. Because English is acquired only through the educational system, it excludes the majority of Kenyans from participating in the development of their own country.
(Kanyoro, 1991, p. 415)

This social climate contributes to an ambivalent attitude to English in Kenya, and suggests that bilingual speakers need to balance carefully their use of English and other languages.

Chapter 5 discusses British colonialism and postcolonial Englishes.

Surveys of the use of English and other languages (reported in Myers-Scotton, 1993b) suggest that most urban Kenyans use their mother tongues at home or with others in the community from their own ethnic group. The mother tongue is important as a means of maintaining ethnic identity and in securing certain material advantages; for example, help from other members of the group in securing employment. People at the top of the socio-economic scale also use some English at home, however, particularly with their children to help them to do better at school. In Nairobi, speakers sometimes switch between their mother tongue, Swahili and English. This is particularly prevalent among children. In fact, a slang variety called Sheng – a mix between Swahili and English – has grown up in certain areas.

Chapter 8 shows how speakers often 'codeswitch' between English and other languages. The chapter includes illustrations from Kenya and Zimbabwe.

At work, speakers may use their mother tongue with people from the same ethnic group, or Swahili with people from other groups. English is used particularly in white-collar occupations. It may be used when communicating with superiors as an indicator of education and authority. And its use among speakers who share a mother tongue may mark out a relationship as one of the workplace.

The use of English as a language of the workplace is discussed in the second book in this series, *Using English: from conversation to canon* (Maybin and Mercer (eds), 1996).

Outside work, Swahili and English are used with people from other ethnic groups. Language choice is linked to education: those who have been educated to secondary level more often report some use of English, along with Swahili. English is also associated with more formal, public interactions.

The use of English in Kenya has both costs and benefits – as illustrated by two incidents recounted by a student at the University of Nairobi:

> (1) My brother was arrested by the police and sent to the chief for making beer without a license. He asked to be forgiven (in the local language) by the chief, who rejected the plea. I went to the chief's center where I found some policemen at the door. Nobody was allowed to enter. I spoke English to one of the policemen and said I wanted to see the chief. The police allowed me in. It was, I strongly believe, my English that gave me the honour to be allowed in. And it was my English, during my talk with the chief, that secured the release of my brother.

> (2) At a beer party near my home, two boys broke into talk in English. The reaction of the old men was bitter and they said, 'Who are those speaking English? Are they back-biting us? They are proud! Push them out.' Although the boys were not addressing the beer party as such, this was regarded as an insult.

> (Cited in Myers-Scotton, 1993b, pp. 30–1)

English and French in Canada

In Canada, both English and French have official status, but the relationship between the two languages is an unequal one. Canada is predominantly English-speaking, with the exception of the province of Quebec and areas along the border in New Brunswick and Ontario. Ronald Wardhaugh (1987, p. 221) calls Quebec 'A French island in an ocean of English' (see Figure 1.3).

English and French in competition

The English and French competed in colonizing the northern part of North America. That competition was ended in 1759 when the English finally conquered the French in a decisive battle on the Plains of Abraham and captured the city of Quebec. Canada came into existence at that time; it was a British possession to the north of those colonies that were soon to break away from the Crown and unite to form a new country, the United States of America. Canada stayed loyal, and gradually expanded to include other British possessions in North America and to fill the prairies to the north of the United States.

Canada actually dates its origin as a virtually independent state to 1867, the year of the British North America Act. This Act of the British Parliament was the last of a series of constitutional arrangements made in London to provide some kind of governing structure for this British colonial possession in North America. The 1867 Constitution established a framework for self-government, but it was actually not until 1982 that the government of Canada and the government of the United Kingdom finally 'patriated' the Canadian Constitution, i.e. gave Canada complete charge of its own constitutional affairs.

(Wardhaugh, 1987, pp. 221–2)

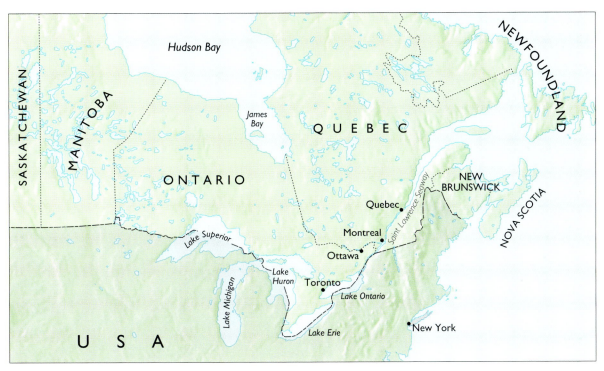

Figure 1.3   Canada: Quebec and surrounding areas

Wardhaugh writes that, with the establishment of Canada as a (virtually) independent state in 1867, French settlers believed they could look forward to an equal relationship with the English. Despite constitutional protection, however, English became the dominant language throughout most of Canada and French speakers found themselves confined increasingly to Quebec. Even here, French language and culture came under threat as the French birth rate fell and new immigrants chose to learn English rather than French.

The 1960s saw increasing political mobilization of French speakers in Quebec. Successive Quebec governments introduced measures to promote the use of French in the province, and in 1976 the separatist Parti Québequois was elected to office. In 1977 the government introduced Bill 101, the Charter of the French Language. Among other things, the bill made French the language of the workplace and imposed tight restrictions on the right to education in English (some of these restrictions were later overturned by the Supreme Court). Outside Quebec, measures were also taken to protect French (e.g. the Official Languages Act of 1969 and the inclusion of certain rights for French speakers in the constitution in 1982). But despite such measures the position of French in Canada, and even in Quebec, was by no means secure. Wardhaugh comments:

> Today, Quebec must be constantly on guard if it is to remain French-speaking. Regularly losing speakers to English, the province must find ways to replace these. What we see in Quebec ... is a kind of organized rear-guard action to preserve French, one which has had both successes and failures, but one from which the French themselves can seek no respite.
>
> (Wardhaugh, 1987, p. 221)

'Of course it's difficult for outsiders to grasp the subtle complexities of the situation here in Québec'

Monica Heller has argued that the major focus of the political mobilization of French speakers in Quebec has been the wish to gain access to economic resources controlled by **anglophones** without sacrificing **francophone** identity:

> … while through the 1950s and 1960s (and even to some extent, in some places, today) francophones who wished to gain access to management positions in private enterprise had to do so through assimilation, the 1960s saw the beginnings of a collective mobilisation designed primarily to achieve that access for the group as a whole, and used both a sense of collective identity and evidence of collective oppression to achieve that mobilisation.
>
> (Heller, 1992, p. 128)

In this context, the use of either English or French may be an overtly political act. Heller discusses the language choices of people who were somehow involved in the process of mobilization – whether as supporters or opponents. She cites the case of a man who arrived at the provincial government office in Montreal to take a French language test (under the provisions of Bill 101, members of certain professions were obliged to take this test in order to continue in their profession):

Man	Could you tell me where the French test is?	
Receptionist	*Pardon?*	Pardon?
Man	Could you tell me where the French test is?	
Receptionist	*En français?*	In French?

The term 'anglophone' (meaning 'English-speaking') derives from French. It is frequently used of English speakers in countries such as Canada where French is also spoken. French speakers are termed 'francophones'; French-speaking areas (both inside and outside France) are referred to collectively as *la francophonie.*

French speech is in italics, and an English translation is given in the right-hand column.

Man   I have the right to be addressed in
                                 English by the government of Quebec
                                 according to Bill 101

Receptionist   [to a third person]
                                 Qu'est-ce qu'il dit?   What's he
                                                                                         saying?

(Adapted from Heller, 1992, p. 133)

In contrast, French speakers in Quebec in the 1970s attempted to challenge the
dominance of English by speaking French where English might be expected.
Heller reports that similar strategies have been used more recently by French
speakers in Ontario. She quotes Louise, for example – a francophone woman
living in Ontario, interviewed in 1989. (This is a verbatim transcript and, like
many research transcripts, it is not punctuated. To anyone not used to seeing
transcribed speech it may look a little odd – and it takes a while to read!)

The French text on the left
is the original interview
text, with Heller's English
translation on the right.
Square brackets [ ]
indicate brief responses
from the interviewer.

… dans les magasins … je fais ma naïve jusqu'au dernier degré 'je ne sais pas l'anglais moi' j'ai pour dire à Orléans à Ottawa tu te fais servir en français [oui c'est vrai] point final [tu peux] c'est moi qui perds du temps je veux dire je perds énormément de temps parce que je la il faut qu'ils aillent me chercher quelqu'un que la je fais ma naïve je vais en tout cas si cela ne fait pas je vais protester 'je veux me faire servir en français' l'épicerie ici e c'est supposé être bilingue tu sais puis quelquefois il y en a qui ne le sont pas puis ils sont insultés parce que la je me rends jusqu'à la direction je leur dis 'ça me prend quelqu'un bilingue' pour {pause} ils sont supposés [mhum] d'avoir quelqu'un là toujours une qui parle tu sais je perds énormément de temps …
(Cited Heller, 1992, p. 131)

… in stores … I act naive to the utmost 'I don't speak English' to say that in Orleans in Ottawa you can be served in French [yes it's true] full stop [you can] it's me who's wasting time I mean I waste enormous amounts of time because I then they have to find me someone I act naive I'll anyway if that doesn't work I'll protest 'I want to be served in French' the grocery here e is supposed to be bilingual you know and sometimes there are some who are not and they're insulted because I then I go all the way to the management I tell them 'I need someone who's bilingual' to {pause} they're supposed to be bilingual you know they're supposed to [mhum] have someone there at all times who speaks you know I waste an enormous amount of time …

It is important to point out that in both these cases the speakers could have used
the other language. The anglophone man was presumably competent in French
since he had come to take a French proficiency test. He is using English as a
language of resistance in a context in which the rights of French speakers are
being asserted. And the French speaker, Louise, is also competent in English – she
has taught both French and English. But she lives in Ottawa, on the border with

Quebec, where francophone mobilization has had its effect and speaking French can be, in Heller's words, 'a major key to upward social mobility'. Heller comments:

> For Louise, and others like her with whom we spoke, French has become valuable, and the source of that value has to do with the creation of resources which francophones exclusively control. It is in her interests to make sure the boundary is maintained.
>
> (Heller, 1992, pp. 131–2)

In other contexts language may be used in a less antagonistic way – for instance, bilingual speakers may switch between English and French to level the boundary between anglophones and francophones.

Franglais in France

France is rather different from both Canada and Kenya, in that English has no official status there. English is taught as a foreign language in French schools, but it is intended mainly for international communication. Furthermore French itself, like English, serves as an international language, spread to various parts of the world by conquest, colonization, and as a language of culture and of diplomacy. This international role of French is in decline, under pressure both from local languages and from English. And within France itself there are fears of increasing linguistic and cultural domination – of 'contamination' by Anglo-American influences.

Activity 1.4   *Franglais*   *(Reading B)*

Please now work through Reading B, '*Franglais*', by Marie-Noëlle Lamy, noting the points she makes about the nature of English borrowings in French, attitudes towards English, and official moves by the French state to restrict the use of English and protect French.

English is now used in a range of cultural contexts (including many that may be considered 'traditionally un-English' (Kachru, 1985, p. 13). Within each of these it will acquire social meanings related to the speakers, contexts and purposes with which it becomes associated. In many contexts (e.g. Kenya, France) there exists a fear of Anglo-American cultural domination, but it cannot be assumed that English always has 'US' or even 'western' associations, or in fact any one set of unambiguous associations. The situation is rather more complex. Kachru comments that in South Asia:

> [English] is used as a tool for propaganda by politically diverse groups: the Marxist Communists, the China-oriented Communists, and what are labelled as the Muslim fundamentalists and the Hindu rightists as well as various factions of the Congress party. Such varied groups seem to recognise the value of English in fostering their respective political ends, though ideologically some of them seem to oppose the Western systems of education and Western values.
>
> (Kachru, 1985, p. 14)

The position of Quebec within Canada is not secure. There were attempts, in the early 1990s, to establish some form of independence for Quebec and in October 1995 (at the time of writing) people in Quebec take part in a referendum on whether to separate from the rest of Canada.

Chapters 3 and 4 discuss how English has borrowed terms from other languages during its history; Chapter 8 discusses the relationship between long-term borrowing and codeswitching between languages.

Examples of franglais *in Paris, Grenoble and Marseille*

Kachru himself sees such diversity ('a unique cultural pluralism' and 'a linguistic heterogeneity') as a benefit. But the examples discussed in this section suggest that the position of English is often problematical and responses to the language ambivalent.

1.5 RESPONDING TO DIVERSITY

It is the language whose possession is going to make the vital difference in the life chances of the peasant in the third world who wants to create in his third world country a society which moves away from the jungle and the poisoned water-hole and so on: this English language which is now indispensable to scientific study round the world. And the other point is of course that it's often a life and death situation where the air traffic controller and the pilot are uncertain about the English that is being used, or the navigator at sea. And I think that these factors that I've outlined to you do indicate the need for some kind of monitoring and control and the laying down of observable standards – available standards – to our children in schools and our people in their workplaces, to foreigners abroad for a recognizable standard form of the English language.

(Honey, unpublished, 1985 television transcript)

[Vladimir Nobokov's] one error lies in arrogating a native-born's right … to do what he likes with the language.

(Graves, 1966, p. 49)

We must note that English does not necessarily mean British English or American English. There are a number of standard Englishes, for there are several English-speaking countries in each of which there is a standard English peculiar to that country.

(Verma, 1982, p. 175)

With the recognition of diversity in English (the diversity of forms that English takes, the diversity of its speakers and the contexts in which it is used) has come the insistence, from many people, on the validity of distinctively different 'Englishes'. S.K. Verma, for instance, is Vice-Chancellor of the Central Institute for English and Foreign Languages in Hyderabad, a national institution that now recognizes Indian English as a valid model for teaching and learning. His article is entitled 'Swadeshi English: form and function' and his use of the term 'Swadeshi English' is indicative of this trend. 'Swadeshi' translates, more or less, as 'home-grown': it is associated with the nationalist movement in India that encouraged the use of local products and materials as a form of resistance to British occupation.

Some examples of English in Bangalore and Mysore (south India)

Verma argues that Indian English is a valid linguistic system, on a par with other varieties of the language:

> Indian English is a self-contained system and follows its own set of rules. This system is closely related to the core grammar of English English. The Englishness of this socioregional dialect lies in the fact that its basic linguistic systems are the same as those of English English. Its Indianness lies in the fact that, within the overall general framework of the systems of English English, it displays certain distinguishing phonological, lexico-semantic, and also syntactic features. In terms of linguistic efficiency, these patterns are as good as any other. They are not corrupt, but rather different forms of the same language.
>
> (Verma, 1982, p. 180)

The argument is not purely a linguistic one. English, in India, is used 'as a vehicle of Indian culture to express culturally determined networks of activities that are typically Indian; for example, the social stratification in India, the caste systems, and a complex network of personal and societal faiths and beliefs' (Verma, 1982, p. 178). While I've used India as an example here, similar views are expressed in other parts of the world where English is used, particularly as a second-language variety. Michael Clyne suggests that English can be regarded as a 'pluricentric' language, that is a language with 'several interacting centres, each providing a national variety with at least some of its own (codified) norms' (1992, p. 1).

Set against this position is a fear that the spread of English will lead to its disintegration: that it will develop into several mutually unintelligible languages (just as Latin developed into French, Romanian, Spanish and other 'romance' languages). Even those who think such a scenario is unlikely, who believe that the need for international communication will act as a brake on disintegration, have sometimes expressed concern about the growing acceptance of distinct

---

Standard English(es)?

Standard English: A widely used term that resists easy definition but is used as if most educated people nonetheless know precisely what it refers to.

(McArthur, 1992, p. 982)

Standard English has been described as a 'prestige variety' of the language; a variety with agreed norms and conventions that can be used as a model for education and for public use (e.g. in the media). The term may also refer to a variety that has been codified; that is, represented in dictionaries and grammars. This suggests that the forms of Standard English should show little if any variation: a standard language has in fact been described as having 'maximal variation in function' but 'minimal variation in form'.

Linguists have distinguished different standard varieties; for example, Standard English English (or Standard English in England), Standard American English, Standard Australian English, Standard Indian English. The term is also applied more or less broadly so that Standard English English, Standard British English and Standard International English are all found in the literature. Standard Englishes, then, cannot be regarded as discrete varieties.

Nor is there a straightforward distinction between standard and 'nonstandard' varieties. There will, for instance, be a great deal of overlap between Standard English English (however this is defined) and other varieties of English found in England.

non-native varieties of English. In his British Council paper 'The English language in a global context', Quirk argued that non-native speakers are well catered-for by 'a single monochrome **standard** that looks as good on paper as it sounds in speech' (1985, p. 6).

Bearing standards: the *English Today* debate

I want to draw together some of the issues discussed in this chapter by considering a recent debate about the validity of both nonstandard and non-native Englishes. One of the protagonists in this debate was Quirk (see above), who published in the journal *English Today* the text of a lecture he had given on variation in English ([1988]1990). In the lecture, Quirk drew a parallel between non-native speakers and native speakers who use a nonstandard variety of English, arguing that both sets of speakers need access to a native standard variety of the language. The publication of the lecture in *English Today* provoked a spate of responses, many of them critical of his position.

Activity 1.5   Standards and standards   *(Reading C)*

Read the extract from 'Language varieties and standard language' by Quirk (Reading C). Try to identify the main points Quirk makes in his argument. How well justified do these points seem to be?

I summarize below some of the responses made to Quirk's argument.

Quirk is arguing against the view that non-native 'Englishes' can be used as models for teaching and learning. He claims this view derives from 'liberation linguistics'. It is promulgated by badly trained teachers and academic linguists who have no experience of English language teaching. Learners of English need a native standard variety to communicate internationally (e.g. with 'the wider English-using community throughout the world', (Reading C, p. 39)); this will also increase their social and geographical mobility and further their career prospects (alternatively, 'low standards … will lock the least fortunate into the least rewarding careers', p. 39).

Underpinning Quirk's argument is his scepticism about the validity of non-native Englishes and about whether they have been or can be standardized. Some research carried out with French (Coppetiers, 1987) has suggested that native and non-native speakers have different intuitions about the language (i.e. they do not always agree about what sentences are possible ones). In an earlier part of his lecture, Quirk uses this evidence as the basis for establishing a fundamental distinction between native and non-native speakers of English and arguing that non-native speakers need to maintain contact with native-speaker models.

Critics of Quirk have taken issue with the nature of the evidence he draws on, the values that underpin his argument, and whether his aims are practically realizable given the diverse contexts in which English is used.

Torkil Christensen (1992), a teacher of English in Japan, is sceptical about the large number of 'half-baked quacks' Quirk seems to encounter and suggests he may have misinterpreted what some of these people said or wrote. Others have questioned the validity of Quirk's straightforward distinction between native and non-native speakers. Paul Christophersen (1990) expresses reservations about the way Quirk draws on a single study (by Coppetiers) to justify this distinction:

> What I am unhappy about is a tendency to assume that there is a
> mysterious, semi-mystical difference between two groups of people,
> natives and non-natives, a difference which affects for ever the way their
> minds work when handling the language concerned ...
>
> (Christophersen, 1990, p. 62)

Christophersen points out that these two groups are not homogeneous. Not all
native speakers share the same intuitions about language, and non-native speakers are a much more diverse group: they have learned English under different
conditions, they use it in different ways and for different purposes. It is not
possible to base generalizations that are meant to apply to millions of people in a
wide variety of contexts upon a single study carried out in a very specific context.

Kachru (1991) similarly argues that non-native speaker intuitions about
English will be linked to the particular social and cultural contexts in which the
language is used. If non-native speaker intuitions differ from those of native
speakers this does not, of itself, suggest that they are invalid and is not an
argument against the development of an institutionalized variety.

One of Quirk's most outspoken critics, Kachru argues that the position taken
by Quirk is an ideological one: it is as much to do with a particular set of social
values as the 'liberation linguistics' he criticizes. Quirk's position is in line with
'deficit linguistics': the view that certain varieties of language (normally those
associated with working-class or minority groups) are inherently inferior to
others.

Kachru accepts that English needs to function as an international language,
but argues that those who make policy decisions about English language teaching
need to take account of the 'realities' of how English is used and how its speakers
feel about it. He stresses the diversity of English language use, as well as some of
the pragmatic constraints on language policy:

- as an international language English is frequently used for communication
  between non-native speakers rather than between native and non-native
  speakers;
- in many countries English is also used as a language of 'intranational'
  communication, in which speakers are exposed to local norms and models
  and the language has acquired local cultural associations;
- in these differing contexts English often forms part of a bi- or multilingual
  speaker's 'repertoire' alongside other languages;
- whether or not it is desirable, on purely practical grounds it is simply not
  possible for non-native speakers to be in constant touch with native models.

Kachru suggests that while Quirk expresses concerns about the use of English, he
takes no account of such sociolinguistic realities.

Quirk and Kachru may disagree about the validity of non-native Englishes,
but they are at one in their support for the language. Tripathi takes issue with both
of them. He is less concerned with the validity of different varieties of English than
with the relationship between English and other languages. He argues that
English is being challenged and replaced by indigenous languages in several parts
of the world:

> The partisans of English keep discoursing on its value as a status symbol
> in countries previously governed by the British, but appear oblivious of
> the resistance it breeds. The factors promoting territorial nationalism
> also encourage linguistic nationalism, the spread of modern education
> and of English itself contributing to this development.
>
> (Tripathi, 1992, p. 9)

The debate surrounding Quirk's paper seems, then, to hinge on different beliefs about processes of standardization and the functions of Standard English, the validity of non-native (and native nonstandard) Englishes, and the values attached to English. These issues are central to any discussion of the history of English and its contemporary position in the world; they resurface in later chapters in this book, and in fact in other books in the series.

Chapter 4 discusses standardization and English in England; and Chapter 5 the development of 'new Englishes' in different parts of the world.

1.6 CONCLUSION

In this chapter I have focused on diversity and change within English: formal differences between varieties of English; differences between speakers; different patterns of use, in different contexts; and different (often ambivalent) social meanings with which the language has been associated.

Linguists tend to rely on certain categories as a basis for discussing diversity and change: they talk about 'Old English' and 'Middle English', 'British English' or 'Indian English', 'Standard English' (or 'Englishes'). Such categories are useful as a starting point for linguistic description and analysis, but I have suggested that they are idealizations. It is difficult to draw definitive boundaries, according to linguistic criteria, around different varieties of English. (There are further discussions and examples of this point in later chapters.) In fact, diversity cannot be considered purely in linguistic terms: people may desire boundaries between varieties, for social and political considerations are of crucial importance in establishing what count as distinct varieties of English.

The spread of English to different parts of the world and its use as an 'international' language have provoked considerable debate: the language may be seen as beneficial, purely instrumental, or a threat. I mentioned that English is regulated in several countries in order to protect other languages and cultures. It has also proved difficult for many linguists to write dispassionately about diversity and change. I have tried to give a flavour of different ideological positions taken by those who study and write about English.

Reading A

THE ENGLISH LANGUAGE TODAY

David Crystal

In the glorious reign of Queen Elizabeth (the first, that is, from 1558 to 1603), the number of English speakers in the world is thought to have been between five and seven million. At the beginning of the reign of the second Queen Elizabeth, in 1952, the figure had increased almost fiftyfold: 250 million, it was said, spoke English as a mother tongue, and a further 100 million or so had learned it as a foreign language.

Thirty-five years on, the figures continue to creep up. The most recent estimates tell us that mother-tongue speakers are now over 300 million. But this total is far exceeded by the numbers of people who use English as a foreign language – at least a further 400 million, according to the most conservative of estimates, and perhaps a further billion, according to radical ones. 'Creep', perhaps, is not quite the right word, when such statistics are introduced.

What accounts for the scale of these increases? The size of the mother-tongue total is easy to explain. It's the Americans. The estimated population of the USA was just under 239 million in 1985, of whom about 215 million spoke English as a mother tongue. The British, Irish, Australians, New Zealanders, Canadians, and South Africans make up most of the others – but even combined they don't reach 100 million. There's no doubt where the majority influence is. However, these figures are growing relatively slowly at present – at an average rate of about half a per cent per annum. This is not where the drama lies.

A much more intriguing question is to ask what is happening to English in countries where people *don't* use it as a mother tongue. A highly complicated question, as it turns out. Finding out about the number of foreigners using English isn't easy, and that is why there is so much variation among the estimates. There are hardly any official figures. No one knows how many foreign people have learned English to a reasonable standard of fluency – or to any standard at all, for that matter. There are a few statistics available – from the examination boards, for example – but these are only the tip of a very large iceberg.

English as a 'second' language

The iceberg is really in two parts, reflecting two kinds of language learning situation. The first part relates to those countries where English has some kind of special status – in particular, where it has been chosen as an 'official' language. This is the case in Ghana and Nigeria, for example, where the governments have settled on English as the main language to carry on the affairs of government, education, commerce, the media, and the legal system. In such cases, people have to learn English if they want to get on in life. They have their mother tongue to begin with – one or other of the local languages – and they start learning English, in school or in the street, at an early age. For them, in due course, English will become a language to fall back on, when their mother tongue proves to be inadequate for communication – talking to people from a different tribal back-ground, for example, or to people from outside the country. For them, English becomes their 'second' language.

Why do these countries not select a local language for official use? The problem is how to choose between the many indigenous languages, each of which represents an ethnic background to which the adherents are fiercely loyal. In Nigeria, for example, they would have to choose between Hausa, Yoruba, Ibo, Fulani, and other languages belonging to different ethnic groups. The number of speakers won't decide the matter – there are about as many speakers of Hausa as there are of Yoruba, for instance. And even if one language did have a clear majority, its selection would be opposed by the combined weight of the other speakers, who would otherwise find themselves seriously disadvantaged, socially and educationally. Inter-tribal tension, leading to unrest and violence, would be a likely consequence. By giving official status to an outside language, such as English, all internal languages are placed on the same footing. Everyone is now equally disadvantaged. It is a complex decision to implement, but at least it is fair.

To talk of 'disadvantaged', though, is a little misleading. From another point of view, the population is now considerably 'advantaged', in that they thereby come to have access to a world of science, technology, and commerce which would otherwise not easily be available to them.

But why English? In Ghana, Nigeria, and many other countries, the choice is motivated by the weight of historical tradition from the British colonial era. A similar pattern of development can be observed in countries which were influenced by other cultures, such as the French, Spanish, Portuguese, or Dutch. French, for example, is the official language in Chad; Portuguese in Angola. But English is an official or semi-official language in over sixty countries of the world – a total which far exceeds the range of these other languages.

Does this mean that we can obtain an estimate of the world's second-language English speakers simply by adding up the populations of all the countries involved? Unfortunately, it isn't so easy. Most of these countries are in underdeveloped parts of the world, where educational opportunities are limited. The country may espouse English officially, but only a fraction of the population may be given an opportunity to learn it. The most dramatic example of this gap between theory and practice is India.

In 1985, the population of India was estimated to be 768 million. English is an official language here, alongside Hindi. Several other languages have special status in their own regions, but English is the language of the legal system; it is a major language in Parliament, and it is a preferred language in the universities and in the all-India competitive exams for senior posts in such fields as the civil service and engineering. Some 3,000 English newspapers are published throughout the country. There is thus great reason to learn to use the language well. But it is thought that those with an educated awareness of English may be as little as 3 per cent of the population. Perhaps 10 per cent or more, if we recognize lower levels of achievement, and include several varieties of pidgin English. In real terms, the English speakers of India may only number 70 millions – a small amount compared with the total population. On the other hand, this figure is well in excess of the population of Britain.

When all the estimates for second-language use around the world are added up, we reach a figure of around 300 million speakers – about as many as the total of mother-tongue users. But we have to remember that most of these countries are in parts of the world (Africa, South Asia) where the population increase is four times as great as that found in mother-tongue countries. If present trends continue, within a generation mother-tongue English use will have been left far behind.

English as a 'foreign' language

The second part of the language-learning iceberg relates to people who live in countries where English has no official status, but where it is learned as a foreign language in schools, institutes of higher education, and through the use of a wide range of 'self-help' materials. There are only hints as to what the numbers involved might be. Even in the statistically aware countries of Western Europe, there are no reliable figures available for the number of people who are learning English as a foreign language – or any other language, for that matter. In a continent such as South America, the total is pure guesswork.

The total most often cited in the mid-1980s was 100 million, based largely on the figures available from English-language examining boards, estimates of listeners to English-language radio programmes, sales of English-language newspapers, and the like. But this figure did not take into account what is currently happening in the country where data about anything has traditionally been notoriously difficult to come by: China.

In China, there has been an explosion of interest in the English language in recent years. One visitor returned to China in 1979, after an absence of twenty years, and wrote: 'in 1959, everyone was carrying a book of the thoughts of Chairman Mao; today, everyone is carrying a book of elementary English'. In 1983, it is thought, around 100 million people watched the BBC television series designed to teach the language, *Follow Me*. Considerable publicity was given in the Western media to the sight of groups of Chinese practising English-language exercises after work, or queuing to try out their English on a passing tourist. The presenter of *Follow Me*, Kathy Flower, became a national celebrity, recognized everywhere. And the interest continues, with new series of programmes being designed to meet the needs of scientific and business users. What level of fluency is being achieved by this massive influx of learners is unknown. But if only a fraction of China's population is successful, this alone will be enough to make the 100 million total for world foreign-language use a gross underestimate.

And why shouldn't they be successful, in China, Japan, Brazil, Poland, Egypt, and elsewhere? There is enormous motivation, given the way that English has become the dominant language of world communication. Textbooks on English these days regularly rehearse the litany of its achievements. It is the main language of the world's books, newspapers, and advertising. It is the official international language of airports and air traffic control. It is the chief maritime language. It is the language of international business and academic conferences, of diplomacy, of sport. Over two-thirds of the world's scientists write in English. Three-quarters of the world's mail is written in English. Eighty per cent of all the information stored in the electronic retrieval systems of the world is stored in English. And, at a local level, examples of the same theme can be found everywhere. A well-known Japanese company, wishing to negotiate with its Arabic customers, arranges all its meetings in English. A Colombian doctor reports that he spends almost as much time improving his English as practising medicine. A Copenhagen university student comments: 'Nearly everyone in Denmark speaks English; if we didn't, there wouldn't be anyone to talk to.'

Statistics of this kind are truly impressive, and could continue for several paragraphs. They make the point that it is not the number of mother-tongue speakers which make a language important in the eyes of the world (that crown is carried by Chinese), but the extent to which a language is found useful outside its original setting. In the course of history, other languages have achieved widespread use throughout educated society. During the Middle Ages, Latin remained undisputed as the European language of learning. In the eighteenth century, much of this prestige passed to French. Today, it is the turn of English. It is a development which could be reversed only by a massive change in the economic fortunes of America, and in the overall balance of world power.

Source: Crystal, 1988, pp. 1–7

Reading B
FRANGLAIS

Marie-Noëlle Lamy

Introduction

'Waouh! Super, ton Walkman CD!' shouts a young character in a French educational cartoon. The cartoon is produced by the local authorities in the French city of Nantes for distribution to teenagers on deprived estates in the area. Its aim is to raise teenagers' awareness of the dangers of receiving stolen goods. To achieve this, it features the story of two young men (one a cunning seller and one an unwitting receiver who gets arrested by the police) drawn and told in such a way as to make its young readers identify with the victim character. As seems clear from the quotation above, using vocabulary and syntax borrowed from English is felt to be a good way of reaching out to the young.

The fashion for English words, or for *franglais*, which is a mixture of English and French, is not new to the French. They have been borrowing from English in this way for at least a century, but there are now fears among those who want to protect French from Anglo-American influences that the trend is accelerating beyond control. In 1964 a French academic called René Etiemble published the results of the check-up he had carried out on the French language in respect of its 'contamination' by English: his book *Parlez-vous franglais?* (Etiemble, 1964) was a serious linguistic analysis, but it was widely read and Etiemble became a household name. Since the 1960s, many have battled against the trend, most recently by drawing on the French tradition of linguistic interventionism and by using the power of the French state.

Borrowing from English

What is borrowing?

One definition of borrowing is what happens when 'language A uses and ends up absorbing a linguistic item or feature which was part of language B, and which language A did not have. The linguistic items or features themselves are called "borrowings"' (Dubois et al., 1973, p. 188).

At its most noticeable, a borrowing is a word or a phrase that 'feels' to you as though it is foreign. This may be a matter of it sounding or looking different, as when English speakers use French phrases like *de rigueur* or *haute couture*. Borrowings may also express a familiar meaning in an unfamiliar way: if, as a French speaker talking in English about corruption, I say 'the fish rots from the head', my remark will be recognized as conveying the same idea as 'the rot starts at the top', but it will sound 'unEnglish'.

However, borrowings only 'feel' foreign if they have not had time to become integrated into the host language. The English language is full of borrowings from Latin (*mansion, cart, street*), or Danish (place names ending in *-by* or *-thwaite*) (Crystal, 1988). But they have been part of the English language so long that no one would now point to them as being foreign.

Types of borrowing

There are many degrees of integration of English borrowings into French. At the least integrated end of the scale, words are used with their original pronunciation (or as close to it as speakers of French can manage), and also with their original meaning and spelling. For example, *un scoop, un squat, un one-man show*.

The highest degree of integration is when the borrowed word loses its spelling and its pronunciation. This can only happen over time. It is the case with French words like *une redingote* (from riding coat) or *un boulingrin* (from bowling green). The French language needs to invent a gender for these guests that come to it from languages that are not gender based, and this it does in ways which are not always predictable. In the examples above, the ending of each word is derived from imitating the original pronunciation and this provides a pretext for assigning gender: French words ending in *-ote* are often feminine, while words ending in *-in* are masculine.

Between these two extremes, there are different ways in which words or phrases can become integrated. Borrowings may retain their spelling (and aspects of their meaning) while the pronunciation is totally gallicized: *une interview* is never pronounced in any other way than (in an approximate rendering) 'intèrviou', and a *rush* (a stampede for some new film or product) is spelt *un rush* but pronounced something like 'reuche'. Sometimes whole phrases and clauses are translated into French: a 'blue-stocking' came into French as *un bas-bleu* at the beginning of the nineteenth century; *ce n'est pas ma tasse de thé* ('it's not my cup of tea') was once felt to be an affectation used only by anglophiles. But now it trips off the tongue, at least in younger social groups.

English borrowings are often abbreviated in French, making them easier to pronounce; *un self* is 'a self-service restaurant', *un fast-food* is 'a fast food restaurant' and *le hard* is 'hard-core pornography' (so *un film hard* is not 'a film that's difficult to understand'!) The meanings of such borrowings may also become specialized: *un clip* is not an extract from any video but 'a music video', while *un kit* is not any object sold in parts, to be assembled by the buyer after purchase, but 'a piece of furniture' bought in kit form.

Sometimes, the French language adds a new sense to the meaning of one of its own native words, under the influence of a similar word that exists in English. For example, *réaliser*: the French meaning of the word was 'to make real'; at the end of the nineteenth century, under the influence of the English verb 'to realize', *réaliser* acquired the meaning 'to understand'.

English borrowings may bear only a trace of their origins. Thus *un smoking*, a word universally accepted by French speakers, is 'a dinner jacket'. The noun *le flip* refers to a (long-term or transitory) feeling of depression, and its associated verb *flipper* means 'to feel depressed'.

In the case of *flipper* a new verb has been created and integrated into the French verb system. Similarly, the verb 'to stress' has found a home within the regular 'first conjugation' of French verbs, yielding everyday phrases like '*je stresse complètement*' (I'm feeling really stressed) and '*j'ai trouvé ça vraiment stressant*' (I found that really stressful).

Finally, fake English words are often adopted by large numbers of French speakers, perhaps in the belief that they really are English, or perhaps because they are perceived to fill a gap in the vocabulary, for example, *un rugbyman* and *un tennisman* (with its feminine *une tenniswoman*). *Le footing* means 'jogging' and is now part of the everyday language of everyone in middle life and younger. The borrowed form may be a genuine English word, but once imported into French, its grammatical function may change: 'parking' becomes *un parking* (a car park) and 'lifting' becomes *un lifting* (a facelift).

The English language as intrusive neighbour

The dictionary definition I mentioned above (Dubois et al., 1973) makes a clear link between attitudes to borrowing and economic and political power, by saying that borrowing 'is necessarily linked to the prestige enjoyed by a language or the people who speak it or, conversely, to the contempt in which language or people are held'. The borrowing of English words and expressions has to be seen alongside the systematic encroachment of English into several parts of French life and culture – a development which may be responded to with enthusiasm, acceptance or outright hostility.

English may be seen as fashionable, particularly by young French people who wish to identify with the prestigious dynamic Anglo-American culture conveyed to them mainly through music and films.

Other groups use English for more utilitarian reasons. For instance, 20,000 members of the staff of IBM France use English as the language of work (*Le Monde*, 1992). International scientific congresses held in France often have to take place in English and budgets are not sufficient to provide interpreting into French. The Institut Pasteur itself has had to change the title of its *Annales de l'Institut Pasteur* to *Research in Macrobiology, Immunology and Virology* publishing articles in English (*Le Monde*, 1990a). There is clearly a feeling among leaders in French industry and research that familiarity with English is a key to staying in the race for world markets. The feeling is shared in other areas, such as the cinema, where producers know that films made in French have little chance of succeeding with Anglo-American audiences, hence the demand made on French actors to use English in French-made productions shot on location in France (*Le Monde*, 1990b).

Among those who fight against the encroachment of English are people who can be described as 'purists', linguistic protectionists who argue for the 'purity' of the French language on aesthetic or cultural grounds. One may sympathize with them, or one may feel that there is no such thing as a pure form of French (or of any other language) and dismiss their arguments as unrealistic. However, contemporary France presents us with examples giving purists a sound economic basis for their concerns: French and English announcements on national French flights; French and English displays on cash dispenser screens in areas of France unlikely to be visited by tourists; French and English messages on the telephone answering machines of national service industries; French and English slogans on French railway tickets; job advertisements for posts in France, aimed at French nationals, published in *Le Monde* – in English! A French Minister for Culture has pleaded for a more energetic response on the part of France to the dominance of English both in the world and within the European Union. 'Japan', he said, '... is developing huge research programmes to make sure that, in a world of machine communication, English doesn't eliminate Japanese'. Similarly, 'we, as members of the European Union, must resist the blandishments of arguments promoting a single vehicular language, which would eventually demote all of our languages except one to the rank of a local dialect' (*Le Monde*, 1994).

The English language and the French state

There is a French tradition of state intervention in matters of language. In the sixteenth century, the Ordonnance de Villers-Cotterêts made it compulsory to use French in political and legal documents and thereby established the dominance of the French language over other languages spoken within the Kingdom of France, such as *Occitan* or *Provençal*. The creation of the Académie Française in 1635 answered a political need for a monarchy seeking to strengthen its control over a linguistically and religiously diverse country. The Académie's role in modern times is less directly felt, although its prestige is still great. More recently, the state has started legislating: the bill, Bas-Lauriol 1975, laid out a number of prescriptions for controlling borrowings from English, but it was never properly implemented.

A law, known as the Toubon law (spring 1995), tackles the problem in the following ways: consumer goods must not be sold without a set of instructions in French; all-English advertisements must not be shown in French cinemas; all-English small advertisements must not be published in the French press; bilingual advertisements and signs must not display the French part of their message in characters smaller than those in the English part. The law doesn't touch airlines or companies trading outside France. Nor does it attempt to interfere with the promotion, in English on French territory, of prestige French products like perfumes. Finally, an early amendment inhibited the law from making it compulsory for all bilingual signs to include a third (EU or regional) language. Unlike its predecessor of 1975, the law has teeth: breaches can be referred by individuals through associations, such as the official pressure group the Commissariat générale de la langue française, direct to the police.

But when the time comes, a body like the Académie des Sciences is prepared to test the law: unable to provide the resources needed to translate conference abstracts from English into French, it considers that 'the only alternative ... is to disobey and see what happens' (cited in *The Times Higher Education Supplement*, 1994).

In this instance, as in many others in the past, resistance to linguistic authoritarianism is likely to be robust. In contrast to the legislative approach, it may be better to look to the advisory approach. Perhaps the most effective aspect of the French state's action has been the creation of the Commissariat, which

publishes (and regularly updates) a *Dictionnaire des néologismes officiels.* Although the dictionary is highly prescriptive in its prohibition against borrowings, it is also constructive in that it offers a wealth of French coinages as alternatives. Some seem doomed in the face of entrenched speech habits (for instance *un bouteur* is unlikely to replace the universally accepted *un bulldozer*), but others are already established (e.g. *un baladeur* instead of *un Walkman*). The successful coinages are those that have been debated, joked about and generally given much planned or unplanned media exposure. As a result, they have come to sound quite natural, no different from words that have evolved organically. The social status of speakers with access to the media has militated against borrowing in the same way as the influence of a prestigious culture militated in its favour in the first instance. The sociolinguistic mechanism can work both ways, even though its work may be considered too slow and too limited by governments struggling to protect French linguistic sovereignty from a dominant foreign economic and cultural power.

References

CRYSTAL, D. (1988) *The English Language,* Harmondsworth, Penguin Books.

DIRECTION DES JOURNAUX OFFICIELS (1988) 5th edn. *Dictionnaire des néologismes officiels,* no. 1468, Paris, Direction des journaux officiels.

DUBOIS J., GIACOMO, M., SUESPIN, L., MARCELLESI, C., MARCELLESI, J-B. AND MÉVEL J-P (1973) *Dictionnaire de linguistique,* Paris, Librairie Larousse.

ETIEMBLE, R. (1964) *Parlez-vous franglais?* Paris, Gallimard.

Le monde (1990a), Paris, 12 January 1990.

Le monde (1990b), Paris, 4 August 1990.

Le monde (1992), Paris, 10 December 1992.

Le monde (1994), Paris, 25 February 1994.

The Times Higher Education Supplement (THES) (15 April 1994).

This reading was specially commissioned for this book.

Reading C

LANGUAGE VARIETIES AND STANDARD LANGUAGE

Randolph Quirk

Reading C is an extract from a lecture given at a language teaching conference in Japan in 1988. A committee of inquiry into the teaching of English in England, the Kingman Committee, had just published its report which argued, among other things, that children need to acquire standard English, this is a matter of 'their educational progress, their career prospects, their social and geographical mobility' (Quirk, 1990, p. 7). Quirk sets this argument against the view, attributed to certain British teachers, that children's capacity to use English effectively 'can and should be fostered only by exposure to varieties of the English language' (Kingman, p. 1, emphasis added) and that 'any notion of correct or incorrect use of language is an affront to personal liberty' (Kingman, p. 3). Quirk terms this position 'liberation linguistics' by analogy with 'liberation theology'.

The lecture continues ...

English in non-English-speaking countries

Let me now turn from the fairly parochial issue of teaching English in Britain to the teaching of English in non-English-speaking countries – where overwhelmingly greater numbers of students are involved. Most of the Kingman Report should surely have no bearing upon *them*. Since students in the Soviet Union or Japan bring little English of their own to the classroom, there can be no question of the teacher performing his or her task by merely exposing them to the 'varieties of English language' around them. They come to learn a totally unfamiliar language, so there can be no question of the teacher rejecting the 'notion of correct or incorrect' use of English. And all the students know perfectly well that, as Kingman says, their command of Standard English is likely to increase their freedom and their career prospects. So of course they – teachers and taught alike – accept the basic conclusion that it is the institution's duty to teach Standard English.

At any rate, that is what one would *expect* to be the position with teaching English as a foreign language, and it is the position that is assumed by most foreign ministries of education and by most foreign students – and their parents.

But the contrast between teaching English to English boys and girls in Leeds and teaching English to Japanese boys and girls in Kobe is not as neat and absolute as I have made it seem. Some schools in London and New York, for instance, have so many pupils from a non-English-speaking background that the techniques and approaches of teaching English as a foreign language have to be adopted – in precisely the same schools and often by the same teachers as those where the ideals of what I've called 'liberation linguistics' are still enthusiastically served up, however much they are just stale leftovers from the 1960s.

Let me give you a New York example. A well-respected educationist wrote an article a year or so ago on the teaching of English to the many thousands of New York children who come from Spanish-speaking homes (Goldstein, 1987). These children, she said, identify far more with the black children in the streets around them than with white children, and for that reason the English they should be taught is not Standard English but what she calls Black English. This is the English that will help them to relate to their peers outside the classroom; and after all, she pointed out, a sentence like 'I don't have none' shows 'a correct use of Black English negation' (p. 432).

Now, that article was published in one of the best known international journals, read by teachers of English not only in the United States but in Italy, Greece, China, and Japan – by the most professionally-minded, in fact, of English language teachers throughout the world. The context in which the article was *written* of course is clear enough, but what about attempts to adapt its message in the very different contexts in which it is *read*?

We must not forget that many Japanese teachers, Malaysian teachers, Indian teachers have done postgraduate training in Britain and the United States, eager to absorb what they felt were the latest ideas in English teaching. Where better, after all, to get the latest ideas on this than in the leading English-speaking countries? The interest in 'varieties of English language', called in question on the first page of the Kingman report, has in fact been widely stimulated, as we know from university theses being written in a whole host of countries: with titles like *Malaysian English, Filipino English, Hong Kong English, Nigerian English, Indian English*.

The countries last mentioned here, of course, are chiefly those where English has had an *internal* role over a long period for historical reasons. English was indeed the language used by men like Gandhi and Nehru in the movement to liberate India from the British raj and it is not surprising that 'liberation linguistics' should have a very special place in relation to such countries. Put at its simplest, the argument is this: many Indians speak English; one can often guess that a person is Indian from the way he or she speaks English; India is a free and independent country as Britain is or as America is. Therefore, just as there is an *American English* (as recorded, for example, in the Webster Collegiate Dictionary), and a *British English* (as recorded, for example, in the Concise Oxford), so there is an *Indian English* on precisely the same equal footing (and of course a *Nigerian English*, a *Ghanaian English*, a *Singaporean English*, a *Filipino English*, etc., etc.).

No one would quarrel with any of this provided there was agreement within each such country that it was *true*, or even that there was a determined policy to *make* it true. So far as I can see, neither of these conditions obtains, and most of those with authority in education and the media in these countries tend to protest that the so-called national variety of English is an attempt to justify inability to acquire what they persist in seeing as 'real' English.

A colleague of mine who this year spent some time working in Kenya told me in a letter: 'There is heated debate here as to whether there is such a thing as "East African English" or whether the local variety is just the result of the increasing failure of the education system.' In his book on English in Nigeria, O. Kujore (1985) says that although earlier observers have talked freely of *Standard Nigerian English*, the fact is 'that any such standard is, at best, in process of evolution'. Similar doubts about Filipino English have recently been expressed in *English Today* [Kapili, 1988] and they confirm my own observations in Manila. It is reported that, not long before her death, Mrs Indira Gandhi returned rather angry from an international conference – angry because she had been unable to understand the English used there by a fellow-Indian delegate. She demanded that her Ministry of Education do something about standards of English.

Within India itself, the status of *Indian English* is the more difficult to establish in that, among the few organizations using the term officially, the Indian Academy of Literature applies it in a purely ethnopolitical sense to literary work in English written by ethnic Indians.

No one should underestimate the problem of teaching English in such countries as India and Nigeria, where the English of the teachers themselves inevitably bears the stamp of locally acquired deviation from the standard language ('You are knowing my father, isn't it?'). The temptation is great to accept the situation and even to justify it in euphemistically sociolinguistic terms.

A few months ago, discussing these matters in the Philippines, I heard a British educational consultant who had worked for a year or so in Manila tell Filipino teachers that there was no reason for them to correct the English of their students if it seemed comprehensible to other Filipinos. Whether the listening teachers felt relieved or insulted I don't know, but of one thing I was sure: the advice was bad. Filipinos, like Indians, Nigerians, Malaysians, are learning English not just to speak with their own country folk but to link themselves with the wider English-using community throughout the world. It is neither liberal nor liberating to permit learners to settle for lower standards than the best, and it is a travesty of liberalism to tolerate low standards which will lock the least fortunate into the least rewarding careers.

Half-baked quackery

When we turn from the special problems of countries like India and the Philippines to countries like Spain and Japan which have little or no legacy of localized English on the streets, in offices, or in markets, we would surely expect to find no such conflicts about teaching Standard English. And so it is for the most part, no doubt. But not entirely. Ill-considered reflexes of liberation linguistics and a preoccupation with what the Kingman Report calls 'exposure to varieties of English language' intrude even here. And this in two respects.

First, the buoyant demand for native-speaking English teachers means that one occasionally finds, in Tokyo or Madrid, young men and women teaching English with only a minimal teacher training, indeed with little specialized education: they're employed because, through accident of birth in Leeds or Los Angeles, they are native speakers of English. Not merely may their own English be far from standard but they may have little respect for it and may well have absorbed (at second or third hand) the linguistic ethos that is simplified into the tenet that any English is as good as any other.

One such young Englishman approached me after a lecture I'd given in Madrid a few months ago. Why, he asked, had I distinguished between the nouns *message* and *information* as countable and uncountable? His students often wrote phrases like *several informations* and since he understood what was meant, how could they be wrong? In some wonderment that I was actually talking to a British teacher of English, I gently explained about Standard English being the norm by which we taught and made judgements. He flatly disagreed and went on to claim that he could not bring himself to correct a Spanish pupil for using a form that had currency in an English dialect – *any* English dialect. 'She catched a cold' is as good as 'She caught a cold', he ended triumphantly and strode away.

Let's hope that such half-baked quackery is rare because the *other* respect in which 'exposure to varieties' is ill-used is not all that rare, I fear. This is where academic linguists from Britain or America, sometimes with little experience of foreign language teaching, are invited to advise on teaching English abroad. If by training or personal interest they share the language ethos that the Kingman Report criticises, their advice – merely a bit controversial in its original British or American educational context – is likely to be flagrantly misleading when exported with minimal adaptation to, say, Japan.

References

GOLDSTEIN, L.M. (1987) 'Standard English: the only target for non-native speakers of English?', *TESOL Quarterly*, vol. 21, pp. 417–36.

KAPILI, L.V. (1988) 'Requiem for English', *English Today*, ET16, vol. iv, no. 4, October 1988.

KINGMAN, J. (1988) *Report of the Committee of Inquiry into the Teaching of English Language*, London, HMSO (the Kingman Report).

KUJORE, O. (1985) *English Usage: some notable Nigerian variations*, Ibadan, Evans.

QUIRK, R. (1981) 'International communication and the concept of nuclear English' in SMITH, L.E. (ed.) *English for Cross-cultural Communication*, London, Macmillan, pp. 151–65.

QUIRK, R. (1988) 'The question of standards in the international use of English' in LOWENBERG, P.H. (ed.) *Language Spread and Language Policy*, Washington DC, Georgetown University Press.

Source: Quirk, [1988] 1990

ENGLISH MANUSCRIPTS: THE EMERGENCE OF A VISUAL IDENTITY

David Graddol

2.1 INTRODUCTION

This chapter does not deal with printed texts in English; a discussion of modern technologies can be found in the fourth book in this series, *Redesigning English: new texts, new identities* (Goodman and Graddol (eds), 1996).

Chapter 1 showed how the term 'English language' embraces a rich diversity of linguistic forms used in different places and contexts and by different people. This chapter and the next three examine the historical dimensions of such diversity. Where did the English language come from? What did it look like in earlier periods of its history? What have been the major influences that have caused the language to develop into its modern forms? This chapter begins with the easiest of these questions – the 'look' of English: what did the language look like in the earliest documents, and how have handwriting and the general appearance of texts changed over time? By exploring the changing appearance of English handwritten texts I also introduce some of the major landmarks in the history of English, many of which are discussed more fully in later chapters.

Chapter 1, and indeed all four books in this series, emphasize the extent to which English is used in different ways in many parts of the world. When we examine the history of English, however – particularly its early history – it is inevitable that the focus of our study is much narrower in scope. It was not until the seventeenth century that English, as a result of colonization in North America and parts of Asia, first became used extensively outside the British Isles. Correspondingly, it is not until Chapter 5, where we investigate the consequences of English colonial activity, that we return to an international perspective.

The seven ages of English

1   *Pre-English period (−c. AD 450)*
Local languages in Britain are Celtic. After the Roman invasion c. 55 BC Latin becomes the dominant language of culture and government. Many communities in Britain are bilingual Celtic-Latin.

2   *Early Old English (450−c. 850)*
Anglo-Saxon invasion c. AD 499 when Romans leave. Settlers bring a variety of Germanic dialects from mainland Europe. First English literature appears c. AD 700. English borrows many words from Latin via the church.

3   *Later Old English (c. 850−1100)*
Extensive invasion and settlement from Scandinavia. In the north of England dialects of English become strongly influenced by Scandinavian languages. In the south King Alfred arranges for many Latin texts to be translated.

4   *Middle English (c. 1100−1450)*
Norman conquest and Norman rule. English vocabulary and spelling now affected by French, which becomes the official language in England. Educated English people trilingual (French, Latin, English). Chaucer.

5   *Early modern English (c. 1450−1750)*
Includes the Renaissance, the Elizabethan era and Shakespeare. The role of the church, of Latin and of French declines and English becomes a language of science and government. Britain grows commercially and acquires overseas colonies. English taken to the Americas, Australia, India. Slave trade carries black speakers of African languages to Caribbean and America, giving rise to English creoles. English acquires a typographic identity with the rise of printing. Many attempts to 'standardize and fix' the language with dictionaries and grammars.

6   *Modern English (c. 1750−1950)*
Britain experiences industrial revolution, and consolidates imperial power, introducing English medium education in many parts of the world. English becomes the international language of advertising and consumerism.

7   *Late modern English (c. 1950−)*
Britain retreats from empire. New standardized varieties of English emerge in newly independent countries. English becomes the international language of communications technology. American English becomes the dominant world variety.

2.2   THE ORIGINS OF WRITTEN ENGLISH

No one is very sure what the 'original' language of Britain was, or even if it is sensible to ask such a question. The early history of Britain is one of successive invasions, of the arrival of new populations who spoke new languages which displaced or mixed with existing ones. In this section I look briefly at the linguistic context in which English first arose and at its first, and largely forgotten, writing system.

The linguistic background

When the Romans first invaded Britain in the first century BC it was inhabited by various Celtic-speaking peoples, some of whom seem to have migrated from what is now France or Belgium. During the Roman occupation (AD 43–410) Latin was the official language – the language of government and commerce – but Celtic undoubtedly remained the vernacular. Lindsay Allason-Jones (1989), in a study of women in Roman Britain, suggests:

> The majority of the native rural population will have continued to speak Celtic dialects as their first language, with enough dog-Latin to get by in trading and in any brushes they might have with officialdom … Contact with merchants and the army helped to spread the Latin language, while those who had had some education or close contacts with officials would have been fluent … By the end of the first century AD the increasingly cosmopolitan flavour of the urban population will have resulted in many languages being heard in Britain with the consequence that a knowledge of Latin would have been essential for efficient communication between people who could have originated as far afield as Scotland, Africa or Turkey. Native Britons will have continued to speak Celtic at home but the increasing number of mixed marriages will have added to the number of families speaking Latin.
>
> (Allason-Jones, 1989, p. 174)

There are several reasons for noting the linguistic situation in Britain in the pre-English period. First, it establishes that Britain was a multilingual and cosmopolitan community well connected with other parts of the world through administration, trade and scholarship. Such contact with other languages is a recurrent feature of the history of English and has had a considerable impact on its grammar and vocabulary. Second, the position of Latin as a **lingua franca** (a language of communication between speakers of different languages), brought by a colonizing power and left to find a new position for itself among local languages when that power withdrew, anticipates the history of English itself as a language of empire in more recent times. Lastly, identification of the languages that were in use in early Britain helps to establish which traditions of writing were current when English first appeared and, therefore, which ones are likely to have influenced the development of writing in English.

An explanation of the term 'Celtic' is given in Chapter 3, section 3.2

Where did English come from?

When, then, did the English language begin? What did the first words look like? The oldest known piece of writing in English (see Figure 2.1) may be a carving on a roe-deer's ankle-bone found in a cemetery site at Caistor-by-Norwich, Norfolk. It dates from c. AD 400 and appears to read *raïhan* (roe-deer). This is only a single word, so it may be disputed that it represents English rather than some other,

Figure 2.1   Runic inscription from Caistor-by-Norwich c. AD 400. This could be the oldest known text in English

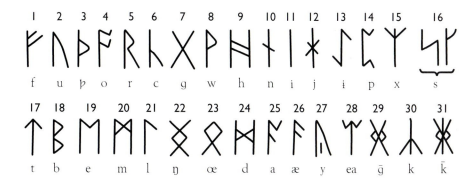

Figure 2.2   The futhorc
(After Page, 1987)

closely related, Germanic dialect. Nevertheless, it demonstrates the **runic script** in which the earliest English was written. This is known as the 'futhorc' after the first few letters of its alphabet (see Figure 2.2). The letters are based on simple lines that can be cut easily with a blade. The origins of the runic writing system are obscure – it appears to be modelled loosely on the Latin or Greek alphabet, but exactly where and when it was devised is unclear. It is known, however, that runes were used in various Germanic languages from the third century AD, and that they were brought to England by people from mainland Europe.

The Anglo-Saxon futhorc

Figure 2.3   One attempt to show the different sources of raiding and settlement in England after the Romans left

The arrival of the futhorc in England provides the first evidence for the existence of the English language. Who brought it, and what was the language (or languages) that came to be transformed into a distinct language variety eventually called 'English'? Clearly these are questions that are of great interest in any history of English but unfortunately there are no straightforward answers.

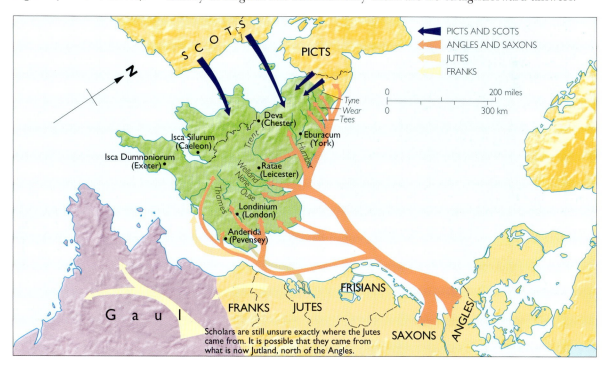

Britain was provided with relative stability and economic growth by the Roman empire for more than three centuries, but the late fourth century was a critical time for the Romans: their territories were increasingly under attack and there was invasion on many sides as a consequence of large-scale movements of peoples across Europe. They eventually withdrew their forces from the further reaches of the empire in order to defend its centre in Italy. In AD 410, when the Roman emperor sent word to the British towns that they should take measures for 'their own defence', it seems that the Roman garrisons had already departed. The bilingual Romano-British communities remained, vulnerable to attack from various sources: some of the Celtic-speaking peoples who had been banished by the Romans to the fringes of Britain now threatened the towns and villas of the 'civilized' south and east, and Germanic-speaking people approaching from the sea began to attack towns and villages with increased ferocity.

Most nations have special stories of their origins and the much repeated account of how the English nation and language came into being derives largely from a historian writing in the eighth century, the Venerable Bede, who wrote (in Latin) a work called *Ecclesiastical History of the English People*.

> ... the Angles or Saxons came to Britain at the invitation of King Vortigern in three longships, and were granted lands in the eastern part of the island on condition that they protected the country: nevertheless, their real intention was to subdue it. They engaged the enemy advancing from the north, and having defeated them, sent back news of their success to their homeland, adding that the country was fertile and the Britons cowardly. Whereupon a larger fleet quickly came over with a great body of warriors, which, when joined to the original forces, constituted an invincible army ... These newcomers were from the three most formidable races in Germany, the Saxons, Angles, and Jutes ...

Figure 2.4   The first page of Bede's Ecclesiastical History of the English People. This is a copy made c. AD 820 of the Latin original completed in AD 731

(British Library)

It was not long before such hordes of those alien peoples vied together to crowd into the island that the natives who had invited them began to live in terror.

(Sherley-Price, 1968, pp. 55–6)

This story provides a simplified account of what was a very complicated situation. Chapter 3 examines how alternative stories can be told, but in this chapter we can note that the English language first appeared in the fifth century AD among a confusion of peoples, origins and languages. Britain then entered a period from which few documentary records survive. When records appear some 200 or so years later, in the form of inscriptions and manuscripts, they indicate that an identifiable language variety has somehow evolved, although still very similar to other Germanic languages such as Old Frisian and with internal dialectal variation between the north and south of England. This language is now called Old English and the people who spoke it are usually referred to as Anglo-Saxons.

Early inscriptions in English

Figure 2.5 illustrates a panel from a whalebone carved box known as the Franks Casket that was carved in the early eighth century in northern England. Around the perimeter of the panel is a runic text which describes the story of Romulus and Remus, the mythical founders of Rome who were, according to legend, suckled by a she-wolf.

Figure 2.5   The Franks Casket was carved in whalebone in Northumbria in the early eighth century

(British Museum)

❖   ❖   ❖   ❖   ❖

Activity 2.1   *(Allow 15 minutes)*

Using the key to the futhorc shown in Figure 2.2, transliterate the first part of the inscription carved on the Franks Casket (shown below) into Old English. Use the exercise to look more closely at the shape of runic letters. How many runic characters seem to be related to the modern English alphabet?

The full inscription reads as follows in modern English: 'Romulus and Remus, two brothers, a she-wolf nourished them in Rome, far from their native land.'

❖   ❖   ❖   ❖   ❖

Runic inscriptions are interesting to the historian of English for several reasons:

- *The range of letters contained in the futhorc*. The Old English futhorc contained, at various times, between 24 and 31 letters, several of which have no equivalent in the modern English alphabet or in the Graeco-Latin alphabet from which the futhorc was descended. Runic inscriptions in Britain thus show the development of a set of letters found only in English.

- *The order in which the letters were conventionally given*. The futhorc takes its name from the first six letters of the series, but the reason for this order is not known. The order was used for learning and memorizing the futhorc itself. The use of a fixed 'alphabetical order' for the purpose of ordering items in a list or for arranging books in libraries did not occur until some centuries later.

- *The shape of the letters*. The angular form of runes was particularly suited to inscription on hard surfaces, such as wood or stone, as opposed to writing with ink on parchment. The shape of the letters thus reflects the technology used to create them. We will see how changes in the implements used for writing in later times have led to changes in the shape of letters.

- *The direction of writing*. The writing on the Franks Casket is read in a circle, so that the text on the lower edge is upside-down. The text on the Ruthwell Cross (see Figure 2.6) runs vertically. Wherever writing is used as decoration (runes figure frequently on jewellery because writing had magical associations) it will, like the panel of the Franks Casket, follow the shape of the design. Writing in early English was not as rigidly left to right, top to bottom, as in later times.

- *The evidence it provides about pronunciation*. The form of the runic alphabet used in Scandinavia was reduced to 16 letters. In England it expanded to 31. The additional letters give clues as to how the pronunciation of English was developing. For example, a general sound change occurred in Old English, causing *k* to be pronounced differently when it occurred before certain vowel sounds. Anglo-Saxon rune masters created a new rune (number 30 in the list in Figure 2.2) to enable them to distinguish between these sounds. The original rune 6 came to be used for the new, softer *ch* sound, and the new rune for the original hard *k*. We examine such changes in pronunciation in English in Chapter 3.

In England runic inscriptions on rocks and large monuments also give evidence of developing dialect differences: unlike small portable items, they were probably constructed near to where they still stand, and so their form of language presumably reflects local usage.

ᚠᚪᚻᚠ ᛁᚳ ᚱᛁᛁᚳᚾᚫ ᚷᚪᚾᛁᛝᚳ

ahof   ic   riicnæ   kyninc

lifted up   I   a great   king

ᚻᛖᚪᚠᚢᚾᚫᛋ ᚻᛚᚪᚠᚪᚱᛞ

heafunæs   hlafard

heaven's   lord

ᚻᚫᛚᛞᚪ ᛁᚳ ᚾᛁ ᚻᚪᚱᛋᛏᚪ

hælda   ic   ni   dorstæ

bow   I   not   did dare

ᛒᛁᛋᛗᚫᚱᚫᛞᚢ ᚢᛝᚷᛖᛏ ᛗᛖᚾ

bismærædu   uŋket   men

mocked   us two   men

ᛒᚪ ᚠᛏᚷᚪᚻᚱᚪ ᛁᚳ ᚹᚫᛋ ᛗᛁᚦ

ba   ætgadræ   ic   wæs   miþ

both   together   I   was   with

ᛒᛚᚪᚻᚫ ᛒᛁᛋᛏᛖᛗᛁᛞ

blodæ   bistemid

blood   bedewed

*Figure 2.6   The Ruthwell Cross was inscribed
c. AD 700 in Latin and in runes with a religious
Anglo-Saxon poem* The Dream of the Rood

Other writing systems used in early Britain

The runes were not the only writing system used in the British Isles at this early time. The 'ogham' script was used for some Celtic inscriptions, mainly in Ireland and Wales. Like the futhorc it was based on angular forms suited to carving in hard materials, but unlike the futhorc the characters appear unrelated to the Greek or Latin script. Inscriptions in ogham often read from bottom to top, or left to right. The ogham script seems not to have influenced the development of English writing.

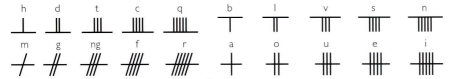

Figure 2.7   The ogham script used for early inscriptions in the Celtic languages

The most widespread writing system in England before the Anglo-Saxon invasion was that used for Latin. Even though the Romans themselves had departed from Britain, Latin continued to be used for many centuries as the main language of writing for religious texts, legal documents and science. This reflected the importance of the church, for whom Latin was the lingua franca and official language. Runic inscriptions in Old English often appeared alongside Latin inscriptions. Both the Franks Casket and the Ruthwell Cross (see Figures 2.5 and 2.6), for example, are bilingual – the Latin is inscribed in Roman script and the Old English in runes.

   By the eighth century the church, rather than the rune masters, effectively controlled the skills of writing and it is not surprising that the first books in English employed the Latin model of writing, with one or two additions to the alphabet to represent sounds not found in Latin. These additional letters, as discussed in the next section, were taken from the futhorc. The runes remained in use for some centuries as magical devices or for secret writing.

Figure 2.8   A typical incised inscription in Latin from a Roman site in the north-east of England

Figure 2.9   A grave slab for Hildithryth, found in an Anglo-Saxon cemetery at Hartlepool, north-east England

Two rather different forms of lettering were used for Latin – an incised form of capital letters used for engraved plaques and monuments, and a handwritten style which we look at more closely in the next section. The form of monumental lettering was remarkably standard throughout the Roman empire. The inscription shown in Figure 2.8, for example, is very similar to inscriptions made at that time in Rome. This form of lettering looks very 'modern' because in later centuries it greatly influenced the form of printed type. Figure 2.9 shows an unusual runic inscription found in the north-east of England which has obviously been cut by a mason who was familiar with the Roman style.

2.3   MEDIEVAL MANUSCRIPTS AND BOOKS

Old and Middle English were largely spoken, rather than written, languages but the only evidence we have of what they were like comes from the relatively few documents and books that have survived to modern times. This, then, is one reason for studying medieval English texts – they represent our only (and unfortunately incomplete) evidence of earlier stages of English. But medieval texts are full of other kinds of interest. Many are beautiful works of art, demonstrating contemporary artistic and cultural values. Their changing character and content provide evidence of the changing institutional and political influences that have helped shape the English language. Lastly, the form of early handwritten texts has influenced the appearance of English texts, including printed texts, up to the present day. Many of the conventions of layout, of spelling and of punctuation, for example, were first worked out in connection with hand-produced manuscripts.

Book production in medieval Britain was an international business. The knowledge of how to create books was acquired by Anglo-Saxon scribes from Irish (Celtic) missionaries, who in turn had learned from Rome. Furthermore, many books were made in England for customers in continental Europe. Hence English books have always been influenced by writing practices in other countries and other languages, and English books and scribal practices have affected practice elsewhere. In this section I focus particularly on those contributions to book and manuscript style that were distinctively English, especially those scribal practices that reflected the special needs of the English language or that in some way influenced its development.

You should bear in mind while reading this chapter that the vast majority of books and manuscripts produced in England before the invention of printing were written in Latin or (in later times) French. Administrative documents were not written in English in any number until the fourteenth century. The story of early written English is one of a local vernacular language struggling to achieve a distinct visual identity and written usage.

Techniques of manuscript production

Early manuscripts were valuable and expensive commodities. Not only was there a scarcity of the skills and knowledge necessary to produce them, but the materials themselves – parchment, ink, tools – were all expensive and their manufacture required skilled labour. This is why book production in medieval times was located almost entirely in monasteries, for whom it was an important industry that helped maintain status and economy. Before labour in England became organized around guilds and it became possible for independent scriveners' (i.e. secular scribes') shops to be set up, manuscript copying and production required the resources of an institution – for the training of scribes, the provision of access to original works and the supply of appropriate working conditions and materials.

Books were copied in the scriptorium – usually sited near the monastery library and often the only heated room in the building. Copyists typically had their own seats at double-sided lectern desks – perhaps with a higher, smaller lectern (like a modern secretarial copyholder) to hold the original. Much of the work was carried out in a standing position and a copyist might be expected to copy around four leaves per day – the speed of production was notably poorer in winter and in northern centres of production, when the daylight hours were fewer and the weather much colder. Some of the copyists speak to us directly in 'colophons' – footnotes added to manuscripts in which copyists identified themselves and perhaps illustrated themselves at work. Both nuns and monks worked as scribes.

The creation of a book involved many people. Several copyists might work on the same book, each responsible for different pages. An assistant might read the original aloud, working from the other side of the desk. When the scribe had finished, the manuscript would be passed to the 'rubricator', who added any headings and initials in red colour. Finally, an artist – the illuminator – would create the elaborate miniature paintings which adorn the finer manuscripts.

As I said earlier, manuscripts provide us with incomplete and indirect evidence of the spoken language. In order to interpret the historical linguistic data they give us, we need understand the division of labour and working conditions involved. The fact that an original was nearly always recited in spoken form during the copying process, for example, is one reason why the spelling in manuscripts often reflected the accent of the copyist instead of maintaining faith with an original. Each copy of a medieval book was slightly different from others, and some copies were made in a different century and country from the original. For example, the page from Bede's *Ecclesiastical History of the English People* shown in Figure 2.4 was produced nearly a century after Bede's original manuscript.

Many of the earliest English manuscripts were created in the north-east of England. Lindisfarne – a small island off the north-east coast, close to the modern border with Scotland – was the centre of the Northumbrian school of scribes and illuminators. This was where Anglo-Saxon scholars were first introduced to the Roman alphabet, through the medium of Latin. Other key libraries and copying centres were established about 70 km away at Monkwearmouth and Jarrow.

The Lindisfarne Gospels, written in Latin by Eadrith, bishop of Lindisfarne c. AD 700, is perhaps the greatest work from the northern scriptoria to have survived from the eighth century. Figure 2.10 shows one of the large decorated initials which begin each of the four gospels after two full pages of decoration. The first words are 'In principio erat verbum et verbum erat apud d(eu)m et d(eu)s [erat verbum]' (In the beginning was the word, and the word was with God and God [was the word]).

This page illustrates several characteristics of early manuscripts produced in England, notably the extent to which writing had become a form of art. Letters are entwined with animal figures and multicoloured tracery, and set out in a way which creates a larger design on the page. The *ci* of *principio* is, like *et*, in the form of a monogram (entwined to create a single graphical device) and a small human face appears within it. A number of tricks are used to ensure that each line fits the

Figure 2.10 (opposite) The opening of the Gospel of St John in the Lindisfarne Gospels, written at Lindisfarne c. AD 700

(British Library)

The word 'rubricator' comes from the Latin *rubrica*, literally 'red earth', which produced the red pigment used to write laws and other important parts of texts.

Square brackets are an editorial convention to show that particular words do not appear in the original document but have been inserted to complete the sense.

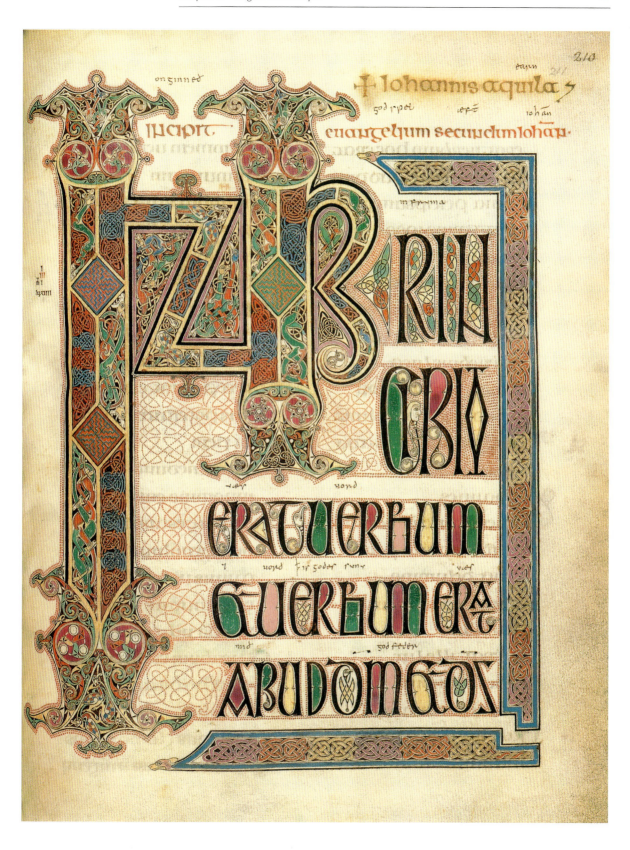

available space. For example, the penultimate line, *et verbum erat*, demonstrates three kinds of shortening: the *et* is monogrammed (a forerunner of the printer's ampersand – &); the *u* and *m* of *verbum* are run together so that they share an upright pen stroke; the *a* of *erat* is placed above the *t*. In the final line the vowels of *deum* and *deus* are omitted, and this is marked by a short line above the words. This last practice was one of many conventions for contracting and abbreviating words available to the scribe.

The lack of gaps between words was common in Latin texts – the inscriptions on neither the Franks Casket nor the Ruthwell Cross, for example, show word spacing. Latin possessed an easily recognizable pattern of word endings which made spaces less important. Writing in English, however, needed spaces since even in Old English word endings were less predictable. Word spacing soon became the norm in English scriptoria even when writing in Latin, and word spacing is used in the main text of the Lindisfarne Gospels.

Word endings in Old English are described in Chapter 3.

Figure 2.12 shows one of the lesser initials in this manuscript and illustrates the script used for the text. (I'll return to the smaller writing visible between the main lines later.) The handwriting is in a form that has come to be called 'insular majuscule', a large **book hand** first developed by the Christian scribes in Ireland. This script is a development of 'uncial' – the standard book hand used throughout the Roman empire in the fourth century AD and for some centuries after. Uncial was the Roman square capital (see Figure 2.8) modified to suit the action of a pen on parchment, as opposed to a chisel on stone. It is what is sometimes called a two-line script – all letters have the same height. When the Roman empire broke up, the different parts of Europe each developed their own 'national hands', and insular majuscule can be regarded as the first distinctively British script.

The word 'national' is placed in quotation marks here because at this time there were no nation states in the modern sense of the term. These emerged during the Renaissance (after c. 1500), as described in Chapter 4.

Figure 2.11   A scribe at work in the scriptorium
(Bibliothèque Nationale)

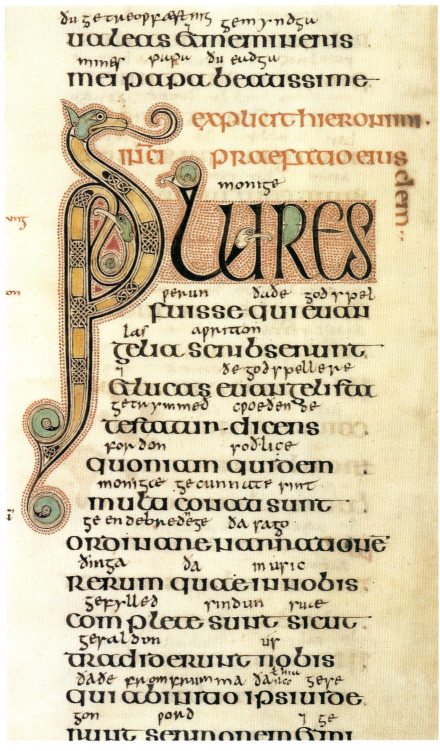

Figure 2.12   *The Lindisfarne Gospels folio 5v, showing the initial 'P' of the word 'Plures' at the start of St Jerome's Preface to the four gospels*

(British Library)

Although some letters (such as *b*) have extensions which rise above the height of other letters (ascenders) and some (such as *p*) have extensions which fall below (descenders), these extensions tend to be truncated, so that the script maintains a two-line character. Insular majuscule was the script used in the Lindisfarne scriptorium for prestigious, ceremonial books.

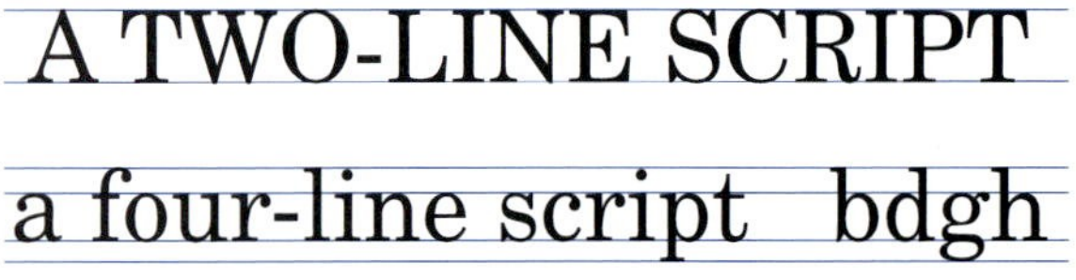

A TWO-LINE SCRIPT

a four-line script   bdgh

Figure 2.13
Two-line and four-line scripts

There was another hand used in ancient Northumbria that was a more cursive and less formal development of the insular majuscule. This hand was called 'insular minuscule', and was a true four-line script.

Insular minuscule began as a documentary hand and was used first for less important items, working drafts, business and legal texts. It was made into an acceptable book hand by the Northumbrian scriptoria, probably because it was quicker, and therefore cheaper, to copy books in it. For example, the scriptoria at Wearmouth-Jarrow were in the habit of using uncial as their main display script (as opposed to the insular majuscule of the Lindisfarne Gospels), but Parkes (1982) has argued that they changed their handwriting to meet the demand from the continent for copies of works by their best-selling author, the Venerable Bede. In other words they developed the insular minuscule into a fast but more presentable hand and began to use it instead of uncial.

Even when insular minuscule had been adopted as the main book hand, uncial might be used for headings and other important sections. In this way, different scripts acquired conventional meanings and the importance of different parts of texts could be signalled by a switch of script (see Figure 2.14). The distinction between a 'display' script for headings and a smaller, less decorative script for the main text anticipates modern typographic practice. The manuscript shown in Figure 2.14 also shows one of the earliest forms of punctuation: the hedera or ivy-leaf which separates the proverb from the commentary.

Within this hierarchy of scripts it was insular minuscule – the most humble of book hands – which became adopted for Old English. This is demonstrated within the Lindisfarne Gospels manuscript itself. An 'interlinear gloss' which provides a word-by-word translation into Old English between the lines of the original was added by Aldred the priest in the tenth century (see Figure 2.12). The text thus bears witness to the bilingual nature of learning and literacy at that period: the importance of Latin as the European lingua franca of Christian religion, science and scholarship, and the developing (but later) recognition of English vernacular as a vehicle of learning. Aldred's vernacular translation is written in a variety of insular minuscule.

Insular minuscule had to be adapted before it could be used for Old English. The Roman alphabet was augmented with extra letters, each with a special name, used to denote some sounds of Old English not found in Latin. The *thorn* (þ), used for the sound *th* in words like *thick,* and *wyn* (ƿ) used for the sound *w,* were taken from the futhorc. Also added was the letter *eth* (ð) used for the sound *th* in words like *the* and a new vowel, *ash* (æ). The letter *g* came to be shaped as ȝ and was called *yogh.* Old English did not use the *j, v, w* of the modern English alphabet, and only rarely *q* and *z.* The Old English alphabet thus included the letters shown in Figure 2.15.

The term 'minuscule' is used for any script formed from 'little' letters, many of which have ascenders and descenders. A 'cursive' script is one in which the letters tend to 'run' into one another.

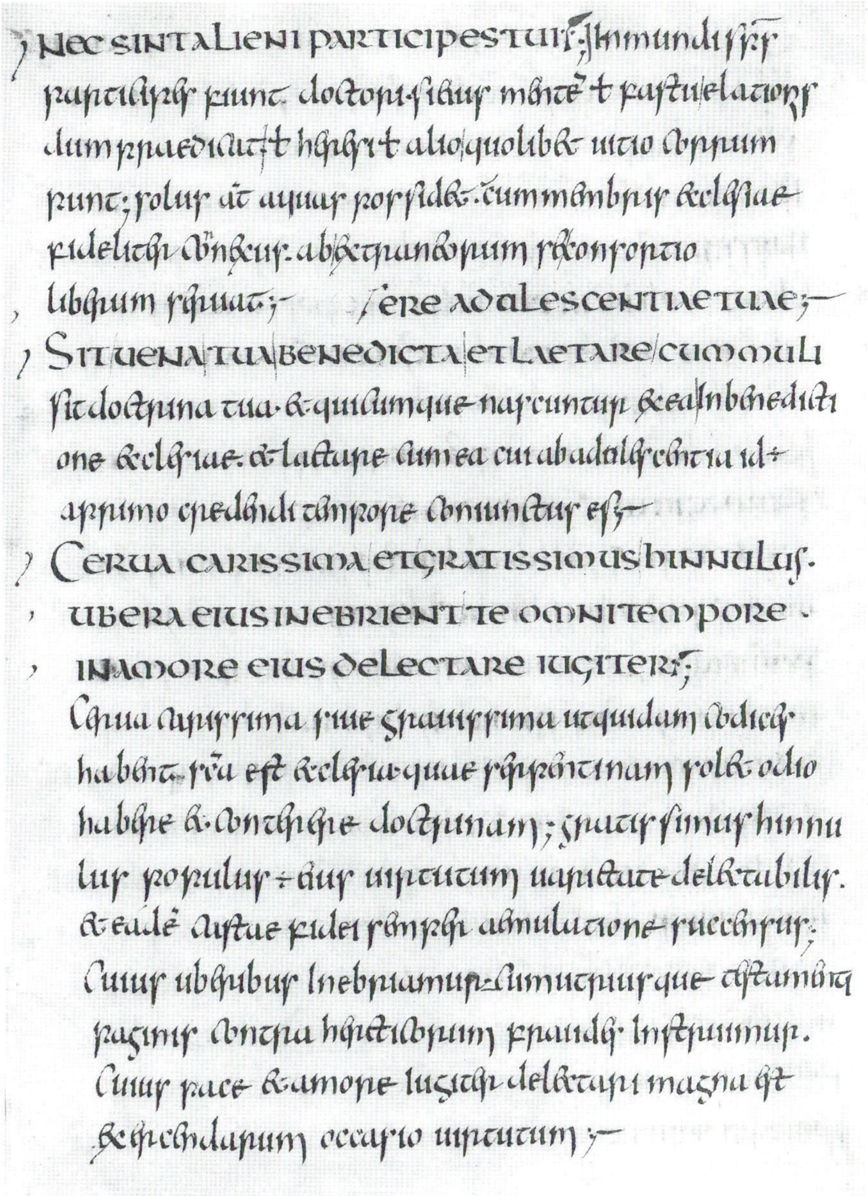

[Manuscript facsimile of Bede's commentary on the Book of Proverbs, written in uncial and insular minuscule script]

Figure 2.14   *Bede's commentary on the Book of Proverbs, in a copy made in the second half of the eighth century at Wearmouth-Jarrow. The proverbs are in uncial and the commentary by Bede is in insular minuscule. Conservation requirements prevent new colour photographs being taken of this manuscript*

(Bodleian Library)

a	æ	b	c	d	e	f	ȝ	h	i	k	l	m
n	o	p	r	s	t	þ	ð	u	ƿ	x	y	

Figure 2.15   *The Old English alphabet*

The earliest Old English writing appeared alongside Latin, and the relative statuses of the languages were signalled through use of script. Figure 2.16, for example, shows a later manuscript detailing the marvels of the east. Distant lands were conventionally described in exotic terms – the far-off isles of Britannia had themselves once been described by the Roman author Tacitus as containing such mythical creatures. Illustrated is a page from this manuscript, written at Winchester or Canterbury c. AD 1040. *The Marvels of the East* is bilingual by design. The (upper) Latin paragraphs are in a 'carolingian' script, whereas the Old English is in an insular minuscule.

The carolingian (sometimes called 'caroline') script was adopted by a decree of Charlemagne in AD 789. This was in part a 'back-to-basics' policy – to reassert earlier cultural values and forms of Roman writing among scripts that had 'degenerated' into a diversity of national hands. It was also politically motivated – an attempt to reintroduce a common book hand throughout western Europe. As it happened, the job of establishing this standard hand fell to Alcuin of York, an English scholar-priest who was then abbot at Tours. Carolingian script was a small, very legible and modern-looking writing which, because of Alcuin's involvement, drew in part on the Anglo-Saxon tradition. Like the insular hands it made no differentiation between capital and lower-case letters: initials were still marked by size and decoration rather than by different shape. Figure 2.17 contrasts the word *gallia* in the two scripts used in the manuscript. Note that the letter *a* in the new carolingian hand (as in the earlier uncial) has the form a, whereas in insular hands (both majuscule and minuscule) it has the form ɑ. In the carolingian script *g* has its modern form, while in the insular miniscule it retains the open (yogh) form (ȝ). Both scripts used the long *s* (ſ). A huge number of religious and classical works were copied into the new carolingian hand, and it became the respectful hand for religious and Latin texts in the ninth and tenth centuries.

Activity 2.2   *(Allow about 30 minutes)*

The manuscripts in Figures 2.12, 2.14 and 2.16 illustrate four styles of lettering: insular majuscule, insular minuscule, uncial and carolingian. Try to write out the four alphabets for yourself. You may find it helpful to prepare a sheet of paper with six columns. In the first two columns on the left write out the modern English alphabet in your own hand, in both capital letters and lower case. Leave space for the extra letters of Old English. Now try to find as many of the letters as possible in each manuscript hand and copy each letter into a column on your sheet of paper. This activity will take some time, but it is a good way of looking closely at the differences between the letter shapes of different hands.

The growth of learning in Old English

The emergence of books written in English was unusual. In no other part of Europe, except perhaps Ireland, did a tradition of vernacular literature emerge so early. Written Old English thus grew up in intimate contact with Latin, with the two languages acquiring a differentiated visual identity which reflected their

Figure 2.16 (above)
The Marvels of the East, written
c. AD 1040 at Winchester or
Canterbury. The text is bilingual –
with Old English below the Latin.
The Latin is written in an English
carolingian, the Old English in an
insular minuscule
(British Library)

Figure 2.17 The word gallia
in Latin (far left) and Old
English (left). Note the
different shape of g and a in
the carolingian and insular
scripts
(British Library)

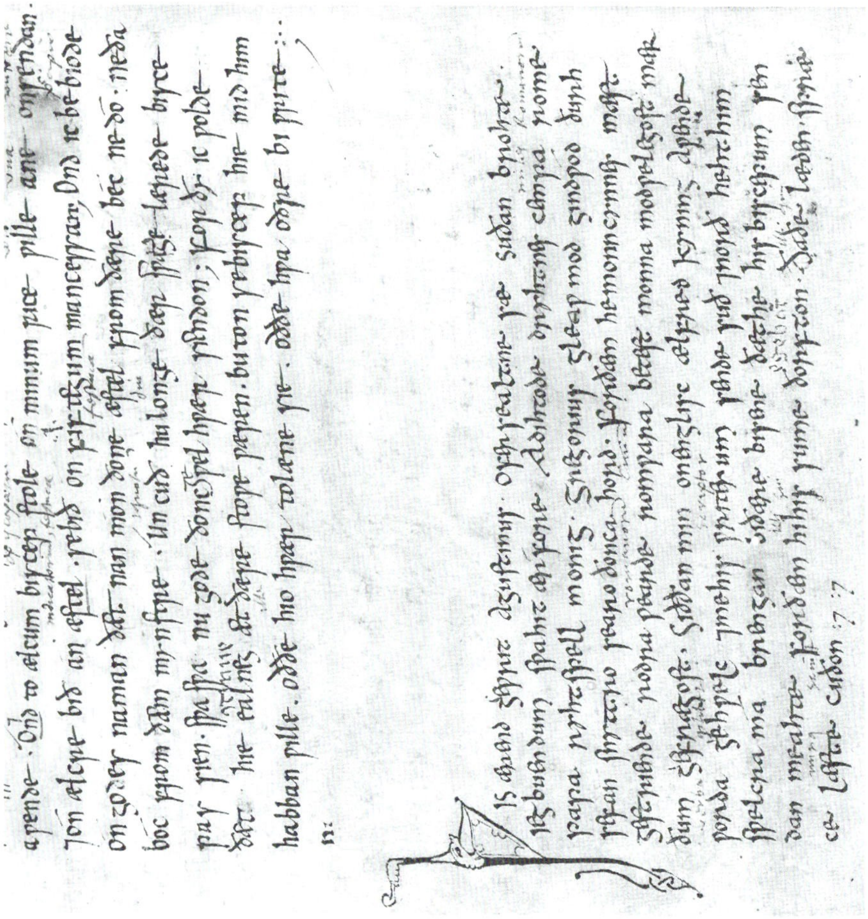

Figure 2.19 A page from the epic Old English poem Beowulf (British Library)

Figure 2.18 Alfred's Preface to his Old English translation of Pope Gregory the Great's Pastoral Care. Written c. AD 890, probably at Winchester (Bodleian Library)

different statuses and functions. In the ninth century, when northern monasteries had been attacked and destroyed – by Viking raiders from Scandinavia, according to many accounts – the focus of book production and learning shifted further south. By the end of the ninth century King Alfred had apparently become concerned about what he perceived as falling standards of literacy and learning, and in c. AD 890 he issued a document known as the Preface to the *Pastoral Care*. The *Pastoral Care* itself was a work composed some 300 years earlier by Pope Gregory the Great, which Alfred translated into Old English. In his Preface he appeals to his bishops to assist in the renewal of learning by translating more works into the vernacular (see Figure 2.18).

From this time on a great many manuscripts and books were written in Old English, and by no means only religious texts. Perhaps the most famous of all Old English literary texts is *Beowulf*, an epic poem concerning the origins of the first English settlers – the Germanic people described by Bede. The poem is known only through a single tenth-century manuscript, but it was probably originally composed in the seventh century (see Figure 2.19).

2.4   THE MIDDLE ENGLISH PERIOD

The eleventh century was a key period in the history of the English language, marking the transition between Old English and Middle English. One of the historical events traditionally regarded as triggering major changes in the English language is the so-called Norman conquest. Chapter 3 examines the linguistic consequences of the conquest more closely, but for now we can note that after the invasion fewer documents were written in English. Some were written in French, which became the fashionable language of the court, but even more striking was the extent to which Latin regained its position as the language of record. One historian of this period remarks:

> On the whole, Norman administrators probably had less experience than Anglo-Saxon ones of written records, and the Normans before 1066 had not shown such a consistent interest as the Anglo-Saxons in recording their history and institutions in literate forms ...
>
> In the eyes of contemporaries on the European continent Latin was the only language of record; a person unfamiliar with it was illiterate.
>
> (Clanchy, 1993, pp. 26–7)

Although manuscripts continued to be made using more or less the same methods as before, there was less use of illustration and more emphasis on the text. Since fewer texts were in English, the carolingian hand became more widely used. One of the best-known texts from this period, written in Latin in the carolingian script, is shown in Figure 2.20. This is the Domesday Book, the great survey of English estates and inhabitants made for William the Conqueror and completed in AD 1086.

The carolingian book hand evolved during the twelfth century into a narrower form in which round strokes became straightened and squared. This script was called 'gothic' or black letter and evolved partly from an increasing need in ceremonial manuscripts for an ornate script that was more economical of space. It also reflected the use of a reed rather than a quill pen and, in large measure, changing aesthetic ideas in which a trend towards tall perpendicular, ornamented

Figure 2.20
An extract from the Domesday Book, written in the carolingian hand, completed in 1086
(Record Office)

forms was apparent in architecture as well as writing. This was the era in which many of the great European cathedrals were built, such as Canterbury and York Minster in England. Frederic Goudy, an American calligrapher and typographer, describes the emergence of gothic lettering as follows:

> Gothic letters are essentially written forms made with one stroke of the slanted pen, and while the Caroline letters written in the same way kept an open, round appearance, in the Gothic, for the sake of greater economy of space, the curves were reduced to straight lines (at first of scarcely varying thickness), making the letters narrower, more angular, and stiffer, until the written page was made up of rows of perpendicular thick strokes connected at the top & bottom by oblique hairlines.

(Goudy [1942] 1963, p. 66)

gothic minuscule

Figure 2.21   Gothic handwriting as reconstructed
by Goudy (1942)
(Goudy [1942] 1963, p. 66)

Commercial manuscript production

Towards the end of the twelfth century the church lost its near-monopoly over the making of manuscripts. Monasteries had for a long time employed secular scribes in order to maintain production, and these scriveners began to form their own guilds (which were an early form of trade union) and workshops. Secular books expanded in number and scribal workshops diversified. The need for such secular workshops arose from the emergence of a merchant class who required official documents to be drawn up. These middle classes also began to demand books – on philosophy, science, logic, mathematics, astronomy.

More authors began to write in the vernacular, though Latin was still the dominant language for scientific writing throughout Europe. They produced works in English on cookery, educational matters, medical manuals and literature. A client who wished to commission, for example, a copy of *The Song of Roland*, might visit a stationer who would act as an agent (a role not dissimilar to that of the modern publisher), and commission a copy with the client's preferred calligraphic style and type of illustration.

The European universities had appeared in the twelfth and thirteenth centuries, and with them a new demand from students. Students could not afford to commission copies, but might hire a book from a workshop and make notes. Increasingly, then, individuals needed to learn the skills of writing in order to create documents for their personal, trade and business use.

Figure 2.22   Part of a specimen sheet of an Oxford scribe c. 1340, displaying to customers of a scrivener's shop the range of gothic scripts in which manuscripts could be commissioned (Bodleian Library)

Ye have bene sike I dar myne hede assure
Or late fed in a feynte pasture
lifte up your hede be glade take no sorowe
And ye shale home ryde with us to morowe
I sey when ye rusted have your fylle
After sorpere slepe wyle do none ylle
Wrap welle your hede with clothes rounde aboute
Stronge notte alle wole make you to route
take a pillowe that ye ly not lowe
Of nede be spare not for to blowe
to holde wynde by myne opynyon
wole engendre collica passyon
And make men to groven on there ropys
When they have fylled wele þer cropys
But towarde nyght ete som fenuele sede
Anyse Comyne or Coryaundre rede
And lyke as I power have and myght
I charge you ryse not at mydnyght
though it be so the moone shyne clere
I wole my selfe be youre orlogere
to morowe erly when I see my tyme
ffor we wole forthe percase afore pryme
And company parde shale do you glade
What loke up youke for be kokes blode
thow shalt be mutye who þ that sey nay
ffor tomorowe anone as yt is day
And that it tyme in the Este to dawe
thow shalt be bounde to a newe lawe
At goynge oute of Caunterbury Toun
And lay afyde thy professyon
thow shalt not chese ne thy sylf withdrawe
yiff ony myrthe be founden in thy mawe
lik the costume of this companye
ffor none so hardy that dare me denye
knyght ne knave Chanon prest ne nonne
to tel a tale playnly as they konne
When I assygne and se tyme oportune
And for that we oure purpos wole contynue
we wole homwarde the same custome use
And thow shalt not platly the excuse
Be nowe wele ware stydye wele this nyght
But for al this be of hert lyght
thy wit shal be the sharper and ye bet
And we anone were to sopere set
And sodede wele unto oure plesaunce
And some afaste with glade contynaunce
Unto bedd gothe every maner wyght
And towarde morow anon as it was lyght
Every pilgryme bothe bet and worse
than bad oure Hoste take anone his horse
When ye sonne rose in the Este ful clere
ffully in purpos to kom to oure dynere

Howe the monke wt ye pilgremes departyde from
Oure Ostynge and broke ther oure faste at Caunbury
And when we weryn fro Caunbury past

Not the space of a bowe draught
Oure Ooste in haste hath my brydele raught
And to me seyde as ye were in game
kome forth Dann Iohn by þ Cristen name
And let us make some maner myrthe or play
Shete youre porelwes sleventy devyse way
Ot is no disporte þ to pathe and þ seye
Ot wole make youre lippes wondre dreye
tele some tale and make therof no tape
ffor by my rouncye thow shal not escape
But preche not of none hohynesse
Gynne some tale of myrthe and of gladnesse
And nod not so with thy hevy heed
tel us some thinge that drawith of to speke
Onely of joye and make no lengere lette
And when I sawghte it wolde be no bette
I obeyed unto his byddynge
And as the lawe me bounde in alle thynge
As I koude with a ful pale chere
My tale I ganne anone as ye shal here

Explicit prologus

Prima pars
Here begynneth the Segge of Thebes ful
lamentably tolde by John lidgate monke of
Bury annexynge it to ye tales of Caunbury

Sirs quod I sith of youre Curtesye
I entered am into youre Companye
And admytted a tale for to tele
By hym that hath power to compele
I mene oure Hoste governere and gyde
Of youre erthone rydynge here besyde
Thogh my wit bareyne be and dulle
I wolle reherce a sorry wonderfulle
tonchynge the segge and destruccyon
Of worthy Thebes the myghty royale Toun
Bilt and bygonne of olde antiquite
Upon the tyme of worthy Iosue
By diligence of kynge Amphion
Cheeff cause first of this foundacyon

A typical literary manuscript from the late Middle English period is shown in Figure 2.23. John Lydgate's *The Siege of Thebes* was composed c. AD 1421 and this manuscript produced about 40 years later as a gift for the king (either Henry VI or Edward IV). The writing is in a gothic hand typical of this period. The miniature painting, contrary to common practice during the Old English period, illustrates the content of the work rather than acting as decoration to the text. The third figure from the left is probably Lydgate himself, and the other figures are characters from Chaucer's Prologue to *The Canterbury Tales* (the second from the left may be Chaucer). This section of Lydgate's text is also a prologue – to a proposed 'additional' tale.

Other features of the manuscript show continuity with earlier traditions: the manuscript divides the page into two columns; there is a rubric which provides a caption to the picture; the initial letter at the beginning of a section is decorated. Some of the special letters used in the Old English manuscript have now been dropped – *yogh* (ȝ) now appears as *gh*, *eth* (ð) has been dropped in favour of *th*, but *thorn* (þ) is still also occasionally used. There is still no punctuation except for a mid point (like a full stop but placed at mid height) marking each half-line. The long *s* (∫) is occasionally used, but not at the end of words.

Punctuation in English

Early manuscripts employed very little in the way of punctuation marks. Scribes used space and decoration to divide texts into structural units, though they sometimes adopted the Latin convention of using points, or stops, to mark breaks within the text. Various kinds of point existed – raised, mid and low – and these typically marked anything from word breaks to paragraphs. The carolingian writing reforms introduced some new marks, thought to have come from musical notation, which helped the reader to adopt an appropriate intonation. Such marks included what became exclamation and question marks. But the majority of modern punctuation marks were introduced into English after the invention of printing.

Until about 1700 such punctuation as existed was designed to help someone reading aloud: marks indicated suitable places for pausing or breathing, or guided the inflection of the voice. Gradually, the practice emerged of using punctuation to mark grammatical structure – such as clauses and sentences – and to guide a reader's interpretation of a text. By the eighteenth century punctuation in English looked much as it does today. There remains an ambiguity in modern English as to whether punctuation should reflect grammatical boundaries or potential reading behaviour.

In the fourteenth century English again began to replace Norman French and Latin as a language of record. Latin, however, continued to be used for many formal legal documents until the eighteenth century, despite various attempts to promote the use of English.

By the fifteenth century economic growth had led to the writing of many more business documents. A clear distinction emerged between the slow, 'print' lettering of the book hands and the faster, more cursive business hands. These business hands were known collectively as 'court hands', and the style of writing as 'bastard' (that is, a cross between a formal book hand and the kind of fast cursive used for personal writing).

2.5 HANDWRITING AFTER THE INVENTION OF PRINTING

The Lydgate manuscript dates from a significant period in English book production, since the earliest printed books had already been made in Germany and the first book to be printed in English was soon to appear, in 1473. The coming of printing had a profound effect on the look of English books and on the status of handwriting. The need for a book hand, for example, all but disappeared, and after the fifteenth century handwriting was used almost exclusively for commercial, legal and personal purposes. By the sixteenth century, in the period of English known as 'early modern English', there was a diversity of hands for such needs, of which two were in common use.

The first was the italic hand. Italic writing became popular in England after about 1550 and was often used for documents in Latin and as a display script in manuscripts written in English – for headings, titles and occasionally for emphasis. It was used especially by women, for whom the alternative hands were thought too closely associated with the male preserve of business. Martin Billingsley, author of *The Pens Excellencie* (1618), commented:

> it is conceiued to be easiest hand that is written with Pen, and to be taught in the shortest time: Therefore it is vsually taught to women, for as much as they (hauing not the patience to take any great paines, besides phantasticall and humorsome) must be taught that which they may instantly learne?
>
> (Cited in Dawson and Kennedy-Skipton, 1968, p. 10)

The usual business hand in the Elizabethan era was a development of the bastard hand called the 'secretary' . This was used not only in England but also in the American colonies, where business and legal interests were fast developing. However, after about 1700 use of the secretary hand everywhere declined in favour of the italic.

The Latin documents produced in various governmental departments had by this time each developed their own more ornamented and distinctive styles. This maintained the tradition of using different scripts for different languages or, rather, for the different functions that different languages served. Hector remarks:

> The departmental set hands were all the products of a more or less self-conscious search for distinctiveness. This fact alone would have prevented them, or any one of them, from setting standards of utility and legibility; and their use for the most formal purposes was bound to result in their being written almost exclusively by a relatively small, and relatively humble, class of specialist clerks and copyists. Their highly mannered style was completely divorced from the circumstances of everyday life, and ... by the middle of the 17th century they had come to be regarded as part of the apparatus of professional mystification.
>
> (Hector, 1966, p. 66)

As handwriting grew in importance as both a business and educational accomplishment, so manuals and handbooks for the teaching of writing proliferated. Such books showed examples of writing by means of copperplate engravings, but this meant that the model scripts they presented reflected the behaviour of an engraving tool rather than a pen; the width of the lines, for example, depended

Figure 2.24   Two examples of Elizabethan handwriting: (top) secretary hand as used by Richard Broughton, 1597; (bottom) italic as used by Lady Lettice Kynnersley, c. 1615

(Folger Shakespeare Library)

This bearer y[ou]r s[er]u[an]t will sufficientlie exemple but you all
this travaill here, w[i]th the circumstance so that therein I will
not trouble you w[i]th any discours: but excuse this longer tarieng
then he was willinge vnto, by reason that in respect of this terme
both m[aste]r Barroll and my selfe happened to some more busines then
we determine so that we can but starte to bespurre &c &c. and trust you
will hold him excused his owne fault is not long that cometh at lengthe.
aboute the compasse of oneEday of July m[aste]r Barroll and I accompanied
w[i]th two youthes my brothers entend to see you, and from thence to
passe at Bridgnorth the uery best time. and to retorne to
passe at Stafford. and from that day till the middes
of August I will remayne at my pleasure we all likinge to make
... reporte of tyme. from the middes of August till mighelmas
... I thinke I shall haue occasion to make a progresse in Southwales
...

Good brother my husband doeth earnestley intreate you. to doo so mu[ch]
for him: as send for my cosen Pettie. and pay him this :5:
which you shall reseue bie this bearer. and I pray you. will
him to make anote vnder his hand. what he hath reseued: I
thank him he is willing to reseue it bie:20: at many til:80:
be run vp: and so I hope my husband will be able to pay it.
the first payment of twenti pound. he geueth at sent James tite:
he had thought to haue com him selfe. but for his trobelsome nighte
loue: good brother will you do somuch for me. she ernest with

Figure 2.25   The engraved frontispiece for Bickham's
The Universal Penman, 1741, with title in ornamented
gothic letters and text in copperplate italic
(Bickham [1741] 1941)

on pressure on the pen rather than the angle at which it was held. People started to use pointed, rather than edged, pens to achieve this effect in handwriting: under pressure on the downward stroke the points of the pen splayed out and so gave extra width. One of the most popular works on writing in the eighteenth century, illustrating this copperplate italic style, was George Bickham's *Universal Penman*. 'Writing is the first step, and essential in furnishing out the Man of Business … In order to write well, there must be Rules given, and much Practice to put 'em into Execution.'

Copperplate was a more open, rounded version of the italic favoured by women but was originally developed by the writing masters of the eighteenth century as a more 'robust and manly' hand suited to English commercial purposes. It became known, indeed, as the 'English round hand' and was used throughout the English-speaking world for over a century. This, then, was the main hand of British colonial administration.

Although the shift to copperplate italic was not strictly a change of script, it marked a radical change in writing behaviour. A quill pen, such as that used by medieval monks, needed to be held vertically so that the ink flowed smoothly. It was held in such a way that it could easily be pulled laterally but very little vertical pressure could be applied. It was more difficult to make upward movements than sideways or downwards ones because the quill nib was more easily pulled than pushed, hence the tendency to create a rounded letter such as 'o' with two downward strokes, lifting the pen from the page. A downward stroke used the full width of the pen nib, whereas a sideways stroke made a thin line. The modulation between thin and thick lines thus arose from the direction of movement, and from the slope of the pen. With copperplate, however, modulation of thickness arose from pressure on the pen, hence both a different kind of pen and a different way of holding it were required.

❖   ❖   ❖   ❖   ❖

Activity 2.3   *(Allow about 10 minutes)*

To do this exercise you might like to use tracing paper.

Below are examples of various styles of writing. Copy each line of text as closely as you can. If possible use a variety of pens such as a traditional-edged fountain pen, a fountain pen with a pointed nib which splays under pressure, and a modern ballpoint or felt-tip pen. Experiment with different pens, and with holding them different ways (in both the medieval manner described above, using directional movement to alter line thickness, and in the modern manner, using pressure on the pen to change line thickness). Observe what happens to the script when you change pen or method. Which scripts can be produced with a modern ballpoint pen?

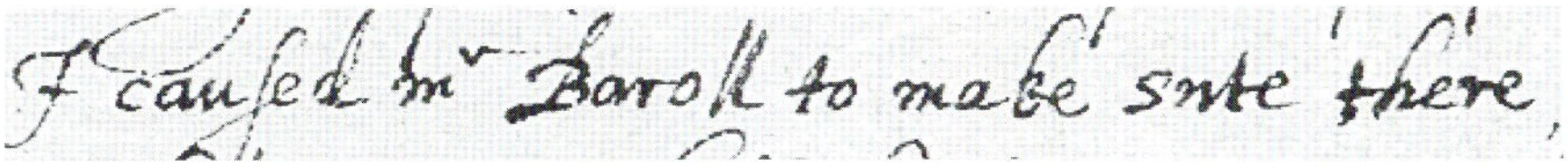

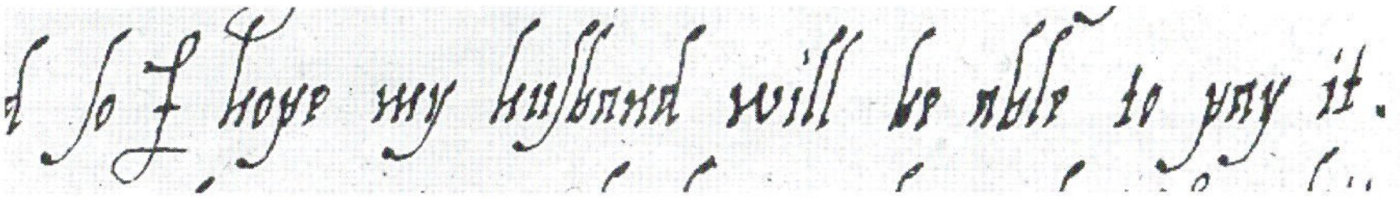

❖   ❖   ❖   ❖   ❖

Writing in the English colonies tended to follow the European models. In America in the eighteenth century writing masters would boast that they could write in 'all the known hands of Great Britain'. One such master was Abiah Holbrook, who died in Boston in 1769. Figure 2.26 shows a reproduction of his writing as it appeared in a book published a century later and reprinted as recently as 1957. It is clear that the 'known hands of Great Britain' included both gothic lettering and copperplate.

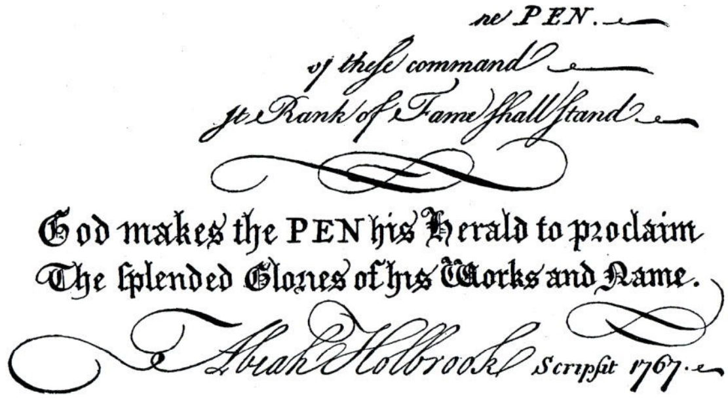

Figure 2.26   The handwriting of Abiah Holbrook, an eighteenth-century writing master from Boston

(Earle, 1899, p. 155)

Handwriting in the nineteenth century

When elementary education became widely available in the nineteenth century young children from all social classes needed to be taught how to write. For the first time writing became a matter for the ordinary citizen, and many made use of it in their later lives for private correspondence and leisure activities. Indeed, schools today remain one of the few institutional locations where extended handwritten documents are to be found.

In the early nineteenth century there was considerable uncertainty as to the form of script that should be taught to children. All subjects in the elementary school had to be taught in ways that maintained both the social order of the classroom and the wider social order based on stable social class relations. For the Victorians, teaching children to write raised a number of moral, economic and political issues: teaching working-class boys a business hand might encourage them to aspire to jobs that were not open to them, yet the teaching of different styles to different children was costly and divisive.

Crellin (1989) suggests that the English educational establishment was reluctant to implement a single, standard script in schools. The reasons for this were partly a political dislike of monopolies – a single script would require the adoption of a standard copybook – and partly a belief in England that writing, like other aspects of education, was an essential aspect of personal development and expression, and should not be regarded as a narrow vocational matter. There was a continuing debate about what style of writing to teach, and whether a single, general purpose style could be envisaged which was suitable for both middle and working classes, and for both boys and girls. One of the most influential styles was created by an Irish philanthropist, Vere Foster. After using his wealth for some time to help young women from poor Irish families to emigrate to America, Foster turned his attention to schools and to the problem of how to improve children's handwriting. As one school inspector remarked of handwriting: 'it enters more largely than any other literary attainment into the qualification of a boy for clerkships and kindred situations; and furthermore, it is the chief test by which the parents judge of their children's progress at school' (cited in McNeill, 1971, p. 129).

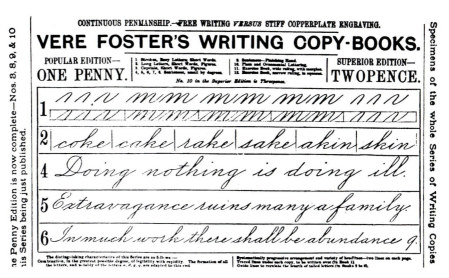

Figure 2.27   An advert for one of Vere Foster's copybooks
(McNeill, 1971, p. 131)

Vere Foster had once worked under the British prime minister, Lord Palmerston, and remembered his insistence on the importance of legible handwriting among government officials.

> As early as 1854, Lord Palmerston had written to Committee of Council asking them to improve the writing taught in schools, Copperplate was becoming narrower and more slanting; its ascenders and descenders had grown even longer until they crossed with lines above and below. It was less legible than the styles of the 18th century, and its fine hairstrokes could not be picked up by the duplicating systems then in use. It was slow. But recruits to the civil service who had come from the classical schools had a style of writing which, though different, was equally unsuitable. It was casually illegible. Palmerston recommended that pupils should be taught 'rather to imitate broad printing than fine Copperplate engraving'. Ten years later there had been no improvement; and the civil service commissioners were obliged to say that in their examinations 'we do not demand or desire that the writing should be of any particular style, provided that it possesses the main characteristics of legibility'.
>
> Palmerston invited Vere-Foster to visit him. He criticised and altered some of the copy lines, and allowed the resulting copybooks to come out in 1865 under the title 'Palmerston Series'. Within three years Vere-Foster was encouraged to carry the reform even further, and the Civil Service Hand had arrived.
>
> Vere-Foster's ... upright, squat and simple style buried Copperplate and The Ladies' Angular Hand in one go ...
>
> Until the enthusiasm for Italic writing in the 1950s, Britain had one common cursive hand. It was a style without the exactness or the beauty of Copperplate. In the hands of different people, it developed all sorts of personal idiosyncracies [sic] of slope or shape.
>
> (Crellin, 1989, pp. 6–7)

Crellin argues that Vere Foster was responsible for the disuse of the 'English round hand' and the creation of a general purpose style of writing – one used by men and women yet showing considerable individual variation. But Vere Foster's solution was not universally accepted; even where it was, the hand taught was still rounded and open. It was, as a result of its roundness, regarded as being more suitable for vocational than for personal use, and this of course meant a hand suited to boys who might expect to gain employment as clerks. There was a resistance to the round hand from girls' schools:

> Female pupils, especially those whose parents are in comfortable circum-
> stances, object to the roundness of style which characterizes the advanced
> or 'finishing' headlines … headlines of angular hand … would render
> those copy-books more popular in Girls' schools than they are at present.
>
> (Cited in McNeill, 1971, p. 136)

We see here how habits of handwriting continued to be stratified by social class and gender. Roundness, as with the earlier secretary hand, was a signifier of trade – a spikier hand was regarded as more fitting for young ladies' personal letter writing.

The quotation from Crellin ends with a reference to a revival of italic handwriting in Britain in the 1950s. In 1952 Alfred Fairbank founded the Society for Italic Handwriting, but this was probably the last high point of the arts and crafts movement, which had started at the beginning of the century among a group of artists and calligraphers who shared a commitment to the maintenance of traditional craft skills in an age of increasing mechanization. An example of Fairbank's model italic is shown in Figure 2.28.

In the seventeenth century it used to be said that one could tell from the handwriting in which department of the government a document had been produced. In other words, slight differences in style were to be explained by the

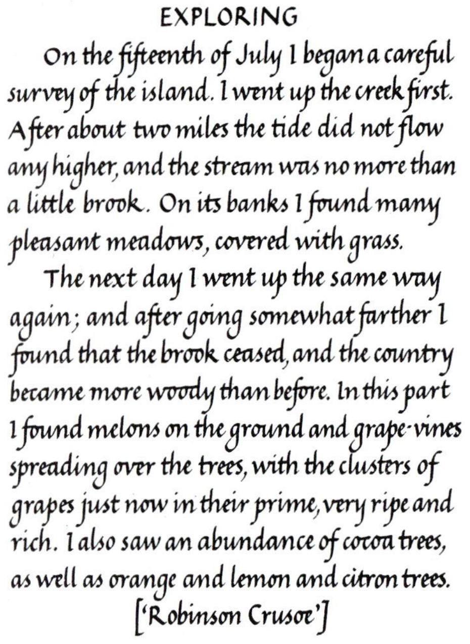

EXPLORING

On the fifteenth of July I began a careful survey of the island. I went up the creek first. After about two miles the tide did not flow any higher, and the stream was no more than a little brook. On its banks I found many pleasant meadows, covered with grass.

The next day I went up the same way again; and after going somewhat farther I found that the brook ceased, and the country became more woody than before. In this part I found melons on the ground and grape-vines spreading over the trees, with the clusters of grapes just now in their prime, very ripe and rich. I also saw an abundance of cocoa trees, as well as orange and lemon and citron trees.

['Robinson Crusoe']

Figure 2.28   Fairbank italic
(Fairbank, 1968, plate 80)

rigorous way in which house styles of different institutions were imposed on individual clerks. The reality, of course, was that the everyday writing of most people showed considerable individual style. Although some consistency in copperplate business hands emerged during the eighteenth century, the legacy of the Victorian education system has been a lack of a single, standard style of handwriting in English schools. School systems in some areas of the USA, Canada and Australia have been more vigorous in demanding a particular form of script. Nevertheless, there is a widespread idea in the English-speaking world that handwritten documents can (and should) betray the identity of an individual more readily than that of the institution within which the writer was trained.

Related to this shift in the perception of handwriting has been a decline in the importance of handwritten English in public communication. By the turn of the twentieth century typewriters were increasingly being used for business correspondence, and handwriting gradually lost even its commercial function in the developed countries. Handwriting in the modern era has thus moved almost completely from the public to the private sphere and is now used primarily for personal writing – notes, drafts of material to be made public in other forms, private letters and diaries. Perhaps the main residual public use of handwriting is for filling in the forms and questionnaires that structure an individual citizen's interactions with the state (e.g. tax forms) and other bureaucratic organizations (such as banks and educational institutions). In these documents the writer is often instructed to use 'block capitals', showing how capital lettering has largely become the modern 'print' style of writing.

Activity 2.4   *(Allow about 5 minutes)*

Can you remember how you were taught to write in school? Do any of the descriptions of technique or style of script given above remind you of your schooling? To what extent were you encouraged to develop your own style?

Try asking these questions of friends and family members. Do any differences emerge which might relate to age, or to the geographical area in which individuals were taught, or to the kinds of school they attended?

2.6   ORTHOGRAPHIES OF ENGLISH: TRADITION AND REFORM

The appearance of words in English reflects the inventory of letters used (the Roman alphabet), the way these letters are shaped in a particular style of handwriting or typeface in printed texts and the way these letter shapes are used in particular words (the spelling). The term **orthography** (literally 'correct writing') embraces all these things.

In this section I discuss changes in attitude towards standard spelling, and the surprising number of attempts that have occurred to reform English orthography, not just by reforming spelling but by making radical changes in the alphabet itself.

Spelling in Old and Middle English

There is a mistaken view that in early times the spelling of English reflected the capricious whims of individual scribes. In fact, spelling in Old English manuscripts was based largely on practice in Latin, with modifications required to accommodate the different sound systems of English. I have already described, for example, how Old English manuscripts adopted some runic characters to represent the sounds which, in modern English, are spelled *th*. Although the spelling of words tended to reflect local dialect features and differed to some extent from one region to another, there was within each dialect area a certain consistency of approach. But it is only from the time of King Alfred that a sufficient number of contemporary Old English texts exist to permit a clear analysis of spelling. At that time spelling seems to have been fairly standardized, and Old English spelling provided a more accurate representation of current pronunciation than present-day orthography does. One reason why a strong standard emerged was because books at that period were being produced from a relatively small area in which there was both little dialect variation and effective institutional control.

Chapter 3 examines the relationship between spelling and pronunciation in Old and Middle English

The Norman invasion led to the collapse of this standard, and to increasing regionalism of spelling. Such regionalism had at least two causes. The first was that English developed striking dialect differences: northern parts of the country continued to be influenced by Scandinavian languages while parts of the south were affected by intimate contact with French. Figure 2.29 shows some of the variation in the Middle English spelling of 'such' in southern England. McIntosh (1969) has suggested that certain differences in spelling, for example the variant spellings of 'such' – *swilk, swich, soch* – indicated differences in pronunciation, even though it is not possible to tell with any precision exactly *what* each pronunciation might have been.

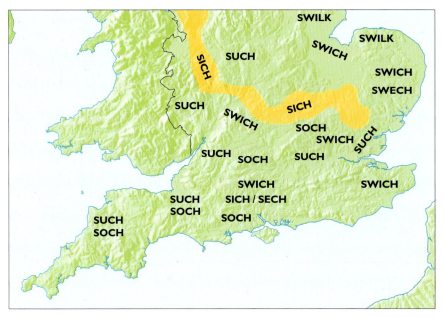

Figure 2.29   *Distribution of different spellings of 'such' in Middle English, according to Samuels* (Samuels, 1969, p. 408)

There were, however, some differences in spelling that did not imply differences in pronunciation; they simply reflected different habits of spelling. This kind of variation was common in Middle English times because English scribal practices were influenced by the practices of French, leading to a confusion of the principles for representing sounds. For example, words such as *cwene* (queen) came to be spelled, according to the Norman French convention, as *quene*, thus introducing *qu* into the spelling repertoire of English. Words spelled with the Old English thorn (þ) were usually respelled by Norman scribes with *th*, and so on. McIntosh (1969) has argued that such differences in spelling should be carefully studied as they can yield valuable information that can help to identify the source of a manuscript.

There is no doubt that the arrival of printing helped consolidate and establish fixed patterns in English spelling, but the process got off to an uncertain start. Caxton, the first person to print books in English, is sometimes credited with standardizing English spelling but this had already been accomplished to some extent by the scriveners' guilds. Printing did, however, have a major standardizing effect in so far as every reader now possessed identical copies of a work.

By the eighteenth century English spelling had reached more or less the state in which we find it today. Unfortunately the fixing of spellings rather than conventions to indicate pronunciation has led to a situation in which English spelling better reflects the pronunciation of several centuries ago than that of the present day. English spelling thus provides a witness to history: to changes in pronunciation; to the changing economics of manuscript production; and to the standardizing effects of printing. It also reflects a number of minor reforms to spelling that have taken place over the last three centuries or so.

The reformers

There have been many campaigns to reform English spelling and indeed the whole orthographic system; a significant number of influential people, including well-known writers, linguists and publishers, have long argued the cause. Many proposals have sought to make English orthography more **phonetic** – that is, to make spelling reflect more closely the pronunciation of modern English, letter by letter.

John Hart, author of several early books on English spelling, argued in 1569 that 'writing should have so many letters as the pronunciation neadeth voices and no more or less'. The orthography of modern English falls a long way short of such an 'ideal' for several reasons:

1   There are far more distinctive sounds (or **phonemes**, see box) in spoken English than there are letters in the Roman alphabet. In the accents of many British speakers, for example, there are around 45 phonemes which need to be represented.

2   Because there are insufficient letters they are not used in a simple way to represent particular sounds: one of the commonest techniques in English orthography is the use of 'digraphs' – two letters together which represent a single sound such as *ch, sh, ee*.

3   Even taking the need for digraphs into account, there is no systematic correspondence between letters and sounds in English. For example, the *c* in 'medicine' and 'medical' are pronounced in different ways. On the

other hand, a *k* sound might sometimes be represented by *k* (as in 'kiss'), sometimes by *c* (as in 'medical'), sometimes by *ch* (as in 'Christian'), and so on.

4   In an ideal phonemic orthography the representation of pronunciation should operate in a linear fashion, but in English spelling you sometimes have to look to the end of a word to work out how an earlier vowel should be pronounced. The most common example is the final 'silent' *e* in words like 'pine' (as opposed to 'pin') or 'tape' (as opposed to 'tap').

Chapter 3 examines more closely the different ways in which English orthography has represented sounds, and some of the changes in pronunciation that have further complicated matters. Here I want to examine the many attempts that have been made to reform English orthography since English spelling became more or less fixed.

Identifying phonemes

A phonemic transcription is one that represents all the significant contrasts between the vowels and consonants of a language. Linguists often use the technique of 'minimal pairs' to identify phonemes. The English words *tin* and *din* are a minimal pair: they are identical apart from their initial sound. Switching these sounds – changing *t* to *d* – produces a different English word. On the other hand, even though the vowel in *tin* is usually longer than the one in *tick* (try saying *tin* and *tick* to yourself, listening carefully to how you pronounce the vowel in each), this is not a phonemic difference because we can't find a minimal pair of words in which switching these shorter and longer variants of *i* creates a different word. Strictly speaking, most so-called phonetic spelling reforms attempt to be phonemic, rather than phonetic. That is, they usually represent significant contrasts rather than minor details of pronunciation and accent.

Activity 2.5   *(Reading A)*

Read 'Extending the Roman alphabet' by David Abercrombie (Reading A), which describes a number of attempts to change both the spelling and alphabet of English during the sixteenth, seventeenth and eighteenth centuries. He argues that the Roman alphabet is not well suited to representing the pronunciation of English and he reviews proposals for alternative, or extended, systems.

Spelling reform faces a number of technical problems, as Abercrombie (1981) describes, but even more intractable are problems connected to culture, politics and economics. There have always been vested interests (in publishing and education, for example) which would be put to enormous inconvenience, discomfort and cost by the introduction of a new orthography. And there is a further problem inherent in any phonetic writing system: how to cater for variation in pronunciation.

English is pronounced in diverse ways – both regionally within Britain (which of all English-speaking countries probably contains the greatest variation of accent) and globally between countries. For example, some English speakers make a distinction between *father* and *farther* by pronouncing an *r* sound in the second word, while others (including speakers of the British accent known as Received Pronunciation) do not make a distinction. So a phonetic spelling system is faced with a difficult choice – does it spell a word like *farther* in a standard way, or does it allow different speakers to spell in accordance with their own accent? If it elects to do the former, then one accent is privileged over others, and people who speak with other accents will either find themselves no better off than before (because for them the spelling system is not phonetic) or be expected to change the way they speak – to adopt the pronunciations represented by the standard writing. If the latter option is followed (as happened to a certain extent with spelling reform in Norway in 1957), then there is no single standard spelling for words, and books may have to be published in a variety of editions.

The American dictionary maker Noah Webster tried to turn these problems to advantage in the late eighteenth century. He argued that American spelling should be reformed in order to create a new visual identity for American English suitable for the newly independent state. Present-day differences in American and British spelling derive largely from Webster's work ([1789] 1991), although they are a great deal less radical than his original proposals.

Activity 2.6   *(Reading B)*

Read the extract from Noah Webster's 'An essay on the necessity, advantages and practicability of reforming the mode of spelling, and of rendering the orthography of words correspondent to the pronunciation' (Reading B). Note the various political, cultural and economic arguments that Webster makes for orthographic reform.

Phonetic spelling reform acquired little institutional support or financial backing in Britain until the middle of the nineteenth century when the publisher Sir Isaac Pitman introduced a system of shorthand writing that he called 'phonography'. The system was intended to facilitate rapid transcription of spoken language, whether for the dictation of business correspondence or for journalists' verbatim notes of interviews. There have been many shorthand systems devised for English (Crystal, 1987, p. 206, suggests there have been more than 400), but Pitman based his on a careful analysis of spoken English. His system was commercially very successful and by the end of the century he claimed that:

> In Great Britain, Pitman's Shorthand is every year more extensively taught and practised; it is used by 95 per cent of newspaper reporters and 98 per cent of shorthand clerks. In the United States, where a number of publishers have issued the system with slight alterations, 97 per cent of the shorthand writers use either Pitman's Phonography or an American presentation of it. The percentage of phonographers in Australia is 96.

> (Pitman, undated, p. iii)

THE SPELER,

Devoated (1) tu the Wŭrship and Lŭv ov the Lord God and Saivier Jesus Christ, az "The Aulmeiti" (Matt. 28. 18-20 ; Rev. 1. 8) ; (2) The Kŭltiur ov the Relijŭs Leif, and thairbei the Ekstenshon ov the Kingdom ov God, or the Chŭrch, konsisting ov aul hu wŭrship the Lord and keep Hiz Komandments ; (3) The Investigashon ov Spiritiual Tru'th ; (4) Speling Reform ; (5) Short·hand ; (6) Pees on Er'th.

KOND'UKTED BEI SER EIZAK PITMAN, BATH.

Preis ½d. ; Poast Paid, 1d. Tú or moar kopiz, Poast Free.

London : Sir Isaac Pitman and Sons.   Bath : Ser Eizak Pitman.   New York : Clarence Pitman, 33, Union Square.

No. 1.	JANIUERI, 1895.	VOL. 1.

SPELING.

A " spel " iz ŭpon the nashon az tu speling. Korekt speling iz sed tu be a mark ov an ediukaited person. Whot iz speling? It iz the plaising tugether ov the leterz that maik a wŭrd. Everi leter haz a naim. The naim ekspresez its sound, if a vowel or vois ; and indikaits the akshon ov sŭm part ov the mou'th that prodiusez it, if it iz a konsonant. Az a konsonant iz not a sound, bŭt meerli the kontakt ov tú parts ov the mou'th, either cheking or propeling a sound, the naimz ov the konsonants ar formd bei meenz ov a vouel preseeding or folo·ing the kontakt ; az f, *ef* ; v, *vee* ; m, *em* ; b, *bee*. The vouel or sound reprezented bei " o " haz for its naim the sound which " o " reprezents, az herd in *no*, *so* ; and the konsonant " p," which iz prodiust bei a preshur ov the lips, seeing that ther iz no sound in the preshur, reseevz a naim bei meenz ov the vouel " ee," and iz kauld *pee*.

The moar efektiuali tu distingwish the " bre'th konsonants " from thair koresponding " vokalz," the vouel yuzd in naiming a non-vokal, or bre'th leter, iz plaist BEFOAR it ; and it iz plaist AFTER the vokal ; as f, *ef* ; v, *vee* ; th (in *thin*), *ith* ; th (in *then*), *thee* ; s, *es* ; z, *zee* ; sh, *ish* ; zh, *zhee*. In naiming the eksplosiv konsonants the vouel iz ŭterd AFTER the kontakt in boa'th keindz ov leterz, vokal and non-vokal ; az, p, *pee* ; b, *bee* ; t, *tee* ; d, *dee* ; and, for eez ov pronŭnsiashon, *ee* iz chainjd to *ai* in ch, *chay* ; j, *jay* : k, *kay* ; g, *gay*. The vouel PRESEEDZ the kontakt in naiming the tú likwidz l, *el* ; r, *ar* ; and the 'three nazalz, m, *em* ; n, *en* ; ng, *ing* (*ing* iz moar eezili spoaken than *eng*.) *W* and *y* hav the vouel that maiks them audibel, az leterz, plaist AFTER, and ar kauld *way*, *yay*. (In the old alfabet *w* iz "dŭbel-yu," and *y* iz "wei.") The aspirait iz konveenientli naimd " aich." The meer ekspŭlshon ov bre'th wud not be herd in speeking ov the leter ; and " haa," or " hay," wud not streik the eer so redili as " aich."

The siks long vouelz, which hav no singel-leter reprezentativ in the komon alfabet, are *aa*, *ai*, *ee* ; *au*, *oa*, *oo*. (At the END ov a wŭrd, *ai*, *au*, ar riten *ay*, *aw*.) The short vouel in *bŭt*, az distinkt from " u " in *put*, iz not reprezented in the komon alfabet. Ther ar aulso siks konsonants that hav no singel reprezentativ seinz or leterz, and tú leterz hav been choazen to reprezent them, naimli, ch, *chay* ; 'th, *ith* ; th, *thee* ; sh, *ish* ; zh, *zhee* ; ng, *ing*. Befoar printing koménst, the skreibz yuzd singel leterz for *ith* and *thee*.

The modern naimz ov the vouelz ar a, *ai* ; e, *ee* ; i, *eye* ; o, *oa* ; u, *yu*. Thay wer formerli kauld, in England, az thay ar now on the Kontinent, a, *aa* ; e, *ai* ; i, *ee* ; o, *oa* ; u, *oo*.

In this eniumerashon ov the naimz ov the leterz we hav inkliuded the 'therteen niu leterz ov the Fonetik Alfabet. Our objekt in this eniumerashon iz, to emfaseiz the fakt that in the hŭndred 'thouzand wŭrdz ov our langwej, oanli about 50, sŭch az " Plato, no, be," *ar pronounst in akordans with the naimz ov the leterz*. Hens the fiutiliti ov teeching children the sound ov·a wŭrd bei ferst naiming its leterz. The cheild shud be given the sound ov the wŭrd *az a hoal*. " Luk and Say " shud be the moto ov the teecher. To pronouns the leterz *bee-ai-tee*, and kaul the wŭrd " bat," when it iz " bait " ; and *see-ai-tee*, " kat," when the naimz ov the leterz maik " sait," oanli konfiuzez the lerner.

Tu sŭkseed in this Reform, it mŭst be diveided intu tú staijez.

RULES of the SPELLING REFORM.

First Stage.—Reject *c* (= *k* or *s*), *q* (= *k*, *qu* = *kw*), *x* (= *ks* or *kz*). Use the other 23 letters thus :—*Consonants* as usual ; and *a*, *e*, *i*, *o*, *u*, SHORT, as in *pat*, *pet*, *pit*, *pot*, *put*. For the remaining 13 sounds, *Italicised* in the following words, use the letters below :

cheap ;	thin, then ;	wish, vision ;	sing.
ch ;	'th, th ;	sh, zh ;	ng.
ch ;	*th, th ;*	*sh, zh ;*	*ng.*

palm, pale, peel ;	pall, pole, pool :	but.
aa, ai, ee ;	au, oa, oo :	ŭ.
aa, ai, ee ;	*au, oa, oo :*	*ŭ.*

For brevity write *a*, *e*, *o*, *u*, for *ai*, *ee*, *oa*, *oo*, at the end of an *accented* syllable, as in *fa*-vor, *fe*-ver, *ho*-ly, *tru*-li, (not *fai*-vor, *fee*-ver, etc.) When "ŭ" is not in stock, print "u."

Write the 5 Diphthongs thus : *ei* (*by*), *ou* (*out*), *iu* (*new*), *ăi* [*ai* in the Second Stage], (*Kaiser*), *oi* (*toil*). When the letters of a digraph represent separate values, interpose a "turned point" (·), as "be·ing" (not *bei-ng*), "short·hand" (not *shor-thand*).

Second Stage.—Each letter has but one sound : Consonants and Diphthongs as above ; *a*, *e*, *i*, *o*, *u*, SHORT, as in *pat*, *pet*, *pit*, *pot*, *put*. For the 13 sounds above, use the following 13 new letters (whose names are below them) : thus making a complete *Phonetic Alphabet* of 24 consonants and 12 vowels, or 36 letters in all.

Є ꞓ;   Ᵹ ꬶ;   ᵭ ᵭ;   Σ ʃ;   Ӡ ʒ;   Ŋ ŋ.

(chay)   (ith)   (thee)   (ish)   (zhee)   (ing)

ᴀ ʙ,   Ɛ ɛ,   Ƒ ị;   Ꝺ ꝺ,   Ꝋ ꝋ,   Ꙋ ꙋ;   Ȣ ȣ.

Ɑ ɑ,   Ɛ ɛ,   Ƒ ị;   Ꝋ ꝋ,   Ꝺ ꝺ,   Ꙋ ꙋ: Ȣ ȣ.

(ah)   (eh)   (ee)   (aw)   (oh)   (ōō)   (ut.)

NOTE : FIRST STAGE.—Write, *if preferred* –At the END of a word, *ay*, *aw*, *ow*, *oy*, for *ai*, *au*, *ou*, *oi*, as in *may*, *law*, *now*, *boy* ; use *u* for *oo* in *truth*, etc. ; *f* (the pronoun) for *ei* ; *yu* for *iu* when initial, as "*yus*" (*use*) ; *n* for *ng*, when followed by *k* or *g*, as *bank* (bangk), *anger* (ang-ger) ; *father*, *old*, etc., for *faather*, *ould*, etc. Use caution, and avoid giving offence. Proper names and addresses should not be altered at present. It is best to adopt phonetic spelling for one's own name if it does not need a new letter. In teaching reading, use the Second Stage.

Tu prodiús a Fonetik, or tru, reprezentashon ov the English langwej ; in ŭther wŭrdz, tu reform the speling on the leinz ov the old alfabet, it iz oanli neseseri to employ eech leter for the sound which it woz intended tu reprezent when ferst plaist in the alfabet, never tu yuz it for anŭther sound, nor tu put a leter in a wŭrd when it iz not pronounst. In the komon speling the siks long vouelz are reprezented in 170 wayz, and the feiv dif·thongz hav 80 reprezentativz, maiking a total of 250 wayz ov speling eleven soundz ! Truli dŭz Max Müller say, " English speling iz a nashonal misfortiun ; it iz ŭnintelijibel, ŭnhistorikal, and ŭnteechabel." Sir C. E. Trevelyan sez, " The English sistem ov speling (I protést agenst its be·ing kauld or'thografi) iz a labirin'th, a kaos, an absŭrditi, a disgrais tu our aij and nashon." The lait Ḍr. Thirlwall, the moast lernèd English Bishop ov this sentiuri, sez, " I luk ŭpon the establisht sistem ov speling (if an aksidental kŭstom may be so kauld,) az a mas ov anomaliz, the groa'th ov ignorans and chans, ekwali repŭgnant tu gud taist and tu komon sens. Bŭt I am awair that the pŭblik kling tu theez anomaliz with a tenasiti propoarshond tu thair absŭrditi, **and ar** jelŭs ov aul enkroachment on ground konsekraited bei preskrip-

---

Pitman was perhaps being a little touchy here about rival systems, but it is nevertheless clear that phonography was far from being a minority, cranky interest. Rather, it had become a writing system for English with international currency and considerable commercial interest.

Pitman's work on phonography stimulated an interest in spelling reform and he began to use the associations and networks that had been established to promote shorthand as a basis for his new campaign. He recognized that a new, phonemically based orthography required extensive research and he collaborated with a phonetician, Alexander Ellis, in devising and refining dozens of alphabets that were phonetically well founded and practical from the points of

Figure 2.30 The first issue of Isaac Pitman's journal devoted to spelling reform

(The Speler, 1895, vol. 1, no. 1)

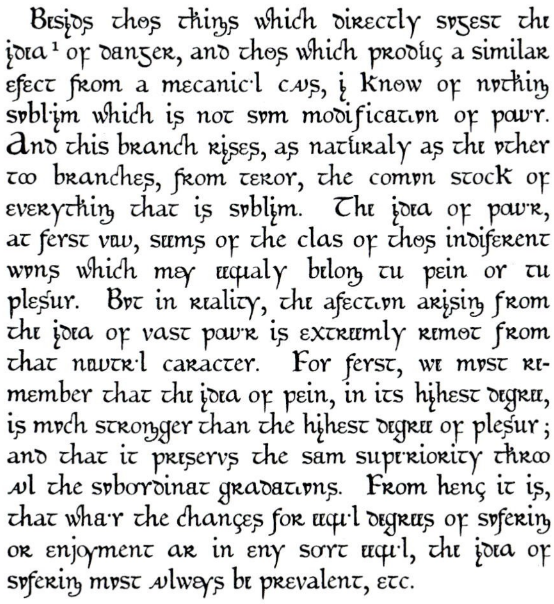

Besjos thos thiŋs which directly sygest the
jora¹ of danger, and thos which produç a similar
efect from a mecanic·l caus, į know of nothiŋ
sublįm which iş not sum modificatıvn of pavr.
And this branch rişeş, aş natüraly aş the vther
too branches, from teror, the comvn stock of
everythiŋ that iş sublįm. The jora of pavr,
at ferst vau, sıms of the clas of thos indiferent
wvns which may ıqualy beloŋ tu pein or tu
pleşur. But in riality, the afectıvn arişiŋ from
the jora of vast pav'r iş extrımly rımot from
that navtr·l caracter. For ferst, wı mvst rı-
member that the jora of pein, in its hįhest dıgrıı,
iş mvch stroŋger than the hįhest dıgrıı of pleşur;
and that it prışervş the sam suprıiority thrœ
·vl the svbordinat gradatıvnş. From henç it iş,
that wha·r the chançeş for ıqı·l dıgrıış of svferiŋ
or enjoyment ar in eny sort ıqı·l, the jora of
svferiŋ mvst ·vlweys bı prevalent, etc.

Figure 2.31
An example of Robert Bridges' simplified spelling from 1913
(Bridges, 1913, pp. 32–3)

view of both writing and printing. Its printing practicability was achieved by a series of publishing ventures, including the *Phonographic Journal* and the *Phonotypic Journal.* By the end of the century Pitman was able to launch the more popular journal *The Speler* (see Figure 2.30).

In the early twentieth century enthusiasm for phonetic spelling was becoming sufficiently great to disturb more conservative minds. The poet Robert Bridges, for example, worried that the fashion for spelling words as they were pronounced would result in 'degraded conversational forms' of southern English being fixed in English orthography. He devised his own proposal, which was to provide a more aesthetically pleasing script suitable for works of literature. Bridges decided to adopt the insular majuscule – the script of the Lindisfarne Gospels – as a model, but in the end made do with 'an old Anglo-Saxon fount, which was lying disused at the Clarendon Press' (Bridges, 1913, p. 19). An example is shown in Figure 2.31.

Yet another literary proposal was facilitated by the playwright Bernard Shaw, an ardent supporter of spelling reform. When he died in 1950 it was found that his will directed a public trustee to seek and publish a new 'Proposed Alphabet' and:

> employ a phonetic expert to transliterate my play entitled *Androcles and the Lion* into the proposed British Alphabet assuming the pronunciation to resemble that recorded of His Majesty our late King George V and sometimes described as Northern English; to employ an artist calligrapher to copy the transliteration for reproduction by lithography, photography or any other method that may serve in the absence of printers' types; to advertise and publish the transliteration with the original Doctor Johnson's lettering opposite the transliteration page by page and a glossary of the two alphabets at the end and to present copies to public libraries in the British Isles, the British Commonwealth, the

American States North and South and to national libraries everywhere in that order.

(Shaw, 1962, p. 9)

An international competition was duly put in hand, resulting in about 450 designs. The winning one is illustrated in Figure 2.32, taken from the edition of *Androcles and the Lion* that was published by Penguin in 1962.

The work by Sir Isaac Pitman and Alexander Ellis in designing a more phonetically transparent orthography led to another quite different project in the 1960s, when Pitman's grandson Sir James Pitman played a key role in implementing a new orthography called the 'initial teaching alphabet', or 'i t a', for use in schools. For a while the scheme gained popularity in several English-speaking countries and was supported by both publishers and education ministries. In an endorsement to one book in the scheme (Downing, 1964), the British minister of education, Sir Edward Boyle, described the introduction of i t a as an 'exciting and important' experiment – 'It is a subject on which there is the possibility of a really dramatic break-through.' No capital letters were used in the i t a – initial letters were indicated in the medieval manner with an enlarged letter. It was intended as an orthography for children's writing as well as for reading, but despite some institutional support the fashion did not last longer than about a decade.

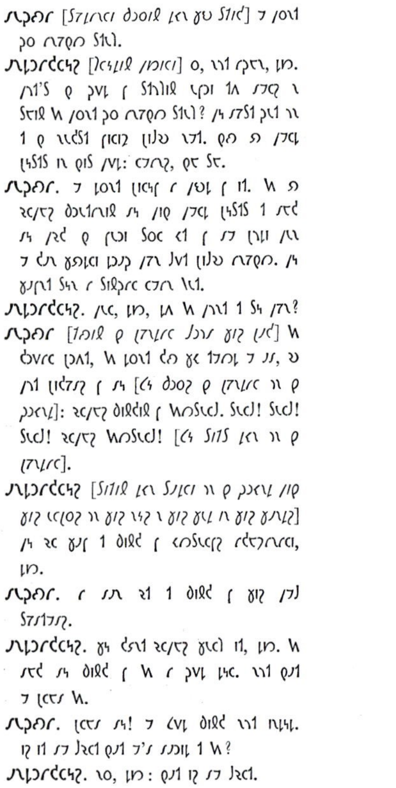

MEGAERA [*suddenly throwing down her stick*] I wont go another step.

ANDROCLES [*pleading wearily*] Oh, not again, dear. Whats the good of stopping every two miles and saying you wont go another step? We must get on to the next village before night. There are wild beasts in this wood: lions, they say.

MEGAERA. I dont believe a word of it. You are always threatening me with wild beasts to make me walk the very soul out of my body when I can hardly drag one foot before another. We havnt seen a single lion yet.

ANDROCLES. Well, dear, do you want to see one?

MEGAERA [*tearing the bundle from his back*] You cruel brute, you dont care how tired I am, or what becomes of me [*she throws the bundle on the ground*]: always thinking of yourself. Self! self! self! always yourself! [*She sits down on the bundle*].

ANDROCLES [*sitting down sadly on the ground with his elbows on his knees and his head in his hands*] We all have to think of ourselves occasionally, dear.

MEGAERA. A man ought to think of his wife sometimes.

ANDROCLES. He cant always help it, dear. You make me think of you a good deal. Not that I blame you.

MEGAERA. Blame me! I should think not indeed. Is it my fault that I'm married to you?

ANDROCLES. No, dear: that is my fault.

Figure 2.32 An extract from Androcles and the Lion *printed in Shaw's alphabet*
(Shaw, 1962, pp. 22–3)

RECEIVED EDUCATED LONDON dt.

1. *Soa· (soa·w) ei sai· (sai·y), mai·ts, you see· nou, dhŭt ei ŭm reit ŭbou·t dhat lit·l gyu·l kum·ing from dhŭ skoo·l yon·dŭr.*

2. *Shee· iz goa·ing doun dhŭ roa·d dhe·r throo· dhŭ red gai·t on dhŭ left hand seid ŭv dhŭ wai·y.*

3. *Shoŏŭr inuf· dhŭ cheild hŭz gon strai·t up tŭ dhŭ doa·ŭr (dau·ŭr, dau·r) ŭv dhŭ rong hous,*

4. *whe·r shee· wil chaan·s tŭ feind dhat drung·kn, def, shriv·ŭld fel·oa (fel·ŭ) ŭu dhŭ nai·m ŭv Tom·us.*

5. *Wee· au·l noa· (noa·w) him ver·i wel.*

6. *Woa·nt dhi oa·ld chap soo·n tee·ch hŭr not tŭ doo· it ŭgen· (ŭgai·n), puo·ŭ thing!*

7. *Luok· ! iz·nt it troo· ?*

Figure 2.33   A.J. Ellis's glossic alphabet from 1890

(Ellis, 1890)

Glossic was a phonetic transcription system invented by Alexander Ellis and used by several writers for the English Dialect Society in the late nineteenth century. Unlike a general purpose orthography which needs to ignore minor, insignificant differences in pronunciation, glossic was created in order to represent fine nuances of accent. Ellis himself used it in his *English Dialects: their sounds and homes* (1890), one of the earliest systematic surveys of British accents (see Figure 2.33). Ellis's glossic fell into disuse but a number of similar phonetic alphabets, many based on the research carried out by Ellis and Pitman, have been used by linguists for similar purposes. In Britain and Australia the International Phonetic Alphabet (IPA) is now the commonest system for making transcriptions of pronunciations in phonetic detail and we use it extensively in this book. Phonetic transcriptions are conventionally placed between square brackets []. A chart of the symbols used in IPA can be found at the end of this book.

2.7   CONCLUSION

The definition of English

This chapter has focused on the materiality of English texts rather than on the abstract linguistic systems which underlie them. There is a long tradition in linguistic study that is concerned with the outward forms of speech (phonetics), but for some reason *visual* manifestations of language have been regarded as somehow less central to linguistic study than *audible* ones.

So one issue raised by this chapter concerns definition: should we consider visual communicative devices used by a text, such as its overall design, handwriting, use of illustration and so on, to be a part of 'the language'? I have tried to show that some aspects of the visual representations of English should be regarded as being just as central to the English language as spoken characteristics.

The historical location of texts

We tend to think of language as something which allows *individuals* to communicate with each other. The language and design of a medieval manuscript, however, is the product of many people. Hence each text can be said to speak with several voices – those of the composer, the copyist(s), the illustrators and rubricators, the later editors and publishers, and sometimes readers who add marginal comments. In any historical account of the English language we need to recognize that not only the language in a larger sense but also individual texts represent the work of many people. For this reason we need to understand a great deal about the political, cultural and economic context in which texts were created in order that we might understand their historical significance, the meaning they might have had for readers, and the evidence they provide of how and why the English language changed.

Trends towards standardization and divergence

Another important theme in this chapter is the idea that homogeneity – in handwriting, in spelling, in book production – represents an institutional achievement. It can be brought about only when many people work to explicit agreed house rules, or when a single person has been trained to follow standard conventions. In the history of English texts we can perceive two divergent tendencies. One is for texts to become less uniform, written in hands which are more idiosyncratic, and designed and spelled in ways which reflect local practices. We can see this in the development of 'national hands' at various times, in the local spelling practices of Middle English scribes, and in the increase in idiosyncrasies. There is, however, a competing trend towards standardization and uniformity – for instance by the imposition of a house style by the institutions which control the production and circulation of texts. The role of the church was apparent in Old English times, and again with the carolingian revival, but printing and schools also had a major standardizing effect on spelling and punctuation in later times. The history of English suggests, however, that there is no inevitable progress towards standardization and uniformity – the two tendencies seem always to be in uneasy competition, as later chapters show.

Reading A

EXTENDING THE ROMAN ALPHABET: SOME ORTHOGRAPHIC EXPERIMENTS OF THE PAST FOUR CENTURIES

David Abercrombie

The most sweeping remedy for the deficiencies of a traditional orthography is to abandon the Roman alphabet altogether, and start again on a fresh basis. Eight such attempts, dating from 1758 to 1962, are shown in Figure 1. They all have the same failing: their sorts [printed characters] are too much alike, and however attractive they may look at first sight, the appearance of words as wholes (on which legibility depends) is not sufficiently distinctive. Only three of them, *a*, *f* and *h*, ever got as far as being printed from type; *f* and *g* were designed for purely scientific purposes.

Figure 1   Various attempts to abandon the Roman alphabet and start afresh

(a)   Honorat Rambaud (1578)

(b)   Robert Robinson (c. 1617)

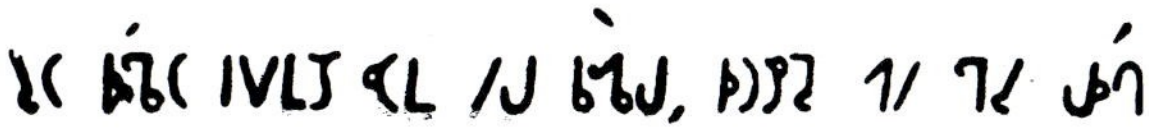

(c)   John Wilkins (1668)

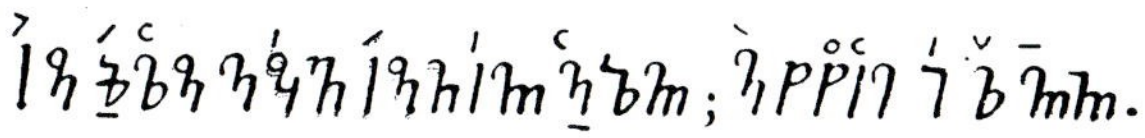

(d)   Francis Lodwick (1686)

(e)   Isaac Pitman (1843)

(f)   A.M. Bell (1867)

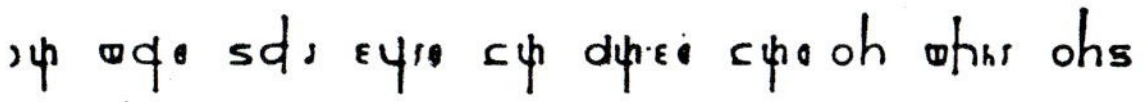

(g)   Daniel Jones and Paul Passy (1907)

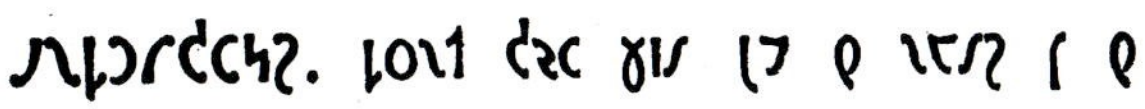

(h)   The Shaw Alphabet, based on Kingsley Read's entry for the Shaw Competition (1962)

There is no doubt, however, that the Roman alphabet is difficult to beat for legibility and beauty, and a better solution is to take it as a basis, and enlarge its scope by various means. Many experiments on these lines have been made in England. Our orthography is one of the least successful applications of the Roman alphabet (Welsh and Spanish, for example, are much more satisfactory), and every schoolchild learns from painful experience how inconsistently our spelling corresponds to spoken reality. Several of our consonant sounds are represented by digraphs, such as *sh wh ng*. Two distinct, though similar, sounds are both written *th* – compare *than* and *thank*. There is no letter, or even digraph, in English for the sound of the French *j*, though we use it in *measure*. Our many vowel sounds are most confusingly dealt with by the five vowel letters *a e i o u* and their combinations: the words *look* and *pull*, for example, contain the same vowel sound, which however is different from that in either *loop* or *dull*. The unjust treatment of English sounds by our traditional spelling probably accounts for the particular fertility of this country in schemes for the augmenting of the Roman alphabet.

One way in which its scope can be enlarged is by the use of diacritics (dots, dashes, and other marks placed under or over the letters). Figure 3 is from the title page of Richard Hodges' *English Primrose* (1644), an ingenious spelling-book, for the use of his pupils, which carried this device to an extreme: it must have been a nightmare for printer and proof-reader. William Johnston published a pronouncing dictionary, in 1764, dedicated to Queen Charlotte in the hope that it might assist her 'in cultivating a right Pronunciation of the English Language'; he made use of italic and black-letter characters, in addition to diacritics (Figure 4).

However, mixtures of fount and diacritics are, on the whole, bad expedients. More satisfactory results are obtained by the introduction of new letters, resulting in an *extended* alphabet, and it is the purpose of this article to examine some little-known typographical experiments on these lines, mostly before the nineteenth century, in England and America.

'Where letters are wanting, nothing seems more natural than to borrow them out of that ancient language that is of the nearest affinity', said Edward Lhwyd, FRS, in 1707, and the Anglo-Saxon þ and ð have been brought in to do duty for the two *th* sounds by many people, from Sir Thomas Smith, Secretary of State to Queen Elizabeth (Figure 5a and b), down to the *Oxford English Dictionary*. ʒ is another Anglo-Saxon letter which has been frequently borrowed.

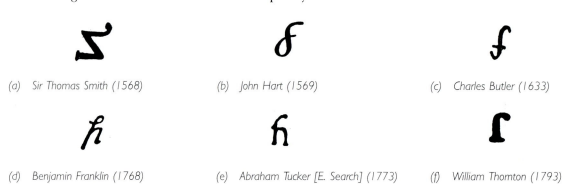

(a)   Sir Thomas Smith (1568)   (b)   John Hart (1569)   (c)   Charles Butler (1633)

(d)   Benjamin Franklin (1768)   (e)   Abraham Tucker [E. Search] (1773)   (f)   William Thornton (1793)

Figure 2   Suggested new letters for the sh sound in hush

THE ENGLISH PRIMRÔSE:

Far furpaſſiñg âl others of this kinde, that ever
grêw in any Engliſh garden : bý the ful
fight whêreof, thêre wil ma-
nifeſtly appêar,

The Ëaſieſt and Speedieſt-way, bóth for the
trúe ſpelliñg and rëadiñg of Engliſh, aṣ
âlſô for the Trúe-writiñg thereof :
that ever was publickly
knôwn tô this day.

Planted (with nô ſmâl pains) bý Richard
Hodǵes, a School-maſter, dwelliñg in South-
wark, at the midle-gate within Moun-
taǵue-clôſe : for the exceediñg grêat
benefit, bóth of his ôwn Coun-
trêy-men and Strángers.

Approved âlſô bý the Learned, and publiſht
bý Âuthority.

If the trumpet give an uncẹrtain ſound, whô
ſhâl prêpârẹ himſelf tô the battel? 1 Cor. 14. 8

LONDON
Printed for Richard Côtes. 1644

Figure 3   From the title page of The English Primrose, by
Richard Hodges, London, 1644

THE

PRÉFACE.

Ẇ̈ERE a pérſŏn éver ſo well
qualified for agreéable cónverſátion, by knówledge and
lẻarning, ſenſe and génius, and
goódneſs of heårt; or wẻre his compóſures
for the públic éver ſo váluable and élegant;
yet if his cónverſátion or diſcóurſes are út-
tered with a broåd, or fóreǐgn áccent; thẻir
obſcúrity, thẻreby occáſiŏned, will grẻatly
obſtrúct the pléaſure and prófit, he woůld
ótherwiſe commúnicate; and the lábour he
cáuſes tô his héãrers tô cómprehénd his
mẻaning, tõgéther with the gráting ſounds
of his lánguage, will néceſſarily in ſŏme
degreé, raiſe thẻir diſlíke.

A 3   Mány

Figure 4   From the Preface to A Pronouncing and
Spelling Dictionary, by William Johnston, London, 1764

(a)   pith   (b)   bathe   (c)   get   (d)   jet   (e)   bide

Figure 5   Specimen words in the extended
alphabet of Sir Thomas Smith, taken from his
De recta et emendata Linguae Anglicae
Scriptione, Paris, 1568

(f)   dish   (g)   cherry   (h)   five

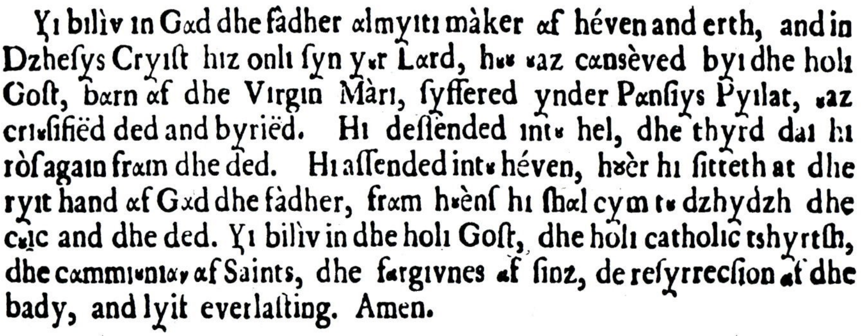

Ɣı bilìv ın Gαd dhe fàdher αlmyıtı màker αf héven and erth, and ın Dzhefɣs Cryıſt hız onlı ſyn yɣr Lαrd, hɣʋ ʋaz cαnsèved byı dhe holı Goſt, bαrn αf dhe Vırgın Màrı, ſyffered ynder Pαnſıys Pyılat, ʋaz crıʋſıfıëd ded and byrıëd.   Hı deſſended ıntʋ hel, dhe thyrd daı hı ròſagaın frαm dhe ded.   Hı aſſended ıntʋ héven, hɣèr hı ſıtteth αt dhe ryıt hand αf Gαd dhe fàdher, frαm hɣènſ hı ſhαl cym tʋ dzhydzh dhe cʋıc and dhe ded. Ɣı bilìv in dhe holı Goſt, dhe holı catholıc tshyrtſh, dhe cαmmıʋnıαʋ αf Saints, dhe fαrgıvnes ʋf ſınz, de reſyrrecſıon αf dhe bady, and lyıt everlaſtıng. Amen.

Figure 6   The Creed, *illustrating one of the phonetic alphabets of John Wilkins. From* An Essay towards a Real Character, and a Philosophical Language, *printed by order of the Royal Society,* 1668

ѳaɒk

(a)   thank

Ð00Z

(b)   those

ſuut

(c)   shoot

Ѳitſ

(d)   which

vꙅri

(e)   very

pɒɒl

(f)   pall

Figure 7   *Specimen words in the extended alphabet of William Thornton, taken from his* Cadmus, *or a* Treatise on the Elements of Written Language, *Philadelphia, 1793*

Greek Letters have also provided extra sorts, especial favourites among the consonants being θ and δ, again for the *th* sounds, and ɛ and ʏ (ligatured o and ʊ) among the vowels. However, most reformers neglected to have their borrowed letters re-cut to accord with whatever roman fount they were using – they simply drew on the nearest Greek fount in size, with poor results aesthetically. John Wilkins, Cromwell's brother-in-law and Bishop of Chester from 1668 to 1672, used peculiar symbols to represent ideas (not sounds) in his *Essay towards a Real Character* (1668), and got James Moxon, the first English writer on typefounding, and author of the *Mechanick Exercises*, to cut them. He took little trouble, however, over the phonetic alphabet in the same book (Figure 6). Although the tailed *y* (representing the vowel in *but*) must have been specially cut, both in upper and lower case forms, no attempt was made to produce suitable forms of α and ʏ , or even to take them from the same fount each time. The carefully designed alphabet of the versatile American Dr William Thornton, however, includes a θ which goes well with roman (Figure 7a). It also includes (Figure 7d) a letter for *wh* borrowed from the gothic alphabet which Bishop Ulfilas invented in the fourth century.

Black-letter founts originally contained numerous abbreviations and contractions used for printing Latin but not employed in English. William Bullokar, an ardent spelling reformer of the second half of the sixteenth century, made

Thæ̢ voͮwel̢ : a. e. i. y. o. b. u. o. ꝏ. ꝏ : ár alͮway ofho̢t found :
ercept : a. e. i. be' dobͬd thus : aa. ee. iy. yi : o̢ that ón of thæ̢ accent
point̢ : ´ : ̎ : ^ : be' fett ouer : a : e : y : o : fo̢ then be' thæ̢ oflonger
found, w̢ytń thus : á : ã : à : and fo of the reff, fo̢ help in eqiuocẏ.

I cal the firff, á : a, with accent : the fecond. á:a, with dobͬl accent :
the thirb, à : a, with fo̢bĕd accent : and fo of other voͮwel̢ fo nóted,
bicau̢ it may help much in eqiuocẏ.

And thæ̢, e. ꝏ. b. u. ár alͮway of long found, ad too thæ̢, æ, and alfo
the half voͮwel̢, l̄. m̄. n. r̄. ár of longer found, then any voͮwel of ho̢t
found.

Ƿen two voͮwel̢ (o̢ half voͮwel̢) com togeder in ón fillabͬl, they
ár caͬd a diphthong, thær-of ther be' in number, vij. ai. ay. ei. ey. oi.
ow. wy : adíng hær-bntoo : ui : feldoom ín ve.

So adíng thæ̢ feuń mirt found̢ (caͬd diphthong̢) befó̢ w̢ytń,
ther ár in englih fpech, rliiij. feueral̄ found̢ in voic, bnder thoom al̄
englih wo̢d̢ and fillabͬl̢ ár founded and fpókń : adíng hær-bntoo
the rár diphthong : uy.

Thæ̢ diphthong̢ haui paier̢ ín found, and ther be' alfo oder diph-
thong̢, but they haui the found of ón of the voͮwel̢ befó̢ faid, al̄
ƿich hal̄ be' wo̢ytń togeder in fqár̢ next bnder : but fo̢ the tým ín
al̄ thæ̢, nót that euery diphthong i̢ of a̢ long tým o̢ longer, then
any long voͮwel : ad hær-bntoo that hal̄ voͮwel̢ may mak a diphthong after, a, o̢ o, r ár paier̢ too the fillabͬl̢ in their fqár̢ folowing.

And hær-ín i̢ too be' nóted, that fo̢ lærnio̢̢, ther i̢ r hal̄ be' a Pamphlet imp̢inted, contefníng b̢efly the effect of this bꝏk, feruíng alfo
fo̢ conferenc' with the old o̢tography hér-after.

Figure 8   The use of black letter for an extended alphabet. From Bullokars Booke at Large for the Amendment of Orthographie for English Speech, *London, 1580*

black letter, and not roman, the basis of his new system; he was thus able to draw extensively on these disused sorts for new letters (Figure 8). Bullokar held the rather extreme view that Sir Thomas Smith and John Hart, his two most notable predecessors, were bound to produce unsatisfactory alphabets for English be-cause they used foreigners to cut their new letters, 'for lack of helpe of skilful men within the realme at that time'. He thanks God that nowadays, however, the printer and workmen are English, and able to help the reformer in fulfilling his aims …

The possibilities in sheer invention of new letters are more limited than one might suppose: an apparently satisfactory new character will often turn out, in use, to be ill-suited to mixture with the rest of the alphabet, or to be too like letters which already exist. Benjamin Franklin, among his many activities, experimented in spelling reform, and his extended alphabet was produced in 1768, though it was not printed until eleven years later. The total effect is very pleasing (Figure 9), but when examined in detail three of the new letters, those for *sh* and the two *th* sounds

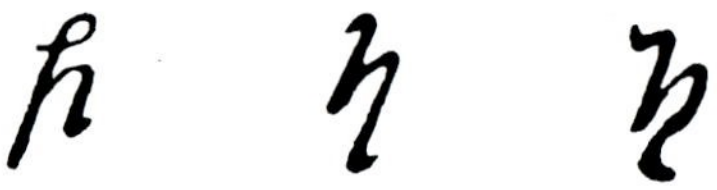

reveal a disturbing similarity both to each other and to h. Franklin was himself a printer, and should have avoided such pitfalls. John Hart, about whom we know little except that he was Chester Herald, had much more success with his new letters, in spite of Bullokar's strictures. His books were beautifully produced: Figure 10 is a page from his treatise on the extended alphabet …

The most profitable source of new letters is neither borrowing, nor outright invention, but modification of existing ones. A number of tolerable sorts can

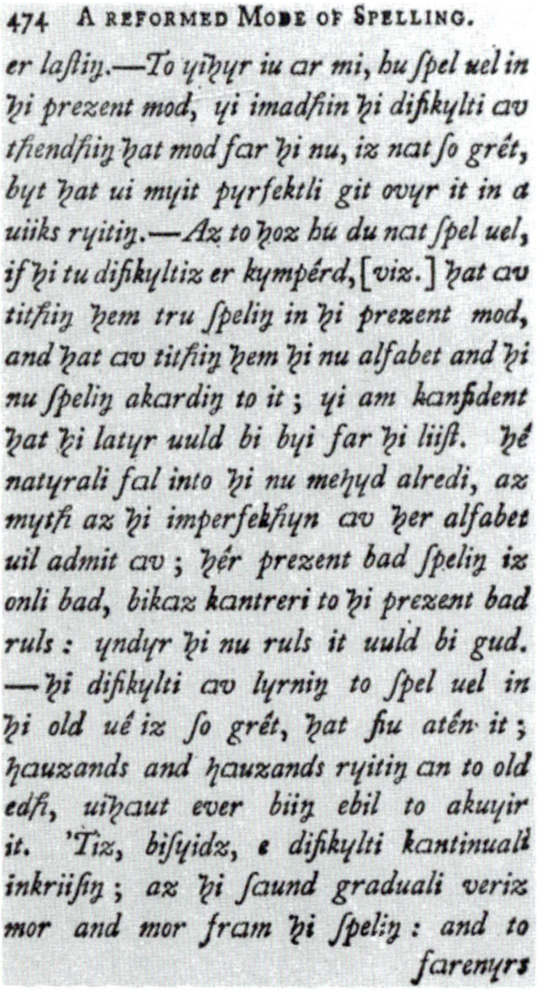

474 A REFORMED MODE OF SPELLING.

er lastiŋ.—To yiɧyr iu ar mi, hu spel uel in ɧi prezent mod, yi imadʃiin ɧi difikylti av tʃiendʃiŋ ɧat mod far ɧi nu, iz nat so grêt, byt ɧat ui myit pyrfektli git ovyr it in a uiiks ryitiŋ.—Az to ɧoz hu du nat spel uel, if ɧi tu difikyltiz er kympérd, [viz.] ɧat av titʃiiŋ ɧem tru speliŋ in ɧi prezent mod, and ɧat av titʃiiŋ ɧem ɧi nu alfabet and ɧi nu speliŋ akardiŋ to it; yi am kanfident ɧat ɧi latyr uuld bi byi far ɧi liiʃt. ɧé natyrali fal into ɧi nu meɧyd alredi, az mytʃ az ɧi imperfekʃyn av ɧer alfabet uil admit av; ɧér prezent bad speliŋ iz onli bad, bikaz kantreri to ɧi prezent bad ruls: yndyr ɧi nu ruls it uuld bi gud.—ɧi difikylti av lyrniŋ to spel uel in ɧi old ué iz so grêt, ɧat fiu atén it; ɧauzands and ɧauzands ryitiŋ an to old edʒ, uiɧaut ever biiŋ ebil to akuyir it. 'Tiz, bisyidz, e difikylti kantinuali inkriiʃiŋ; az ɧi saund graduali veriz mor and mor fram ɧi speliŋ: and to farenyrs

Figure 9 A page in the extended alphabet of Benjamin Franklin, from Political, Miscellaneous and Philosophical Pieces, London, 1779

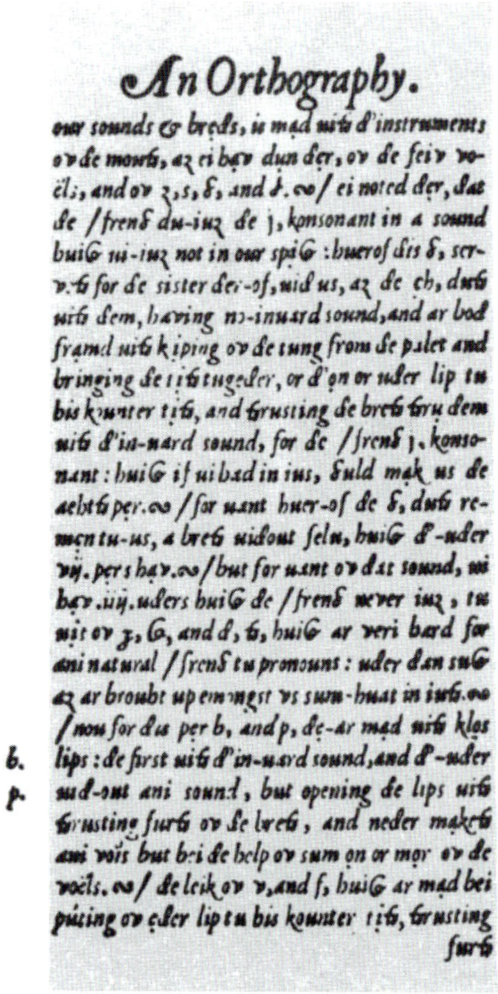

An Orthography.

our sounds & breðs, is mad wið ð'instruments ov ðe mouð, az ei hav dun ðer, ov ðe feiv voëls, and ov z, s, ʃ, and ȝ. ∞ / ei noted ðer, ðat ðe / frenʃ du-iuz ðe j, konsonant in a sound huiç wi-iuz not in our spiç: huerof ðis ʃ, serv.ð for ðe sister ðer-of, wið us, az ðe ch, duð wið ðem, having no-inward sound, and ar boð framd wið kiping ov ðe tung from ðe palet and bringing ðe tið tugeðer, or ð'on or uðer lip tu his kounter tið, and ðrusting ðe breð ðru ðem wið ð'in-ward sound, for ðe / frenʃ j. konsonant: huiç if wi had in ius, ʃuld mak us ðe aeihtð per. ∞ / for want huer-of ðe ʃ, duð remen tu-us, a breð widout selu, huiç ð'-uðer viij. pers hav. ∞ / but for want ov ðat sound, wi hav .iij. uðers huiç ðe / frenʃ never iuz, tu wit ov ȝ, ç, and ð, ð, huiç ar veri hard for ani natural / frenʃ tu pronouns: uðer ðan suç az ar brouht up emongst vs sum-huat in iuð. ∞ / now for ðe per b, and p, ðe-ar mad wið klos

b. lips: ðe first wið ð'in-ward sound, and ð'-uðer

p. wid-out ani sound, but opening ðe lips wið ðrusting furð ov ðe breð, and neðer makeð ani vois but bei ðe help ov sum on or mor ov ðe voëls. ∞ / ðe leik ov v, and f, huiç ar mad bei puting ov eiðer lip tu his kounter tið, ðrusting

furð

Figure 10 A page from An Orthographie, conteyning the due order and reason, howe to write or paint thimage of mannes voice, most like to the life or nature, by John Hart, London, 1569 immediately be obtained by inversion: ə ч ɯ ɔ ʎ ʌ, and frequent use has been made of these, together with the less satisfactory ʁ ʃ ɿ ʍ ʞ ɟ ᵷ. The Anti-Absurd Alphabet (1845) of Major Beniowski, a Polish enthusiast for the reform of English spelling, relied entirely for new letters on inversion (Figure 11). Inverted upper-case J, reduced in size to range with the short letters, was used by William Thornton for *sh* (Figures 2f and 7c).

Reversed letters have also occasionally been tried, a successful example being Sir Thomas Smith's reversed z for *sh* (Figures 2a and 5f). A less obviously useful specimen is a reversed h which, together with several inverted letters, was used by an amusing early eighteenth-century writer who signed himself G.W. and who was possibly an Exeter schoolmaster called John White (Figure 12).

Structural modification is another possibility. Removal of the dot from i produces ı (used, for example, by Smith Figure 5e, Wilkins Figure 6), but does not make for legibility. Nevertheless, it forms part of the official Turkish alphabet, introduced in 1928. Bars or dashes added to letters were the main standby of Charles Butler, who published in the early seventeenth century an English grammar, and works on bees and the principles of music, in an extended alphabet

---

xxvi

kichen kitchen	rəp rope
selʌr cellar	sponj sponge
stabl stable	sʌdl saddle
stən stone	mȝntin mountain
nʌpkin napkin	chɔk chalk
kʉp cup	hej hedge
kʌndł candle	plȝ plough
snʉferz snuffers	nʉt nut
tongz tongs	whɛl wheel
ʌshez ashes	sʉ sea
smək smoke	wav wave

the lɔrd'z praer.

Ȝɪ fʌther, which ʌrt in hevn, hʌlǝɛd bʉ (b'e) thy nam : thy kingdom kʉm : thy wil bʉ (b'e) dʉn in erȝh ʌz it iz in hevn ; giv ʉs this da Ȝr dalʉ (dal'e) bred : ʌnd fɔrgiv ʉs Ȝr trespʌsez, ʌz wʉ (w'e) fɔrgiv them thʌt trespʌs ʌgɛnst ʉs : ʌnd lɛd (l'ed) ʉs not intu tcmta-shon : bʉt dʉliver (d'eliver) ʉs from ʉvl ('evl) : fɔr thyn iz the kingdom, the pȝer, ʌnd the glərʉ (glər'e) fɔr ever ʌnd ever : amen.

the gospel ʌkɔrding tu

sant mʌ ʇhiu.

chʌpter 2.

1. nȝ when jɛzʉs woz bɔrn in beȝhlehem ov
   1. Now when Jesus was born in Bethlehem of

jiudɛʌ in the daz ov herod the king, bʉhɔld,
Judea, in the days of Herod the king, behold,

thar kam wyz men from the ʉst tu jeruzʌlem.
there came wise men from the east to Jerusalem.

2. saing, whar iz hʉ thʌt iz bɔrn king ov
   2. Saying, where is he that is born king of

the jiuz ? fɔr wʉ hʌv sɛn hiz stʌr in the
the Jews? for we have seen his star in the

ʉst, ʌnd ʌr kʉm tu wʉrship him.
east, and are come to worship him.

3. when herod the king hʌd herd thʉz ʇhingz,
   3. When Herod the king had heard these things,

hʉ woz trʉbled, ʌnd ɔl jeruzʌlem with him.
he was troubled, and all Jerusalem with him.

Figure 11   Facing pages from the Anti-absurd or Phrenotypic Alphabet and Orthography for the English Language, *by Major Beniowski, London, 1845*

(22)

We are not awar ſlau muh our deſcitful let-trz, ſlindr uthr Learning, and refining Inglifh, and ſlau tru letrz would furthr it.

Mad C w"ɔ ſ ſpelz found ɔe sam, *Stilo novo.*

Betráz q h and k.

Deſetfule deniz its nam,

And ſ doɔ it betra.

Diſſembliʌ C wiɔ nidles vot,

Ov ridiʌ brex ɔe nec.

Unles it ſlav a proper nam,

And ſpelliʌ ſuits wiɔ C.

C ȝiʌz an il exampl,

And iz a tripl tnaʌ : CCC ERAS. Ad.

On guſtis it doɔ trampl,

Scab'd for aol ſler aolz braʌ.

Ov ſierz ɔe blind ledr iz :

De ded ɔe liviʌ rul. ARISTOF.

And ʍot a tirſum taſc iz ɔis

To wat upon a Fuul ?

Larg ſlauſn ſlav wi in larg taunz,

And largr hevnle buux :

Larg Cots and Tlox ſlav wi and ɔaunz,

Aʊr fit in letr ſtox.

It nivr iz tuu lat to ɔriv,

Nor to iuvenſoʌz ad :

For Silvr auns wi raɔr ſtriv,

Dʌn maʌe paundz ov Led.

Nʌu ɔat I ma u trule ſi,

Sertante to mi ſa :

If lic u ſim and no frend be,

Non ledz mi wurſr wa.

In cruuced waz ɔis aol iz il,

Men tno not ɔat ɔʌ er. (ſir.

And ɔat men luv darcnes ſtil, ſo fʌot in endleſs

As c t and h do fuul our erz ovr and ovr in hatch and catch, &c. ſo dodh D (non without deſet) in Wedneſday, Hedg, Judg, ſpring, grudg, badg,

Figure 12 Verses from Magazine, or Animadversions on the English Spelling, by G.W., London, 1703

(a) English   (b) orthography

(c) which   (d) though

Figure 13 Specimen words in the extended alphabet used by Charles Butler in his English Grammar, Oxford, 1633

(a) New letters used by Thomas Spence in his Grand Repository of the English Language, a pronouncing dictionary published in Newcastle in 1775, enlarged from the copperplate frontispiece

Impropriety, (IMPRⱭPRIITE) n. unfit-neſs; inaccuracy.

Impròve, (IMPRⱭDV) v. to make better.

Impròvident, (IMPRⱭVIDINT) q. not pro-vident.

Imprüdent, (IMPRUDINT) q. indiſcreet.

I'mpudent, (IMPIDINT) q. fhameleſs.

(b) Some entries from Spence's dictionary

Figure 14

(Figure 13). He also used an inverted t, and a modified long ∫, with a bar added (Figure 2c). Sir Thomas Smith produced an extra e letter by adding a stroke (Figure 5g). William Thornton tried a square o (Figure 7f).

New sorts can be obtained by ligaturing existing letters. Thomas Spence, who had a stormy political career at the end of the eighteenth century, produced ten by this means for use in his pronouncing dictionary (which was the first to use a scientifically exact notation). It is of particular interest that, although they are not very distinguished, the new letters were cut in Newcastle by Thomas Bewick (Figure 14b).

An extended alphabet was elaborated by Alexander Gill, teacher of Milton and headmaster of St Paul's from 1608 to 1635 ('a very ingeniose person' wrote Aubrey, 'notwithstanding his whipping-fitts'). Two versions are illustrated in Figure 15. The earlier contains numerous new letters, mostly modifications of existing ones, the modifications being added in red ink after the book was printed. The later version, with four new letters only, was less ambitious.

One of Gill's new letters, it will be noticed, was for the consonant v in *haven*. This reminds us that in his day u and v were merely alternative forms of the same letter, both being used for the vowel and the consonant (*uvula* was printed *vuula* in normal practice); the modern differentiation of u for vowel and v for consonant was not established until about 1630. Gill makes u and v into separate letters, but uses them both for vowel sounds. Sir Thomas Smith also produced a new letter for the consonant v (Figure 5h); John Hart, however, as will be seen from Figure 10, anticipates modern usage, and he was apparently the first in England to observe it. The two letters i and j have a similar history. Gill uses j as a vowel symbol, and he, Smith and Hart all use the Anglo-Saxon ȝ for the consonant *j*.

A third letter of the alphabet also originally had two alternative forms – s ∫. They were never differentiated into separate letters, though Edward Capell, the

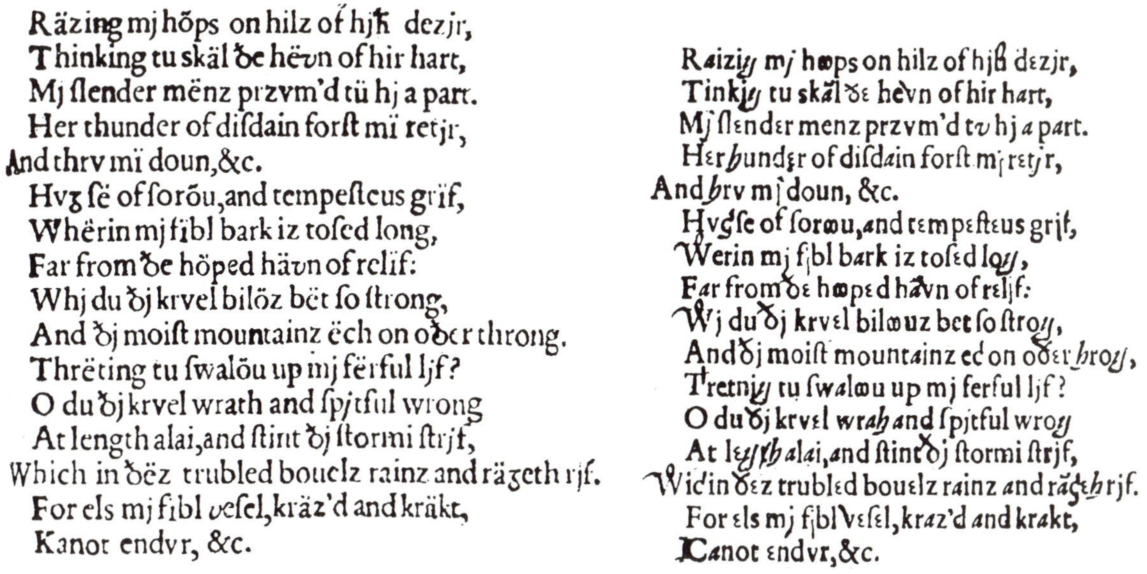

(a)   A passage from 1st edition, London, 1619

(b)   The same passage from 2nd edition, London, 1621

Figure 15   Lines from Spenser's Faerie Queene in the alphabet used by Alexander Gill in his Logonomia Anglica, 1619

eighteenth-century editor of Shakespeare, attempted to introduce a distinction between the two forms. He used short s whenever it had the soft sound z, but long ſ when it had the hard sound ss; uſe and *use* were therefore distinguished as noun and verb. The idea, however, never caught on, and was abandoned at the beginning of the nineteenth century – fortunately, for it is too like f to be a useful member of the alphabet.

The invention of new letters is of considerable importance to phoneticians, spelling reformers, and governments who wish to provide illiterate peoples under their rule with alphabets; and it is still a matter of general interest, as the publicity given to Bernard Shaw's will showed. The early experiments illustrated above are not easily accessible, but they are of more than antiquarian interest. Since the establishment of phonetics as a science, about a hundred years ago, innumerable extended alphabets have appeared, and there is probably more awareness nowadays of the importance of legibility, appearance and the needs of the printer; but no fresh principles in the invention of new letters have emerged.

References

BELL, A.M. (1867) *Visible Speech: the Science of Universal Alphabetics,* London, Simpkin, Marshall & Co.

BENIOWSKI, Major (1845) *The Anti-absurd or Phrenotypic Alphabet and Orthography for the English Language,* London, published by the author.

BULLOKAR, W. (1580) *Booke at Large, for the Amendment of Orthographie for English Speech,* London, Henry Denham.

BULLOKAR, W. (1585) *Aesop's Fables,* London, Edmund Bollifant.

BUTLER, C. (1633) *The English Grammar, or the Institution of Letters, Syllables, and Words, in the English Tongue,* Oxford, William Turner, for the author.

CAPELL, E. (1760) *Prolusions; or, select Pieces of antient Poetry,* London, J. & R. Tonson.

FRANKLIN, B. (1779) *Political, Miscellaneous, and Philosophical Pieces,* London, J. Johnson.

GILL, A. (1619) *Logonomia Anglica,* London, John Beale; 2nd edn 1621.

HART, J. (1569) *An Orthographie, conteyning the due order and reason, howe to write or paint thimage of mannes voice, most like to the life or nature,* London, William Seres.

HODGES, R. (1644) *The English Primrose,* London, Richard Cotes.

JOHNSTON, W. (1764) *A Pronouncing and Spelling Dictionary,* London, printed for W. Johnston.

JONES, D. AND PASSY, P. (1907) *Alphabet phonétique organique,* supplément au *Maître Phonétique.*

LHWYD, E. (1707) *Archaeologia Britannica,* Oxford, printed at the Theatre for the author.

LODWICK, F. (1686) 'An essay towards an universal alphabet', *Philosophical Transactions,* no. 16, pp. 126–37.

MOXON, J. (1683) *Mechanick Exercises,* London, printed for Joseph Moxon.

PITMAN, I. (1843) 'Phonographic alphabet number 9', *Phonographic Journal,* no. 2, p. 107.

RAMBAUD, H. (1578) *La Declaration des Abus que lon commet en escriuant*, Lyon, Jean de Tournes.

ROBINSON, R. (1617) *The Art of Pronuntiation*, London, printed by Nicholas Okes.

SEARCH, E. (pseud., i.e. Abraham Tucker) (1773) *Vocal Sounds*, London, Jones, sold by T. Payne.

SHAW, B. (1962) *Androcles and the Lion, an Old Fable Renovated, with a Parallel Text in Shaw's Alphabet*, Harmondsworth, Penguin.

SMITH, T. (1568) *De recta et emendata Linguae Anglicae Scriptione*, Paris, Robert Stephan.

SPENCE, T. (1775) *The Grand Repository of the English Language*, Newcastle upon Tyne, T. Saint, for the author.

THORNTON, W. (1793) 'Cadmus, or a Treatise on the Elements of Written Language', *Trans. Am. Philosophical Soc.*, no. 3, pp. 262–319.

W., G. (1703) *Magazine, or Animadversions on the English Spelling*, London, printed for the author.

WILKINS, J. (1668) *An Essay towards a Real Character, and a Philosophical Language*, London, printed by order of the Royal Society.

Source: Abercrombie, 1981, pp. 207–44

Reading B

AN ESSAY ON THE NECESSITY, ADVANTAGES AND PRACTICABILITY OF REFORMING THE MODE OF SPELLING, AND OF RENDERING THE ORTHOGRAPHY OF WORDS CORRESPONDENT TO THE PRONUNCIATION

Noah Webster

It has been observed by all writers on the English language, that the orthography or spelling of words is very irregular; the same letters often representing different sounds, and the same sounds often expressed by different letters. For this irregularity, two principal causes may be assigned:

1   The changes to which the pronunciation of a language is liable, from the progress of science and civilisation.

2   The mixture of different languages, occasioned by revolutions in England, or by a predilection of the learned, for words of foreign growth and ancient origin.

But such is the state of our language. The pronunciation of the words which are strictly *English*, has gradually been changing for ages, and since the revival of science in Europe, the language has received a vast accession of words from other languages, many of which retain an orthography very ill-suited to exhibit the true pronunciation.

The question now occurs; ought the Americans to retain these faults which produce innumerable inconveniences in the acquisition and use of the language, or ought they at once to reform these abuses, and introduce order and regularity into the orthography of the AMERICAN TONGUE?

Let us consider this subject with some attention.

Several attempts were formerly made in England to rectify the orthography of the language. But I apprehend their schemes failed of success, rather on account of their intrinsic difficulties, than on account of any necessary impracticability of a reform. It was proposed in most of these schemes, not merely to throw out superfluous and silent letters, but to introduce a number of new characters. Any attempt on such a plan must undoubtedly prove unsuccessful. It is not to be expected that an orthography, perfectly regular and simple, such as would be formed by a 'Synod of Grammarians on principles of science', will ever be substituted for that confused mode of spelling which is now established. But it is apprehended that great improvements may be made, and an orthography almost regular, or such as shall obviate most of the present difficulties which occur in learning our language, may be introduced and established with little trouble and opposition.

The principal alterations, necessary to render our orthography sufficiently regular and easy, are these:

1   The omission of all superfluous or silent letters; as *a* in *bread*. Thus *bread, head, give, breast, built, meant, realm, friend,* would be spelt, *bred, hed, giv, brest, bilt, ment, relm, frend*. Would this alteration produce any inconvenience, any embarrassment or expense? By no means. On the other hand, it would lessen the trouble of writing, and much more, of learning the language; it would reduce the true pronunciation to a certainty; and while it would assist foreigners and our own children in acquiring the language, it would render the pronunciation uniform, in different parts of the country, and almost prevent the possibility of changes.

2   A substitution of a character that has a certain definite sound for one that is more vague and indeterminate. Thus by putting *ee* instead of *ea* or *ie*, the words *mean, near, speak, grieve, zeal,* would become *meen, neer, speek, greev, zeel*. This alteration could not occasion a moment's trouble; at the same time it would prevent a doubt respecting the pronunciation; whereas the *ea* and *ie* having different sounds, may give a learner much difficulty …

3   A trifling alteration in a character, or the addition of a point would distinguish different sounds, without the substitution of a new character. Thus a very small stroke across *th* would distinguish its two sounds. A point over a vowel, in this manner ä, or ȯ, or ᴛ, might answer all the purposes of different letters. And for the diphthong *ow*, let the two letters be united by a small stroke, or both engraven on the same piece of metal, with the left hand line of the *w* united to the *o*.

These, with a few other inconsiderable alterations, would answer every purpose, and render the orthography sufficiently correct and regular.

The advantages to be derived from alterations are numerous, great and permanent.

1   The simplicity of the orthography would facilitate the learning of the language. It is now the work of years for children to learn to spell; and after all, the business is rarely accomplished. A few men, who are bred to some business that requires constant exercise in writing, finally learn to spell most words without hesitation; but most people remain, all their lives, imperfect masters of spelling, and liable to make mistakes, whenever they take up a pen to write a short note. Nay, many people, even of education and fashion, never attempt to write a letter, without frequently consulting a dictionary.

But with the proposed orthography, a child would learn to spell, without trouble, in a very short time, and the orthography being very regular, he would ever afterwards find it difficult to make a mistake. It would, in that case, be as difficult to spell *wrong*, as it is now to spell *right*.

Besides this advantage, foreigners would be able to acquire the pronunciation of English, which is now so difficult and embarrassing, that they are either wholly discouraged on the first attempt, or obliged, after many years labor, to rest contented with an imperfect knowledge of the subject.

2   A correct orthography would render the pronunciation of the language, as uniform as in the spelling books. A general uniformity thro the United States, would be the event of such a reformation as I am here recommending. All persons, of every rank, would speak with some degree of precision and uniformity. Such a uniformity in these states is very desirable; it would remove prejudice, and conciliate mutual affection and respect.

3   Such a reform would diminish the number of letters about one sixteenth or eighteenth; this would save a page in eighteen; and a saving of an eighteenth in the expense of books, is an advantage that should not be overlooked.

4   But a capital advantage of this reform in these states would be, that it would make a difference between the English orthography and the American. This will startle those who have not attended to the subject; but I am confident that such an event is an object of vast political consequence. For, [sic]

The alteration, however, small, would encourage the publication of books in our own country. It would render it, in some measure, necessary that all books should be printed in America. The English would never copy our orthography for their own use; and consequently the same impressions of books would not answer for both countries. The inhabitants of the present generation would read the English impressions; but posterity, being taught a different spelling, would prefer the American orthography.

Besides this, a *national language* is a band of *national union*. Every engine should be employed to make the people of this country *national*; to call their attachments home to their own country; and to inspire them with the pride of national character. However they may boast of Independence, and the freedom of their government, yet their *opinions* are not sufficiently independent; an astonishing respect for the arts and literature of their parent country, and a blind imitation of its manners, are still prevalent among the Americans. Thus an habitual respect for another country, deserved indeed and once laudable, turns their attention from their own interests, and prevents their respecting themselves ...

But America is in a situation most favourable for great reformations; and the present time is, in a singular degree, auspicious. The minds of men in this country

have been awakened. New scenes have been, for many years, presenting new occasions for exertion; unexpected distresses have called forth the powers of invention; and the application of new expedients has demanded every possible exercise of wisdom and talents. Attention is roused; the mind expanded; and the intellectual faculties invigorated. Here men are prepared to receive improvements, which would be rejected by nations, whose habits have not been shaken by similar events.

Now is the time, and *this* is the country, in which we may expect success, in attempting changes favourable to language, science and government. Delay, in the plan here proposed, may be fatal; under the tranquil general government, the minds of men may again sink into indolence; a national acquiescence in error will follow; and posterity will be doomed to struggle with difficulties, which time and accident will perpetually multiply.

Let us then seize the present moment, and establish a *national language* as well as a national government. Let us remember that there is a certain respect due to the opinions of other nations. As an independent people, our reputation abroad demands that, in all things, we should be federal; be *national*; for if we do not respect *ourselves*, we may be assured that other nations will not respect us. In short, let it be impressed upon the mind of every American, that to neglect the means of commanding respect abroad, is treason against the character and dignity of a brave independent people.

Source: Webster [extracts from the appendix to *Dissertations on the English Language*, 1789] 1991, pp. 83–93

3 THE ORIGINS OF ENGLISH

Dick Leith

3.1 INTRODUCTION

In this chapter I examine the history of the English language in its first thousand years of existence – from its original appearance in England in the fifth century AD, as a consequence of the Anglo-Saxon invasions, to the introduction of printing in the fifteenth century. I show how English has changed over the years and how it has been influenced by other languages spoken by later settlers; that is, the Scandinavian languages spoken by Viking invaders who settled in England between the eighth and eleventh centuries, and the French of the eleventh-century Norman invaders. I also discuss how various other languages have affected the development of English at different times, in particular Latin, which was used for many centuries by intellectuals and the church. I shall thus describe the history of contact between English and other languages.

This book is concerned not just with the linguistic form of English but also with political and cultural issues associated with its use by different kinds of people around the world. The early part of the history of the language necessarily focuses on its use in the territory which is now known as England. You might think that describing this history is a straightforward task – one which does not raise some of the complex political and cultural issues associated with later periods in English (such as the era of colonial expansion dealt with in Chapter 5). In this chapter, however, I argue that telling any history is like telling a story which both describes events and gives them a particular interpretation and value (see the box below on 'Stories and histories'). It is therefore important to ask yourself, in connection with any narrative, 'Who is telling this story?', 'Whose perspective does it represent?'

I argue here that the most familiar story of the English language, as customarily told by linguistic historians, was mainly constructed in the nineteenth century, and that it draws particularly on nineteenth-century ideas of national identity. Indeed, the very idea of national identity is largely a construct of nineteenth-century nationalism, something that is discussed further in Chapter 4. Such nationalism assumes the existence of an unchanging national 'essence' residing in a shared ethnic origin, a fixed territory and a common language. It may be significant that this familiar story of the origins of English and its subsequent development was created during the height of the British empire, when Britain controlled many colonial territories around the world. English, however, is no longer the language of a British colonial power. It may be time for a more critical examination of the traditional nineteenth-century account.

This chapter thus has two main functions. It describes what we know about the English language in its early stages of development; and it looks at how this evidence has been drawn upon to tell particular narratives about the history of English.

Stories and histories

What is the difference between a story and a history? Is one fictional and the other based on fact?

Traditional folk tales told in the western world (whether fact or fiction) all share some basic features of plot structure and character roles. This emerged in a study of 100 folk tales conducted by Propp (1958). Propp identified some recurrent character roles (such as *villain* and *hero*), and argued that all plots shared the same underlying structure (including the sections *preparation, complication, transference, struggle, return* and *recognition*).

Recently, linguists have argued that when people describe real events – whether in personal anecdotes or in newspaper stories – they tend to adopt a similar structure. For example, in the fourth book in this series, Goodman and Graddol (eds) *Redesigning English: new texts, new identities,* the linguist Allan Bell examines the narrative structure of news stories. In the second book in this series, Maybin and Mercer (eds) *Using English: from conversation to canon,* Janet Maybin describes in Chapter 1 how 'we hardly ever report someone else's exact words when we are relating an incident or anecdote; we paraphrase and reframe them to make a particular point and to show ourselves in a particular light'. By including certain evaluations of events, we can use narratives to construct the world in particular ways and to develop our own sense of identity.

One of the arguments in this chapter is that history is a kind of story about the past, and it is therefore not surprising to find it is given a narrative structure which conforms to the generic western model. Furthermore, histories are like anecdotes in that they may contain particular evaluations of events which help construct a particular identity for the story-teller and others. The way the 'story of English' has been told thus inevitably reflects the interests and motives of those who tell it. In this chapter we examine who has been cast as the 'hero', and what has been seen as the 'complication' and 'struggle' which needed to be overcome. We also look at variants of the story that have a 'happy ending' (the language which flourished in Old English times, but which had to struggle to overcome the complication of the Norman conquest and triumphantly returns as the 'world language') as well as those which have a sad ending (a language which had a golden age but which became corrupted by the influence of other languages).

Differences between stories are not a conflict about what 'really' did and did not happen so much as a matter of differences in interpretation and evaluation. This approach to history allows us to see it as something which is constantly created and re-created, and which reflects the particular cultural values and interests of those who tell it and the times they live in. We need, therefore, to examine any 'story of English' critically. From whose position is the story told? Are there alternative ways of telling it that reflect different viewpoints?

3.2   STORIES OF ENGLISH

About two thousand years ago there was a place in what is now the north of England which the Celtic Britons named *Caer Ebruac.* Then the Romans came and named it *Eboracum.* About 400 years after that the Anglo-Saxons came, and named it *Eoforwic.* And about 400 years after

that, the Vikings came, and named it *Jorvik*. From this we have today's form, *York*.

In the brief history given here of the place-name York we also have a potted history of all the peoples involved in the formation of the English language before the Norman conquest in 1066: Celts, Romans, Anglo-Saxons and Vikings. We can find here a story of contact between speakers of different languages. The Romans, who spoke Latin, heard the Celtic form *Ebruac* and changed it to *Ebor*. This form in turn perhaps reminded the Anglo-Saxons of their word for 'boar', which was *eofor* (pronounced something like 'ever', but with the first syllable close to 'air'). They added to it the form *wic* (pronounced like 'witch'), a common element in English place-names that originally may have meant a dairy-farm. The Vikings, who spoke a language similar to that of the Anglo-Saxons, substituted their own form *vik* for *wic* and pronounced *eofor* in their own way (deleting the 'f' and shifting the stress, to sound like 'your').

Stories are also often told in order to make some sort of point. The point of my story is that the 'English' place-name York bears the traces of four different languages spoken by four different peoples. Stories are also usually built around a central character. In the case of a language, this may need to be a whole people. Of the four different peoples mentioned above it is the Anglo-Saxons who are now seen as occupying this main character role. It is the language of the Anglo-Saxons that is often said to constitute the 'core' of English. Apart from most of the proper names, and the word 'place' (which comes from French), all the words in my story of the history of the place-name York were actually chosen on the grounds of their Anglo-Saxon origin. 'Two', for instance, was *twa*, and 'thousand' was *þusend*. So I have been able to tell this story about contact with other languages in a way which gives a privileged position to the Anglo-Saxon element in English.

There is a tradition in English thought, which flourished in the nineteenth century, that glorifies the Anglo-Saxons and their language. It was then that the systematic study of the history of the English language began – at a time when ideas about national identity and Britain's place in the world were undergoing significant change (partly as a result of the experience of the British empire). One outcome of this has been to equate Anglo-Saxons with 'Englishness', as though national character, as well as language, had a racial origin.

This emphasis on the Anglo-Saxons as the central 'character' in the story of English was not always made. In 1783, for instance, the writer of one dictionary, Lemon, claimed that 'the groundwork of our modern English tongue is Greek' (quoted in Crowley, 1989, p. 41). Such references to the so-called classical languages of Europe (i.e. ancient Greek and Latin) were made because they enjoyed the greatest prestige, and it used to be thought by some historians that the Anglo-Saxons were little more than barbarians.

In Chapter 4, I come back to the eighteenth-century idea that the era of classical Greek and Latin, rather than that of Old English, was a 'golden age'. That chapter also discusses more fully the emergence of nineteenth-century ideas about national identity. The important point to note here is that the most familiar 'story of English' to be found in the majority of textbooks today dates back to the nineteenth century. Only very recently have scholars begun to explore what other ways can be found of explaining and interpreting the known historical data.

A confusion of names

The different people, languages and territories involved in the early English period are referred to by a bewildering variety of names. This is partly because historians are not very sure exactly who was who, so they use different terms to describe them. But there were genuinely many different peoples and language varieties which contributed to the development of English and which were given different names by speakers of different languages. Indeed, the names used to describe people, places and languages often reflect the viewpoint from which the story is told. Described below are the five major linguistic influences on English.

Celtic

This term describes the people and language that existed in Britain before the Roman invasion in the first century BC. Modern Welsh and Gaelic (spoken in Wales and in Ireland and Scotland, respectively) represent the two main branches of Celtic: Brythonic and Goidelic. At the time of the Anglo-Saxon invasions, Goidelic was restricted to Ireland and the Celtic language spoken throughout the mainland was Brythonic. In discussions of early history, the terms 'British', 'Briton' and 'Brittonic' imply Celtic people and their languages as opposed to Anglo-Saxon people and Old English.

Latin

The Romans first introduced Latin to Britain when they invaded Britain in the first century BC. Even after the Roman legions left, in the early fifth century AD, Latin remained an important influence on the English language right up until the eighteenth century, mainly through the church and the institutions of law, education and science.

Anglo-Saxons

These were the settlers/invaders who arrived in Britain in the fifth century AD from northern Germany and whose language formed the basis for English. A variety of terms are used to describe these people, most commonly 'Angles', 'Saxons' and 'Jutes'. The generic term 'Anglo-Saxon' is used in this chapter to describe the people and culture once they settled in Britain. Although their language is sometimes also called 'Anglo-Saxon', in this book the term used is 'Old English'. Names such as 'Mercia', 'Northumbria', 'Wessex', and 'Kent' refer to Anglo-Saxon kingdoms.

Scandinavian

The Scandinavian invaders arrived from the eighth to the eleventh centuries and are sometimes also referred to as the 'Vikings' or 'Norse'. The most significant settlement in northern and eastern parts of England was by the Danes; in the north-west of England and in Scotland it was by Norwegians.

French

The Norman invasion of the eleventh century introduced a variety of French (Norman French) to Britain. Varieties of French remained an important linguistic influence on English up to modern times.

The nature of evidence

It seems appropriate at this point to enquire into the beginnings of the story of English. How, or where, do we start this story? With the territory on which it was first spoken, or with which it came to be identified? With the people who first spoke it? Or is it possible to start with the language itself, without making any reference to land or people?

External and internal evidence and external and internal history

The history of any language includes both a linguistic history (the nature of the grammar and vocabulary at different points in time) and an account of who spoke the language, where and when. The first kind of history is often called the **internal history**, and the latter the **external history**. Just as there are two dimensions to the history of a language, so there are two kinds of evidence. Broadly speaking, we can distinguish between linguistic evidence as such – often called **internal evidence** – and non-linguistic historical information – often called **external evidence**. Internal evidence comes mainly from texts and documents which provide examples of the language at known points in time. External evidence typically comes from archaeological sites or contemporary written histories.

Evidence is one of the most important problems in writing the history of a language. There are problems concerning the availability of evidence, the relationship between internal and external evidence, and the interpretation of whatever evidence exists.

One problem with beginning the story of English with the language itself (i.e. starting with the internal history) is that there is no evidence of it before written texts in Old English were first produced in England in the eighth century. Some historical accounts do, however, start with this 'prehistory' by attempting to reconstruct those languages spoken on the European continent that were the precursors of English. One of the great achievements of the nineteenth-century language scholars – who were known as 'philologists' – was to show the regular patterns of relationship among languages of the same 'family'. English was established as a Germanic language, which in today's context means that it shares important characteristics with German, Dutch, Danish, Norwegian and Swedish. Philologists studied the oldest forms of all these languages and argued that they all derived from a common ancestor before written records began.

On the other hand, if we start our story with either the territory or people (i.e. with an external history) we risk the suggestion that the language 'belongs' to either one. The problems implied by this will emerge in due course. However, I begin my account in the next section with aspects of the external history.

3.3   BEGINNING THE STORY: PROBLEMS OF EXTERNAL HISTORY

The central questions in the external history of early English relate to where the first speakers of English came from and where they settled. Reading A is an account of the origins of English up to the Norman conquest of 1066 by the contemporary linguist David Crystal. It is taken from his book *The English Language* (1988). He has already established that the roots of English were not 'native' to the British Isles, that the language originally came from what is now northern Germany.

Activity 3.1   *(Reading A)*

Read 'The story of Old English' by David Crystal (Reading A), which gives a very useful background to the origins of English. I suggest that you first read through this quickly, noting the general account of Old English which Crystal gives. Then re-read the extract more carefully in order to answer the questions given below.

- Note the effects that the following groups of people had on the creation and development of Old English and their role in the history of England, according to Crystal: the Romans, the Celts, the Anglo-Saxons, the Christian missionaries and the Danes.
- What group of people does Crystal consider played the central role in the formation of Old English?
- Does Crystal consider there to be a clear line of descent from Old English to modern English?
- What does Crystal have to say about King Alfred?
- Does Crystal rely mainly on external or internal evidence? Can you find examples of both?

Comment

Throughout this chapter we return to this issue of the role of different settlers/invaders in the development of the English language. Below I explore the types of evidence that Crystal uses and what conclusions this leads him to draw.

The extract from Crystal is primarily an *external* history dealing with such matters as invasions and the introduction of writing, using mainly external evidence. But you should note that in his account of the early Anglo-Saxon period – which he describes as a 'dark age' – Crystal draws on internal evidence such as vocabulary and place names. He appears to use this internal evidence to serve two purposes. First, it shows that at one level of structure – vocabulary – the language of the Anglo-Saxons was not entirely Germanic, since it absorbed words from Latin and Celtic and was later supplemented by words from the Scandinavian language spoken by the Viking invaders. The internal evidence thus provides indirect evidence for a story of **contact**.

The second purpose is more complicated. The vocabulary and place-name evidence is actually being used here in the virtual absence of evidence from external sources about the Celtic presence in Britain in the early Anglo-Saxon period. So telling this part of the external history depends on internal evidence, and its interpretation. Because so few words were adopted by the Anglo-Saxons from the Celts, Crystal infers that the latter people were entirely dominated. He says that 'We do not know if many Celts stayed in the east and south of England, but if they did, they would have soon lost their identity within the dominant Anglo-Saxon society'. This interpretation depends on making an assumption that the less powerful social group adjusts to the norms, linguistic and otherwise, of the more powerful one. This would appear to be supported by the fact that the external evidence we have of the dominant position of the Vikings in northern England during the eighth to eleventh centuries is matched by the internal evidence of the substantial adoptions from Scandinavian languages into English in this period.

The external evidence

Given the problems involved in interpreting external history from internal (i.e. linguistic) evidence, we need to ask how far we can establish the story from external evidence alone? I will start by considering what is perhaps the most famous piece of external evidence, Bede's *Ecclesiastical History of the English People*, which he wrote in Latin in the eighth century and which was translated into Old English in the ninth century.

You may remember from Chapter 2 Bede's story about the three different tribes – the Angles, Saxons and Jutes – who settled in different parts of what is now called England and southern Scotland (see Figure 2.3). According to Bede each tribe spoke its own dialect, derived from its area of origin on the European mainland. These dialects later became identified with the different Anglo-Saxon kingdoms of Mercia and Nothumbria (settled by the Angles), Kent settled by the Jutes, and Wessex settled by the Saxons (there were also the smaller kingdoms of East Anglia, Essex and Sussex).

Bede, however, was writing nearly 300 years later than the events he describes. He makes no mention of the possibility that the Romans themselves may have used Germanic mercenaries on British soil in defence of their province. He says nothing about the tribe known as Frisians who were among the Germanic invaders and his account suggests that the names 'Angles', 'Saxons' and 'Jutes' were mutually exclusive, which may not have been the case. You may remember from Reading A that Crystal takes the same view as Bede, claiming that the 'main dialect divisions reflect the settlements of the invading tribes, with their different linguistic backgrounds'. Some language scholars have argued that the distinctive dialects used by the Anglo-Saxons were forged not on the continent but in the territory now called England. DeCamp, for example, argued that:

> the origins of the English dialects lie not in pre-migrational tribal affiliations but in certain social, economic, and cultural developments which occurred after the migration was completed. This does not imply that the continental Germanic dialects are irrelevant to the genesis of English dialects ... Only those influences, however, which were felt after the migrations were relevant to the formation of the English dialects; for I believe that these dialects originated not on the continent but on the island of Britain.
>
> (DeCamp, 1958, p. 232)

Exactly what happened during this period which led to the regional differences in Old English is thus obscure. But we know that in more recent times there have been perhaps similar linguistic consequences of migration, settlement and the building of new communities. In Chapter 5 we discuss what happened in colonial times when people speaking different kinds of English migrated to America and created a new, shared form of language. Chapter 7 describes a modern-day study of the accents of settlers in the new city of Milton Keynes.

Bede, of course, could not have known what linguists now know about processes of language change. It is possible that he was trying to explain the contemporary division into kingdoms and dialects in terms of stories about settlement history that had been passed down through the ages. So he may have 'tidied up' the picture in order to construct a coherent history that also empha-sized the role of the Anglo-Saxons and minimized the influence of the Celts on the English language.

It is also noteworthy that Bede was writing an *ecclesiastical* history. Bede himself was a churchman and it was the Roman Catholic church, rather than the monarchies, that had the strongest institutions at this time. It has recently been suggested that the boundaries between the dialects of Old English, though corresponding roughly with those of the ancient kingdoms, might best be seen as ecclesiastical (Hogg, 1992, p. 4). Writing itself was for a long time the preserve of the church, with its various dioceses dividing up the land into geographical segments. We must remember that our evidence of Old English dialects comes from written texts, and we do not know how well these reflected the spoken languages of the areas where they were written.

The case of Bede demonstrates an important principle in respect of documentary evidence: we need to take account of *who* authors are, their social position, when they were writing and their reasons for writing in the first place.

Bede's *History* is the earliest English account. There is, however, an even earlier Celtic account, *On the Ruin and Conquest of Britain*, written in the 540s by Gildas, which Bede drew on. The accounts by Bede and by Gildas provide rather different perspectives on the external history of English. Seen from the point of view of the Welsh, the invasion of the Anglo-Saxons was a disaster. In the Celtic version of the story, it could be argued that the Anglo-Saxons are cast as the 'villain' rather than the 'hero'. Gildas wrote: 'All the greater towns fell to the enemy's battering rams; all their inhabitants, bishops, priests, people, were mown down together … Horrible was it to see …' (Williams, 1985).

Activity 3.2   *(Allow 10–15 minutes)*

The (translated) words from Gildas given above are quoted by the modern Welsh historian Gwyn Williams in his book *When was Wales?* (1985). Below is Williams's account of the Anglo-Saxon invasion and settlement.

While reading the account consider how far Williams adopts the perspective of Gildas in respect to how he views the Anglo-Saxons. What language does he use to describe the Anglo-Saxons? According to Reading A, Crystal believes that within the areas dominated by the Anglo-Saxons, the Celts 'would soon have lost their identity'. He goes on to state that 'the Celtic language of Roman Britain had hardly any influence on the language spoken by the Anglo-Saxons'. Do you think Williams agrees with this view of the conquest of the Celts? Read the extract now.

> After Gildas the curtain comes down. From the late sixth century the mixed peoples of the east, generically labelled Anglo-Saxons and organizing themselves in kingdoms, resumed their advance. It was a long, slow, piecemeal business; some of the advances may not represent straightforward conquests and there is evidence of the transient existence of peoples who were literally mixed. But it was remorseless … After a battle near Bath in 577, the kings of Gloucester, Bath and Cirencester were gone and Saxon power reached the Bristol Channel, to press on into the south-west. Almost a century later, in a bewildering maze of triangular struggles between Mercians, Northumbrians and West Britons, the newcomers entrenched themselves on the northern shores of the Irish Sea. It took another century to establish the power of Mercia in the Midlands. Britain, in its shifting form, and uniquely in Europe, fought the barbarians for nearly four hundred years before it was lost. It was late in the eighth century that Offa of Mercia, first of the Saxon kings

to adopt imperial styles, drove his Dyke from sea to sea, to shut out the West Britons from their inheritance as 'foreigners' – the Welsh [the word 'Welsh' derives from an Old English word meaning both 'foreigner' and 'slave'].

East of a line from the Yorkshire Wolds to Southampton, there is precious little evidence of British [Celtic] survival, even in river names. West of that line, however, into the upland watershed, there is much evidence. Place-names remain strongly Celtic, though often transmuted; Brittonic [the language of the Celts], now rapidly changing and splintering into different languages – one of them Cymraeg, or Welsh – survived as a subject tongue. Early laws of the kingdom of Wessex make specific provision for a whole British hierarchy within its society. Further west still beyond this line and up to the rooted Celtic lands of north-west Britain, Wales and Cornwall, British survival under Saxon control seems to have been substantial, perhaps even massive. As English settlement inched up to the Wye and the line of the Southern Dyke, there may have been almost as much fusion as conquest.

It was in these latter regions that the rising kingdoms of Northumbria, Mercia and Wessex took shape between 600 and 800. And it was in those districts that a recognizable Wales was defined.

(Williams, 1985, pp. 26-7)

Comment

For modern Welsh historians such as Gwyn Williams, the growth of importance of the English language is still perceived negatively since it has contributed to the erosion of the Welsh language and Celtic culture. In that respect, Gywn Williams seems to align himself with the Celtic tradition (based on Gildas) rather than the Anglo-Saxon one (based on Bede).

Williams draws on various kinds of external and internal evidence to cast doubt on the account of conquest and destruction of the Celts by the Anglo-Saxons. He emphasizes the possibility of cultural 'fusion' and also the lengthy resistance (spanning four centuries) that the Celts put up against the Anglo-Saxon invasions. This in turn plays down the 'achievement' of the Anglo-Saxons and the humiliation of the Celtic ancestors of the Welsh. The line from the Yorkshire Wolds to Southampton referred to by Williams in the extract above corresponds to the area of earliest settlement shown on Figure 3.2.

The early laws of Wessex, which form part of his external evidence, established that the 'wergild' (the compensation to be paid to a slain man's kindred) payable for a Welsh man was much lower than for an Anglo-Saxon. For example, the lowest class of Anglo-Saxon required a wergild of 200 shillings, whereas that for even a landowning Welsh man did not exceed 120 shillings, as the extract from the law (AD 688–94) below shows:

if   a Welsh   man   have   a hide of land,   his wergild is   120   shillings;
Gif Wilisc mon hæbbe hide londes, his wer bið CXX scillinga;

if   he   the   half   have,   80   shillings;   if   he   none
gif he þonne healfe hæbbe, LXXX scillinga; gif he nænig

have,   60   shillings
hæbbe, LX scillinga

The Wergild'

(Cited in Whitelock, 1967, p. 53)

While this law shows that the Welsh were considered of inferior status, it also means they must have been living among the Anglo-Saxons and have had a distinct identity.

The external evidence is too limited to establish the facts about the Anglo-Saxon invasion and settlement. This is why Williams, like Crystal, turns to internal evidence. I look at the nature of the internal evidence, particularly that provided by place-names, below.

The internal evidence

Some of the early adoptions from Celtic were used in place-names, which are especially difficult to interpret (partly because they were first written down long after the period of naming). These often refer to natural features such as rivers, hills and woods. Celtic forms were frequently combined with Anglo-Saxon ones, and sometimes both elements denote the same thing: *Brill* (in Buckinghamshire) combines Celtic *bre* (hill) with Old English *hyl* (hill).

Often included among these Celtic words is *combe*, denoting a valley. This is discussed in 'Place-name evidence'.

Place-name evidence

The photograph shows the village of Long Compton in Warwickshire, taken from the north-eastern side of the combe (shown in the foreground). The high ground in the distance is the southern side of the combe (which marks the border with Oxfordshire).

The village of Long Compton in Warwickshire

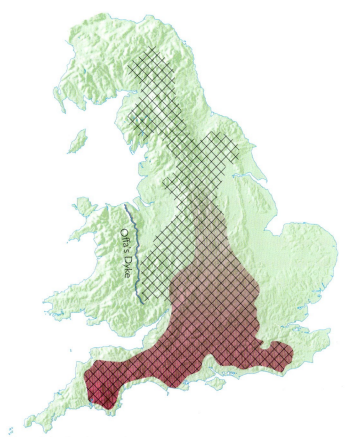

Figure 3.1   Distribution of combe *as a place-name element*

In modern Welsh *cwm* means 'valley'. But there is also an Old English word *cumb* ('cup' or 'vessel'). So place-names such as Pyecomb in Sussex or Long Compton in Warwickshire could derive from either Celtic or Old English, or perhaps the Anglo-Saxons decided to adapt the meaning of their own word *cumb* once they had heard the Celtic word used.

Recently, place-name scholars have started to investigate the actual places or sites where certain names are used (Gelling, 1984). *Cumb* seems to denote a broad, bowl-shaped valley with three fairly steep sides. The name is most common in south-west England, suggesting that it could be an adoption from Celtic. Figure 3.1 shows some of the complex problems involved in interpreting the evidence of its distribution.

The cross-hatched areas denote land hilly enough for *combe* to be a relevant name (the areas now known as Wales and Cornwall were not settled by the Anglo-Saxons). The shaded area denotes the distribution of *combe*. Notice that it is rare in the north and also in the area of the Welsh border (where we might expect it). Was the Celtic term used in these areas? Or if the term is derived from Old English, was it known to the Anglians who settled in the north and Midlands? Was it no longer used when Anglo-Saxons settled the Welsh border areas?

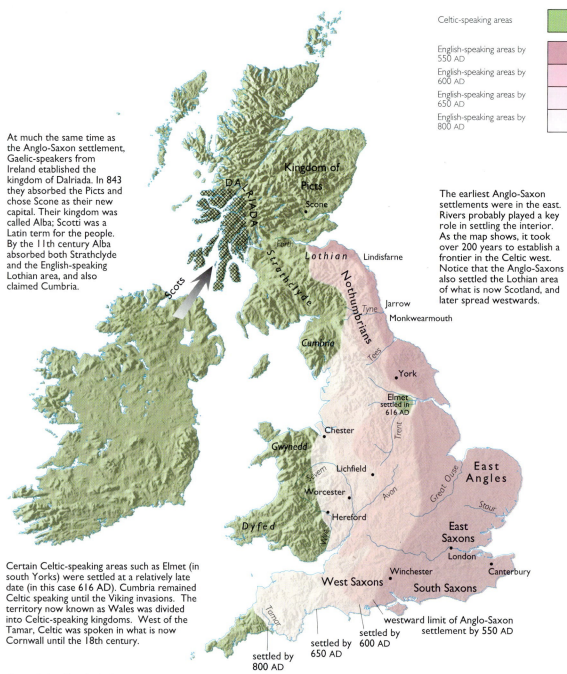

At much the same time as the Anglo-Saxon settlement, Gaelic-speakers from Ireland etablished the kingdom of Dalriada. In 843 they absorbed the Picts and chose Scone as their new capital. Their kingdom was called Alba; Scotti was a Latin term for the people. By the 11th century Alba absorbed both Strathclyde and the English-speaking Lothian area, and also claimed Cumbria.

The earliest Anglo-Saxon settlements were in the east. Rivers probably played a key role in settling the interior. As the map shows, it took over 200 years to establish a frontier in the Celtic west. Notice that the Anglo-Saxons also settled the Lothian area of what is now Scotland, and later spread westwards.

Celtic-speaking areas

English-speaking areas by 550 AD

English-speaking areas by 600 AD

English-speaking areas by 650 AD

English-speaking areas by 800 AD

Certain Celtic-speaking areas such as Elmet (in south Yorks) were settled at a relatively late date (in this case 616 AD). Cumbria remained Celtic speaking until the Viking invasions. The territory now known as Wales was divided into Celtic-speaking kingdoms. West of the Tamar, Celtic was spoken in what is now Cornwall until the 18th century.

Figure 3.2   The Anglo-Saxon settlement

The problem of interpreting place-name evidence shows some of the difficulties in interpreting the internal evidence in general. In the past, the fact that so few words seem to have been adopted from the Celts was taken as evidence to support the view that this people were either slaughtered, put to flight, or enslaved by the conquering Anglo-Saxons. But recent archaeological findings suggest relations between the two peoples were often characterized by overlap and fusion (Myres, 1986). In other words, external evidence tends to support the version of events described by Gwyn Williams.

Place-name evidence also raises a problem of a different order. Above I referred to it as an example of 'internal' evidence. However, we need to draw on so much non-linguistic evidence to interpret place-names that we might justifiably wonder how 'internal' to the language such names are.

This is part of a larger problem which we will meet again in this book. What exactly counts as part of the language? Where does the boundary lie between linguistic and nonlinguistic, between internal and external? The lack of any simple answer to this question is one reason why it is difficult to define the boundaries of the English language itself.

King Alfred

I would like to turn now to the role of King Alfred. If you remember, I asked you to look at what Crystal has to say about this West Saxon king in Reading A. You may have noticed that he mentions King Alfred in three different contexts. The first has to do with commissioning the translation of Latin texts into the West Saxon dialect of Old English. According to Alfred himself, the reason for this was the decline in knowledge of Latin and the destruction of Latin texts as a result of the Viking invasions. The second and third concern the dominance of Wessex and the West Saxon dialect in the late Anglo-Saxon period, which was the legacy of Alfred once he had overcome the Vikings.

It is very common to find this emphasis on **standardization** in histories of English. It involves what we can call a 'progressive' story; that is, progressing from humble origins to a more developed present (rather like a fairytale). And the desire to find evidence of standardization has tempted scholars to seek it in the West Saxon dialect of Old English. As Crystal says, a great deal of material written in other dialects was translated into West Saxon. By the end of the Anglo-Saxon period writers from as far apart as York (in the kingdom of Northumbria) and Canterbury (in Kent) were writing in West Saxon. So that particular dialect has sometimes been seen as a standard in Old English, albeit in the very restricted sense of a written (i.e. not spoken) norm.

This seems to me to be part of a tradition begun in the nineteenth century which glorifies Alfred as the embodiment of 'Englishness': if he had not suc-ceeded in single-handedly defeating the Vikings, England would have become part of Scandinavia. Alfred is therefore a 'national' hero, and his promotion of English (rather than Latin) is a sign of this national consciousness. Just as he centralized English rule under the West Saxon dynasty, so he took the first step in centralizing the language, by promoting one dialect at the expense of the others.

One problem with this view of Alfred is that his victory over the Vikings, as Crystal tells us, was not final. At the end of the tenth century fresh Viking raids led to the installation of a Danish dynasty as kings of England between 1016 and 1042. This view can also be challenged on other grounds. Alfred's writing programme depended on a great deal of help from Mercia, which was also making its own, independent, translations into the Mercian dialect during this time. If indeed there was a West Saxon standard, it came later and was associated less with the monarchy than with the influential Benedictine monasteries of the tenth century.

Of the seven kingdoms (names in capitals) three dominated the
Anglo-Saxon period: Northumbria in the 7th century, Mercia (with its
dyke marking the Welsh border) in the 8th and Wessex from the 9th.

Figure 3.3
The Anglo-Saxon kingdoms

The scriptorium (see Chapter 2) at Winchester (Alfred's capital) seems to have
made considerable efforts in regularizing spellings, but the language was very
different from that of King Alfred's time.

Alfred's promotion of writing and learning can be interpreted in a different
way: as part of his strategy to establish himself as a king in the image of the Roman
emperors. For this, the king needed the support of the church, which at this time
was a stronger institution than any 'monarchy', and the promotion of learning
(including commissioning translations) was one way of gaining this. In fact,
Alfred was so successful in this that he not only founded a dynasty with its own
mint, laws and county administration that controlled the whole of England, but it
is *his* perspectives that have been widely accepted by later historians. It is possible
that he commissioned the writing of *The Anglo-Saxon Chronicle*, which provides an
account of Anglo-Saxon history from a Wessex point of view. And according to the
Oxford English Dictionary, the word *Englisc* (English) was first used to denote both
people and language under his auspices. Alfred's use of this term perhaps reflects
his claim to the territory originally settled by the Anglians and later overrun by the
Vikings, before being defeated by his armies. Finally, the view that the Vikings

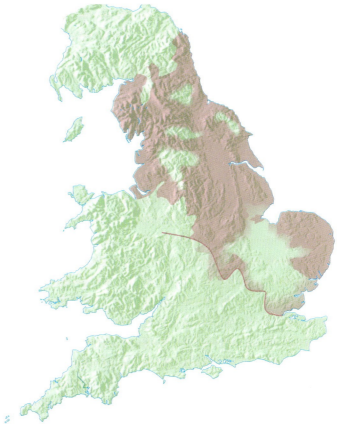

The southern limit of the Danelaw was the Roman road known as
Watling Street, running from London to north Wales (marked in
purple). North of that line the Danes ruled until the West Saxon kings
re-conquered the Danelaw in the 10th century. The pink coloured
portion represents the area where place-names derive from the
language spoken by the Vikings – Danes in the east, Norwegians in the
west. Vikings from Norway also settled in Ireland, the north-east and
west of Scotland, and around the coast of Wales.

Figure 3.4   The Danelaw

were the chief reason for the destruction of manuscripts, which has become the
accepted one, is essentially Alfred's (Crystal, for example, writes, 'Doubtless many
manuscripts were burned during the eighth-century Viking invasions'). It again
may reflect contemporary propaganda aimed at placing the Scandinavian settlers
in a poor light.

So we can see that although there are a large number of facts that historians
agree on, there are various ways of linking these facts together to tell a coherent
story. We can begin to see how the dominant story of English is one which – not
unexpectedly – embodies the perspective of those English speakers who held
political and cultural power. This is a theme that I return to in Chapter 5 when I
examine the colonial spread of English to other parts of the world.

So far we've looked at some of the problems involved in ordering an external
account of Old English. Now let's see what the language itself looked like.

3.4 THE INTERNAL HISTORY: AN EXAMPLE OF OLD ENGLISH

The most obvious kind of evidence available for looking at the internal history of Old English (i.e. its linguistic history) is the internal evidence provided by written texts. We deal here with an extract from a story told by the Anglo-Saxons themselves about the poet Caedmon. It is taken from the same text discussed above, Bede's *Ecclesiastical History of the English People*, one of the works selected by Alfred for translation into Old English from the original Latin. As an example of ninth-century West Saxon it therefore gives us *internal* evidence about a dialect of Old English. Caedmon was supposed to be the first man to adapt the ancient Anglo-Saxon poetic form – traditionally used to celebrate the deeds of pagan heroes – for the expression of the Christian message. The gift of verse is miraculously given him one night when, according to his custom, he absents himself from feasting and revelry because he has no performance skills.

Below is a translation of the extract. Read this now before going on to look at the Old English version in Activity 3.3.

> When he did that on one particular occasion, left the house with the party and went out to the cattle shed (whose care was entrusted to him that night) and at the appointed time he laid down his limbs in rest and fell asleep, then there stood before him a certain man in a dream and he hailed him and greeted him and called him by his name: 'Cedmon, sing me something.' And he answered and said: 'I don't know how to sing; and that's why I went out from this party, and came away here, because I didn't know how to sing.' Again, he who was speaking with him said: 'Nevertheless, you can sing for me.' Then he said: 'What have I to sing' He said: 'Sing to me about the creation.' When he had received this reply, he began to sing at once lines and words in praise of God the creator which he had never heard before, their order is this:
>
>> Now we have to praise the guardian of the heavenly kingdom, the power and the conception of the creator, the deeds of the father of glory, as he, the eternal lord, established the beginning of every wonder. He, the holy creator, first shaped heaven as a roof for men on earth. Then mankind's guardian, almighty and eternal lord, afterwards adorned the fields for men.
>
> Then he arose from that sleep and all those things that he had sung in his sleep he had fixed in memory, and quickly he added to those words many words in the same metre of song dear to God.
>
> (Cited in Burnley, 1992, pp. 28–31)

Activity 3.3 *(Allow 10–15 minutes)*

The nineteenth-century philologist Walter Skeat argued that the language of the Anglo-Saxons was the 'same language' as modern English, that is that there is a continuous development from Old English to modern English. You will see that this early West Saxon text is 'glossed' between the lines by modern English, much as the Anglo-Saxons themselves glossed Latin texts (see Chapter 2, section 3). This enables you to match each Old English word with its modern gloss.

Have a close look at Figure 3.5 now. Can you make any sense of it?

Caedmon's Story in Old English

The following lines are from the original Old English version of the story of Caedmon from Bede's *Ecclesiastical History of the English People*. Above each line is a word for word translation. We have used modern punctuation and capitalization to make it easier for you to see the sentence structures. The asterisks in lines 16–24 show the breaks between the verse half-lines of the poem.

1 When he that on a certain occasion did, that he left the house of the
   þa he þæt þa sumre tide dyde, þæt he forlet þæt hus þæs

2 feast and out was going to of cattle the shed whose
   gebeorscipes ond ut wæs gongende to neata scipene, þara

3 care to him was that night entrusted when he there at
   heord him wæs þære neahte beboden, þa he ða þær in

4 the appointed tide his limbs in rest laid down and fell asleep
   gelimplice tide his leomu on reste gesette ond onslepte

5 then stood him a certain man below in (a) dream and him hailed and
   þa stod him sum mon æt þurh swefn ond hine halette ond

6 greeted and him by his name called: 'Caedmon sing me
   grette ond hine be his noman nemnde: 'Cedmon sing me

7 something'. Then answered he and said: 'Not know I not (how)
   hwæþwugu'. þa ondswarede he ond cwæð : 'Ne con ic noht

8 to sing' and I because of this from this feast out went
   singan ond ic for þon of þeossum gebeorscipe ut eode,

9 and here came because I nothing to sing not know how'. Again he
   ond hider gewat, for þon ic naht singan ne cuðe '. Eft he

10 said, he who with him speaking was: 'However you can for me
   cwæð, se ðe mid hine sprecende wæs: 'Hwæðre þu meaht me

11 sing?' Then said he 'What shall I sing?' Said he:
   singan?' þa cwæð he: 'Hwæt sceal ic singan?' Cwæð he

12 'Sing to me (about the) Creation'. Then he this answer received, then
   'Sing me frumsceaft.' þa he ða þas andsware onfeng þa

13 began he at once to sing in praise of God the Creator these
   ongon he sona singan in herenesse Godes Scyppendes þa

14 lines and these words which he never (had) heard whose order
   fers ond þa word þe he næfre gehyrde, þæra endebyrdnesse

15 this is:
   þis is :

16 now (we) must praise of heaven's kingdom the Guardian
   Nu sculon herigean * heofonrices Weard

17 of the Creator's power and his conception
   Meotodes meahte * ond his modgeþanc

18
the work of the Father of Glory   as he of wonder every
weorc   Wuldorfæder, * swa he wundra gehwæs

19
eternal Lord   the beginning established
ece Drihten, * or   onstealde.

20
He first   made   on earth for men
He ærest sceop * eorðan bearnum

21
heaven   as a roof   the holy Creator
heofon to hrofe, *   halig Scyppend

22
then   the world   of mankind   the Guardian
þa middangeard * monncynnes Weard

23
everlasting Lord   afterwards adorned
ece   Drihten, * æfter   teode

24
for men the earth   God Almighty
firum   foldan, * Frea ælmihtig

25
Then arose he from   that sleep   and all   that   he   sleeping   song
þa aras he from þæm slæpe , ond eal þa þe he slæpende song

26
firmly in memory   had   and to those words   at once many   words in
fæste in gemynde hæfde, ond þæm wordum sona monig word in

27
the same   metre of God worthy   songs   added.
þæt ilce gemet Gode wyrðes songes to geþeodde.

Figure 3.5   The story of Caedmon from Bede's Ecclesiastical History of the English People

Comment

You may well have found the text completely unintelligible. Some degree programmes which study the history of English actually require students to learn the language of the Anglo-Saxons as though it were a foreign language. The language itself used often to be called 'Anglo-Saxon' in order to draw attention to the differences from modern English; scholars such as Skeat, however, preferred the term 'Old English', to stress the similarities, and it is this term which modern linguists also prefer. In the section below we look at a small selection of the text's linguistic features to see whether this term, which emphasizes the continuity between old and modern forms of the language, seems justified.

One problem for the modern reader is actually recognizing the continuity between the Old English words and the modern glossed ones. Let's start with vocabulary, and then examine sounds and grammar.

Old English vocabulary

The continuity mentioned above is often obscured by the changes in spelling. If for instance you rewrite þ and ð as th, and æ as a, you'll find some words become instantly recognizable: *þæt, þis, æfter,* or at least close to their modern form, as in *fæste* (fast) and *wyrð* (es) (worth). Adding two more rules (*hw* = *wh*, *ht* = *ght*) and we get *what* from *hwæt* and *night* from *næht(e)*. So there may be more continuity than appears at first sight.

The vocabulary of English has been greatly enlarged since Anglo-Saxon times, however, by adoptions from other languages (often carrying with them the spelling conventions of those languages). Many of the words in Figure 3.5 are no longer used today, but others are still used in senses different from those in the extract. *Tide* in line 1, for instance, may make us think of the sea, but its meaning here is the same as that in the proverb 'Time and tide wait for no man'. In Old English *tide* meant 'time', but it later came to denote a particular time or occasion (as in 'Whitsuntide') and it is possible that the modern sense 'the time the sea either comes in or goes out' derives from this. Another Old English word, *tima*, retained the meaning of time in the more general sense.

Two other words, *neata* and *scipene*, you might be tempted to describe as obsolete. But if you have any knowledge of rural speech in England you may recognize the first word in the East Anglian form *neat-house* (cattle-shed) and the second in *shippon*, a word with the same meaning as *neat-house* used in dialects of south-western England and parts of the north. So Old English words are often retained in specialized varieties of English such as regional dialects. In fact, many philologists of the nineteenth century were deeply interested in dialects because they saw them as 'survivals' of earlier forms of English.

Old English sounds

So far we have looked at some aspects of the vocabulary and the spelling of an Old English text. Is there anything we can say about the *sounds* represented by those spellings? The answer is yes, but first it's necessary to stress that we can never prove how the Anglo-Saxons pronounced certain sounds. What we can do is make an informed guess based on different types of evidence.

Scholars have always assumed that the Old English spelling is a closer representation of pronunciation than is the case with modern English. It follows from this that in Old English 'silent letters' were unlikely, and that a change of sound will be reflected by a change in spelling. Another assumption is that spellings had the sound-values originally associated with spoken Latin (it was, after all, the Latin alphabet that the Anglo-Saxons learned). If these assumptions are valid, quite a lot of information about possible Old English pronunciations may be inferred from spellings. But we also need to know the Old English *system* of spelling. And as well as having unfamiliar spellings, Old English also used familiar spellings to represent unfamiliar sounds, or sounds in unfamiliar positions.

Let's demonstrate this with the letter *h*, familiar both to us and to the Anglo-Saxons. As you can see from Figure 3.5 it occurs initially in Old English in words like *he*, and it seems reasonable to assume that it sounded much like the modern sound /h/. But if you consider the use of *h* elsewhere in modern English, you may find that it's most often used in combination with other letters, such as *th, ph* (and also *gh*, which is either no longer sounded or is pronounced /f/). So *h* either represents a sound by itself, or in combination with other letters represents different sounds. But in Old English the letter occurs in quite different combinations and contexts from modern English. It occurs initially before other consonants, as in *hwæt, hrofe*, but also as a separate consonant sound (much as in *he*, perhaps). It also occurs at the end of words, as in *þurh*, again as a separate sound related to /h/, but probably closer to the /x/ in Scots *loch* or German *doch*. And in a word like *ælmihtig* (almighty) the *h* may have sounded like the 'ch' in German *nicht*.

So far our account is oversimplified because the Anglo-Saxons had more than one system of spelling, depending on *where* texts were written. Caedmon's poem,

Chapter 2 describes the importance of Latin in Anglo-Saxon manuscript production.

Sounds given between slashes, for example /h/, are phonemic transcriptions. See the box in section 2.6 for details of phonemes.

for instance, was also written down in the eighth-century Northumbrian dialect. In it we find the spellings *uard* and *barnum* instead of *Weard* (line 16) and *bearnum* (line 20). This may be because the sound /r/ in the West Saxon dialect influenced the pronunciation of the preceding vowel, making it a *sequence* of vowels, perhaps pronounced [ɛə] as in 'wear' today (what linguists call a **diphthong**). We have no way of knowing precisely why this should have been so – perhaps /r/ was pronounced differently in different parts of England, as it still is today (see Chapter 7) – but we can find similar instances in modern British English where the same consonant sound has influenced vowels differently in different dialects. In southern English pronunciation *water*, for instance, rhymes with 'caught a', whereas in some northern dialects it rhymes with 'matter'. The sound /w/, which is made by *rounding* the lips, has in the south influenced the pronunciation of the following vowel, which also is rounded, whereas in the north what was probably the original pronunciation, the short *a* has been retained.

Activity 3.4   *(Allow about 10 minutes)*

The most significant differences in pronunciation between Old and modern English concern vowels. Here we shall consider just two vowel sounds. First, pronounce to yourself the following two groups of words:

* holy, so, arose
* out, thou, house

Are the sounds spelled *o* in the first group the same? Similarly, do the sounds spelled *ou* in the second line also form a group with the same sound? And in each case, is the sound a single vowel sound or a diphthong (that is, does the tongue move as you pronounce the *o* and *ou*? You might have to slow the pronunciation right down to feel this). Now look again at Figure 3.5 and find the Old English equivalents of these words, noticing how they are spelled.

Comment

You probably found that the words in the first group shared the same vowel, as did those in the second, although different from that for the first group. In many varieties of English they are both diphthongs, although the actual quality of sounds varies enormously. But the *o* in the first group can also be a simple long vowel for many speakers.

The Old English equivalents of these words are respectively *halig, swa, aras,* and *ut, þu* and *hus.* Notice that in both Old and modern English forms there is a *pattern* in the spelling: where we get *o* and *ou* today we often get *a* and *u* ([a:] and [u:]) in Old English. This actually over-simplifies the picture, but it will do for the present discussion.

Spelling patterns can help us postulate what Old English might have sounded like if we take them together with another kind of evidence, that of modern dialect pronunciation. The kind of vowel assumed for Old English in words such as *hus* can still be heard in Scotland and some northern dialects of England. Similarly, *a* has developed differently in the same areas, retaining a *front* articulation in the north, but developing a back one, either a long vowel or a diphthong, further south.

Chapter 7 discusses the boundary of this pronunciation in more detail.

So far we've dealt briefly with aspects of spelling, vocabulary and sound. It's now time to examine the last level: structure.

Old English grammar

In this section, I look at two related aspects of grammar – word order and inflections (word endings).

Word order

Activity 3.5   *(Allow 10–15 minutes)*

Look at the first six lines of Figure 3.5 and compare the word order in the gloss with that of the translation. List the differences in terms of the position of the verbs. Can you find a pattern in them?

Comment

You will have found that the words are often in a sequence different from that found in modern English; for example, *ond ut wæs gongende to neata scipene* (and out was going to of cattle-shed) places *ut* in front of the verb phrase *wæs gongende*, instead of after it, the preferred order in modern English. As you read on, however, you may notice that it is often the whole verb phrase that is positioned differently from today. It is often put last, as in *ond hine be his noman nemnde* (and him by his name called). The position of the verb in the sentence tends to vary across the different languages of the world. Speakers of English today usually put the verb immediately after the subject of a sentence, and before any direct object; modern English is accordingly described as a subject-verb-object (SVO) language. In the last example above, the order is subject-object-verb (SOV).

There was greater freedom in word order in Old English, in comparison with modern English. This freedom is skilfully exploited in Caedmon's poem (see lines 16–24). To understand this, however, we need to know that Anglo-Saxon verse was based not on rhyme (as became common in later times) but on a combination of stressed syllables (usually four per line) and **alliteration** (repetition of initial consonants). If you look again at the poem you'll find that it is set out in half-lines, with a clear gap in between, with each linked by alliteration. In the example below (line 21) the alliterating sounds are italicized and the stressed syllables are in bold type:

> ***heo**fon to **h**rof*e   ***ha**lig **Scypp**end*
> heaven as a roof   the holy creator

If we put this together with the preceding line (line 20) and compare them with the modern translation we see how radically different the word order is from that of modern English:

> He ærest sceop   eorðan bearnum
> He first made   on earth for men
>
> heofon to hrofe   halig Scyppend
> heaven as a roof   the holy creator

Perhaps the most natural modern English word order would be: *He, halig Scyppend, ærest sceop heofon to hrofe bearnum eorðan* (He, the holy creator, first made heaven as a roof for men on earth).

It is important to add that such strange-seeming word-order patterns also occur alongside sequences which are much the same as those found in modern English. If you look at the dialogue section in the story, '*Cedmon, sing me hwæþwugu*' (Caedmon, sing me something) is virtually identical with modern English apart from the word *hwæþwugu*. You now know that *hwæt* is the Old English form of 'what', and once you learn that the Old English spelling *sc* corresponds with modern English *sh*, the actual word order in the clause '*Hwæt sceal ic singan?*' ought to present no problems. It's therefore possible to say, with Skeat, that there are clear lines of continuity between Old and modern English. But it's also possible to paint a very different picture, as the next section suggests.

Inflections

One reason why word order was freer in Anglo-Saxon times was that relationships between words could also be signalled by the actual 'shape' taken by individual words. If you look at line 26 of Figure 3.5, for instance, you'll see that one of the words we can recognize, *word* (word), has two shapes: *word* and *wordum*. The *-um* ending means the same as the modern preposition 'to', and also tells us that the form is plural. So in studying Old English it's very important to learn what endings can be added to a particular word, and what meanings are attached to them.

These endings are known as **inflections**. Inflections are not unknown in modern English. One example is the *-s* which is added to the end of many nouns to make them plural. But the Anglo-Saxons had a much richer range of inflections, to mark what linguists call **case**. If we take a noun such as *drihten* (lord) in line 19 we would find that an *-e* inflection occurs when the word is functioning as an indirect object, as in 'to the lord', for example; whereas an *-es* ending denotes what is called the 'possessive' case, as in 'of the lord'. And there is a different range of inflections for the plural cases.

In describing Old English, and indeed other inflected languages, it has long been the custom to use the terminology of Latin grammar. The indirect object case, for instance, is known as the 'dative'; the possessive as the 'genitive'. When a noun is being used as the grammatical subject of a sentence it is in the 'nominative' case; when it is the direct object it is in the accusative case. It is also customary to set out all this information about case endings in the following kind of table:

	Singular		Plural	
Nominative	drihten	the lord (subj.)	drihtnas	the lords
Accusative	drihten	the lord (obj.)	drihtnas	the lords
Genitive	drihtnes	of the lord	drihtna	of the lords
Dative	drihtne	to the lord	drihtnum	to the lords

Linguists speak of this kind of display as a **paradigm**. One of the complications a student of Old English encounters is that there are a number of different paradigms (each with different systems of case inflections) according to whether a noun is classified as 'masculine' (as in the case of *drihten*) or 'feminine' (as in *scipene*, line 2 of Figure 3.5) or 'neuter' (as in *hus*, line 1). And to make matters even more complicated, case endings vary not only in respect of gender but also according to whether a noun is classified as 'strong' or 'weak'. *Noma* (name), for instance, is masculine like *drihten* but has different endings because it is weak rather than strong (as in *noman* in line 6). (Think of the terms 'masculine', 'feminine', 'neuter', 'gender' 'strong' and 'weak' as purely grammatical ones, referring only to patterns of inflection.)

Activity 3.6   *(Allow about 5 minutes)*

If all this terminology is new or confusing for you, it's worth reflecting on the different forms a personal pronoun such as *he* has in most varieties of modern English.

Nominative	he	e.g. *he* ate it
Accusative	him	e.g. I ate *him*
Genitive	his	e.g. I ate *his* apple
Dative	him	e.g. I gave the apple to *him*

However, the Anglo-Saxons had four forms for the pronoun *he*. They all occur in the first six lines of Figure 3.5. Look back at the Caedmon text and make a list of them.

Comment

Three of the Old English forms will already be familiar to you: *he, his, him.* But where today we would use *him* for a direct and also indirect object (as in 'I gave the book to him') the Anglo-Saxons used *him* only in the latter case, that is, the dative. The accusative form was *hine,* which still survives in some dialects of south-west England.

Inflections in Old English were added to adjectives as well as nouns. And as in modern English, they were also added to verbs. But while most modern varieties of English have two forms in the present tense of verbs such as 'to sing' (as in 'sing', 'sings') they had four in Old English. The paradigm looks like this:

	Singular		Plural	
1st person	ic singe	I sing	we singaþ	we sing
2nd person	þu singest	you sing	ge singaþ	you sing
3rd person	he singeþ	he sings	hie singaþ	they sing
	heo singeþ	she sings		
	hit singeþ	it sings		

Notice that there is one third person singular ending *-eþ*, and a plural one *-aþ* (remember that the þ was later respelled as *th*). Notice also the forms of the pronouns, and the fact that Old English makes a distinction between a singular *you* (later *thou*) and plural *you* (later *ye*). A more archaic translation of these forms would be 'thou singest, ye singeth'.

The evidence of tenth-century Northumbrian texts such as the Lindisfarne Gospels (discussed in Chapter 2) suggests that by this time the inflectional system sketched above was in the process of change. In the next section we investigate why this happened.

3.5   WHY DID THE GRAMMAR OF OLD ENGLISH CHANGE?

The examples of Old English in the last section show how different Old English was compared with modern English. Not only have individual words changed in spelling and pronunciation, but key features of grammar have altered too.

Indeed, the very *kind* of language has changed – from being an inflectional language, with relatively free word order, to one with more characteristics of an isolating language in which grammatical relations are signalled by word order rather than inflections. For that reason, modern English has a more fixed word-order pattern than Old English.

Change in language has been an important object of enquiry for linguistic scholars since the early nineteenth century. But whereas philologists were interested in establishing the *facts* of change, it is only relatively recently that the question of *why* languages change has been investigated. This process remains mysterious, however, not least because of the multiplicity of factors which appear to influence it. For instance, we know that a variety of nonlinguistic (external) factors can lead to language change; the effect of repeated invasions on the vocabulary of English is one clear example. But many linguists have long argued that there also exist *internal* reasons for linguistic change. That is, the grammar of English may have had some kind of built-in instability which made certain kinds of change likely. Or there may be universal tendencies which make all languages evolve in similar ways. Let's now look at various external and internal explanations for why the inflectional system of Old English disappeared.

Internal causes of change

For the nineteenth-century philologists and many modern linguists, change in language is purely internal. The philologists thought of language as an organism, which could mutate and develop rather like a flower or tree. So change in language could be seen as an example of a change in nature: it is part of the nature of an oak tree, for instance, to grow leaves in spring and then lose them in autumn. The language scholar's job, then, is to describe as accurately as possible the structure of a given language so that its internal 'natural' laws of development can be discovered.

One such law states that over the centuries the stress in English speech has tended to fall increasingly on the first syllable of words. A consequence of this is that the inflected syllables at the end of words are more weakly stressed, and the vowel is likely to be reduced to what linguists call a **schwa** sound (represented phonetically as [ə] as in modern English 'sof*a*'). If the distinctive vowel sounds of different inflectional endings are all reduced to [ə], then the endings become redundant.

Modern linguists tend to think of language not as an organism but as a *system.* Part of this approach focuses on the way knowledge about a language is stored in the minds of speakers. And part of that knowledge in respect of Old English, as you now know, concerns the patterns of inflection. You may remember that in certain of the noun paradigms mentioned above not all cases had distinctive endings. This has led some linguists to argue that the Old English inflectional system was inefficient and was therefore, as the linguist Roger Lass has argued, 'ripe for analogical re-modelling' (1992, p. 104). This means that speakers themselves start to regularize the paradigms, and one way of doing this is simply to delete endings.

If you look back at the case endings for *drihten* (see the section 'Inflections') you'll notice that there is no distinction between nominative and accusative in either singular or plural. The case of a neuter noun such as *hus* is even more extreme. As the paradigm shows, not even the singular and plural forms for these cases are distinguished:

	Singular	Plural
Nominative	hus	hus
Accusative	hus	hus
Genitive	huses	husa
Dative	huse	husum

One problem with purely internal accounts of linguistic change such as those of the philologists and modern linguists described here is that they are not explanatory enough. For instance, inflections have been retained in other Germanic languages even where stress is similarly on the initial syllable. And focusing on a language rather than its speakers begs the question as to how or why a change is adopted. It is worth pointing out here that all linguists tend to agree that linguistic change cannot be brought about by an individual speaker alone. Although as individuals we are free to change whatever we like – as children and imaginative writers continue to demonstrate – such changes cannot be considered part of a language until they have passed into wider usage. So the question then arises: if one person starts using the language in a novel way – by pronouncing a word ending differently, or using a word in a new sense – why should other people start doing the same?

External causes of change

Any answer to this must take account of social relations between speakers, and this by definition forms part of the realm of the external. In recent years linguists with a special interest in language in relation to society – **sociolinguists** – have shown that linguistic changes are often associated with particular groups in society, and that people tend to adopt changes introduced by more powerful or prestigious groups. In Chapter 7, for example, we look at the work of Labov in this area. Any adequate account of linguistic change must make some reference to different groups within society, their relative status, and the patterns of contact existing among them.

The fact that inflectional breakdown seems to have begun in Northumbria has encouraged some sociolinguists to ask what existed in the external social context in that area to trigger the change. If you look back at Figure 3.4 you'll see that it's in the north-eastern half of England that the Vikings settled. One vital aspect of this immigration from Scandinavia was that it went on long after Alfred's accommodation with the Danish King Guthrum – in fact, until about the middle of the eleventh century. And during the latter century it is likely that Scandinavian speech was quite prestigious, particularly as the king of England between 1016 and 1042 was actually Danish. It is not known how long the Scandinavian languages continued to be used in England, partly because there is no evidence that they were used to produce written texts. The linguistic historian Kastovsky (1992) argues that the large number of adoptions into English of Scandinavian vocabulary and grammatical forms evidenced by texts of the thirteenth and fourteenth centuries suggests that by this time Scandinavian languages had been abandoned in favour of English.

It is also impossible to say whether the Anglo-Saxons and the Vikings found their respective languages mutually intelligible – Old Norse and Old English were, after all, related Germanic languages. It's therefore possible that numbers of speakers of both languages gradually became bilingual. Kastovsky (1992, p. 329) argues that at first there may have been greater pressure on the English to learn Scandinavian than vice versa, since the Vikings were invaders and because of the prestige factor mentioned earlier. If this were true, the English would have encountered many Scandinavian words which linguists, at any rate, can relate to similar words in Old English. You will recall that the Anglo-Saxon word for 'heaven' was *heofon*; the Scandinavian was *himinn*. But although the Vikings used a similar range of inflections their actual forms were different: the nominative plural of *himinn*, for instance, was *himnar*. Perhaps what happened between the two groups of people was a process in which the inflectional differences between the languages were resolved by largely doing away with them altogether.

In this view, the breakdown of inflections owes as much to processes of contact between speakers of different languages as it does to pressures of a purely internal kind. We have no direct evidence of this actually happening during this period, but what we do know is that such processes of inflectional simplification are real, and characteristic of contact situations in other places today, as we discuss in later chapters. So it may not be unreasonable to apply it to the past.

So far we've looked at Old English: where it came from, what it was like, how certain aspects of it changed, how the process of change might be explained. We now move on to a different period of the English language, that known as 'Middle English'.

This explanation of why English changed is similar to that used to explain how pidgins arise in some language-contact situations. We discuss English pidgins and how they arise in Chapter 5.

3.6   THE NORMAN CONQUEST AND THE INFLUENCE OF FRENCH

You will remember that in Reading A Crystal ends his account of Old English with the Norman conquest of 1066. In that year a French-speaking dynasty from the dukedom of Normandy was installed in England. This external event has been seen for a very long time as decisive, not only for the history of England (and consequently Britain) but for the English language as well. For scholars who have viewed the history of England and English as one of unbroken progress, the conquest has often been a milestone on the road to 'civilization', playing a key role in the development of modern English. But another view, perhaps more widely held, sees the events of the conquest in terms of (an at least temporary) decline: as the wrecking of a relatively sophisticated 'native' Anglo-Saxon culture by a 'foreign' and tyrannical French one, so that the continuity of English culture was ruptured and the continued existence of the English language threatened.

This latter view of events may be almost as old as the conquest itself. It is the story known as the 'Norman yoke'. Versions of this were intermittently kept alive during the Middle Ages, probably because it was politically useful for certain groups within English society (including the monarchy itself). It again assumed importance during the English Civil War of the seventeenth century. By the late eighteenth century it seems to have become part of a common patriotic mythology that was anti-French. It was on these ideas that Sir Walter Scott drew in his novel *Ivanhoe*, first published in 1815:

> At court, and in the castles of the great nobles, where the pomp and state of a court were emulated, Norman-French was the only language employed; in courts of law, the pleadings and judgements were delivered in the same tongue. In short, French was the language of honour, of chivalry, and even of justice, while the far more manly and expressive Anglo-Saxon [Old English] was abandoned to the use of rustics and hinds [farm-servants], who knew no other.
> (Scott, [1815] 1986, p. 9)

We have already seen that anyone telling the 'story of English' needs to create a narrative, based on known facts, which follows the conventions of storytelling. Stories require heroes and perhaps villains. They need to have an ending – preferably a happy one. I have been arguing in this chapter that the way the story of English is traditionally told positions the English people and language as the hero, which triumphs (that is, emerges as a standard language used throughout the world) against all difficulty and danger. The idea of the 'Norman yoke' suggests that the French people and language represent the 'villain' of the story, who creates the 'danger' or 'complication' which every hero must overcome.

Whatever view of the conquest is taken, one of its effects we can be sure about. It brought about a period of close contact and often bitter rivalry between the English and the French which in some respects has lasted into the present century. Ideas about 'Englishness' often reflect whatever is considered to be 'not French', and these ideas have varied a great deal over such a long span of history. In general, attitudes to French and France can be characterized as ambivalent: hostility mixed with admiration.

But these effects had less to do with the immediate aftermath of the conquest than with later developments. For in comparison with the Vikings, the Norman invaders were few in number and were spread rather thinly across the country. Not only is there evidence to suggest that Scott's picture was too black and white, it is arguable that the most important source of French influence was not the Norman French of the invaders but another dialect, the more prestigious central French of the French king's court in the area of Paris. Furthermore, it is less a matter of *spoken* French than its written varieties.

The main reason for this is that in 1204 the dukedom of Normandy was gained by the king of France. The kings of England were therefore no longer also dukes of Normandy, and contacts with Normandy gave way to contact with the French court.

French in England after 1066

In this section we look at the evidence for the use of French in England in the period between the Norman conquest and the fourteenth century, when the use of French began to die out. The picture is actually very complicated. We need to bear in mind the geographical, social, institutional and temporal dimensions of French use; the possible extent of French–English bilingualism; and within that last category, the *direction* of language learning – speakers of English learning French, speakers of French learning English.

Let's start by reminding ourselves of the contexts mentioned by Scott: the king's court, the nobles' castles, the courts of law in which Norman French was the language of 'honour', chivalry and justice. First, the king's court. It is certainly true that for 300 years after the conquest all the kings of England spoke French as their first language; some knew no English at all (although William the Conqueror himself is supposed to have tried to learn, and failed). The court patronized literature in French and in general was heavily influenced by French culture. But by the fourteenth century kings were usually bilingual.

A further linguistic consequence of the conquest, as Scott suggested, concerned the language of law. But according to Clanchy (1993, p. 45), the Norman kings also greatly expanded the uses of writing for bureaucratic purposes in general. Some of this was in Latin, whereas in pre-conquest times English would have been used. But a great deal of administrative writing was increasingly undertaken in French. This was so much the case that until the fourteenth century English was actually a minority written language within England.

As for the Norman landowning nobility, the picture is more complicated. In a recent survey the linguistic historian David Burnley finds contemporary evidence suggesting that many people of this rank learned English quite soon after the conquest. But 'equal competence in both languages was rare' (Burnley, 1992, p. 424). One occupational group likely to be bilingual to a degree consisted of those known as *latimiers* (interpreters), who mediated between the Norman landowners and the labourers (Scott's 'rustics and hinds' who needed to know no other language than English).

One institution not mentioned by Scott was the church (where the senior positions at least were awarded to Normans). Here some bilingualism seems to have been essential, since it was the duty of the clergy to preach to an English-speaking congregation. And for a monolingual speaker of English to rise in the church hierarchy bilingualism was also necessary, at least as far as written French was concerned.

Rather paradoxically, it seems that once the dynastic link with Normandy had been broken in 1204 and England had acquired greater autonomy, the influence of French in England grew stronger. If the nobility was to remain French-speaking it had to learn central French with the help of tutors. French came to be associated with social aspiration, and could also be learned by people who had previously known only English. I deal with French in educational institutions in a later section. Meanwhile, let's see how French affected the English language.

The influence of French on English vocabulary

The most obvious effect of French on English is at the level of vocabulary. A great many French words were adopted into English and such words have often been seen in a negative light. If you look back at the Scott extract, you'll see that he characterizes Anglo-Saxon as 'far more manly and expressive' than French. Elsewhere in *Ivanhoe* he presents the issue in terms of social stratification. In a famous conversation the jester Wamba discusses with a swineherd the naming of animals reared to be eaten. A 'swine' (from the Old English word for 'pig') becomes, says Wamba, 'pork' (from the French) 'when she is carried to the castle hall to feast among the nobles' (Scott, [1815] 1986, pp. 14–15).

This conversation shows a further aspect of the process of adoption: English acquired a layer of French words to refer to things (in this case livestock) that already had names. The new French words were also associated with the new masters and the uses to which they put things. (In fact, adoptions from French rarely seem to refer to things or concepts unknown to the English.)

In more recent times French adoptions have been associated with inflated words of more than one syllable. Referring to this as an 'alien' habit, a conservative British prime minister, Baldwin, said in a speech three years before the General Strike of 1926 that the 'salvation' for Britain (and indeed for the whole world) lay not in French-derived polysyllables such as *proletariat* but in monosyllables such as 'faith', 'hope', 'love' and 'work' (Crowley, 1989, p. 255). But there is an irony in Baldwin's argument. For although 'hope', 'love' and 'work' are all Old English words, 'faith' was actually adopted from French in the twelfth century. So not all French adoptions can be seen as merely reflecting Norman power, and not all were words of more than one syllable.

The earliest adoptions after the conquest were from Norman French. Examples are *duc, cuntess, curt* (duke, countess, court), *messe, clerc* (mass, scholar) and *werre, pais* (war, peace). They could be said to reflect the dominance of the Normans in powerful institutions such as the royal court and the church. These early adoptions in some cases coexisted with their central French counterparts adopted at a later date. So we have Norman French *warden, convey, gaol*, beside central French *guardian, convoy, jail*. More often that not the central French words belonged to the written medium, mainly of the fourteenth century (see below). It has been estimated that by this date about 21 per cent of the English vocabulary derived from French, in comparison with about 9 per cent soon after the conquest (Burnley, 1992, p. 432). But most of these words were relatively 'exotic', belonging to the specialist discourses of church, law, chivalry (knightly behaviour) and the running of country estates. By far the most frequently occurring words were still of Germanic origin. We demonstrate some of these points in the extracts in the next section, where we see what English looked like in the so-called Middle English period.

3.7   EXAMPLES OF MIDDLE ENGLISH

Linguists have traditionally dealt with the idea of Middle English as though the English language developed through three stages: old, middle and modern. By contrasting each stage, they have presented the history of English as a movement from a highly inflected and stable language, through a period of inflectional breakdown and instability, to the final attainment of a standardized language. This history – a period of calm disrupted and then restored – is one way of creating a clear story from the known facts, but it is a narrative which embodies many value judgements. For example, French is regarded as having a negative effect on English – it has been cast in the role of the villain. The idea that a codified 'standard' language is the triumphant happy ending to the story embodies a value judgement of a different kind – that diversity and variation are less desirable than a unified standard form.

One reason why Middle English has been seen as unstable is that the activities of the Winchester scriptorium in the late West Saxon era (see Chapter 2) were discontinued after the Norman conquest. This is partly why the conquest has often been seen as so disruptive. Most students of Middle English have been struck by the enormous variability in written texts (in comparison to those in Old English), from different areas, at different times. But instead of seeing this as a sign of instability, we could see it more as a flowering of regional diversity – as assertion of local identity and cultural independence from a centralizing power. We find that in studying Middle English, it really matters *where* a text was written.

My first example demonstrates the uneven effect of the Norman conquest on the English language. It is an extract from a poem written about 130 years after the invasion, probably in a part of south-eastern England (perhaps what is now known as Surrey). It is evidence of one abrupt break with the past: the adoption of the French tradition of verse, which uses rhyme rather than stress and alliteration. The poem, which is known as *The Owl and the Nightingale*, shows how this tradition had been thoroughly assimilated by at least one poet writing in this variety of early Middle English. (I have translated those words which might be problematic.)

I   was in   a   summer valley
Ich was in one sumere dale

in   a   very hidden corner
In one suþe diȝele hale

heard   I   held great debate
Iherde ich holde ꞡrete tale

an owl   and   a   nightingale
An hule and one niȝtingale

that pleading was stiff and firm and strong
þat plait was stif and starc an strong

sometimes   soft and loud in between
Sumwile softe an lud among

(Cited in Bennett and Smithers (eds), 1968)

I haven't punctuated the extract, since modern editions of the poem punctuate it in different ways. You'll probably find it much easier to deal with than the Old English text about Caedmon. It's important to point out that any word-order deviations from modern English are dictated by the need to rhyme. Notice that though _yogh_ (see Chapter 2) is retained (as in 'diȝele'), _æ_ is replaced by _a_ in 'was' and 'þat'.

We can make out a case for saying that the language of this extract has been greatly affected by the Norman conquest, but it's still possible to argue that it also shows a great deal of continuity with Old English. It's probable, for instance, that _lud_ (_hlud_ in Old English) was still pronounced as a long [uː] sound, much as in Old English. Look back at the Caedmon poem (Figure 3.5): does the alliteration in _stif an starc an strong_ (in the piece above) remind you of anything in Old English verse? Moreover, in this extract, the only word borrowed from French is _plait_, 'pleading', appropriately enough a legal term, reflecting the dominance of the Normans in the institution of law.

One final point of interest concerns the existence of two different forms for the indefinite article: _an_ and _one_. The Old English form was _an_, with the vowel of _halig_. In the south of England this vowel tended to be rounded and spelled with an _o_, hence _one_. (In the north of England, however, it remained unrounded, as in the next extract.) But occasionally it was also shortened, from 'long _a_' to 'short _a_', hence _an_. So the quality of vowel in the older pronunciation is kept in the shortened form.

The next example is from about a century later, and from the north of England. It is a verse fragment from York, dated 1272:

alas   who shall these horns   blow
wel qwa sal thir hornes blau

holy   cross (on) thy day
haly Rod   thi day

now is he dead and lies low
nou is he dede and lies law

(who) was wont to blow   them always
was wont to blaw thaim ay

(Cited in Milroy, 1992b, as cited in Dickens and Wilson, 1956, p. 118)

While it shows the influence of French versification, this fragment contains no adoptions from French. And unlike the previous extract, it shows that the Old English _a_ (as in _haly_) has not been rounded in this part of England. In fact, it shows a different kind of influence – that of the Scandinavian languages spoken by the Vikings (York itself was a Viking centre).

The form _thaim_ (them), for instance, was borrowed from Old Scandinavian _þeim_, to replace the Old English forms _hem_ etc. found in the Caedmon text (and preserved as *hi* elsewhere in *The Owl and the Nightingale*). The form with *th*, as in *them*, gradually spread southwards and westwards in the course of time, replacing the older *h-* forms. A similar pattern occurs with the third person singular verb inflection *-s*, as in *lies*. You may remember that in the West Saxon Caedmon text the ending was *-þ* (again, still preserved in *The Owl and Nightingale*). In the late Northumbrian Lindisfarne Gospels, however, the *-s* form was already being used. Like the *them* form, it has since gradually moved south and been adopted into the variety of English that is used today in print.

Two final points to make about this fragment illustrate important features of the language in the Middle English period. Two spelling conventions, *s* for *sh* (as in *sal*) and *q* for *wh* (as in *qwa*) are exclusively northern, and have remained in use today in texts written in Scots (see next chapter). And notice that 'blow' has two spellings, *blau* and *blaw.* Consistent spelling wasn't seen as important at this time as it is today: this is one reason why scholars have often thought of Middle English as unstable. But in fact such inconsistency remained a feature of handwritten texts until well after the introduction of printing in 1476, as Chapter 2 shows.

There is no evidence that regional differences in English (as exemplified above) were generally seen as a problem by contemporary observers. But by the fourteenth century a conscious interest was being taken in them. The diversity in English pronunciation, especially regarding the north and south, seemed 'a great wonder' to one contemporary observer, John Trevisa. In a famous passage from his translation (in 1384) of a text called *Polychronicon* originally written in Latin in 1327 (see the section on 'English and education' below), he characterizes the speech north of the River Humber (especially at York) as *scharpe, slitting, frotynge and vnchape,* by which he meant that it was shapeless and grated like the sound of ripping cloth (Burnley, 1992). For southerners such as Trevisa this attitude to northern speech seems to have stemmed from a sense of cultural superiority. The north was less populous and poorer; parts of it even shared certain administrative arrangements and customs with Scotland (and until 1157 was actually claimed by that kingdom). To northerners, on the other hand, southern English was difficult to understand but was also an emblem of governmental power. For by the fourteenth century a new 'centre' had emerged in England – the south-east around London. Here the king held his court, and a commercial capital had emerged.

Although it is the linguistic differences between north and south that were remarked on, the dialect of the West Midlands was also highly distinctive. Below is an extract from the *Ancrene Wisse*, written perhaps in a Herefordshire priory at around 1230. Its language is so close to a number of others produced in the same area that scholars have assumed the existence of a scriptorium in this area exercising a form of written standardization. The text aims to instruct a small group of wealthy women dedicated to a life of religious devotion.

1   therefore my   beloved sisters   above all things   be   diligent to have   (a)
     Forþi mine leoue sustren, ouer alle þing beoð bisie to habben

2   pure   heart   what is (a)   pure   heart?   I   it   have   said before that is
     schir heorte. Hwet is   schir heorte? Ich hit habbe iseid ear: þet is

3   that you   nothing neither want   nor   love   except God   alone and the
     þet ȝe na þing ne wilnin ne ne luuien bute Godd ane, ant te

4   very   things   for (the sake of) God   that   help   you   toward him   for   God   I
     ilke þinges   for   Godd, þe helpeð ow toward him. For Godd, ich

5   say   love   them   and   not   for   themselves
     segge, luuien ham, ant nawt for hamseoluen.

The language has often been seen as much closer to Old English than other texts of the same period. For instance, the plural of 'sisters' with -*n*: in Old English -*n* was the plural ending of weak nouns; it has since become quite widespread for marking plurals in regional dialect, as in *housen* ('houses'). In line 2 the form *hwet* (instead of *hwæt*) derives from a sound-change in the Old English dialect of Mercia in which many instances of [æ] were raised to [e]. Also in line 2 the initial *i* in *iseid* derives from the Old English form *ge-* which marked a past participle. In line 3 *luuien* derives from Old English *lufian* which belonged to a class of 'weak' verbs with *i* in the infinitive form. In line 5, *ham* shows that the Old English *h*-forms of the personal pronouns have not yet been replaced by the Scandinavian *þ* forms.

3.8   ENGLISH IN THE LATER MIDDLE AGES

Consider the following list of events:

1362	Statute of Pleading decrees law-suits should be in English
1380	Grammar school masters advised to translate Latin into French as well as English
1380s	New Testament translated into English
	Chaucer writes *Canterbury Tales* in English
1399	First king of England since 1066 (Henry IV) to speak English as a first language

These events show that by the last half of the fourteenth century English was becoming used more widely in those domains which had been hitherto dominated by French. But how do we explain this process?

Histories of English have tended to explain it as an expression of English *national* identity. In this view, 'England' was a unity, a central aspect of that unity being the English language. As Baugh and Cable write in their revised and widely used history of English (1978, p. 148), English was being restored 'to its rightful place as the language of the country'.

I want to argue that this statement may reflect the inherited preoccupations of the nineteenth century more than those of the fourteenth. It might be safer to speak here of *patriotism*, based on hostility towards the French, rather than nationalism in its fuller, nineteenth-century sense, in which language is seen as the decisive component of a unified national identity (there is more about nationalism and the English language in the next chapter). It certainly seems difficult to find a general sense of unity throughout English society at this time. Let's look at different institutions in turn, starting with the law.

English and the law

It is true that in the preamble to the Statute of Pleading, widespread ignorance of French is mentioned as one justification for using English in law. But the Statute also mentions the 'great mischiefs' that arise from ignorance of the law in general. So rather than seeing the Act as empowering all the realm's subjects by using the common language, we can also see it as seeking to ensure that the government's laws were obeyed at a time of great social upheaval. For the Statute closely followed a second outbreak of the plague known as the Black Death, which had so reduced the rural population that labour had become scarce. Landowners could no longer make the traditional demands on labourers, who in turn could now actually bargain with them for wages. One outcome of such changes in social relations was the so-called Peasants' Revolt in 1381.

Interesting light is cast on this change in the legal process by the recent discovery of records of a bigamy trial held at York in 1364. The judge dismissed the testimony of a witness on the grounds that the latter's language often shifted between northern English, southern English and Scots (the witness had spent his childhood in southern Scotland). The judge thought this a sign of dishonesty, suggesting that as far as the law was concerned, variation in English could be seen as a problem, at least for the accused (Bailey, 1992, p. 25).

English and the church

The church was another institution facing acute divisions in the last half of the fourteenth century. A group known as Lollards preached against what they saw as corrupt church practices. They had substantial support among the lower classes, and to appeal to these much theological writing was done in English. We can see the English translation of the New Testament in this light, rather than as exemplifying 'national' pride in the English language.

English literature

Literature is the one institution in which nineteenth-century ideas about national identity have been most thoroughly projected on to earlier periods of history. The fourteenth-century poet Chaucer, author of the widely acclaimed *Canterbury Tales*, has often been celebrated as embodying the spirit of Englishness. But this privileging of imaginative writing as the supreme kind of language (and therefore the embodiment of the nation) was not that of Chaucer's own contemporaries. In fact, most imaginative writing at this time was still produced anonymously (as in our two extracts discussed above). It was not until Caxton's promotion of Chaucer as someone who made English 'ornate and fayr' that our modern habit of naming imaginative writers and remembering their work began. And in Caxton's time the word 'literature' – a fourteenth-century adoption from French – meant 'learned writing' in general: the specialization in meaning to works of the imagination belongs to the nineteenth century.

English and the court

Although French was used at the royal court throughout the fourteenth century most courtiers, including the king himself, seem to have been bilingual. The status of French at court was complicated by the fact that from 1337 England was at war with France for over a century (during the Hundred Years War). Any French or French-speaking favourites of the king might be targeted by jealous rivals, and language became an issue whenever anti-French patriotism was aroused. This feeling was most likely among the emerging wealthy merchant class.

English and education

The history of English teaching is discussed in a later book in this series, *Learning English: development and diversity* (Mercer and Swann (eds), (1996).

The final institution to deal with is education. Although the study of Latin remained central to the curriculum, English replaced French as the medium of instruction in the course of the fourteenth century. A major source of evidence for this process is the *Polychronicon*, mentioned earlier. As well as translating this John Trevisa added his own comments; he notes, for instance, that one year after the first occurrence of the Black Death an Oxford grammar schoolmaster, John of Cornwall, first introduced English as the medium of education. That this was unpopular in some quarters is suggested by the concern about French recorded in 1380 (see the list of dates at the beginning of this section).

Some further interesting additions occur in another translation of *Polychronicon* made in about 1440 by one Osbern Bokenham, an Augustinian friar from Suffolk. This translation was called *Mappula Angliae* and was written for the most part in a dialect of the south-east Midlands. The following extract develops the theme of Anglo-French linguistic relations in reference to education.

❖ ❖ ❖ ❖ ❖

Activity 3.7 *(Allow about 15 minutes)*

Read the extract from Bokenham's *Mappula Angliae*. I have glossed the difficult words; most of them are adoptions from either French or Latin (it's sometimes difficult to tell which). Some, like *corrupcioun* (corruption), *famylyar* (familiar), *conquerour*, *gramer* (grammar), *custom*, *nacyons* (nations), *seconde*, *cause*, *nobyll*, *maner* (manner), *courtis* (court), *rurales* (country people), *honorable*, *labouryd*, *processe* and *barbarizid*, have become thoroughly assimilated into English, only their spellings pose problems for the modern reader. Others, like *commixtion* (mixing), *augmentacioun*, *encrees* (increase), *decre* (decree), *ordynaunce* (ordinance), *consuetude* (practice) and *construyn* (interpret) are either more learned or more obscure in terms of spelling. Try to summarize Bokenham's argument.

1	<small>this corruption their mother-tongue</small> And þis corrupcioun of Englysshe men yn þer modre-tounge,
2	<small>said mixing Danes</small> begunne as I seyde with famylyar commixtion of Danys firste
3	<small>Normans took great augmentation increase</small> and of Normannys aftir, toke grete augmentacioun and encrees
4	<small>after coming things</small> aftir þe commyng of William conquerour by two thyngis. The
5	<small>decree order said</small> firste was: by decre and ordynaunce of þe seide William con-
6	<small>grammer schools against practice</small> queror children in gramer-scolis ageyns þe consuetude and þe
7	<small>nations their left</small> custom of all oþer nacyons, here owne modre-tonge lafte and
8	<small>Donatus in interpret</small> forsakyn, lernyd here Donet on Frenssh and to construyn yn
9	<small>do Latin way</small> Frenssh and to maken here Latyns on þe same wyse. The
10	<small>lords' sons</small> secounde cause was þat by the same decre lordis sonys and
11	<small>noble</small> all nobyll and worthy mennys children were fyrste set to
12	<small>learn before could English</small> lyrnyn and speken Frensshe, or þan þey cowde spekyn Ynglyssh
13	<small>writings contracts kinds of pleas</small> and þat all wrytyngis and endentyngis and all maner plees
14	<small>disputes</small> and contrauercyes in courtis of þe lawe, and all maner rek-
15	<small>reckonings accounts household should done</small> nyngis and countis yn howsoolde schulle be doon yn the same.
16	<small>seeing country people so that seem</small> And þis seeyinge, þe rurales, þat þey myghte semyn þe more
17	<small>estimable more easily</small> worschipfull and honorable and þe redliere comyn to þe

> 18   famyliarite of þe worthy and þe grete, leftyn hure modre
>   *acquaintance*
>
> 19   tounge and labouryd to kunne spekyn Frenssh: and thus by
>   *strove*   *learn*
>
> 20   processe of tyme barbariȝid thei in bothyn and spokyn
>   *mangled*
>
> 21   neythyr good Frenssh nor good Englyssh.
>   *neither*

(Quoted in Burnley, 1992, p. 172)

Comment

A point central to this extract (and also to Trevisa's translation of *Polychronicon*) is that if you went to a grammar school in England before the fourteenth century you would have learned through the medium of French, not English. Accordingly, French became associated with social aspiration for some sections of the monolingual English-speaking community. The suggestion is that bilingualism operated in the opposite direction – English to French – from that discussed in relation to the court above.

You might have found it noteworthy that a mid-fifteenth-century text is still exploiting a rich vein of anti-French feeling. But when Bokenham was writing, England had been at war with France for over 100 years. And in fact the 'decre and ordynaunce' (referred to by Bokenham) which William the Conqueror is supposed to have enacted to undermine the English language – one of the causes of 'corrupcioun' – was actually a forgery of the fourteenth century.

This notion of corruption in language is worth comment. It depends in turn on the idea of purity. Although extremely familiar to us, the idea of a pure language was probably not something that most people in the Middle Ages would have taken for granted. Indeed, the English language itself seems never to have been an object of attention before the fourteenth century. This was partly because English was not a taught language. Latin, on the other hand, had to be taught, even if it was to become the natural language of scholarship, and of thought, in the life of an individual. Medieval Latin was a living language for anyone connected with the upper echelons of the church, and this meant most educated people. Those few children able to attend a school in the Middle Ages would have studied Latin, through the medium of French; the textbook of Latin grammar they used, by Donatus, had been written, in Latin, in the fourth century AD (Bokenham's *lernyd here Donet* (line 8) means 'learned their Donatus').

Greek ideas about language

One idea central to Greek thought about language was that of the barbarian. The ancient Greeks tended to define themselves in terms of language, and referred to other peoples as *barbarians* (unable to speak Greek, such peoples could only make 'baa-baa' noises!). Another idea was that the older Greek language of the so-called heroic age depicted in the great epics of Homer was more 'pure', and therefore better, than later forms of Greek. From the Greeks, then, came the idea that a given language could be either pure or impure; impurity being the result of mixture and change over time.

Latin ideas about grammar were largely based on those of the ancient Greeks. The box 'Greek ideas about language' (page 129) summarizes these.

The argument in the Bokenham extract above seems to be reactivating the idea of corruption as it came down through the Latin grammarians, and applying it to linguistic change – seen here as a process of degeneration. For in trying to be 'more worschipfull and honorable' certain 'rural' English people were abandoning their French, with the result that they had become what some people today might term 'semi-lingual', speaking 'neythyr good Frenssh nor good Englyssh'. Instead, they 'barbarizid' both languages; Bokenham's use of the term is the first recorded in the technical Latin sense.

A final point about the extract's argument is that it represents a perspective on linguistic history which has since become very common. Rather than triumphantly emerging as the standard language, here the story of English since the Norman conquest is one of decline from a purer state (much as the Norman yoke story is one of a more general decline). And Bokenham attributes the decline to contact between English and other languages. In contrast to the progressive story mentioned earlier, the decline story tends to lament rather than celebrate.

The English of official documents

By Bokenham's time, English was increasingly becoming the automatic choice for documents emanating from the crown. But it was a particular variety of English, essentially a London variety of the south-east Midlands dialect. A written form of this was developed by scribes working in that part of the royal administration known as Chancery. Chancery English – as the variety of English used for *written* documents of a very specific kind was called – was to a large extent less subject to the kind of internal variation characteristic of earlier kinds of Middle English.

Chancery English was to some extent a particular sub-variety of the east Midlands dialect, reflecting immigration into London by the merchant class from that area. It used the form *such* ('such', from Old English *swylc*), for instance, whereas earlier sub-varieties of east Midlands used in London had either *swic* or *sich* (to rhyme with 'stitch'); see Chapter 2, Figure 2.29. The fact that many Chancery forms are the same as those used in print today has encouraged many scholars to describe this variety as the precursor of standard English. It is certainly true that the Chancery scribes, like the scribe of the late West Saxon dialect, seem to have been concerned about eliminating variations in spelling, especially where these were based on local or individual pronunciations. Documents passed to them for copying were respelled according to their own conventions. The practice of regularizing spellings is part of the process of standardization: in fact, spellings are probably the easiest aspect of language to standardize.

Activity 3.8   *(Allow about 10 minutes)*

If you have any knowledge of written legal English, the following example of a Chancery document may seem familiar. (It entrusts Sir John Talbot with the post of chancellor of Ireland, a territory claimed by the English crown since 1171.)

- Note any differences from modern English spelling. Look particularly at the ends of words, at places where today we might use a different letter.

- Does Chancery use the same stock of letters as modern English?

The kyng by þadvise and assent of the lordes spirituell and temporell beying in this present parlement woll and grantith þat þe said Sir John Talbot haue and occupie the saide office of Chauncellor of Irelond by hym self or by his sufficient depute there after the fourme of the kynges lettres patentes to hym made þerof. The which letters patentes been thought gode and effectuell and to be approved after the tenure of the same. Also þat þe grete seal of þe saide lond belongyng to þe saide office, which þe said Thomas hath geton von to hym by delyuered to þe said Sir John Talbot or his sufficiente depute hauing power of hym to resceive hit.

Comment

You may have noted that final *e* (a relic of the old inflectional system) is retained in, for example, *fourme* (form) and *saide* (said) and that *l* at the end of words is doubled (*spirtuell*). The letter *y* is often used where today we would have *i*, and *v* is used at the beginnings of words where today we have *u*. But notice also that *þ* is retained initially alongside *th*. Some of these variations persisted into the printed literature of the fifteenth century.

This east-Midlands variety of English is traditionally seen as that from which a standard of English emerged.

3.9   CONCLUSION

In this chapter I have tried to show:

- How English developed from complex patterns of contact between Anglo-Saxons, Celts, Vikings and (with their ongoing relations with France) Normans; how it was a minority written language in the early Middle Ages, and how by the fifteenth century it had largely replaced French and Latin in official documents (although Latin remained in use for scholarly writing).

- How we can trace continuity (and in the case of grammar, discontinuity) between Old English and modern English (including its regional dialects) from a range of Anglo-Saxon and Middle English texts.

- How from the earliest times English has varied, both regionally (especially from north to south) and stylistically (from poems to royal documents), and how this variability can be seen as a central part of the story of English.

- How the history of English is beset by problems of evidence (both external and internal) its availability and interpretation.

Overall, I have argued that scholars in the past have tended to see the history of Old English from a West Saxon perspective, and the history of Middle English from the perspective of an emerging 'standard' based on written east Midlands usage.

This is partly because the available evidence is patchy (most surviving Old English texts are West Saxon) but also because evidence has been selected and interpretations shaped to suit particular stories, the most popular now being based on ideas about national identity, with a particular ending, the emergence of a standard variety.

Finally, throughout this chapter I have focused on 'England', with only the briefest nod towards Wales, Scotland and Ireland. English was spoken in these territories during the periods we have examined here, but the English language in these other parts of Britain has its own, complicated histories and is dealt with in Chapter 5.

Reading A

THE STORY OF OLD ENGLISH

David Crystal

Before the Anglo-Saxon invasions, the languages of Britain were Celtic, spoken in many dialects by people who had themselves invaded the islands several centuries before. Many Celtic tribes had in turn been subjugated by the Romans, but it is not known just how much Latin – if any – was spoken in daily life in the province. When the Roman legions left, in the early fifth century (to help defend other parts of the Roman Empire), the only permanent linguistic sign of their presence proved to be the place names of some of their major settlements – such as the towns now ending in -*chester* (derived from the Latin word for 'camp', *castra*), and a small number of loan words, such as *stræt* (street, road).

The linguistic effects of the Anglo-Saxon wars were just as clear-cut. Many Celtic communities were destroyed, assimilated, or gradually pushed back westwards and northwards, into the areas we now know as Cornwall, Wales, Cumbria, and perhaps also Scotland. Here the Celtic dialects were to develop in separate ways, resulting in such modern languages as Welsh and Gaelic. We do not know if many Celts stayed in the east and south, but if they did, they would soon have lost their identity within the dominant Anglo-Saxon society. One thing is clear: the Celtic language of Roman Britain had hardly any influence on the language spoken by the Anglo-Saxons. Only a handful of Celtic words came into English at the time – such as *crag, combe* [valley], *bin, cross, brock* (badger), and *tor* (peak). And there are even very few Celtic place-names in what is now southern and eastern England (though these are much more common in Cornwall and Devon, and of course in Wales and Scotland). They include such river names as *Thames, Avon* (from the word for 'river'), *Exe, Usk,* and *Wye.* Town names include *Dover* (water), *Pendle* (*pen* is 'top' in Welsh), and *Kent* (whose meaning is unknown).

There is a 'dark age' between the arrival of the Anglo-Saxons and the first Old English manuscripts. There are a few scattered inscriptions in the language, dating from the sixth century, and written in the runic alphabet which the invaders brought with them, but these give very little information about what the language was like. The literary age began only after the arrival of the Roman missionaries, led by Augustine, who came to Kent in AD 597. Large numbers of Latin manuscripts were produced, especially of the Bible and other religious texts.

Old English manuscripts also began to be written. The earliest texts are glossaries of Latin words translated into Old English, and a few early inscriptions and poems, dating from around AD 700. But very little material remains from this early period. Doubtless many manuscripts were burned during the eighth-century Viking invasions. The main literary work of the period, the heroic poem *Beowulf,* survives in a single copy, made around AD 1000 – possibly some 250 years after it was first composed. Most extant Old English texts date from the period following the reign of King Alfred (849–899), who arranged for many Latin works to be translated – including the Bede *Ecclesiastical History.* But the total corpus is extremely small. The total number of words in the Toronto corpus of Old English texts, which contains all the texts (but not all the alternative manuscripts of a text) is only three and half million – the equivalent of about thirty medium-sized modern novels.

The texts which have survived come from all over the country, and from the way they are written they provide evidence that there were several dialects of Old English [although they were predominantly written in West Saxon]. There was no single system of spelling at the time. Scribes would spell words as they sounded, and these spellings suggest different accents. Thus in the south-east of the country, the word for 'evil' was written *efel*, whereas in other places it was written *yfel*. Hundreds of such spelling differences exist.

The main dialect divisions reflect the settlements of the invading tribes, with their different linguistic backgrounds, and these divisions are still apparent in the country today. The area occupied by the Angles produced two main dialects: *Mercian* was spoken in the Midlands, roughly between the River Thames and the River Humber, and as far west as the boundary with present-day Wales; *Northumbrian* was spoken to the north of Mercian, extending into the eastern lowlands of present-day Scotland, where it confronted the Celtic language of the Britons of Strathclyde. *Kentish*, spoken by the Jutes, was used mainly in the area of present-day Kent and the Isle of Wight. The rest of England, south of the Thames and west as far as Cornwall (where Celtic was also spoken), was settled by Saxons, the dialect being known as *West Saxon*. Most of the Old English manuscripts are written in West Saxon, because it was the kingdom of Wessex, under King Alfred, which became the leading political and cultural force at the end of the ninth century. However, modern standard English is descended not from West Saxon, but from Mercian, as this was the dialect spoken in the area around London, when that city became powerful in the Middle Ages.

There is a clear line of descent from Old English to the English of the present day, in sounds, spelling, grammar, and vocabulary. About a third of the words we use on any page are of Old English origins. But what of the other two-thirds?

The history of English is one of repeated invasions, with newcomers to the islands bringing their own language with them, and leaving a fair amount of its vocabulary behind when they left or were assimilated. In the Anglo-Saxon period, there were two major influences of this kind.

- The Christian missionaries [arriving from Rome from AD 597 onwards] not only introduced literacy. They also brought a huge Latin vocabulary, some of which was taken over into Old English. The Anglo-Saxons had encountered Latin before, in Europe, when several Latin words entered their language – such as *weall* ('wall'), *stræt* 'street', *ceap* ('bargain', 'cheap'), and *win* ('wine'), and they brought these words with them to Britain. But there were only a few dozen such words. By contrast, the missionary influence resulted in around 450 new words coming into the language, mainly to do with the church and its services, but including many domestic and biological words. The vast majority have survived in modern times. At the same time, many Old English words were given new meanings – *heaven, hell, God, gospel* ('good news'), *Easter, Holy Ghost, sin* – and there were several other usages, most of which have not survived (such as *Scyppend* 'shaper', meaning 'creator').

- The second big linguistic invasion came as a result of the Danish (Viking) raids on Britain, which began in AD 787 and continued at intervals until the beginning of the eleventh century. Within a century, the Danes controlled most of eastern England. They were prevented from further gains by their defeat by King Alfred in 878 at Ethandun (modern Edington, in Wiltshire). A treaty was then drawn up in which the Danes agreed to settle only in the north-east third of the country – east of a line running roughly from Chester to London – an area that was subject to Danish law, and which thus became known as the Danelaw. In 991 a further invasion brought a series of victories for the Danish army, and resulted in the English king, Æthelred, being forced into exile, and the Danes seizing the throne. England stayed under Danish rule for twenty-five years.

The result of this prolonged period of contact was a large number of Danish settlements with Scandinavian names. There are over 1,500 place-names of Scandinavian origin in England, especially in Yorkshire and Lincolnshire. Over 600 places end in -by, the Danish word for 'farm' or 'town' - *Derby, Grimsby, Rugby,* etc. Many of the remainder end in -*thorp* ('village'), as in *Althorp* and *Linthorpe,* -*thwaite* ('an isolated area'), as in *Braithwaite* and *Langthwaite,* or -*toft* ('a piece of ground'), as in *Lowestoft* and *Nortoft.* Many Scandinavian personal names (e.g. surnames ending in -*son,* such as *Davidson* and *Henderson*) are also found in these areas.

In the long term, over 1,800 words of definite or probable Scandinavian origin entered the language during this period, and are still to be found in present-day standard English. Several thousand more continued to be used in regional dialects, especially those of the north-east. In fact, hardly any of these words actually turn up in Old English manuscripts, which shows the time it takes for words to become established, and to be used in literature (among the exceptions are *law* and *riding,* as in the 'West Riding' of Yorkshire, from *priding* – a third part). Most of the words doubtless became established during the tenth and eleventh centuries, but written evidence for them is largely lacking until the thirteenth century, at the beginning of the Middle English period. Among these are most of the words which use *sk* sounds – *skirt, sky, skin, whisk,* etc.

The closeness of the contact between the Anglo-Saxons and the Danish settlers during this period of 250 years is clearly shown by the extensive borrowings. Some of the commonest words in English came into the language at the time [from Danish], such as *both, same, get, give,* and *take.* Three of the Old English personal pronouns were replaced by Scandinavian forms (*they, them, their*). And – the most remarkable invasion of all – the invading language even took over a form of the verb *to be,* the most widely used English verb. *Are* is of Scandinavian origin.

The Anglo-Saxon age was a time of enormous upheaval. Each invasion, whether physical or spiritual, was followed by a long period of social change which left its mark on the language, especially on the vocabulary. But none of the linguistic changes were as great as those which followed the most famous invasion of all, led by Duke William of Normandy in 1066, and which came to identify the second main period in English language history, Middle English.

Source: Crystal, 1988

MODERNITY AND ENGLISH AS A NATIONAL LANGUAGE

Dick Leith and David Graddol

4.1   INTRODUCTION

This chapter describes some key developments in the English language from the end of the fifteenth century to the nineteenth century. It was during this period that English became standardized, and much of this chapter is taken up with consideration of how the idea of a 'standard' form of English, which could serve as a 'national' language of first England then Britain, arose.

As in previous chapters, we examine here both changing linguistic characteristics and the wider social context within which English developed. That context was by any account remarkable. The sixteenth and seventeenth centuries form the period of English known as 'early modern'. It was the time in which Shakespeare, Dryden and Samuel Pepys lived, creating what many people today still regard as the 'great works' of English literature. It was also the era when Europe, as a whole, developed a radically new political and economic form, that of autonomous nation states each with a 'national' language.

This period was the one in which the English language was first taken overseas, to the new colonies in the Americas and Asia. In other words, just as it became a national language it became an international one as well. We focus in this chapter, however, on the development of English in England. Chapter 5 examines the expansion of English beyond England – to other parts of the British Isles and overseas.

4.2   MODERNITY AND THE RISE OF A NATIONAL LANGUAGE

It was not only the language which became 'modern' during the period we discuss in this chapter, but the whole of European society. England, like many parts of Europe, can in many ways be said to have made the transition from a medieval to a modern society during the sixteenth and seventeenth centuries, and that process was both complex and traumatic. For some, those who enjoyed the new wealth and intellectual liberation brought about by the growth of a market economy and the breaking away from the authoritarian dogmas of the Catholic church, it was a period of great excitement and opportunity. For many, such as the peasants who lost access to the land which provided them with a living, it was an oppressive period of poverty and social problems.

Modernity, in the sense that has come to be used by cultural theorists today, is both a state of mind and an economic and social condition. As a state of mind, it implies an intellectual outlook based on self-knowledge and rational argument rather than subservience to dogma or belief in magic. As a social condition, modernity implies particular forms of social relation based on forms of capitalism. Whether or not modernity is itself a transient condition is a moot point. In recent decades the political and economic structure of Europe has been undergoing another transformation, one which may prove to be as radical as that in the early modern period.

'Modernity' as we use the term in this chapter thus refers to ideas about social identity and language that are associated with wider intellectual and political developments in Europe, particularly during the period 1500–1900. Modernity, in this sense, has also been experienced in other parts of the world where European culture was a major influence in social and economic development – most notably North America. In many ways, modernity can be regarded as a defining characteristic of 'the west'.

The Renaissance

The origins of this period of social upheaval lie in the intellectual movement that came to be known as the Renaissance or the 'revival of learning'. Starting in Italy in the fifteenth century and gradually spreading across Europe, the Renaissance was a time when scholars rediscovered the works of 'classical' scholars of Greek and Roman times. The invention of printing made it possible for these works to be distributed widely and read by a greater range of people than would otherwise have been possible. Among the readers of the classical texts were the new merchant classes who had money but not, by and large, the kind of education which allowed them to read Latin.

Printers required capital to set up their equipment, buy paper and materials and pay hired labour. They therefore needed to maximize the size of their local market, and this is one reason why the development of printing stimulated rapid growth in translations of classics into local languages. As we see in the next section, the translation and publishing of books in English by William Caxton (c. 1422–91), the first English printer, was to have a profound standardizing effect on the language.

The growth of capitalism

As international trade grew, so did banking and other financial services such as stock exchanges. For instance, Henry VIII of England (1509–47) borrowed £1 million on the Antwerp market in the last four years of his reign. With the growth of capitalism, new social class relations began to take shape. England, for example, was a major wool exporter but now began to manufacture and export cloth rather than the raw material. When the medieval 'guilds' controlled the supply of labour in the large towns many merchants moved their operations to rural areas, where it was easy to find people willing to undertake spinning and weaving in their own cottages for low wages. Increasingly merchants centralized production in 'manufactories' where workers could be supervised and where the complex division of labour could be managed. In the same way as the physical landscape of England was transformed when open land was enclosed by landlords for sheep rearing, so the social landscape took on a new shape as peasants increasingly became hired labourers and factory workers.

The growth of a market economy caused prices to rise throughout Europe. In Britain, basic commodities such as cereals and clothing are known to have quadrupled in price by 1600 while average wages only doubled. Entrepreneurs engaged in the new trade and industries became rich, but those on fixed incomes suffered and poverty emerged as a major social problem. Thus one of the key features of the age was the restructuring of English society along lines of social class. As we discuss below, during the following centuries there arose new attitudes towards 'social correctness' and forms of English that indicated a speaker's social position.

The Reformation

The Reformation is the name given to the breaking away, in many parts of northern Europe, from the Roman Catholic faith and from the institutional authority of the Roman Catholic church. Throughout the period covered by Chapter 3 societies in western Europe owed allegiance to the Roman Catholic church, under the central authority of the Pope. By the sixteenth century, however, many of the tenets of the Catholic faith were being challenged by people who came to be called Protestants (who, to put it simply, favoured a less elaborate form of worship based on individual faith). Although originally a matter of religious doctrine, the challenge was championed by certain European leaders whose ambition was to set up states independent of the Pope's authority. In the early 1530s, Henry VIII declared himself (rather than the Pope) head of the English church. The new technology of printing again played a central role in spreading these ideas, and the publication of an English translation of the Bible in the mid sixteenth century has often been regarded as a decisive moment in the creation of standard English.

The rise of humanist science

The Reformation led to a generally freer climate with regard to the pursuit of analytical studies involving the natural world. Scholars everywhere became more prepared to regard aspects of the human condition as the products of humans rather than of God. Language was one of many fields of scholarship which benefited from this 'humanist' enterprise, as scholars began to write treatises on language, construct grammars of English and compile dictionaries.

A remarkable expansion of knowledge occurred during the early modern period, partly as a result of European exploration of the world (most notably the Americas), partly as a result of the sudden growth in scientific research. Indeed, the early modern period of English stretches from Copernicus's calculation in the early 1500s that the sun, rather than the earth, was the centre of the solar system to Isaac Newton's investigations into the properties of gravity and light. This was the period in which science in its modern sense emerged: the idea that knowledge resulted from the 'proof' of hypotheses based on careful experimentation and empirical observation. But the discussion of such discoveries required a vast number of new words, and the new forms of reasoning and argument required innovation in the grammatical resources of English.

The process of standardization

The period in which modern English arose was thus characterized by interconnected and fundamental changes in the structure of society. The key linguistic process associated with these social changes is **standardization**: English was transformed from a vernacular language into one with a standardized variety that could be identified with England as a nation state.

A **standard language** is one that provides agreed norms of usage, usually codified in dictionaries and grammars, for a wide range of institutional purposes such as education, government and science. Sociolinguists tend to use the term **Standard English** to denote the primarily written, especially printed, usage of educated people.

In standardization, there are four main processes (which may happen simultaneously):

1   *Selection*: of an existing language variety as the basis. The variety selected is usually that of the most powerful or socially influential social or ethnic group.

2   *Codification*: reduction of internal variability in the selected variety, and the establishment of norms of grammatical usage and vocabulary. Since standard languages are rooted in written forms, standardization often also involves the establishment of a standard spelling for words.

3   *Elaboration*: ensuring that the new language can be used for a wide range of functions. This may involve the extension of linguistic resources; for example, new specialized vocabulary or even new grammatical structures.

4   *Implementation*: the standard language must be given currency by making texts available in it, by discouraging the use of alternative language varieties within official domains, and by encouraging users to develop a loyalty and pride in it.

Standardization thus has two main dimensions: as the sociolinguist Einar Haugen puts it, its goals are 'minimal variation in form, maximal variation in function' (Haugen [1966] 1972, p. 107).

A number of languages have been turned into standard, national languages in the twentieth century as the result of deliberate policy and **language planning**; for example, Swahili in Tanzania, Putongua in China, Bahasa Indonesia and Tok Pisin in Papua New Guinea. Standardization in English, however, was only partly a deliberate process. It resulted from a combination of social and economic conditions, though, as we will see, it was helped along by the activities of a large number of people. It is also important to note at the outset of this chapter that standardization in English has been only partly achieved. Indeed, Milroy and Milroy (1985, p. 24) suggest that no 'spoken language can ever be fully standardized'. Standard English remains something of an ideal, an imaginary form of English that is often rhetorically appealed to but never clearly identified. Standardization is thus not simply a linguistic fact but an ongoing process and an ideological struggle.

Sociolinguists have only recently begun to study how reduction in variation in form (Haugen's first dimension) arises in speech communities without formal intervention by governments or language planners. Le Page and Tabouret-Keller (1985, p. 187) propose a phenomenon that they call **focusing**. A focused linguistic community is one in which there is a strong sense of norms. There are four key 'agencies' of focusing:

1   close daily interaction in the community;

2   the mechanisms of an education system;

3   a sense of common cause or group loyalty, perhaps caused by perception of a common threat;

4   the presence of a powerful model, such as the usage of a leader, a poet, a prestige group or a set of religious scriptures.

The concept of focusing is applied in the course of the discussion of standardization in English that follows.

4.3   CAXTON AND THE CONSEQUENCES OF PRINTING

The invention of printing in Europe and its introduction by Caxton to Britain played a crucial role in the development of Standard English.

nobles and vplapnes cam to his scole for to lerne.
n these dapes p Saturne began thus to floure a was
rr. pere of age and his broder .rl. Dranus their fader
by a sekenes that he had dped and deptid out of this
world leupng his wpf Desta endewed largelp of
possessions. his deth was noyous and sorowfull to
Desta his wife. whyche causid her to wepe out of
mesur and his sones and doughtirs also thep dide his
obsequye reuerentlp in fulondpng of grete and bittir
sorow. the obsequye don ther weppng and sorow
yet during vesta saw that Tptan her eldest sone pre-
tended to haue and enioye the succession of his ffader
she on a day callid her der sone Saturne wpth Tptan and other of the Contre and there rehercede a said
vnto them that her pong sone Saturne shold succede
and hiue the herptages of her husbond Tptan herpng
the wpll of hps moder redoublid hps sorow and cau
sid hpm to wepe grete plente of teeris and knelpde to
fore his moder humblp and sapde in thps wpse Moder
p am rpght infortunate whan pe wpll that mp right
patrpmonye be put from me And that naturelli me
ought to haue by rpght sholde be gpuen fro me and
yat beause p p am not so well formede of membres
as mp broder satorne ps whiche sorow is to me pas
spng noyous pe wil putte from me mp ffortune and
burthe whiche pe may not do by lawfull reson p am
pour first sone pe haue norpsshid me wpth psubstace
of pour bloode as pour chplde born in pour belp.ir. mo
nethes Also p am he that first dwellid and enhabited
pour fempnyn chambres s lone to fore me toke there
onp seafpng whan p toke that tho pe gaf me pour due

Figure 4.1 The first book ever printed in English was The History of Troy, *translated from the French and printed by Caxton in 1473. The black-letter typeface copied the style of gothic handwriting common in the Protestant countries of northern Europe*

(John Rylands University Library of Manchester)

Activity 4.1 *(Reading A)*

Reading A, 'Caxton on dialects', is taken from a book by the linguists Roy Harris and Talbot Taylor called *Landmarks in Linguistic Thought* (which immediately gives you the authors' perspective on Caxton's significance).

Read this piece, then re-read it, noting what the authors have to say about the following issues:

1 the origin of the concept of 'national language';

2 the problems posed by the lack of a fixed form for such languages;

3 how Caxton solved the problem for England;

4 the mixed attitudes towards the new 'national languages';

5 the Renaissance 'attitude' to language in relation to nationhood.

Comment

The concept of 'national language' originated in the European Renaissance, but the new national languages lacked a fixed form: regional dialects proliferated, linguistic change was rapid, and there was a relative lack of conventionalized spellings and authoritative sources. All these factors posed problems for printers. Caxton solved this problem for England by default – by printing the dialect of the south-east Midlands. Contemporary attitudes to national languages were confused: it was *politically* necessary to defend them, but they were widely felt to be inferior to classical Greek and Latin. Finally, language was seen by many Renaissance thinkers as an instrument to be shaped to suit the 'national' purpose.

You might have wondered about the authors' interpretation of Caxton's little story reproduced at the beginning of the reading. Theirs is actually the most usual interpretation. The story is seen as authoritative evidence of linguistic disorder (and therefore justifying the argument that English was in need of standardization). But you may have felt that too much fuss has been made about the eggs example. After all, aren't there plenty of similar examples of 'non-communication' in English today despite the process of standardization that has since occurred?

One conclusion we could draw is that all Caxton is doing is highlighting the fact that language – *any* language – is variable, and that this at times might cause problems for users. But we could also see Caxton as manipulating this example to suit his commercial interests. His argument that the English and their language were as variable as the effects of the moon makes a fanciful appeal, perhaps, to the idea of a readership united by a single characteristic. And the kinds of people able and interested enough to buy printed books were the newly literate middle class, who would be precisely the ones to identify with the mercer's sense of linguistic put-down.

There are also some points to add in relation to the introduction of printing technology and its cultural significance. Caxton certainly helped to familiarize people with variants of the east Midlands dialect by establishing that dialect as the medium of print: *I* rather than *ic(h)*, for instance, or *home* rather than *hame*. One consequence of this was that other dialects tended no longer to be printed (one exception is discussed below). So a printed norm based on usage in only one part of the territory became the 'national' norm too. Caxton effectively accomplished the first stage of standardization by selecting one variety (east Midlands English).

Printing also made it possible for identical material to be read by people throughout an entire territory *simultaneously*. This became especially true when newspapers were first introduced during the eighteenth century. Print therefore can assist the first of the focusing agencies listed at the end of section 4.2: 'daily interaction', albeit of a very restricted type, throughout a community is made possible, even though this is actually limited to the literate and wealthier community. In this way, print can also be seen as instrumental in *creating* images of a 'national' community. Without it, it is difficult to imagine the existence of distinct nations in the modern sense.

4.4   THE ELABORATION OF ENGLISH

As Harris and Taylor (1980) say in Reading A, language during the Renaissance period generally became the object of attention and debate. There is plenty of evidence to show that for the first time in its history English was evaluated as a medium of serious communication, and its forms and structures scrutinized.

Literary English and the growth in English vocabulary

Caxton had effectively selected a variety of English as suitable for publishing, but there were many who considered English still unsuitable for literary or scholarly use, areas of life in which Latin and Greek were regarded as the perfect instruments. The Renaissance had done much to make the works of classical authors more easily available; for example Roger Ascham, who was tutor to Queen Elizabeth (r. 1558–1603) and later her Latin secretary, is quoted in Reading A:

> … And as for ye Latin or Greke tonge, euery thyng is so excellently done in them, that none can do better. In the Englysh tonge contrary, euery thinge in a maner so meanly, both for the matter and handelynge, that no man can do worse.

There arose among a group of English authors the idea that the English language could be *made* more perfect, that it could be turned into as 'eloquent' a language as classical Latin. 'Eloquence' was a concept first associated with the ancient Greeks. Eloquence made a language more persuasive, and persuasion was central to the Greek ideal of the democratic city states such as Athens. The concept was important to the Romans too, who applied it to the writing of literature as well as public speaking. One linguistic dimension of eloquence was *copiousness*: the language needed enough words to represent every idea. In fact, it needed more than this: in order to prevent repetition of the same word, a variety of synonyms were needed to provide stylistic variation. This could be achieved either by greatly increasing the word stock or by increasing what was called 'significancy' – the ability of words to mean more than one thing (polysemy). At the sentence level eloquence also required the use of rhetorical structures, such as 'antithesis' in which oppositions are carefully balanced against each other.

How, then, could English be made more eloquent so that it could take over from Latin in the writing of poetry and literature, and so that a 'national' literature could be created which expressed the emerging cultural identity of England? There were three principal means of creating new vocabulary: words could be invented, using existing principles of word formation; words could be adopted from Latin or Greek; or obsolete English words could be brought back into use, perhaps with new meanings. English writers enthusiastically supported the project to increase the English lexicon. It is estimated that during the period 1500–1700 over 30,000 new words were added to the English vocabulary. The process reached its peak in the early 1600s when, on average, over 300 new words were recorded each year (see Figure 4.2).

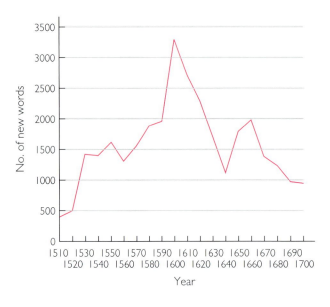

Figure 4.2 Growth in the English vocabulary 1500–1700

(Adapted from Görlach, 1991, p. 137)

A contemporary scholar, John Wilkins (1614–72), described the expansion of vocabulary and the mechanisms employed to achieve it:

> Since Learning began to flourish in our Nation, there have been more than ordinary Changes introduced in our language; partly by new artificial *Compositions*; partly by *enfranchising* strange forein words, for their elegance and significancy, which now make one third part of our Language; and partly by *refining* and *mollifying* old words, for the easie and graceful sound by which means this last century may be conjectured to have made a greater change in our tongue, than any of the former, as to the addition of new words.

(Wilkins [1668] 1968, p. 8)

The many Latin words introduced into English during this period made the new literary language difficult for many readers to understand. Among the earliest dictionaries of English were lists of such 'hard words', as they were called.

In addition to the introduction of new words during this period, existing words acquired more meanings (see Figure 4.3), thus increasing significancy.

At the level of the sentence, eloquence was achieved by imitating the rhetorical structures of Latin. An example is actually shown by Ascham himself (see the quotation above and in Reading A), who uses the antithetical style. We might therefore wonder whether he was only *affecting* to complain about English, as a kind of clever joke against the detractors of the language.

Many authors were, in fact, ambivalent in their attitude to the changes in English. On the one hand Latin and Greek were the perfect languages and so anything borrowed from them must surely be to the advantage of English. On the other hand there had emerged a competing, nationalist discourse in which words of Anglo-Saxon origin were to be preferred over 'foreign' ones. Chaucer, who had been praised by Caxton in his printed edition of *The Canterbury Tales*, was referred to by the sixteenth-century poet Edmund Spenser as 'the well of English

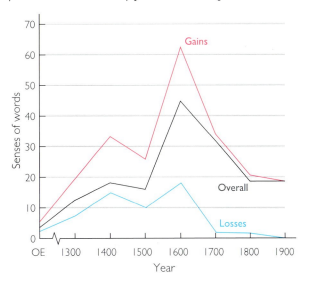

Figure 4.3   Growth in the multiple meanings of words in early modern English. The accretion and obsolescence of independent senses of eight polysemous words: draught, form, sense, set, stock, trade, train, wit

(Adapted from Görlach, 1991, p. 199)

undefylled' (undefiled). Such writers had thus established a 'golden age' of English literature and for them it was better to rehabilitate archaic words than borrow from Latin. The 'hard words' created by borrowing from Latin were stigmatized by such writers as 'inkhorne' terms.

Terrible, windy words from Latin

The Elizabethan dramatist Ben Jonson has a character in his play *The Poetaster* (1601) forced to expel the following 'terrible, windy words': *conscious, defunct, incubus, inflate, reciprocal, retrograde, spurious, strenuous*. How widely used are these words today?

By the end of the sixteenth century, however, many literary men thought that English, through the works of poets like Spenser, had achieved literary greatness. In 1592 the writer Thomas Nashe, for instance, credited the 'Poets of our time' with having:

> cleansed our language from barbarisme and made the vulgar sort here in London ... to aspire to a richer puritie of speech ...
> (Cited in Bailey, 1992, p. 37)

The language of Shakespeare

English in Shakespearian times was in a state of transition. The word endings of the older language – which helped distinguish between noun, adjective and verb, had largely been lost, but the stricter conventional word order which a non-inflected language needs in order to make clear word relationships (such as which noun is the subject and which the object of a verb) had not yet become fully established. This provided a resource for ambiguity which poets of the time fully exploited. They were helped further by the fact that rigid conventions of spelling and punctuation were not yet in place. Anne Ferry describes one strategy used by Shakespeare:

> ... a characteristic of sixteenth-century English is the relative fluidity of its grammar. Principal parts of speech seem to have been more readily interchangeable and in some ways that are no longer possible. Such interchanges were particularly common between adjectives and nouns, adjectives and adverbs, verbs and adverbs, but even nouns and verbs exchanged functions. For instance, in Shakespeare's Sonnet 105 the poet prays, 'Let not my loue ... as an Idoll show.' The grammatical construction makes 'doll' a noun, 'show' a verb. Yet the ear catches a lurking possibility that 'show' is a noun and 'Idoll' an adjective (which would now invariably be distinguished to the eye by the spelling *idle*), a possibility to which Elizabethan readers might be alerted [because] they more often read aloud or experienced words as they sound, and that adjective-noun combinations like idle show were a specially prominent feature of this poetry.
> (Ferry, 1988, pp. 2–3)

Some of this ambiguity has been lost to modern readers, used to more conventional word order and using modern editions in which orthography has been standardized. However, further ambiguities not available to contemporary audiences have since become available as many of the words used by Shakespeare have acquired new senses and connotation.

Several aspects of the verb phrase in Shakespearian writing are typical of sixteenth-century English. Use of the *do* verbal auxiliary was not yet common, nor were progressive verb forms:

> Even the casual reader of Elizabethan English is aware of certain differences of usage in the verb which distinguishes this part of speech from its form in later times. These differences are sometimes so slight as to give only a mildly unfamiliar tinge to the construction. When Lennox asks in *Macbeth, Goes the King*

hence today? we have merely an instance of the more common interrogative form without an auxiliary, where we should say *Does the king go?* or *Is the king leaving today?* Where we should say *has been* Shakespeare often says *is: Is execution done on Cawdor?* and *'Tis unnatural, Even like the deed that's done;* or *Arthur, whom [who] they say is killed tonight.* A very noticeable difference is the scarcity of progressive forms. Polonius asks, *What do you read, my Lord?* – i.e. *What are you reading?* The large increase in the use of the progressive is one of the important developments of later times.

(Baugh and Cable, 1978, p. 245)

Shakespeare used a wide vocabulary, including many of the latest innovations by other authors (such as *antipathy, critical, demonstrate, dire, emphasis, horrid, prodigious, vast*) and many of his own making (he is credited with coining words like *accommodation, assassination, dislocate, obscene, pedant, reliance, submerged*). Some historians claim he also supplemented his vocabulary with dialectal words from the Warwickshire area:

> … Shakespeare's vocabulary betrays his Warwickshire roots. In his work we find words like *ballow*, a North-Midlands word for cudgel; *batlet*, a local term, used until recently, for the bat to beat clothes in the wash; *gallow*, meaning to frighten; *geck*, a word for a fool, which was also used by George Eliot in *Adam Bede*; *honey-stalks*, a regional word for the stalks of clover flowers; *mobled* for muffled;

> *pash*, meaning to smash; *potch*, to thrust; *tarre*, to provoke or incite; and *vails*, a Midland term for perks or tips.

(McCrum et al., 1992, p. 100)

Finally, Shakespeare has become so well known throughout the English-speaking world, that many modern speakers of English have some familiarity with sixteenth-century English. Many expressions and idioms, for example, are based on Shakespeare:

> If you cannot understand my argument, and declare 'It's Greek to me', you are quoting Shakespeare; if you claim to be more sinned against than sinning, you are quoting Shakespeare; if you recall your salad days, you are quoting Shakespeare; if you act more in sorrow than in anger, if your wish is father to the thought, if your lost property has vanished into thin air, you are quoting Shakespeare; if you have ever refused to budge an inch or suffered from green-eyed jealousy, if you have played fast and loose, if you have been tongue-tied, a tower of strength, hoodwinked or in a pickle, if you have knitted your brows, made a virtue of necessity, insisted on fair play, slept not one wink, stood on ceremony, danced attendance (on your lord and master), laughed yourself into stitches, had short shrift, cold comfort or too much of a good thing, if you have seen better days or lived in a fool's paradise – why, be that as it may, the more fool you, for it is a foregone conclusion that you are (as good luck would have it) quoting Shakespeare.

(Bernard Levin, cited in McCrum et al., 1992, p. 98)

Activity 4.2   *(Allow 15–20 minutes)*

Below is an extract from *The Arte of English Poesie*, one of the most famous contributions to the debate about the merits of English as a medium for poets. Published in 1589, it is attributed to George Puttenham.

You'll probably find the language of this extract a lot easier than any of the texts so far, but you may have problems recognizing certain words because many spelling conventions (the use of *u* and *v*, for instance, as in *vnciuill* (uncivil) are similar to those mentioned at the end of Chapter 3. And in three words – *natiō, corruptiō* and *mās* (man's) – the *n* is indicated by a line above the preceding vowel.

Read the extract through fairly quickly, then re-read it. We don't expect you to understand every word, but we do expect that you'll find it a lot easier the second time. As you re-read it, think about the following questions.

1   What are the main points that Puttenham makes in this section?

2   Puttenham uses the words 'language' and 'speech'. What does he seem to
     mean by them? Can you think of a modern word to characterize what
     Puttenham calls 'language'?

3   Why do you think modern historians of English have considered this extract
     to be so significant?

But after a speach is fully fashioned to the common vnderstanding, and
accepted by consent of a whole countrey and natiō, it is called a language,
and receaueth none allowed alteration, but by extraordinary occasions
by little and little, as it were insensibly bringing in of many corruptiōs that
creepe along with the time; of all which matters, we haue more largely
spoken in our bookes of the originals and pedigree of the English tong.
Then when I say language, I meane the speach wherein the Poet or
maker writeth be it Greek or Latine, or as our case is the vulgar English,
and when it is peculiar vnto a countrey it is called the mother speach of
that people: the Greekes terme it *Idioma*: so is ours at this day the Norman
English. Before the Conquest of the Normans it was the Anglesaxon, and
before that the British, which as some will, is at this day, the Walsh, or as
others affirme the Cornish: I for my part thinke neither of both, as they
be now spoken and pronounced. This part in our maker or Poet must be
heedyly looked vnto, that it be naturall, pure, and the most vsuall of all his
countrey: and for the same purpose rather that which is spoken in the
kings Court, or in the good townes and Cities within the land, then in the
marches and frontiers, or in port townes, where straungers haunt for
traffike sake, or yet in Vniuersities where Schollers vse much peeuish
affectation of words out of the primatiue languages, or finally, in any
vplandish village or corner of a Realme, where is no resort but of poore
rusticall or vnciuill people: neither shall he follow the speach of a craftes
man or carter, or other of the inferiour sort, though he be inhabitant or
bred in the best towne and Citie in this Realme, for such persons doe
abuse good speaches by strange accents or ill shapen soundes, and false
ortographie. But he shall follow generally the better brought vp sort,
such as the Greekes call [*charientes*] men ciuill and graciously be-
hauoured and bred. Our maker therfore at these dayes shall not follow
Piers plowman nor *Gower* nor *Lydgate* nor yet *Chaucer,* for their language is
now out of vse with vs: neither shall he take the termes of Northern-men,
such as they vse in dayly talke, whether they be noble men or gentlemen,
or of their best clarkes all is a matter: not in effect any speach vsed beyond
the riuer of Trent, though no man can deny but that theirs is the purer
English Saxon at this day, yet it is not so Courtly nor so currant as our
Southerne English is, no more is the far Westerne mās speach: ye shall
therfore take the vsuall speach of the Court, and that of London and the
shires lying about London within lx. myles, and not much aboue. I say not
this but that in euery shyre of England there be gentlemen and others
that speake but specially write as good Southerne as we of Middlesex or
Surrey do, but not the common people of euery shire, to whom the
gentlemen, and also their learned clarkes do for the most part con-
descend, but herein we are already ruled by th'English Dictionaries and
other bookes written by learned men, and therefore it needeth none
other direction in that behalfe. Albeit peraduenture some small admoni-
tion be not impertinent, for we finde in our English writers many wordes
and speaches amendable, and ye shall see in some many inkhorne termes
so ill affected brought in by men of learning as preachers and

schoolemasters: and many straunge termes of other languages by Secretaries and Marchaunts and trauailours, and many darke wordes and not vsuall nor well sounding, though they be dayly spoken in Court. Wherefore great heed must be taken by our maker in this point that his choise be good.

(Puttenham [1589] 1936)

Comment

1 Puttenham is discussing which *kind* of English is appropriate for poets (or 'makers') to use. The most eloquent variety, he argues, will not be found in ports or remote villages, nor on the northern or western peripheries, but within a radius of 60 miles ('lx myles') around London. But this geographical dimension is complicated by three further factors. First is an occupational factor: avoid the 'affectation' of university scholars who use 'inkhorne' terms (as discussed above). Bear in mind that the dictionaries 'written by learned men' to which he refers would have been lists of so-called hard words. Secondly, there is a temporal factor: he refers, significantly enough, to the English authors Chaucer, Gower and the anonymous author of *Piers Plowman* (all from the fourteenth century) and Lydgate (fifteenth century) as representing not a golden age but merely a bygone past. Thirdly, and above all, there is a social factor (look at the usage of the gentry at court).

2 Puttenham seems to use 'language' to denote a particular linguistic variety rather than, as today, a group of related varieties or dialects (the term 'dialect', Greek in origin, was actually first used in English about the time Puttenham was writing). He introduces the notion of 'hierarchy' in his discussion of linguistic varieties, with 'language' at the top. In this he seems to be anticipating one meaning of the modern term Standard English.

3 This point follows on from the last. Historians of English have generally argued that this extract is evidence for the existence of a Standard English when Puttenham was writing. The passage shows clearly that dialect speech is a sign of social status, and that the upper-class usage of the London area was considered prestigious. But there are problems with using the term Standard English here. The *written* norm that Puttenham says even non-Londoners use is not the same as a spoken one, and a spoken norm may be a matter of vocabulary, grammar or (perhaps) pronunciation. Puttenham lumps these together: at one point he is discussing accent ('ill shapen soundes'), at another, vocabulary. And what are we to make of his description of south-eastern courtly language as 'naturall, pure, and the most vsuall'? As the usage of a tiny minority, it can hardly be the most 'usual' of the country, and Puttenham later says that northern speech is the 'purer English Saxon'.

These apparent confusions are not so surprising if we remember that Puttenham was not writing a sociolinguistic description of sixteenth-century English but a manual for *poets*. He was courting favour at the royal court by recommending that poets should use the language of courtiers. In so doing he introduced a crucial association between ideas about the 'best' English usage and social exclusiveness. As we shall see, this association has remained an issue ever since.

Changes in word order

In early modern English there were few radical changes in grammar, but certain patterns became more common while others fell into disuse. Figure 4.4 shows one of these changes: the rise of the use of *do*, particularly in questions, as an alternative to inversion of the word order (e.g. 'do you see?' rather than 'seest thou?'). Görlach (1991, p. 119) comments: 'these figures show the increasingly functional distribution of *do*, which is likely to be connected with the increasing rigidity of fixed word order in the sixteenth/seventeenth centuries'.

Differences in verb forms including *do* are discussed in more detail in Chapter 6, section 6.3.

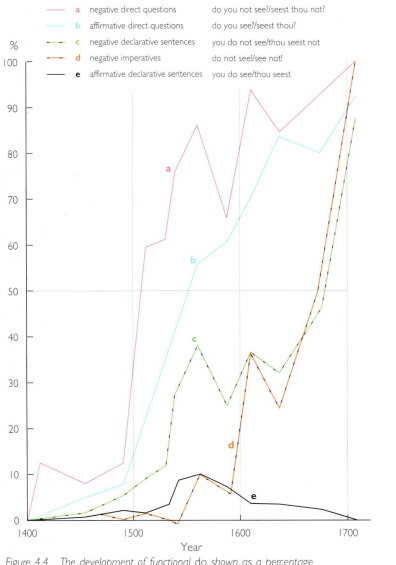

Figure 4.4   The development of functional *do* shown as a percentage
(Adapted from Görlach, 1991, p. 118)

The Reformation and its linguistic consequences

During the sixteenth century it seems that English writers developed a stronger loyalty and pride in the English language. This was no doubt helped by the Reformation, an event not mentioned in Reading A. The Reformation affected England after Henry VIII declared himself head of the English church. Two important results of this action were a radical change in the status of the clergy and an enormous growth in the power of the monarchy. Another was religious conflict and persecution that lasted for generations, giving rise to a definition of 'Englishness' that was Protestant, upright, industrious and defensive towards the outside world.

In terms of the agencies of focusing, this defensiveness can be related to the sense of an external threat which stimulates feelings of a common cause (see item 3 in the list of agencies of focusing at the end of section 4.2). The monarchy encouraged the view that England stood alone against hostile Catholic powers, and so the boundaries of England as an independent realm, in both space and time, became the object of attention. Maps of the present and surveys of the past were made. The language of England – its regional diversity and Anglo-Saxon past – became the object of antiquarian study. This was helped in the late 1530s by Henry VIII's closure of the (Catholic) monasteries – institutions that housed many of the manuscripts on which our knowledge of Old English depends.

Another, more famous linguistic consequence of the Reformation was the translation of the Bible into English, first carried out in 1526. A slightly later translation, together with the Book of Common Prayer in 1549, became the focus of the service in the new Church of England, breaking the long association between Christianity and Latin. The English Bible – which could now be widely disseminated in print – became an important focusing agency in itself (see item 4 in the list at the end of section 4.2). The Authorized Version of the Bible, published in 1611, was by the eighteenth century regarded by some as a kind of 'classical' variety of English, representing a golden age of usage.

In general, the political significance of translation seems to have been grasped by the monarchy as a means of asserting its authority. The Catholic church had its own body of laws in Latin, a language that was incomprehensible to most people in England. To translate these laws into English could be a symbolic challenge to papal authority and Henry VIII was probably behind the translation of many legal texts. Ancient governmental statutes in Latin (such as the Magna Carta of 1215) were also translated, helping to give the impression of a distinctively English, as opposed to international, law.

One effect of the Reformation, then, was to focus on English as opposed to Latin and other European languages.

4.5   THE CODIFICATION OF ENGLISH

In the course of the sixteenth century English became the object of serious academic study by people with practical interests who were responding to the political, cultural and religious controversies of their times (as seen in the previous section). One such practical interest arose because English had now become a language taught in school (see item 2 in the list of focusing agencies at the end of section 4.2).

One of the first grammars in English was William Lily's *A Shorte Introduction of Grammar*. Although known as 'Lily's Grammar', the book was actually put together from various sources after his death in 1523 (see Figure 4.5). This was one of the first books in English to become 'authorized' by King Henry VIII – it remained the 'national grammar' for several centuries and versions of it were used in English schools down to the nineteenth century. Although written in English it was essentially a grammar of Latin, but it provided the basic introduction to grammar that all the English writers of the early modern period, including Shakespeare, Spenser and Ben Jonson, were brought up on. As one editor has commented, 'This was the introduction to the classics of Rome for those who were to create the classics of England' (Flynn, in Lily [1542] 1945, p. xi).

The grammatical analysis described by Lily was already an ancient one. The earliest Greek grammar, written by Dionysius Thrax around 100 BC, identified eight 'parts of speech'. Since grammar was considered a universal structure which, like rhetoric, could be applied to any language, this number of parts of speech was sought in other languages, such as Latin (by Donatus in the fourth century AD) and then later in English. Lily therefore established not only an English terminology for grammatical ideas but also a grammatical analysis of English, closely modelled on that of Latin. Thus began a tradition of writing grammars of English that followed Latin models, a tradition that was not entirely broken until the nineteenth century.

The first grammar to attempt a description of the English language in English was Bullokar's *Bref Grammar for English*, published in 1586. One of its purposes, like Lily's Grammar, was educational – to 'rationalize' English spelling, vocabulary and grammar. In this respect its conception of grammar differed from that of modern linguistics. In fact, grammar for Bullokar meant the 'art of writing', its

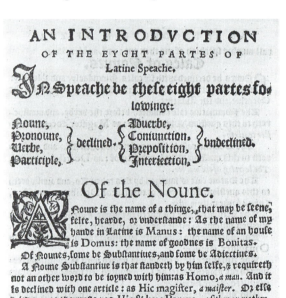

Figure 4.5   A page from Lily's A Shorte Introduction of Grammar, published in 1542, which established grammatical terminology in English. The book is also interesting typographically: black-letter type, which had largely been replaced in English books by roman type, is retained here for English. Latin words are set in roman type and English translations in italic

(Folger Shakespeare Library)

meaning in ancient Greek (Bullokar [1586] 1977). This conception dominated European thinking about grammar until well past Bullokar's time, and has had vital implications for education and the processes of standardization, as we will see.

Such a grammar served more than an educational purpose; it could be seen as symbolic of the dignity of English by other Europeans. As Harris and Taylor argue in Reading A, the writing of grammars for European languages had become politically expedient by Bullokar's time. Any European state desiring autonomy needed to have its own grammar of the so-called national language.

The issue of pronunciation in the sixteenth century

The extract from Puttenham in section 4.4 above shows that although there may have been a *general* curiosity about English during the sixteenth century there was also a particular focus on just one variety of it. This was due partly to an obsession with social status. As the strength of the monarchy grew, so did the significance of the royal court. Hierarchy was a key concept not only linguistically but also socially. High social status was something to be signalled through dress, manners, behaviour and speech (Stallybrass and White, 1986).

One reason for this concern with hierarchy – or 'degree', as it was often called – was that society was felt to be changing at a rather uncomfortable rate. In such situations people often hang on to what they know, even though it may no longer match social reality. As the box below shows, the terminology used to denote different social orders was itself out of date.

The terminology of 'degree'

Since the eleventh century society had been divided into three 'estates' who had clear social functions: *clerkes* (who prayed and wrote), *knyghtes* (who fought) and *laborers* (who worked). These categories were seen as ordained by God. But they were out of date in the reality of medieval life: how, for instance, did merchants in the towns fit in? By the sixteenth century this categorization was even more obsolete. The clergy had become a 'profession' much like any other. 'Knights', moreover, no longer had their original role, and a new one, as 'gentlemen' – based on ownership of wealth, and the kind of breeding suitable for government – was evolved by social commentators (Wrightson, 1991). The problem with the category of 'gentleman' was the set of criteria used for distinguishing it. Conservative social theorists might cling to the older type of 'prominent', landowning aristocrat, but in the sixteenth century wealth could be gained from other sources, such as trade. By the end of that century any attempt to sustain a rigid system of status terms had given way to a more informal system, in effect sorting the 'haves' from the 'have nots' – the latter often denoted by the term the 'common (or vulgar) sorte'.

As Puttenham's text suggests, there was a courtly interest in relating varieties of English to different social strata. But another, practical reason for postulating a hierarchy of language varieties was that schoolchildren in England were now learning to read and write English. Educators were acutely aware of the relationship between how English was written and how it was pronounced, and if you bear in mind what was discussed in the last two sections, it is not surprising that the relationship came to be conceived in terms of a recommended pronunciation. The term used at the time to denote this concern was **orthoepy**.

Some historians of English seem to have assumed that during the sixteenth and following centuries there existed an accent with the same kind of status and stability as modern Received Pronunciation (RP). We argue below that this is very unlikely (although some sixteenth-century orthoepists probably desired one!). Nevertheless, certain pronunciations (especially southern ones) were clearly more prestigious than others. When Merchant Taylor's School, in London, was visited in 1562 by inspectors, they faulted the teachers 'that being northern men born, they had not taught the children to speak distinctly, or to pronounce their words as well they aught'.

A number of quite sophisticated descriptions of English vowels were made during the sixteenth century but in some key respects these various descriptions do not agree with each other. This could mean either that one or more of the accounts was wrong, or that the disparity can be used as evidence of considerable diversity in pronunciation. Let's illustrate this by thinking about the pronunciation of certain vowels today, all of which are made with the *front* of the tongue raised.

Activity 4.3   *(Allow 5 minutes)*

Pronounce to yourself the words *mite*, *meet*, *meat* and *mate*. Are all four vowels different, or are some the same? Are any of them diphthongs? (You might need to re-read Chapter 3, section 3.4 to refresh your memory on this point.)

Comment

We expect you pronounced *meet* and *meat* the same, probably with long vowels [iː]. For most speakers of English, *mite* will have a diphthong. *Mate* will either have a different diphthong or a long vowel which is different again. Whatever your pronunciation, it is likely to be different from that prevailing in the sixteenth century, as we discuss below.

In the Middle Ages it seems that these sounds had all been long vowels, with *mite* sounding like today's *meet*; *meet* sounding like *mit* with a lengthened vowel; *mate* sounding rather like *mat* with a lengthened vowel; and *meat* with a vowel somewhere in between *meet* and *mat*. By the sixteenth century the vowel in *mite* had become a diphthong and the vowel of *meet* raised to the position previously occupied by *mite*. In addition to these differences, however, *meat* in some contemporary accounts had the same vowel as *meet*, while in others it was distinguished (as the different spelling suggests). So if sixteenth-century speakers of English were asked to carry out Activity 4.3 some would group *meat* with *mate*, others would group it with *meet* and some, it seems, would pronounce all three words differently, as in the older pattern.

It is this older, three-way distinction that is described by one of the most famous sixteenth-century orthoepists, John Hart. Hart was an official at the royal court, and his account may represent the usage of the traditional landowning gentry rather than that of the newly enriched merchant class. Or he may even have been *recommending* this pattern in the face of extensive linguistic variation and change, where the sons of tradesmen pronounced *meat* like *mate*, and where the lower class rhymed *meat* and *meet* – which, incidentally, is the modern pattern (Labov, 1978).

The Great Vowel Shift is
discussed more fully in
Chapter 7.

This complex reorganization of vowel sounds also involved the raising of
vowels in words like *moon* and the diphthongization of the vowel in words like *loud*
(see Chapter 3, section 3.4). Since it involved so many sounds, it is traditionally
known as the **Great Vowel Shift**. One final and vital point is that at this time the
great vowel shift was essentially a shift in *London* pronunciation, occurring among
people living in the capital. Since then, the shift has gradually influenced the
dialects of other areas and its effects are still being felt today. In some areas,
however, certain pronunciations remain unaffected by it. The vowel of *house, out*,
etc., as discussed in Chapter 3, still retains its older undiphthongized pronunciation in some dialects of northern England, and is a stereotype of modern Scots.

It is important to remember these regional variations in English today
because many historians of the language have presented the effects of the Great
Vowel Shift as establishing 'modern' English. According to Baugh and Cable, it
brought 'pronunciation within measurable distance of that which prevails today'
(1978, p. 250). This is one example of how variability in English sounds during the
modern period has been downplayed in order to focus on the development of a
particular variety – the usage of the capital city.

4.6   PURITANISM AND THE RISE OF SCIENCE

During the sixteenth century many of the requirements of standard language had
been put in place: the vocabulary of English had been greatly elaborated; a new
and flourishing English literary tradition had arisen; and scholars had begun to
write grammars of English, proposals for spelling rationalization and handbooks
for pronunciation. During the seventeenth century these projects were taken
forward, and the longer term effects of the Reformation were felt throughout
English society. The Protestant spirit of intellectual independence encouraged a
rapid growth in scientific discovery in England and an associated expansion of
English to cater for new forms of writing. Latin as the language of scholarship was
all but abandoned by the end of the century.

For some influential English people the reforms of the church instituted after
Henry VIII's break with Roman Catholicism did not go far enough. These people
favoured an even 'purer' form of worship, and they came to be known as Puritans.
Their vested interest in the idea of an essentially 'English' church led some
towards the study of Anglo-Saxon culture, which they celebrated as a golden age
of freedom and equality disrupted by the 'Norman yoke' (as discussed in Chapter
3, section 3.6). Many Puritans championed English over Latin, and favoured a
'plain' English purged of Latinate eloquence.

It is hardly surprising, then, that many Puritan scholars were involved in the
study of Old English manuscripts. They also took an interest in English dialects.
The Puritan John Ray, a famous botanist, for example, published in 1674 his
collection of dialect words as an aspect of a locality's 'natural history'. Dialects
were of interest to some Puritans because of their association with the Old English
rather than Latinate component of the English vocabulary. In fact, dialects were
defended by some as evidence of the 'copiousness' of English. But dialects have
wider relevance too. In the course of the seventeenth century several different
Puritan sects emerged, drawing support from across the entire social spectrum.
Ordinary Puritans would have spoken regional dialects. So the Puritan perspective on language, and with it a grasp of history and a wide social base, created the
possibility for an understanding of English as a 'national' language capable of
uniting *all* English people in the eyes of God.

Puritanism and the politics of pronoun usage

By the 1640s the Puritan perspective had become highly political. The growing power of the monarchy had been challenged by Parliament, and during the Civil War that followed (see box), Puritans played an active role on the parliamentary side. Pamphlets circulated by certain Puritan sects argued not only that the king was a tyrant like the Norman conquerors, but that ownership of any kind of property, including land, was morally wrong. These radical arguments did not prevail among the wealthier parliamentarians, and although, as we see below, the arguments themselves survived (see Alexander, 1982), the sects who upheld them were increasingly marginalized.

The English Civil War

Parliament clashed with the king over the scope of his powers. Hostilities started in 1642. After numerous battles Charles I was defeated in 1645. After a great deal of debate the king was executed in 1649, and a 'commonwealth' was declared. But the monarchy was restored in 1660.

For one Puritan sect, the Quakers, egalitarian ideas were inseparably linked to language use. The sect's founder, George Fox, used his knowledge of Old English to argue in favour of keeping the older form of the second person pronoun, *thou* (usually replaced by *you* today).

Activity 4.4   *(Allow about 15 minutes)*

Re-read Chapter 3, section 3.4 and then the three quotations given below:

1   Hwæðre þu meaht me singan.
    (However, you can sing for me.)
    (See Chapter 3, Figure 3.5, line 10, where Caedmon is asked to sing.)

2   If we speak to our inferior, we must use a certayne kynde of modest and civill authoritie, in giving them playnely to understand our intent and purpose. A Marchant [merchant] having many servantes, to his chiefest may speake or wryte by thys terme, *you*: but to them whome he less esteemeth, and are more subject to correction, he maye use this term, *thou*, or otherwise at his discretion.
    (Sir Thomas Fulwood, *The Enimie of Idelness*, 1568, emphasis added)

3   ... when the Lord sent me forth into the world, he forbade me to put off my hat to any, high or low; and I was required to 'thee' and 'thou' all men and women, without any respect to rich or poor, greater and small.
    (*Journal of George Fox*, 1675)

Can you trace a pattern in the development of *thou*? In your experience, how is the form used today?

Comment

In the first quotation the only possible form is *þu* (thou), since this was the singular form, and it is only Caedmon who is being addressed. The second quotation clearly shows, however, that by the sixteenth century the use of *thou* could reflect relationships of power. A merchant could address a clear subordinate with *thou* and reserve *you* for others (and, incidentally, expect to be addressed with *you* by a subordinate). This usage was rejected in the following century, as shown in the third quotation, by George Fox (who in fact insisted on 'theeing and thouing' the judge when on trial for his beliefs – today many Quakers still use *thee*). These pronouns were discarded only recently in poetry and liturgy, and they are retained in some regional dialects.

As you know, in Old English *þu* was the pronoun for 'you'. There was also another form, *ʒe* (modern *ye*: it is the *accusative* form of this that gives us the modern *you*), which referred to a plural 'you'. By the thirteenth century, perhaps as a result of influence from French usage, this distinction had given way as follows: the singular forms came to mark either a relationship of power (as explained above) or familiarity (also solidarity) among people who knew each other well (as in modern dialect usage); the plural forms came to be used, in addition to their obvious function, to signify respect (plural marking had come to be associated with high social status, as in the continuing use of *we* rather than *I* by members of the English royal family). By the sixteenth century this new pattern was itself giving way to one in which *you* was becoming the norm with a singular addressee, at least among certain groups in London and the south-east of England.

As in all examples of linguistic change, it is hard to pinpoint exactly the mechanism of change. Why, for instance, did the habit of using *thou* to mark a power relationship die out altogether? Baugh and Cable (1978, p. 242) explain the mutual use of *you* in all contexts as a 'general concession to courtesy'. This

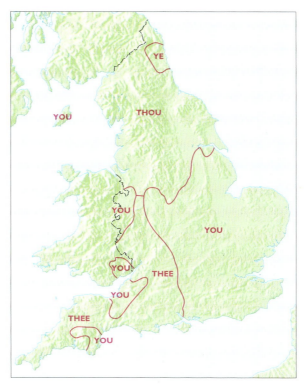

Figure 4.6   The pronouns thou *and* thee *are still used in some regional English dialects in England*

kind of explanation, which is very common, associates *you* usage with democracy and egalitarianism. Abandonment of the *thou* of power is attributed to the widespread adoption of these 'modern' ideas. But as we've seen, these ideas were marginalized during the seventeenth century. They re-emerged in the following century in a very different political context, and only became widely adopted when linked to the ideology of nationalism. Finally, why did the familiar use of *thou* die out in lower-class speech in south-east England? Perhaps usage of *thou* in general acquired unfavourable associations from Quaker usage: old-fashioned, politicized, rural, *regional*. It is noteworthy that Quaker strongholds were in the north and south-west of England, so that their religious (and political) preference for the older pronoun overlapped with dialect usage.

It is also noteworthy that many histories of English have overlooked the regional survival of *thou* and *thee*. Once again, Baugh and Cable (1978, p. 242) state that they 'are in ordinary use today only among the Quakers'. In this statement we see the narrowing of focus to supposed 'standard' usage seen as constituting *the* history of English. Both the *idea* of a standard language and the notion that the 'official' history of the language should be a history of the 'standard' language are key modernist ideas. (Note that *standard* is in quotes here because the extents to which a standard language existed and was used were and are matters of ideological debate.)

The rise of science

During the seventeenth century scholars pursued an idea already anticipated by Bullokar in his *Grammar*: if English was to be the medium of learning it would be much easier for people to learn Latin *after* they had learned the structure of English rather than the other way round, as had been the custom. This objective influenced the way grammars came to be written. For instance one mid century Puritan grammarian, John Wallis, rejected the idea that grammar should start with the categories established for Latin. This should start instead with 'what was there', on the grounds that this might be worth studying for its own sake.

This attitude is generally known as 'empiricist'. Obedience to the authority of the Catholic church and classical thinkers was replaced by relying on the evidence provided by the senses. This kind of thinking was held to be the basis of what today we know as 'science'. Many Puritans were attached to the details of science, which in the seventeenth century were not opposed to those of religion as they were later to become in the minds of many. Indeed, the scientist worked to the greater glory of God by helping to reveal to humanity the beauty and sophistication of the created universe – of which language was a part.

❖ ❖ ❖ ❖ ❖

Activity 4.5   The development of scientific English   *(Reading B)*

Now read 'The development of scientific English' by David Graddol (Reading B) which describes the effect of the scientific discoveries of the seventeenth century on written English. This reading provides a more detailed case study of how English was 'elaborated' in order to make it suitable for use in a new domain of communication hitherto dominated by Latin. Many of the grammatical characteristics of written English that we take for granted today emerged during this process.

❖ ❖ ❖ ❖ ❖

John Wallis (1616–1703)

One of the last of the Renaissance scholars, John Wallis, published a grammar of English in 1653, *Grammatica Linguae Anglicanae*, which is widely regarded as the first systematic attempt to describe the structure of English in its own terms – rather than imposing the categories and terminology established for Latin. The grammar itself was one of the last of the scholarly treatises to be written in Latin.

Wallis was an Oxford don who, like many other Renaissance scholars, was occupied in a wide range of activities. He was mainly a mathematician, the inventor of the mathematical sign for infinity. As a geometrician he tried his hand at architecture, designing the self-supporting roof of the Sheldonian Theatre in Oxford. Wallis also developed a considerable reputation during the English Civil War for his ability to decipher secret messages, and devised a system for the teaching of the deaf. Together with another Oxford scholar interested in linguistic matters, John Wilkins, Wallis was a founding member of the Royal Society.

Non ignoro alios ante me hoc aliquando aggreſſos eſſe, et aliquid etiam non contemnendum praeſtitiſſe, nempe Doctorem *Gill* Latine, *Benjaminum Johnſon* Anglice, et nuper non male *Henricum Hexham* Belgice (quem tamen mihi non prius videre contigit quam totum opus conſummaveram, et quidem ultimae paginae, editionis primae, ſub prelo erant). At nemo eorum, quantum ego exiſtimo, illa inſiſtit via quae huic negotio maxime eſt accommodata: omnes enim ad Latinae linguae normam hanc noſtram Anglicanam nimium exigentes (quo etiam errore laborant fere omnes in aliis modernis linguis tradendis) multa inutilia praecepta

An extract from John Wallis's Grammatica Linguae Anglicanae *published at Oxford in 1653, which is often regarded as the first systematic grammar of English*

(Kemp, 1972, p. 108)

4.7   THE DISCOURSE OF STANDARDIZATION IN THE EIGHTEENTH CENTURY

Puttenham's hierarchical view of language was developed by many observers during the eighteenth century, but in the very different social and cultural context of a literate middle class based partly in the London coffee-houses. Here language, politics and the history of literature were among the topics discussed, and essays on these subjects were published in several newly established periodicals. It was in this context that the word 'standard' seems first to have been applied to issues of language. Significantly, however, its most common meaning seems to have been 'level of excellence'. A writer in 1711 shows how the Greeks 'brought their beautiful and comprehensive Language to a just Standard' (quoted in the *Oxford English Dictionary* (Simpson and Weiner (eds), 1989) as '1711 Shaftesbury Charact (1732) III. 138'). Also significant is the continued association of the word with the classical languages, and the fact that it denoted a standard of *literary* correctness or excellence. In the following year, however, the clergyman and writer Jonathan Swift applied the term to English. He wanted to refine the language 'to a certain standard' (Crowley, 1989, p. 93).

Commentators like Swift were very concerned to protect English against the charge of 'barbarism'. The way to do this was to 'fix' the language so that it no longer varied and changed. One mechanism was to emulate states like France and Italy and set up an academy to regulate usage (you might find it useful to re-read Reading A at this point). But the idea, most famously proposed by Swift himself in 1712, came to nothing. Another course was to write a definitive dictionary, of the kind attempted by Dr Samuel Johnson in 1755, which we discuss below.

The desire for linguistic order did not arise simply from a desire to emulate the classical languages. Writers like Swift were anxious to preserve the *political* order with which they identified. For these writers the fixing of the language was to help safeguard what Swift called the 'civil or religious constitution'. As Dr Johnson wrote some 40 years later: 'tongues, like governments, have a natural tendency to degenerate: we have long preserved our constitution, let us make some struggles for our languages'.

A major reason for making this link between language and society was the memory of the Civil War. The philosopher Thomas Hobbes (a Royalist) had claimed to find a 'breakdown' of language during the war: 'one man calleth *Wisdome*, what another calleth *feare*; and one *cruelty*, what another *justice* … Without agreement on the commonwealth, nor society, nor contract, not peace.' If language was breaking down, Hobbes argued, it was a sure sign that society too was breaking down. These kinds of association between the condition of the language, the political constitution (or state) and the issue of social cohesion have endured in Britain ever since.

Let's now consider these points in relation to one of the most influential books in the history of English, Johnson's *Dictionary*.

Activity 4.6   *(Allow 30 minutes)*

Bearing in mind Johnson's words quoted above, read the five extracts from the Preface to his *Dictionary* given in Figure 4.8. As you read, consider the questions below.

- What are the problems Johnson sees in writing a dictionary of English? What help, if any, was available to him?

- What kind of English usage does he include, and what does he exclude?

- What 'story' of language seems to guide him? And what does he have to say about change in language?

- What are his views on translation and academies?

*Figure 4.7
An eighteenth-century
coffee-house*

(Mary Evans
Picture Library)

1   When I took the first survey of my undertaking, I found our speech copious without order, and energetick without rules: wherever I turned my view, there was perplexity to be disentangled, and confusion to be regulated; choice was to be made out of boundless variety, without any established principle of selection; adulterations were to be detected, without a settled test of purity; and modes of expression to be rejected or received, without the suffrages of any writers of classical reputation or acknowledged authority.

Having therefore no assistance but from general grammar, I applied myself to the perusal of our writers; and noting whatever might be of use to ascertain or illustrate any word or phrase, accumulated in time the materials of a dictionary, which, by degrees, I reduced to method, establishing to myself, in the progress of the work, such rules as experience and analogy suggested to me; experience, which practice and observation were continually increasing; and analogy, which, though in some words obscure, was evident in others.

2   So far have I been from any care to grace my pages with modern decorations, that I have studiously endeavoured to collect examples and authorities from the writers before the restoration, whose works I regard as *the wells of English undefiled*, as the pure sources of genuine diction. Our language, for almost a century, has, by the concurrence of many causes, been gradually departing from its original *Teutonick* character, and deviating towards a *Gallick* structure and phraseology, from which it ought to be our endeavour to recal it, by making our ancient volumes the ground-work of stile, admitting among the additions of later times, only such as may supply real deficiencies, such as are readily adopted by the genius of our tongue, and incorporate easily with our native idioms.

But as every language has a time of rudeness antecedent to perfection, as well as of false refinement and declension, I have been cautious lest my zeal for antiquity might drive me into times too remote, and croud my book with words now no longer understood. I have fixed *Sidney*'s work for the boundary, beyond which I make few excursions. From the authours which rose in the time of *Elizabeth*, a speech might be formed adequate to all the purposes of use and elegance. If the language of theology were extracted from *Hooker* and the translation of the Bible; the terms of natural knowledge from *Bacon*; the phrases of policy, war, and navigation from *Raleigh*; the dialect of poetry and fiction from *Spenser* and *Sidney*; and the diction of common life from *Shakespeare*, few ideas would be lost to mankind, for want of *English* words, in which they might be expressed.

3   Nor are all words which are not found in the vocabulary, to be lamented as omissions. Of the laborious and mercantile part of the people, the diction is in a great measure casual and mutable; many of their terms are formed for some temporary or local convenience, and though current at certain times and places, are in others utterly unknown. This fugitive cant, which is always in a state of increase or decay, cannot be regarded as any part of the durable materials of a language, and therefore must be suffered to perish with other things unworthy of preservation.

4   Total and sudden transformations of a language seldom happen; conquests and migrations are now very rare: but there are other causes of change, which, though slow in their operation, and invisible in their progress, are perhaps as much superiour to human resistance, as the revolutions of the sky, or intumescence of the tide. Commerce, however necessary, however lucrative, as it depraves the manners, corrupts the language; they that have frequent intercourse with strangers, to whom they endeavour to accommodate themselves, must in time learn a mingled dialect, like the jargon which serves the traffickers on the *Mediterranean* and *Indian* coasts. This will not always be confined to the exchange, the warehouse, or the port, but will be communicated by degrees to other ranks of the people, and be at last incorporated with the current speech.

5   The great peſt of ſpeech is frequency of tranſlation.   No book was ever turned from one language into another, without imparting ſomething of its native idiom ; this is the moſt miſchievous and comprehenſive innovation ; ſingle words may enter by thouſands, and the fabrick of the tongue continue the ſame, but new phraſeology changes much at once ; it alters not the ſingle ſtones of the building, but the order of the columns.   If an academy ſhould be eſtabliſhed for the cultivation of our ſtile, which I, who can never wiſh to ſee dependance multiplied, hope the ſpirit of *Engliſh* liberty will hinder or deſtroy, let them, inſtead of compiling grammars and dictionaries, endeavour, with all their influence, to ſtop the licence of tranſlatours, whoſe idleneſs and ignorance, if it be ſuffered to proceed, will reduce us to babble a dialect of *France*.

Figure 4.8   Extracts from the Preface to Dr Johnson's Dictionary, *taken from the fourth edition of 1773*

Comment

From the first extract we get a glimpse of Johnson's classicizing desire for perfection in language: English has no 'settled test of purity'. To make matters worse, there was nothing except 'general grammar' to help him. Virtually all the dictionaries available to Johnson were specialist ones: lists of so-called hard words (adoptions from Latin and Greek), bilingual dictionaries and so on. So he had to scrutinize the work of writers. The second extract tells us that he favours the writing not of the present but of the past, notably of the late sixteenth or seventeenth centuries. (Notice that he quotes Spenser's phrase about the 'wells of English undefiled'.) This was a golden age for Johnson, from which the language had degenerated, partly because of influence from French ('Gallick'); but note that his remark about a 'time of rudeness antecedent to perfection' suggests yet another linguistic story: that a language may first blossom and then decay. We can call this a *cyclical* view of language. But it is important to note that Johnson refers only to writing of a certain kind: *literature*, by which he meant writing such as theology (Hooker) and scripture (the Bible), or scientific and governmental works (Bacon and Raleigh), as well as literature in the narrower sense more commonly used today. The third extract shows that he excludes the (presumably spoken) usage of the 'laborious [working] and mercantile part of the people' on the grounds that this usage does not last. Mercantile matters are also singled out in the fourth extract: it is 'commerce', rather than 'conquests and migrations', that 'corrupts' English; and in the final extract he also blames translation. His opposition to an academy is based on a notion of 'liberty' that he sees as essentially English (as opposed to the fanatical adherence to tyrannical laws, seen as an attribute of the French).

❖   ❖   ❖   ❖   ❖

The doctrine of correctness

Johnson's *Dictionary* was followed by several 'grammars' of English which recommended certain grammatical usages as 'correct'. For instance, the cumulative negative construction such as the one in the Caedmon text – *Ne con ic noht singan* (I don't know how to sing) (see Chapter 3, Figure 3.5) – was deemed illogical, therefore incorrect. It contained two negative particles, *ne* and *noht*, which in accordance with the laws of algebra must cancel each other out. So the correct (modern) form ought to be 'I don't know how to sing', with just one negative particle (*n't*).

These arguments, a further aspect of the eighteenth-century discourse of standardization, were sometimes given a divine justification. In an earlier section we discussed the idea that everything in nature was an expression of God's order. If the way a society is organized – its 'constitution', to use Johnson's word – can be claimed as part of nature, then it too reflects God's will. The 'genius' of English – to quote Johnson again – reflected the English way of life, and part of this genius was its grammar. To deviate from correct grammar, then, was to displease God. The grammarian Robert Lowth, who was to become a bishop, and for whom the English translation of the Bible was the 'best standard of our language', thought that correct grammar was next to godliness. His grammar, first published in 1762, ran to 22 editions in 30 years (Lowth [1762] 1968).

The doctrine of correctness was also applied to pronunciation in the form of pronouncing dictionaries. A very famous one was John Walker's *A Critical Pronouncing Dictionary* of 1791, which listed 'rules ... for attaining a just pronunciation' of English (Walker [1791] 1968). Walker acknowledged the range of dialectal pronunciations throughout England but confined his attention to Londoners, 'who, as they are the models of pronunciation to the distant provinces, ought to be the more scrupulously correct'. His 'Fourth Fault' of Cockney, the lower-class dialect of London, was '(n)ot sounding *h* where it ought to be sounded, and inversely. Thus we not infrequently hear, especially among children, *heart* pronounced *art*, and *arm, harm*.' He ends this discussion by saying that Cockney 'though not half so erroneous as that of ... any of the provinces, is, to a person of correct taste, a thousand times more offensive and disgusting'.

Modern linguists would characterize Walker's tone here as **prescriptive**: he is telling people what he feels they should say. It seems likely, however, that pronouncing words like *arm* with initial *h* arise precisely because some speakers have been made to feel anxious about 'correct' pronunciation. If they do not customarily pronounce initial *h* (there is evidence for *h*-less pronunciation as far back as the Middles Ages; see Milroy, 1992) they will not know which words (e.g. *heart*) are supposed to have it, and which do not (e.g. *hour*). So they 'hypercorrect', by adding initial *h* to any word which starts with a vowel.

4.8   STANDARD ENGLISH, DEMOCRACY AND THE STATE

The nineteenth century in Britain was a period of extraordinary technological and social change. The industrial revolution gave rise to a growing middle class who were unsure of their social position and behaviour and who looked to grammars and pronouncing dictionaries for help. During this century schooling also became more widespread, and linguistic correctness became a most important mark of education. It was at this time that the term Standard English first came to be used, and increasingly so in connection with spoken as well as written English. In the second half of the century, in particular, there were many British people who felt a sense of national identity and confidence as never before: the British colonies in India and elsewhere became incorporated into the British empire under Queen Victoria; British technological invention led the world; private enterprises and corporations were creating wealth which might benefit all sectors of society.

During this period a large number of national institutions and societies – public bodies outside the control of central government – were established which helped to consolidate and regulate national culture and science in a manner that was, by now, typically English. In this last section we want to look at the role of these bodies in creating a standard, national language, and at some of the social and intellectual movements which helped to create an opposing force – towards regional rather than national pride and celebration of dialect rather than standard speech.

Dialect speech and the discourse of democracy

The eighteenth-century distinction between polite and vulgar effectively disparaged all popular, dialectal speech. Words like 'offensive' and 'disgusting' (as used by Walker to describe cockney speech) were commonplace at this time. Such views were reinforced by the increase in educational provision during the nineteenth century. The wealthy were able to send their sons to the new fee-paying 'public schools' – a practice made possible by the construction of the railways. These schools promoted a highly focused form of pronunciation which became known as Received Pronunciation (RP). Compulsory state education was introduced in 1870 and one of its aims was the teaching of 'Standard English'. If this had been successful, it would for most pupils have meant the eradication of their local dialects. This 'national' educational policy was applied in all parts of Britain; the local speech of Scotland, for example, was regarded as a dialect of English (for an alternative view of its status, see Chapter 5).

There was, however, an opposing attitude towards English dialects which saw them as the authentic source of English culture and language, unadulterated by the social effects of industrialization and urban living. During the 1760s writers had drawn attention to the 'popular' traditions of verse that had existed in medieval times, or that had since coexisted with the literature of the 'polite'. This stimulated interest in the idea of literature of, and for, the common people, an interest culminating in the poet Wordworth's famous preface to his *Lyrical Ballads* in 1802. These poems were not aimed at satisfying the taste of the 'polite' reader; instead they celebrated the 'rustic life' of ordinary people whose feelings were supposedly untainted by social vanity. Above all, though not written in the dialect of Wordworth's Cumberland home, they purported to use the very language of ordinary people. Wordworth's sentiments were possible because a reaction to the discourse of standardization had taken place.

From the 1840s onwards there emerged a flourishing literature in dialect in various parts of industrialized northern England (Joyce, 1991). Significantly, this literature was both printed and sold by local publishers. Many of the dialect writers were workers and they were often self-educated in the new textile factories of Lancashire and Yorkshire. By the 1850s industrial cities such as Manchester had their own local newspapers, and were fiercely proud of their manufacturing traditions. Much of the literature reflects a regional 'patriotism', with a strong antipathy towards the south-east of England.

This tradition of writing lasted well into the twentieth century. Below is an extract from a poem, 'In Praise o' Lancashire', published in 1923. It celebrates the working people of Lancashire who, unlike the 'chirpin' Cockneys of London, have made their county the 'engine-heause' (house) of Britain. As well as fighting for their country they have also fought for 'freedom', by agitating for representation in Parliament and building trade unions. The poem embodies a working-class conception of manliness and ends with a celebration of the dialect as an expression of solidarity:

So give us th' good owd dialect,	(old)
That warms eaur hearts an' whums,	(our, homes)
That sawders us together,	(solders)
An' that cheeans us to eaur chums.	(chains)
It may be rough-and-ready stuff,	
An' noan so fal-lal smart,	(not, high-falutin')
But it's full o' good an' gumption,	(vigour)
And it's gradely good at th' heart!	(properly)

Dialects were seen by some scholars as making an important contribution to the 'national language'. We can find this perspective among some language scholars in the nineteenth century. Max Müller, Professor of Comparative Philology at Oxford University, wrote in 1862 that 'The real and natural life of language is in its dialects.' But the importance of dialect was usually seen in the light of what it preserved from the past. Even the most systematic dialect scholars such as A.J. Ellis (see Chapter 2, section 2.6) saw dialect as being on the verge of extinction, to be replaced by what other scholars such as Walter Skeat (see Chapter 3, section 3.4) called the 'standard or literary language'. This replacement was seen as not only inevitable but progressive, since dialects (despite their historical significance) were usually seen as hindering wider communication and as 'holding back' their speakers' education. Various 'external' changes, such as the development of railways (making communications easier and faster) and the depopulation of rural areas (reducing the number of the dialect speakers), were seen as assisting the process.

A final point about dialect in the nineteenth century is that it was understood to be essentially rural. But one reason for rural depopulation was the rise of manufacturing industry – the so-called industrial revolution – which forced people to move from the countryside to work in factories in towns and cities. This 'working class', as these people had come to be called, were often seen by the class above them as a threat. In fact, some observers even saw them as barbarians, with all the accumulated meanings of that term: outsiders, destroyers of 'culture', cruel, little better than savages. This was especially the case with the poor of London. In 1902 the sociologist C.F.G. Masterman, in a book appropriately entitled *From the Abyss*, wrote of their 'bizarre and barbaric revelry' (quoted in Crowley, 1989, p. 217). The London poor were regarded by many middle-class people as 'inarticulate', so the term 'dialect' was considered too good for them. Even today, urban working-class speech – often regarded simply as 'bad English' – continues to be the image of unacceptability for many people. It was only from about the middle of the twentieth century that the term 'dialect' came to be used by language scholars to include the local speech of towns and cities. This was a significant innovation, making it more difficult to dismiss dialect as merely obsolescent.

The *Oxford English Dictionary*

The issue of what constituted the national language was debated by those scholars involved in compiling the *Oxford English Dictionary* (OED), widely seen as the finest achievement of the philological method and as a work of the greatest authority.

In the case of the OED, the issues of what to include and how to present information were considered in great detail by the members of the Philological Society who prompted the dictionary. In a Proposal of 1858 there were five main points:

1   it should be exhaustive;

2   all English books should be admitted as authorities;

3   there should be a chronological limit as to the earliest texts from which quotations would be drawn;

4   it should chart the history of each word, its form and senses;

5   it should show the origins of each word and its relationships with words in other (related) languages.

The criterion of exhaustiveness (point 1) was, in the end, sacrificed by the decision to make dialect vocabulary a separate project. In 1873 the English Dialect Society was set up specifically to compile a dialect dictionary, which was published in 1898. The final decision to focus on one variety of English at the expense of the others – an issue central to this chapter – is summed up in this sentence from the Proposal: 'As soon as a standard language has been formed, which in England was the case after the Reformation, the lexicographer is bound to deal with that alone.' For the compilers of the dictionary this meant in practice the 'standard literary' language. Why this limitation? Why such a forceful word as 'bound'?

In the course of the nineteenth century English literature had become the object of academic study. There were political reasons for this. By appealing to a shared literary past, so the argument went, the growing gulf between the urbanized working class and the social groups above them could be bridged. According to one contemporary commentator the study of 'native literature' from past to present was the 'true ground and foundation of patriotism' (quoted in Crowley, 1989, p. 123). So, as Tony Crowley argues, the OED also reflected the era's preoccupation with nationalism. One problem, however, was that the records demonstrating this literary past were scattered and incompletely understood. It was necessary for scholars to find the texts in the first place, explicate their language and then publish them. The dictionary depended on this research, which was helped by the formation of the Early English Society in the 1860s and by numerous other specialist societies such as the New Shakespeare Society, established in 1873.

In respect of point 3 of the Proposal, it was originally intended to go no further back than the emergence of an 'English type of language', which was supposed to date from about 1250. Some language scholars at this time argued that since Old English was 'unintelligible' to the modern reader, the new dictionary should avoid quoting words from the Anglo-Saxon period. On the other hand, there was to be no chronological limit as far as the *origins* of words were concerned (point 5). The idea was to take a word back as far as it could go, even to the reconstructed 'Old Teutonic' originally spoken by the Germanic ancestors of the Anglo-Saxons. In this respect the historical boundaries between English and other languages were blurred.

So the new dictionary was to be primarily historical: it was to show where the English vocabulary came from, how it had changed over the centuries and how the meanings of words had changed. Let's demonstrate this with two examples from the second (1989) edition of the OED, in the light of the relevant points made in the Proposal.

Activity 4.7   *(Allow 5 minutes)*

Examine the opening part of the OED entry for the word *folk* given in Figure 4.9. What do you think is intended by listing all the different 'forms' (see point 4 of the Proposal). Can you guess what the capitalized abbreviations (e.g. OS, ON) stand for?

Comment

The listed forms are the various spellings of the word in the different centuries denoted by the numbers (1 means eleventh century, etc.). As for the abbreviations, all stand for Teutonic (Germanic) languages closely related to English: OFris is Old Frisian; OS is Old Saxon; OHG and MHG are Old and Middle High German; ON is Old Norse. Notice that an 'original' Old Teutonic form has been suggested; the asterisk means this is a reconstructed rather than a recorded form.

folk (fəʊk). Forms: 1–2 folc (*pl.* folc), 2 folche, *Orm.* follc, follk, 3 folck, *south.* volck, 3–4 folc, *south.* volc, volk, 3–6 folke, 3–8 fok(e, (5 fokke), 6 folck(e, 8 *Sc.* fouk, 3– folk. Also 3–4 *wk. gen.* folken(e. [OE. *folc* str. neut. = OFris. *folk*, OS. *folc* (Du. *volk*), OHG. *folc* neut., masc. (MHG. *volc* neut., masc., mod.Ger. *volk* neut.), ON. *folk* neut., people, army, detachment (Sw., Da. *folk*):—OTeut. *folkoⁿ. The original sense is perh. best preserved in ON.; cf. OSl. *plŭkŭ* (Russ. *polk*) division of an army, Lith. *pulkas* crowd, which are believed to be early adoptions from Teut.

The view of some scholars, that the Teut. word and the L. *vulgus* both descend from a common type *qolgos, is very doubtful.]

1. a. A people, nation, race, tribe. *Obs.* exc. *arch.*

So far we have said nothing about the 'senses' of words mentioned in point 4 of the Proposal. In the case of *folk*, this is of great interest for our discussion. The first sense was taken over by the Latin adoption *nation*, which later came to yoke it with the idea of 'independent state'. During the nineteenth century *folk* was revived in a spirit of Anglo-Saxonist antiquarianism to denote the 'common people' in formations such as *folklore*.

❖ ❖ ❖ ❖ ❖

Our second example (in Activity 4.8) relates back to section 4.7 on correctness.

❖ ❖ ❖ ❖ ❖

Activity 4.8   *(Allow 15 minutes)*

Refute was adopted from Latin in the seventeenth century. How would *you* define its meaning? Make up a sentence illustrating its use. Now compare what you've written with the meanings listed in the OED entry in Figure 4.10. Notice how the different meanings are illustrated by means of quotations. Which meaning is closest to your own illustrative sentence?

refute (rɪˈfjuːt), *v.* [ad. L. *refūtāre* to repel, repress, rebut: see RE- and CONFUTE *v.* Cf. F. *réfu-er* (*c* 1549 in Godef.).]

† **1.** *trans.* To refuse, reject (a thing or person). *Obs. rare.*
1513 BRADSHAW *St. Werburge* I. 1535 Her royall dyademe and shynynge coronall Was fyrst refuted for loue of our sauyoure.

2. To prove (a person) to be in error, to confute.
1545 JOYE *Exp. Dan.* Argt. 5 b, Which reiecteth and refuteth the iewes and vs castinge away god and his gospel as thei did. **1579** FENTON *Guicciard.* III. (1599) 116 He refuted the Admirall, who..assayed to qualifie indirectly the wills of the councell. **1641** HINDE *J. Bruen* xxii. 68 Who might also have received their answer and beene evidently refuted to their faces, if they had but observed his ordinary practices. **1692** WASHINGTON tr. *Milton's Def. Pop.* M.'s Wks. 1738 I. 544 That you, my Countrymen, refute this adversary of yours yourselves. **1768** tr. *Rollin's Anc. Hist.* (ed. 5) I. p. xlix, In his second [book], wherein he refutes his brother Quintus. *refl.* **1869** *Daily News* 14 Dec., But Mr. M. is good enough, for all practical purposes, to refute himself.

3. To disprove, overthrow by argument, prove to be false: **a.** a statement, opinion, etc.
1597 HOOKER *Eccl. Pol.* v. lxxx. §7 It is some greife to spende thus much labour in refuting a thing that hath so little grounde to vpholde it. **1664** POWER *Exp. Philos.* I. 39 An errour so gross and palpable, that it needs not the Microscope to refute it. **1710** LADY M. W. MONTAGU *Let. to Bp. Burnet* 20 July, They bring them a thousand fallacious arguments, which their excessive ignorance hinders them from refuting. **1780** COWPER *Table-t.* 104, I grant the sarcasm is too severe, And we can readily refute it here. **1838** LYTTON *Alice* II. vii, Unconsciously his whole practice began to refute his theories. **1875** JOWETT *Plato* (ed. 2) I. 194 They can refute a propostion whether true or false.

b. an imputation, accusation, etc.
1611 SPEED *Hist. Gt. Brit.* IX. xxiv. §231 Which imputation in sundry languages he refuted in Print. **1725** POPE *Odyss.* VIII. 270 Well thy gen'rous tongue With decent pride refutes a public wrong. **1784** COWPER *Task* II. 824 Let the arraigned Stand up unconscious, and refute the charge. **1838** THIRLWALL *Hist. Greece* V. 375 The plan which he has suggested..is the surest way to refute such calumnies. **1875** MANNING *Mission H. Ghost* x. 277 Would you not seek everywhere for proofs to refute the accusation?

4. *absol.* To demonstrate error.
1742 YOUNG *Nt. Th.* VII. 1343 Instead of racking fancy, to refute, Reform thy manners, and the truth enjoy. **1805** *Med. Jrnl.* XIV. 174 Those, whose only object is to cavil where they cannot refute.

¶ **5.** *trans.* Sometimes used erroneously to mean 'deny, repudiate'.
1964 C. BARBER *Ling. Change Present-Day Eng.* v. 118 For people who still use the word in its older sense it is rather shocking to hear on the B.B.C., which has a reputation for political impartiality, a news-report that Politician A has *refuted* the arguments of Politician B. **1978** *Observer* 7 May 4/9 Mr O'Brien, who was first elected general secretary three years ago, refutes the allegations. **1979** *Daily Mail* 17 Feb. 15/3 He refuted allegations that she took her own life because of police harassment. **1980** *Bookseller* 19 July 257/1, I refute Mr Bodey's allegation that it is our policy not to observe publication dates, and to display new titles in newsagents immediately on receipt from the publisher.

Hence **reˈfuted** *ppl. a.*, **reˈfuting** *vbl. sb.*
c **1555** HARPSFIELD *Divorce Hen. VIII* (Camden) 239 In the refuting of which impure and unchaste proviso..I trust the reader will bear with me. **1638** R. BAKER tr. *Balzac's Lett.* (vol. II.) 33 Such of their objections, that seeme worth the refuting. **1646** SIR T. BROWNE *Pseud. Ep.* I. viii. 30 He often..seems to confirme the refuted accounts of Antiquity. **1780** COWPER *Progr. Err.* 550 His still refuted quirks he still repeats. **1818** in Lady Morgan *Autobiog.* 241 Commonplaces, repeated a hundred times over with a refuted tone.

Comment

It would not be surprising if your definition came close to the fifth definition, since this usage is quite widespread today. It is interesting, however, that a supposedly objective document such as the OED lists this as 'erroneous', presumably because the older meanings are felt to be more correct (see Figure 4.11, taken from Dr Johnson's *Dictionary*). The doctrine of correctness, discussed above in relation to grammar and pronunciation, has also influenced the way we think about the meanings of words. One of the problems with seeing words from the perspective of origins is that we tend to assume that a word has an 'essence' located in its oldest meaning and form. So the history of any word's meaning is in danger of becoming a story of *decline* from a golden age.

> *To* REFU'TE. *v. a.* [*refuto,* Lat. *refuter,* Fr.]   To prove
> falfe or erroneous.   Applied to perfons or things.
>   Self deftruction fought, *refutes*
>   That excellence thought in thee.   *Milton's Par. Loft.*
>   He knew that there were fo many witneffes in thefe two
> miracles, that it was impoffible to *refute* fuch multitudes.
>   *Addifon.*

Figure 4.11
Refute from Johnson's Dictionary taken from the fourth edition of 1773

4.9   CONCLUSION

We have tried to show that during the so-called modern period English has been developed as the language of an autonomous state, and that it has been seen as expressive of English nationality. But we have also tried to show that the concept of the national language is problematic. On the one hand it can be seen as *inclusive*, although this raises the issue of where the boundaries of the language actually are (as in the case of Scots, discussed in Chapter 5); on the other hand it can be seen as *exclusive*, based on the usage of an elite located in the south-east of England. It is the second meaning that is associated with the term Standard English.

We have suggested that the history of English during the entire modern period may be explored in relation to the concept of *focusing*. We have looked at the introduction of printing, and later at different 'powerful models' (classical, literary, biblical, the usage of a prestigious social grouping) which influenced thinking about English at various times. Some of these models, as in the debates about the meaning of Standard English, appear to pull in different directions. We have also examined aspects of formal education (from the elitist ideas of sixteenth-century orthoepists to the systematic introduction of state schooling in the nineteenth century, with its emphasis on Standard English).

We have noted the sociolinguistic processes that have led to standardization and towards the creation of a more unified and 'rational' language, and we have also seen that there were opposing tendencies, such as regional pride and interest in local dialects. The existence of such competing forces – which some scholars have called 'centripetal' (pulling in to the centre) and 'centrifugal' (tending to pull away from the centre and fragment) – is one reason why a single, homogeneous variety of English will never be achieved.

Reading A

CAXTON ON DIALECTS

R. Harris and T.J. Taylor

And certaynly our language now vsed varyeth ferre from that whiche was vsed and spoken whan I was borne. For we Englysshe men ben borne vnder the somynacyon of the mone, whiche is neuer stedfaste but euer wauerynge, wexynge one season, and waneth and dyscreaseth another season. And that comyn Englysshe that is spoken in one shyre varyeth from a nother. In so moche that in my dayes happened that certayn marchauntes were in a shippe in Tamyse for to haue sayled ouer the see into Zelande, and for lacke of wynde thei taryed atte Forlond, and wente to lande for to refreshe them; And one of theym named Sheffelde, a mercer, cam in-to an hows and axed for mete; and specyally he axyd after eggys: And the goode wyf answerde, that she coude not speke no Frenshe. And the marchaunt was angry, for he also coude speke no Frenshe, but wolde haue hadde egges, and she vnderstode hym not. And thenne at laste a nother sayd that he wolde haue eyren: then the good wyf sayd that she vnderstod hym wel. Loo, what sholde a man in thyse dayes now wryte, egges or eyren. Certaynly it is harde to playse eueryman by cause of dyuersite and chaunge of langage.

(Prologue to *Eneydos*, William Caxton, 1490)

The linguistic mentality of modern English is one in which English, French, German, Spanish, Portuguese, Italian, Dutch, etc. are all recognized as established national languages. Each has its own literature, history and grammar. Each is backed by the authority of an independent state. Each is the official medium of communication for all legal and constitutional purposes within certain political frontiers. This state of affairs, which Europeans nowadays take for granted, and which leads them to treat languages as national badges of affiliation, came into being only at the Renaissance. Throughout the Middle Ages, linguistic thought in Europe had been moulded by the intellectual predominance of the two great languages of antiquity. Greek, although few could read it and even fewer speak it, was identified with the primary sources of European culture: it was the language of Homer, of Plato, of Aristotle, of Demosthenes. Latin, on the other hand, was the international working language of European education and administration: it was the language of law, of government, of the universities and of the Church. The eventual end of the long reign of Greek and Latin, together with the accompanying rise in status of the local European vernaculars, marked a most important watershed in the history of the western linguistic tradition.

William Caxton (c. 1422–91), the first English printer, translated and published a number of French works, including the *Eneydos*, from his Prologue to which the above excerpt is taken. The fact that Latin is a moribund language and European culture no longer has a genuine *lingua franca* presents Caxton, as printer and publisher, with an opportunity but at the same time with a difficult linguistic choice.

For any writer of the 15th and 16th centuries the only viable alternative to writing in Latin was to write in one or other of the current European vernaculars. But half a century after Caxton English writers were still apologizing for writing in English; for example, Roger Ascham, in his treatise on archery (1545) thinks it necessary to explain as follows:

... And as for ye Latin or Greke tonge, euery thyng is so excellently done in them, that none can do better. In the Englysh tonge contrary, euery thinge in a maner so meanly, both for the matter and handelynge, that no man can do worse.

(*Toxophilus* Dedication)

The question of the 'inferiority' of the vernacular languages was a much laboured Renaissance debating point. But a much more mundane, practical problem was foremost in the mind of the first English printer. What most worried Caxton was the fact that English, unlike Latin, had no recognized common usage. It varied considerably from one part of the country to another, causing practical difficulties of everyday communication, as Caxton's anecdote about the merchant who wanted eggs illustrates. To put this problem in its historical perspective one must remember that when Chaucer, whose works were among those which Caxton printed, wrote *The Canterbury Tales* a hundred years earlier, the language of government in London was still officially French. ... The century in which Caxton set up the first printing press in Westminster (c. 1476) was the first century in which the English language in England was no longer in competition with French.

Although Caxton specifically addresses the problem of linguistic variation in English, and offers the quaint explanation that the English are destined to linguistic vacillation because they are born under the sign of the moon, he would have been unobservant not to notice in the course of his long residence on the Continent that 15th-century French was no more uniform than 15th-century English. Every country in Europe was a linguistic patchwork of dialects, and would remain so for many generations after Caxton's death. But Caxton's observation is of historical significance because, for the first time, this is seen as a problem.

The lack of uniformity in English usage posed in fact more than one problem for Caxton. In a country where some people say *egges* but others say *eyren*, and those who say one do not understand those who say the other, it is a problem for any publisher who wishes to sell books to as many people as possible to know which among the conflicting dialects will be most widely understood. But even if that problem is soluble, there is a further question to be faced; namely, how to spell the dialect you have chosen to print, given that there is no accepted assignment of letters of the alphabet to the various competing dialectal pronunciations. These difficulties are further complicated if, as Caxton recognizes, the dialects themselves are caught up in a process of change.

... He ... observes that English had undergone considerable modifications during his own lifetime. Perhaps his awareness of those changes was enhanced by the fact that he had spent much of his earlier career as a merchant and diplomat abroad and was struck by the disparity when he eventually returned to the country of his birth. Finally, it must be borne in mind that the problems relating to English usage which Caxton faced could not be solved by consulting dictionaries or grammars of the English language, because in Caxton's day English, unlike Latin, had no dictionaries or grammars.

The uncertainties of linguistic usage which Caxton found himself wrestling with were in certain respects by no means new. From antiquity onwards, scholars had recognized that vacillations might arise because of linguistic clashes between different *dialects,* different *orthographies*, and different *generations*. The dialect problem, the orthographical problem, and the problem of linguistic change arise from conditions which are endemic in every literate society once it reaches a certain size and phase of development. What was novel about Caxton's dilemma (although not unique to Caxton's particular case) was that these old problems were brought into much sharper focus than ever before by the invention of printing. Printing was the technological foundation of the European Renaissance, and the most radical innovation in human communication since the invention of writing. Caxton is a man caught at the crossroads of history in more senses than one. He is trying to introduce and popularize a new technology which is destined to revolutionize the availability of information in civilized society. The political and educational consequences of this new technology will be profound. But this profoundly important initiative is being undertaken in the most linguistically adverse circumstances possible. For what has just broken down is the universal linguistic viability of Latin; and in England there is no comparably stable language to take its place. Printing is a communications technology which demands uniformity, and in Caxton's England, to say nothing of the rest of Europe, there was none.

Printing is the classic case of a technical innovation which necessitates rethinking basic assumptions about society, and in this particular instance about society's linguistic organization. Caxton's historical problem as England's first printer arose from the fact that he was committed to a technology which did not make it possible, as it had been when every readable document was laboriously hand-copied, to make individual alterations to individual copies. Printing means mass replication. It also means replication at great speed (relative to the speed of producing hand-written copies). These two factors – exact mechanical replication and speed of production – combine to afford unprecedented marketing possibilities for the product. They also combine to expand potential readership out of all (previous) recognition. But these possibilities are thwarted if the linguistic condition of society is such that linguistic fragmentation (for whatever reason) is valued above uniformity. One of the paradoxes of the Renaissance is that 'Caxton's problem' would never have arisen if printing had been invented two hundred years earlier. For then Latin would still have reigned unchallenged as the official language of Europe.

In Caxton's remarks we see no indication of a realization that either he himself or the technology he was introducing were to play a key role in solving the problem of linguistic diversity which he so clearly perceived. By deciding, for better or for worse, to adopt the dialect of London and the South-East as the English for his books, Caxton took a decisive step forward in establishing that particular variety as 'the English language'. In retrospect, Caxton seems to have forged history's answer to his own question.

A rather different but related problem was that faced by European writers educated to revere the Classics, but politically motivated to claim that their own vernacular was linguistically on a par with any other European language, including the great languages of Greece and Rome. This problem was bound to induce a kind of linguistic and cultural schizophrenia, of which du Bellay's *Deffence at Illustration de la Langue Francoyse* (1549) is a prime example. In the *Deffence*, du Bellay is driven to admit that the French of his day is lacking in the means of expression required to analyse, discuss and articulate all the ideas which civilized society needs. Nevertheless, he maintains that this is not the fault of 'the French language' as such. The French language may yet produce its Homers, Demosthenes, Virgils and Ciceros [the great literary figures of Greece and Rome].

> And if our language be not so copious and rich as the Greek or Latin, that must not be imputed to it as a fault, as if of itself it could never be other than poor or sterile: but rather must one attribute it to the ignorance of

our ancestors, who ... have left our language so poor and bare ... But who would say that Greek and Latin were always in the state of excellence wherein they were seen in the time of Homer and of Demosthenes, of Virgil and Cicero?

(*Deffence*, Chapter III)

Du Bellay's *Deffence* was written barely more than half a century after Caxton's Prologue to *Eneydos*. Its tone is apologetic: but the apologia in retrospect rings false. Du Bellay must have sensed that history was on his side; and on the side of the European vernaculars. There could be no nostalgic going back to a European linguistic mentality dominated by Latin and Greek. The interesting aspect of this linguistic attitude is its insistence that we – the linguistic community – constantly make, amend and improve our language: it is not our linguistic inheritance which determines the limits within which we may think and express ourselves. In this respect du Bellay marks an advance over Caxton: 'Caxton's problem' is still a problem of choice within the limits set by existing alternatives. 'Du Bellay's problem' is quite different – it opens up a linguistic horizon of endless possibilities. Learning from the past does not restrict us to the limitations of the past. To learn is already to transcend the limits of what was learned. The development of a language is not like a natural growth: it is an instrument human beings use, consciously, to advance into the future.

This typically Renaissance view of language as a communicational instrument which human beings are free to alter, adapt and embellish as they see fit marks a definitive rejection of medieval scholastic attitudes to language. ... For du Bellay, as for many Renaissance men of letters, it is as obvious that a language can be altered and improved by human design as that a nation can rise by its own efforts to heights of supremacy. Du Bellay's *Deffence* is a manifesto of patriotism more than a treatise of linguistic theory, but it is none the less significant for that.

A similar spirit of linguistic patriotism was beginning to emerge in other European countries. In the *Deffence*, in fact, du Bellay is merely copying and adapting to the needs of French a case which had recently been put forward by the Italian writer Speroni in his *Dialogo delle Lingue* (1542). Du Bellay's examples and even his phraseology in the *Deffence* are taken straight from Speroni. This fact itself highlights another paradoxical aspect of the Renaissance: willingness to learn from other countries, and in particular emulation of antiquity, went hand in hand with a pre-eminent insistence on establishing the claims of one's own culture as inferior to none.

In the formation of this new national consciousness the role played by the languages of Europe was perhaps more important than any other, in part because the geography of Europe does not lend itself to setting up obvious administrative or military boundaries, as the Romans had discovered centuries earlier. For the first time it became essential to have a national language in order to secure proper recognition as a nation. A hotchpotch of regional dialects would no longer do. For the first time dictionaries and grammars of the vernacular languages begin to appear alongside dictionaries of Greek and Latin. Moreover these new dictionaries and grammars are not meant for foreigners. The task of the vernacular grammarians and lexicographers is seen as being to 'fix the language'; that is to eliminate vacillations and inconsistencies of the kind which perplexed Caxton, and impose linguistic uniformity. After centuries of linguistic fragmentation, Europe has at last awoken to a new sense of connection between linguistic identity and political identity.

References

The Prologue to Caxton's translation of *Eneydos* is reprinted in W.A. Craigie, *The critique of pure English from Caxton to Smollett* (Oxford: Clarendon Press, Society for Pure English Tract LXV, 1946), and also in W.F Bolton, *The English language* (Cambridge: Cambridge University Press, 1966).

The standard edition of du Bellay's *Deffence* is that of H. Chamard (Paris: Didier, repr. 1970). The French text is translated by G.M. Turquet (London: Dent, 1939).

There is an article by W.K. Percival on 'The grammatical tradition and the rise of the vernaculars' in Sebeok, 1975.

Source: Harris and Taylor, 1980, pp. 86–93

Reading B
THE DEVELOPMENT OF SCIENTIFIC ENGLISH

David Graddol

World science is dominated today by a relatively small number of languages, including Japanese, German and French, but it is English which is probably the most popular global language of science. This is not just because of the importance of English-speaking countries such as the USA in scientific research; the scientists of many non-English-speaking countries find that they need to write their research papers in English in order to reach a wide international audience. Given the prominence of scientific English today it may seem surprising that no one really knew *how* to write science in English before the seventeenth century. Before that, Latin was regarded as the lingua franca for European intellectuals.

Why science came to be written in English

The European Renaissance is sometimes called the 'revival of learning', a time of renewed interest in the 'lost knowledge' of classical times. At the same time, however, scholars also began to test and extend this knowledge. The emergent nation states of Europe developed competitive interests in world exploration and the development of trade. Such expansion, which was to take the English language west to America and east to India, was supported by scientific developments such as the discovery of magnetism (and hence the invention of the compass), improvements in cartography and – perhaps the most important scientific revolution of them all – the new theories of astronomy and the movement of the earth in relation to the planets and stars developed by Copernicus (1473–1543).

   A study of how Copernican theory came gradually to be accepted across Europe would illustrate how closely entwined were the various strands of the Renaissance process. Copernicus was one of the first generation of scholars who were able to publish and circulate their ideas to a wide audience by means of the printed book. The printing trade itself had an economic interest in translating such works into the national languages – in England there were many potential purchasers who did not understand Latin. But the spread of Copernican ideas was not welcomed by the Catholic church. Indeed, the whole project of humanist science, based on the intellectual independence of the scientists, free to test ideas empirically and by rational argument, was potentially subversive of the authority of the church, the transnational institution which had for so many centuries been the focus of learning in Europe. When Galileo dared to admit that he believed in Copernican theory the Pope issued anti-Copernican edicts restraining Italian scientists from publishing or teaching theories which appeared to contradict the biblical account of the cosmos. The church effectively stifled the new science in Italy.

In England the eleven years of Puritan government which followed the Civil War may well have helped to produce an intellectual climate of democracy, anti-authoritarianism, independence of mind, in which a distinctively British form of science – which stressed the importance of empirical method, simplicity, utility and attention to detail – arose.

The Royal Society

England was one of the first countries where scientists adopted and publicized Copernican ideas with enthusiasm. Some of these scholars, including two with interests in language – John Wallis and John Wilkins – helped found the Royal Society in 1660 in order to promote empirical scientific research.

Across Europe similar academies and societies arose, creating new national traditions of science. The scholars of many of these countries, such as France, Italy and Spain, published in their national languages. But those countries which found themselves on the periphery of the great expansion in scientific learning were faced with a difficult choice: if they wished to ensure that their own scholarly institutions were able to exchange knowledge internationally, then they were forced to adopt one of the international languages of science. This helps to explain why Latin persisted as a lingua franca alongside national languages for some time. The use of an international language, however, cut off the fledgling scientific institutions from their own national audiences, inhibiting the diffusion of the new learning among their populations. Some countries, such as Sweden, adopted a bilingual policy: two scientific academies were founded at the start of the eighteenth century, one of which used Latin as its official language, the other Swedish. The language dilemmas that faced such countries then continue to face them today, but now English has taken over the role of Latin.

In the initial stages of the scientific revolution most publications in the national languages were popular works, encyclopedias, educational textbooks and translations. Original science was not done in English until the second half of the seventeenth century. For example, Newton published his mathematical treatise known as the *Principia* in Latin, but published his later work on the property of light – *Opticks* – in English.

There were several reasons why original science continued to be written in Latin. The first was simply a matter of audience. Latin was suitable for an international audience of scholars, whereas English reached a socially wider but more local audience. Hence popular science was written in English.

A second reason for writing in Latin may, perversely, have been a concern for secrecy. Open publication had dangers in putting into the public domain prelimi-nary ideas which had not yet been fully exploited by their 'author'. This growing concern about intellectual property rights was a feature of the period – it reflected

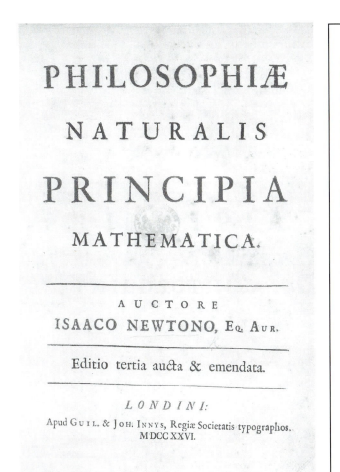

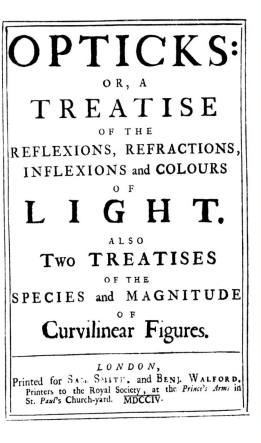

Figures 1 and 2   In the interval between the publication of Newton's Principia Mathematica (first published 1667; the title page from the third amended edition is shown here) and his Opticks (1704), original science came to be written in English
(Figure 1: British Library; Figure 2: Newton, 1704)

both the humanist notion of the individual, rational scientist who invents and discovers through private intellectual labour, and the growing connection between original science and commercial exploitation. There was something of a social distinction between 'scholars and gentlemen' who understood Latin, and men of trade who lacked a classical education. And in the mid seventeenth century it was common practice for mathematicians to keep their discoveries and proofs secret, by writing them in cipher, in obscure languages, or in private messages deposited in a sealed box with the Royal Society. Some scientists might have felt more comfortable with Latin precisely because its audience, though international, was becoming increasingly socially restricted. Medicine and surgery clung the most keenly to Latin as an 'insider language'.

But a third reason why the writing of original science in English was delayed may have been to do with the linguistic inadequacy of English in the early modern period. English was not well equippe l to deal with scientific argument. First, it lacked the necessary technical vocabulary. Second, and in some ways more interestingly, it lacked the grammatical resources required to represent the world in an objective and impersonal way, and to discuss the relations, such as cause and effect, that might hold between complex and hypothetical entities.

Fortunately, several members of the Royal Society possessed an interest in language and became engaged in various linguistic projects. One, the most ambitious, was to create a new, universal language which would incorporate the new scientific taxonomies in its vocabulary structure, permit logical argument, and be politically and religiously neutral. Perhaps the best known of these enterprises was the 'Real Character' of John Wilkins.

The Royal Society played with the idea of forming a committee which would act as a lead body in establishing new forms of English, like the language academies of other European countries. In 1664 the society voted that there be a committee for improving the English language. Although this proposal came to little, the society's members did a great deal to foster the publication of science in English and to encourage the development of a suitable writing style. Many members of the Royal Society also published monographs in English. One of the first was by Robert Hooke, the society's first curator of experiments, who described experiments with microscopes in *Micrographia* (Hooke [1665] 1961). This work is largely narrative in style, based on a transcript of oral demonstrations and lectures.

In 1665 a new scientific journal, *Philosophical Transactions*, was inaugurated. This was perhaps the first international English language scientific journal and it encouraged the development of a new genre of scientific writing, that of short, focused accounts of particular experiments. One historian suggests that foreign scholars frequently complained about the use of English for the *Philosophical Transactions*, 'being clumsy in the English language' (Hunter, 1989, p. 250).

The seventeenth century was thus a formative period in the establishment of scientific English. In the following century much of this momentum was lost as German established itself as the leading European language of science. It is estimated that by the end of the eighteenth century, 401 German scientific journals had been established as opposed to 96 in France and 50 in England (Houghton, 1975, p. 19). However, in the nineteenth century scientific English again enjoyed substantial lexical growth as the industrial revolution created the need for new technical vocabulary and new, specialized, professional societies were instituted to promote and publish in the new disciplines.

The creation of scientific English

I have claimed that the English language had to be made capable for scientific discourse, a project which was to take at least 300 years. The creation of scientific English was a part of a wider Renaissance project of elaborating the English language so that it could be used in a wide range of communicative domains. One of the first arenas to benefit had been literary language. However, the over-ornate style which had become common in literary discourse was not regarded as suitable for precise, unambiguous description and clear logical argument. An early history by one of the founding members of the Royal Society, Thomas Sprat, indicates something of the Puritan aversion to the 'eloquence' of the times. '*Eloquence*,' he

MICROGRAPHIA:

OR SOME

Physiological Descriptions

OF

MINUTE BODIES

MADE BY

MAGNIFYING GLASSES.

WITH

OBSERVATIONS and INQUIRIES thereupon.

By R. HOOKE, Fellow of the ROYAL SOCIETY.

Non possis oculo quantum contendere Linceus,
Non tamen idcirco contemnas Lippus inungi. Horat. Ep. lib. 1.

LONDON, Printed by *Jo. Martyn*, and *Ja. Allestry*, Printers to the
ROYAL SOCIETY, and are to be sold at their Shop at the *Bell* in
S. *Paul's* Church-yard. M DC LX V.

Figure 3   Hooke's Micrographia *was one of the first scientific treatises written in English*
(British Library)

(1)   Numb. 1.

PHILOSOPHICAL
TRANSACTIONS.

Munday, March 6. 1665.

The Contents.

An Introduction to this Tract. An Accompt of the Improvement of Optick Glasses *at* Rome. *Of the Observation made in* England, *of a Spot in one of the Belts of the Planet* Jupiter. *Of the motion of the late* Comet *prædicted. The Heads of many New Observations and Experiments, in order to an Experimental* History of Cold; *together with some* Thermometrical Discourses and Experiments. *A Relation of a very odd Monstrous* Calf. *Of a peculiar Lead-Ore in* Germany, *very useful for Essays. Of an* Hungarian Bolus, *of the same effect with the* Bolus Armenus. *Of the New American Whale-fishing about the* Bermudas. *A Narative concerning the success of the* Pendulum-watches *at Sea for the* Longitudes; *and the Grant of a* Patent *thereupon. A Catalogue of the* Philosophical Books *publisht by Monsieur de* Fermat, *Counsellour at* Tholouse, *lately dead.*

The Introduction.

Hereas there is nothing more necessary for promoting the improvement of Philosophical Matters, than the communicating to such, as apply their Studies and Endeavours that way, such things as are discovered or put in practise by others; it is therefore thought fit to employ the *Press*, as the most proper way to gratifie those, whose engagement in such Studies, and delight in the advancement of Learning and profitable Discoveries, doth entitle them to the knowledge of what this Kingdom, or other parts of the World, do, from time to time, afford, as well
A   of

Figure 4   Philosophical Transactions, volume 1, number 1
(Cambridge University Library)

said, 'ought to be banish'd out of all *civil Societies*, as a thing fatal to Peace and good Manners' ([1667] 1959 p. 111). He suggested that the society had:

> been most vigorous in putting in execution, the only remedy that can be found for this *extravagance*: and that has been, a constant Resolution to reject all amplifications, digressions, and swellings of style: to return back to the primitive purity, and shortness, when men deliver'd so many *things*, almost in an equal number of *words*. They have exacted from all their members, a close, naked, natural way of speaking; positive expressions; clear senses; a native easiness: bringing all things as near the Mathematical plainness, as they can: and preferring the language of Artizans, Countrymen, and Merchants, before that, of Wits, or Scholars.
>
> (Sprat [1667] 1959, p. 113)

It is worth noting that the motivation for neologism in science was rather different from that in literary genres. Whereas literary English sought synonyms in order to provide alternative forms of expression (eloquence), science required a precise and standardized language in which, ideally, there were only as many words as things.

Terminology

One of the pressing linguistic needs of the new scientific community lay in terminology. This lack was felt keenly by the early translators of classical works. In this situation any translator is faced with several choices:

1   the Latin term can be 'borrowed' in its entirety into English, adapted to English morphology;

2   the Latin word can be translated element for element into English (what is technically known as a *calque*);

3   a new English word can be invented;

4   an existing word can have its meaning extended so that it acquires a special-ized, technical, as well as everyday sense.

All these techniques were used to develop scientific English, but by far the commonest was the first: the simple adoption of the Latin term. One of the earliest attempts to render a technical discussion into the English language is a Middle English translation by Chaucer from a Latin work *Compositio et Operatio Astrolabii* by the eighth-century Arabian astronomer, Meeahala. In many ways it was no more than an instruction manual, though one written for a young boy – probably Chaucer's own son – who had not yet learned Latin. In the first part of this treatise on the *Astrolabe* Chaucer takes care to introduce a number of terms taken from Latin, such as 'altitude':

> Thyn astrolabie hath a ring to putten on the thombe of the right hond in taking the height of thinges. And tak kep, for from henes forthward I wol clepen [call] the heighte of any thing that is taken by the rewle 'the altitude', withoute moo wordes.

> (Chaucer, *Astrolabe*, I.l., in Robinson, 1966, p. 546)

Chaucer's willingness to borrow from Latin was in contrast to the Old English period, when the vocabulary of English was still almost entirely Germanic in origin and the *calque* was a more popular strategy. For example, the Old English scholar Aelfric translated the grammatical term *praepositio* as *foresetnys*, a term which was later replaced by a Latin loan: the OED attributes *prepisicion* to Wycliffe in 1388.

Not all the science that was translated into English originated from European scholars. As Chaucer's work shows, Muslim science was important in the medieval world, as was that of ancient Greece. Several of the words to be translated from Latin were thus already loans from Arabic or Greek. Examples of Arabic terms from astronomy include *azimuth, zenith, nadir;* from mathematics *algebra, cipher, zero* and – from the name of a Muslim mathematician, al-Khwarizmi – *algorithm;* from alchemy *alcohol, alkali.* From Greek came many terms in geometry, such as *diagonal, hypotenuse, pentagon, polynomial.*

In the second half of the seventeenth century English scientists were them-selves increasingly responsible for discoveries and inventions. As the horizons of knowledge expanded, particularly in botany, geography and chemistry, new forms of classification and nomenclature arose. There were so many new things to be described and new concepts to be communicated that the vocabulary of English again needed to be enhanced in a systematic manner.

Latin remained an important resource for neologisms in this period for several reasons. One was that new concepts were invented by the discoverers and theorists – the leading-edge scholars who were familiar with Latin and found in its inflectional system a production morphology for the creation of adjectives and nouns (particularly those based on the name of the discoverer). But the use of Latinate neologisms also provided something close to shared vocabulary between scientists in different countries. The national languages thus provided a matrix into which a common technical vocabulary could be inserted, just as today many languages have adopted a common technical vocabulary based on English.

The liberal incorporation of Latin words into English texts, however, was not without its problems. One of the purposes of publishing works in English was to make them available, for both educational and commercial reasons, to a wider national audience. But the use of so many strange and foreign words could have the effect of making them inaccessible.

Grammar

One form of neologism is the extension in the use of an existing word to a new word class. For example, a noun can be used as a verb, or a verb as a noun. Shakespeare frequently made nouns behave as verbs. For example, King Lear describes his daughter Cordelia (Act 1, scene 1) as 'Unfriended, new-adopted to our hate,/Dower'd with our curse, and stranger'd with our oath'. Renaissance science seems to have encouraged the transformation of verbs to nouns. Such changes are not just stylistic: whether an idea is presented in language as a 'process' (verb) or a 'thing' (noun) may be important. Shakespeare was a dramatist and no doubt wished to portray the world as consisting of happenings. The project of humanist science can, at one level, be regarded as one which imposed order on the fluid experience of the world: a reconceptualization of the world as consisting of 'things', of objects of study. The language of Shakespeare and of science thus provide alternative modes of construing the world.

In a study of scientific language from Newton's *Opticks* to the present day, Halliday (1993) schematically describes the evolution of scientific discourse and its mode of representing the world in the following way. He suggests that the preferred grammatical format for describing physical phenomena was originally in the form of:

a happens; so x happens

Gradually, through the centuries, there is a movement towards the form:

happening a is the cause of happening x

In the first grammatical structure, events are described by means of a verb in a conventional narrative form. In the later structure these events have become expressed through nominal (i.e. noun) forms. These noun phrases grow in length and complexity, whereas verbal forms become fewer.

The linguistic sleight of hand by which events and processes are represented in language as states or things (i.e. as noun or noun phrases) Halliday calls 'grammatical metaphor'. Such language not only allows the natural world to be objectified but also enables the scientist to develop a complex, and at times abstract, argument. It allows, for example, a complex phenomenon to be 'packaged' linguistically as one element in a clause so that the whole can be positioned within an unfolding argument. It is a feature of English grammar that noun phrases can be extended in this way whereas verb phrases cannot. In the following extract from *Electricity and Magnetisim* (1675) by Robert Boyle (a founding member of the Royal Society), the author uses four noun phrases in the second sentence: 'the modification of motion in the internal parts', 'the Emanations of the Amber', 'the degree of it', and 'the Attraction'.

> it has been observ'd, that Amber, &c. warm'd by the fire, does not attract so vigorously, as if it acquire an equal degree of heat by being chaf'd or rub'd: So that the modification of motion in the internal parts, and in the Emanations of the Amber, may, as well as the degree of it, contribute to the Attraction.

> (Boyle [1675] 1927, pp. 8–9)

In such constructions the verb does not describe a process in the world but rather proposes a relationship *between* such processes, either causative or logical. Thus scientific discourse typically uses verbs to express logical relations and argument, and nouns to represent entities and processes in the world. Halliday suggests that this is how Renaissance scientists came to be able to conduct the new science, which brought together experimental method with theoretical interpretation, in English: 'up to that point, doing and thinking remain as separate moments in the cultural dynamic: in "science" the two are brought together' (Halliday, 1993, p. 67).

It was not until the late nineteenth century that realist scientific discourse could be said to have been perfected. By then it had become common for scientists to avoid the use of the first person ('I') even when describing experimental method. Newton, by contrast, began his account of Experiment 1 in the *Opticks*: 'I took a black oblong stiff paper ... this paper I view'd through a prism of solid glass.' The world as construed by scientific English had by the start of the twentieth century achieved complete objectivity or, one might say, 'thinginess': it existed 'out there' independently of the agency or examination of the scientist.

There are, however, linguistic costs attached to such grammatical structures, as Halliday points out. In English the verb phrase provides the richest mechanism for describing relationships between entities. Hence the use of long nominal expressions means that the precise relations between entities *within the phrase* cannot be made explicit. Halliday identifies some of the ambiguities in one text as follows:

> What is *lung cancer death rates*: how quickly lungs die from cancer, how many people die from cancer of the lung or how quickly people die if they have it? What is *increased smoking*: more people smoke, or people smoke more? What is *are associated with*: caused by (you die because you smoke), or cause (you smoke because you are – perhaps afraid of – dying?) We may have rejected all but the right interpretation without thinking – but only because we know what it is on about already.

> (Halliday, 1993, p. 68)

Hence scientific English often requires a certain knowledge and understanding of the subject matter: it may be better at high-level, abstract argument than at low-level, explicit description.

Just when realist scientific discourse had been achieved, many scientists began to become unhappy with the Newtonian view of the world. Theories of relativity and thermodynamics began to challenge the Newtonian certainties. English is again coming to be regarded as 'insufficient to the task' by some scientists precisely because it construes the world as objective and static. Halliday suggests that scientific discourse may become more verbal in the future:

> Newtonian science has to hold the world still, to anaesthetize it so to speak, while dissecting it – if you are trying to understand something, then in the early stages of your enquiry it is helpful if it does not change while you are examining it. Of course, reality does change while you are looking at it, and twentieth century science is coming to terms with this; so the grammar of scientific discourse in the next 500 years or so will probably be very different from what it is now – perhaps more like that of spoken language with its clauses rather than expanded nouns.
>
> (Halliday, 1993, pp. 131–2)

References

BOYLE, R. ([1675] 1927) *Electricity and Magnetism*, Old Ashmolean Reprints, 7, series ed. R.W.T. Gunther, Oxford, Oxford University Press.

HALLIDAY, M.A.K. (1993) 'On the language of physical science' in HALLIDAY, M.A.K. and MARTIN, J.R. (eds) *Writing Science: literacy and discursive power*, Basingstoke, Falmer.

HOOKE, R. ([1665] 1961) *Micrographia or Some Physiological Descriptions of Minute Bodies made by Magnifying Glasses with Observations and Inquiries thereupon*, preface R.W.T. Gunther, New York, Dover; first published London, Royal Society.

HOUGHTON, B. (1975) *Scientific Periodicals: their historical development, characteristics and control*, London, Clive Bingley.

HUNTER, M.C.W. (1989) *Establishing the New Science: the experience of the early Royal Society*, Woodbridge, Boydell.

ROBINSON, R.N. (1966) *The Works of Geoffrey Chaucer*, 2nd edn, Oxford, Oxford University Press.

SPRAT, T. ([1667] 1959) *History of the Royal Society by Thomas Sprat*, ed. J.I. Cope and H.W. Jones, St. Louis, Washington University Press.

This reading was specially written for this book.

5 ENGLISH – COLONIAL TO POSTCOLONIAL

Dick Leith

5.1   INTRODUCTION

The previous two chapters have described the history of English within England, from the first arrival of Germanic immigrants on British shores in the fifth century AD, through to the twentieth century. This chapter describes the 'expansion' of English: how it became established as the first language – or one of the languages – of many communities outside England. I argue that this process occurred first *within* the British Isles, as English became more widely used in Ireland, Scotland and Wales where Celtic languages were extensively spoken. Later, it spread to many other parts of the world as colonies of English speakers were established in places such as the Americas, Africa, India and Australia.

An important theme of this chapter is one of **language contact**. As we have seen from earlier chapters, English within England was shaped by repeated contact with other languages – particularly Latin, Scandinavian languages and French. During the process of expansion, English again came into contact with other languages (such as Celtic within Britain, or native American languages in America). Furthermore, in several of the overseas colonies people speaking different varieties of English settled together. Here I describe some of the linguistic consequences of such contact, and how new varieties of English, with distinctive grammar, pronunciation and vocabulary, have emerged in different parts of the world.

As in previous chapters, I provide a social and cultural analysis of the spread of English and of the political contexts in which it occurred. Central to the process of expansion, over several centuries, was the experience of **colonization**: the establishment of communities of English speakers, sometimes forcibly, who maintained economic and cultural links with England and who positioned themselves in a relation of power with pre-existing inhabitants.

A second theme in this chapter, then, relates to the varying experience of colonization in different parts of the world, the complex issue of cultural identity and divided language loyalties associated with colonization and the different symbolic roles that English has subsequently played in the emergence of new national identities.

5.2   THE COLONIAL EXPERIENCE

David Crystal (in Reading A in Chapter 1) estimated that between the end of the reign of Elizabeth I (1603) and the beginning of the reign of Elizabeth II (1952) the number of mother-tongue English speakers in the world increased from 5–7 million to around 250 million, of whom four-fifths lived outside the British Isles. This growth was largely due to the colonial expansion of England which began in the sixteenth century.

It is possible to argue (as I do in this chapter) that the process of colonization began even earlier than that within the British Isles themselves, when English first became established as the main language of the Celtic-speaking territories of

Ireland, Scotland and Wales. In this way, it can be argued that the spread of English has been closely associated with a colonial process from the twelfth to the twentieth centuries.

There was no single, universal colonial experience. Each colony provided a unique context politically, socially and linguistically. Nevertheless, it is possible to discern a common sequence of events in many of those colonies where English emerged as a main language: first, an original settlement by English speakers; secondly, political incorporation; thirdly, a nationalist reaction which sometimes, but not always, led to independence. Each stage had linguistic implications, and I deal with them in turn.

Colonization

In three areas of the British Isles – Ireland, Scotland and Wales – Celtic languages (Irish, Gaelic, Welsh) continued to be widely spoken long after the Germanic invasions of the fifth century which established English in England. Although I argue that the spread of English within Britain was part of a colonial process, it was not a simple matter of one nation state – 'England' – setting up a colony in another. As you will recall from Chapter 4, it was only during the Renaissance that nation states took form in Europe. How, then, can the spread of English in the twelfth century be regarded as a colonial process?

According to the historian Robert Bartlett (1993) the peripheral areas in Europe – which include the Celtic territories of Britain – were colonized during the Middle Ages from what he calls the 'centre', formed by Latin Christendom (Figure 5.1). Following their conquest of England in 1066, the Norman monarchs encouraged the colonization of first Wales and then Ireland by awarding land to knights in return for subduing the local population (the situation in Scotland was slightly different, as we discuss below). The colonists were of mixed origins (some, for instance, were Flemings from Flanders), but shared a commitment to Christianity as defined by the Pope. The linguistic outcome of this stage was the introduction of varieties of English (and other languages such as French and Flemish) into these territories.

Colonies were first established beyond the British Isles at the end of the sixteenth century. One motive for colonization was economic: companies run by capitalist entrepreneurs were granted a monopoly over a certain commodity by the monarch, who was able to gain by taxing the profit made in trading it. But the new colonies were useful for social reasons too. In England, economic problems such as unemployment and inflation combined with population growth to create a large class of dispossessed 'vagrants' and political dissidents; these could help solve the problem of providing labour in colonies overseas. Finally, there were also political reasons. As already mentioned, colonization was a Europe-wide phenomenon. It was partly motivated by rivalries among European states: at first the Portuguese and Spanish, then the Dutch in the seventeenth century, the French in the eighteenth, and, by the end of the nineteenth century, the Germans. We shall see below how the history of English in the colonies needs to be understood against this background.

Since the process of colonization beyond the British Isles lasted more than 300 years and affected four continents, it is very difficult to make generalizations about its character. In this chapter I have identified and illustrated three types of English colony, each with its own linguistic consequences.

In the first type, exemplified by America and Australia, substantial settlement by first-language speakers of English displaced the precolonial population. In the

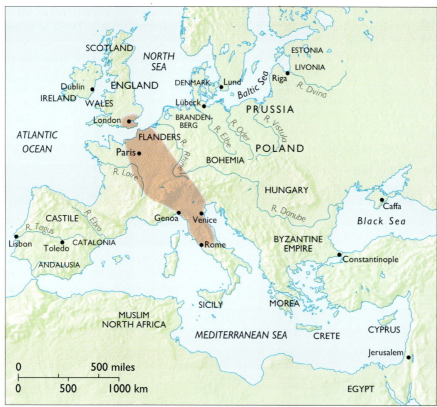

Figure 5.1 The 'centre' in medieval Europe

(Adapted from Bartlett, 1993, p. xvi)

The shaded area includes four key centres: Rome (Christian authority), France (centralized political power and intellectual life), the coastal cities of northern Italy and northern Europe (finance), and Flanders (manufacture). From these centres the culture of towns, stone castles and armoured, mounted knights seeking landed estates with their armed followers, was gradually imposed on the European periphery. Caffa (now called Feodosiya) was one of the many colonies established in the south-eastern periphery by Genoa. In the north-western periphery, this process of colonization affected all the Celtic territories of the British Isles.

second, typified by Nigeria, sparser colonial settlements maintained the pre-colonial population in subjection and allowed a proportion of them access to learning English as a second, or additional, language. There is yet a third type, exemplified by the Caribbean islands of Barbados and Jamaica. Here, a pre-colonial population was *replaced* by new labour from elsewhere, principally West Africa. The linguistic consequences of this third type were the most complex, as I explain later in the section on pidgins and creoles.

Political incorporation

As colonies developed and became of greater strategic importance to England, the English government took greater responsibility for their administration. The Celtic territories were the first to experience **political incorporation** in this way. In 1536, for instance, 'England' as the name of the **state** also included Wales. In dealing with Scotland, however, the English government revived the old term 'Britain'. Both territories were formally joined as 'Great Britain' in 1707. Ireland was formally incorporated in 1800 as part of what had come to be called the

'United Kingdom'. For the greater part of the nineteenth century all these territories were officially 'British', and many individuals from Ireland, Scotland and Wales played an active part in forming the British empire overseas. And in all of them, broadly speaking, English came to be identified as the language of the state.

Originally, colonists were subjects of the English monarchy, economically dependent on, and controlled by, 'the mother country'. Linguistically, this meant that the usage of England remained a powerful model. But political incorporation beyond the British Isles took a looser form than in the case of the Celtic territories described above. It was not until the nineteenth century that the British government rather than the various trading companies assumed the administration of the remaining colonies, creating the 'British empire'. And by that time the issue of political incorporation had been complicated by nationalist reaction.

Nationalist reaction

The political incorporation of communities that feel they have a distinct cultural identity provides fertile ground for the emergence of **nationalist reaction**. From the late eighteenth century onwards, different forms of nationalist activity characterized political life in many of the areas colonized by the English. Language figured prominently in such nationalist reaction: in some cases, the precolonial language provided a focus for the assertion of a separatist identity, in others this role was played by English itself.

For example, by the end of the nineteenth century the newly emerging **nationalisms** in Ireland, Scotland and Wales were beginning to fear for the survival of the Celtic languages, and campaigns were mounted to promote them. One consequence of this is that they became *taught* languages, learned by many people who otherwise knew only English. Another consequence was that they became increasingly sentimentalized, as much by the English as by the Celts themselves. The Victorian educationalist and literary scholar Matthew Arnold, for instance, spoke of the 'lively Celtic nature' expressed by Irish and Welsh writing. The Celts and their languages were conceived as artistic, even feminine, in contrast to the efficiency and manliness of Englishness and English (recall Scott's characterization of English, discussed in Chapter 3, section 3.6).

Overseas, nationalist reaction began with North America in 1776. Political independence was achieved by armed force and the new state declared itself a republic. Fearing this might be a precedent, the British government offered a form of self-government to the United States's neighbour, Canada, in 1867. Dominion status, as this was called, was similarly granted to other, more recent colonies with substantial settlement from the British Isles: Australia (in 1901), New Zealand (in 1907) and South Africa (in 1910, but complicated by the presence of a large Dutch settlement). In 1931 the dominions were linked to Britain under its monarchy in the 'Commonwealth'.

The history and status of English in Canada is discussed in Chapter 1.

In the dominions, nationalist sentiment has tended to take a cultural rather than political form. It is most clearly seen, perhaps, in debates about literature. National and linguistic identities are often created in relation to other, more powerful ex-colonies: Canada in relation to the USA; New Zealand to Australia.

Movements for *political* independence, on the other hand, emerged in India and many of the new African colonies during the twentieth century. The language of these movements was also English, even though this was a *second* (or at least additional) language for most of the inhabitants.

Some linguistic consequences of colonization

One of the more striking linguistic consequences of colonization has been the appearance of new varieties of English worldwide. Some of these remain local languages of relatively low social status. Others have become codified, standardized and adopted by newly independent states as an official or main language. In this section I briefly review some of the linguistic processes which have been associated with colonization.

The colonial process brought English into contact with a variety of other languages and it did so within particular relations of power. Indeed, an important part of any definition of colonization must relate to the pattern of social, economic and political inequalities which privileged the English language and those who spoke it. The colonial conditions of language contact played an important role in shaping the new varieties of English that emerged.

In North America and Australia, where Europeans largely displaced the precolonial populations, the influence of the original local languages on English was slight – usually restricted to the adoption of words relating to phenomena new to the Europeans, such as local cultural practices, animals and geographical features. It was rare, in this kind of colony, for phonological or grammatical features of precolonial languages to be adopted into English.

The social conditions in such colonies did, nevertheless, give rise to forms of linguistic change, as I outline below.

Dialect levelling and focusing

In all the colonies – from the first established in Ireland in the twelfth century to much later ones, such as Australia where settlement was first established in the late eighteenth century, English-speaking settlers formed a diverse group of people. Many came from lowly social positions in England but found themselves in a position of power in relation to the original, precolonial populations. Some were economic migrants from rural communities (the outstanding case of this is probably the migration from Ireland to North America during the Irish famines of the nineteenth century). Some were political or religious refugees (such as the Protestants who created some of the first North American colonies in the seventeenth century). The restructuring of social identity is a typical colonial process and applies to both the incoming European community and to members of the precolonial population who become incorporated into the colonial system. Ambivalent cultural and linguistic loyalties commonly arise.

The mixed demographic background of early settlers suggests that the varieties of English taken to the colonies were diverse and often nonstandard. When speakers of different varieties of English are brought together in a new community, either as a result of resettlement or because patterns of communication are restructured, a process of **dialect levelling** often occurs. That is, differences between speakers tend over time to become eroded.

This tendency is encouraged by **focusing agencies**, such as education, or the speech of one particular social group within the community emerging as a powerful and high-status model. In those colonies which retained close trading links with England, the prestigious English of London and the south-east of England often formed such a model. Political incorporation also raised the status of Standard British English in many colonies as higher-status English speakers were typically sent overseas as representatives of the British government.

Nationalist reaction, and the seeking of independent political and cultural identity, sometimes had the opposite effect by encouraging the identification and

The concept of focusing is discussed in Chapter 4.

codification (particularly in spelling books and dictionaries) of a local variety of English. This sometimes created a cultural and political tension over the legitimacy of a local variety of English. Ambivalent attitudes to local forms of English are still evident in many of the former colonies.

The creation of new varieties

The processes I have described are ones which tend to produce uniformity from a pattern of difference. There were, however, other tendencies that led to **internal differentiation**. As colonies expanded and became more established, different areas usually developed a sense of local cultural and linguistic identity. This might be reinforced by contact with local languages, by new kinds of social hierarchies (often positioning precolonial people as low status), or by different forms of continuing relationship with Britain.

The most complex linguistic situation was found in those colonies where bilingual communities were created. This was the case in India and West Africa, where a relatively small number of Europeans imposed political and economic control over precolonial populations. Here, the English language came into the most intimate contact with other languages and new, sometimes radically divergent, forms of English arose. When a language is imposed on a community as part of a colonial process, speakers tend to incorporate many linguistic features from their first language when speaking the new, imposed one. Such a widespread influence, which might include the adoption of a phonological system or set of grammatical patterns, is sometimes described as a **substrate**.

At first, this might occur simply because local people learn English as a second or additional language, and knowledge of their first language interferes in a systematic way with their English. However, as time goes on, a new variety of English establishes itself, acquires a stability and coherence, and becomes the target language learned by young people. At that point we can describe the emergent variety of English as possessing a distinct identity and, typically, as having a generally understood social status within the community.

A good example of a linguistic substrate is provided by Hiberno-English (also called Irish English), the variety that arose in Ireland as a consequence of contact between English and Irish. In this, several grammatical structures and features of accent seem to be the result of an Irish substrate, even though very few speakers of Hiberno-English learn Irish as their first language.

Perhaps the extreme consequence of language contact, where only the vocabulary appears to be English and the grammar is derived from elsewhere, can be found in the English pidgins and creoles which have appeared in many parts of the world since the seventeenth century. Many of these are a linguistic legacy of the slave trade which brought speakers of African languages to the American colonies, and speakers of Oceanic languages to Australia. I discuss these more fully later in the chapter.

5.3 THE SPREAD OF ENGLISH WITHIN THE BRITISH ISLES

I have argued that the global spread of English began within the British Isles, towards the end of the twelfth century. In this section I take Ireland and Scotland as case studies, arguing that many aspects of the growth of English usage in these formerly Celtic-speaking areas can be seen as an early colonial process which in some ways provided a model for later English colonization overseas. The new varieties of English which arose in these areas have also been influential in the development of English beyond the British Isles, since Irish and Scottish emigrants formed a substantial proportion of some English colonies.

I examine the stages of colonization, political incorporation and nationalist reaction experienced in each territory, and then discuss some of the linguistic consequences for English.

Figure 5.2 Anglo-Norman expansion in the British Isles

The Gaelic-speaking Scottish monarchy (vertical hatched area) offered sanctuary to English refugees from William the Conqueror and, in the 12th century, land to Anglo-Norman families. New burghs (towns) became centres of English usage. The English attempt to conquer the Scots, begun by Edward I, failed at Bannockburn in 1314.

Norse hegemony over the west and north of Scotland was ended in 1263. The present border with England was contested until the 16th century.

⚝ Norman castles of the 11th century

⚝ Castles established under Henry I (1100–1135)

⚝ Castles established under Henry II (1154–1189)

⚝ Castles established under Edward I (1272–1307)

□ Boroughs/burghs

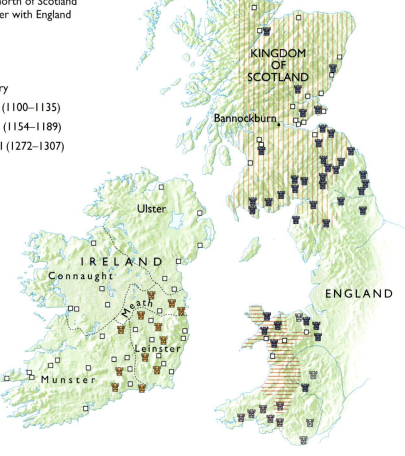

Anglo-Norman influence in Ireland began in 1167 under Henry II. Dublin was occupied and by 1250 only the north-west remained in Irish hands. English was established in the boroughs. But during the next 200 years the Irish re-asserted control, leaving only the Pale - a small area around Dublin - in English hands.

The process of castle-building along the Welsh border was begun by William the Conqueror. Under Henry I, English- and Flemish-speaking settlers were planted in the south-west. Edward I overcame Welsh resistance in the north-west and in 1284 established the Principality of Wales (horizontal-hatched area). The rest of the territory was divided into earldoms and lordships subject to the English crown.

The colonization of Ireland

The first colonies were established in the south-east of Ireland towards the end of the twelfth century. English law was introduced to protect the colonists and disadvantage the Irish. New towns or boroughs – which were a distinctive form of Anglo-Saxon settlement that contrasted with local dispersed habitations – were built and became centres of Anglo-Norman influence (records from the late twelfth century show immigration to Dublin, Ireland's capital, from towns in the south-west of England and Wales). A century later two-thirds of Ireland had been conquered after military campaigns against the Irish earls (princes).

It is a feature of colonial activity that personal identities and loyalties change. By the fourteenth century, it seems, many of the colonists had married among the Irish and adopted the 'manners, fashion' and, significantly, 'the language of the Irish enemies', in the words of a Statute of 1366. This process continued, so that by the late fifteenth century English control was limited to a small area around Dublin known as 'the Pale'.

English control, however, was reasserted during the sixteenth century, reflecting the monarchy's preoccupation with territorial boundaries. Henry VIII's Proclamation of 1541 urged that 'the king's true subjects' in Ireland 'shall use and speak commonly the English tongue'. The Protestant Reformation (discussed in Chapter 4, section 4.2) gave a new twist to Anglo-Irish relations, since the Irish continued to practise Roman Catholicism. Under Elizabeth I (1558–1603) England was at war with Catholic Spain and Irish Catholicism was seen as treachery. An English army was sent to overcome the resurgent Irish chieftains. In the course of long and bitter fighting the invading English defined the enemy as the opposite of all those qualities claimed for the Protestant English. According to the attorney general for Ireland, Sir John Davies, in 1610 the 'wild' Irish did not 'build houses, make townships … or improve the land as it ought to be' (quoted in Stallybrass, 1988). They were also described as filthy, long-haired and promiscuous. The Irish were eventually defeated, their land confiscated and awarded to fresh colonizers. Many of these colonizers in the north-east of Ireland were Scots, who gave rise to the linguistic area known today as Ulster Scots (see Figure 5.3). Among the other colonizers were the poorest sections of the English population

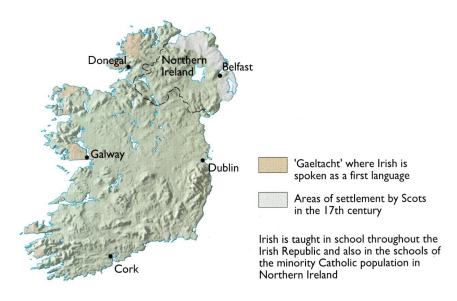

Figure 5.3   The linguistic situation in Ireland

'Gaeltacht' where Irish is spoken as a first language

Areas of settlement by Scots in the 17th century

Irish is taught in school throughout the Irish Republic and also in the schools of the minority Catholic population in Northern Ireland

in London, encouraged to go to Ireland because the government feared they would be 'seditious' if they stayed in England (Stallybrass, 1988).

Political incorporation

The new colonists of the seventeenth century clung to their Protestant, non-Irish identities, while the Irish were resettled in the poorer west of the country. Anti-English sentiment among the Irish was strong enough to support any cause that threatened the British state, especially if a Catholic power were involved in that cause. But by the end of the eighteenth century the new democratic and nation-alist ideas discussed in Chapter 4 had fuelled a movement for independence from English rule which also took root among sections of the Protestant population. It was after an uprising in 1798 that Ireland was incorporated into the United Kingdom by the Act of Union of 1800.

Nationalist reaction

It has been estimated that by 1800 English was the first language of half the population of Ireland. In the course of the nineteenth century Irish was increas-ingly abandoned. Three reasons have been suggested for this (Harris, 1991b, p. 38). One of these was depopulation. Famines in the 1840s greatly reduced the Irish-speaking population, either by death or emigration (principally to America). Another reason was the introduction of universal English-language education. The final one is significant in the context of ideas linking nationalism and language. English, not Irish, became the language of the two institutions which claimed to speak on behalf of the Irish population: the Catholic church and the independence movement. The latter gathered pace in the course of the century, culminating in the establishment of the Irish Free State (Irish Republic) in 1921, whereby 26 counties in southern Ireland gained independence from the United Kingdom. Northern Ireland remains part of the UK.

Before the seventeenth century, Irish was the first language of the whole population. Today it is used as a first language by only about 2 per cent of the population of the Irish Republic, although it remains the 'national' and 'first official language'. As such it is a compulsory subject in secondary schools and is cultivated as the language of literature, broadcasting and government publica-tions. English is recognized in the Irish constitution as a 'second official language' but in practice is used alongside Irish. Despite the fact that an overwhelming proportion of Irish people have chosen to speak English in their daily lives, they often explicitly express loyalty to the *idea* of Irish as part of their 'national' identity.

This language loyalty, and the role of Irish in the Irish Republic today, can both be seen as the result of nineteenth-century language nationalism. By 1893 three organizations had been set up to revive the Irish language (which, like regional dialects in England, was seen by some as obsolescent). They were largely led by literary figures and intellectuals, often from the upper class, for whom the Irish language was linked to the images of both an ancient literary culture and the non-literate usage of the peasantry in the west. For these movements, language was at the heart of Celtic culture: remove the language, and everything else dies.

Some features of Irish English

In time, there emerged a distinctive form of English spoken in Ireland, now known as Hiberno-English or Irish-English. This was influenced in various ways by the Irish language which was the first language of many of its original speakers. Irish English gradually became the form of English learned by monolingual English speakers in Ireland.

According to the linguistic historian Bliss, Hiberno-English is relatively uniform throughout much of the west and in the area colonized by the English (Bliss, 1984; see also Filppula, 1991). He explains this uniformity as resulting from the original pattern of contact, but adds that over the centuries the influence from Irish has actually increased, rather than diminished. This influence can be felt primarily at the level of pronunciation. For example, Irish speakers tend to pronounce /t/ (as in *tin*) with the tip of the tongue placed against the top front teeth, rather than against the ridge behind the teeth, as in most varieties of English spoken in England. One consequence of this 'dental' pronunciation of /t/ is that the contrast with /θ/ (as in *thin*) tends to be lost, so that *tin* and *thin* sound the same. The explanation for another characteristic is more speculative. Bliss hypothesizes that the reason the stress on some words, such as *deficit* and *intricate,* is often on the second syllable rather than the first is due to Irish schoolteachers in the so-called Hedge schools, set up during the eighteenth century by the Irish themselves. The teachers were actually fluent in many languages (including Greek and Latin) but were largely self-taught. Therefore they would have only *seen* words like these in books rather than heard them spoken, and could only guess at their pronunciation.

Reading C in Chapter 6 discusses sentence structure in Irish English.

The influence of Irish on the *grammar* of Hiberno-English is more controversial. Chapter 6 examines some of the variation in grammar between varieties of English more systematically. Here, I just mention one grammatical construction characteristic of Hiberno-English, exemplified by the following expression, recorded in Wicklow near Dublin (Filppula, 1991, p. 55):

It's looking for more land a lot of them are.

This structure is technically known as 'clefting'. In standard British English it might be translated as 'A lot of them are looking for more land.'

Many commentators have claimed that this construction reflects a similar one in Irish. However, Irish has not been spoken in Wicklow for more than 200 years, so if this is a consequence of language contact it suggests there is a uniformity in Hiberno-English based on Irish substrate. This, however, is not the only possible explanation. Many grammatical patterns in Hiberno-English may derive not from contact with Irish, but from the many different regional varieties of seventeenth-century English taken to Ireland by colonists which have become obsolete (or at least very scarce).

Recent research on Hiberno-English suggests that it may be less uniform than was originally thought. And the problems of deciding the source of specific characteristics discussed are instructive for a number of reasons. First, it may be that no *single* explanation for a linguistic feature is possible: a source in Irish, say, may be reinforced by a similar construction in a variety of English. Secondly, how are we to evaluate pronunciations such as *intricate* with the stress on the second syllable? As 'mistakes', or simply local variants? Both these issues are ones we shall encounter again in connection with new varieties of English in other parts of the world.

Colonization in Scotland

So far I have described Scotland as a Celtic territory, and this is true in several respects. When the Romans left Britain, much of the area now known as Scotland was inhabited and controlled by Celts closely related to those encountered by the

Anglo-Saxons (see Chapter 3). The language they spoke was Brythonic Celtic, an ancestor of modern Welsh (they are sometimes referred to as 'Strathclyde Welsh'). In the northern and eastern area were the Picts – another Celtic group about whom little is known.

You will remember (see Chapter 2, section 2.2) that the reason the Romans abandoned Britain was connected with the large-scale migrations of peoples that had begun in northern Europe. The invasion of England by Germanic settlers (the Anglo-Saxons) was itself a part of this migrational pattern, which continued during the following centuries (AD 400–800). Scotland experienced invasion and settlement from three sides during this period. The first people to arrive (in the fifth century, at the time the Anglo-Saxons were first landing in eastern England) were yet another group of Celts from Ireland, who settled in the western area. They spoke a Goidelic Celtic language closely related to Irish, which became the ancestor of Scottish Gaelic.

By the seventh century, the Anglo-Saxons of Northumbria had expanded northwards into southern Scotland, gradually spreading westwards to south-western Scotland. The fact that *The Dream of the Rood* was inscribed on the Ruthwell Cross near Dumfries (see Chapter 2, Figure 2.6) is testimony to the fact that a variety of English has been spoken in southern Scotland for almost as long as in England.

The third wave of invasions came later, from Scandinavia in the eighth century. The northern islands of Shetland and Orkney, together with part of the Scottish mainland, became a central part of the Viking world, linking Norway with Iceland. The people in this area remained Norse-speaking until around the sixteenth century and the regional dialects in this area today possess a Scandinavian substrate seen most clearly in vocabulary and pronunciation.

By the tenth century there were thus five linguistic groups in Scotland (the remains of the original Pictish people and of the Welsh people, the newer Scottish Gaelic people, the Anglo-Saxons of Northumbria who settled in southern Scotland, and the Norse-speaking people in the northern extremities).

The argument that Scotland experienced colonization is thus more complex than in the case of Ireland. Of the five tenth-century linguistic groups, the dominant one was the Scottish Gaelic. They had by then developed a centralized Gaelic-speaking monarchy which controlled even the south-eastern, Northumbrian-speaking area. In fact, in contemporary accounts these Gaelic people and their language were referred to as 'Scots' or 'Scottish'.

The next development, as in Ireland, was Anglo-Norman colonization, but unlike the Irish case, this came about because of an invitation rather than by conquest. The Scottish kings welcomed refugees from the Norman conquest after 1066 and were so attracted by what they saw as the superior military technology of the Anglo-Normans that they gave lands to individual knights (partly in the hope of strengthening the power of the monarchy). Another aspect of Anglo-Norman culture – town-building – was also adopted. New towns were established and populated with English-speaking merchants. As in Ireland, towns came to be associated with 'Inglis' (the name given to English by the Scots) and by the thirteenth century the royal court itself spoke Inglis.

An attempt at military conquest, however, was made by the English at the end of the thirteenth century. After crushing the Welsh, Edward I of England pursued a claim to the throne of Scotland, but under his son, Edward II, the English forces were finally defeated at the battle of Bannockburn in 1314. This stimulated a fierce patriotism, based on hostility to England, among sections of the Scottish nobility. After Bannockburn, Scotland can be described as a 'state' independent of England for nearly 300 years, with its own educational, administrative and legal institutions.

During this period Inglis was cultivated as the language of the Scottish state, based at Edinburgh. From 1494, in fact, Inglis came to be referred to as 'Scottis' or 'Scots', reflecting the fact that it, rather than Gaelic, was now regarded as the state language. A flourishing literature in this language developed. Both Scots and English, however, seem to have been understood in Scotland. In the sixteenth century English influence was also associated with the Reformation. Prot-estantism was received enthusiastically in Scotland, but the Bible used there was printed in English, not Scots.

Political incorporation

The process of political incorporation began when Elizabeth I of England died childless in 1603. James VI of Scotland was invited to become King James I of England. One effect of this unification of the crowns, however, was that James resided in England rather than Scotland. The two territories were united formally as the state of Great Britain in 1707, a settlement which divided the Scots. But Scotland retained its distinctive educational and legal practices, many of which continue today.

In the process of political incorporation it was English rather than Scots that came to be prestigious in Scotland. 'Scotticisms' were even used as examples of incorrect pronunciation by orthoepists (specialists who study pronunciation) such as John Walker, in a dictionary published in 1791 (discussed in Chapter 4, section 4.7). During the eighteenth century the idea of educated speech in Scotland was based on the 'polite' usage of London and the south-east of England, and this attitude has persisted till the present day. But as in the case of regional dialects in England, Scots continues to be used among the working class, espe-cially in rural areas. And it has been maintained as a *literary* medium by sections of the Scottish intelligentsia, for whom Scots expresses a cultural identity distinct from England. Other kinds of writing in Scots have also been maintained in newspapers printed and published in Scotland, especially in the northeast (Donaldson, 1986).

Nationalist reaction

It seems that Scottish 'national' identity can be associated with either highland (Gaelic) or lowland (formerly known as Inglis) culture. Transcending this differ-ence, however, is a widespread sense that to be Scottish is to be *not* English (although some Scots are also proud to be both Scottish and British).

Gaelic culture has remained strongest in the mountainous and peripheral areas of Scotland known as the Highlands and Islands. In this area a Gaelic culture similar to that of Ireland survived until the defeat of the highland chieftains during a rebellion of 1745. In the following 100 or so years the highlands were forcibly depopulated, the number of Gaelic speakers fell dramatically and a Gaelic revivalist movement similar to that in Ireland was created. Today, Gaelic as a first language is virtually limited to speakers in the Hebridean Isles, especially the outer ones.

The process described above, which produced widespread Gaelic/English bilingualism, can be seen as Anglicization. In many respects it paralleled the situation in Ireland: the destruction of the Gaelic culture was accompanied by a supremacist attitude which saw the Gaelic-speaking highlanders as savages.

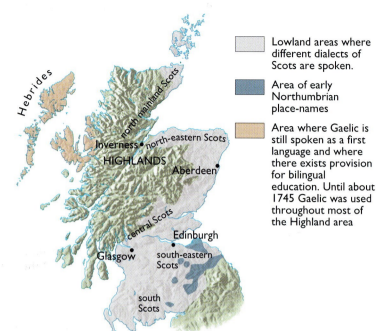

Figure 5.4   The linguistic situation in Scotland

But it is important to note that this attitude did not only come from the government in London. It was most vigorously held among the Scots of the towns and cities in the lowlands. More Scots actually fought on the government side in the 1745 rebellion than on that of the rebels.

Lowland nationalism looks to the Scots language as a symbol of cultural identity. But how far is it appropriate to see this as a language distinct from English, and a possible candidate for being Scotland's 'national' language?

These questions have been aired increasingly as the twentieth century progresses. Scottish nationalism has emerged as a political force, and throughout Scotland today there is widespread disenchantment with what are seen as the effects of the 1707 Union (to which some Scots had been opposed at the time). Some measure of independence for Scotland is now on the political agenda, and recent years have seen a vigorous market for books and pamphlets on Scottish identity. Now that Britain is part of the European Union, Scottish identity is often being recast as *European* rather than British.

The case for Scots as the national language of a newly independent Scottish state is based on a nationalist interpretation of its history and is eloquently presented in a pamphlet entitled *Why Scots Matters* by the Scottish language scholar Derrick McClure (1988). McClure argues that although Scots was originally a variety of Northumbrian English, it became the language of an independent state in the late Middle Ages. Its relationship with English at this time can be seen as similar to that of Portuguese and Spanish, or Swedish, Danish and Norwegian today: closely related linguistically, but each identified with a separate state. Like English and the other languages mentioned, Scots has its own range of dialects, each with its own spelling conventions. Assuming that a state represents the whole people (the 'nation'), the language of that state deserves to be distinct from that of other nations. The best way of symbolizing Scottish distinctiveness is thus through Scots.

Some problems with this view of history will be familiar from our discussion of English in Chapters 3 and 4. One is its dependence on the idea that *literature* is the crucial use of language. Another is the association of spoken Scots with the *rural* working class, and the tendency among Scots to disparage the lower-class usage of Scottish cities (Aitken, 1984). But on the other hand, Scots language activism has also been forward-looking. Scots is now on the curriculum in some Scottish schools; it is a subject studied in a number of Scottish universities; and attempts are being made to develop it as the medium for other kinds of writing.

The Bible in Scots

An interesting example of this wider written usage is the Scots translation of the New Testament of the Bible first published in 1983 (Lorimer (tr.), 1988). A major argument used by language activists throughout the British Isles is that a vernacular translation of the Bible is a key instrument of *focusing* (see Chapter 4, section 4.2). The survival of Welsh, for instance, has sometimes been attributed to the fact that a Welsh Bible was published during the Reformation.

Activity 5.1   *(Allow 10 minutes)*

The first extract below is from 1 Corinthians 14, verse 14, which discusses the 'monie [many] different languages i the warld [world]'. Read it carefully, making a note of any word you don't understand. Then read the second extract which is the equivalent passage from the Authorized Version of the English Bible (here verse 11). How would you compare the effects of the different versions? List any differences in spelling you notice.

- But gin I am no acquent wi the langage o a man I speak wi, my speech will be like the cheepin o a spug tae him, an his will be like the chitterin o a swallow tae me.
- Therefore if I know not the meaning of the voice, I shall be unto him that speaketh a barbarian, and he that speaketh *shall* be a barbarian unto me.

Comment

You probably had difficulty with *spug* (house-sparrow). *Chitterin* could be 'chattering'. The Scots translation, with its concrete references to the chirping house-sparrows and chattering swallows, could be seen as a good example of the 'expressiveness' that has often been associated with the language. However, any such differences may not reflect intrinsic qualities of the two language varieties – it may be more a matter of the style of translation. I discuss this more fully below.

An earlier, unpublished draft of the Scots Bible was much closer to the more abstract wording of the Authorized Version:

I will be like a barbarian tae him an he will be like a barbarian tae me.

There is a classical precedent for the more concrete version: in Greek (the original language of the New Testament), 'foreign languages were proverbially compared to the twittering of birds' (Lorimer (tr.), 1988, p. xxi).

The problem with claiming that one language is 'more expressive' than another is that such comparisons are usually made with only one variety of a given

language in mind. If the 'Standard English' of government documents is compared with, say, a poem in Scots, the latter is almost bound to feel more 'expressive'; but as the example above shows, it is possible to say much the same thing in
different ways in Scots.

Another distinctive feature of the Scots Bible lies in the spelling. Scots, unlike
English, lacks a highly standardized spelling system. (The printed Scots of the
north-east, for instance, *looks* different in many ways from that of central Scotland,
mainly because it is based on differences in speech.) You might have noticed
certain spellings such an *an* (and) and the *-in* of *cheepin*. These have a long history
in written Scots, but one interesting point about them is that they could also
represent relaxed *English* pronunciation. Keeping them in printed Scots helps
ensure it has a different look from English. This may prove to be an effective
weapon, for if you can show that the *language* is different, you can also argue that
the *people* are different, providing you also make the nationalist assumption that
each people has its own distinctive language.

5.4 THE SPREAD OF ENGLISH BEYOND THE BRITISH ISLES

The establishment of English-speaking colonies in North America at the beginning of the seventeenth century was the first decisive stage in the colonial
expansion of England which made English an international language. The first
English settlers, however, were by no means the first Europeans to set up colonies.
South America was the first to be 'discovered' by Europe – in the late fifteenth
century by the Portuguese and Spanish. This is a useful reminder that other
European languages often came into contact with English in the colonies and
influenced its development. The much later colonization of Australia in many
ways followed a pattern similar to that in North America. In both cases, large-
scale immigration of English-speakers and other Europeans displaced existing
populations.

English in North America

The first English attempt at settlement in North America, in 1584, proved a
failure, but in 1607 a second expedition established the colony of Jamestown in
Virginia and was followed by several others, of which the most famous was the
group on board the *Mayflower* who became known as the 'pilgrim fathers' and
who settled in Plymouth, Massachusetts, in 1620. Their colony was perhaps the
most successful at attracting settlers: within 20 years a further 25,000 Europeans
had migrated to the area.

The Pilgrims, like many of the early English settlers, sought religious freedom
(one effect of the Reformation, discussed in Chapter 4, was the persecution of
Puritans as well as Catholics). Pennsylvania, further south, was settled originally by
a Quaker colony, but attracted English and Welsh settlers of various religious
denominations too. In each direction there were colonists from other European
states: French to the north and north-west, Dutch to the west.

The pattern of colonization in the southern areas differed slightly from that
of the north. In contrast to the northern smallholdings, huge plantations and
estates developed in the south, growing rice at first and later cotton. These
colonies were settled by a high proportion of people from the south and west of

The names of some precolonial peoples are shown thus: Crow. In Africa, many of these peoples were organized in relatively centralized kingdoms. Unlike the French and Spanish, English-speaking colonists in America settled in dense numbers and tended eventually to displace precolonial inhabitants. In the Caribbean, however, the Arawaks were virtually wiped out by the earliest Spanish colonists.

Figure 5.5   The Atlantic slave trade and colonization in America and the Caribbean

England (many of them deportees and political refugees). Labour for the plantations was supplied by slaves who were transported from Africa (I discuss the role of the slave trade in English colonies more fully in section 5.5). In South Carolina by 1724 slaves outnumbered free people by three to one. These estates formed the nucleus of what has come to be known as the American south.

The complex relationship between North American settlement and the slave trade, showing some of the main West African languages which were to influence the new forms of English that became spoken by slaves in North America and the Caribbean, is shown in Figure 5.5. This map also shows the major precolonial languages spoken in North America. You may like to refer back to this map during the discussion of West Africa (later in this section) and the development of English pidgins and creoles (section 5.5).

Any linguist examining the early period of settlement is faced with two main questions. First, how and when did American English become differentiated from British English and recognized as an independent variety? Secondly, how did internal dialect differences in American English arise? These two questions are similar to ones which I asked in relation to the first Anglo-Saxon settlement of England and the emergence of Old English.

The variety of English which was implanted in North America was that of the early modern period, described in Chapter 4. It has sometimes been claimed that many of the differences between American and British English can be explained in terms of a 'colonial lag', that the language of colonial settlers is more 'conservative' than that of the country they left. Thus, some features of American English, such as the widespread pronunciation of /r/ in words like *cart* and *far,* might be attributed to the fact that /r/ in such words was generally pronounced in Elizabethan English. Although the speech of Londoners later became 'r-less', this was too late to influence the speech of those who had already left.

Chapter 7 has more to say on the pronunciation of 'non-prevocalic' /r/.

The problem with this explanation is that in some areas on the east coast – among them the oldest settlements – there has long been an r-less tendency. This area seems to have maintained close cultural and trade links with England and the British model of speech remained a powerful model of social correctness. Other, more inland communities seem not to have maintained such close ties with England. Hence this feature, at least, of modern dialect variation is better explained by different patterns of contact with England *after* the first settlement.

You may recall that this is the same explanation put forward by David DeCamp (1958) for the pattern of Old English dialects (see Chapter 3, section 3.3). The original Germanic settlers of England came from different locations (you will perhaps remember the story of the Angles, Saxons and Jutes) and the question arose as to whether the dialect areas which emerged in England derived from the patterns of first settlement (that is speakers of different language varieties settling in different areas). DeCamp argues that English dialect variation was 'made in Britain' after the first settlement and reflected differences in the extent of continuing links with continental Europe.

It might be supposed that in North America some dialect variation arose from contact with different indigenous languages. The influence of precolonial languages on American English, however, has been surprisingly slight. Different settlements had various motives for contact with the precolonial population; some tribes had more interest in it than others. Some Puritan colonists wanted to convert the local people, or to enlist their help as household servants, so schooling was arranged for them and parts of the Bible were translated into their languages. But the native Americans were reluctant to have their identities changed in this way, and as the colonies expanded westward, they were pushed in the same direction.

Sociolinguists, such as Carver, 1992 (see box on 'Indian words in American English'), use the same assumption to explain the limited influence of precolonial languages on American English as was discussed in relation to the lack of Celtic influence on Old English: that the language of a conquered people has little effect on that of the conquerors.

Another phenomenon which may have affected both Old English and the English of the American colonies is that of dialect levelling. This process seems to occur whenever a new community is formed containing speakers of many closely related language varieties (we look at a recent study of accent in a new town in England in Chapter 7). British English, because of its continued prestige, seems

Indian words in American English

The colonists encountered a strange landscape and unfamiliar forms of wildlife for which they had no English names. When, for example, they came upon a furry, cat-sized creature with a masklike marking, they were at a loss as to what to call it. They naturally adopted the Indian name, which for Europeans was difficult to pronounce. Captain John Smith spelled it *rahaugcum* and *raugroughcum* in his account (1608) of the Virginia colony. He was trying to write the Algonquian word *ārā'kun* from *ārā'kunem*, literally, 'he scratches with his hands', which probably alludes to the raccoon's habit of scrabbling for crabs and other titbits along stream bottoms. The name was also used in the New England colonies and was spelled *rackoone* or *rockoon*. By 1672 the current spelling was established and the Indian word was fully assimilated into colonial English.

…

Although numerous Indian languages were spoken on the North American continent, only one language group, the Algonquian, is the nearly exclusive source of the Indian words borrowed by the colonists. This huge group of tribes included the Arapaho, Blackfoot, Cheyenne, Cree, Delaware, Fox, Micmac, Ojibwa or Chippewa, and Penobscot, each speaking a different Algonquian dialect.

About half of all the 300 or so American Indian loanwords current today entered the language in the seventeenth century, including *caribou, hickory, hominy, moccasin, moose, possum, papoose, persimmon, pone, powwow, skunk, squash, squaw, terrapin, tomahawk, totem, wigwam* and *woodchuck* …

A colonial Indian from the colonial era would probably not recognize any of these words because they were radically changed in the course of being adopted into American speech. Algonquian has many sounds and sound combinations that were completely foreign to English speakers, making them difficult to pronounce. Often the words were abbreviated or clipped (*hominy* from *rockahominy, squash* from *asquutasquash, hickory* from *pawcohiccora*). Sometimes the Indian word was changed by folk etymology, an attempt to make sense of a new and unusual-sounding word by analysing it (incorrectly) in terms of known words. For example, the Indian word *muskwessu* or *muscassus* became *muskrat*, a musky-smelling rodent; *otchek* or *odjik* became *woodchuck*; and *achitam* became *chipmunk*.

The influence of the Indian culture was not negligible when we take into account the numerous combinations in which these loanwords occur (e.g. *skunk*-cabbage, *skunk* bear, *skunk* weed), not to mention the couple hundred or so combinations made with *Indian* (e.g. *Indian pony, Indian mallow*). In addition, there are many expressions derived from features of Indian life: *on the warpath, peace pipe, to bury the hatchet, to hold a powwow, Indian summer, pale face, brave* (noun), *firewater, Indian file, Indian giver, happy hunting grounds, Great Spirit, medicine man, war paint, war dance, to scalp* and *a ticket scalper.*

In the larger picture, however, given that the Americans Indians were reduced to a conquered people, it is not surprising that their languages had a relatively slight influence on American English, aside from the large number of place names that are of Indian origin (over half of American state names, for example, are Indian loanwords). Moreover, all the American Indian loanwords are nouns, which indicates a casual rather than a true mingling of the two cultures.

(Carver, 1992, pp. 134–5)

to have acted as a focusing agent in America. Hence American speech tended to level out in the direction of the educated usage of London and south-east England, even though the speech of the majority of the early settlers was nonstandard.

As English settlements in North America became more established, there arose another tendency towards internal differentiation. The different economy of the southern area, for example, gradually pulled its culture and speech habits in a different direction from that of the north. So emerged one of the major modern dialect boundaries of the United States: that between northern and southern speech. For instance, the English dialect forms of *see* in the past tense were not levelled. *Seed*, as in 'I seed' (derived from adding a 'weak' ending 'd'), is common in the south, whereas *seen*, as in 'I seen' (originally a 'strong' past tense form co-occurring with *saw*), is used in the north. As these local economies developed, and conflicts of economic interest with England grew, the colonists became increasingly aware of the linguistic differences among themselves. Once the colonies were independent of England in 1783, this became a burning issue for some of the founders of the new republic such as Noah Webster.

'Strong' and 'weak' verbs are discussed further in Chapter 6

Chapter 2 contains a reading from Webster (Reading B) in which he discusses the need for linguistic uniformity. You may wish to look through the final section of this reading to remind yourself of the points Webster makes.

For Webster, America in 1783 was no longer a colony but it was not yet a nation. A written constitution defined it politically as a republican state (more precisely, a federation of individual states), but national unity had to be worked for, and a crucial arena for this was language. Even if American speech was diverse, linguistic uniformity could follow from the achievement of a distinctive *visual* identity through spelling, which in turn could influence speech over the generations. In wanting to make American English look different from the English of England, Webster drew on some of the ideas about language, especially Puritan ones, which I discussed in Chapter 4, section 4.6.

Taking a cyclical view of linguistic history, Webster argued that the golden age of language in England was past; America's was in the future. It would be based, however, on the more 'Saxon' elements in the language, and spelling would reflect the pronunciation of words more clearly. In this respect Webster was guided by an antipathy to what he saw as the class-bound perspective of Dr Johnson (who, incidentally, opposed American independence). Johnson's fondness in his dictionary for spellings that revealed a word's origins in Latin, Greek or French (thereby masking its pronunciation) was seen as elitist. For example, Webster objected to the spelling *realm*. But Johnson would have approved of it, since the a occurred in the source language, French. In an interesting development of Puritan thought, Webster saw the dialects of England as a legacy of its class system. America, by contrast, would be classless and would create its own language based on the usage of its independent 'yeomen'. This would contrast strongly with the quality of pompousness that Webster found in Johnson's own prose.

Webster was therefore keen on linguistic levelling, but not so much as a spontaneous process as from a programme of focusing based on the printed word. One difficulty with this was the fact that publishing, especially of literature, was controlled by Britain throughout much of the nineteenth century. However, in many ways Webster's own dictionary, together with a keen interest in universal education, did provide a powerful model for American usage.

The nationalist ideal of linguistic uniformity in American English has, however, not been completely achieved. One reason is that the processes of internal differentiation mentioned above have not diminished. The economic and cultural division between north and south led to the Civil War of the 1860s, which ended with the north victorious. In part, the war was a confrontation between the forces of political centralization, represented by the north, and those of regional autonomy. Ever since, the south has often been represented as a bastion of older, agricultural, hierarchical values outside those of mainstream America. Its dialect has also been vigorously defended. In a book of his published lectures, one of the most influential of twentieth-century literary critics, Cleanth Brooks, asks whether the language of the south had any future. Its 'most dangerous enemy', he says, 'is not education properly understood, but miseducation: foolishly incorrect theories of what constitutes good English, an insistence on spelling pronunciations, and the propagation of bureaucratese, sociologese, and psychologese, which American business, politics and academies seem to exude as a matter of course' (Brooks, 1985, p. 53).

Another source of differentiation is the sheer diversity in the American population since the late eighteenth century. Figure 5.6 shows the progress of settlement west of the early colonies. By the mid nineteenth century, settlers had advanced as far west as the Mississippi, their numbers swelled by thousands of land-hungry Scots Irish from Ulster. By the end of that century the west too had been settled, partly by millions of immigrants from various parts of Europe. A levelled form of pronunciation, known as 'general American', is associated with these states. Theoretically, the newcomers were to form what is often called the 'melting pot' of American society, in which ethnic origin is subsumed by a common American citizenship; in practice, however, new composite identities such as 'Irish American' and 'Italian American' have been created, and European cultural practices maintained.

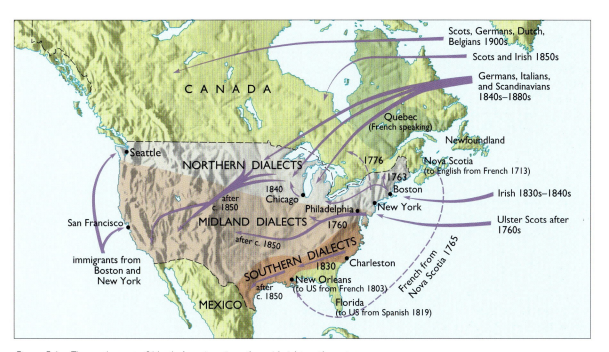

Figure 5.6   The settlement of North America since the mid-eighteenth century

Processes of naming in American English

Wherever colonies are established, settlers have to create new names – for places, for geographical features, for existing inhabitants and their languages, for new animals and experiences. Examining the naming practices often gives an insight into the changing identities and cultural loyalties of settlers, and into their relationships with other speakers of other languages. As we saw in Chapter 3, section 3.3, in connection with the original invasion and settlement of England by the Anglo-Saxons, names often embody a particular cultural and political perspective: the Anglo-Saxons called the Celts 'Welsh', which meant 'foreigner' or 'slave', even though the Celts were the displaced, original inhabitants.

The first settlers in America named their settlement Jamestown, after King James I, and the region was called Virginia, after the recently deceased Queen Elizabeth (the Virgin Queen). Later colonists in the north-west of America named their settlements after their original towns and villages in East Anglia, in England. Perhaps such naming was a way of preserving something of their English identity. But in other ways naming was innovative. The settlers used English words in new senses to name aspects of their new environment. *Creek*, for instance, in England generally meant a saltwater inlet; gradually the colonists extended it to mean a freshwater stream – a development described as 'barbarous' by an observer from England in 1735 (Bailey, 1992, p. 123). Similarly, *bluff* traditionally referred to a steep rise of land along the seashore, but in America it came to mean the steep bank of a river, and eventually a grove of trees rising from the flat prairie.

The early colonists adopted about 150 words from the Algonquian family of languages to name aspects of native culture, such as *moccasin, papoose, squaw*. All these innovations have become quite generally adopted in America.

In the westward expansion of the late eighteenth century relations with the native Americans were much more hostile; only about another 150 words were adopted, all from the same language family. But places, including states (*Mississippi* means 'great river') and cities (*Chattanooga* signifies 'rock rising from a point'), were often given native names. Already by 1789 Webster had written: 'It is remarkable, that almost all the rivers in America, as well as many places, preserve the names given them by the natives of the country. This is paying a tribute of respect to the Indians, who formerly possessed these fertile regions' (quoted in Simpson, 1986, p. 209). But the fashion for using native American names coincided with the act of dispossessing the indigenous peoples of their land: was it based on respect, guilt, or sentimentality? It is interesting to note that when the Anglo-Saxons invaded England, river names were among the few Celtic words to be adopted by the newcomers.

In a yet later stage of settlement, many new words were adopted from the European languages of the nineteenth-century and early twentieth-century immigrants. Often these name cultural practices introduced to American society. For example, many have to do with ways of preparing food, such as *pizza* (Italian) and *hamburger* (German).

The cultural politics of naming remains a sensitive issue. American society today includes many groups who maintain a distinct ethnic and cultural identity, and the names used to describe them have often reflected the attitudes and values of the dominant, white culture. There is a tendency now to resolve the difficult question of 'from whose position should they be named?' by allowing people to name themselves. For example, African Americans have been successful in persuading other Americans to shift the vocabulary used to describe them (Bailey, 1992, p. 212) and the term 'negro', in widespread use before the 1960s, is rarely heard today.

In the course of the twentieth century some observers have come to see this ethnic diversity as a threat to the nation. Recent Spanish-speaking immigrants (often illegal entrants) from Mexico have confronted the states of Texas and California with the language of the earliest European colonists in America and reminded them that the USA has no official 'national' language in the legal sense (legislation on this issue has actually been called for). And despite civil rights legislation, a substantial proportion of the black population, the descendants of slaves, still feel less than full American citizens. Black English shares many features with the American south, but also with many creoles. The latter association has often been stressed by blacks themselves, as a means of claiming a separate, 'African' identity through language. This issue is discussed further in a later section.

English in Australia

The English settlement of Australia occurred nearly two centuries later than that of America. Penal colonies on the south-east coast of Australia were founded in 1788. Many of the convicts, once freed, became smallholders. They gradually coined a vocabulary to name new colonial identities and distinguish themselves from the precolonial Aboriginal population: 'currency' meant a non-Aboriginal born in Australia, 'native' Australian a *white* Australian actually born in the country, 'sterling' someone born in Britain who was not a convict. There was a diversity of non-British-born 'free settlers' from Europe and south-east Asia. The attitudes to the British state of these various settlers might best be described as ambivalent. Throughout much of the nineteenth century there was a vigorous anti-British sentiment; in recent years republicanism has gained ground.

The convict population came mainly from London and the south-east of England. Australian pronunciation is very close to Cockney, except that initial /h/ (at the beginning of words) is sounded. It seems that originally this was not the case, but that /h/ was introduced as a result of substantial settlement from Ireland (Trudgill, 1986). This would be another instance of levelling, as discussed in the last section. Throughout much of its history Australian pronunciation has been stigmatized as slovenly, which is not surprising given the social origins of the settlers and the fact that settlement took place when prescriptive attitudes to language were becoming the official orthodoxy (see Chapter 4). As a result, Received Pronunciation (RP) has been perceived as a norm in the education system.

Recent research on pronunciation in the cities, however, suggests that in at least one respect this has changed. Colonization in Australia took place at a time when the vowel in words such as *after, grasp, dance* was being lengthened in London and the south-east of England. Originally these words had the same vowel as in cat, and this pronunciation is common in the north and Midlands of England today. The lengthened pronunciation is also still quite common in East Anglia and the south-west of England. But a further change then took place in London, and subsequently in received pronunication. The lengthened vowel came to be pronounced with the back of the tongue, rather than the front as in the vowel of cat. According to research by Bradley (1991) pronunciation of words such as these tends to vary in Australia today, but there is no overall tendency towards lengthening, – rather the reverse. In this respect, Australian English is becoming less like RP, suggesting perhaps a desire among speakers to differentiate themselves from models associated with Britain.

Activity 5.2 *(Reading A)*

The distinctiveness of Australian English has also been seen in relation to vocabulary. Reading A is part of the Introduction to the *Australian National Dictionary* (AND), published in 1988, together with the entries for some of the words it mentions.

Turn to this reading, noting its discussion of what I shall call **delineation**: how to define a variety of English such as that of Australia so that it appears as a distinctive symbol of a nation state. Notice how the dictionary tries to do this. Notice also the kinds of sources used. The entry for *stock* shows the range of new compounds coined in Australian English, as discussed in paragraph 3. Finally, does anything strike you as interesting about the ways in which *business, clever* and *koori* are used?

Comment

You may have noticed that Australianisms are defined in relation to the usage of America (a powerful influence on English internationally) and New Zealand (Australia's nearest neighbour). The dictionary also depends on *written* sources. One implication of this is that many words will have been used in Australia earlier than the first date of actual record. In the case of words like *port*, a suitcase (from *portmanteau*), recorded in written sources since 1898, it means that crucial information about their regional distribution and their use in different contexts is not available. This would require systematic research on *spoken* Australian which has not yet been done.

The Aboriginal usages show how the meanings of 'English' words may be 'Aboriginalized', adapted to a different cultural milieu (that of Aboriginal folklore and medicine). The significance of *koori*, perhaps, is that it is an Aboriginal word largely used by the Aborigines to name themselves (similarly 'Eskimos' in Canada are now generally referred to as *Inuit*).

Finally, you may have noticed that in discussing the 'Australianness' of a word or what a word refers to, the editor argues that 'the words added to a language by a people are an index of their history and culture' (paragraph 8). You might remember that this link has been mentioned before. The assumption is that a distinctive culture will have distinctive words, so the more distinctive words you can find, the more evidence you have of a distinctive culture. This issue is often raised in relation to a desire for 'authenticity' in postcolonial varieties of English. A concern aired by Americans after independence, and in ex-colonies elsewhere ever since, is that the language of England is an unsuitable vehicle for the authentic expression of postcolonial experience. Usually it is in *literature* that this issue is raised. Here, however, the concern is expressed through the production of a 'national' dictionary. As we saw in Chapter 4, a dictionary has often been seen as a 'monument' to both language and nation, and interest in new varieties of English has been greatly stimulated by the publication of dictionaries such as the AND.

English in West Africa

Earlier I identified three types of English colony. America and Australia represented the first group I mentioned: the wholesale immigration of native-speaking English settlers who displaced the local, precolonial population. I want now to move on to an example of the second type of colony, where sparser colonial settlements maintained the precolonial population in subjection.

At much the same time as the Australian penal colonies were established, different kinds of settlement were set up in West Africa. Sierra Leone, where the first European slaving expedition occurred in the sixteenth century, was settled by escaped and (after 1807) freed slaves. A little later, Liberia was established by the USA for ex-slaves. The significance of these ventures was the association of slaves with an African 'homeland', an association based on the notion of 'descent' from African tribes. One eventual outcome of this development was the sense of common cause between black people in both America and Africa. This commonality was aided in the British colonies by the fact of a shared language English.

New British colonies were established in Africa after 1880. Between that date and the end of the century virtually the entire continent was seized and shared out among the European powers. In West Africa, however, there was no substantial settlement by people from the British Isles. Instead, the new colonies were *administered* by a small number of British officials. The population remained overwhelmingly African, with a small number receiving education in English from missionaries, and a larger number using English-based pidgins in addition to the languages they already spoke.

During the nineteenth century Britain came to see the role of colonies such as those in Africa as that of producing raw materials, while Britain remained the source of manufacturing. The precolonial populations were not given any rights as far as the vote and compulsory education were concerned, despite the fact that these had been granted to the working class in Britain. These economic and political arrangements were justified by appealing to contemporary theories of racial difference. The precolonial populations were classified as dark-skinned, and considered to be at a lower stage of cultural and intellectual development than white Europeans. Colonial service could therefore be conceived as a duty and as a way of demonstrating 'manliness', a key aspect of nineteenth-century Englishness.

The system described above is often referred to by the word **colonialism**. First used in the nineteenth century, it reflects changes in the relationship between Britain and its colonies as they were incorporated into what was called the British empire. The term is more loaded than 'colonization', partly because it has been used most frequently by those who were opposed to it, on the grounds that it amounted to exploitation of the weak by the powerful. In one respect it names the process from the point of view of the less powerful, and has often been used pejoratively. In fact, the *Oxford English Dictionary* (Simpson and Weiner (eds), 1989) has a citation for the word in 1957 as 'the commonest term of abuse nowadays throughout half the world'.

According to the African linguist Ali Mazrui, British colonialism, with its emphasis on the difference between the subject black population and its white rulers, set the tone for colonialism in Africa in general (Mazrui, 1973). And according to him, it was in the British colonies that Africans led the struggle for independence. This was partly because they felt a solidarity with the black ex-slaves in the United States, involved in their own struggles for full citizenship. A movement known as pan-Negroism emerged, based on what was seen as a shared ethnic identity. This gave way to pan-Africanism, an anti-colonial struggle for blacks in Africa alone. Mazrui argues that the language of both of these movements was English, and that this may have led Africans in French colonies to feel somewhat excluded from them.

Why was it English that was so bound up with the anti-colonial struggle? For Mazrui, the fact that the African elite could enjoy higher education in (English-speaking) North America as well as Britain meant that their attitudes were partly shaped by the issue of black emancipation there. But he also discusses the possibility that in the French colonies Africans, at least in theory, were considered citizens of France itself. Accordingly, they viewed the French language with affection. In the British colonies, on the other hand, attitudes to English seem to have been more pragmatic (as perhaps was also the case in nineteenth-century Ireland).

But there are other ways in which the movement for African independence and the English language have been linked. These have to do with supposed properties of the language itself. Edward Blyden, a black man born in the Caribbean in 1832 and later a professor of languages in Liberia, argued that English was best suited to unify Africans because it 'is a composite language, not the product of any one people. It is made up of contributions by Celts, Danes, Normans, Saxons, Greeks, and Romans, gathering to itself elements ... from the Ganges to the Atlantic.' In other words, it is the very impurity and hybridity of English that makes it so useful. In addition, the diversity of African society, symbolized by the huge numbers of different languages spoken (often by one individual), is seen as a problem for the cause of independence.

Observers have often explained this diversity as produced by 'tribalism'. For promoters of independence, this tribalism needs to be replaced by a different, European concept: that of nationalism – a state with fixed territorial boundaries that represents the interests of, and has legitimate control over, its people.

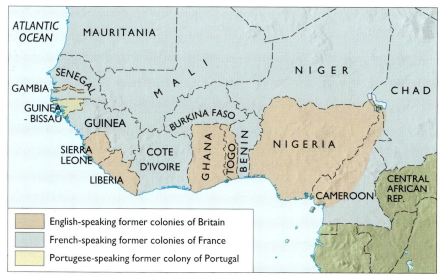

Figure 5.7
English-speaking West Africa

During the early 19th century Britain established coastal colonies in Gambia, the Gold Coast (later Ghana), and the Lagos area of Nigeria. Sierra Leone became a colony for freed slaves (like Liberia, set up by the Americans, which was independent by 1847). In the European 'Scramble' for Africa from 1880 onward, French and British rule was extended throughout the territories indicated, and Germany acquired Cameroon and Togo (later shared between Britain and France). Apart from Portugese Guinea-Bissau, all these territories gained independence between 1957 and 1968.
All the English territories are multilingual: 237 languages are spoken in Cameroon, and over 390 in Nigeria. Some African languages are used on the radio, on television, in the written press, in education and in administration. English, however, is used in all or most of these institutions in every former colony.

In this view, learning English helps Africans to recreate their identities as members of *nations* rather than tribes. It has sometimes been claimed that British colonialism has helped Africans to 'modernize' themselves by introducing them to the English language and, in so doing, to a new culture with concepts such as 'freedom' and 'national identity'.

This view raises a number of problems. For example, it claims that a particular language encodes particular ways of thinking. Many Africans have themselves expressed it, often in debates about the role of English in postcolonial society. Many writers of literature have argued that English is an inadequate medium for the expression of an authentically 'African' experience. Others, however, have argued that the postcolonial African identity is a hybrid one, and that an African exposed to the English language and to concepts derived from European experience is no less 'African' than any other. So it is the task of the writer to create a kind of English capable of expressing the 'authenticity' of Africa. We see an instance of this below in relation to English in Nigeria, an area of West Africa colonized after 1884, which achieved independence in 1960.

The use of English by postcolonial writers is discussed in the second book in this series, *Using English: from conversation to canon* (Maybin and Mercer (eds), 1995).

Activity 5.3   *(Reading B)*

Reading B, 'Identifying Nigerian usages in Nigerian English' by Ayọ Bamgboṣe, discusses some of the problems of identifying and describing characteristics of one of the 'New Englishes' which have arisen in English colonies where many speakers of precolonial languages acquired English as a second or additional language. Please read it now. What differences and similarities are there between this and the patterns of linguistic contact described earlier in this chapter?

Comment

One issue the author discusses has already been raised in this chapter: the problem of delineation. Another is the question of 'interference' from substratum languages which I discussed earlier in relation to Ireland. But this question is more complicated in Nigeria, since at least 390 African languages are spoken there. Interestingly enough, Bamgboṣe deals with the same grammatical construction 'clefting' (although he doesn't mention it by name). I explain his argument below.

Chapter 7 contains further discussion of stress-timed and syllable-timed languages.

All languages have ways of drawing attention to one part of an utterance at the expense of other parts, in order to achieve emphasis. In areas where English is spoken as a first (Bamgboṣe uses the term 'native') language, emphasis is usually achieved by syllable stress. In '*John* did it' greater stress is put on *John* than on the other words in the utterance, so it stands out. But this device is only possible in those varieties of English which are **stress-timed**, which means that they have an alternating pattern of stressed and unstressed syllables. In languages where syllables are pronounced with an even rhythm, other ways of achieving emphasis must be found, and one way of doing this is by means of a grammatical construction such as clefting. This in effect divides the utterance into two and introduces a new subject, it, to the first part. Presumably this construction has become part of Nigerian English because stress-timing is rare (if it exists at all) in Nigerian languages. But it is also worth pointing out that clefting is also an option in first-language varieties of English, especially in writing, where it is often recommended as a way of avoiding italics for emphasis. So its presence in Nigerian English might also have been reinforced by its association with the *written* English of formal education. The same explanation may hold in respect of the stress patterns of words in Nigerian English discussed on the same page (you may recall the discussion of Hiberno-English in this respect).

Finally, Bamgboṣe's reference to the Nigerian novelist Amos Tutuọla needs some comment. He cites Tutuọla's phrase 'born and die babies' as an example of 'substandard' English. But in a footnote to the original paper he explains this as referring to African beliefs about babies which 'die and return, usually to the same parents'. In this respect, Tutuọla is trying to use English to represent concepts for which he feels there is no English expression. Does this mean that English is capable of representing African experience 'authentically'? Many of Tutuọla's readers have found these usages poetic rather than substandard. To use Bamgboṣe's terms, what is 'deviant' from one perspective may be 'creative' from another.

5.5   THE DEVELOPMENT OF ENGLISH PIDGINS AND CREOLES

There is a significant omission in my discussion of English colonization so far, and that is the role of the slave trade which brought Africans to America and elsewhere to supply cheap labour for the developing colonies. The long-term effect of the slave trade on the development of the English language is immense. It gave rise not only to black English in the United States and the Caribbean, which has been an important influence on the speech of young English speakers worldwide, but also provided the extraordinary context of language contact which led to the formation of English **pidgins** and **creoles**. Here then I shall look at the third type of English colony that I've identified: where a precolonial population is replaced by new labour from elsewhere, principally West Africa.

The origins of the slave trade belong to the earliest stages of colonial activity. In 1562 an Elizabethan Englishman called Sir John Hawkins sailed with three ships and 100 men to the coast of West Africa and captured 300 Africans 'partly by the sworde, and partly by other meanes' (in the words of a contemporary account). He sold them in the Caribbean, filled his ships with local hides, ginger, sugar and pearls, and returned to England 'with prosperous successe and much gaine to himself and the aforesayed adventurers [London merchants]'. This venture marked the beginnings of the British slave trade (Walvin, 1993, p. 25).

The Africans Hawkins took were from a place that is known today as Sierra Leone. It is possible that they had already had contact with the Portuguese, who had been trading in the area for about a century (Le Page and Tabouret-Keller, 1985, p. 23). We don't know what languages they spoke, or even whether they had any language in common (in Sierra Leone today 18 languages are spoken), but it is possible that they had some knowledge of a simplified language used between Africans and the Portuguese for the purposes of trade. This kind of makeshift language is called a 'pidgin' (originally the name of a Chinese-English trading language). Throughout the world people have shown remarkable ingenuity in creating such languages for limited forms of interaction where no shared lingua franca (or common language) is available. The oldest known pidgin is called 'Sabir'; this was based on Mediterranean languages and used during the crusades in the eleventh to thirteenth centuries. Pidgins typically have a small vocabulary and little grammatical complexity, and often depend heavily on context for understanding. They occur when limited communication is required (often for reasons of trade) between speakers who have no language in common.

One trade controlled by the Portuguese was the shipment of slaves from Africa to the islands of the Caribbean colonized by the Spanish. They used their pidgin in dealing with African middle-men, who traded slaves (captured from other tribes) in return for other goods. In selling his slaves to the Spanish colonists of Hispaniola (later Haiti) Hawkins was taking trade from the Portuguese; but it seems that the Portuguese-based pidgin was used widely enough to survive the successful attempts by both the English and Dutch to capture the slave trade (Le Page and Tabouret-Keller, 1985, pp. 29–30).

The Atlantic slave trade

Slavery had been practised by the Greeks in the classical era, by the Anglo-Saxons, and by Scots raiding northern England during the Middle Ages. The trade in slaves from Africa, however, seems to have been started by the Muslim Arabs of the eastern Mediterranean. This trade was taken over in the fifteenth century by Portuguese seafarers and, later, by the Dutch to supply slave labour for sugar plantations newly established across the Atlantic on Caribbean islands. When the *British* slave trade was ended in 1807, nearly 12 million Africans had been shipped across the Atlantic (many millions dying in the process).

The slave trade was made possible by the capital accumulated by merchants in European cities. This could finance trading expeditions for luxuries only obtainable outside Europe, and the establishment of plantations to cultivate them. This created an increasing demand for addictive luxuries, such as tea, coffee and sugar. In the Caribbean, labour for the plantations was at a premium because the precolonial populations, Arawaks and Caribs, had been wiped out on many islands. They were replaced by convicts and servants from England and Ireland, but these could not guarantee either a plentiful enough or a permanent workforce. Human labour had therefore to be treated as a commodity, and Africans could be so treated because they were thought to be not only 'heathen' but beyond the reach of Christian conversion. They were usually characterized as lazy, unreliable and worthless by their 'owners'.

The profits from the sugar trade were enormous and maintained the high living standards of both colonial planters and shareholders in England. The latter discussed their business affairs in the London coffee-houses. According to the historian James Walvin (1993), the coffee-houses themselves depended on the import of luxuries such as tea, coffee and sugar which the slave trade alone made possible.

It is possible that on Hispaniola, Hawkin's slaves substituted Spanish words for the Portuguese ones in their pidgin, and thus created a Spanish-based pidgin. Or perhaps they were resold, as often happened, to another set of colonists in a different Caribbean territory. Lack of evidence makes it very difficult to keep track of every shipment of slaves. What we do have, from such contemporary accounts as Ligon's *A True and Exact History of the Island of Barbados* (1647), is a description of slaving practice and estimates of numbers in one of the earliest of the British colonies in the Caribbean, Barbados.

Barbados had been colonized in 1627. With Dutch help, settlers from the British Isles sowed tobacco and other crops. The labour was supplied by Awaraks from the Dutch colony, and later by convicts, political undesirables and the poor from the London area, the west of England and Ireland (Le Page and Tabouret-

Keller, 1985, pp. 38–9). In the 1640s the fertile soil was turned over to sugar cane, and the British population was eventually outnumbered by slaves. According to Ligon, they were 'fetch'd from several parts of Africa, who speak severall languages, and by that means, one of them understands not another' (Ligon, 1647, p. 46).

Perhaps it is this statement of Ligon's that has encouraged linguists to take the view that '(t)he policy of the slave traders was to bring people of different language backgrounds together in the ships, to make it difficult to plot rebellion' (Crystal, 1988, p. 235). If this view is accepted then pidgin would have been the only form of communication available to slaves on the new plantations, and over the generations the African languages they spoke would have been abandoned. But since pidgin had only been used for very simple kinds of interaction, its vocabulary and grammar would have been limited. So it would have needed extending and adapting. Once it had been passed on to the children of the slaves, and used by them as a first language, it would have become a *creole*.

Creoles have emerged in many parts of the world and linguists have long been puzzled why so many of them seem to share many grammatical characteristics. One theory is that they all had a common root in some unknown trade language. This idea, partly through lack of evidence, has lost favour in recent years. An alternative explanation has been put forward: that similarities among creoles are due to an innate 'bio-programme' for language. According to this view, creoles provide a unique insight into the basic nature of human language capacity.

Activity 5.4 *(Reading C)*

Reading C, 'Creole English' by Suzanne Romaine, is taken from the entry for *creole* in the *Oxford Companion to the English Language*. Read it now, noting the main features of creoles. In particular, what makes a creole an *English* creole? And what stages of development do creoles pass through?

Comment

An English creole is a language which is formed when an English pidgin becomes a first language, and thus extended in the ways required by a native speaker to communicate in a wide variety of contexts. An English creole possesses a very different grammar from other varieties of English – at the syntactic level it has more in common with creoles of other languages than with Standard English. It is called an English creole because its *vocabulary* has been based on that of English. Hence English is what Suzanne Romaine calls the 'lexifier' language.

Figure 5.8 shows some of the places where English-based pidgins and creole langues are found.

The first stage of creole development is typically pidginization. **Creolization** occurs as this develops into a full language, acquired by children as their first language. In many parts of the world, particularly the Caribbean, continued contact with standard forms of English give rise to **decreolization** – a convergence with the lexifier language. This typically gives rise to a **post-creole continuum** – a diversity of language usage from a near-standard form of English (known as the **acrolect**) to the most divergent, creole forms (known as the **basilect**).

Figure 5.8 (opposite) Some of the world's English-based pidgins and creoles

Note: the distinction between a pidgin and a creole is not always clear. For example, Bislama is often referred to as a pidgin, although it is an official language of Vanuatu and seems to be creolized in urban areas.

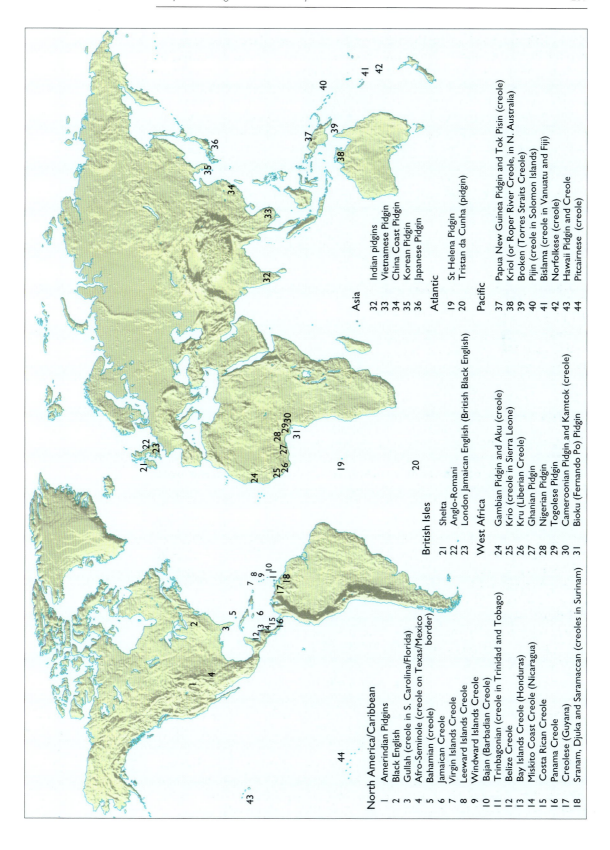

North America/Caribbean

1 Amerindian Pidgins
2 Black English
3 Gullah (creole in S. Carolina/Florida)
4 Afro-Seminole (creole on Texas/Mexico border)
5 Bahamian (creole)
6 Jamaican Creole
7 Virgin Islands Creole
8 Leeward Islands Creole
9 Windward Islands Creole
10 Bajan (Barbadian Creole)
11 Trinbagonian (creole in Trinidad and Tobago)
12 Belize Creole
13 Bay Islands Creole (Honduras)
14 Miskito Coast Creole (Nicaragua)
15 Costa Rican Creole
16 Panama Creole
17 Creolese (Guyana)
18 Sranam, Djuka and Saramaccan (creoles in Surinam)

British Isles

21 Shelta
22 Anglo-Romani
23 London Jamaican English (British Black English)

West Africa

24 Gambian Pidgin and Aku (creole)
25 Krio (creole in Sierra Leone)
26 Kru (Liberian Creole)
27 Ghanian Pidgin
28 Nigerian Pidgin
29 Togolese Pidgin
30 Cameroonian Pidgin and Kamtok (creole)
31 Bioku (Fernando Po) Pidgin

Asia

32 Indian pidgins
33 Vietnamese Pidgin
34 China Coast Pidgin
35 Korean Pidgin
36 Japanese Pidgin

Atlantic

19 St Helena Pidgin
20 Tristan da Cunha (pidgin)

Pacific

37 Papua New Guinea Pidgin and Tok Pisin (creole)
38 Kriol (or Roper River Creole, in N. Australia)
39 Broken (Torres Straits Creole)
40 Pijin (creole in Solomon Islands)
41 Bislama (creole in Vanuatu and Fiji)
42 Norfolkese (creole)
43 Hawaii Pidgin and Creole
44 Pitcairnese (creole)

Creolization happened in many parts of the English-speaking Caribbean, but it seems unlikely to have occurred in Barbados (the island described by Ligon). There the slaves may have learned the local English from the convict and servant population, which shows features associated with Hiberno-English and the English west country. For instance, *thing* may be pronounced with the initial /t/, and the forms of verbs may show the west country use of *do*: *she do tell me* instead of *she tells me*. The slaves at first were outnumbered by the British population, with whom they worked and lived closely; children of mixed parentage were born, and these formed a new class of free tradesmen and merchants with some basic education (highly prized on the island). Since Barbados is small and flat, communications were good and assisted the kind of 'close daily interaction' necessary for the formation of a relatively 'focused' Barbadian (Bajan) English.

Creolization does seem to have occurred, however, in Jamaica. This island was captured from the Spanish in 1655, rapidly turned over to sugar production, and settled by English-speakers from Barbados and other Caribbean islands such as St Kitts and Nevis (settled in the 1620s), and by convicts from Britain. By 1673 these seem to have been matched in number by African slaves, but by 1746 the latter outnumbered the former by over ten to one, and the owners of the plantations (which were often very large) lived in perpetual fear of slave revolt. For if the slaves were kept separate linguistically, it did not prevent them from rebelling, despite the severest punishments.

In what language did the slaves plot their revolts? Did they develop their creoles to create meanings unavailable to the slave-owners? Or did they retain their African languages? It is noteworthy that if they did abandon the latter, they did so while still retaining their culture of religious, medical and artistic practices. They also often hung on to their names, despite the fact that they were renamed by the planters as a mark of ownership (Walvin, 1993, p. 63). On the other hand Wolof, an African language spoken today in Senegal and Gambia, is said to have been quite widely spoken in the slave-owning southern states of America during the eighteenth century (McCrum et al., 1992, p. 226), where conditions seem to have been much less conducive to its retention than in Jamaica. For in America plantations were generally smaller than in Jamaica, slaves were often resold or moved from one plantation to another and, above all, owners soon preferred to produce new slaves from within the existing slave community, rather than continue to import them from Africa (so contact with African languages from freshly imported slaves would have been lost).

Whether or not the African languages were abandoned, it seems that their influence can be traced in creoles. Words such as *adru* (a medicinal herb) from Twi, *himba* (edible wild yam) from Ibo, and *dingki* (funeral ceremony) from Kongo have all been found in Jamaican Creole.

Activity 5.5 *(Allow 5–10 minutes)*

Re-read the last sentence in the paragraph above. In the light of my discussion of slave culture and language, do you think there is anything especially appropriate about these Africanisms? Now look at Figure 5.5 to find out where Kongo, Twi, Ibo and Jamaican Creole are spoken. What does this suggest about the source of slaves?

Comment

The Africanisms refer to knowledge and practices the slaves brought with them to Jamaica. They also show the vast 'catchment area' for the slave trade. The English at first preferred slaves from the Gold Coast (now Ghana), but by the second half of the eighteenth century most of the slaves came from further east and as far as Angola. When it is known that in Ghana today at least 46 languages are spoken, it is possible to infer that the slave traders hardly needed to ensure that slaves speaking the same language were kept separate.

Jamaican Creole also has words from Portuguese (*pikni*, 'a small child'), Spanish (*bobo*, 'a fool'), French (*leginz*, 'a bunch of vegetables for a stew'), Hindi (*roti*, 'a kind of bread'), Chinese (*ho senny ho*, 'how's business?') and even Arawak, the language of the precolonial population who had been exterminated by the time English was first spoken in Jamaica (*hicatee*, 'a land turtle', adopted via Spanish). The English element includes dialect words now scarcely heard in England (for example, *higgler*, 'a market woman'). An eighteenth-century account of Jamaican speech also notes the presence of nautical terms such as *berth* (office), *store* (warehouse), *jacket* (waistcoat), *windward* (east) and *leeward* (west), suggesting that the 'maritime' speech of English seamen (drawn from a mix of dialects of British English) may have influenced the formation of an English-based pidgin (Bailey 1992, p. 126).

Since the nineteenth century formal education, officially based on the teaching of 'Standard' English, has been available in Jamaica. But, as in the case of Ireland, access to the prescribed linguistic model, especially in relation to speech, has been limited. New varieties of Jamaican speech that can be described as more standardized, however, have been evolved alongside Jamaican Creole. This is the process that linguists call de-creolization. Individual Jamaicans are said to move along a continuum with creole at one end and more standardized English at the other. As in many other parts of the Caribbean, use of creole is firmly linked to a sense of local identity.

5.6   CONCLUSION

In this chapter I have discussed the spread of English from England, first to other parts of the British Isles and then to other areas of the world. I have identified the processes of colonization, political incorporation and nationalist reaction, suggesting that these take different forms in different contexts and have different linguistic consequences. By way of illustration, I took several countries as case studies: Ireland and Scotland in the British Isles; the USA and Australia as examples of countries in which English speakers largely displaced the precolonial population; Nigeria as an instance of a country that was more sparsely settled by English speakers, but where a proportion of the precolonial population had access to English as an additional language; and the Caribbean (in particular, Jamaica), where a displaced population was replaced by people who spoke different languages, brought in initially as slaves, and where communication between these people and English speakers resulted in the development of a pidgin language that subsequently creolized. In each case I have discussed the changing role of English in emerging national identities.

I suggested that the varieties of English that have arisen in these different places have been shaped by contact: contact with other languages, as well as between the varieties of English used by settlers. I discussed some of the linguistic characteristics of these varieties, and their possible origins, focusing mainly on vocabulary (grammar is discussed in the next chapter and pronunciation in Chapter 7).

If you bear in mind the discussion in Chapter 3 of the different kinds of story which have been told about the history of English, you probably won't be surprised to learn that the worldwide spread of English has often been told as a progressive, even triumphalist story, reflecting the glory and international superiority of England and Englishness. But just as the Welsh took a different view of the 'triumph' of the Anglo-Saxons (see Gildas's account in Chapter 3, section 3.3), so it is possible to regard the global success of English as the result of centuries of exploitation and oppression. For many users of English today, the story might feel more like one of imposition.

But it is also possible to see English as having become a genuinely 'world' language, transcending all differences of culture, race and belief. It is worth noting that it is North America, with far more speakers of English than the British Isles, that has probably played the major role in spreading the language. While some people might regard the influence of the United States as a new form of cultural imperialism, there is also a sense in which 'ownership' of English has finally passed out of the hands of the 'native-speaking' countries: it has become a resource to be exploited, culturally and commercially, by many countries across the world.

Because of the huge scope of the subject dealt with in this chapter, I have selected a limited number of case studies that illustrate the main developments in the global spread of English. Throughout the chapter I have tried to emphasize the range of meanings English has for its speakers, and for those who come into contact with it. Such meanings will not always be clearly delineated, and individuals may well have rather ambivalent attitudes towards English. This continues a theme that runs through the book, and that is developed further in later chapters.

Reading A

EXTRACT FROM THE
AUSTRALIAN NATIONAL DICTIONARY

W.S. Ramson (ed.)

Introduction

For the purposes of this dictionary an Australianism is one of those words and meanings of words which have originated in Australia, which have a greater currency here than elsewhere, or which have a special significance in Australia because of their connection with an aspect of the history of the country. The aim of the dictionary is to provide as full an historical record of these as possible.

In the simplest analysis Australian English, the English used by Australians, differs from that used elsewhere in the ways and to the extent that the circumstances of life in this country and the history of its people have been distinctive. Most obviously, there are words and meanings of words which have originated in Australia because of the need to give a name to a bird, a plant, an artefact, or a feature of the landscape encountered here for the first time: the application of a largely descriptive nomenclature to species of indigenous flora and fauna, and the borrowing from Aboriginal languages of terms for Aboriginal implements and weapons are illustrations of this.

But Australian English reflects also the composition of the immigrant population and an experience which while in part distinctive was in part common to other British colonies. Regional dialect and slang words which have remained non-standard in Britain became generally current in Australia. Occupational vocabularies, made up in part of traditional, often dialect, terms, in part of new terms required by new circumstances, acquired greater prominence: some mining terms, for instance, obtained general currency when gold-mining, in several parts of the new world, became a popular as distinct from a specialized pursuit. Words necessary to describe the opening up of an unfamiliar country, often originating in another colony or common to more than one, became part of an active vocabulary in Australia, of a largely passive one in Britain. Words formed from standard elements, as compounds formed on main elements like *bullock, canvas, cattle, sheep,* and *stock,* acquired a special significance because of the importance of the activity with which they were associated.

It is a reasonable presumption that a word recorded by the *Oxford English Dictionary* and its four-volume Supplement (OED(S)) or the *English Dialect Dictionary* (EDD) as British regional dialect is rightly so described even if it can be antedated in Australian use. In many instances, also, a substantially earlier American history establishes an American origin for a word borrowed into Australian. But it would be hazardous to argue an Australian origin for *round up* or *puncher* (as in *bullock puncher*) simply on the ground that both are recorded earliest in Australia. And, in fields like gold-mining, sheep-raising, shearing, and Services speech, New Zealand and Australia have so many words in common that the location of the earliest written evidence may well be fortuitous. It has therefore seemed best to interpret 'Australianism' liberally, not making undue claims but including in the dictionary many words which are of undoubted significance in the Australian context but about the precise origin of which there remains uncertainty.

The first stage in the compilation of any dictionary on historical principles is the establishment of a bibliography of sources and the implementation of a reading programme …

In the *Instructions* [for the reading programme] readers were asked to be alert to:

words and phrases they believed were Australian

words and phrases in occupational vocabularies, especially those used 'on the job'

words and phrases in other specialized vocabularies

names for animals, birds, fish, plants, and geographical features

words and phrases apparently borrowed from Aboriginal languages

colloquial expressions

proverbial expressions and catch-phrases

familiar words and phrases used in unusual ways

family or local expressions

words and phrases not in common use, especially those which appear obsolete

words and phrases which others have found unfamiliar.

…

Also [note] that common names in natural history checklists are included only if there is adequate evidence of sustained popular use.

…

A selection was then made of those citations which most fully represented a word's life and most definitively and vividly illustrated its use and meaning. In the case of names of flora and fauna the selection was intended to include descriptive material and in many cases to substantiate the particular uses of names which have often been used loosely. Particular care was taken to select citations which established the Australianness of the word or its referent, not crudely in a quest for colour but in the recognition that, as the words added to a language by a people are an index of their history and culture, so the actual context of use provides evidence of their social and cultural attitudes and preoccupations.

…

The essence of an entry in an historical dictionary is its set citations: these establish the chronology of a word's use, substantiate the definition or definitions, and illustrate the range of registers within which a word has been used. We have taken the view that, while it is sometimes a proper part of the descriptive process to use a subject label to indicate that a word is restricted to a particular field of activity, there is a danger that using labels to indicate register can be over-interpretative and over-restrictive. This seems particularly true of Australian English, which allows easy movement between formal and informal usage. It should be clear from the citations if a word belongs mainly to colloquial use or to the slang of a particular group, and equally clear if it is for some reason taboo in some contexts. Labels like *coarse, colloq., derog., slang* and *vulgar,* which tend unnecessarily to categorize, have therefore been omitted. Inclusion of words that many will find offensive does not mean that the editors endorse the sentiments they frequently express: our responsibility has been to record the language as it has been used and to supply the evidence of this use in citations which enable users of the dictionary to form their own judgements about both the words and their users.

business. *Aboriginal English.*

1. Traditional lore and ritual; the exercise of this. Also *attrib.*

1943 W.E. HARNEY *Taboo* 170 'That not proper wind, but blackfellow business.' Blackfellow business! Some native in another tribe had cast some magic and sent this wind to destroy the tribe. **1961** F. DE GRYS *Cobba Cobba* 113 Whitefella Aspros were not likely to be much good for a headache caused by too much Blackfella Business. **1974** J. BERN *Blackfella Business* 26 Blackfella business is the expression of Aboriginal consciousness in general. **1977** J. & P. READ *View of Past* 12 Aug. (1978) 308 (typescript), A lot of these girls here are all, all educated when there are business ceremonies, ceremonial things, our custom way... They still join in. **1978** *Alywarra Land Claim: Transcript of Proc.* 9 Oct. 416 Do they also own the business and the story to that place? **1983** NATHAN & JAPANANGKA *Settle down Country* 114 Because of 'sorry business' [*sc.* mourning ceremonies] the people had moved from their normal site. **1985** I. WHITE et al. *Fighters & Singers* 13 They might make him a man .. this year at business time up here.

2. In the collocation **Sunday business,** an exclusive ritual (see quots. 1949 and 1962). Also **Sunday business ritual.**

1949 HARNEY & ELKIN *Songs of Songman* 143 The women .. go off to 'dance', that is perform their secret corroboree, their 'Sunday Business'. **1962** D. LOCKWOOD *I, Aboriginal* 32 Henceforth the ceremony was strictly men's Sunday-business .. in which [the women] could not take part. **1964** —— *Up Track* 124, I have seen dozens of corroborees and a few big Sunday Business rituals among today's aborigines. **1978** J. & P. READ *View of Past* 227 They going to be shown all that Sunday business .. do you reckon?

clever, *a. Aboriginal English.*

1. Wise; learned in traditional lore. Esp. in the collocation **clever man.** See KORADJI.

1909 *Folklore* (London) XIV. iv. 487 A 'doctor' or clever blackfellow can sometimes go and see a Wahwee. **1935** *Oceania* VI. 33 Several men had the reputation of being 'clever' men. **1944** A.P. ELKIN *Aboriginal Men High Degree* (1946) 85 Amongst these people there was a class of 'clever' men who specialized in meditation, hypnotism, thought-transference and 'seeing' what was occurring at a distance. **1947** *Oceania* XVII. 330 The two women, who were 'clever', and possessed a certain amount of magical 'power', had used .. a decoy. **1965** R. ROBINSON *Man who sold Dreaming* 12 The clever-feller is a witch-doctor, a rain-maker, one who can cast spells .. an old man who has specialised in magic. **1977** J. BARKER *Two Worlds* 71 They were just ordinary Aborigines and not reputed to be witch doctors or clever men. **1985** T. WISE *Self-Made Anthropologist* 246 At times, he seemed to think that many clever men used the knowledge that there was a certain element of faith on their viewers' part.

2. *Transf.* and *fig.*

1972 *Bulletin* (Sydney) 24 June 59/1 As widely reported, the clever-feller-money-magicians (who are *usually* right) are predicting a further 0.2 percent cut in the long term bond rate. **1986** HERCUS & SUTTON *This is what Happened* 229 There was a white cleverman at Port Augusta—white people call him 'doctor'.

Examples of entries from the Australian National Dictionary: business, clever koori, and compounds formed with stock.

koori /'kʊri/, *n.*[1] Also **koorie** and formerly **coorie, kuri, kurri.** [a. Awabakal (and other n. N.S.W. languages) *guri* man.] An Aboriginal (now used chiefly by Aborigines). Also *attrib.*

1834 L.E. THRELKELD *Austral. Grammar* 87 *Ko-re*, man, mankind. **1845** C. HODGKINSON *Aust., Port Macquarie to Moreton Bay* 54 They .. informed me that the Bellengen corees (black fellows), were belcoula, (not angry). **1892** J. FRASER *Aborigines N.S.W.* 2 The kuri, or 'blackman' is usually kind and affectionate to his jin, 'wife'. **1966** M. BROWN *Jimberi Track* 40 At any moment the dogs were liable to be sent racing through the camp, or some koorie or other set screaming. **1970** R. ROBINSON *Altjeringa* 30 These wild Kurris were runnin' out of the scrub. **1973** D. WOLFE *Brass Kangaroo* 306 You should get rid of the white bosses here and let us koories run the station. **1977** K. GILBERT *Living Black* 201 How many Kooris, town or mission, would be prepared to come out here and put up signs saying 'This is an Aboriginal Burial Ground. Keep Off. This is a Sacred Area.' Who'd be in it? **1985** J. MILLER *Koori* 218 Since I believe in Koori land rights and no dams on the Franklin River, that makes me a black, greenie, pinko.

koori, /'kʊri/, *n.*[2] [a. Panyjima *kurri* marriageable teenage girl.] A young Aboriginal woman.

1908 *West Austral.* (Perth) 22 Feb. 12/3 Do you remember .. there was a coorie and two piccaninnies. .. What was her age? About ten or eleven. **1968** D. O'GRADY *Bottle of Sandwiches* 28 The only women around the place were the gins and coories of his Aboriginal stockmen. **1985** MARIS & BORG *Women of Sun* 94 If you were a koori, what chance did you have of finding a job?—except .. cleaning up whitefeller's dirt?

2. Special Comb. **stock agent,** one who deals in the buying and selling of stock; **boot** *obs., stockman's boot,* see STOCKMAN 2; **boy,** an Aboriginal male employed to look after stock; **country,** an area in which stock-raising is the principal industry; an area suitable for this; **driver** *obs.,* DROVER 1; **-driving** *vbl. n.,* DROVING 1; **establishment,** a sheep or cattle farm; **horse,** a horse trained to work with stock; **house** *obs.,* a building in which stock is accommodated; **hut** *obs., stockman's hut,* see STOCKMAN 2; **inspector,** an official employed to ensure that regulations concerning stock are complied with; **market** *obs.,* a place where sheep and cattle are sold; trade in sheep and cattle; **master, proprietor** *obs.,* STOCKHOLDER; **property** *obs., stock establishment;* **reserve,** *travelling stock reserve,* see TRAVELLING STOCK 2; **-rider,** STOCKMAN 1; so **-ride** *v. intr.;* **-riding** *vbl. n.* and *attrib.;* **route,** *travelling stock route,* see TRAVELLING STOCK 2; also *attrib.;* **run,** see RUN *n.*[2] 2; **saddle,** a heavy saddle made for a stock horse; **station** *obs.,* see STATION 2 a. and 3; **water,** water suitable for stock; **woman,** STOCKHOLDER; a woman employed to tend stock.

Our perception of the vocabulary of Australian English as an entity has made us wary also of using regional labels for many items in the colloquial vocabulary which are commonly supposed to be localized in their use. With the names of species flora and fauna the evidence is sometimes unequivocal and attributions can be given with confidence. And in the case of a small number of items of peripheral interest – the names given to glasses of beer, for example – the written evidence is adequate. But for many more interesting items, words like *port* for instance, the evidence is unconvincing: we have frequently allowed popular opinion a voice in a citation but until there is a survey of regional usage which takes account of the spoken as well as the written word – and such a survey is a natural consequence of the completion of this dictionary – it must remain opinion.

The dictionary's concern is with the English used by or accessible to the majority of Australians. It thus necessarily takes account of what is referred to in AND as *Australian pidgin*, the language of contact between European settler and Aboriginal, used particularly in the earlier part of the nineteenth century and now largely obsolete, and what is referred to as *Aboriginal English*, that set of terms which is used mostly by Aborigines and which relates to their attitudes and concerns, made up partly of standard English words like *business* and *clever*, which have been given new meanings, partly of Australian pidgin words which have outlived the stigma attaching to a contact language, and partly of words originating in Aboriginal languages, especially words like *koori*, which manifest a pride in Aboriginality. In both cases, what is offered in AND is a preliminary account – in the case of pidgin because what is recorded is that which has at least in part been absorbed into Australian English, in the case of Aboriginal English because, while its spoken life is undoubtedly vigorous, its emergence into written English is mostly late.

Source: Ramson, 1988, pp. vi-viii, 124, 150, 354 and 635

Reading B

IDENTIFYING NIGERIAN USAGES IN NIGERIAN ENGLISH

Ayọ Bamgboṣe

An inevitable point of departure in describing usage in a second-language situation is a conscious or unconscious comparison with a native variety of the language concerned. This is precisely what has been done in the description of Nigerian English. Labels such as 'same', 'different', or 'similar' must be justified in terms of observed usages in the varieties to which they are applied. Three approaches may be identified: the interference approach, the deviation approach, and the creativity approach.

The interference approach attempts to trace Nigerian usages to the influences of the Nigerian languages. This approach is certainly most relevant as far as the phonetics of Nigerian English is concerned. But as I have pointed out elsewhere, even at this level there are 'features which are typical of the pronunciation of most Nigerian speakers of English' (Bamgboṣe 1971, p. 42) irrespective of their first-language background. Besides, a typical pronunciation may result from a factor other than interference. For example, most speakers of English from the eastern part of Nigeria pronounce the possessive 'your' as [jua] or [ja], even though all the languages in that area have the sound [ɔ]. The prevalence of this pronunciation is no doubt due to its widespread use by teachers and generations of pupils who have passed through the same schools.

The interference approach is even less justifiable in lexis and syntax. Adekunle (1974) attributes all of standard Nigerian English's Nigerian usages in lexis and syntax to interference from the mother tongue. It is quite easy to show that while some usages can be so attributed, the vast majority, at least in Educated Nigerian English, arise from the normal process of language development involving a narrowing or extension of meaning or the creation of new idioms. And most such usages cut across all first-language backgrounds. For example, when 'travel' is used in the sense 'to be away', as in *My father have travelled* (= My father is away), it is not a transfer of a first-language expression into English, but a modification of the meaning of the verb 'to travel'.

One final objection to the interference approach is that not all cases of interference can validly be considered Nigerian usages. Some clearly belong to the level of pidgin English. For instance, the absence of a gender distinction in third-person pronominal reference may result from first-language interference, e.g. *He talk say* (= He/She says that ...), but it is unlikely that this will be considered a feature of any variety of Nigerian English.

The deviation approach involves a comparison of observed Nigerian usage with Native English, and the labelling of all differences as 'deviant'. Such deviance may result from interference, or from an imperfect attempt to reproduce the target expressions. For example, *Borrow me your pen* (= Lend me your pen) is clearly a case of interference from a first language which makes no lexical distinction between 'lend' and 'borrow'. On the other hand, the pluralization of 'equipment' in *We bought the equipments* indicates a failure to grasp the distinction between countable and mass nouns.

There are two main weaknesses in the deviation approach. First, it tends to suggest that the observed usage is 'imperfect' or 'non-standard' English. The fact that some so-called deviations have now achieved the status of identifying markers of a standard Nigerian English tends to be overlooked in a description that lumps all divergences together as deviant usage. Second, the deviation approach ignores the fact that certain characteristic Nigerian usages in English result from the creativity of the users.

The creativity approach tends to focus on the exploitation of the resources of Nigerian languages as well as English to create new idioms and expressions. According to this approach, a usage which might otherwise have been classified as resulting from interference or deviation is seen as a legitimate second-language creation. Thus, from the expression *She has been to Britain* a noun, *been-to*, has been created to describe anyone who has travelled overseas, particularly to Britain.

The main advantage of the creativity approach is that it recognizes the development of Nigerian English as a type in its own right. But not all cases of usage in Nigerian English can properly be regarded as arising from creativity. Besides, certain usages motivated by creativity are, at best, substandard English. Amos Tutuọla's novel, *My Life in the Bush of Ghosts*, is a good example of this. The incidents in the novel take place 'in those days of unknown year' when 'slave wars were causing dead luck to both young and old'; and the hero visits 'Deads'-town' and sees 'born and die babies' as well as 'triplet ghosts and ghostesses' [see Tutuọla 1954, pp. 17, 18, 62 and 63].

The above discussion shows that while each approach throws some light on the nature of Nigerian English, none is by itself adequate to characterize the whole spectrum of Nigerian English. Besides, not every feature thrown up by each approach necessarily exemplifies Nigerian English. A combination of all approaches is therefore required, and a certain amount of subjective judgement regarding acceptability will be required in determining what falls within or outside the scope of Nigerian English.

...

Some typical features of standard Nigerian English

In order to illustrate such features as I consider typical, I provide (below) examples based on my general observation of the use of English by [educated Nigerian] speakers. I believe these features cut across different first-language backgrounds, and no amount of drilling or stigmatization is going to lead to their abandondment.

...

Morphology and Syntax

These are generally the same as in standard English, except for features such as the following: 1) Peculiar word formation may occur with plurals (e.g. *equipments, aircrafts, deadwoods*), antonyms (*indisciplined*), and adverbials (*singlehandedly*). 2) Dropping of 'to' from the infinitive after certain verbs; e.g. *enable him do it.* 3) A preposition may be employed where Native English will avoid or will use a different preposition; e.g. voice out instead of 'voice' (I am going to voice out my opinion), *discuss about* instead of 'discuss' (We shall discuss about that later), *congratulate for* instead of 'congratulate on' (I congratulate you for your brilliant performance). 4) A focus construction is often used, involving the subject of the sentence as focus and an anaphoric pronoun subject, e.g. *The politicians and their supporters, they don't often listen to advice. A person who has no experience, can he be a good leader?*

Lexis and semantics

As has often been observed, most differences between Nigerian English and other forms of English are to be found in the innovations in lexical items and idioms and their meanings. Following are some of the features concerned. 1) New lexical items may either be coined from existing lexical items or borrowed from the local languages or from pidgin, either directly or in translation. For examples of coinage, consider *barb* (to cut [hair]) from 'barber', *invitee* (guest) from 'invite', *head-tie* (woman's headdress), and *go-slow* (traffic jam). Loanwards and loan translations are generally drawn from different aspects of the cultural background, including food, dress, and customs for which there are quite often no exact equivalent lexical items in English; e.g. *akara balls* (beancakes), *juju music* (a type of dance music), *bush meat* (game), *tie-dye cloth* (cloth into which patterns are made up by tying up parts of it before dyeing), and *white-cap chiefs* (senior chiefs in Lagos whose rank is shown by the white caps they wear). 2) Some lexical items acquire new meanings; e.g. a *corner* becomes a 'bend in a road', *globe* is an 'electric bulb', *wet* means 'to water (flowers)', and a *launcher* is someone called upon to declare open a fund-raising function. *Locate* means 'to assign to a school or town' and is used when speaking of newly qualified teachers. *Land* is 'to finish one's intervention or speech', *environment* is a 'neighborhood', and *bluff* means 'to give an air of importance'. 3) Other lexical items have retained older meanings no longer current in Native English. *Dress,* 'move at the end of a row so as to create room for additional persons', is a retention of the earlier meaning recorded by the *Shorter Oxford English Dictionary:* 'to form in proper alignment'. *Station,* 'the town or city in which a person works', is a retention of the earlier meaning recorded by the same source: 'the locality to which an official is appointed for the exercise of his functions'. 4) Certain idioms acquire new forms or meanings. To *eat one's cake and have it* is an inversion of 'to have one's cake and eat it' (Example:

You can't eat your cake and have it). *As at now* replaces 'as of now' (Example: As at now, there are only two men available). 5) Some totally new idioms are developed; e.g. *to take in* for 'to become pregnant'. (Example: She has just taken in). *Off-head*, 'from memory', is similar to standard English *offhand* (Example: I can't tell you the number off-head). To *take the light* means to make a power cut (Example: Has the national Electrical Power Authority (N.E.P.A.) taken the light again?). And *social wake-keeping* refers to feasting, drumming, and dancing after a burial (Example: There will be social wake-keeping from 10 p.m. till dawn).

Context

Even when lexical items or idioms have roughly the same meanings as in Native English, they may be used in completely different contexts. Examples which have been given in the literature include the use of *sorry* as an expression of sympathy, for example, to someone who sneezes or stumbles, or *wonderful* as an exclamation of surprise. To these may be added the use of *please* as an indication of politeness (for example, in a formal or official letter), *Dear Sir* for opening a personal letter to someone older than oneself, and *my dear* for addressing practically anyone, including strangers.

References

ADEKUNLE, M.A. (1974) 'The standard Nigerian English', *Journal of the Nigeria English Studies Association,* vol. 6, no. 1, pp. 24–37.

BAMGBOSE, A. (1971) 'The English language in Nigeria', in SPENCER, J. (ed.) *The English Language in West Africa,* London, Longman, pp. 35–48

TUTUOLA, A. (1954) *My Life in the Bush of Ghosts,* London, Faber & Faber.

Source: Bamgbose, 1982, pp. 102–7

Reading C
CREOLE ENGLISH

Suzanne Romaine

In sociolinguistic terms, [creole] languages have arisen through contact between speakers of different languages. This contact first produces a makeshift language called a *pidgin*; when this is nativized and becomes the language of a community, it is a creole … They are usually given labels by sociolinguists that refer to location and principal *lexifier language* (the language from which they draw most of their vocabulary): for example, *Jamaican Creole*, in full *Jamaican Creole English*, the English-based creole spoken in Jamaica …

Creole English

There are many English-based creoles. In West Africa, they include *Aku* in Gambia, *Krio* in Sierra Leone, *Kru English* in Liberia, and *Kamtok* in Cameroon. In the Caribbean and the neighbouring mainland they include *Bajan* in Barbados,

Creolese in Guyana, *Miskito Coast Creole* in Nicaragua, *Sranan* in Surinam, *Trinbagonian* in Trinidad and Tobago, and the creoles of the Bay Islands of Honduras. In North America, they include *Afro-Seminole, Amerindian Pidgin English,* and *Gullah.* In Oceania, they include *Bislama* in Vanuatu, *Broken* in the Torres Straits, *Hawaii English Creole, Kriol* in Northern Australia, *Pijin* in the Solomon Islands, and *Tok Pisin* in Papua New Guinea. It has been argued that *Black English (Vernacular)* in the US has creole origins since it shares many features with English-based creoles in the Caribbean. In the UK, *British Black English,* spoken by immigrants from the Caribbean and their children, has features inherited from Caribbean English Creole.

Shared features

Typical grammatical features in European-based creoles include the use of pre-verbal negation and subject-verb-object word order: for example (from Sranan in Surinam), *A mo koti a brede* He didn't cut the bread. Many use the same item for both existential statements and possession: for example, *get* in Guyanese Creole *Dem get wan uman we get gyal pikni* There is a woman who has a daughter. They lack a formal passive: for example, in Jamaican Creole no distinction is made in the verb forms in sentences such as *Dem plaan di tri* (They planted the tree) and *Dem tri plaan* (The tree was planted). Creoles tend to have no copula and adjectives may function as verbs: for example, Jamaican Creole *Di pikni sik* The child is sick. Most creoles do not show any syntactic difference between questions and statements: for example, Guyanese Creole *I bai di eg dem* can mean 'He bought the eggs' or 'Did he buy the eggs?' (although there is a distinction in intonation). Question words in creoles tend to have two elements, the first generally from the lexifier language: for example, Haitian Creole *ki koté* (from *qui* and *coté*, 'which' and 'side') meaning *where*, Kamtok *wetin* (from *what* and *thing*) meaning *what*. It has been claimed that many syntactic and semantic similarities among creoles are due to an innate 'bioprogram' for language, and that creoles provide the key to understanding the original evolution of human language.

Creolization

The process of becoming a creole may occur at any stage as a makeshift language develops from trade jargon to expanded pidgin, and can happen under drastic conditions, such as where a population of slaves speaking many languages has to develop a common language among slaves and with overseers. In due course, children grow up speaking the pidgin as their main language, and when this happens it must change to meet their needs. Depending on the stage at which creolization occurs, different types of structural expansion are necessary before the language can become adequate. In the case of Jamaican Creole, it is thought that a rudimentary pidgin creolized within a generation, then began to *de-creolize* towards general English. Tok Pisin, however, first stablized and expanded as a pidgin before it became creolized; in such cases, the transition between the two stages is gradual rather than abrupt.

The term is also applied to cases where heavy borrowing disrupts the continuity of a language, turning it into a creole-like variety, but without a prior pidgin stage. Some researchers have argued that Middle English is a creole that arose from contact with Norse during the Scandinavian settlements [eighth to eleventh centuries] and then with French after the Norman Conquest [eleventh century]. In addition to massive lexical borrowing, many changes led to such simplification of grammar as loss of the Old English inflectional endings. It is not, however, clear that these changes were due solely to language contact, since other languages have undergone similar restructurings in the absence of contact, as for example when Latin became Italian.

De-creolization is a further development in which a creole gradually converges with its superstrate or lexifier language: for example, in Hawaii and Jamaica, both creoles moving towards standard English. Following the creolization of a pidgin, a *post-creole continuum* may develop when, after a period of relatively independent linguistic development, a post-pidgin or post-creole variety comes under a period of renewed influence from the lexifier language. De-creolization may obscure the origins of a variety, as in the case of American Black English.

Source: McArthur (ed.), 1992, pp. 270–1

6 VARIATION IN ENGLISH GRAMMAR

Linda Thomas

6.1 INTRODUCTION

From previous chapters in this book you will already have gained an idea of the considerable variation that exists between the 'Englishes' that are spoken and written in different parts of the world. Chapter 5 discussed the historical development of different varieties of English, and also gave examples of the characteristics of some of these varieties. There was a particular focus on vocabulary, though other aspects of language were also mentioned. This chapter looks in more detail at **grammar**: at how the words of different varieties are made up (or the different forms certain words may take); and at the ways in which words combine with one another to make meaningful sentences.

From your reading of earlier chapters you'll appreciate that there are certain difficulties in this enterprise: there are no definite boundaries between different varieties, and it is by no means clear even how much to include within the term 'English' (i.e. where English stops and another language begins). Here we cast our net fairly wide, including examples from the range of Englishes discussed in previous chapters: 'traditional' dialects in the UK including those influenced by other languages (such as Irish English); other 'native-speaker' varieties (such as US English); 'non-native' varieties that are affected by other languages spoken in the area (e.g. Indian English); and some pidgin and creole varieties. However, the aim is not to provide a 'menu' of the grammars of different Englishes but to focus on particular features of English that have been found to vary and to try to give a flavour of how these have been described and analysed by linguists.

6.2 VARIETIES OF ENGLISH

Linguists interested in grammatical variation make certain broad distinctions, for instance between 'standard' and 'nonstandard' English and between different geographical varieties. This is made problematical by the lack of clear boundaries between different varieties, discussed in earlier chapters. Before looking in more detail at grammatical description I briefly review some of these problems, referring back to discussions in previous chapters where this is relevant.

Standard and nonstandard Englishes

Chapter 4 discussed the development of a standard variety of English in England – a variety that was focused and that showed minimal variation between different geographical areas. Standard English is the variety that is taught in schools, used in the media and codified in dictionaries and grammars. It is associated with 'middle class' or 'educated' speakers.

Examples of varieties of English

The day me da landed home way the job me ma seen him comin' out the window an' she knew he had got it before he come inte the house because of the way he was walkin' an' on account of the fact that he had only been left home a wee bit over an' hour, for if he hadn't of got it, she reckoned, he wouldn't have been rushin' home in such a hurry te tell us the bad news.

(Molloy, 1985, p. 22)

De whole talk start when Maggie say she don't see why the government mus' borrow money if dey have so much money in de country. She say as far as she concern she does always follow wha' she granmudder used to tell she: 'Never ah borrower or ah lender be,' an' 'We ants never borrow we ants never lends.' So she say if money eh no problem, why we mus' go an' borrow from foreigners.

(Cited in Winer, 1993, p. 183)

The first extract comes from a book written in a variety of English found in Belfast, Northern Ireland; the second from an article written in an English-based creole spoken in Trinidad. Both are unusual, in that books and articles are normally written in a standard variety of English: there are some noticeable differences between the forms of English used in these extracts and Standard English.

First, the spelling has been adapted in an attempt to reflect local pronunciation. Some words also reflect the local dialect: 'wee' in the first extract means 'little', and 'landed' is used in the sense of 'arrived'. There are grammatical differences too. Notice, for instance, the nonstandard forms of some past tense verbs: in the first extract, 'seen' rather than 'saw' and 'come' rather than 'came'; and, in the Trinidad example, the fact that the verb is not marked for past tense (e.g. 'start' rather than 'started'). There are further differences in verbs in the Trinidad extract; for example, in 'she does … follow' the word 'does' is not used for emphasis: it signifies habitual action. Also, in this variety there are differences in pronoun forms: for instance 'used to tell *she*' rather than 'her'. At the level of sentence structure, the Trinidad extract shows some differences in word order, as in 'why we mus' go' rather than 'why must we go'.

It is possible to identify differences between **standard** Englishes that are spoken in different parts of the world (e.g. between Standard English English, Standard Scottish English and Standard US English), but there are relatively few differences between these varieties. There is much greater regional variation between **nonstandard** varieties of English. However, you'll also be aware that the distinction between 'standard' and 'nonstandard' is not as hard and fast as it appears. In England (for instance) the speaker of a nonstandard variety is not using a totally different system from a standard speaker: these are interlinking systems which may have more similarities than differences.

The standard forms that have been codified tend to come from written English: spoken English is more variable and it is spoken English that is frequently the object of study by those interested in language variation. But it is not easy to establish distinctions between spoken Standard and nonstandard English (for instance, between 'colloquial' forms of language used by speakers of standard English and 'nonstandard' forms).

Differences between speech and writing are considered further in the second book in this series, *Using English: from conversation to canon* (Maybin and Mercer (eds), 1996).

Furthermore, several nonstandard forms are now common in different geographical areas: some nonstandard features are widespread and can be said to belong to a general nonstandard dialect rather than to a specific regional variety.

Geographical varieties of English

The geographical labels that we often use to identify different Englishes conceal a great deal of variation. Even in relatively limited geographical areas there will be differences in the types of English spoken. Joan Beal (1993) lists several features of Tyneside English (spoken in the counties of Northumberland and Tyne and Wear, in the north-east of England), but she concedes that 'the reader is unlikely to encounter anybody who will use all of these features all of the time' (p. 191). There is local geographical variation 'especially in an area in which there is a stark contrast between the Tyneside conurbation, the small mining towns of mid-Northumberland, and the isolated rural communities of north Northumberland' (p. 191). Social factors also play a part in that people of higher social status tend to use fewer local forms of language. And context is important – people may avoid local features on more formal occasions. Beal comments:

> A vast amount of research would be needed in order to quantify the amount and type of variation for each feature, so for the time being I have presented these features as if they were invariable. It is important to remember that this is an idealization.
>
> (Beal, 1993, p. 192)

Detailed information on the distribution of grammatical features is also lacking in other varieties. John Harris (1993) notes that different dialects of Irish English share linguistic features that distinguish them from other varieties. But while a great deal is known about the regional distribution of pronunciation features, information on grammatical features is 'more or less impressionistic'.

Chapter 7 has more to say about the detailed charting of regional variation in pronunciation features, and about social variation. Chapter 8 looks at variation across different contexts.

There remains the issue of deciding where one variety stops and others begin – something that Jim Miller discusses in relation to Scottish English:

> Specifying Scottish English can seem as tricky as the party game in which, blindfold, you have to pin the tail on the drawing of a donkey. For example, many words that Scots consider typically Scottish are common to all varieties of Northern English and some occur quite far away, such as *bide* (= 'stay'), which turns up in Hardy's novels. Another example is the use of *though* at the end or in the middle of a clause and used by the speakers to concede that such-and-such is indeed the case in spite of their expectations to the contrary: e.g. *It's cauld the day, though* ('It's cold today but who would have expected it'). This construction is very frequent in the speech of Scottish speakers, but it occurs outside Scotland; and is given in the Longman *Dictionary of Contemporary English*.
>
> The solution to the problem of shared vocabulary and constructions is not to throw away the concept of Scottish English but to accept that the geographical varieties of nonstandard English should be viewed as intersecting sets of constructions. Scottish English may share one construction with Tyneside English, a second with Hiberno-English and a third with the West Midlands, but it may be alone in possessing all three constructions. On a wider scale, we would have to recognise that Scottish English shares constructions with the English of Canada and the southern United States.
>
> (Miller, 1993, p. 99)

*The standard English (and clothing style) of the opinion poll taker contrasts here with the Creole (and clothing style) of the working class citizens. **Bush** here is any rural area, considered more self-sufficient for food. Two negators are present: **cyah** 'can't' [kjǎ:]. and **eh** 'don't'; the **nuh** here is emphatic. The sentence pattern with initial copula is clear in **Is 4 years now ah unemployed** 'it is 4 years now (that) I am/have been unemployed'. Creole pronunciation is reflected in the spellings **somewey** 'somewhere' and **wo'k** 'job', the latter representing the more Creole [wʌk] rather than TE [wɜːk]. **Child** is a term of address usually used between females.*

Standard English and Creole in Trinidad

(Reproduced in Winer, 1993, p. 233)

Standard English as a basis of description

In practice, descriptions of regional or nonstandard varieties of English tend to focus on those constructions that differ from a standardized variety of the language. I follow this convention here, because it is consistent with the literature I am drawing on and because it is difficult to describe a range of different grammatical constructions without taking something as the basis of comparison. For the purposes of this chapter I use the term 'Standard English' to refer to the standard English of England (which differs in some respects from other standardized varieties).

Chapter 7 discusses similar issues in relation to accent in which one variety, Received Pronunciation, is frequently taken as a basis of comparison.

This approach does, however, raise certain issues which it's important to bear in mind: it means that different varieties are necessarily defined in relation to a standard. Grammatical accounts tend to focus on just those features that differ from the standard, rather than including what is often a large body of features held in common. They are extremely partial, seeking to highlight and explain difference rather than to provide a comprehensive grammar of a variety. This way of describing variation may also suggest that there is a 'core' of English (exemplified in the standard variety) from which other varieties deviate to a greater or lesser extent.

Varieties of English are, then, idealizations. As well as discussing the different forms of some English grammatical constructions this chapter illustrates the way different varieties of English have been constructed by those who study them.

A note on grammatical description

A relatively small number of terms are used here to help with grammatical description. These include terms referring to certain common word classes, as in the following example:

Determiner	Adjective	Noun	Verb	Determiner	Noun
That	small	mouse	ate	the	cheese

Some terms in the example such as **adjective, noun** and **verb** will be familiar to many readers. **Determiner** may not be: it refers to words such as *the, a(n), that, those, this, these, my, some* which occur before a noun (or an adjective and noun) and, according to David Crystal (1992, p. 99) which '"determine" the way in which the noun is to be interpreted – *a car* vs *the car* vs *my car* etc'.

Sentences such as the example above are made up of groups of words termed phrases: it's possible to identify 'that small mouse' and 'the cheese' as **noun phrases** ('a sequence of words including a noun which can be substituted for a single noun in any sentence', Graddol et al., 1994, p. 79), and 'ate' as a **verb phrase**. Verb phrases may be more complex; for instance, they may consist of one or more **auxiliary verbs** and a **lexical verb**, as in the following examples:

	Auxiliary verb	Lexical verb	
The mouse	will	eat	the cheese
	may	eat	
	has	eaten	
	may have	eaten	

In the sections which follow, I look first at aspects of the verb phrase; then the noun phrase; and finally overall sentence structure. I introduce further grammatical terms as these are required: the discussion does not provide anything like a comprehensive description of English grammar (for an example of this, see Quirk et al. (1985), *A Comprehensive Grammar of the English Language*, which I refer to from time to time), but it does at least give an indication of what a grammatical description looks like.

Grammatical examples

Grammatical accounts are sometimes based on linguists' intuitions: linguists invent sentences to test, or illustrate, a point of grammar, assuming that their intuitions of what counts as a grammatical sentence correspond with those of other speakers. There is a danger here in that linguists' (and others'!) intuitions about sentences don't always correspond with the ways people actually use language. Here I resort to invented examples when I need to illustrate something like a grammatical category. Most of the time, however, I deal with attested examples – that is, those that have been used by speakers (or occasionally writers) of English.

6.3   THE VERB PHRASE

Differences in verb forms

There are several differences in the *form* verbs may take in different varieties of English. For instance, Table 6.1 shows different forms of the present tense in Standard English and in two regional varieties of British English. From this table, we can see that there is only one present-tense form in traditional varieties spoken by some people in south-west England and in East Anglia, whereas the standard variety distinguishes between the third-person singular (*she, he* and *it* forms) and other verb forms in the present tense.

Table 6.1   Varying forms of the present tense

South-west England	East Anglia	Standard English
I loves	I love	I love
you loves	you love	you love
she, he, it loves	she, he, it love	she, he, it, loves
we loves	we love	we love
they loves	they love	they love

(Cheshire and Milroy, 1993, p. 16)

In Chapter 3 (section 3.4), you saw how Old English had a whole series of **inflections**, or verb endings, that changed according to the subject of the verb (distinctions were made between the 'first-person singular subject' (*I*), the 'second-person singular subject' (*you*) and so on). These inflections have been lost, by and large, in modern English but there seem to have been different patterns of development; Cheshire and Milroy (1993, p. 17) comment: 'Because non-standard varieties of English have not been codified, they have sometimes been affected by processes of language change that have not influenced the development of Standard English. In some cases, this means that the rules for the non-standard feature are more regular than the rules for Standard English'.

Other varieties of English also show differences in present-tense verb forms. For instance, in Singapore (as in East Anglia) the third-person marker is not regularly used and is usually absent from colloquial speech. It may be, as John Platt (1991) has suggested, that this is due to the influence of the local languages, Chinese and Malay, which do not mark verbs according to subject. But this process also occurs elsewhere when speakers of other languages learn English, irrespective of whether these other languages themselves mark verbs according to subject.

'Strong' verbs and 'weak' verbs

Strong (or irregular) verbs indicate such things as tense by a change of vowel (e.g. I *sing*, I *sang*, I have *sung*), in contrast to weak (regular) verbs, which add an inflection (I *jump*, I *jumped*, I have *jumped*).

In Old English, strong verbs could have four different forms; for example, *helpan* ('help') had e in the present tense, two past-tense forms (*healp* and *hulpon*), and *holpen* as a 'past participle'. Like many Old English strong verbs, *help* has become regularized in modern English (*help, helped, helped*).

There are also differences in other verb forms. Old English had an extensive system of strong-verb forms, many of which were subsequently lost as the language developed and changed. Many contemporary varieties of English have simpler strong-verb systems than the standard: for instance, nonstandard dialects in Britain have forms such as *I do, I done, I have done;* and *I go, I went, I have went.*

Examples of strong verb forms

Table 6.2 below compares some strong verb forms in Tyneside English, Irish English and the standard variety. The 'base' form is that used in the present tense (e.g. 'I *break* things all the time'); 'past' refers to the past tense ('I *broke* it yesterday'); the 'past participle' is used in constructions such as 'I'm afraid I *have broken* it'. How many of the nonstandard forms have you heard in use?

Table 6.2   Examples of strong verb forms

Tyneside			Irish			Standard		
Base	Past	Past participle	Base	Past	Past participle	Base	Past	Past participle
break	broke	broke	break	broke	broke	break	broke	broken
bite	bit	bit	bite	bit	bit	bite	bit	bitten
go	went	went	go	went	went	go	went	gone
sing	sang	sang	sing	sung	sung	sing	sang	sung
do	done	done	do	done	done	do	did	done
come	come	came	come	come	come	come	came	come
run	run	ran	run	run	run	run	ran	run
beat	beat	beat	beat	beat	beat	beat	beat	beaten
give	give	give	give	give	give	give	gave	given

(Based on Harris, 1993, and McDonald, 1981, cited in Beal, 1993)

Harris (1993, p. 152) suggests that the simplification of the strong verb system was advanced in both literary and vernacular varieties of English by the eighteenth century. It was subsequently reversed, in part, in the standard system but not in nonstandard dialects. Harris (p. 152) compares the Irish English example 'He *would a went* on his own' ('He *would've gone* on his own') with Jane Austen's '... the troubles we *had went* through' (*Sense and Sensibility*).

Viv Edwards (1993) suggests that this process of simplification continues to affect some verb forms in Standard English, with many speakers now unsure of the distinction between 'past tense' and 'past participle' forms such as *drank/drunk* or *swam/swum.*

To have and *to do*: lexical and auxiliary verbs

So far I've focused on the different forms verbs may take, but there are also differences in how verbs are used. Something that has been particularly well documented is the variable use of the verbs *have* and *do*, both of which may function as lexical or auxiliary verbs (see page 226).

Activity 6.1   *(Allow about 10 minutes)*

Which of the following sentences would you normally use, and which seem strange or unlikely?

(a) Have you been there?
  Had you been there?

(b) Have you any money?
  Have you got any money?
  Do you have any money?

(c) Had you any money?
  Had you got any money?
  Did you have any money?

(d) Have you a good time?
  Do you have a good time?

(e) Had you a good time?
  Did you have a good time?

(f) Have you your lunch at home?
  Do you have your lunch at home?

(g) Had you your lunch at home?
  Did you have your lunch at home?

Comment

Compare your intuitions about your own usage with the account, by Arthur Hughes and Peter Trudgill, of British and North American usage quoted below.

Table 6.3   Use of *have* in different standard varieties of English

		1	2	3	4	5
(a)	Have you been there?	I	I	I	I	I
	Had you been there?	I	I	I	I	I
(b)	Have you any money?	I	I	0	0	0
	Have you got any money?	I	I	I	I	0
	Do you have any money?	0	0	0	I	I
(c)	Had you any money?	I	I	0	0	0
	Had you got any money?	I	I	I	I	0
	Did you have any money?	I	I	I	I	I
(d)	Have you a good time?	0	0	0	0	0
	Do you have a good time?	I	I	I	I	I
(e)	Had you a good time?	I	0	0	0	0
	Did you have a good time?	I	I	I	I	I
(f)	Have you your lunch at home?	0	0	0	0	0
	Do you have your lunch at home?	I	I	I	I	I
(g)	Had you your lunch at home?	?	0	0	0	0
	Did you have your lunch at home?	I	I	I	I	I

I = occurs

0 = does not occur

Column 1 gives the usage typical of perhaps most Scottish and Northern Irish speakers; column 2, the usage of many northern (particularly Lancashire, but not Liverpool) and older southern English speakers …; column 3, the colloquial usage of most younger southern English speakers; column 4, the usage of certain younger educated British speakers, particularly in formal styles – which may show American influence; column 5 shows typical North American usage.

(Hughes and Trudgill, 1987, pp. 25–6)

One test frequently used by linguists to determine whether a verb is an auxiliary or a lexical verb is whether it uses the auxiliary *do* to form negative and interrogative constructions. This test can help identify two uses of *have*.

Have *as auxiliary verb*	Have *as lexical verb*	(*compare* own)
she has eaten chips	she has a large house	(she owns ...)
she hasn't eaten chips	she doesn't have a large house	(she doesn't own ...)
has she eaten chips?	does she have a large house?	(does she own ...?)

As you can see from Table 6.3, however, usage varies – in fact the use of *have* is one feature that distinguishes different standard varieties of English; in 'You *had* a good time', for instance, 'had' looks like a lexical verb, but you can see from example (e) in Table 6.3 that in Scotland and Northern Ireland it may behave like an auxiliary (forming an interrogative by changing places with its subject, the pronoun *you*, rather than using the auxiliary verb *do*). Hughes and Trudgill also suggest there are age differences: some forms in some varieties are preferred by younger speakers and others by older speakers.

Chapter 7 discusses how differences between age groups are often taken as indicators of language change.

THE VERB " TO HAVE "

AFFIRMATIVE

Singular.	*Plural*.
I have	we have
you have	you have
he, she, it has	they have

I have a book; you have a book; so we have two books. Tom has a red book; Mary has a blue book. All the students have books. The teacher has a wrist-watch[1]; it is three o'clock by the watch. The classroom has one door and two windows. The windows are open but the door is shut. Tom has a pen to write on the paper. Mary has a pencil to write in the book.

Question.	*Answer*.
Have I a book ?	Yes, you have a book.
Have you a book, Tom ?	Yes, I have a book.
Has Tom a book ?	Yes, he has a book.
Has Mary a book ?	Yes, she has a book.
Have we a classroom ?	Yes, we have a classroom.
Have the two boys books ?	Yes, they have books.

INTERROGATIVE

Singular.	*Plural*.
have I ?	have we ?
have you ?	have you ?
has he ?	have they ?
has she ?	
has it ?	

Figure 6.1   Everything you wanted to know about have
(Eckersley, 1937)

Many nonstandard varieties use different forms for these two functions of *have*. For instance, the form *have* may be used throughout the present tense for the auxiliary verb, whereas *has* is found for the lexical verb.

Do itself doesn't function just as an auxiliary verb. It may also be a lexical verb, as in 'He's *doing* very well in school'. In this case also, some varieties of English use different forms of the verb depending on whether it is functioning as an auxiliary or lexical verb. In several varieties in the UK, (particularly in the south of England) the form *do* is found for the auxiliary verb and *does* for the lexical verb. In Australia, Inner Sydney English includes a further distinction between negative and positive forms, as in 'It *don't* look all that good, *does* it?'

Harris (1993, p. 153) also cites differences in past-tenses forms of *do* in Irish English:

He *done* it

He *didn't* do it

Did he do it?

He broke the window, so he *did* (i.e. not 'so he done')

Tense and aspect

Tense and aspect

The grammatical categories of **tense** and **aspect** are closely related in English.

Tense is used to locate an event or situation in time. While English has two tense forms (a present and a past, as in *play, played*), a wider range of distinctions may be made with the help of auxiliary verbs.

Aspect provides information such as whether an event or situation is continuing, or completed; or whether it's a one-off event as opposed to one that is habitual, or repeated. Standard English has two aspects: the *perfective* (e.g. 'I *have read* the book') and the *progressive* (e.g. 'I *am reading* the book').

Tense and aspect may combine to produce more complex forms (e.g. 'She *had been reading* the book').

Tense and time

> We used to do some queer things then, but we were happy, man, aye, we were happy. Once a rag man says to me … Hey sonny … What? … He says, your hanky's hanging out … hanky… wey, you never had a hanky then. You used to wipe your nose like that, you know. It was my shirt tail hanging out of a hole in my pants … aye he says … your hanky's hanging out.
>
> (Cited in Hughes and Trudgill, 1987, p. 73)

The words above are those of a male speaker from Newcastle on Tyne in the northeast of England. He is using a device that is found very frequently in English: the 'present-tense' form *says* to relate past events in a story. This is often referred to as the historic present – it's an example of the lack of one-to-one correspondence between verb *tenses*, on the one hand, and reference to *time* (past, present and future events) on the other. There are other examples. The present tense may be used for habitual actions, as in 'I *go* to London everyday', or for future time reference 'Your train *leaves* at three o'clock' (*will leave* is also possible).

Some varieties use a construction with *will* when Standard English would prefer the present tense, for instance Indian English 'When you *will arrive*, please visit me' (cited in Trudgill and Hannah, 1994, p. 110).

As far as the past-tense verb form is concerned, as well as indicating simple past time (as in 'I *painted* a picture') it may be used for:

- unreal or hypothetical situations:
  'If you *came* over, we could play chess';

- 'impossible' wishes:
  'I wish I *had* a million pounds';

- reported speech:
  'She said she *loved* me madly'
  (where the words actually spoken would have been 'I *love* you madly').

(Based on Palmer, 1984)

Past time is often signalled by adverbial expressions, such as 'yesterday' or 'two days ago'. In Jamaican English and other varieties based on this (e.g. London Jamaican), the past tense need not be used when there is an adverbial that indicates a reference to past time 'He *walk* home yesterday'.

Other varieties frequently rely on adverbial and other contextual information, rather than the past-tense form, to indicate past time:

It was during that time these people *make* some arrangement ...
[West African English]

Before I always *go* to that market [Malaysian English]

Last time she *come* on Thursday [Singaporean English]
(Cited in Platt et al., 1984, pp. 69–70)

Some of the other languages of the regions in the above examples do not mark verbs for tense, and it's possible that they have influenced the structure of the English variety. Platt et al. (1984) suggest that it is thus 'quite common to "set the scene" by specifying that something took place in the past and then to use all the verbs unmarked for past tense' (p. 70). You may remember this also happened in the Trinidadian Creole extract quoted at the beginning of this chapter.

Lise Winer points out that in Trinidadian Creole whether an unmarked verb form is interpreted as referring to past or present events depends on whether the verb is 'stative' or 'nonstative'.

Stative and nonstative verbs

Stative verbs are those concerned with states of affairs, or perceptual states (such as *believe, like, know, want*), as opposed to *nonstative* or *dynamic* verbs concerned with actions, processes or events.

She contrasts the following examples:

Hayden write di letter (= past)
(Hayden wrote the letter)

Di child want food (= present)
(The child wants food)
(Winer, 1993, p. 22)

Tense and time, then, do not have a very firm relationship in English, and the precise nature of the relationship differs in different varieties: in some 'new Englishes' usage may be influenced by other languages spoken in the area.

Other temporal relationships in English can be indicated by combinations of tense and aspect (which we look at in more detail next). But these also vary considerably between different varieties of English. I give some examples below of variations in what have been termed the 'present perfective' aspect and the 'progressive' aspect.

Aspect: some uses of the 'present perfective'

Present perfective

We can gain an indication of the use of the perfective aspect by focusing on one form, the 'present perfective'. This is the construction made up of *have* plus the 'past participle', for example, 'I *have eaten*'. It is used in 'relating a past event/state to a present time orientation' (Quirk et al, 1985, p. 1992).

Examples from Standard English illustrate this definition. For instance, the present perfective may indicate a state leading up to the present, or an event or series of events leading up to the present:

That house *has been* empty for ages

Have you (ever) *been* to France?

It may indicate the recency of an event:

Have you *heard* the news? The president *has resigned*

or, with certain verbs, that the result of an action still obtains:

My mother *has recovered* from her illness

(All the examples are Standard English usages cited in Quirk et al., 1985, pp. 192–3)

You can gain a sense of the meaning of the present perfective by contrasting it with past-tense forms ('The house *was* empty …'; 'My mother *recovered* …').

The perfective aspect is relatively infrequent in English. Quirk et al. point out that a study of a large (computerized) corpus of English found approximately ten per cent of verb phrases were perfective.

Languages mark perfective aspect in different ways, for instance Table 6.4 shows that Malay and Hokkien Chinese use the forms *sudah* (meaning 'completed', 'finished') and *liáu* (meaning 'finished already'), respectively, to show a completed action.

Table 6.4   *Finish*: Malay and Hokkien Chinese

Malay	saya sudah makan	I have/had eaten
Literal translation	I finish eat	
Hokkien	Goá chiáh pá liáu	I have finished eating
Literal translation	I eat full already	

(Platt et al., 1984, pp. 70–1)

Which of the following sentences do you think you would be most likely to say?

I went to the exhibition last year

I have been to the exhibition last year

Standard English English would tend to use the simple past verb form *went* with time adverbials such as 'last year', but other varieties, including Scottish and Irish English, US and Caribbean English and Indian English, will often use a present perfective form, such as *have been*. On the other hand, Standard English English prefers the present perfect for recently completed events, or with *yet:*

So you*'ve* finally *arrived?*

Have you *bought* one yet?

Contrast this with the following example from American English:

So you finally *arrived*

and another example from Irish English:

Did you *buy* one yet?

In some varieties of English (e.g. Malaysian English, Singaporean English) adverbs may be used to mark aspect:

My father already *pass away*

(contrast *has passed away* in Standard English)

This is similar to the way aspect is marked in Malay and Hokkien.

Irish English marks several different tense and aspect distinctions that correspond roughly to the present perfective in Standard English. A well known example (Harris, 1993, p. 141) is the so-called 'hot-news' perfective:

She's *after selling* the boat

(She's *just sold* the boat)

Harris (1993, p. 141) suggests this construction is almost certainly a straight borrowing from Irish:

Tá sí tréis an bád a dhíol

(Be she after the boat selling)

Harris's full set of 'perfective' forms are illustrated below.

Perfect Irish English forms

Resultative

(= past event with present relevance)

I've it pronounced wrong

(I've pronounced it wrong)

used only with 'transitive' verbs (ie verbs that have a direct object – 'it' in this case).

I'm not too long left

used for 'intransitive' verbs.

Extended now

(= an event that began in the past and persists into the present)

I *know* his family all my life

(I *have known* …)

(Adapted from Harris, 1993, pp. 160–1)

Hot news

(= an event that occurs just before the moment of speaking)

He *is after eating* his dinner

(He's *just eaten* his dinner)

or

He *is after* his dinner.

Indefinite since-time

(= an event occurring in an unspecified period leading up to the present)

I *never saw* a gun in my life nor never saw one fired

(I have *never seen* …)

He argues that, while the hot-news construction can be clearly traced to Irish (Gaelic), the origins of the other four are less easy to determine. They may have parallels in Irish but they are also based on older patterns of English which have now largely disappeared.

The similarities between Irish and English have thus been 'reinforcing' or 'preservative', maintaining the older forms and providing an illustration of the way in which different processes can interact to affect the grammatical construction of a language variety.

Aspect: Variation in the 'progressive'

Progressive aspect

As its name suggests, the 'progressive aspect' … indicates a happening *in progress* at a given time. Compare:

> Simple present: Joan *sings* well.

> Present progressive: Joan *is singing* well.

These two sentences have the same tense, but different aspects. Notice the difference this makes to the meaning: *Joan sings well* refers to Joan's competence as a singer (that she has a good voice – a relatively permanent attribute); *Joan is singing well* refers to her performance on a particular occasion or during a particular season.

(Quirk et al., 1985, p. 197)

Like the perfective, the progressive aspect is also subject to variation. Though slightly more prevalent in the north of England, a widespread feature of nonstandard varieties in the UK is the use of the past participle forms *sat* and *stood* with progressive *be*, where the standard variety would be more likely to have *sitting* and *standing*:

> She *was sat* there
> (She *was sitting* there)

Cheshire et al. (1993) have recorded the use of *sat* and *stood* in both educated spoken and written English and suggest that 'their occurrence in written English points once again to the difficulty of identifying clearly the features that are characteristic of nonstandard English rather than standard English' (p. 71).

There are also differences in the way progressive aspect is used. For instance, its use with 'stative' verbs:

> I *was knowing* it

> I *am believing* it

> I *wasn't liking* it

> I *am having* a cold

would not normally be found in Standard English but this is a normal feature of many other varieties (for example Irish English, Scottish English, Indian English, Singaporean English, East and West African English). Such constructions may sometimes be influenced by other languages spoken alongside English; but they may also be the result of speakers simply 'overextending' the use of progressive aspect to conditions where it wouldn't apply in Standard English.

In their book *A History of the English Language*, Baugh and Cable comment on the relative recency of many aspect forms:

> Where we should say *has been* Shakespeare often says *is: Is execution done on Cawdor?* and *Tis unnatural, Even like the deed that's done*; or *Arthur, whom* [who] *they say is killed tonight*. A very noticeable difference is the scarcity of progressive forms. Polonius asks, *What do you read, my Lord?* – i.e. *What are you reading?*
>
> (Baugh and Cable, 1978, p. 245)

Baugh and Cable chart the history of progressive aspect:

> In Old English such expressions as *he wæs lærende* (he was teaching) are occasionally found, but usually in translations from Latin. In early Middle English, progressive forms are distinctly rare, and although their number increases in the course of the Middle English period, we must credit their development mainly to the period since the sixteenth century. The chief factor in their growth is the use of the participle as a noun governed by the preposition *on* (*he burst out on laughing*). This weakened to *he burst out a-laughing* and finally to *he burst out laughing*. In the same way *he was on laughing* became *he was a-laughing* and *he was laughing*. Today such forms are freely used in all tenses (*is laughing, was laughing, will be laughing*, etc.).
>
> (Baugh and Cable, 1978, p. 291)

'Passive' forms (constructions with *is being* or *was being*) were an even later development:

> In the last years of the eighteenth century we find the first traces of our modern expression *the house is being built*. The combination of *being* with a past participle to form a participle phrase had been in use for some time. Shakespeare says: *which, being kept close, might move more grief to hide* (*Hamlet*). This is thought to have suggested the new verb phrase. The earliest instance of the construction which has been noted is from the year 1769. In 1795 Robert Southey wrote: *a fellow, whose uppermost upper grinder is being torn out by a mutton-fisted barber*. It seems first to have been recognized in an English grammar in 1802. As yet it is generally used only in the present and simple past tense (*is* or *was being built*). We can hardly say *the house has been being built for two years*, and we avoid saying *it will be being built next spring*.
>
> (Baugh and Cable, 1978, p. 292)

Chapter 4 discusses some of the characteristics of Shakespeare's language.

We should not leave this section on English aspectual distinctions without mentioning a distinction which is available to many nonstandard speakers, but not to standard speakers. This is the ability to use verb forms to indicate actions or events that are *habitual* or *repeated*. In Somerset, in the south-west of England, the auxiliary verb *do* is used to indicate habitual events:

> We did come back then and we did have a glass or two of cider, and then we did go and have a bit of breakfast, come out again and then we did have another drink before we did start off.
>
> (Cited in Ihalainen, 1991, p. 154)

Irish English has a similar feature, using *be* or *do be*.

> Even when I be round there with friends I be scared
>
> He never be's sick or anything
>
> He does be late for dinner sometimes
>
> He does plough the field for us
>
> (Harris, 1993, p. 162)

Harris (1993) points out that there is a difference between 'habitual *be*' in 'They *be* shooting and fishing out at the forestry lakes', and progressive aspect 'They *are* shooting and fishing out at the forestry lakes', where the latter, although expressing continuous or incomplete action, fails to express the repetitive nature of these events.

Some other varieties have alternative means of indicating a current habitual action. Speakers of colloquial Singaporean and Malaysian English have the form *use to*

> My mother, she *use to* go to Pulau Tikus market
> (meaning: and still does)
>
> (Platt et al., 1984, p. 71)

So the tense/aspect system in English is not the same for all speakers. Different elements of verb structures are present in different combinations to signify different meanings and are subject to different grammatical constraints. Some of these structures are exclusive to varieties other than Standard English English and they create meanings or shades of meanings which are not available in a similar form in the standard.

Modal auxiliary verbs

Modal auxiliaries in Standard English English

Modal auxiliary verbs are *will, would, can, could, might, shall, should, must, ought to* and marginally *need/dare/used to*.

These express a range of meanings, including volition, prediction, possibility, obligation:

> You *can* read this chapter
>
> You *might* read this chapter
>
> You *will* read this chapter
>
> You *should* read this chapter
>
> You *must* read this chapter

Different meanings can sometimes be ascribed to the same verb form: 'You *can* read this chapter' may either mean that you have permission to read it, or that you have the ability to read it.

The kinds of constructions we have looked at so far have been concerned with actions, events and so on and their relationship to points in time. The modal auxiliaries provide a means for expressing the likelihood or possibility of a state of affairs. There is considerable variation in the use of modal verbs in English.

Even among standard varieties there are different preferences for usage and changes in the system can be observed. We can take the distinction between *will* and *shall* as one example of this. In 1926, H.W. Fowler noted: 'there is an inclination, among those who are not to the manner born, to question the existence, besides denying the need, of distinctions between *shall* and *will*' (Fowler, 1926, p. 526).

Fowler was attempting to maintain a distinction between *shall* and *will*, but he seems to have been fighting a losing battle. Commentators at the time mention the lack of *shall* in Scottish, Irish, 'provincial', and 'extra British' usage. And Fowler himself is able to quote several examples 'from newspapers of the better sort' in which 'one or other principle of its use has been outraged'; for instance:

> But if the re-shuffling of the world goes on producing new 'issues', I *will*, I fear, catch the fever again.
>
>   I am confident that within three years we employers *will* be reaping benefit from it.

(Cited in Fowler, 1926)

(In each case *shall* would be preferred for 'plain future' reference in the first person: that is, after *I* or *we*.)

As well as ongoing change, and different preferences, within Standard English, varieties of English also differ from each other in their use of modal verbs. One or two examples will give a flavour of this:

- In Indian English, *could* and *would* may be found, rather than *can* and *will*, as in 'We hope that you *could* join us'; Trudgill and Hannah argue that *could* and *would* are seen as more tentative and therefore more polite. *May* is also found as the polite form for the expression of obligation: 'These mistakes *may* please be corrected' (= *should be* in Standard English) (Trudgill and Hannah, 1994, p. 109).

- In Standard English, *must* has two main meanings:

  conclusion:
  'You *must* be exhausted' (judging by your appearance)

  obligation:
  'You *must* be at the airport by nine' (or your ticket will be given to a standby passenger)

But the use of *must* is more restricted in Scots/nonstandard Scottish English. It is found for 'conclusion' meanings but *have to* and *need to* are preferred for 'obligation' (Miller, 1993, p. 117). Miller reports that 'even Scottish University undergraduates (and some English ones too!) have no clear intuition about the obligation *must*' (p. 117).

- 'Double modal' constructions, such as 'He *will can* help us tomorrow' are not found in Standard English English. But this example is found in Scottish English and it means 'He will be able to help us tomorrow' (Miller, 1993). Beal (1993) reports similar double modal constructions in Northumberland and Tyneside and they can also be found in the English of the southern USA. Miller suggests that the history of immigration from Scotland to the USA provides a possible link between these two varieties and points therefore to the lengthy history of this nonstandard construction.

Fowler's *Dictionary of Modern English Usage* has been the basis of many prescriptions about 'correct' English. It is discussed further in Chapter 9.

Activity 6.2   *(Reading A)*

Now work through Reading A, 'Modals on Tyneside'. This is an extract from Beal's work on the grammar of Tyneside English, which I have referred to at several points in this chapter. It allows you to look at one variety in a little more detail and see a whole range of ways in which the use of modals within it differs from that of Standard English.

Asking questions

I mentioned earlier that auxiliary verbs inverted, or changed places with their subject noun phrase to form a question, whereas for lexical verbs auxiliary *do* was 'imported' to fulfil this function. The verbs *have* and *be* are unusual in that they can change places with their subject even when they don't appear to be acting as auxiliaries.

Some interrogative or question structures in Standard English English

Shona can play the piano	Can Shona play the piano?
Shona has played the piano	Has Shona played the piano?
Shona is playing the piano	Is Shona playing the piano?
Shona plays the piano	Does Shona play the piano?
You have some money	Have you any money?
The world is flat	Is the world flat?

It is usual in the grammar of Standard English English for inversion to occur only in a 'direct question', such as those above, and not in an indirect question such as 'She wants to know whether the world is flat'

But question formation differs in different varieties of English. For instance, in some (including Irish, Scottish and Tyneside English) subject–verb inversion is allowed in indirect questions to produce constructions such as the following (from Tyneside) 'When he discovered I wasn't at school he wanted to know *what was the matter*' (cited in Beal, 1993, p. 204) where Standard English would have *what the matter was*. In the Indian English recorded by Platt et al. (1984, p. 127) direct and indirect questions could follow the opposite pattern from Standard English English, with direct questions such as 'What *you would like* to eat?' and an indirect question such as 'I asked Hari where *does he work*'.

The Trinidadian Creole example quoted earlier illustrates a further case in which there is no inversion between the auxiliary verb and subject, where there would be in Standard English: 'So she say if money eh no problem, why we mus' go an' borrow from foreigners'.

Another type of question that is particularly prone to variation is the 'tag question'. This is the question structure tagged on to the end of a main clause, as in 'You are staying, *aren't you?*'.

Activity 6.3   *(Allow 10 minutes)*

Can you see any pattern in the way the following tag questions are constructed; for instance, how does the verb in the tag relate to that in the main clause? Which examples do you think you might hear from other speakers in the area where you live? Which do you think you might use?

1   So that's your little game, is it?
2   Are you still working at Woolies, are you?
3   She has gone home, is it?
4   You did see it, didn't you?
5   She can come, can she not?
6   She can come, can't she?
7   You're going tomorrow, isn't it?
8   You didn't see it, did you?
9   She can't come, can she not?
10 She can't come, can't she not?
11 He isn't going there, isn't it?

(Examples from Milroy and Milroy, 1993; Trudgill and Hannah, 1994; Platt et al., 1984)

Comment

Standard English English has quite a limited range of tag constructions in comparison with some nonstandard varieties and quite a complex one in comparison with others. Questions (4) and (8) exemplify the most common structure in standard English: (4) with a positive main clause and a negative tag predicts the answer *yes*; (8) with a negative main clause and a positive tag predicts the answer *no*. (Of course this is simplifying the situation somewhat since patterns of intonation will also affect how these utterances are interpreted.) A less common construction for Standard English English is (1), where a positive tag question appears with a positive main clause (Quirk and Greenbaum (1973) suggest that this type of construction may imply suspicion or sarcasm). In all cases the verbs in the tag question (*did* and *is*) echo the auxiliary *do* or the verb *be* in the main clause.

Item (2), in which a positive main clause (a question) occurs with a positive tag, is a Scottish English construction not found in Standard English English. It also expects the answer *yes*. This construction is also found in Tyneside English.

Lines (5), (6), (9) and (10) come from Tyneside English ((6) would also be found in Standard English) and the relationship between them is complex. Beal (1993) suggests that in the case of (5) and (9), the speaker is requesting information. With (6) and (10), the speaker is asking for confirmation (presumably of something already known or suspected).

Questions (3), (7) and (11) exemplify 'invariant tags': that is, the form of the tag remains the same (*is it* or *isn't it*) regardless of the auxiliary used in the main clause. This construction occurs in several varieties, including Welsh, Indian, West African and Malaysian and Singaporean English. Both positive and negative tags are free to appear in combination with either a positive or a negative main clause, to seek information or confirmation. The examples above are by no means exhaustive. Other invariant tags include *not so* ('He loves you, *not so?*') and *no* ('You sent there yesterday, *no?*'). The invariant tag is the same as that found in several other languages, including Hindi and Urdu *na?* and French *n'est-ce pas?*

There are several aspects of the verb phrase that are subject to variation in English. I have tried to give an indication of the kinds of feature that vary, and the different forms these features may take. I have also mentioned some explanations offered by linguists for such variation: for instance, the suggestion that nonstandard varieties sometimes continue developments that have been slowed down by standardization; and that other languages spoken in a particular region may affect the variety of English that is spoken there.

6.4   THE NOUN PHRASE

The extract from Trinidadian Creole quoted in section 6.1 illustrated one highly variable feature of English grammar: the pronoun system. I look further at this, but first I consider another aspect of the noun phrase that has been studied by linguists interested in variation: the use of determiners.

Determiners

Activity 6.4   *(Allow about 5 minutes)*

Look at the list of sentences below. Which do you think you might use and which would not be possible in your variety? Are there any differences in meaning between the sentences in each group?

1   (a)   She is an engineer
      (b)   She is the engineer
      (c)   She is engineer

2   (a)   She likes butter
      (b)   She likes the butter

3   (a)   They are on their way to the church
      (b)   They are on their way to church

4   (a)   They are on their way to the bank
      (b)   They are on their way to bank

My comments follow.

The determiners illustrated in Activity 6.4 are the 'definite article' (*the*) and the 'indefinite article' (*a* or *an*). Use of the articles is fairly complex: it's one of the things learners of English as a foreign language often find difficult, and it also varies between different varieties of English.

The indefinite article *a* (or *an*) is often used on first reference to someone or something, so 'she is an engineer' may highlight *engineer* as something new (i.e. information that hasn't already been referred to) and a point of interest. *The*, on the other hand, refers to something definite: in this case, a particular engineer who has probably already been referred to.

Usage varies, however. For instance, in some varieties *the* is found for indefinite reference, such as in this example from Irish English 'He's *the* quare singer' ('He's a remarkable singer') while the English of West Africa, India or Singapore may have no article 'He is teacher'.

In this case, other languages spoken in the region may influence the English construction. For instance, Platt (1991) suggests that Chinese and Malay may have an influence on this kind of structure in the case of Singaporean English, since these languages do not have the same kind of definite/indefinite system as that found in Standard English English.

'Butter' in (2a) would be termed a 'non-count noun' with 'generic' reference: it denotes something viewed as an inseparable whole; it would not be used in this sense in the plural form (compare 'She likes literature' or 'She likes music'). It is 'generic' in that it refers to butter in general. In this case, it would not be used in Standard English with the definite article. So (2b) means something rather different: it refers to some particular butter, rather than butter in general. Here again, however, usages varies. For instance, both Irish and Scottish English may use the definite article for non-count nouns with generic reference, as in 'He has *the measles*' and 'He's a terrible man for *the drink*'.

Non-count nouns themselves differ in different varieties. For example, *furniture* would normally be a non-count noun in Standard English. But in the English of India and Ghana, *furniture* appears as a 'count noun' (like *tomato*, or *chair*). So forms such as *a furniture* and *furnitures* are found (Ahulu, 1994).

The construction in (3b) seems to refer to the institution embodied in the noun *church* rather than to a specific church (contrast (3a)). This construction is possible for certain other nouns, for example, 'She is in hospital'.

But Scottish English, along with American English, uses the definite article (*the church, the hospital*) with this 'institutional' meaning. The English of West Africa and India, on the other hand, sometimes applies the 'institutional' meaning to a wider range of institutions, such as *bank* (as in (4b)).

Definitely Scottish

A well known characteristic of Scottish English is the use of *the* with nouns denoting institutions, certain illnesses, certain periods of time and with quantifiers such as *both* and *all*.

(a)   the day [= today], the morn [= tomorrow], the now [= now]

(b)   She has the hiccoughs/the shivers/the 'flu/the measles/the chickenpox.

(c)   They are at the kirk [= at church] at the school/in the jail/in the hospital/at the college.

(d)   in the house [= at home], through the post [= by post], up the stair [= upstairs], down the stair, over the phone [= by phone]

(e)   The bouncer throws the both of them out.

(f)   Cathy helps Trisha ... and the both of them get on really good.

(g)   The hale three of them's back on it [= the whole three, all three].

Phrases such as *at the school* and *in the hospital* do not necessarily refer to a specific school or hospital as they would in standard English but are equivalent to *in school* and *in hospital*.

(Miller, 1993, p. 289)

Pronouns

Pronoun systems are interesting: there are both striking similarities and differences between languages, and within English itself; and pronoun sets and their uses also exhibit a good deal of variation.

Pronouns are often thought of as a category of word which 'stands for' (*pro*), or refers to, a noun:

> Where's *Jenny?*
>
> *She* (= Jenny) is in the kitchen

Strictly speaking, however, *she* is referring back to a noun phrase here – and, as you saw above, noun phrases can be far more complex:

> Where's the flying elephant with the big pink floppy ears?
>
> *She* (= the flying elephant with big pink floppy ears) is in the kitchen

Pronouns can also replace entire clauses, as in:

> The flying elephant with the big pink floppy ears is cooking the dinner
>
> I don't believe *it* (= the flying elephant with the big pink floppy ears is cooking the dinner)

There are different types of pronoun in English; for example:

- possessive:
  'This book is *mine*'

and

- reflexive:
  'Jenny kicked *herself* for making the same mistake again'

Pronouns are also the only word class in English where there is a remnant of case marking: in standard English, the personal pronoun system has subject pronouns (*I* like Jo) and non-subject pronouns (Jo likes *me,* Jo gave the book to *me*).

Pronouns may refer to noun phrases (and other constituents) within a text, but they also have a 'deictic' function: they can refer to 'spatial, temporal, social or personal aspects of a situation' (Mühlhäusler and Harré, 1990, p. 9), that is, to the real world rather than just the linguistic context. Pronouns may be purely deictic, as in the following dialogue:

> A   I've got to go home
> B   What is it?
> C   My daughter's locked herself out

Here *it* refers to some problem or issue that, B assumes, must be behind A's need to go home. The 'spoof' film *Airplane* uses the textual and deictic aspects of pronoun reference to good effect with jokes along the lines of:

> A   This woman has to be gotten to a hospital
> B   What is it?
> C   It's a large building with doctors and nurses in it

The notion of 'case' is discussed in Chapter 3.

Pronoun systems may contain different numbers and types of pronoun. This allows them to make different distinctions in terms of who or what they refer to. Table 6.5, for example, compares the subject and non-subject pronouns found among certain speakers on Tyneside and in Standard English.

Table 6.5 Personal pronouns in Tyneside English and Standard English English

Person		Tyneside		Standard	
		Subject	Non-subject	Subject	Non-subject
Singular	1st	I	us	I	me
	2nd	ye	you	you	you
	3rd	she	her	she	her
		he	him	he	him
		it	it	it	it
Plural	1st	us	we	we	us
	2nd	yous	yous/yees	you	you
	3rd	they	them	they	them

(Adapted from Beal, 1993, p. 205)

❖ ❖ ❖ ❖ ❖

Activity 6.5 *(Allow 5–10 minutes)*

Using the data in Table 6.5, compare the personal pronouns found in Tyneside English with those found in Standard English English. What differences are there between the two sets of pronouns?
My comments follow.

❖ ❖ ❖ ❖ ❖

Although the pronoun system found among certain Tyneside speakers is distinctive, it does share some patterns with other nonstandard dialects. For example, the use of *us* rather than *me* as a first-person 'non-subject' pronoun (as in 'Give *us* a kiss') is found in several other varieties. Tyneside English carries this usage further with its plural pronouns. Forms such as: '*Us*'ll do it' and 'They beat *we* four nil!' have been found in Tyneside English, effectively reversing the 'subject' and 'non-subject' pronoun forms found in Standard English.

This correspondence between nonstandard 'subject' pronouns and standard 'non-subject' pronouns is not uncommon. There was an example in the Trinidadian Creole cited at the beginning of this chapter: 'She does always follow wha' she granmudder used to tell *she*', and the following examples come from London Jamaican (cited in Sebba, 1993, p.16), and Somerset (cited in Ihalainen, 1991, p. 106) respectively:

> Me was trodding down de road and me come across me bredder 'e – me ask 'im for some money an 'e na got.
> You got to take he right out of your herd. You got to send he in, have'm slaughtered. He is no good.

Me in London Jamaican and *she* in Trinidad English-based Creole may be found in both subject and non-subject positions (so the distinction made in standard English is absent here).

It has been claimed that, in dialects such as Somerset, the use of pronouns such as *he* in non-subject position is reserved for emphasis. Ihalainen, however, suggests that in his data this usage is 'quite frequent and in casual speech almost the rule' (1991, p. 106).

A further area of comparison is that of the second-person pronouns, singular and plural. You may remember from Chapter 4 that English originally had a distinction between singular *thou* and plural *you*, which has since been lost in the standard variety. Some traditional dialects of English have retained singular *thou*, but many other varieties have filled the gap with an alternative plural form *yous*. The distinction between *you* and *yous* is present in areas of north-east and north-west England, Scotland, Northern and Southern Ireland, parts of North America and Australia. This enables a distinction to be made which is absent in Standard English. Milroy and Milroy quote an informant from Belfast:

> So I said to our Trish and our Sandra: 'Yous wash the dishes'. I might as well have said: 'You wash the dishes', for our Trish just got up and put her coat on and went out.

(Milroy and Milroy, 1985, p. 25)

In the southern states of America, the plural may be made with *y'all* to distinguish it from the singular *you*.

Many languages use the plural forms of pronouns as a 'polite' form of address when referring to only one person, a possibility that has been lost in Standard English (contrast French where *vous* functions as both plural and a 'polite' form, indicating social distance). Mühlhäusler and Harré (1990, p.132) suggest that the following factors influence pronoun choice where a polite form is available: 'rank, status, office, generation, formality, informality, public discourse, private discourse, intimacy, social distance, high degree of emotional excitement'.

They compare Japanese with English. Japanese possesses a complex system of honorific terms of address which reflect the social system. Unlike English, speakers are constrained to make social distinctions by pronoun choice and such social distinctions are encoded in the grammar of the language.

Examples of different pronouns forms in Japanese

A wide range of pronoun forms is used. Among the first-person forms, we find:

watakushi	very formal male; less formal female
watashi	formal male; neutral female
atakushi	rare male; snobbish female
atashi	chiefly female, colloquial
washi	dialectal, chiefly male, older generation
boku	exclusively male, proscribed in talking to superiors
ore	colloquial male

Among the second-person forms, we find:

anata	standard, polite, not used to superiors
anta	informal
sochira	polite, very formal
kimi	chiefly men to men of equal or lower status
omae	informal, colloquial, somewhat pejorative
kisama and *temē*	derogatory, very impolite

(Crystal, 1987, p. 99)

Reasons for the loss of asymmetrical forms of address in English are socially complex; see Chapter 4.

Such comparisons provide an interesting example of the distinction between a linguistic resource and a grammatical constraint. Although the polite form of the pronoun is largely lost in English, status can be signalled in other ways if a speaker so chooses (for example, by adding other forms of address such as 'madam' or 'sir'). But the issue can also be 'fudged' because the term *you* is neutral – there is no other pronoun choice. In Japanese, on the other hand, even use of the most neutral term in the pronoun set signals social meaning since one form has been *chosen* at the expense of another (more or less polite) form. Mühlhäusler and Harré further suggest that 'native speakers of English can adjust to a more rapid process of social change than can speakers of languages in which the overlap between social conventions and rules of grammar is more extensive' (1990, p. 143).

A further distinction is possible in certain varieties of English, between what is termed 'inclusive' and 'exclusive' reference. For instance, if a colleague said to you 'We are responsible for the latest mistake', several interpretations are possible. The people responsible could, in principle, be your colleague and you; your colleague, you and some other(s); or your colleague and some others but not you (in practice, it would probably be clear from the context who was responsible). But languages such as Ojibwa, spoken in North America, would leave no doubt. Ojibwa has different forms of pronouns according to who is included: *ninuwi*, for instance, means 'he and I', and *kinuwi* means 'you, he and I' (Robins, 1989). Australian Creole, spoken by some Aboriginal speakers, has a similar distinction between 'inclusive' and 'exclusive' *we* reflecting the structure of Aboriginal languages; while Fijian English distinguishes between *us two* (termed a dual-inclusive form) and *us gang* (corresponding to other uses of *we*) (see Siegel, 1991). It is of course possible to signify more exact reference in other varieties of English, as in the famous opening line of the three witches in *Macbeth*, 'When shall we three meet again', but it is not a grammatical requirement to do so.

Pronoun systems, then, show considerable variation and the differences between them are quite complex. I have tried to give a flavour of this and also suggested possible origins of such variation. In some cases, varieties of English have retained older pronoun forms which have been lost in Standard English; in others, varieties have fewer distinct pronoun forms than Standard English, probably continuing the process of regularization; but it's also possible for varieties to create new distinctions, some of which may be based on the structure of other local languages.

❖ ❖ ❖ ❖ ❖

Activity 6.6 *(Reading B)*

You may remember from Chapter 5 (section 5.6) that **pidgin** languages are often said to have simplified grammars. But the terms 'simple' and 'simplification' are in themselves problematic, partly because their usage has been imprecise and partly because they may have connotations of 'naivety'. In describing pidgin languages, 'simplification' is now primarily used to denote the increasing regularity of the grammatical system, but the term may be used differently by different writers. Simplification is, in any case, not always easy to assess.

You should now read 'Bislama Pronouns' (Reading B). In this reading, Jeff Siegel uses the terms 'simple' and 'complex' in relation to the number of distinctions available in the pronoun system of an English-based pidgin, Bislama, spoken in Vanuatu in the South Pacific (Siegel refers to English as the 'lexifier language' for Bislama). In comparison with Standard English, Bislama has fewer distinctions in one area of the pronoun system and more distinctions in another. As the pronoun system indicates, Bislama is very different from Standard English, and is commonly regarded as a distinct language.

This reading also allows you to review many of the grammatical distinctions discussed in this section.

❖ ❖ ❖ ❖ ❖

Chapter 5 discussed the development of pidgins and creoles.

Bislama in Vanuatu

The constitution of Vanuatu states: Lanwis blong Ripablik blong Vanuatu, hemia Bislama. Trifala lanwis blong mekem ol wok blong kantri ya, i gat Bislama mo Inglis mo Franis – The language of the Republic of Vanuatu is Bislama. There are three languages for conducting the business of the country, Bislama, English and French.

(McArthur, 1992, p. 131)

6.5   SENTENCE STRUCTURE

So far, we have looked at some of the kinds of variation that exist at phrase level; that is, at aspects of the verb phrase (constructions involving auxiliary and lexical verbs) and noun phrase (determiners and pronouns). But I mentioned earlier that variation also occurs at clause or sentence level: in the way words, phrases and clauses are put together.

Subjects, verbs and objects

English is often described as a **subject-verb-object** (**SVO**) language, in that the usual (or 'unmarked') sequence in a sentence follows this order:

S	V	O
My aunty	caught	the flu
The toad	ate	the fly
The elephant	cooked	the dinner

There are six possible subject, verb and object combinations: SVO, SOV, VSO, VOS, OSV, OVS. In practice, however, most languages follow either the SVO or the SOV construction.

While SVO is the usual sentence construction in English, other constructions are possible. To mark emphasis, subject and verb can be inverted as in the following VSO constructions:

Was he angry!

Am I bored!

And set expressions such as:

Here comes Jo

regularly place the subject after the verb.

Consider the following sentence pairs:

1   (a)   There are fairies at the bottom of my garden

   (b)   Fairies are at the bottom of my garden

2   (a)   There's a fly in my soup

   (b)   A fly is in my soup

Sentences (1a) and (2a) practically have the status of clichés, but they also illustrate something about how English works. It is frequently the case in English that the subject of a sentence contains 'given' information; that is, information already known from preceding sentences, or from the immediate context, or from shared knowledge. The rest of the sentence gives 'new' information. While (1b) and (2b) are perfectly grammatical, they may seem a bit awkward. It would be unusal to place a word or phrase such as 'Fairies' or 'A fly', which look as if they are providing new information, in a position where definite or given information is expected. The use of *there*, as a 'dummy subject', avoids this awkwardness.

There may appear with a singular verb (*there is*) or a plural verb (*there are*) depending on whether the 'notional' subject is singular or plural. But there are no hard and fast rules about this.

Many varieties of English have the singular form of verb regardless of the status of the notional subject:

There'*s* fairies at the bottom of my garden

There *was* five of us there

A prescriptive grammar would deem this feature unacceptable, but it is difficult to term it 'nonstandard' since it is an attested part of the informal speech of educated English speakers, often used as the yardstick for defining standard spoken English. It serves as a further illustration – recall 'was sat' (p. 235) – of how problematical defining 'standard' versus 'nonstandard' English really is.

Another type of dummy subject can be seen in *it* constructions, such as:

It is raining

It's time to go.

Dummy *it* and *there* are necessary in English because English favours subject–verb constructions, and declarative sentences without a subject are not normally grammatical. Not all languages follow this rule. Italian, for instance, can produce sentences like:

Piove

E pericoloso sporgersi

which literally translated become:

*Is raining

*Is dangerous to lean out

Asterisks (*) denote sentences regarded as ungrammatical or that are not found.

Pro-drop Languages

Italian can appear without pronoun subjects in cases other than dummy *it* and *there*. It has been referred to as a 'pro-drop' language. Such languages typically have a richly inflected verb system where person is indicated by the verb ending. In Italian, it is possible to say *lui parla* ('he speaks') but more usual to say simply *parla*. The corresponding English translation 'speaks' is not generally possible.

However, there are exceptions to be found in the 'new' Englishes; Platt et al. give the following examples (1984, p. 117):

Here is not allowed to stop the car [Hong Kong]

Is very nice food [Uganda]

No. Is not the same [Nigeria]

Is not very interesting, this programme [Malaysia]

Platt et al. suggest that for some varieties of English, this construction may result from the influence of background languages which do not require a 'dummy'.

There are several constructions that may be used in English to make part of a sentence more prominent. For instance, consider these two sentences:

(a)   Jo loves fish

(b)   It is fish that Jo loves

Sentence (b) is an example of '*it*-clefting': it is a means of marking the focus of information ('it is fish'). It appears more in written English and less in spoken, where patterns of stress and intonation are more likely to be used to change focal prominence. At least that is the case in Standard English English. In Irish English, clefting features much more frequently. Filppula (1991) and Harris (1991a) make several comparisons between Irish (Gaelic) constructions, and the Irish English preference for cleft constructions.

They argue, first, that some features of English which might be used to highlight elements in a sentence, such as intonation or change of word order, are not possible in Irish. However, there does exist in Irish a construction similar to the English cleft sentence which is its principal means of marking information focus. A second (related) point is that the range of constituents which can be placed in focal position is wider in Irish English than in Standard English English, corresponding with the range to be found in Irish. So, for example, the cleft construction:

It's looking for more land a lot of them are

(compare: A lot of them are looking for more land)

is acceptable in Irish English, but would not be acceptable in other English varieties (see Filppula, 1991).

A third point in the argument is that the range of functions which the Irish English cleft sentence serves is wider than that of English English, and in line with those found in Irish. It seems plausible, then, that it is the influence from Irish which leads Irish English speakers to have a preference for the cleft construction and so use it more frequently. Furthermore, Filppula's data suggest that Irish English clefting occurs more often in areas where the influence of Irish is stronger and more recent – as in the counties of Kerry and Clare – and less often where influence is weaker and less recent – as in Dublin, where there are no longer any native speakers (Filppula, 1991). This feature of Irish English provides an ideal illustration of the kinds of influences that may come from background languages during the spread of English into a region.

Activity 6.7   *(Reading C)*

Now read 'Sentence structure in Irish English' by John Harris (Reading C). He discusses further examples of *it*-clefting, and also 'left-dislocation' (when a constituent of a sentence is moved, from its expected position, to the left or towards the front of the sentence).

Note that terms such as *it*-clefting and left-dislocation suggest that some sort of process has taken place. The implication is that there is a 'normal', or unmarked, word order which has been disrupted. These terms (like many recent grammatical terms) may also seem unfamiliar or even exotic, but the meaning will be clear if you look at Harris's examples first and then at the surrounding discussion.

6.6   CONCLUSION

In this chapter we have looked at just a few aspects of English grammar, focusing on grammatical features that have been found to vary between different varieties of English. I conceded at the outset that, as earlier chapters have shown, there are not really discrete varieties of English. There is a great deal of overlap between them, but studies of language variation tend to focus on differences and how these may have come about.

I pointed out that standardized varieties of language tend to show only limited variation, and that most studies of variation have been based on nonstandard varieties. I also suggested that the boundary between 'standard' and 'nonstandard' is by no means clear – I mentioned some features that are identified as nonstandard but that are also used regularly by 'educated' speakers.

There are several reasons – social, linguistic, historical, geographical – for the wealth of diversity and variation in English. Many of these are discussed in previous chapters and this discussion continues here. In the constructions looked at, some were the result of different patterns of development (for instance, certain linguistic features may be retained in a nonstandard variety long after they have ceased to exist in Standard English – the singular and 'familiar' pronoun *thou* is an example); alternatively, a nonstandard variety may have continued a process of change that has become 'frozen' or slowed down by standardization (such as the loss of inflections in the present tense of verbs).

Migration patterns also affect the distribution of different forms of English. I mentioned that the presence of 'double modals' in parts of the USA could be traced back to a Scottish influence.

In some cases, English has been affected by other languages with which it has come into contact (and sometimes supplanted): for instance, Irish English shows the influence of Irish (Gaelic); while many 'new Englishes', such as Indian English or Singaporean English, have incorporated features from other languages spoken in the region.

Another process which affects variation is that of analogy, or overextension of a particular construction (I suggested that constructions such as 'I *was knowing* it' could result from the overextension of 'progressive aspect' to conditions where it wouldn't occur in Standard English).

Sometimes the same feature occurs in different varieties for different reasons; the absence of the third-person -*s* form in the present tense of verbs is probably due to the influence of other languages in Singapore, but to the process of inflection loss in some dialects in England. But we can't always be certain about the origins of grammatical constructions. The use of progressive aspect with verbs such as *know* may be an overextension, but one that has been influenced by local languages; and some of the different 'perfective' forms found in Irish English may derive from older forms of English that have been reinforced by the influence of Irish.

The grammars of different varieties of English make different sets of distinctions: there are different tense and aspect relations in different Englishes, and pronoun systems also distinguish different sets of people and relationships. Pronouns provided us with a good example of the difference between a linguistic resource and a grammatical constraint: where a language variety does not make certain distinctions in its pronoun system, there are plenty of linguistic resources available to make the distinctions in alternative ways (the use of titles may substitute for 'polite' pronoun forms). But the absence of distinctions that are encoded in the language also allows speakers to fudge the issue.

At the beginning of this chapter I mentioned two important points for those studying different varieties of English: not everyone in a geographical area speaks in the same way, and the same person will use different forms of language on different occasions. Linguists interested in grammatical variation have sometimes looked at patterns of use across different social groups in the same region. Various models of social variation have been established, such as the notion of a continuum of varieties running from Standard English through to a localized vernacular. Linguists have also studied variation in the grammar of individual speakers. But a problem sometimes encountered is the relative infrequency of some grammatical constructions, which may make it difficult to investigate general social patterns. Several major studies of social and contextual variation have focused on pronunciation features. We therefore look at these topics in detail in the next chapter, in relation to accents of English. Chapter 8 examines further the use of different varieties of English in different contexts.

Reading A
MODALS ON TYNESIDE

Joan Beal

The use and nature of modal verbs in Tyneside is markedly different from that of Standard English in several important ways.

First, *may* and *shall* are hardly ever used in Tyneside English (as also in Scots English), and have no important part to play in the grammar. As in many other nonstandard dialects, *can* is used rather than *may* to express permission, but in Tyneside, even the sense of possibility normally expressed by *may* is carried by *might* instead, as in

> Mind, it looks as though it might rain, doesn't it?

> (McDonald, 1981, p. 284)

There is, therefore, no strictly grammatical need for *may* in Tyneside, as it has no function that cannot equally well be performed by *can* or *might*. If it is used at all, it is as an ultra-polite and formal stylistic variant of *can*. *Shall*, likewise, rarely occurs in Tyneside: for the expression of futurity, *will* or *'ll* are used. This is also true of most dialects of English, where *will* varies with *shall* even in standardized varieties. However, in most dialects, *shall* is used in first person questions, such as 'Shall I put the kettle on?' In Tyneside, as in Scots and Irish English, *will* is used even here, thus 'Will I put the kettle on?'

Secondly, there is a rule of Standard English that only one modal verb can appear in a single verb phrase. Thus 'He must do it' is grammatical whilst '*He must can do it' is not. Indeed, Standard English has developed a whole battery of 'quasi-modal' verbs to 'stand in' for modals where the meaning requires them but the above rule forbids them. The meaning of the sentence would therefore be expressed in Standard English as 'He must be able to do it'.

> The asterisk (*) is a convention used by linguists to denote a sentence which is ungrammatical [or not found].

In Tyneside English, the rule inhibiting double modals does not apply so long as the second modal is *can* or *could*. Thus the asterisked sentence would conform to the rules of Tyneside English. These double modals are also found in Scots and some American dialects, but more combinations of modals are allowed in these dialects than in Tyneside. Furthermore, more combinations are allowed in the dialects of rural Northumberland than in those of urban Tyneside. For instance, the combination of *would* and *could* appears in the urban area – but only in a negative form – whilst in rural Northumberland the positive form may be found. Examples from McDonald (1981, pp. 186–7) are:

(1) I can't play on Friday. I work late. I *might could* get it changed, though.

(2) The girls usually make me some (toasted sandwiches) but they *mustn't could have* made any today.

(3) He *wouldn't could've* worked, even if you had asked him.
    (Tyneside)

(4) A good machine clipper *would could* do it in half a day.
    (Northumberland)

Thirdly, in Standard English, certain adverbs are placed *before* main verbs but *after* modals, thus 'I only asked' and 'I can only ask'. In Tyneside English, adverbs may be placed before *can* and *could*. Examples from McDonald (1981, p. 214) are:

(1) That's what I say to people. If they only could walk a little bit, they should thank God.

(2) She just can reach the gate.

Fourthly, in Tyneside, as in other nonstandard dialects of English, *can* and *could* are used in perfective constructions where Standard English has *be able to*:

(1) He cannot get a job since he's left school.

(2) I says it's a bit of a disappointment, nurse. I thought I could've brought it back again.

(McDonald 1981, pp. 215–6)

These sentences could be 'translated' into Standard English respectively as:

(1) He has not been able to get a job since he left school

(2) I thought I would have been able to bring it back again

Fifthly, there are several cases in which a modal or quasi-modal verb has a meaning in Tyneside different from its Standard English meaning or where a different modal is used to express the same meaning. It is important for the outsider to be aware of these differences; after all a double modal immediately strikes a non-Tynesider as odd, and alerts him to the need for careful interpretation, but where a familiar syntactic structure has a different meaning, it may turn out to be a 'false friend'. For example, in a sentence with the meaning 'the evidence forces me to conclude that ... not', Standard English would use *can't*, whilst Tyneside would use *mustn't*. Thus:

The lift can't be working (Standard)

The lift mustn't be working (Tyneside)

...

On the other hand, where Standard English uses *mustn't* to mean 'it is necessary not to ... ', Tyneside uses *haven't got to*. Here, misunderstandings could easily arise: a Tynesider saying:

You haven't got to do that!

means, not that you are not obliged to do it, but that you are obliged *not* to do it!

References

McDONALD, C. (1981) 'Variation in the Use of Modal Verbs with Special Reference to Tyneside English', unpublished PhD thesis, University of Newcastle.

Source: Beal, 1993, pp. 194–7

Reading B
BISLAMA PRONOUNS

Jeff Siegel

One commonly cited feature of pidgin languages is that they are 'simplified' or 'reduced' in comparison with their lexifiers. The lexifier is the language that has provided most of the lexicon, or vocabulary, to the pidgin; for example, English is the lexifier for varieties of pidgin English. If we compare a pidgin with its lexifier in an area of grammar, we would expect to find simplification involving a reduced number of grammatical distinctions, and therefore a smaller number of grammatical forms needed to mark these distinctions.

A typical example is found in the pronoun system of Cameroon Pidgin English (CP) (Todd 1984, p. 7), a variety of West African Pidgin English, spoken in Ghana, Nigeria and Cameroon. The CP pronoun system, unlike that of English, does not make distinctions in gender and case. So, while Standard English has separate pronouns for female, male and neuter third-person subjects – *she, he* and *it* – CP has only *i*, which can mean 'she', 'he' or 'it' according to the context. And while Standard English has separate pronouns for different cases – for example, *they, them* and *their* in third-person plural – CP normally uses only one form, *dem*.

At first glance, simplification can also be found in the pronoun system of Bislama, a dialect of Melanesian Pidgin, spoken in the South Pacific country of Vanuatu. (The other dialects of Melanesian Pidgin are Tok Pisin, spoken in Papua New Guinea, and Pijin, spoken in the Solomon Islands.) As in CP, gender is not distinguished in Bislama; the pronoun *hem* (or sometimes *em*) can mean 'she', 'he' and 'it'. So the sentence

Hem i stap long haos

can have three different meanings, depending on the context:

He's in the house

She's in the house

It's in the house

Also, case is not distinguished; *olgeta* is used for 'they', 'them' and 'their', as in the following sentences:

Olgeta oli save ple ragbi	They can play rugby
Mi bin singaotem *olgeta*	I called them
Haos blong *olgeta* i bon finis	Their house has burned down

So it seems that Bislama has a pronoun system which is 'simpler' than that of Standard English. However, this is not the full story. The pronoun system of Bislama makes some other distinctions that are not made in English. For example, while Standard English has only one second-person pronoun, *you*, which can be either singular or plural, Bislama has four different second-person pronouns: *yu* (singular 'you'), *yutufala* (dual 'you two'), *yutrifala* (trial 'you three'), and *yufala* (plural 'you all'). Thus Bislama pronouns make a four-way distinction in number – singular, dual, trial and plural – while Standard English pronouns sometimes make no distinction, as with *you*, or at the most only a two-way distinction – singular and plural – as with *I* versus *we*.

Bislama also makes another distinction not found in English with regard to 'inclusiveness'. It has two sets of first-person non-singular pronouns, 'inclusive' versus 'exclusive', all corresponding to English *we*. Whereas the sentence:

The girls said to Miriam 'Fred invited us to the party!'

could have two possible meanings in English:

1   Fred invited us (including you) to the party

2   Fred invited us (but not you) to the party

in Bislama there would be no such confusion. There is a first-person inclusive plural pronoun *yumi* ('we or us, including you') and a first-person-exclusive plural pronoun *mifala* ('we or us, not including you'). So the two meanings would be expressed in Bislama in different ways:

1   Fred i bin singaotem *yumi* long lafet

2   Fred i bin singaotem *mifala* long lafet

Here is a chart of all the pronouns found in Bislama:

	Singular	Dual	Trial	Plural
1st person inclusive		yumitu(fala)	yumitrifala	yumi
1st person exclusive	mi	mitufala	mitrifala	mifala
2nd person	yu	yutufala	yutrifala	yufala
3rd person	hem/em	tufala	trifala	olgeta

So, while it is true that the Bislama pronoun system is simpler than that of English in its lack of gender and case distinctions, at the same time it is more complex in its inclusiveness and number distinctions. Simplification is not straightforward; one language may be simpler than another in some aspects, but more complex in others.

How can we explain such complexity in a pidgin language? First of all, Bislama is no ordinary pidgin: it is an expanded one – whose functions have been extended to cover nearly all those of a normal language, except being transmitted as the mother tongue of a speech community. Like other dialects of Melanesian Pidgin, Bislama is used as the daily means of communication in urban areas; it is used in radio broadcasting and parliamentary debates; it has become a written language and is used in newspapers, government pamphlets and Bible translations. Bislama is unique, however, in having been declared the national language in Vanuatu's constitution.

Functional expansion is often accompanied by grammatical expansion, and in terms of grammatical complexity, expanded pidgins are often indistinguishable from creoles and other languages which are transmitted as mother tongues. The lexifier language is sometimes a source of grammatical expansion, but another source is the 'substrate' languages – the mother tongues of the pidgin's speakers. Substrate influence, as it is called, is most likely when there are commonalities among the substrate languages.

In the case of Bislama, the substrate languages all belong to the Oceanic subgroup of the 'Austronesian' family [the Oceanic group contains about 300 languages spoken over most of New Guinea and the islands of Melanesia, Micronesia and Polynesia], and the pronoun systems of most of them make the same distinctions in inclusiveness and number. For example, Tangoan, spoken on

Tangoa, a small island off the coast of Santo in north-western Vanuatu, has the following system of subject pronouns (Camden, 1979, p. 88):

	Singular	Dual	Trial	Plural
1st person inclusive		enr̄arua	enr̄atolu	enr̄a
1st person exclusive	enau	kamamrua	kamamtolu	kamam
2nd person	egko	kamimrua	kamimtolu	kamim
3rd person	enia	enrarua	enratolu	enra/enira

The same distinctions are found in Raga, spoken on the north-eastern island of Pentecost (Walsh, 1978, p. 190), Paramese, spoken on the central island of Paama (Crowley, 1990, p. 227), and Old Anejom, spoken on the southern island of Aneityum (Lynch, 1991, p. 190).

Thus it is clear that the forms of Bislama's pronoun system are derived from its lexifier language, English, but the grammatical distinctions are from its Oceanic substrate languages.

References

CAMDEN, W.G. (1979) 'Parallels in structure of lexicon and syntax between New Hebrides Bislama and the south Santo language spoken at Tangoa' in *Papers in Pidgin and Creole Linguistics*, no. 2, Canberra, Pacific Linguistics A-57.

CROWLEY, T. (1990) *Beach-la-mar to Bislama: the emergence of a national language in Vanuatu*, Oxford, Clarendon.

LYNCH, J. (1991) 'A century of linguistic change in Anejom' in BLUST, R. (ed.) *Currents in Pacific linguistics: papers on Austronesian languages and ethnolinguistics in honour of George W. Grace*, Canberra, Pacific Linguistics C-117.

TODD, L. (1984) *Modern Englishes: pidgins and creoles*, Oxford, Blackwell.

WALSH, D.S. (1978) 'Tok Pisin syntax – the Eastern Austronesian factor' in *Papers in pidgin and creole linguistics*, no. 1, Canberra, Pacific Linguistics A-54.

This reading was specially commissioned for this book.

Reading C
SENTENCE STRUCTURE IN IRISH ENGLISH

John Harris

In this [reading], we examine very briefly a number of grammatical devices in Irish English whose function it is to help organize the presentation of information in spoken discourse. We'll look specifically at some of the grammatical means available to Irish English speakers for focusing attention on particular sentence constituents and for making explicit the distinction between given and new information. (Briefly, given information is that which is already supplied by the previous context of speaking; new, as the term suggests, refers to information not previously provided.)

The initial unit of a clause is often referred to as the theme, which can be described as 'the communicative point of departure for the rest of the clause'. Typically, the theme contains given information which is completed by new information presented in the remainder of the clause. However, by giving intonational prominence to clause-initial position, it's possible to make the theme the focal point of new information. In English statements, it is of course the clause subject that normally appears in this position. But speakers have recourse to a number of grammatical fronting operations which have the effect of shifting a sentence constituent out of its 'normal' or expected position and into the theme slot. One of these is left-dislocation, whereby the targeted constituent is simply fronted to theme position, e.g. *I'd call it daylight robbery → Daylight robbery I'd call it.* Another is clefting, whereby a clause is split into two portions, each with its own verb. One version of this produces a so-called *it*-cleft: the first subclause is introduced by *it is/was* followed by the fronted element; the second resembles a *that* relative clause. For example: *I saw Joe yesterday → It's Joe (that) I saw yesterday.* In some types of Irish English, these devices are used much more frequently than is usual in standard speech. Moreover, the grammatical conditions under which the operations are permitted to apply in Irish English differ in several important respects from standard usage.

Left-dislocation

In standard usage, detachment of an object or adverbial complement from its verb through left-dislocation tends to be disfavoured or sounds archaic. This sort of fronting is, however, quite common in many types of Irish English, e.g.:

> A story now he told me when he was young.

> Too much motors you'd be meeting.

> In some building he is working.

> [Cited in Filppula, 1986]

A strikingly nonstandard feature of left-dislocation in some varieties of Irish English is the tendency for a fronted noun phrase to leave a pronoun 'trace' or 'shadow' of itself in its 'normal' position. For instance:

> Anything you wanted you could a got it.

with left-dislocation of the object noun phrase *anything you wanted* and shadow *it*. (The corresponding sentence without left-dislocation would be *You could a got anything you wanted*.) Similarly:

> That baby from it was born her mother had it.

(Compare this with *Her mother had that baby since it was born*.) The same phenomenon appears to be involved in nonstandard relative clause structures with shadow pronouns … For example, in

> This girl I was actually travelling with, her mother is in hospital.

we have left-dislocation of *this girl I was actually travelling with* plus shadow *her*. (Compare this with the standard order, without fronting: *The mother of the girl I was actually travelling with is in hospital*.)

it-clefting

Irish English has fewer restrictions than standard English on the type of sentence constituent that can be fronted by means of *it*-clefting. For instance, in standard usage clefting is generally not permitted to break up subject–complement structures [these are expressions such as *my cat* in the sentence: *Bridget is my cat*; or *flat* in the sentence: *It was flat*. They are said to 'complete' the meaning of the subject (*Bridget* or *It*)] This constraint is not binding on Irish English, as the following sentences illustrate:

> It's flat it was.
>
> It's asleep he is.
>
> [Cited in Henry, 1957]

Unlike standard usage, Irish English also permits clefting of a verb phrase, as in:

> It's looking for more land a lot of them are.
>
> [Cited in Filppula, 1986]

> Was it drinking she was?
>
> It must be working for her he was.
>
> [Cited in Henry, 1957]

The fronting of the logical subject of an existential *there* sentence through clefting is generally not acceptable in standard English. (*There's a fly in my soup* is an example of this type of sentence, with *a fly* as logical subject. We wouldn't normally expect *It's a fly there is in my soup* in standard usage.) Not so in Irish English:

> It was a kind of a house built of strong timber was there one time.
>
> [Cited in Filppula, 1986]

References

FILPPULA, M. (1986) *Some Aspects of Hiberno-English in a Functional Sentence Perspective*, University of Joensuu Publications in the Humanities, 7 Joensuu, University of Joensuu.

HENRY, P.C. (1957) *An Anglo-Irish Dialect of North Roscommon*, Dublin, University College.

Source: Harris, 1993, pp. 173–5

ACCENTS OF ENGLISH

Susan Wright

7.1 INTRODUCTION

> You may laugh, but surveys prove that most of the English population
> equate good articulation with higher IQs, better looks, cleanliness, sex
> appeal and reliability. It's called Received Pronunciation.
> (Lette, 1993, pp. 97–8)

> The English have no respect for their language and will not teach their
> children to speak it … it is impossible for an Englishman to open his
> mouth, without making some other Englishman despise him.
> (Shaw, [1910] 1972)

Although the first quotation is from a work of fiction, its substance is so familiar
that many people will have no difficulty accepting it as real. The Australian
heroine, Madeline, is being given a short, sharp lesson in the manners and
customs of the English middle class. The aim of the lesson is not purely informa-
tive; it is designed to persuade the pupil to change her own articulation habits –
her accent – in order to conform with and fit into the society on whose fringes she
is hanging.

The desirable accent held up as a model is **Received Pronunciation** (**RP**), a
social rather than regional British English accent which has also been called 'The
Queen's English' and 'BBC English', and which, Madeline's adviser confidently
asserts, is endowed with a whole set of positive associations. By implication, other
English accents are less well endowed, a sentiment echoed by George Bernard
Shaw in his play *Pygmalion,* from which the second quotation is taken.

The notion of 'good articulation' is rather problematical. In the sense used in
Lette's quotation it might cover the pronunciation of consonants and vowels (the
sound segments of a language), but it would take far more than a change in
articulation, in this sense, for an Australian English speaker to sound like a posh
'Brit'. Indeed, one of the most striking things about Australian English may not be
its articulation at all, but its intonation.

In this chapter I discuss the various component parts that can be said to make
up an English **accent**: its consonants and vowels, as well as other distinctive
features such as patterns of intonation. I also discuss how accents vary regionally
and across different social groups, and how accents change. Finally, I return to the
issue with which I began: the kinds of social judgements that are frequently made
about different accents and their speakers.

7.2 THE MAKING OF AN ENGLISH ACCENT

The use of RP as a basis for description

It is quite usual for people to assert that they themselves have 'no accent'; indeed,
this distinction appears to be the basis of how accent has traditionally been
described. For example, British linguists often use Received Pronunciation as a

kind of descriptive guide to the contrasts and similarities between accents, as though RP itself was an accentless norm or standard. RP is one of the most comprehensively described English accents because early twentieth-century British linguists attempting to arrive at a description of the sounds of English were essentially describing their own accent. Daniel Jones, for instance, widely considered to be the leading phonetician in the first part of the twentieth century, initially based his description of Received Pronunciation on his own speech. Jones concedes this in his 1907 volume, *Phonetic Transcriptions of English Prose*, though later works expand the definition to cover the pronunciation used by the 'educated classes' in southern England. Jones's work was *pre*scriptive as well as descriptive: the 'standard pronunciation' was intended as a guide for those learning English as a foreign language, and for native speakers who wanted to learn 'correct' pronunciation. He also worked as a member of the BBC Advisory Committee on spoken English and was influential in the selection of RP as a norm for announcers on BBC radio. (The part played by Jones in 'theorizing' a spoken standard of English has been well documented by Tony Crowley, 1989, pp. 165–74.)

Linguists now would claim not to attach the social and personal significance to RP (and RP speakers) that society in general appears to do. Most linguists treat RP simply as one of a variety of accents, neither better nor worse than any other accent of English. Yet RP surfaces silently as the basis of linguists' **phonemic descriptions** of English, and this has led to other accents being described in terms of their distance from an RP standard. In this context of linguistic description RP is essentially abstract, or an idealization, but it is a model of the sound system of English with which many readers will be familiar. For this reason, this chapter follows suit in using an abstract RP as a model for description.

We should concede that in practice RP also refers to a real accent, which is as unstable as any other. As the British phonetician John Wells (1982, pp. 279 ff.) points out, RP is no 'homogeneous invariant monolith' – there is considerable variation among its speakers and consequently there is variation in the pronunciation of RP.

A phonemic description provides an account of the distinctive sound units (**phonemes**) that make up a language's sound system. You will already have met this notion in earlier chapters. See, for instance, Chapter 2 section 2.6.

RP and the Queen's English

Janet Holmes, a New Zealand linguist, discusses below the origins of RP. She reports a frequent claim that 'received' comes from 'received at court':

> In earlier centuries you could tell where an English lord or lady came from by their regional form of English. But by the early twentieth century a person who spoke with a regional accent in England was most unlikely to belong to the upper class. Upper-class people had an upper-class education, and that generally meant a public (i.e. private!) school where they learned to speak RP. RP stands, not for 'Real Posh' (as suggested to me by a young friend), but rather for Received Pronunciation – the accent of the best educated and most prestigious members of English society. It is claimed the label derives from the accent which was 'received' at the royal court, and it is sometimes identified with 'the Queen's English', although the accent used by Queen Elizabeth II is a rather old-fashioned variety of RP.
>
> (Holmes, 1992, p. 143)

By contrast, the *Oxford English Dictionary* (OED) suggests that 'received' is used in the now rather old-fashioned sense of 'generally accepted'. The first use of the term is attributed to A.J. Ellis in 1869, with linguists generally settling on this usage in the 1930s.

received (rɪ'siːvd), *ppl. a.* [f. prec. + -ED¹.]

1. a. Generally adopted, accepted, approved as true or good.

b. Of language or pronunciation: *received pronunciation*, the pronunciation of that variety of British English widely considered to be least regional, being originally that used by educated speakers in southern England; also, the 'accepted', standard pronunciation of any specified area, Received Standard; *Received Standard* (*English*), the spoken language of a linguistic area (usu. Britain) in its traditionally most correct and acceptable form. Hence in other derived uses.

[**1818** *Trans. Amer. Philos. Soc.* I. 259 According to its most generally received pronunciation, it is more properly a diphthong.] **1869** A. J. ELLIS *On Early Eng. Pronunc.* I. 13 The alphabet required for writing the theoretically received pronunciation of literary English. **1874** —— *Ibid.* IV. 1095/1 The tip of the tongue for received English is not so advanced towards the teeth or gums, as for the continental sound. **1882** —— in *Trans. Philol. Soc.* 21 We say they are dialectal forms of the received *down*. **1889** [see *RP* s.v. *R II. 2 a]. **1890** *Dialect Notes* I. 26 For the study of pronunciation the received spelling is very ill adapted. **1913** H. C. WYLD in *Mod. Lang. Teaching* IX. 261/2 When he speaks of *Standard English*, he is, I believe, referring to what I now call *Received Standard*. **1914** M. MONTGOMERY in *Ibid.* X. 11/2 Yet in that country [*sc.* Germany], as time goes on, a process of assimilation towards a single 'Received Standard' is said to be growing more, rather than less, marked. **1932** D. JONES *Outl. Eng.* xviii. 148 In Received English there are six affricates which may be represented phonetically by.. diagraphs. **1932** *S.P.E. Tract* XXXVII. 542 These authors.. define the 'Received Pronunciation' as that of 'the great public schools, the Universities, and the learned professions'. **1936** *Trans. Philol. Soc.* 80 My own recollection of this opposition to Received Speech is that the dialect speaker acquires a consciousness of 'correctness' in speech accompanied by a powerful objection to being caught..'talking fine'. **1937** D. JONES in *Le Maître Phonétique* Apr. June (Suppl.), I take the view that foreigners learning English should be free to choose whatever pronunciation they prefer. Many naturally choose what has been termed 'received' pronunciation (R.P.), as being a widely understood type of English. **1940** J. H. JAGGER *Eng. in Future* i. 15 The influence of the various forms of Modified Standard—to accept Professor Wyld's terms—upon each other and upon Received Standard. **1962** A. C. GIMSON in R. Quirk *Use of Eng.* 281 *Received Pronunciation*, or RP, suggesting.. the result of a collective social judgment rather than of a conscious, prescriptive agreement. **1964** C. BARBER *Ling. Change Present-Day Eng.* ii. 20 The influence of the mass-media and of mass-education.. does not necessarily produce speakers of Received Standard English. **1969** S. POTTER *Changing Eng.* i. 14 Other cities, notably Edinburgh and Dublin, have their received pronunciations, and so have other regions of the English-speaking world. **1973** G. W. TURNER *Stylistics* v. 147 Even now 'received pronunciation' will help its user to obtain credit when ordering goods by telephone. **1974** J. I. M. STEWART *Gaudy* x. 179 There is no such thing as an Oxford accent, since what phoneticians call Received Standard English came into existence without the university's playing any very identifiable part in the process.

'Received pronunciation'

(Simpson and Weiner (eds), 1989)

The connection – or otherwise – between RP and the Queen's English has been investigated by Katie Wales (1994):

> If the Queen's English is synonymous with 'The Queen's English', the converse is not exactly true: not all users of the latter speak and sound like the Queen … There is no doubt that RP is itself the accent of a rather 'exclusive' group, despite the fact that it serves as a model of educated British English throughout the world for foreign learners of English. Some estimates of the speakers of RP are as low as 3–5% …
>
> Three varieties of RP usually distinguished: 'general' or 'mainstream', used as the teaching model; 'conservative' RP spoken by the older generations, and 'advanced' RP spoken by the younger. The accents of the Queen and Princess Margaret, like the Queen Mother, can be associated with conservative RP, which sounds to many ears decidedly old-fashioned, reminiscent of the pre-war spoken English of BBC broadcasting, British films and Pathé newsreels. So older royalty will say /haɪs/ for /haʊs/ *house*; /ɔːf/ for /ɒf/ *off*; /'lendskeɪp/ for *landscape*; and /sendst/ for /sændhɜːst/ *Sandhurst*; /'paːlɪs/ for /'paʊələs/ *powerless*; and /rɪ'feɪnd/ for /rɪ'faɪnd/ *refined*. Stress falls on the first syllable in words like *formidable*, *temporarily* and *fragmentary*. Conservatism, of course, is what is traditionally expected of the monarchy generally; and the fact that the Queen in her Christmas broadcasts sounds like a pre-war BBC recording is no doubt because of the unbroken tradition of such royal broadcasts since George V first spoke to his people on the *wireless* in 1924 at the British Empire exhibition at Wembley, millions of people thus hearing 'The King's English' for the first time. There is also created as a result a sense of 'distance' between royalty and commonalty. But this conservatism and distance tend to appear negative, rather than positive, as the 1990s progress; and the Queen's accent open more and more to ridicule, to accusations of being 'affected'.
>
> (Wales, 1994, pp. 4–5)

English phonemes

When considering the ways in which accents vary it is conventional to look at the range of distinctive sounds or phonemes they possess, the distribution of these phonemes and how they are actually realized, or pronounced.

English accents may be considered to have different phonemic systems. Scottish English has a phoneme that is not found in other varieties of English, though it does exist in other languages. It is the consonant sound at the end of *loch* (technically described as a 'voiceless velar fricative' and transcribed as /x/). This sound, or something very similar, occurs in modern German *Bach* (stream). The words *loch* and *lock* form a **minimal pair** in Scottish English (in that they are identical in all respects except one – the final consonant), illustrating the existence of two distinct phonemes /x/ and /k/. By contrast, other varieties of English lack this distinctive sound, so that the word *loch* is pronounced exactly the same as *lock*.

Table 7.1   The phoneme inventory for consonants in RP

/p/ poppy	/f/ fife	/h/ ha-ha
/b/ bible	/v/ verve	/m/ mimic
/t/ totter	/θ/ thigh	/n/ nine
/d/ dad	/ð/ they	/ŋ/ singing
/k/ kick	/s/ sea-sick	/l/ loyal
/g/ gag	/z/ zoos	/r/ rarer
/tʃ/ church	/ʃ/ shush	/j/ yo-yo
/dʒ/ judge	/ʒ/ azure	/w/ wayward

(Graddol et al., 1994, p. 51)

Perhaps the phonemic differences between accents of English are more strikingly illustrated by comparing the vowel systems of some varieties. Table 7.2 gives a list of RP vowels.

Table 7.2   The phoneme inventory for vowels in RP

/iː/ peat	/ʊ/ put	/ɪə/ pier
/ɪ/ pit	/uː/ pool	/eə/ pear
/e/ pet	/ɜː/ pearl	/ʊə/ poor
/a/ dad	/eɪ/ pail	/ə/ banana
/ʌ/ putt	/əʊ/ pole	
/ɑː/ father	/aɪ/ pile	
/ɒ/ pot	/aʊ/ foul	
/ɔː/ caught	/ɔɪ/ foil	

(Adapted from Graddol et al., 1994, p. 51)

Note: The : marker in /uː/, etc. indicates a long vowel (the distinction between long and short vowels is less relevant to certain other varieties of English). Vowels that have two symbols, such as /əʊ/, are **diphthongs**. Put simply, a diphthong is made up of two vowel sounds that glide together as they are articulated. You may be able to feel this if you say the vowel in 'pile' very slowly.) The /ə/ symbol refers to *schwa*, a vowel that occurs in unstressed syllables in words such as 'police', 'remarkable', etc.

Activity 7.1   *(Allow about 5 minutes)*

Look carefully at Table 7.2. You will see that this presents twenty different, or contrasting, vowel sounds in RP. How do you pronounce the words listed? Are the vowels in each of these words all pronounced differently in your variety of English, as they are in RP, or do some sound the same? (Bear in mind that we are focusing here on the number of *distinct* vowel sounds in an accent, not on subtle differences in the pronunication of a vowel. Your own variety may make different distinctions from those in Table 7.2; for instance, you may use additional phonemes not found in RP.)

Comment

The vowel systems of different Englishes will have some things in common but they may also differ in terms of their phonemic contrasts. We can illustrate this with some examples from Scottish English and the variety of English spoken in the south-west United States (see Table 7.3). Both these varieties, like RP, have separate phonemes in words like *peat, pit, pet and putt*. But they make different contrasts between the words *dad, father, pot* and *caught* (to simplify the comparison I have omitted the RP 'long vowel' markers here).

Table 7.3   A comparision between three different vowel systems

	RP	Scottish English	SWAm (= South-West US English)
dad	a	a	a
father	ɑ	a	ɑ
pot	ɒ	ɔ	ɑ
caught	ɔ	ɔ	ɑ

Scottish English has a single phoneme accounting for the vowels in *dad* and *father*, in contrast to the distinctions made in RP and SWAm. And whereas RP has a three-way contrast of the vowels in *father, pot* and *caught*, Scottish English has a two-way contrast (*father* vs *pot* and *caught*) and SWAm has the single phoneme /ɑ/ in all these words. We can say that each accent has a vowel system of a slightly different 'shape' from the others. They do not share the same distinctions.

The problem with any comparison of this sort is that it is still necessarily an abstraction. It cannot capture subtle differences in the pronunciation of the same phoneme, as it occurs in different words or as it is pronounced by different speakers. But a phonemic account does provide a starting point from which we can go on to look at such differences.

The distribution of phonemes

Try saying the word *cart* to yourself. And now *carry*. You will almost certainly pronounce an /r/ sound in the case of *carry* but, depending on where you come from, you may or may not pronounce an /r/ in *cart*. Two accents may have the same phoneme (/r/ in this case) but differ in terms of the distribution of this phoneme – that is, the contexts in which the phoneme occurs.

A distinction is often made in English between so-called **rhotic** and **non-rhotic** accents. Speakers of both types of accent will pronounce the /r/ in words like *round* and *carry* (where it occurs before a vowel). Speakers of rhotic accents will also pronounce an /r/ when it is not followed by a vowel (as in *car* or *cart*). This latter type of pronunciation is often referred to by the rather ungainly term **non-prevocalic /r/**. (You will also find the term 'postvocalic /r/' in the literature used to mean the same as non-prevocalic.)

Figure 7.1 illustrates this distinction in traditional regional varieties of English in England. (We return later to the different /r/ sounds shown in Figure 7.1.)

The rhotic/non-rhotic distinction has also been used to distinguish between accents outside England (see Wells, 1982, p. 76). For instance, many US, Canadian, Irish and Scottish accents (what Lass, 1987, calls 'northern hemisphere extra-territorial Englishes') may be broadly identified by the presence of non-prevocalic /r/. In addition, some accents vary with respect to whether /r/ is consistently pronounced. Jamaican English is an example of a so-called semi-rhotic variety where /r/ may be pronounced at the end of words (*car*, *far*), but not when it comes after a vowel but before a consonant (*cart*). I look again at non-prevocalic /r/ in section 7.4.

> Non-prevocalic /r/ is part of most people's stereotype of a North American accent. And it is strongly associated with particular styles of American popular music, as Chapter 8 illustrates.

The phonetic realization of phonemes

I mentioned earlier that phonemes were essentially an abstract concept and that the same phoneme could be pronounced, or 'realized', differently in different accents. Staying with the example of /r/ pronunciation, what this means is that the actual physical articulation and resulting sound (the auditory impression) of one speaker's pronunciation of the abstract phoneme /r/ may differ from another speaker's. This **phonetic** level takes us away from the comparatively abstract comparison of accents in terms of systems, towards the phonetic reality of actual pronunciation. (Remember from Chapter 2 that the linguistic convention is for phonetic descriptions to appear in square brackets while phonemic descriptions appear in obliques.) If you look at Figure 7.1 again, you will see that this illustrates four different pronunciations of /r/ in traditional varieties of English. But this is not the whole picture; there are further pronunciations of /r/ which distinguish speakers in terms of age and, to some extent, social class. As the British sociolinguist Peter Trudgill (1974) found in his study of young speakers in Norwich, England, in the early 1970s, a pronunciation of /r/ that makes a word like *rabbit* sound close to *wabbit* is spreading in both working-class and middle-class urban accents in the south and east of England. This particular /r/ is pronounced by squeezing the sound out between the bottom lip and the top teeth, rather than between the lips like /w/. The short-hand, technical description of this articulation is 'labio-dental approximant' and it is represented phonetically as [ʋ]. Variation in /r/ pronunciation is also characteristic of accents of English outside the British Isles, such as South African English (see Lanham and McDonald, 1979).

A phoneme may be pronounced differently depending on its position in a word. To take the /l/ sound this time, in RP, the /l/ in *leaf* and *feeling* sounds different from the /l/ in *feel*. When /l/ occurs at the beginning of a word or between two vowels, it is articulated with the tongue tip touching the alveolar ridge just behind the teeth, and is known as a 'clear' /l/. When it occurs at the end of a word, at the same time as the tongue tip makes contact with the alveolar ridge, the back of the tongue bunches up towards the velum or soft palate. This creates a

> *Figure 7.1 (opposite) Different pronunciations of /r/ in England.*
>
> *Several different ways of pronouncing /r/ in the words* farmer *and* Friday *can be found. The black hatching shows where 'non-prevocalic /r/' is not pronounced in the first syllable of* farmer.
>
> (Survey of English Dialects, QVIII.4.7)

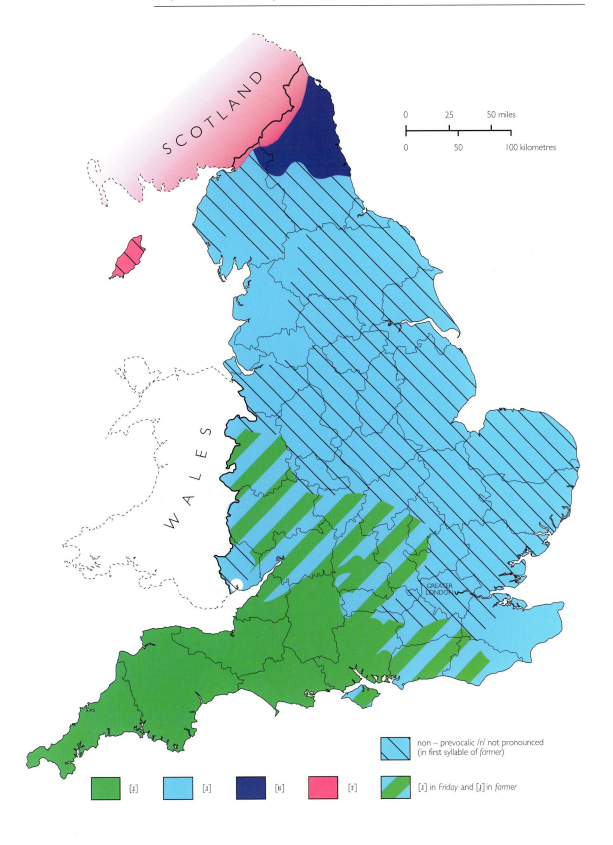

non – prevocalic /r/ not pronounced
(in first syllable of *farmer*)

[ɾ]   [ɹ]   [ʁ]   [r]   [ɹ] in *Friday* and [ɾ] in *farmer*

different 'dark' sound quality. So these two pronunciations of /l/ have come to becalled 'clear' and 'dark' /l/, respectively, as illustrated in Figure 7.2a and b.

Not all accents of English show this contrast. Indeed, speakers of Lancashire English typically use dark /l/ no matter where /l/ occurs in a word, as do most American English speakers and almost all Australian English speakers. By contrast, many Irish English speakers use clear /l/ wherever the sound occurs.

In some accents, dark /l/ might be 'vocalized'. In this pronunciation, the tongue tip does not touch the alveolar ridge, leaving the sound to be shaped only by the bunching tongue (see Figure 7.2c). The resulting sound impression has been compared with the quality of [w]; it is actually strongly vowel-like (comparable with the RP vowel in *good*), hence the term 'vocalized /l/'. In Scotland, working-class Glaswegian has vocalized /l/ when the sound occurs in certain positions, as in the words *well* and *million*.

Overview

To give a brief review: I have discussed the way accents of English vary with respect to their sound segments, that is their consonant and vowel sounds. Linguists tend to distinguish between accents in terms of:

- the different phonemes they possess (e.g. the different vowel systems of RP, Scottish English and south-west US English);
- the distribution of these phonemes, or the different environments in which they occur (e.g. the distinction between rhotic and non-rhotic accents);
- and at a rather less abstract level, in terms of differences in how these phonemes are pronounced or 'phonetically realized' (the so-called clear and dark /l/ distinction).

As I suggested in the introduction, however, there are other ways in which accents differ. An accent may be more striking for its intonation, rhythm or voice quality than for the sound of its vowels and consonants. Some of these features are discussed now.

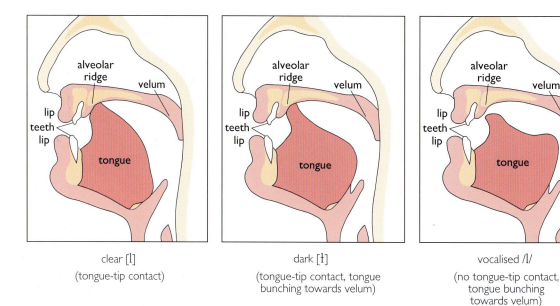

clear [l]
(tongue-tip contact)

dark [ɫ]
(tongue-tip contact, tongue bunching towards velum)

vocalised /l/
(no tongue-tip contact, tongue bunching towards velum)

Figure 7.2a–c Clear and dark /l/ and vocalized /l/

Some prosodic features of English accents

The term **prosody** includes features such as **rhythm** (the use of stress to mark prominent syllables in an utterance) and **intonation** (changes in pitch). These are also sometimes known as 'suprasegmental' features because they operate above the level of individual sound segments (i.e. vowels and consonants). Although they make an important contribution to the overall sound of an accent they are rather difficult to describe clearly and accurately. One reason is that they interact in quite complex ways.

Intonational groups

In continuous speech it is possible to distinguish intonational groups. The length of intonational groups is generally restricted by the fact that they are usually said in one breath, and the boundaries between groups usually come at a point where there is a major break in grammatical structure. Here is an example:

[When I went to London] [I wanted to go to the zoo]

Intonational groups provide units for the analysis of rhythm and intonation. The example below identifies the *nucleus* (the last stressed syllable which also carries the main pitch movement) and parts of the utterance that precede this: the *head* (running from the first stressed syllable up to the nucleus) and *pre-head* (an initial, unstressed item).

Pre-head	Head	Nucleus
I	*wan*ted to *go* to the	zoo

(Note: stressed syllables are italicized.)

It would also be possible to place the nucleus elsewhere – for example by placing the main stress on 'go' for emphasis. Any syllables after the nucleus are known as the 'tail'.

(Adapted from Graddol et al., 1994, p. 60)

The fact that speakers are easily able to identify meaningful contrasts between distinct prosodic patterns indicates that prosody is part of the system of language. Different varieties of English tend to use rhythm and intonation contrasts to mark much the same differences in meaning, although the actual patterns used may vary from variety to variety. So the prosodic systems of different accents are clearly not identical.

It is often very hard to isolate the source of the prosodic distinctiveness of an accent. For example, Caribbean English – notably Jamaican English – is, almost stereotypically, considered to be 'rhythmical'. There are several interacting features which contribute to this impression. First, many words tend to receive stress on their final syllables, in contrast to the initial stress of RP; for instance, 'cele*brate*' rather than '*cele*brate'. Further, speakers of Caribbean English tend not to reduce vowel quality in unstressed syllables: the two syllables in the word 'police' sound equal, instead of the first syllable being reduced to a *schwa* sound [pəliːs]. This gives an impression that syllables have equal length, and sometimes equal weight. A wide pitch range is also used in intonation nuclei to differentiate salient or important words from others. So distinctive stress assignment, combined with markedly wide pitch patterns, creates the unique intonation of Caribbean English.

The rhythmic profile of an accent may be created by prosodic features in combination with the pronunciation of vowels or consonants. For example, Adam Brown (1988) discusses how Singaporean English accents strike the listener as 'staccato' in effect. This impression derives partly from the precise cutting-off of successive words from one another, combined with the assignment of more or less equal length to each syllable to create a consistent pace. But it is also partly to do with the extensive use of the sound known as a 'glottal stop' [?], both between words and to replace certain consonants at the ends of words. (The glottal stop is sometimes represented in writing as an apostrophe, as in *wha'* for 'what' or *bu'er* for 'butter'). The staccato profile is thus constructed out of a range of different features; 'rhythm' is not a simple matter.

'Stress-timed' and 'syllable-timed' Englishes

English is sometimes said to be a **stress-timed** language, in that stressed syllables occur at regular intervals, regardless of the number of intervening unstressed syllables. For instance, in:

(a) *No cat caught a mouse*

(b) *No cat caught any mice*

roughly the same amount of time elapses between the two stressed syllables *caught* and *mouse/mice*, despite the extra syllable in (b). By contrast, in **syllable-timed** languages, roughly equal time would be given to each syllable (see Graddol et al., 1994, pp. 51–6).

In fact, varieties of English spoken in many parts of the world are better described as syllable-timed. This would apply to the English spoken in, for example, the Caribbean, India, several African countries and Singapore.

One accent in which a distinctive intonation feature has been studied in some depth is Australian English. The feature is a high rising tone (HRT) or, as Gregory Guy and Julia Vonwiller label it, Australian questioning intonation (AQI). Despite the label, AQI occurs as a rising intonation at the end of a declarative sentence; it does not necessarily indicate that the speaker is asking a question. In the following example from Guy and Vonwiller, the symbol ↑ is used to indicate AQI. The speaker is an upper-working-class teenage girl.

> Oh, occasionally Mrs L– used to blow up kids when they hadn't done anything. And once, a girl and I were walking down the stairs, and she touched a doorknob or something, 'cause she didn't realise what was *wrong with it* ↑ And it fell *off* ↑ and she got the cane for *breaking it* ↑ And I knew very well she *hadn't broken it* ↑And I tried to tell the teacher. The teacher was really mean, you know.
>
> (Cited in Guy and Vonwiller, 1989, p. 23)

Actually, HRT, or something like it, is notable in other varieties of English too. While it does not occur frequently or typically in RP, Guy and Vonwiller remark that it does occur in the varieties of English spoken in Tyneside, Liverpool, Manchester, Glasgow and Birmingham, although it does not have the same communicative function in these accents that it does in Australian English. It is also heard in several parts of North America.

Guy and Vonwiller have investigated the different communicative meanings of this intonation pattern by examining a range of situations and samples of spoken language. They argue that spoken texts that are complex in structure and meaning require the speaker to monitor the listener. One way in which the speaker can check whether the listener is following the strand of talk, for example in narrative texts and in descriptions, is to incorporate AQI into the tone of voice itself. So AQI serves as a monitoring strategy. But AQI also has what they call an 'interactional' meaning in a conversational setting. A speaker might use AQI to indicate to her interlocutor that she is not ready to give up her turn in the conversation, but that she is continuing with what she is saying.

Guy and Vonwiller were also interested in uncovering what they label the 'sociosymbolic' meaning of AQI; that is, the social evaluation of the intonation pattern as 'prestigious' or 'nonstandard'. They found that most Australians don't associate it with high social status, don't consider it suitable for high-status occupations, and think it is more typical of young people.

Activity 7.2   *(Reading A)*

Now work through Reading A, extracts from Guy and Vonwiller's paper 'The high rising tone in Australian English'. In these extracts the authors argue that AQI is an example of language change in progress: it is a relatively new change that is currently spreading among speakers in Sydney, where the study was carried out.

You should note down the evidence Guy and Vonwiller draw on to support their argument. (Guy and Vonwiller use the term 'tone groups' as their unit of analysis. These are similar to what I referred to above as 'intonational groups'.) In sections 7.3 and 7.4, I have more to say about many of the issues they discuss.

Voice quality in English

Distinctive intonation patterns are tied up with the distinctive sound quality of a voice. Individual speakers might sound 'nasal', 'breathless' or 'adenoidal', and indeed some accents strike listeners in the same way. Linguists call this impression of a voice's overall shape **voice quality**. The basis of a voice quality is 'articulatory setting': the physical arrangement of different parts of the vocal tract as people speak. Australian English is an accent in which intonation and voice quality are perceived to be strongly tied together. Wells (1982, p. 604) reports that HRT or AQI is often, although not universally, associated with a nasal voice quality; intonation and voice quality are not inseparable though they might be perceived as such.

In England, one of the most striking voice qualities is that associated with local Liverpool English. (Beatles devotees will recognize the distinctive Merseyside voice quality in the sound of such classics as *Love Me Do!*) This voice quality has been described as 'adenoidal'. Knowles (1978, p. 89) relates this to a particular setting of the vocal tract (not to obstructed nasal passages, as has sometimes been suggested). He notes that 'the centre of gravity of the tongue is brought backwards and upwards ... the pharynx is tightened and the larynx is displaced upwards'. Basically, the back of the tongue bunches and is raised in the direction of the soft palate. The combination of a highly distinctive voice quality with high rising tones gives Merseyside speakers a particularly vivid prosodic profile, which perhaps is a more striking identifier of Liverpool English than any vowel or consonant values.

Listeners respond very clearly and often emotively to the voices of different speakers and to the voices associated with particular accents. An interesting impression of an RP voice in the 1950s is presented by a BBC journalist, René Cutforth. He provides a mental sound picture of a friend of his, a journalist:

> … her mode of speech is of that strangulated kind usually to be found among dons at the older universities. It is as if even in such a trivial expression as 'Good morning' for instance, the voice were in labour with some fine point of discrimination … It is a very special, very English voice: it sounds like all the self-conscious superiorities of both caste and intellect rolled together.
>
> (Cutforth, 1955, p. 146)

Cutforth's description highlights the fact that hearers respond powerfully to voice quality as part of the overall impression of an accent. (He does not say whether the speaker remained on friendly terms with him!)

This discussion of accent has given us a framework that we can use to talk about different accents of English. I want now to look first at regional variation: how accents vary and change across geographical areas.

7.3 REGIONAL VARIATION IN ACCENT

> The science of speech. That's my profession: also my hobby. Happy is the man who can make a living by his hobby! You can spot an Irishman or a Yorkshireman by his brogue. *I* can place any man within six miles. I can place him within two miles in London. Sometimes within two streets.
> [Professor Higgins, Shaw's phonetician in *Pygmalion*]
> (Shaw, [1910] 1972, pp. 678–9)

Most people tend to associate accents of English with different English-speaking areas. But when we come to consider specifically *regionally* differentiated varieties of English, we also confront the issue of **dialect**. The difference between accent and dialect seems relatively simple to describe: accent consists of pronunciation; dialect consists of grammar, words and their meanings, and pronunciation. However, as mentioned in Chapter 1, it is difficult to draw precise boundaries between them, and the question of where accent ends and dialect begins may be answered differently depending on the situation and region being examined. There is plenty of anecdotal evidence to indicate that a single speaker may be capable of controlling the continuum of dialect in his or her own speech. So the formal speech of a Geordie from the north of England may be marked by the distinctive pronunciation features of 'Tyneside English', but in casual talk (say, in a close family setting, or with friends) it will have vocabulary, word forms and grammatical constructions that – in addition to the Tyneside accent – mark the variety of English as being rooted in Tyneside.

Mapping regional accents: isoglosses

One way of taking account of the continuous nature of the differences between accents and dialects of different regions is to draw up separate geographical boundaries for each relevant linguistic feature giving each one its own **isogloss** – or boundary marker – showing where one variant (a particular pronunciation, grammatical form, vocabulary item, etc.) gives way to another. Isoglosses for different accent and dialect features will not coincide exactly, but will cross one another and overlap to create a bundle of isoglosses which together create a continuous boundary showing how one dialect or accent shades into another.

Figure 7.3 (opposite) An isogloss bundle in the north of England. The key shows pronunciations found above and below each isogloss

(Open University, 1987, p. 18)

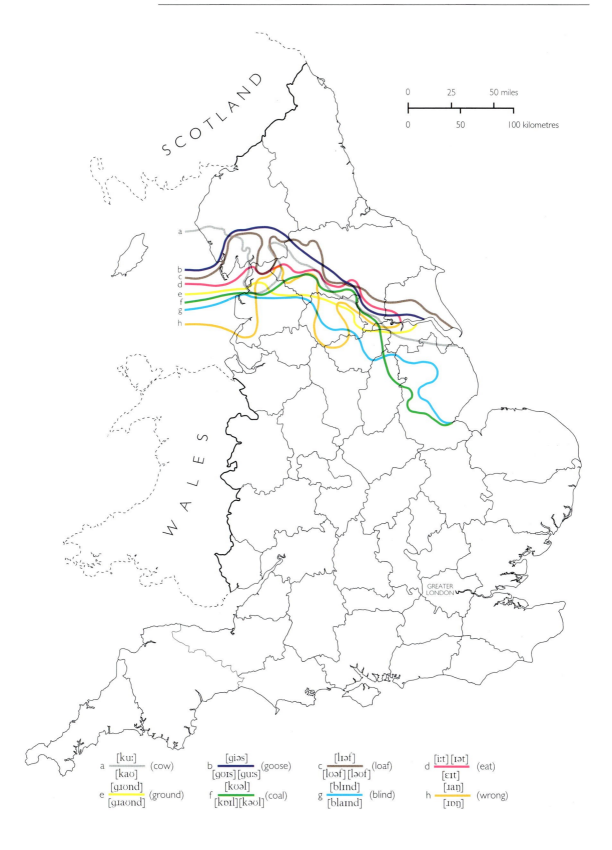

SCOTLAND

WALES

GREATER
LONDON

0   25   50 miles

0   50   100 kilometres

a [kuː]
   ───── (cow)
   [kaʊ]

b [ɡiəs]
   ───── (goose)
   [ɡʊɪs] [ɡuːs]

c [lɪəf]
   ───── (loaf)
   [lʊəf] [ləʊf]

d [iːt] [ɪət]
   ───── (eat)
   [ɛɪt]

e [ɡɹɒnd]
   ───── (ground)
   [ɡɹaʊnd]

f [kʊəl]
   ───── (coal)
   [kɒɪl] [kəʊl]

g [blɪnd]
   ───── (blind)
   [blaɪnd]

h [ɹaŋ]
   ───── (wrong)
   [ɹɒŋ]

Some phonological isoglosses that are used to divide northern and southern English accents into two broad groups are illustrated in Figure 7.3.

Although the pronunciation differences illustrated in Figure 7.3 are modern ones, they are useful in providing a starting place for the reconstruction of earlier patterns of variation: they actually represent the present-day consequences of a set of changes, called the 'Great Vowel Shift', affecting vowel pronunciation in England from around the fifteenth century.

In the Middle English period, the long vowel that is now pronounced in a word like *food* (/uː/) in RP was the typical pronunciation in a word like *cow*. And the present day RP vowel (/iː/) in a word such as *team* occurred in the word *blind* in Middle English. If you look carefully at Figure 7. 3, you'll see that the isoglosses (a) and (g) distinguish an area in the north of England which retains pronunciations for *cow* and *blind* that are remarkably similar to those that were current in most Middle English dialects, including southern and Midlands varieties. In the south and Midlands areas of England, the present-day pronunciations of *blind* and *cow* are closer to RP.

But the map doesn't show all of the changes that make up the Great Vowel Shift. For instance, the pronunciation of the vowels in words such as *sweet*, *clean*, *stone*, *name* and *moon* in Middle English was very different from their present-day RP pronunciations.

What occurred was a systematic shift affecting the long vowels of English. They became 'closer' (i.e. articulated with the tongue raised higher in the mouth). Those that were already close (where the tongue could not move any higher) became diphthongs. Some of these vowels went on to experience further changes in their pronunciation.

Figure 7.4 illustrates diagrammatically the initial raising and diphthongization of the vowels. Table 7.4 sets out resulting changes in pronunciation up to the present day.

We have already mentioned these historical changes – see Chapter 3, section 3.4, on pronunciations in Old and Middle English and Chapter 4, section 4.5, for a discussion of the Great Vowel Shift.

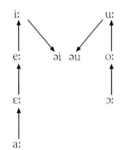

Figure 7.4 A diagrammatic representation of the Great Vowel Shift from Middle English to early modern English

(Adapted from Wells, 1982, p. 185)

Table 7.4 Pronunciation changes resulting from the Great Vowel Shift

	Middle English (c. 1100–1450)	Early modern English (c.1450–1600)	Present-day English
blind	iː	əi	aɪ
sweet	eː	iː	iː
clean	ɛː	eː	iː
stone	ɔː	oː	əʊ
name	aː	ɛː	eɪ
moon	oː	uː	uː
cow	uː	əu	aʊ

(Adapted from Gimson, 1989, p. 82)

The vowel shift seems to have been a kind of chain reaction. For example, once people began to say the vowel in *sweet* with a quality approaching the current RP /iː/ pronunciation, so they began to say the vowel in *blind* (which used to be pronounced /iː/) differently.

Of course, despite the apparent neatness of the chain reaction idea, the vowels did not all begin to be pronounced differently at exactly the same time. There is some evidence to suggest that the vowels in *sweet* and *moon* shifted before the others did. It is also likely that vowels initially changed their form only in certain words and then in more and more as the new pronunciations spread through the language. Chambers and Trudgill (1980) have documented the gradual diffusion of more recent sound changes through the vocabulary of English: a process they refer to as **lexical diffusion**.

If the vowel shifts did not all take place simultaneously, they also took different lengths of time to affect different regions of England and become established in these regions' accents. It seems that it was people in the south-eastern part of the country who first began to change the way they pronounced vowels like those in *sweet* and *moon*, and then those in *blind* and *cow*. It may be that the movement of wealthy and influential people from East Anglia and Kent to London in the fifteenth century helped the spread of the innovative pronunciations to London accents. From London, the innovation was then carried westwards and northwards as speakers with the new pronunciations moved around the country.

The Great Vowel Shift had a considerable impact on the pronunciation of English in different parts of England. It has given rise to a division between northern accents – which have kept some of the old pronunciations – and the rest. Look at Figure 7.3 again. What the isoglosses tell us is that the changes moved steadily northwards, but that they petered out by the time they got to a line running across the country from the River Humber in the east to the River Ribble in the west. Communities north of this line retained some of the old pronunciations and their accents remain unaffected by all the innovations represented by the Great Vowel Shift.

The spread of accents from place to place

The mechanism by which new pronunciations spread from community to community across the country is called **regional diffusion**. The geographical spread of a linguistic innovation depends on the movement of people and the continuing contact between those on the move and the speech communities they pass through. The information that enables linguists to construct an isogloss may be collected at intervals over time, to build up a picture of change in progress. For instance, if a linguistic innovation is diffusing across a region through time, it should be possible to map the change in progress at any particular point in time.

Let us consider a case of a **vowel merger** (when two vowels merge to become a single vowel): the progressive merger of the vowels in words like *cot* and *caught* or *hock* and *hawk* in general American English. The resulting merger of these two vowels sounds similar to the vowel in RP *father* [ɑː]. The regional diffusion of this development is quite complicated to plot, but it is possible to put together the comments and findings of a range of researchers to present a picture of how far the merger has got. The dialects which have merged vowels in *cot* and *caught* are represented in the shaded area in Figure 7.5.

According to the US linguist Walt Wolfram (1991, p. 54), the merger is a feature of the accents of 'the Boston area in Massachusetts, a region centred

C	Connecticut
D	Delaware
M	Maryland
Mass	Massachusetts
NH	New Hampshire
NJ	New Jersey
RI	Rhode Island
V	Vermont
WDC	Washington District of Colombia

Figure 7.5   The merger of the vowels in cot *and* caught *in American English*
(Source: Wolfram, 1991, p. 77)

around Pittsburgh Pennsylvania and a vast area of the western United States'. The distinction between the vowels in *cot* and *caught* is retained consistently (in most phonetic environments) in the accents of a majority of English speakers in the east (New York City, western New England, Philadelphia in Pennsylvania, Baltimore in Maryland), and in those of middle-aged and older speakers in the Midwest (for instance, Iowa and Ohio). But the distinction has now almost disappeared in the speech of young people in the Midwest. According to William Labov (1992) the merger radiates from two centres. The first is around Boston in eastern New England, extending into the north but not far to the south. The second is around Pittsburgh, extending northwards into the upper Ohio valley. The western extension covers most of the west, with a transitional area running through Wisconsin, Minnesota, Iowa, Kansas, Arkansas and then southward to the southernmost portions of New Mexico and Arizona. Wolfram (1991, p. 88) reports that this merger is not primarily a metropolitan phenomenon in the west, noting that speakers from Los Angeles and San Francisco do not typically use this form. However, it is observable that young speakers in these two cities do, which suggests that while the merger is predominantly a regional phenomenon, age is an influential, complicating factor.

This change is interesting because the USA has, until recently, traditionally been assumed to be a speech area without much regional variation compared with, say, Britain. The same has been assumed for South African English.

Lanham and McDonald's sociohistorical description of South African English (1979) illustrates the interaction of social and regional factors in different varieties of this form of English. They show how the settlement of different regions in South Africa in the nineteenth century by different social groups from

England has contributed to present-day patterns of social and regional variation. The English accent of the eastern Cape (also called 'extreme South African English') is the accent of the white native English-speaking working class (descended from the first English settlers – artisans and labourers – whose passage to South Africa was assisted by the colonial government in 1820). The Natal English accent, locally prestigious and also termed 'respectable South African English', is associated historically with the middle-class English settlers of the mid nineteenth century who became owners of the sugar plantations of Natal. In the South African national context, these two regional accents tend now to be associated with two distinct social classes. However, middle-class English speakers who were born and grew up in the eastern Cape will speak extreme South African English, and working-class English speakers from Natal may well speak so-called respectable South African English.

There are varieties of English that are influenced by regional factors of a particular type. For example, the principal influence on the pronunciation of English in India is the sound system of the country's indigenous languages. Indian languages have influenced the prosody of Indian English and the pronunciation of vowels and consonants (such as the articulation of consonants like /d/ and /t/ with the tongue tip slightly curled over backwards on the alveolar ridge – termed 'retroflex articulation'). The influence of the principal languages of different regions on the pronunciation of English has resulted in the regional variations of Indian English, so that it is possible to tell whether an Indian English speaker comes from, say, Bengal or Tamil Nadu.

In the Indian situation, accents of English develop in the context of extensive language contact and considerable bilingualism. English is not the first language of the majority of speakers and its pronunciation is strongly shaped by the phonetics of the first language. By contrast, English is now the first language of most people in Wales, although it has not been the dominant language for the majority of speakers for very long and Welsh has experienced a revival in recent years. Welsh phonological features strongly colour the pronunciation of English in the region. The most striking 'Welsh' characteristic of the English spoken in much of Wales is its 'sing-song' or 'musical' intonation. This is created by prosodic features involving stress and timing.

In these countries – India and Wales – the linguistic situation that existed before the introduction of English is a key factor in shaping the accent that develops as English gains new speakers in these areas, both first-language and second-language.

New accents in new places

But what happens when English speakers from a number of different places end up forming a new community, for instance in a new town? I have talked a bit about Australian English and about South African English. These two varieties are now different from British accents of English, even though their input accents were British. What happened in the emergence of distinct accents of English in Australia and in South Africa was that features of the early British regional accents combined with features that grew up on their own in the new place. The result is a variety that is typically or characteristically Australian and South African, respectively. Of course, it is possible to trace their similarities and contrasts – after all, they are varieties of the same language!

The British sociolinguist Paul Kerswill has been investigating the birth of an accent in the new town of Milton Keynes in Buckinghamshire, England.

Activity 7.3   *(Reading B)*

To look further at the miracle of accent birth, work through Reading B, 'Milton Keynes and dialect levelling in south-eastern British English', by Paul Kerswill. You should note the results of his study, and how he arrives at his conclusions.

It is also worth paying attention to the research methodology. There is quite a lot of detail on this, and it will give you some idea of techniques many linguists have used to investigate variation and change in English.

Comment

Kerswill establishes that there is indeed a new accent developing in Milton Keynes – but it shares common features with accents used elsewhere in the south-east of England. He relates these findings to a more general process of **dialect levelling**, in which differences between dialects in the south-east are gradually being ironed out.

Kerswill finds that it is his twelve-year-old informants who are in the vanguard of the linguistic change. He suggests that younger children are still following their parents' pronunciation, whereas the older children – a group for whom approval and acceptance by their peers is most important – are converging on a new pronunciation.

The methodology adopted in this study consisted of identifying a set of **sociolinguistic variables**, or features of language that are used variably in a community, and investigating how the different forms, or variants, of these variables are used by different groups of speakers and in different contexts. As such, this methodology has much in common with other research designed to investigate social variation in accent (and other aspects of language). This is a topic I turn to in section 7.4.

7.4   SOCIAL VARIATION IN ACCENT

Social groups and speaking styles

For most people, the most significant thing about accent is the way it enables us to identify a speaker as a member of a particular group; for instance, a social class, an age group, a group of men or women, or an ethnic group. Sociolinguists use categories (or **social variables**) like class, age, sex and ethnicity to describe what defines a collection of speakers as a speech community. (Recall that Guy and Vonwiller appealed to the social dimensions of age, sex and class in working out which Sydney residents used AQI most frequently. Kerswill focused on age and gender in his Milton Keynes study.) This approach was pioneered by the American linguist William Labov in the 1960s.

The relationship between an accent and a particular social group is, of course, rarely static. The results of Labov's investigation of the variable pronunciation of non-prevocalic /r/ in words like *car* and *part* by New York City speakers suggested that the ways in which an accent varies across members of a society, group by group, reflect the social organization or stratification of that society. Further, he argued that linguistic change in progress shows up because it disrupts the usual patterns of variation.

Section 7.2 discussed the geographical distribution of non-prevocalic /r/. Here I look at how, within a geographical area, the pronunciation of non-prevocalic /r/ can be associated with particular social groups.

Labov divided his informants into six different groups, principally on the basis of socio-economic class. He noticed that his upper-class informants pronounced non-prevocalic /r/ most consistently. By contrast, the lower-class informants had the least /r/ pronunciation of all the socio-economic groups. In New York City non-prevocalic /r/ was associated with high social status and prestige.

People vary their pronunciation to some extent from situation to situation. Labov collected samples of his informants' pronunciation from five different **speaking styles**.His notion of style has a special sense: it is based on the degree of attention a speaker pays to his or her speech. Labov's styles were graded as follows:

least attention	casual speech (life and death narratives)
	careful speech (interview answers)
	reading style
	word lists
most attention	minimal pairs

Labov's stylistic inventory – the list of styles above – divides into the quite different activities of 'conversation' and 'reading'. He expected that high proportions of a 'prestige' pronunciation would occur in the recordings of the highly formal reading tasks (including reading minimal pairs, word lists and whole passages), and that unplanned, conversational speech would be the least likely to show a high proportion of a prestige feature. The underlying argument is that a speaker is likely to be consciously aware of prestige accent features and so will use them in speaking styles demanding a high degree of attention.

Figure 7.6 is a hypothetical example of what you might find in a situation of stable stratification, taking into account the expected stylistic variation for each social group. You can see here that 'lower-class'speakers would be expected to pronounce /r/ least frequently across all styles and that the percentage of /r/ pronunciations would increase the higher you go up the 'social class' scale. There would also be a difference between styles, with speakers from each social group pronouncing /r/ more frequently as styles became more formal, according to Labov's classification.

Note: In the /r/ index, a score of 100% would indicate that speakers always pronounced non-prevocalic /r/; 50% that they pronounced it in 50% of cases; 0% that they never pronounced it.

Labov's actual findings were slightly different (see Figure 7.7). This graph has become something of a classic in sociolinguistic research, and you will find it reproduced in several sociolinguistic textbooks.

Activity 7.4   *(Allow 10–15 minutes)*

Look carefully at Figure 7.7.

1   How is non-prevocalic /r/ actually distributed among the speakers and styles in Labov's study?

2   In particular, how does Figure 7.7 differ from the hypothetical distribution in Figure 7.6?

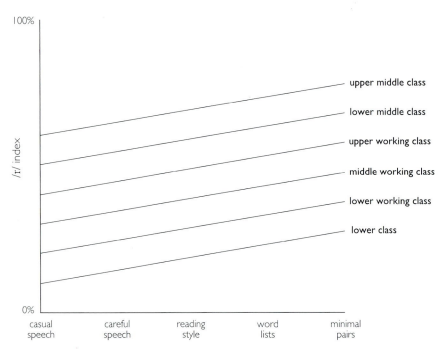

Figure 7.6 *Stable sociolinguistic stratification (use of non-prevocalic /r/ according to socio-economic class and style)*

(Based on Coates, 1986/93, p. 63)

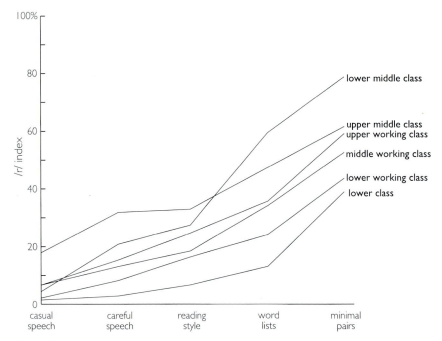

Figure 7.7
Change in progress (use of non-prevocalic /r/ according to socio-economic class and style)

(Adapted from Labov, 1968, p. 114)

Comment

Figure 7.7 shows a similar general trend to that in Figure 7.6, though the pattern is rather less neat. Actual social classes are not homogeneous and informants will not behave exactly as predicted. But the most noticeable feature is that lower-middle-class informants use a higher proportion of non-prevocalic /r/ in the more formal reading situations than the speakers in the social group above them: the upper middle class. This shows up in the 'lower-middle-class' line crossing over the 'upper-middle-class' line. Labov termed this 'cross-over' effect **hypercorrection**, in that the lower-middle-class speakers actually go beyond the speech of the upper middle class, which they are targeting. He interpreted this pattern to indicate that the lower-middle-class speakers – conscious of the prestige value of non-prevocalic /r/ pronunciation in their society – were anxious to show this awareness. Consequently, they maximized their use of this pronunciation in situations in which they paid considerable attention to their speech. The motivation he offers for this linguistic behaviour is that lower-middle-class speakers are insecure and, in many cases, aspire to be accepted and recognized as members of the upper middle class.

Social aspects of accent change

Labov argued that Figure 7.7 illustrated language change in progress: the pronunciation of the non-prevocalic /r/ is spreading. He also argued that this change was the result of conscious behaviour, categorizing it as 'change from above' (i.e. above the level of consciousness). The opposite, 'change from below' (i.e. below the level of consciousness), describes a linguistic change that is the result of unconscious behaviour. The spread of AQI, discussed by Guy and Vonwiller, is an example of change from below. The nature of the spread or diffusion of the change that Labov observed is social, as it percolates through the social classes, from the upper to the lower middle class (activated by the behaviour of the lower middle class in taking up a feature associated with the class above them). The diffusion of the feature through the speech of a particular social group is stylistic: it first appears in the most formal, reading styles and then it gradually percolates into the speaking styles, first the formal and then the casual.

Our discussion of social variation and change in accent has so far focused on social class as the principal determining factor. But the category of social class is broad and rather vague. It embraces a range of different people and is not as homogeneous as certain stereotypes would lead us to believe. For example, it is possible that middle-class women might behave differently from middle-class men, as far as language is concerned. And in fact Labov's New York City findings suggest that it was lower-middle-class *women* who were instrumental in the diffusion of /r/ pronunciation in the community. Labov argued that these women were particularly conscious of the prestige value of /r/ and that they worked hardest to assimilate upper-middle-class speech. He based his thesis on two observations. First, he noticed that his female informants appeared to hypercorrect more frequently than his male informants. And secondly, when asked about their own sense of their /r/ usage, the women frequently reported that they used non-prevocalic /r/ more often and more consistently than they actually did. He concluded that lower-middle-class women were in the vanguard of socially motivated linguistic change.

This interpretation of sex differences has been quite influential in the sociolinguistic study of change. For example, Guy and Vonwiller infer from the fact that Sydney women use AQI more than twice as often as men that they must be leading its spread in the Sydney speech community.

Deborah Cameron and Jennifer Coates (1988) offer a critical account of the role of women in the situations of linguistic change investigated by Labov. While they concede that the research appears to demonstrate women initiating changes in the direction of prestige norms, they question the status of the male norms in terms of which the women's behaviour is examined (Cameron and Coates, 1988, pp. 16 ff.).

Gender and accent

Debates about gender and language use have highlighted several problematic areas in sociolinguistic research such as that carried out by Labov. For instance, research often shows women using more 'prestige' pronunciations than men from the same social class, and this seems consistent with Labov's finding that women are in the vanguard of linguistic change in the direction of more 'prestige' variants. Researchers often seek explanations that apply to women as a group – for example, that women are more 'status conscious' than men. Problems with this include:

- Women were traditionally assigned to a social class on the basis of their husbands' jobs, incomes, etc. rather than independently. This begs the question of whether they were in fact members of 'the same social class'.

- Men have sometimes been taken as the norm, so that women's pronunciations are perceived as divergent and in need of explanation.

- Women themselves are not a homogeneous group: remember that Labov found it was one subset, the 'lower-middle-class' women, who were instrumental in linguistic change.

- Not all research has found sex differences in the expected direction (the Sydney women in Guy and Vonwiller's study were adopting a feature also associated with working-class speech). More recent research points to the influence of women's and men's lifestyles, and the people they meet and interact with, upon their language use.

This suggests that, in any discussion of social variation, we need to look carefully at the assumptions made by researchers: at how they assign people to social groups, and at how they analyse and interpret linguistic evidence.

Although breaking down the large category of class into different sexes and even age groups might go some way towards identifying the social locus of change, this process does not help to discover the role of different people – individuals – within the group. So there remains the problem of identifying the innovators and initiators of linguistic change.

The challenge of identifying the actual site of change has led several researchers to adapt and develop Labov's methods and categories. Barbara Horvath (1985) found the category of social class too vague and undifferentiated when she set out to investigate the accents of social groups in Sydney, Australia. So she decided to use a different method of analysis, termed 'principal components analysis'. (Kerswill also used this method to analyse the data collected in Milton Keynes.) The method is rather complex, but its main value is that it allows a researcher to consider a whole set of social variables all at once. This technique enabled Horvath to avoid having to specify a single variable (such as socio-economic class, or age or style) as a determinant of linguistic behaviour. Instead, a *combination* of variables can be used to account for patterns of linguistic variation. Horvath's method demonstrated how social class (defined by occupation alone) and ethnic origin (Anglo, Greek, Italian) interact to influence the language of Sydney speakers. She also found that the different generations in immigrant communities differed in their speech. This age factor interacted with class as well.

Work carried out by James and Lesley Milroy in Belfast in Northern Ireland also challenges the tenets of Labovian sociolinguistics. Lesley Milroy points out (1987, p. 105) that the relationship between linguistic and social structure is not necessarily best examined by an exclusive exploration of variables such as age or class. The notion of **social network** provides another way of investigating how speakers use language variation (consciously or unconsciously) to signal different kinds of social identity and social aspiration. Rather than grouping speakers into predetermined categories such as social class, the social network situates an individual within the sum of his or her relationships, both formal and informal, with other people. These relationships may be contracted via friendship, family, work, neighbourhood or ethnicity.

Social networks

Social networks are a way of measuring the closeness of relationships within a community. A researcher drawing on social networks would note the range of contexts in which one individual regularly encounters another (termed 'plexity') and the extent to which the members of a social circle are in contact with one another (termed 'density'). A 'multiplex' network is one in which, for example, the same people encounter one another at church and at social gatherings as well as at work. This relationship contrasts with a 'uniplex' one in which, for instance, one individual does not see another outside of the workplace. A 'dense' network is one in which everybody knows and interacts regularly with everybody else.

Networks may be close-knit with dense and multiplex ties, in that the same individuals regularly meet in a range of different contexts, or they may be relatively loose-knit, where members are linked only by 'uniplex' ties and have several 'outside' ties with other communities.

The Milroys adopted social network theory in order to describe the nature of the Belfast community whose language they were investigating. Belfast is a place where traditional distinctions based on socio-economic class are considerably complicated by differences based on religious affiliation and factional politics. Historically, areas of the city have tended to be categorized depending on whether their residents are mainly Catholic or Protestant, rather than whether they might be described as working-class or middle-class. In this particular situation, Labov's a priori application of social class is inappropriate since the community itself resists such pigeon-holing. However, this particular instance does not mean that social class is never an important factor in accounting for linguistic variation.

The Milroys found that particular kinds of networks will either inhibit or advance linguistic variation and change in a community. For instance, groups like the men of the Ballymacarett district of Belfast, who worked in the local shipyard and whose relationships were typically dense networks bound by strong ties, were more likely to enforce the prevailing linguistic norms in the community and were less likely to tolerate or encourage change. In this they differed from the Ballymacarett women, who often travelled outside the area to work and had fewer local ties. This sex difference was to some extent reversed in another area studied, the Clonard, where many younger women worked together and had close ties in the community.

Dense, multiplex networks, then, seem to act as brakes on linguistic innovation. By contrast, weak ties between individuals seem to facilitate the spread from network to network of linguistic innovations, such as new pronunciations or new words. The Milroys argue that the peripheral members of a community who themselves have ties with other communities (through work, study or friends) effectively conduct or carry innovation into a community. These conclusions complement Labov's arguments about change in progress, but provide far more information about the site of change, as well as possible explanations for change.

While Horvath's revision of sociolinguistic methods concerns the ways in which language data are analysed, the Milroys revised the ways that language data are collected. Recall that Labov organized his data into a single continuum of style, defined in terms of degree of attention the informants paid to their speech. One of the problems with this predetermined stylistic scale is that it doesn't really represent a *continuum* embracing casual as well as formal speaking styles. There is, for example, a clear contrast between the styles of speaking and reading. We might argue that talking differs radically from reading, as the latter requires certain formally learned skills. A group's linguistic behaviour might vary because some people are more competent readers than others and not because they are treating the tasks as stylistically different. In addition, since the sociolinguistic interview is a highly artificial speech situation, it is virtually impossible for interview material to be treated as natural speech. (It may of course be thought of as representing a particular style of speaking, namely interview style.)

Labov recognized a further problem that he termed 'the observer's paradox': the informants' speech will necessarily be affected by the mere fact that they are being observed and recorded.

Lesley Milroy made considerable efforts to lessen the danger of the researcher's interference by ensuring that her Belfast informants treated her initially as 'a friend of a friend', and then, as they became more familiar, as an acquaintance or friend. More importantly, to acquire examples of speech that was as natural as possible, the gathered samples included conversations between individuals in different social settings, groups and occasions. Here, the aim was not to differentiate styles using an artificial and unmeasurable device such as level of attention. Instead, the research drew on the common-sense recognition that people's accents vary according to context.

Context is highly complex, including factors such as topic of conversation, audience and purpose of communication. It is considered further in Chapter 8.

In this section, we have considered ways in which people's accents vary, depending on a range of social factors. Sociolinguists have traditionally been interested in examining the influence of factors like social class, sex and age on accent variation and, ultimately, on linguistic change. Such categories may enable large-scale patterns and general trends to be identified, but they cannot shed any light on the precise mechanisms of linguistic change. The Milroys' work in Belfast was an attempt to do this: to identify how change comes about within a community.

You may find it useful to review Readings A and B, looking at what evidence they provide about variation and change in English accents, in the light of having read this section.

7.5   EVALUATING ACCENTS

In section 7.4, we considered the ways in which the social structure of a speech community may be reflected in the patterns of speech in that community. However, if we wish to understand how this connection between language and society operates, we need to consider the speakers' perspective on this issue. The point is that accents are socially differentiated because 'speakers' attach different social meanings to them – in often unpredictable and uneven ways.

And so we are in a position to return to the issues mentioned at the beginning of this chapter. However odd or idiosyncratic the quotations from Lette's novel and Shaw's preface to *Pygmalion* might appear, they happen to reflect what some English speakers think about the ways in which English is spoken and the prestige attached to certain accents, such as RP in England.

Activity 7.5   *(Allow 15 minutes)*

Read the following poem, 'Them and [uz]', by Tony Harrison. Unusually for poetry, it includes International Phonetic Alphabet (IPA) symbols to represent different sounds associated with contrasting accents. You may wish to refer to the IPA chart at the back of this book to identify these sounds.

As you read, consider the attitudes being described and satirized in the poem.

- What is the poet's attitude towards RP?

- How does this differ from the attitudes suggested in the quotations from Lette and Shaw at the beginning of this chapter?

By the way, can you identify the regional English accent being posed against RP?

Them & [uz]

I

αἰαῖ, ay, ay! ... stutterer Demosthenes
gob full of pebbles outshouting seas –

4 words only of *mi 'art aches* and ... 'Mine's broken,
you barbarian, T.W.!' He was nicely spoken.
'Can't have our glorious heritage done to death!'

I played the Drunken Porter in *Macbeth*.

'Poetry's the speech of kings. You're one of those
Shakespeare gives the comic bits to: prose!
All poetry (even Cockney Keats?) you see
's been dubbed by [ʌs] into RP,
Received Pronunciation, please believe [ʌs]
your speech is in the hands of the Receivers.'

'We say [ʌs] not [uz], T.W.!' That shut my trap.
I doffed my flat a's (as in 'flat cap')
my mouth all stuffed with glottals, great
lumps to hawk up and spit out ... *E-nun-ci-ate!*

II

So right, yer buggers, then! We'll occupy
your lousy leasehold Poetry.
I chewed up Littererchewer and spat the bones

into the lap of dozing Daniel Jones,
dropped the initials I'd been harried as
and used my *name* and own voice: [uz] [uz] [uz],
ended sentences with by, with, from,
and spoke the language that I spoke at home.
RIP RP, RIP T.W.
I'm *Tony* Harrison no longer you!

You can tell the Receivers where to go
(and not aspirate it) once you know
Wordsworth's *matter/water* are full rhymes,
[uz] can be loving as well as funny.

My first mention in the *Times*
automatically made Tony Anthony!

(Harrison, 1987, pp. 122–3)

Comment

The poem is a vigorous riposte to those 'nicely spoken' keepers of English culture
and letters. Harrison, from Leeds in Yorkshire in the north of England, sets a
scene in which he is called upon to recite something from 'our glorious heritage'.
He barely has time to utter four words before his pronunciation is ridiculed as
barbaric. The agent of his humiliation persists, claiming that poetry must be
enunciated; in other words, recited in RP accent. This provokes a furious and
eloquent retort that the greatest English poets, like Shakespeare, Keats and
Wordsworth, would not have been RP speakers.

Finally, Harrison alludes to the association of RP with the British establishment and its institutions by referring to the broadsheet newspaper *The Times*.
Somewhat ruefully, he observes that the establishment will not even allow his
name (never mind his accent!) to remain as he wishes.

While Tony Harrison mounts a strong defence of his local accent, others have
succumbed to pressure to change the way they speak, albeit sometimes with mixed
feelings. Take the following testimony of a young woman originally from Derby in
the north of England, who changed her accent to match her move from her local,
working-class community to London:

> Leaving one's class was to be both admired and scorned. My mother
> described its pejorative connotations as typified by a change of accent
> which she referred to as 'lasting and pasting'. The fear in the working-
> class morality of putting on airs and graces was the fear of being found to
> be an impostor. The terror was not a simple matter of working-class pride.
> It was all right to talk like that if you had a right to belong to that class. In
> 1983, I lasted and pasted it. Few [in Derby] would have recognised my
> accent as local. In London they still constantly remark on my 'northern
> accent', as though it were a mark of quaint and charming working-class
> authenticity.
>
> (Cited in Walkerdine, 1985, pp. 74–5)

The 'lasting and pasting' she refers to is the use of the long /ɑː/ of RP *bath* and
grass in place of what Harrison calls the 'flat cap' *a* /a/, an almost stereotypical
marker of northern accents. The journalist Nancy Banks-Smith worked on a
different feature in the attempt to get rid of her Lancashire accent:

> When I went to Roedean [a girls' private school in southern England] I was put in a cupboard and told to say:
>
>> It was eight bells ringing
>> And the morning watch was done
>> And the gunner's lad was singing
>> As they polished every gun
>
> until I dropped every last g. I came out of that cupboard talking like a duchess. The unforeseen result was that I noticed for the first time that my parents had Lancashire accents and found them horribly embarrassing. Now my accent is a horrible embarrassment to my children, who pretend I've called to collect for the Distressed Gentlefolks Association and just leaving.
>
> (N. Banks-Smith, *Guardian*, 30 October 1991)

What Banks-Smith is talking about is dropping the pronunciation of the consonant /g/ at the end of the *-ing* syllable (represented by the single phoneme /ŋ/ in RP) which is, as she sees it, an obvious giveaway of her Lancashire accent. It is striking that she contrasts her embarrassment at her parents' accents with her own children's embarrassment at hers. The implication of her reference to the 'Distressed Gentlefolks Association' seems to be that she has acquired a version of RP that is distinctly old-fashioned, compared with her children's accent.

Of course, because most people's attitudes are very ambivalent, it is hard to interpret popular attitudes to language, and more precisely to accent. For one thing, although RP might appear to be the most prestigious accent of English, not all speakers of English would agree with this claim. Many non-native speakers in Africa and South Asia have equivocal, but often negative, attitudes towards RP. In his study of English in Ghana, K.A. Sey reports that while 'educated' Ghanaian English is acceptable, 'the type that strives too obviously to approximate to RP is frowned upon as distasteful and pedantic' (Sey, 1973, p. 8). And the Nigerian linguist Ayọ Bamgboṣe (1971, p. 41) comments that his compatriots 'consider as snobbish any Nigerians who speak like a native speaker of English'. In the past, RP was highly valued by Indian speakers of English, so that in the experience of Braj Kachru 'to have one's English labelled *Indian* was an ego-cracking linguistic insult'. But the situation has changed considerably, so that Kachru is now able to report that (mainly young) Indian English speakers are more willing to tolerate and accommodate Indian English than before (Kachru 1992, p. 60).

This is in contrast to New Zealand, for example, where the sociolinguist Janet Holmes reports how her compatriots express negative attitudes to their own accent, calling it a 'harsh and horrid brogue' by contrast with what they judge to be the 'pure English' of England (Holmes, 1992, p. 354).

Of course, for many speakers of English in India and Africa the experience of the British colonial past and its politics is woven inextricably into attitudes towards English, and especially British English: non-native speakers of English may have mixed feelings, even downright negative ones, about the RP accent in particular. It is also traditionally, even commonly, the case for native English speakers – deliberately or unconsciously – to react negatively to non-native accents of English. Kachru captures this reciprocal antipathy in the colonial context rather neatly: 'The second language user never seemed to win in this see-saw of attitudes. If he gained "native-like" competence he was suspect; if he did not gain it he was an object of linguistic ridicule' (Kachru. 1986, p. 22).

Chapter 9 considers further the issue of 'good' and 'bad' English.

The task of measuring people's subjective attitudes and emotions about accents has absorbed sociolinguists for a long time. The US dialectologist Dennis Preston has been gathering data from southern Indiana speakers and south-east

Michigan speakers about the comparative 'correctness' and 'pleasantness' of the accents of the other states in the USA. His aim is to gain a sense of the 'folk concepts' which 'represent strongly held, influential beliefs in the linguistic life of large and small speech communities' (Preston, 1993, p. 375) by getting ordinary people to draw perceptual maps of the country, differentiating between areas of good and bad English. Figure 7.8 shows southern Indiana speakers' ratings of US accents in terms of their 'correctness'. From the data, the areas most associated with incorrect English are the south and New York City; neighbouring areas receive only slightly higher ratings. Southern Indiana itself receives a reasonable rating, but Washington DC, Connecticut, Delaware and Washington state are regarded as superior.

Apart from asking people outright what they think of a particular accent, the most common method of gauging subjective reactions is to ask people to rate speakers talking in different accents in terms of a set of personal qualities. These might include honesty, friendliness, intelligence, self-confidence, sense of humour, ambition, sincerity, likeability, fluency and attractiveness – character traits rather than qualities that could be used to describe an accent. This is based on the premise that there is a powerful link between attitudes towards an accent and attitudes towards the speakers of that accent. (Such work was pioneered by the British social psychologist Howard Giles and his associates; see for instance Giles and Powesland, 1975.)

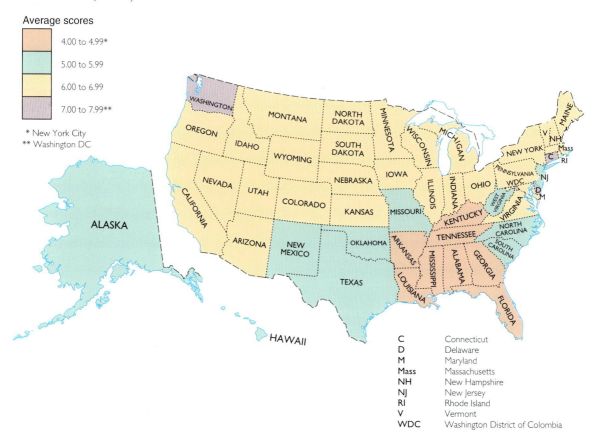

Figure 7.8   *Southern Indiana speakers' ratings of 'correct' English on a scale from 1 (least correct) to 10 (most correct)* (Adapted from Preston, 1993, p. 349)

Listeners are expected to make their judgements of a speaker on the basis of the sound of the voice, but there are numerous difficulties with this sort of test, not the least of which is determining precisely what the listener is reacting to: voice pitch or timbre, voice quality, rate of speaking or accent. And as we have seen, accent includes features beyond mere pronunciation.

In recent studies of the social evaluation of varieties of Australian English, speakers of 'cultivated Australian' were always rated higher than speakers with 'broad' accents. And cultivated Australian speakers tended to be rated higher on 'intelligence, competence, reliability, honesty and status than broad speakers, although the latter were evaluated as higher on humorousness and talkativeness' (Ball et al., 1989, p. 94).

So while Australians do not judge the broad accent very highly in terms of status or prestige, they judge it more positively in other respects.

It is worth thinking about people's attitudes to accents in the light of the investigations of researchers such as Labov, Kerswill and the Milroys. One conclusion we might draw is that English speakers associate particular accents with social class as well as with geographical region. This was demonstrated in the findings of a BBC radio survey of British listeners' attitudes towards different regional accents. Asked to match occupation (ranging from chimney sweep through car salesman to bank manager) and particular character traits (honesty, trustworthiness, friendliness) with different accents, the majority of respondents placed RP at the top of the social scale and labelled it as most honest. By contrast, they placed local Liverpool (Scouse) at the bottom of the social scale, and Cockney as the least attractive in terms of character.

Howard Giles's research on British English suggests that listeners' perceptions of accent are actually rather ambivalent. He found, like Ball in Australia, that RP-accented speakers were perceived more favourably in terms of 'competence' (ambition, intelligence, self-confidence, determination and industriousness), but that speakers using certain regional accents were perceived more favourably in terms of 'personal integrity' and 'social attractiveness' (seriousness, talkativeness, good-naturedness and sense of humour). There are, then, certain costs as well as benefits in the use of RP in Britain and elsewhere.

7.6   CONCLUSION

In this chapter I have discussed some of the characteristics of an English accent, showing how different accents can be contrasted in terms of their phoneme systems (the consonants and vowels of English); the distribution of phonemes (where they are used); and how phonemes are realized or pronounced. I have also discussed the importance of features that operate above the level of the phoneme: prosodic features such as intonation and rhythm, and voice quality.

A major theme of the chapter has been the inherent variability of English accents. I have discussed how accents differ regionally and socially, and how language change is bound up with such variation – the focus on change in this chapter continues a theme that has run through several earlier parts of the book. I have discussed some of the origins of contemporary variability: the regional diffusion of new pronunciations (e.g. the Great Vowel Shift in England, the *cot/caught* merger in the USA); patterns of settlement in former colonies (e.g. South Africa); and the influence of other languages (Indian languages in India, Welsh in Wales). Several of the studies mentioned in this chapter also show how change spreads through different social groups – in practice, social and regional factors are inextricably linked. The two readings – from Guy and Vonwiller, and Kerswill, respectively – provide more detailed examples of how linguists have investigated variation and change in English accents; both show linguists acting rather like detectives, trying to piece together evidence to account for change in progress.

A second theme, and again one that is important throughout this book, is that of identity: accents provide a way of marking one's identity as a member of a social group, or groups. And accents carry important social meanings. I have suggested that, within any community, one can identify general patterns in how people perceive and evaluate accents but also that in practice these attitudes are likely to be rather more ambivalent than may at first be apparent.

This theme of identity is continued in the next chapter, where we discuss how individuals vary the way they speak – their accents, but also other aspects of language – in different contexts.

Reading A

THE HIGH RISING TONE IN AUSTRALIAN ENGLISH

Gregory Guy and Julia Vonwiller

The development of AQI

[To answer questions about the origins and spread of any linguistic form we need to ask the question: 'Who uses it and how much?' The social dimensions of age, sex, and class are important for investigating change in progress.] These dimensions are relevant because of the way linguistic innovations spread through society. New items in a language diffuse across a speech community in a wave-like fashion, starting with a few social groups in the community and then gradually being adopted by others (Labov, 1981; Bailey, 1973). This means that at a given point in time a distinctive, uneven social distribution should exist, with some advanced groups using the new form extensively while other conservative groups may not yet be using it at all. Therefore, looking at the use of a form by age, sex, and class groups will give us a cross-sectional picture of the innovation in mid-flight through social space.

The age distribution is the most crucial. Most speakers of a language appear to become relatively fixed in many linguistic traits by the time they develop their adult linguistic system. In other words, they do *not* go on changing the way they speak – by adopting new pronunciations, or new grammatical constructions – after the age of about eighteen to twenty (Labov, 1981). Thus the only age group which is always ready to adopt new forms is the young: children and teenagers …

This is what we find for AQI [Australian questioning intonation]. Table 1 … shows the percentages of AQI use … for speakers from different age groups … This intonation clearly predominates among the young, with a maximum in the older teenagers who use the intonation at ten times the rate found for speakers over the age of forty. Young adults fall into an intermediate position. The slight drop-off in younger teenagers probably suggests that at this age children are still influenced somewhat by the non-AQI-using speech of their parents.

This age pattern supports the hypothesis that AQI represents a recent innovation, probably arising within the last twenty to thirty years in Sydney. But the age pattern alone is not conclusive, since the same pattern would obtain if AQI were something that everyone used as a teenager, but then gave up as they grew older. So we also need to look at the class and sex distributions, and at the diachronic evidence [i.e. evidence over time].

Table I AQI use in four age groups

Age group	Instances of AQI	No. of tone groups	% AQI [per tone group]
11–14 yrs	79	5,032	1.6
15–19 yrs	306	15,067	2.0
20–39 yrs	24	4,386	0.5
40 + yrs	49	19,642	0.2

(Source: Adapted from Guy et al., 1986)

Table 2 AQI use by sex

Sex	Instances of AQI	No. of tone groups	% AQI [per tone group]
Male	561	53,769	1.0
Female	1,163	53,916	2.2

(Adapted from Guy et al., 1986)

The sex distribution of AQI in Sydney is shown in Table 2, which draws on an even larger corpus than Table 1. Women use the form about twice as frequently as men.

So this dimension offers further support for … the hypothesis that AQI is a recent, and ongoing, innovation.

The last social dimension we shall consider is social class. … Leading researchers [agree] that internally developed, untargeted linguistic innovations, as in Labov's 'change from below' (1966, p. 224) characteristically originate in the broadly defined working class (Labov, 1980, 1981; Kroch, 1978; Guy et al., 1986). The reasons for this are complex but they have to do with the social solidarity of the innovators and with the apparent resistance to linguistic change shown by higher status, non-innovating groups. In any case, as Kroch (1978) notes, no case has been found in which the highest status group originates a systematic linguistic change.

Given these facts, we would expect an innovation to show a characteristic uneven social class distribution, with a peak rate of usage in the working class. The data … given in Table 3, show that the social class distribution of AQI follows exactly this pattern, with the working class speakers using AQI at an average rate which is two to three times that of the middle class.

Table 3 AQI use by social class

Social class	Instances of AQI	No. of tone groups	% AQI [per tone group]
Middle	273	36,852	0.7
Upper working	673	39,518	1.7
Lower working	778	31,315	2.5

(Adapted from Guy et al., 1986)

All of the social dimensions of interest, therefore, show the characteristic 'finger-prints' of change in progress. This suggests that the use of a high rising tone in declaratives … is a new development in Sydney English, and did not exist earlier than about twenty to thirty years ago. But to be absolutely confident of this one would still like to have some concrete diachronic evidence on this point, some data to examine from Sydney speakers several decades ago …

[Fortunately we have such data in the form of a sample of sixty-five boys and girls, recorded by Mitchell and Delbridge (1965a and b) at three Sydney high schools around 1960. In this sample the occurrence of AQI amounted to 0.3 per cent], less than one-sixth of the frequency of AQI use that today's older teenagers are showing (see Table 1). Consequently the counter-hypothesis stated above, that perhaps all Sydney speakers use AQI as teenagers and then stop using it as adults, is essentially disproved. Teenagers in 1960 didn't do this. Rather, the data support our basic hypothesis about the age grading and change in progress. The 0.3 per cent of AQI usage found among the older Sydney teenagers recorded in

1960 corresponds very closely to the 0.2–0.5 per cent rates of usage found among the two adult groups recorded in 1980. As the teenagers of 1960 are today all in their late thirties or early forties, this comparability of figures suggests that, regarding AQI, these people *did* become fixed in their linguistic usage upon reaching adulthood, and that the focal point of innovation has remained with the younger members of the speech community across the last several decades. Adults do not introduce new forms of this sort, but tend to stick with the way they learned to say things when they were children or teenagers.

The ... age, sex, and class patterns of distribution, and the diachronic evidence from the Mitchell and Delbridge data, all combine to create a very strong case that AQI is a recent change, and one that is still underway, still spreading. This in itself is a remarkable finding, since it constitutes possibly the only known case of intonational change. This is because most of our knowledge about language change is based on written records, and intonation is very poorly represented in all traditional writing systems. Intonations probably change as often as any other linguistic feature, but unless they are 'caught in the act', they become essentially unrecoverable. AQI, therefore, appears to be the first intonational change to be caught in this way, and therefore constitutes an important addition to our knowledge of language change.

...

As to where it came from, linguistically speaking, it seems to us that AQI is best understood as an extension with a modified meaning of the ordinary English usage of HRT-in-declarative as a device for asking questions. This has been an intonational option in all English dialects for, one assumes, a long time. If one says 'You're letting your hair grow?', the syntax is declarative, but the intonation is interrogative, having the effect of questioning the propositional content of the utterance, creating a *yes/no* question with the meaning 'Is it true that ...?' The syntax and the intonation involved in AQI are the same as this; what makes AQI different is just its meaning. Instead of questioning propositional content, AQI questions the listener's *state of understanding*. AQI therefore asks 'Do you understand?' This seems to us to be a modest and natural extension of the meaning of the HRT-in-declarative construction, and the most likely source of the AQI in use in Sydney today.

References

BAILEY, C.J. (1973) *Variation and Linguistic Theory*, Washington DC, Center for Applied Linguistics.

GUY, G., HORVATH, B., VONWILLER, J., DAISLEY, E. and ROGERS, I. (1986) 'An intonational change in progress in Australian English', *Language in Society*, vol. 15, pp. 23–51.

KROCH, A.S. (1978) 'Towards a theory of social dialect variation, *Language in Society*, vol. 7, pp. 17–36.

LABOV, W. (1966) *The Social Stratification of English in New York City*, Washington DC, Center for Applied Linguistics.

LABOV, W. (ed.) (1980) *Locating Language in Time and Space*, New York, Academic Press.

LABOV, W. (1981) 'What can be learned about change in progress from synchronic description?' in SANKOFF, D. and CEDERGREN, H. (eds), *Variation Omnibus*, Edmonton, Alberta, Linguistic Research.

MITCHELL, A.G. and DELBRIDGE, A. (1965a) *The Speech of Australian Adolescents*, Sydney, Angus Robertson.

MITCHELL, A.G. and DELBRIDGE, A. (1965b) *The Pronunciation of English in Australia*, Sydney, Angus Robertson.

Source: Guy and Vonwiller, 1989

Reading B

MILTON KEYNES AND DIALECT LEVELLING IN SOUTH-EASTERN BRITISH ENGLISH

Paul Kerswill

The role of dialect contact in language change

English, like all living languages, has undergone change throughout its history. Language change does not always occur at the same rate, however, and it is reasonable to suppose that the speed of language change depends in no small measure on the social changes affecting the speakers of the language. Here, I look at one kind of social change – the increase in geographical and social mobility of recent years – and consider its possible effects on the pronunciation of British English.

From the point of view of language change, it is probably the geographical aspect of mobility that has the more far-reaching effect. As people move to new areas, they may form social and ethnic groups with distinct ways of speaking, as in the case of immigrants from overseas. Migration within a single language area, such as Britain, leads to prolonged contact between speakers of different dialects of the same language (termed 'dialect contact' – see Trudgill, 1986).

In the south-east of England, as elsewhere, there has long been geographical and social mobility, leading (we must presume) to dialect contact. Mobility has increased markedly since the Second World War, and has probably led to the fact that young people in the south and south-east are beginning to sound more and more like each other. (This reduction of differences between dialects has been termed 'dialect levelling'.) Such mobility is perhaps typified by the rise of 'new towns', including Hemel Hempstead, Stevenage, Peterlee, Telford and Milton Keynes – all of which were established as a matter of government policy.

Below I describe a study I carried out with a colleague, Ann Williams, in Milton Keynes, the most recent and fastest expanding of these new towns. Our intention in the study was to see if there is evidence for the rise of a 'new dialect' in Milton Keynes, distinct from those of other places and from those of the people who moved into the town.

The Milton Keynes study

The role of children in the formation of new dialects

The Milton Keynes project follows a research tradition established by William Labov, who with his 1966 New York City research published the first systematic large-scale study of urban speech. However, the approach we took in the Milton Keynes project necessarily differed from Labov's. A tenet of his methodology is that by comparing the speech of older and younger people we can get a 'snapshot' of language change. In Milton Keynes this is clearly not possible, since there are few older 'native' inhabitants. In any case, our aim was a different one, as I suggested above.

Instead, we focused mainly on children, in whose speech we might expect to find evidence of a new dialect: children's speech is less fixed, more malleable than that of adults, most of whom will only change their speech in minor ways when they move to another area. It is the children of the in-migrants who, on encountering age-mates in nursery and at school, will have to 'settle on' a set of features that will be characteristic of speech in the new town.

A crucial further question is at what age children begin and complete their convergence on a new dialect. Most of us can tell anecdotes of young children losing their parents' accents on associating with other children, and of teenagers picking up strong local accents as they come under peer pressure to conform in all matters of behaviour. These changes in children's speech are part of what we can term 'sociolinguistic maturation': how do children acquire the sociolinguistic skills adults have that enable them to speak in different ways according to context? The project aimed to throw some light on this issue.

Choice of location

Milton Keynes is in the county of Buckinghamshire in England, close to the borders with two other counties, Bedfordshire and Northamptonshire. It lies near the towns of Bedford and Northampton, some 90 kilometres north-west of London. Milton Keynes was designated a new town in 1969, when there was already an existing population in this area of around 44,000 living mainly in the towns of Wolverton and Bletchley. By the 1991 census, the population had risen to 176,330. Table 1 shows where the new arrivals came from. Over three quarters were from the south-east, and nearly half of these were from London. Obviously, this fact will have repercussions for any 'new dialect' we might find in the town.

Table 1 Percentage of resident households moving to Milton Keynes since its designation as a new town, in 1969

Area of previous residence	% households
London	35.2
Immediate sub-region (approx. 15 minute drive)	3.4
Rest of Buckinghamshire	5.2
Rest of Bedfordshire/Northamptonshire	9.8
Rest of south-east	22.6
Total from south-east	76.2
Rest of England	16.2
Rest of UK	3.7
Overseas	3.9
Total	100.0

(Milton Keynes Development Corporation (MKDC), 1990, p. 31)

Methodology

Sociolinguistic variables

In the Milton Keynes project, we investigated ten sociolinguistic variables: in this case, speech sounds that had different pronunciations within the speech community. Five of these variables are discussed in this reading; they are summarized in Table 2. (I follow the usual practice of putting sociolinguistic variables in curved brackets.)

Table 2   The sociolinguistic variables used in the study

Consonants

(t)	word medial 't' which is often replaced by a glottal stop [ʔ], as in *letter*, *bottle*, ([leʔə], [bɒʔl])
(th)	word initial, word medial, word final voiceless 'th', as in *three*, *nothing*, *tooth*, where the dental fricative [θ] can be replaced with the 'f' sound [f].

Vowels

(ou)	the 'diphthong' vowel in *coat*, *moan*, etc. The second part of this diphthong can be 'fronted' (pronounced further forward in the mouth), to give the impression of received pronunciation '*kite*' or '*mine*'. Fronting may lead to '*Coke*' resembling '*cake*' in RP.
(u:)	the long vowel in *move*, *shoe*, etc., which can be fronted to a vowel close to that of French *tu* or German *grün*.
(au)	the diphthong in *house*, *now*, etc.; this can have a wide range of pronunciations in south-east England, ranging from the vowel [ɛɪ], which resembles the vowel in RP *rain*, through an RP [aʊ], to a broad London [ɛː], which resembles the vowel in RP *scar*ce.

Speakers

In selecting our speakers, we decided to focus on children from three age groups: four-year-olds (when children are still largely under the influence of their caretakers' speech), eight-years-olds and twelve-year-olds (when they are verging on adolescence, with its associated peer group structures and orientation away from parental values). Additionally, we interviewed one caretaker for each child – in almost every case the mother. Once we had obtained the relevant permissions, we arranged recordings in one nursery and two schools in two of the earliest housing estates of the post-1969 new town. Our final sample consisted of 48 children who were either born in Milton Keynes or who had arrived there by the age of two. The children were equally divided between the sexes and the age groups, so that there were eight children in each group or 'cell' (i.e. eight girls aged four, eight aged eight, and so on). Sex and age were, then, the primary 'social variables' of the study. We felt that social class was less relevant to the central aims; it was held roughly constant by virtue of the fact that the schools and the nursery shared the same, fairly homogeneous catchment area.

The recordings

The recordings were divided into two main sections: elicitation tasks and spontaneous speech. The elicitation tasks were intended to elicit particular words which contained our target sociolinguistic variables; some were reading lists, others games such as quizzes, 'spot-the-difference' pictures and map-reading tasks. The spontaneous speech was obtained by interviewing the children about their school, friends and homes and by making recordings in the playground using radio microphones. The children's caretakers were also interviewed.

In analysing these speech samples, we noted down all the occurrences of different variants (i.e. actual pronunciations) for each sociolinguistic variable. We could then quantify our data and carry out various forms of statistical analysis.

Interpreting the results

Is there a distinctive Milton Keynes dialect?

There are a number of expectations that one might have of the emerging Milton Keynes dialect. For instance, it might resemble the traditional dialect of the area; or it might reflect the range of accents of the new inhabitants of the city (so, given that about 75 per cent of the incomers are from the south-east, three-quarters of the emerging dialect features might be from the south-east, with the remainder divided between the other areas represented). Table 3 shows neither of these to be the case. The children's accents differ, in many respects, from those of the original inhabitants of Milton Keynes and the nearby area. Furthermore, in the speech of the children with parents from outside the south-east, there is practically no trace of the parents' accents. In fact, every one of the Milton Keynes children's pronunciation features, both old and more recent, is also found in London and elsewhere in the south-east.

Table 3 A comparison between pronunciations in Stewkley near Milton Keynes (recorded in the 1950s); among elderly Milton Keynes residents (recorded in 1991); and among Milton Keynes children (recorded in 1991)

	Stewkley 1950s	Elderly MK 1991	MK children 1991
arm	arrm	arrm	ahm
three	three	three	free
feather	feather	feather	fevver
night	noit	noit	naa-it
round	raind	raind	round
fill	fill	fiw	fiw
woman	umman	woman	woman
letter	le'er	le'er	le'er

Note: 'Arrm' indicates that the 'r' is pronounced. 'Le'er' indicates a glottal stop for 't'. The information for older speech is from the *Survey of English Dialects* (SED), which investigated Stewkley in the 1950s, and from six elderly people we recorded who were born within what is now Milton Keynes.

So far, the impression we get is that the new Milton Keynes 'dialect' is simply 'Cockney' (or London dialect) transported; indeed, some residents talk about 'Milton Keynes Cockney'. Perhaps what lies behind this phrase is the recognition that Milton Keynes speech is not *exactly* Cockney, but has a 'flavour' of it. So what pronunciation features are the children converging towards?

We can start with a vowel variable, (ou) – (the diphthong in words such as *home, go, boat, know, don't*, etc). I indicated in Table 2 that the second part of this could be 'fronted', so that the word *Coke* might be mistaken for *cake*. We quantified

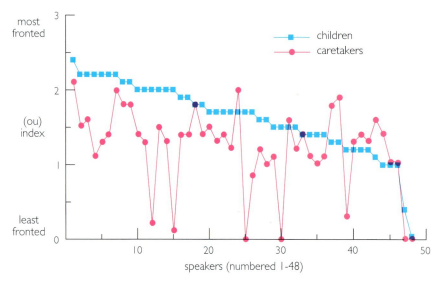

Figure 1   Association of children's (ou) scores with those of their caretakers

the fronting of (ou) on a four-point scale running from 0–3. Figure 1 shows the degree of fronting for the forty-eight children, with each child's score plotted against that of her or his caretaker. This shows that the children on average 'front' their vowels considerably more than the adults. The figure confirms my earlier suggestion that the children's speech is different from that of their parents. The children's pronunciations are also far less variable than the adults'. Fronted (ou) is, then, likely to be a characteristic of the new Milton Keynes dialect.

It's important to point out that this new feature, along with most of the other new features we have studied, is also found across broad swathes of southern England. For instance (ou)-fronting is observable in Reading, 90 kilometres to the south, as well as in Cambridge, 80 kilometres to the east. What we are observing is the convergence of accents, not just in the new town melting pot but throughout the south-east of England – as mentioned above. I return to this point below.

Who leads in the development of a new dialect?

We turn now to a consideration of which age group leads in linguistic developments, including the formation of a new dialect. We can again take the data for (ou) and compare it with that for (uː), the vowel in *move, spoon*, etc. As with (ou), (uː) is also being fronted. Figure 2 shows the percentage use among women and girls of 'fronted' pronunciations of both vowels in the words *home* and *move*. The patterns are not identical for each vowel, but it is clear that the oldest girls have by far the greatest degree of fronting, with the younger ones having scores similar to those of the caretakers. A likely explanation for this pattern is that the youngest girls still follow their mothers as far as these vowels are concerned, while the oldest, near-adolescent girls are converging on a different pronunciation.

New dialect formation and sociolinguistic maturation

It is apparent, then, that it is older children who do most of the sociolinguistic 'work' in new dialect formation. How does this relate to sociolinguistic maturation? We can now return to the variable (t), which we have defined as the

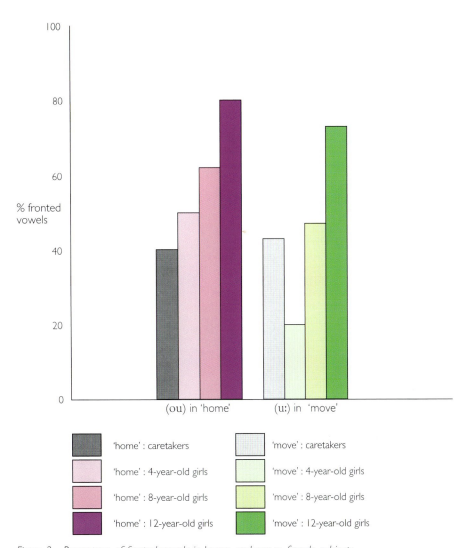

Figure 2   *Percentage of fronted vowels in* home *and* move, *female subjects*

alternation of [ʔ] and [t] within a word such as *letter*. Figure 3 shows the percentage use of the [t] pronunciation in three different elicitation tasks (reading and
other tasks designed to elicit particular words), with the speakers divided according to sex and age group. Note first the fairly small differences between the tasks,
with the most formal, the reading task, having the highest use of the 'standard'
pronunciation [t] overall (the four-year-olds are, of course, omitted from this
task). Secondly, it is striking how the girls consistently have a much higher score
than the boys of the same age. This finding is consistent with much sociolinguistic
research, which shows that female speakers often use more 'standard' features
than male speakers. Thirdly, and most significantly for our discussion here, it is
the oldest age group that has the highest frequency of [t]. We can assume that
elicitation tasks will encourage a rather formal speaking style, in which adults will
feel the need to use features characteristic of careful and standard speech. It is the
oldest children who seem to be adhering most closely to this expectation. The
connection between this finding and new dialect formation is this: older children

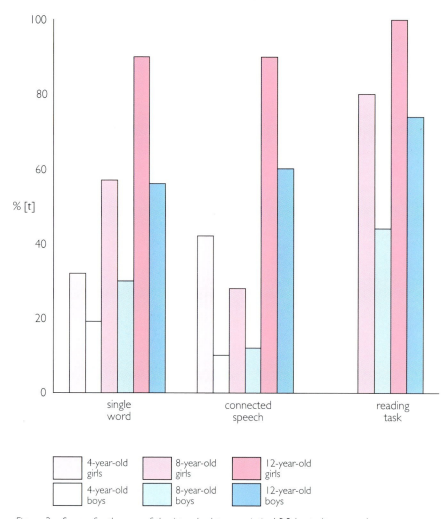

Figure 3   Scores for the use of the 'standard pronunciation' [t] by task, sex and age

demonstrate patterns characteristic of adult communities in terms of linguistic variation – here, style-shifting patterns. In a new community, it is they, by contrast with younger children, who are the first 'natives' to establish these patterns. We can couple this with the fact that the older children are linguistically more alike than the younger children and thus may well foreshadow what the 'new' accent will sound like. These results – the style-shifting patterns and the degree of linguistic similarity – allow us to suggest that the older children's speech quite closely represents the characteristics of the new 'speech community'.

Implications

Dialect levelling in the south-east of England

I suggested earlier that we may be witnessing the spread of a relatively uniform pattern of speech across south-eastern England. If so, this means that many features of the 'new' dialect we have been discussing in this chapter are in fact common to a much wider area than just the one town. Let us consider one further

variable, the vowel (au), as in 'h*ou*se', 'r*ou*nd', 'n*ow*', etc. In the south-east of
England, this vowel shows a large number of regional variants, Table 4 shows that
the caretakers bring to Milton Keynes several different variants, all of which are
found in the south-east. Interestingly, the children seem to favour the regionally
neutral, RP-like variant, [aʊ], not the more regionally marked forms of their
parents. Significantly, this vowel is gaining ground very strongly elsewhere too; for
example, in Reading it has all but replaced the local vowel [ɛɪ], which is a striking
feature of the old accent there.

Table 4
Percentage use of different pronunciations of the vowel in *house, round*, etc. (interviews)

	[hɛːs]	[haːəs]	[hæʊs]	[haʊs]
Children	11	8	13	66
Caretakers	12	17	39	31

Note: [hɛːs] represents a broad London monophthong; [haːəs] is a slightly diphthongized version of it.
[hæʊs] is a diphthong starting with the vowel of 'hair' and finishing with the vowel of 'pull'. [haʊs]
represents an RP-like form.

This and other variables, including (ou) and (uː) as well as the use of [f] for 'th' in
three, thin, etc., provide evidence of dialect levelling in the south-east: differences
are becoming less and less marked, so that it is today more difficult to tell apart
young speakers from Southampton, Reading, London and Cambridge than it was
thirty years ago. Despite these strong tendencies, it is unlikely that regional
differences will disappear altogether, since language differences have always been
part of the armoury human beings use to maintain their own distinct social
identities.

Milton Keynes, Estuary English and changes in spoken English

Several commentators have referred to a phenomenon known as 'Estuary
English' (Rosewarne, 1984, 1994; Coggle, 1993). This is the notion that there is an
increasingly widespread way of speaking 'Standard' English (without nonstandard grammatical features) that contains a number of south-eastern pronunciations, such as the glottal stop and the vocalized 'l'. The Estuary English phenomenon is an old one, since people have long been shifting to Standard English while
retaining parts of their local pronunciation. What is new is the increasing acceptability of this form of speech in the media and the professions, where it is replacing
RP, much to the annoyance of several newspaper columnists.

It is tempting to suppose that what we have observed in Milton Keynes is a
form of Estuary English, since both are geographically levelled forms of speech.
This is misleading, since young people native to Milton Keynes between them
presumably cover a range of speech types, both nonstandard and standard, that is
similar to that found in other towns. If the Milton Keynes nonstandard speakers
do sound more Estuary English-like than their compeers elsewhere, this is because of the special sociolinguistic situation there, involving much more intensive
dialect contact than in other parts of the south-east. What we see is possibly a sign
of future changes in English: new towns are perhaps in the vanguard of the dialect
levelling found in England as a whole.

Acknowledgement

Data for this reading is derived from the project 'A new dialect in a new city: children's and adults' speech in Milton Keynes', funded by the Economic and Social Research Council, 1990–4, ref. R000232376. Principal investigator: Dr P. Kerswill; Research Fellow: Dr A. Williams. Further information on the project can be found in Kerswill (1994), and Kerswill and Williams (1992, 1994).

References

COGGLE, P. (1993) *Do You Speak Estuary?*, London, Bloomsbury.

KERSWILL, P.E (1994) 'Babel in Buckinghamshire? Pre-school children acquiring accent features in the new town of Milton Keynes' in MELCHERS, G. and LENNARTS-SON, L. (eds) *Nonstandard Varieties of Language*, Acta Universitatis Stockholmiensis, Stockholm, Almqvist and Wiksell.

KERSWILL, P. E. and WILLIAMS, A. (1992) 'Some principles of dialect contact: evidence from the new town of Milton Keynes' in PHILIPPAKI-WARBURTON, I. and INGHAM, R. (eds) *Working Papers 1992*, Department of Linguistic Science, University of Reading.

KERSWILL, P.E. and WILLIAMS, A. (1994) 'A new dialect in a new city: children's and adults' speech in Milton Keynes', final report and summary of research submitted to the Economic and Social Resource Council.

LABOV, W. (1966) *The Social Stratification of English in New York City*, Washington DC, Center for Applied Linguistics.

MILTON KEYNES DEVELOPMENT CORPORATION (MKDC) (1990) *Milton Keynes Population Bulletin 1990*, MKDC.

ROSEWARNE, D. (1984) 'Estuary English', *The Times Educational Supplement*, 19 October 1984.

ROSEWARNE, D. (1994) 'Estuary English: tomorrow's RP?', *English Today*, vol. 10, part 1, pp. 3–8.

TRUDGILL, P. (1986) *Dialects in Contact*, Oxford, Blackwell.

This reading was specially commissioned for this book.

8 STYLE SHIFTING, CODESWITCHING

Joan Swann

8.1 INTRODUCTION

Elizabeth	Do not really wish to marry? I? I will marry. I have said so. I hope to have children, otherwise I shall never marry.
[Mary and Elizabeth come together]	
Mary	Indeed I wish that Elizabeth was a man and I would willingly marry her! And wouldn't that make an end of all debates!
La Corbie	But she isny. Naw, she isny. There are two queens in one island, both o' the wan language – mair or less. Baith young … mair or less. Baith mair or less beautiful. Each the ither's nearest kinswoman on earth. And baith queens. Caw. Caw. Caw.
	…
La Corbie	*[Rhyming]* Ony queen has an army o' ladies and maids
	That she juist snaps her fingers tae summon.
	And yet … I ask you, when's a queen a queen
	And when's a queen juist a wummin?
[She cracks her whip, and the hectic and garish but proud Elizabeth bobs a curtsy, immediately becoming Bessie.]	
Mary	Bessie, do you think she'll meet me?
Bessie	Aye, your majesty, she'll meet wi' ye face to face at York, an' you're richt, gin ye talk thegither it'll a' be soarted oot. If ye hunt a' they courtiers and politicians an' *men* awa!
(Lochhead, 1989, pp. 15–16)	

In Liz Lochhead's play about Mary Queen of Scots the same actor plays Elizabeth I of England and Bessie, a maid to Mary. A change of language marks a change of persona. The change is deliberate, practised and explicit – heralded by La Corbie and the crack of a whip. It is also, you might say, pretence. The actor is actually neither Elizabeth nor Bessie, she is simply playing a couple of parts.

In this chapter I explore how speakers routinely draw on different varieties of English, or on English and other languages, to communicative effect – albeit rather less dramatically and without the aid of a script. I look at variation within English, which has often been represented as a range of speaking styles associated with different contexts. And I also look at how speakers switch between languages, or language varieties, during the course of a single interaction.

I suggest that, in both cases, questions of social **identity** are at issue. Previous chapters have discussed the social meanings associated with different languages, or language varieties: how the language variety you use conveys certain information about you, such as where you come from and what kind of person you are. But language diversity and variability do not serve simply as social indicators: they also constitute a resource that can be drawn on by speakers, to represent different aspects of their identity or to balance competing identities.

While a great deal of work on speakers' variable language use has been concerned with social issues, the way speakers manage switches between languages also has implications for grammar. How does the grammar of English and other languages allow you to switch from one to another? What happens when you switch between English and another language with a very different grammar? I explore such issues briefly below.

Finally, I try to draw together some different theories of speakers' variable language use.

8.2   STYLISTIC VARIATION IN ENGLISH

'By gum, tha's got a reet rum
session ahead o' thee, an' as I
were only saying t' Bishop o'
Sheffield t'other day ...'
(Guardian, 6 November 1984, p. 1)

The Bishop of Sheffield had referred, in a meeting, to social and regional divisions in Britain and suggested that the Queen should have a greater presence in the north.

My sister, she's a right little snobby ... if she came here now she'd speak plain English, but she can speak Patois better than me. She speaks it to me, to some of her coloured friends who she knows speak Patois, but to her snobby coloured friends she speaks English. She talks Queen English, brebber. She's the snotty one of the family.

(Cited in Edwards, 1986, p. 121)

Activity 8.1   *(Allow 5 minutes)*

Spend a few minutes thinking about the various contexts in which you use spoken English during the course of a day. Forgetting for the moment about any other languages you may speak, are there any differences in the type(s) of English you use in different contexts?

Comment

The answer you give to this activity will clearly depend upon your own circumstances. I find that, in general, I use a more standard variety of English at work than at home. But 'work' and 'home' aren't really two discrete contexts. At work I need to take part in meetings, to talk about work topics on the phone, to chat to colleagues over lunch. Talk at home could involve colleagues who are also friends and it may involve a variety of different topics – including what has been happening at work.

   The way people talk will differ according to several contextual factors (where speakers are, who they are speaking to, what they are speaking about). It will differ along several linguistic dimensions (pronunciation, grammatical structures, choice of words). Furthermore, although speech variation has often been related to the formality of a context (so that a meeting is more formal than a chat over lunch), degree of formality alone isn't enough to explain variation. I come from Newcastle-on-Tyne, in the north-east of England, and my daughter comments that I use many more 'Geordie' (Newcastle) pronunciations when talking on the phone to my parents than when chatting at home in Milton Keynes.

I want to go on now to look at how linguists have attempted to document and explain this kind of variability in speech. I draw on the notion of **style** to refer, initially, to aspects of dialect and accent: to the way in which the pronunciations, choice of words and grammatical features associated with different varieties of English are used variably by speakers in different contexts.

   Linguists investigating **stylistic** (or **contextual**) **variation** in this sense usually identify a set of **sociolinguistic variables** and see how these are realized (i.e. what form they take) in different contexts. Some of the studies of English accent discussed in Chapter 7 identified a stylistic continuum that was associated with degree of formality: speakers used more 'prestige' or high-status features in more formal contexts, and more vernacular features in more informal contexts. Here, I extend this earlier discussion by looking at further examples of research on speaking style. These confirm that speakers draw on different forms of English in different contexts, but they also suggest that there is no single stylistic continuum: speaking style is better regarded as multidimensional.

For discussion of other aspects of style, such as the notion of literary style in English, see the second book in this series, *Using English: from conversation to canon* (Maybin and Mercer (eds), 1996).

Chapter 7 discusses the use of 'sociolinguistic variables'; the chapter also contains a preliminary discussion of speaking style drawing on the work of William Labov in the USA.

Style and audience

Researchers have traditionally isolated certain features of context in order to examine how these relate to speaking style. Allan Bell, for instance, developed a theory of **audience design** which suggests that the person or people you are speaking to will have the greatest effect on the type of language you use. Bell studied the varieties of English used by newsreaders on New Zealand radio stations and found that their pronunciation differed on different stations. (The study was carried out in the 1970s but is discussed in several more recent publications – see for instance Bell, 1991.)

Bell investigated several sociolinguistic variables, including how speakers pronounced the /t/ in words like *writer* and *better* (in New Zealand English this may have a standard [t] prounciation, technically a voiceless alveolar plosive; or it may be voiced, so that the words begin to sound like 'rider' and 'bedder').

Bell discovered that what he termed the more 'formal' [t] pronunciation was used more often on a station with a mainly 'educated' or 'professional' audience, less on 'general audience' stations, and least on rock music stations. Furthermore, some newsreaders worked for more than one station, and in this case their pronunciations differed on different stations: they seemed to converge on a 'station style'. Bell claims that it is the different audiences for each station that affect newsreaders' speech, while other factors, such as the topic mix of the news and the studio setting, remain constant.

Radio stations might seem to be rather a special context, because speakers are speaking on behalf of a station rather than in their own voices. But there is a great deal of evidence now that in face-to-face interactions speakers use different varieties of English depending on the person they are speaking to. The British linguist Peter Trudgill (1986) discusses a particularly striking example of this in his own speech. As part of a sociolinguistic survey of English in Norwich in the east of England, Trudgill interviewed a range of informants from different social backgrounds. Later, he returned to this data to analyse his own speech, comparing his pronunciation with that of his informants. Like Bell, one of the variables Trudgill looked at was the /t/ sound: in Norwich, as in several other parts of the UK, the pronunciation of /t/ in words such as *better* or *bet* may move towards a glottal stop [?] (often represented in writing as *be'er*).

Figure 8.1 shows Trudgill's results for this variable. In most cases he tended to use slightly more glottal stops than the informant he was speaking to. He attributes this to his age: he was 24 at the time, younger than these informants, and glottal stops are used more frequently by younger speakers. Although numbers are small, he also seems to have used a higher number of glottal steps when talking to his male informants – a finding consistent with some other research that has shown speakers of both sexes use more nonstandard features when talking to men than to women. The overall pattern of his speech, however, is remarkable for the way in which it mirrors that of his informants.

Nikolas Coupland (1984) found something very similar when he analysed the speech of an assistant in a travel agency in Cardiff, in Wales. He found, again, that her pronunciation of certain sounds mirrored that of her clients. In fact, he comments that the assistant's pronunciations were almost as good an indicator of the social class and educational background of her clients as the pronunciations of the clients themselves.

Both Trudgill and Coupland argue that these speakers were 'converging' towards the speech of their interlocutors: they were trying to sound similar to them. This notion of speech convergence derives from a theory concerned with motivations for stylistic variation known as **accommodation theory**. The theory suggests that speakers will **converge** towards their interlocutor when they wish to reduce social distance, or get on with one another. They will **diverge** (i.e. become linguistically less similar) when they wish to emphasize their distinctiveness or increase social distance. It seems plausible to argue, in each of these cases, that the speakers wish to get on with their interlocutors because they need something from them: custom in the case of the travel agent; co-operation in carrying out the

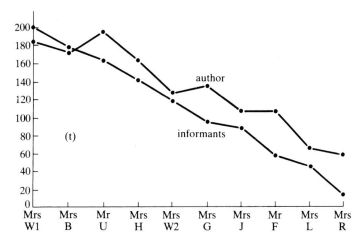

Figure 8.1   Variable (t): selected scores in Norwich study (Trudgill, 1974)
(Trudgill, 1986, p. 8)

interview in the case of the researcher. (Accommodation theory is consistent with Bell's theory of audience design. I return to both these theories in section 8.4.)

Style and other factors

In the research I have discussed so far the assumption was that speakers were in the same place, talking about similar topics – only the audience differed. Other research has set out to construct contexts so that the influence of different factors (including audience) may be examined. This was something attempted by Viv Edwards and her co-researchers in their study of the speech of young black people in Dudley, in the west Midlands area of England. Edwards's research (Edwards, 1986) was conducted as a set of interviews, with informants recorded in small single-sex groups in a researcher's flat. Within these constraints, five different 'situations' were created:

1	Formal interview with white researcher	Group interviewed about education by older white researcher, smartly dressed and referred to as 'Mr Sutcliffe' by other researchers.
2	Formal interview with black fieldworker	Group interviewed by a black fieldworker of the same sex as group members; researcher uses a questionnaire and asks about interests and leisure pursuits.
3	Informal conversation with white student	Group left alone with Jeremy, a young white student from the same area. Jeremy is casually dressed and explains he is not part of the research team, but interested in some of the things they have been discussing.
4	Discussion by black peer group	Group left alone to talk about questionnaire they will be asked to complete later. Questions cover attitudes to mainstream white society; treatment of young black people by police, etc.
5	Informal conversation with black fieldworker	Group with black fieldworker in conversation over biscuits and drinks towards the end of the session.

Edwards was interested in the extent to which speakers used a variety they termed 'Patois' (sometimes also called 'British black English'), in these different contexts. She identified a number of features that varied (i.e. that occurred as either 'English' or 'Patois' variants). The entire list of variables is shown in Table 8.1. Some of these are pronunciation features; for example, whether the first sound in 'then' is pronounced *th* or *t* (phonetically [ð] or [t]). But most are features of grammar; for example, whether a speaker says 'John *swims* fast' or 'John *swim* fast'.

Different terms are used for the varieties of English spoken by black people in Britain, as well as in the USA, and these have often aroused controversy.

Table 8.1 Linguistic variables in the Patois index

1. *Dentals*
   English variants: /θ,ð/, e.g. /θin, ðen/ — thin, then
   Patois variants: /t, d/, e.g. /tik, dat/ — thick, that
2. *Vowels*
   English variants: /ʌ/ (Received Pronunciation), /ʊ/ (West Midlands), e.g. /rʌn/, /rʊn/ — run
   Patois variant: /o/, e.g. /fon/ — fun
3. *Third person singular present tense verbs*
   English variant: John *swims* fast; Kevin *eats* a lot
   Patois variant: John *swim* fast; Kevin *eat* a lot
4. *Plurals*
   English variant: six *cars*; all the *books*
   Patois variant: six *car*; all di *book*
5. *Simple past tense*
   English variants: Winston *saw* the boy; Beverley *walked* away
   Patois variant: Winston *see* di boy; Beverley *walk* away
6. *Copulas* (before adjectives and verbs)
   English variants: The man *is* happy; John *is* coming
   Patois variants: Di man *happy*; John *a come*
7. *First person singular pronoun*
   English variant: *I* feel happy
   Patois variant: *me* feel happy
8. *Third person singular pronouns*
   English variant: *he* put it away
   Patois variant: *im* put it away
9. *Third person plural pronouns*
   English variants: *they* like the baby; look at *their* hats
   Patois variant: *dem* like di baby; look at *dem* hat
10. *Infinitives*
    English variant: John asked *to* see it
    Patois variant: John aks *fi* see it
11. *Negatives*
    English variant: The boy *doesn't* see it
    Patois variant: Di boy *no want* it

(Edwards, 1986, p. 80)

Edwards noted how often English or Patois forms were used by different speakers and in different situations. The average scores for use of English/Patois variants in each situation were as follows (Edwards, 1986, p. 81):

Situation	1	2	3	4	5
Average score	94.43	87.05	92.37	56.71	69.89

Note: figures are expressed as a percentage, where a score of 100 would mean use of only English variants and a score of 0 would mean use of only Patois variants.

Activity 8.2   *(Allow 5–10 minutes)*

How does the young people's speech seem to vary in the five contexts just discussed? What might explain this variation?

Comment

The first thing that strikes me is that audience seems to have an effect; in particular, the presence or absence of a white interlocutor affects the speakers' use of Patois features. Situation 3, the conversation with Jeremy, the white student, is designated informal but elicits very few Patois features – almost as few as the formal interview with the white researcher.

But the format of the interaction also seems to affect people's speech. In situation 2, a formal interview, there is far less use of Patois than in situation 5, an informal conversation, although the same person (a black fieldworker) is involved in each case.

Patois features occur least of all in situation 1, the formal interview with the white researcher; they occur most in situation 4, the informal conversation with no outsider present.

I would also want to point out that while these results seem quite clear-cut, the contexts are rather artificial and we have no guarantee that the young speakers interpreted the situations in the same way as the researchers.

Finally, the results I've quoted are average figures: there were considerable differences between speakers (e.g. some used more Patois features throughout than others) and between the incidence of different features.

Edwards's research, like that of Bell, Trudgill and Coupland, is mainly quantitative; she identifies linguistic features that can be counted up to allow a numerical comparison between their use by different speakers and in different contexts. But she also presents us with case studies, which give a fuller account of individual speakers' use of language.

Below are extracts from the speech of two informants: Don, who is particularly hostile towards mainstream white society and whose life 'centres very firmly on the black community'; and Darleen, who has more connections within the white community and more limited knowledge of several aspects of black language and culture (Edwards, 1986). The author's commentary is included with the extracts of speech.

> After completing the questionnaire … Don offers his candid opinions to the black fieldworker and the other participants:
>
>> Dem [the questions] alright in a way, right. Dem reasonable. Dem coulda be lickle better, but dem reasonable. Me na bex (angry) wid dem, dem alright … When white people ready fi write some rubbish bout black people, dem can do it, dem can do it, right. So dat's why me say dem reasonable. Notn wrong wid dem.
>
> This short extract illustrates a wide range of [Patois] features … The phonology is consistently Patois; he uses Patois pronouns *mi* and *dem*; adjectival verbs *bex, reasonable* and *alright*; *fi* before an infinitive; and *no* in negative constructions. …
>
> [Don's] most 'English' performance … is in the formal white interview. When talking about the origins of black culture, for instance, he says:

I say it come from Africa really. It started from dere tru slavery. Dat's di way I see it. It started from there, yeah. But those kids what born over here right, they don't want to admit it. Like Paddy, they don't want to admit it right that our culture started from Africa.

Don's language in this situation is highly variable. Whereas in black peer group conversation he shows an overwhelming preference for Patois variants, in the white interview he chooses a much higher proportion of English variants including inflected past tenses, negatives with *don't* and copulas. While he still uses Patois features like dental stops (*tru, dere, di*) and adjectival verbs (*born*), the number and range of these features is very limited.

...

[Darleen's English is marked] by a high incidence of specifically Black Country dialect forms such as *her, wor, cor, ay* and copulas in *(a)m* [e.g. *you'm out* in the extract below]. In describing facilities for young people in Dudley, for instance, she says:

Just walk up the streets and you'm out of Dudley, know what I mean? In Birmingham, I don't know, I just get round a nice shop – I'm lost in it. But if you just walk up the High Street you'm out ... The other best thing in Dudley is the Trident Centre, that's what I think, there by Sainsbury's. You can sit down there. I said to Michael today, 'That's the best thing in Dudley, ay it?'

The only time when Darleen uses Patois is when left alone with her friends. ... She shows only a narrow range of Patois features, making variable use of Patois dentals and vowels and uninflected nouns and verbs. Otherwise Patois is limited to *mi, im, dem* and the continuative particle *a* [the particle marking continuous duration of action, as in the extract below]:

Wa happen? Me a go say you a go get what you a look for?
(*What happened? I'm going to say that you're going to get what you're looking for.*)

She is very aware of the limitations in her Patois:

Tell the truth, we'm very up on our English. We talk slang sometime in Patois ... If I was in Jamaica now I'd be brought up to talk like that, but it's a white community.

(Edwards, 1986, pp. 88–92)

There is a danger, when presenting a generalized and quantitative account of speaker style, of seeing speakers as responding somewhat mechanically to context. Edwards's case studies suggest that things are more complex: that one needs to take account of speakers' feelings about language and about the contexts in which they are speaking. This is borne out by one or two other studies, such as some research carried out by Jenny Cheshire on the speech of young, white working-class speakers in Reading, in the south-east of England. Like Edwards, Cheshire was interested in the incidence of nonstandard grammatical features, but these were features associated with Reading vernacular English, such as the nonstandard present-tense verb forms in the following examples:

I starts Monday, so shut your face

You knows my sister, the one who's small

They calls me all the names under the sun

(Cited in Cheshire, 1982)

Cheshire found that, on the whole, her young informants used fewer vernacular features when they were recorded at school than when they were recorded in a local adventure playground. But speakers differed in the extent to which they adapted their speech in the school context. She suggests that differences between speakers have to do with their familiarity with school and knowledge of school conventions (for instance, that Standard English is associated with talk in the classroom), and also with how they feel about school (so that pupils who identify with the school culture, or who get on with a teacher, are more likely to adapt their speech and produce fewer nonstandard forms). Speakers, then, are making their own constructions of context: it is their perceptions of, and feelings about, people and situations that affect the way they speak. Nor are contexts fixed. Cheshire (1982, p. 125) comments that speakers continually reassess the context and adjust their speaking style accordingly.

Michael Huspek, similarly, had to take account of his informants' feelings about people and events in his study of the speech of lumber workers in a large industrial city in north-west USA. Huspek worked with a group of lumber workers for 28 months over a four-year period, and recorded several interviews with them. From these he was able to identify features that varied according to the linguistic context and to the topic the men were talking about (Huspek, 1986). One feature he identified was *-in/-ing* as a verb ending; for instance, whether a speaker said 'sitt*in*' or 'sitt*ing*'. This feature has often been selected as a sociolinguistic variable in English as it has been found to vary widely between different speakers and in different contexts. Huspek found that the men he studied most frequently used the *-in* variant, but did introduce *-ing* forms in certain circumstances. In the following passage the speaker switches from an informal to a more formal register to talk about a scientific topic (this switch is marked by the use of some *-ing* forms, shown in italics):

> I myself think it's where our source of energy is gonna come from. And nuclear power. I think we're gettin' into an area where we don't know that much about. And I myself feel we're gonna start sump'm that we're not gonna be able ta stop. Say a chain reaction, or somebody *splitting* some atom or other, that's gonna start *chain-reacting* an' it's not gonna be able to get stopped.
>
> (Huspek, 1986, p. 154;
> spelling conventions and use of italics are Huspek's)

Huspek argues that the *-ing* form may also be used in relation to someone who is respected by the speaker: 'His engine was purr*ing* just like a kitten'. But also, presumably ironically, it may signal disrespect or resentment, as in the following example:

> We were jus' sittin' there on the beach tokin' away on this big doobie y'know when along comes this straight guy jogging along. He was all really decked out, y'know. He had lotsa bucks too. Y'know, I mean you could tell it by his clothes an' like that. So Jerry yells over at 'im: 'Hey man, you're doing real fine!'
>
> (Cited in Huspek, 1986, p. 155)

Huspek argues that the *-ing* variant is recognized as a prestige form, hence it is used when workers discuss the actions of 'high-prestige others'. But the workers' feelings about such people are somewhat ambivalent and so the 'prestige' form does not have entirely positive connotations.

The story so far

I've tried to select a range of studies that examine different features of English, that focus on different contexts, or aspects of context, and that, to some extent at least, employ different methods of investigating style. But this evidence still presents us with a rather limited picture of style in English. The evidence suggests that speakers vary the way they speak depending, at least, upon:

- the person or people they are speaking to (different clients in a travel agency);
- the setting (in school or an adventure playground);
- the format of the interaction (an interview or informal conversation);
- the topic being discussed (a switch to a scientific topic may produce a change in speaking style).

But evidence from any one study is extremely partial and what is found depends upon how the research is constructed – or what the researcher sets out to look for. However, the studies themselves do show that even more factors need to be taken into account, for instance the following.

- I've already suggested that these studies, perhaps necessarily, employ a simplified model of context; that speakers are not merely responding to predetermined contextual features such as audience, setting and topic but to their own interpretations, or constructions of context. Different aspects of context will be more or less salient for different speakers. Nor should speaking style be seen simply as responsive: in using certain pronunciations when speaking about scientific research (for instance) speakers are also establishing this as a certain kind of topic (e.g. formal, high-status).
- Each study has investigated variables that have 'prestige' and 'vernacular' forms. These have a cluster of associations. For instance, prestige varieties of English are associated with speakers and listeners with high socio-economic status and with settings and topics that have been characterized as formal, and perhaps also 'high-status' (e.g. school setting, scientific topic). Vernacular varieties are set in opposition to these at the other end of the spectrum. We are presented with a unidimensional picture of style in that speakers' variable use of language is seen to run along a single stylistic continuum.

    But it's also apparent from the studies that rather more is going on. Trudgill, in discussing his own variable pronunciation, mentions the potential influence of gender reflected in his use of more glottal stops to male than to female interlocutors. It is likely that he is responding to more than one aspect of his informants' social identities. In Edwards's study of speech in Dudley there are two vernaculars, Patois and local Black Country speech; Edwards contrasts only 'Patois' and 'English', but within the 'English' category speakers probably have access to more and less standard forms. Here again, style is likely to operate in more than one dimension, allowing speakers access to a more complex range of social meanings.
- Saying that styles have certain associations may suggest that their meanings are obvious or unambiguous. But one cannot simply 'read off' a certain meaning from a speaker's style. Huspek (1986), for instance, suggests that the same pronunciation feature (-ing) could convey either 'respect' or 'disrespect': you need a certain amount of contextual knowledge to interpret the use of different linguistic features.
- Studies of style, like studies of other aspects of variation discussed in Chapters 6 and 7, tend to isolate and quantify a small number of linguistic features.

The second book in this series, *Using English: from conversation to canon* (Maybin and Mercer (eds), 1996), discusses the interplay between verbal and nonverbal features in English conversations, interviews and other types of interaction.

However, in varying the way they speak people will draw on a whole set of features, including those that are less easy to measure (e.g. tone of voice). These will combine with, or be counterbalanced by, other nonverbal features (e.g. posture, facial expression); in practice, linguistic choices play a part in highly complex negotiations of social meanings.

Some research has adopted a more complex model of style, seeing this as multidimensional and as representing different, perhaps competing, aspects of social identity. I look at examples of this in the following section.

Multistyle

> … the individual creates for himself [sic] the patterns of his linguistic behaviour so as to resemble those of the group or groups with which from time to time he wishes to be identified, or so as to be unlike those from whom he wishes to be distinguished.
>
> (Le Page and Tabouret-Keller, 1985, p. 181)

R.B. Le Page and Andrée Tabouret-Keller's work was carried out in multilingual communities, including several Caribbean countries, but their ideas have also influenced researchers with an interest in monolingual stylistic variation. They suggest that the desire to identify with, or distinguish oneself from, particular social groups is a major factor influencing speakers' choice of language variety. But they also allow for fluctuating patterns of usage (the phrase 'from time to time' is important here) and for the fact that speakers may have various (perhaps conflicting) motivations to speak in certain ways.

Trudgill (1983) draws on these ideas in order to analyse the way British rock and pop singers in the 1950s modified their pronunciations when singing in ways that were different from their usual speaking styles. The overall effect of this was to make the singers sound more 'American'. Trudgill compares this with other singing styles, such as folk singers attempting rural accents and reggae singers sounding more Jamaican.

The variable use of 'non-prevocalic' /r/ in American English speech is discussed in Chapter 7, section 7.4.

Trudgill argues that US singers also modified their accents. The target in this case was the pronunciation used by southern or black singers, because 'it is in the American South and/or amongst Blacks that many types of popular music have their origin' (Trudgill, 1983, p. 146). British singers were probably also aiming at this target, but they didn't always make it. For instance, British singers tended to pronounce an /r/ non-prevocalically in words such as 'girl' in imitation of US pronunciation; but US singers, who would use /r/ in this position in their speech, tended to omit it in singing in imitation of the target southern variety.

Slanging in Singapore

Americanized pronunciations occur in several contexts. For instance, in Singapore some individuals may adopt salient features of American English to transmit a westernized identity. The features most commonly adopted are non-prevocalic /r/, and the replacement of intervocalic /t/ with /d/ in imitation of the US 'tap' pronunciation. This adoption of an Americanized accent, as opposed to a Singaporean accent, is called 'slanging' in Singapore. Those who do this have been satirized in comic books and in sketches.

(I am grateful to the sociolinguist Anthea Fraser Gupta for this observation.)

Trudgill found that, among British rock and pop groups, patterns fluctuated with different trends in pop music. An interesting pattern emerged in the 1970s with the advent of punk music, associated with urban working-class life and anti-mainstream values. When singing, punk-rock singers adopted certain low-prestige southern English features that they did not necessarily use in speech. Such features were used alongside 'American' pronunciations, although they were in conflict with them:

> For [many punk-rock singers] there is a genuine split in motivation. The conflict is between a motivation towards a supposedly American model, and towards a supposedly British working-class model – which can be glossed as a conflict between 'how to behave like a genuine pop singer' and 'how to behave like a British urban working-class youth'. The combination of linguistic forms that is typically found in punk-rock singing is an attempt to find a balance between the two.
>
> (Trudgill, 1983, p. 159)

Activity 8.3   *(Reading A)*

Now read 'Hark, Hark, the Lark: multiple voicing in DJ talk', by Nikolas Coupland (Reading A). This is a study of one speaker, Frank Hennessy (FH), a disc jockey in Cardiff, Wales, and how he uses accent during his radio programme.

Coupland's study is useful at this point because it both builds on and extends much of the work discussed above. Coupland is interested in stylistic variation; he begins by identifying a set of sociolinguistic variables (in this case, pronunciation features) and goes on to see how these are realized in different contexts. He assigns each pronunciation a numerical score, according to whether it is more or less vernacular.

But Coupland's analysis departs in significant ways from many previous studies, and takes account of most of the points I made on pp. 310–311. As you work through the reading I suggest you note particularly the results of Coupland's analysis and the interpretations he offers; for example:

- the notion of 'micro-contexts'; how FH's speaking style can be related to these;
- Coupland's insistence on the creativity of this process (e.g. FH as the 'orchestrator of contexts', p. 329; his 'stylistic creativity', p. 329);
- the different sets of pronunciation features drawn on by FH (from Cardiff English and other varieties) and the interplay of meanings this gives rise to;
- Coupland's concluding discussion of Cardiff English as a 'voice' – a way of speaking that has complex associations drawn from other speakers and other contexts, and that can be manipulated by speakers to express different identities and relate to listeners in different ways.

Many of these points recur in sections 8.3 and 8.4 of this chapter.

Coupland refers to FH's status as a 'performer' and it's interesting that many ideas about speaking style have come from research on 'performers' of one sort or another, including newsreaders, pop singers and DJs. Such cases highlight the problematical nature of audience, as this has traditionally been investigated by

The use of English in the media is discussed further in the fourth book in this series, *Redesigning English: new texts, new identities* (Goodman and Graddol (eds), 1996).

sociolinguists. You may, for instance, question who the audience actually is that is being addressed in Coupland's study. Coupland himself has conceded that further work is needed on style in a wider range of contexts.

8.3   SWITCHING IN AND OUT OF ENGLISH

Je suis une Canadienne-française I guess

(I'm a French-Canadian I guess)

(Cited in Heller, 1990, p. 67)

So far I have focused on style as a phenomenon that operates *within* English. But for a great many speakers English is only one of a number of languages at their disposal. In bi- and multilingual communities, style may be expressed by the selection of one language in preference to another. Chapter 1 discussed both patterns of language use, and the social meanings associated with English and other languages in several bilingual contexts. I suggested there that, by opting for English or another language, speakers were tapping into a whole set of social meanings with which the language has become associated. But bilingual speakers need not keep their languages separate. One possibility open to them is to **codeswitch** – to switch back and forth between languages, thus capitalizing on the associations of each language, or 'keeping a foot in each camp'.

> Compare the examples of bilingual codeswitching here with the interesting illustration of switching between scripts in Bede's Commentary on the Book of Proverbs, Chapter 2 Figure 2.14.

A large amount of research on bilingual codeswitching has looked at the use of English alongside other languages. This no doubt reflects researchers' own backgrounds and the dominance of English within academic life, as well as the prevalence of English as a second (or third, etc.) language in so many parts of the world. Researchers have been interested both in the meanings and functions of codeswitching and in how switching works linguistically. I consider both aspects in the sections that follow.

Why switch?

Activity 8.4   *(Readings B and C)*

Reading B, 'Strategic ambiguity: code-switching in the management of conflict', is from Monica Heller's paper on codeswitching in Canada; Reading C, 'Codeswitching with English: types of switching, types of communities', is from Carol Myers-Scotton's paper on codeswitching in Zimbabwe and Kenya. (Remember that Chapter 1 discussed patterns of language use in Canada and Kenya; you may find it useful to refer back to this.)

Read both of these now, noting down what each researcher has to say about motivations for codeswitching. My comments are in the text which follows.

Both readings suggest that, like the use of different speaking styles by monolingual speakers, bilingual codeswitching is meaningful: it fulfils certain functions in an interaction. Myers-Scotton's **markedness model** suggests that particular codes (in this case, languages) are associated with, and therefore expected in, particular contexts (her example 1 shows the use of Swahili with a security guard and English with a receptionist). Codeswitching itself may be the unmarked (expected)

choice in certain contexts (as in Myers-Scotton's examples 2 and 3; Heller's example 1 also seems to fall into this category).

A speaker's choice of language has to do with maintaining, or negotiating, a certain type of social **identity**. The use of a particular language also gives access to rights and obligations associated with that identity. Codeswitching between languages allows speakers (simultaneous) access to rights and obligations associated with *different* social identities. Heller argues that in Canada codeswitching can allow speakers access to 'situations defined by the other language' (and, ultimately, to certain material benefits) without having to relinquish their identity as, respectively, English- or French-speakers (she uses the terms 'anglophones' and 'francophones'). It is also useful to the 'marginal' speakers in Heller's example 1 who wish to avoid categorical alignment with one group or another. Myers-Scotton's examples of 'unmarked switching' from Kenya and Zimbabwe (examples 2 and 3, respectively) show speakers balancing different aspects of their identity by switching between an African language and English.

Switching may sometimes operate to initiate a change to relationships, or to make salient different aspects of the context (for instance, Myers-Scotton's example 4, of 'marked' (or unexpected) switching, in which a switch to English communicates authority; and Heller's example 2 in which Albert switches to French to open the meeting).

Codeswitching is useful in cases of uncertainty about relationships: it allows speakers to feel their way and negotiate identities in relation to others (see, for instance, Myers-Scotton's illustration of 'exploratory switching' (example 5) in which a young man attempts to negotiate higher status through English).

While both readings focus on the relationship between codeswitching and social identities, Heller also points out that switching may fulfil specific functions in an interaction (for example, as a conversation management device or a means of managing personal relations).

Researchers interested in the meanings or functions of codeswitching have sometimes tried to establish social meanings at a very general level. One of the best known examples of this is the distinction identified by John Gumperz (1982) between 'we' codes (associated with home and family) and 'they' codes (associated with more public contexts). In many bilingual and multilingual contexts it would be easy to suggest that English functions as the 'they' code because it is often associated with education, formality, and public rather than private arenas. This, however, suggests a view of meaning as something rather fixed and static. It is clear from the two readings you have just studied that codeswitching needs to be interpreted in context. Myers-Scotton points out that in Kenya English can encode both social distance and solidarity, depending on the context. Meanings are also subject to change: Heller points out that new communication practices have developed in the Canadian company she studied because of changes in the position of English in relation to French. Finally, within any one context meanings are by no means unambiguous. In fact, one of the values of switching is that it permits a certain amount of ambiguity in contexts and in relations between people.

Codeswitching may also be used to deliberate effect, as in the example of a Tamil/English pun in Figure 8.2.

The research by both Heller and Myers-Scotton looked at switching between English and other (distinct) languages, but switching also takes place between more closely related varieties. The following example, from research carried out by Mark Sebba, shows Brenda (B), a seventeen-year-old of Jamaican parentage,

தள்ளினா என்னவாகும்?

[pinnale = behind
pin + ale = with a pin]

(Bus-ai pinnale tallina ennvakum?)
(If you push the bus from behind, what will happen?)

Pin வளையும்.

(Pin valaiyum.)
(The pin will bend.)

Figure 8.2   A codeswitching pun in Tamil and English
(I am grateful to Nadaraja Pillai for this example.)

switching from London English to 'Creole' (a London variety based on Jamaican Creole) to create an impression of a character in a narrative. (Transcripts of spoken language are not always easy to read! In this case the list of trancript conventions set out in the margin should help.)

Transcription conventions

- each line of the transcript is numbered for ease of reference

- deep brackets [indicate overlapping speech

- (.) means a brief pause; (0.8) means a timed pause (0.8 seconds)

- switches to Creole are in italics

1	B	now 'e ad everyfing if you was to sit down an
2		'ear that guy speak (.) ['e (was going) to Jamaica
3		['e was ni:ce (0.8) 'e was ni:ce
4	B	'e was going to *build 'is place* (0.6)
5		[*'im a build 'is business (1.0)*
6	?	[ye:h 'e was NI:CE man
7	B	an' it's the type of guy like that (0.6) I want

(Sebba, 1993, p. 113)

Brenda is talking about a man who is the type of man she would like to marry. She begins talking in London English about his plans to go to Jamaica, then switches to Creole. She switches back to London English to describe her own feelings. Sebba cites an earlier commentary he made on this extract, arguing that the switch to Creole creates, or 'animates', the character Brenda is describing:

> The switch to Creole occurs before the first instance of '*build 'is*' and this could be taken as a direct quotation of the man's words, rendered in Creole because he is apparently a Jamaican: cf. Brenda's 'if you was to sit down an' ear that guy speak'. More interestingly, however, this switch somehow indexes a culture for which this goal stands as an ideal: building your own place is a plausible goal in the Jamaican culture but very unusual in Britain, especially for a black person.
> (Sebba, 1993, p. 121)

Sebba found that young British black speakers switched routinely between Creole and London English in conversation with one another. He suggests, like Heller and Myers-Scotton, that codeswitching is related to different aspects of a speaker's identity – it gives them 'a foot in each camp'. It is also possible to attribute meaning to particular switches. During mainly Creole conversation, a switch to English may be used for an aside. By contrast, a switch from English to Creole marks out a sequence as salient: it stands out; it is the part of the utterance that other parties in the interaction respond to.

In the following extract, Brenda has recounted to friends how she rebuffed the advances of a boy at a party who had been told by another boy that Brenda 'had called him and wanted him'. Here, she adds that she did agree to dance with the boy but she had nothingelse in mind.

B	1	then I just laughed (0.6) and then 'e – 'e just pulled me for a
	2	dance – I didn't mind dancin' [wiv 'im 'cause *me know say, me*
(J	3	⌞ yeah)
	4	*no 'ave nothin' 'inna my mind* [but to dance, and then we
(J	5	⌞ yeah)
	6	star%ed to talk and all the rest of [it and tha%s [it *full stop*!
(J	7	⌞yeah ⌞yeah)
(2.0)	8	
J	9	'e was a nice guy, but differently, right

(Adapted from Sebba, 1993, p. 111)

Transcription conventions

- each line of the transcript is numbered for ease of reference
- % represents a glottal stop
- deep brackets [indicate overlapping speech
- (.) means a brief pause; (0.6) means a timed pause (0.6 seconds)
- switches to Creole are in italics
- J's occasional contributions of 'yeah' have been placed in brackets because they give conversational support rather than being turns in their own right.

The salient parts of Brenda's story occur in the switches to Creole in lines 2 and 4 and line 6, where she explains why she agreed to dance. Sebba suggests rather tentatively that while speakers use both Creole and English at home and among peers to discuss a range of topics, Creole may feel closer to the 'heart and mind' and thus may impart greater salience to an utterance.

Codeswitching approaches have tended to be used to look at the variable language use of bilingual or bidialectal speakers where, even when two varieties are related, switches are relatively easy to identify. But, in practice, the distinction between (bilingual or bidialectal) codeswitching and (monolingual) style shifting becomes rather blurred. There is a problem, discussed in earlier chapters, of establishing clear linguistic boundaries between 'varieties' and attributing features unambiguously to one or another. Furthermore, as Coupland showed in Reading A, it's possible to apply an approach that looks very like an analysis of codeswitching to style shifting within English. Sebba's data is also quite similar to Edwards's examples of the use of Patois and English in Dudley. Edwards isolated certain features and counted up how often they were realized as Patois or English variants, thus allowing her to make a numerical comparison between the language used by different speakers and in different contexts. Sebba, on the other hand, focused on how his speakers drew strategically on English and Creole during conversations. Sebba comments on the analysis by Edwards 'it tells us whether that person uses many or few Patois features overall in their talk, but nothing about how he or she uses Patois and English as part of a communicative strategy' (Sebba, 1993, p. 36).

Quantitative analyses of style and qualitative analyses of codeswitching can therefore be regarded as different methods, underpinned by different views of what is important about language as much as responses to different sorts of data.

Switching and grammar

The examples of codeswitching cited in this chapter and its associated readings show that, as well as fulfilling a number of social functions, switching can take a variety of different forms. Speakers may switch from one language to another at a clause boundary, or a long sequence in one language may be followed by a switch to another. But often switches occur within a clause and involve a more intimate mix of two or more languages. This poses an interesting question about grammar: when switches occur between two language varieties with distinct grammars, what is the grammar of the whole utterance? Are both grammars somehow involved, or does one win out – and if so, which one?

In the following examples, in the transcription English is always in normal type, a second language in italic; a third language is in small capitals. The English translation is on the right.

> *J'ai la– la philosophie ancienne on va dire, que, tu sais, si tu as faim,* get off your ass and go and work, *tu sais?*

> I have the– the old philosophy, let's say, that, you know, if you're hungry, get off your ass and go and work, you know?

[Switching between French and English in Canada]
(Poplack et al., 1988, p. 53)

> *Yahāā kii* kampani*yāā* ejenTo *kō baRaa paesaa detii hāe.*

> Companies here give a lot of money to the agents.

[Switching between Hindi and English in India]
(Kumar, 1986, p. 201)

> NINDANGA NA KAKAMEGA, *watu huko wanatumia Kiswahili,* English, *na Luyia.* You know, this is a Luyia land and therefore most of the people who live in rural areas do visit this town often. *Kwa hiyvo huwa sana sana wanatumia Kiluyia na Kiswahili. Lakini wale ambao wanaishi katika* town *yenyewe, wanatumia Kiswahili sana.*

> To start with Kakamega, people there use Swahili, English and Luyia. You know, this is a Luyia land and therefore most of the people who live in rural areas do visit this town often. Therefore they use Luyia and Swahili very much. But those who live in the town itself, they use Swahili very much.

[Switching between Luyia, Swahili and English in Kenya]
(Myers-Scotton, 1993a, p. 4)

Activity 8.5   *(Allow about 10 minutes)*

How do the switches into English differ in the examples above? What seems to happen to the grammar of the English switched items in each case?

Comment

In the switch from French to English, whole clauses are switched. English grammar is observed within the switched text.

In the Hindi/English example, single words from English are switched. The spellings 'kampani' and 'ejent' suggest that these words are drawing on the Hindi sound system. Neither word has the English plural marker *s* but they each have a Hindi morpheme attached to them. (In fact, *ō* and *yāā* are plural morphemes in Hindi.) An English speaker unfamiliar with Hindi might not even recognize these words as English.

The third example involves three languages, Luyia, Swahili and English. A whole English sentence is switched, which retains its own grammar. Later, the word 'town' is switched. Since conventional spelling is used it is not clear whether this shows traces of the Swahili sound system.

These switches may look different, but while switching occurs at different points in an utterance, and involves different linguistic items, it is not random: switches follow certain patterns and so are subject to grammatical constraints. Over the years, a great deal of research effort has gone into determining these constraints. The problem has been that while researchers can provide 'local' accounts of constraints (that is, accounts that work for the data they have collected) other researchers, working with other types of data (perhaps from different languages), have found counter examples that break these local rules.

I mentioned above one general hypothesis: the grammars of both (or all) languages used in an interaction somehow determine when a switch may take place. This was in fact suggested by Shana Poplack (1980), who argued that a switch from one language to another would occur at points where the surface structure of the two languages map on to each other (this she termed the 'equivalence constraint'). She gave the following example from English and Spanish (Figure 8.3).

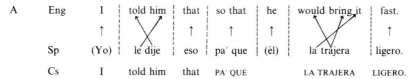

Figure 8.3   Permissible codeswitching points

[Note: the pronouns *yo* and *él* are in brackets because they may be omitted in Spanish.]

(Poplack, 1980, p. 586)

Here the vertical lines show points at which a switch is possible from English to Spanish, or vice versa. Switches here would not violate the word order of either language. Between these lines, however, the order of constituents is different for each language (I am using 'constituents' here in the sense of components, or items that make up a larger unit). The arrows show the correspondence between English and Spanish constituents: *le*, for instance, is the equivalent of 'him'. But *le* precedes the verb in Spanish whereas *him* comes after the verb in English. A switch between *told* and *him* (e.g. saying 'told *le*') would not, therefore, be possible. The third line (Cs) shows where the speaker actually switched from English to Spanish.

Poplack's constraint looks plausible, but unfortunately there are counter-examples. Myers-Scotton cites the following from Swahili and English:

B *Unaweza kumpata amevaa nguo   nyingine* bright   You can find
                          clothes other   bright   her wearing
                                                      other bright
                                                      clothes

C *Anaonekana kama ni mtu   innocent*   He looks like
                    person innocent   [he] is an
                                            innocent
                                            person

(Myers-Scotton, 1993a, pp. 28–9)

In example B *bright* follows Swahili word order, coming after *nguo* (whereas it would need to precede the noun 'clothes' in English). Similarly, *innocent* follows Swahili word order in example C. Such examples are not uncommon in Myers-Scotton's data and have also been found by other researchers.

Myers-Scotton also provides counter examples to another constraint suggested by Poplack, the 'free morpheme' constraint:

D   *Hata siku hizi ni-me-decide*   [But] even these days I have
    kwanza kutumia sabuni ya miti.   decided first to use bar soap [in a
                                       conversation about buying
                                       detergent]

(Myers-Scotton, 1993a, p. 4)

Here the phrase '*ni-me*-decide' is the equivalent of 'I have decided'. *Ni* is the pronoun 'I', and *me* gives the verb 'decide' a particular tense (= have decided). Both *ni* and *me* are 'bound morphemes' in Swahili; that is, they cannot occur on their own. Both must be attached to the verb 'decide'. (Rules are different in English: for instance, *I* occurs as an independent item, but the past-tense marker *-ed* must be attached to a verb and can't occur on its own.) According to the free morpheme constraint, this example would not count as switching, because it involves attaching Swahili bound morphemes to an English root, 'decide'. *Decide* has been integrated into the morphology of Swahili. It would probably count as a borrowed item, rather than a codeswitched item. (The Hindi/English example I cited at the beginning of this section also violates the free morpheme constraint.)

Myers-Scotton's own explanation of codeswitching constraints is more comprehensive and would cover all the examples I have cited so far. Her explanation is termed the 'matrix language frame model'. She argues that within any stretch of codeswitching one language can be seen as the main language. This is the **matrix language**, in that it provides a frame into which items from the other language, or languages, may be embedded. It is the grammar of the matrix language that affects the form of codeswitching. When single words from another language are embedded the matrix language word order applies, and the matrix language also supplies what Myers-Scotton terms 'syntactically relevant morphemes'.

Examples B and C above demonstrate the word order (strictly, morpheme order) principle. Below is a further example, along with an illustration of what a counter example would look like.

Example E is an actual utterance, in which an English switched item fits in with Swahili word order:

E   *Ni-ka-wa-ona* workers *wa-nene sana*   And I saw [some] very
                           fat   very   fat workers
(Myers-Scotton, 1993a, p. 91)

A potential counter-example, showing English word order, could be as in example F (such examples did not occur in Myers-Scotton's data):

F   **Ni-ka-wa-ona sana wa-nene* workers*

The question of syntactically relevant morphemes is more complex. Myers-Scotton distinguishes 'content morphemes' (typically nouns, most verbs, adjectives) and 'system morphemes', which signal grammatical relationships rather than carrying semantic content (in English, items such as determiners (*the, a, all, any*); verb endings (such as *-ed, -ing*); and the verb *be*). Myers-Scotton argues that any system morphemes that signal relations between items in a sentence must come from the matrix language (the 'system morpheme principle'). So, example G below is possible but H would not occur:

G   *Yule mtu ni mtoto   w-a* boss   That person is the
                 child   of   boss's child

H   **Yule mtu ni* the boss's *mtoto*

(Myers-Scotton, 1993a, p. 109)

In the examples above, English words are used but they are not following the grammar of English: they have been temporarily assigned the grammar of another language. But on other occasions English switched items do retain their own grammar. This usually occurs when sequences of words – 'embedded language islands' – are embedded in the matrix language. In example I 'this evening' is part of an island following English word order (the matrix language is Swahili):

I   *Wache mimi nielekee tauni,*   Let me go so that I may reach
    tukutane this evening ...   town, let's meet this evening ...
(Myers-Scotton, 1993a, p. 140)

It is also possible to say '*evening* hii'. This would not be an island. It follows Swahili word order and consists of an English embedded item followed by a Swahili system morpheme (*hii* = this). Other Swahili–English combinations are not possible: 'jioni *this*' (*jioni* = evening) violates the system morpheme principle and '*this* jioni' violates both the system morpheme principle and the word order principle.

Myers-Scotton's explanation is one that I find attractive because it can account for a wide variety of codeswitching between different languages. (I have included examples here from her own research on African languages and English, but if correct her theory should be valid for all languages.) It also covers some switches that are not included *as switches* in other frameworks. (For instance, single words that fit in with the morphology of the matrix language have sometimes been relegated to a separate category of 'nonce', or one-off, borrowings.)

Codeswitching and borrowing

The inclusion of one-word switches within her framework allows Myers-Scotton to posit a connection between codeswitching and **borrowing**. Codeswitched items are regarded as belonging to another language, so that someone who codeswitches has to have access to two linguistic systems (though this doesn't imply they are equally competent in both languages). Borrowed items, on the other hand, are felt to have become part of the matrix language. All languages have borrowed terms (for example, English has *amateur* from French; Swahili has *baisikeli* (bicycle) from English). Terms such as *baisikeli* fill a gap in the matrix language, but languages also borrow when they have equivalent terms of their own (for instance, 'town' in Swahili). Myers-Scotton argues that words such as *baisikeli* (she terms these 'cultural borrowings') enter the language abruptly as the need for them arises, whereas words like 'town' ('core borrowings') enter gradually, via codeswitching: they are subject to the same social motivations and grammatical constraints. As they become used more frequently, they are on their way to becoming borrowings, sometimes displacing original terms. There is, therefore, a continuum operating between codeswitching and borrowing, rather than a cut-and-dried distinction between the two.

Chapters 3 and 4 point to the large number of borrowed terms acquired by English during its history (the term 'adoption' is used in these chapters). Chapter 1 discusses attitudes in France towards borrowings from English.

In this section I've pointed out that embedded items may show greater or less integration into the structure of the matrix language, in terms of phonology, syntax and morphology (and that researchers have used such formal criteria to distinguish between different types of embedded items, for instance, to determine whether or not they count as codeswitching). I'd like to conclude the discussion with a brief look at some research carried out by Rajeshwari Pandharipande in Maharashtra, a state in northern India. Pandharipande was interested in the extent to which English switched items were integrated into Marathi grammar, as in the following example:

J   [English switch containing Marathi suffix]

to office *cyā* work   *sāṭhii ālā   hotā*   He had come for
he office of   work   for   came was   some office work

K   [English switch without Marathi suffix]

to office work *sāṭhii ālā hotā*   He had come for
                                                   some office work

(Adapted from Pandharipande, 1990, p. 20)

In the above lines, example J follows the Marathi construction *kāryālayā cyā kāmā* (literally 'office of work'), whereas the switch in example K retains English grammar, 'office work'.

Pandharipande points out that in the community she studied English is associated with 'modernity'. Speakers frequently switch between Marathi and English when topics such as modern technology, higher education and media are discussed. But the degree of integration of English switched items is also important in this respect. In contexts in which modernity is particularly salient, English embedded items tend to retain more of their English form (word order and morphology). In contexts where modernity is less of an issue, or where other factors are important, English items take on more structural features from Marathi. Pandharipande's research therefore takes us back to the social meanings of codeswitching, showing how they may affect the linguistic form of an utterance.

8.4   DESIGNER ENGLISH?

I suggested earlier that qualitative studies of codeswitching highlighted speakers' strategic use of different language varieties – and that this was masked in quantitative studies totalling the occurrence of linguistic variants in different contexts. Quantitative comparisons seem to downplay any notion of individual agency: this is simply much less visible than in stretches of transcript showing how speakers utter certain words and phrases and how these are responded to by others. But despite these methodological biases, many interpretations of all studies of speaker style (I use this as a generic term to include monolingual style shifting and bilingual codeswitching) have seen this as a relatively creative enterprise: speakers, to a large extent, are able to design their speech to take on particular identities.

This suggests that speaker style has its origin in variation between groups of speakers (the patterns of social variation discussed in Chapters 6 and 7). There is some evidence for this view: research in English-speaking communities (and no doubt others) has found that most linguistic features that show variation vary between social groups as well as stylistically. Some show only social variation, but none shows only stylistic variation. Furthermore, with rare exceptions, stylistic variation is always less extreme than social variation. Bell (1984, p. 153), in a review of this research, comments 'The explanation is that style variation … derives from and mirrors the 'social' variation. As is the habit of mirrors, the reflection is less distinct than the original: style differentiation is less sharp than the social'.

Features that show stylistic variation are subject to evaluation by speakers (that is, when asked, speakers will make evaluative judgements about them so they are aware, at some level at least, of their connotations and associations). Therefore, the argument goes, they are able to draw on them to communicate social meanings.

Myers-Scotton's markedness model (which has been applied to variation in the speech of monolingual as well as bilingual speakers) seems to allow a more dynamic relationship between individual speaking style and established social meanings. She argues that speakers are aware of patterns of language use that are unmarked or expected in particular contexts from their experience of taking part in similar interactions. They usually choose a speaking style that fits in this context – that is consistent with the relationship they would expect to hold with other participants. But even here they are being creative in the limited sense of choosing one option, the unmarked pattern. In so doing, they are helping to re-establish this as 'normal' or expected. Sometimes they may make a marked choice in an attempt to redefine a relationship. For Myers-Scotton, this is equivalent to saying: 'Put aside any presumptions you have based on societal norms for these circumstances. I want your view of me, or of our relationship, to be otherwise' (1993b, p. 131). Of course, such a marked choice may not succeed in redefining a relationship because it may be contested by others.

The work on bilingual codeswitching discussed here, as well as some studies of monolingual style shifting (such as Trudgill's study of British pop groups and Coupland's study of the Cardiff DJ) have focused on the role of style in managing or (re)negotiating speakers' social identities. Other interpretations have seen style as primarily a response to an audience. In section 8.2, I mentioned two theories that took this approach: audience design and accommodation theory. These theories are consistent with one another, so here I discuss them together.

Accommodation theory developed from the work of the social psychologist Howard Giles and his associates in the 1970s. It has been enormously influential. I mentioned earlier some initial premises of accommodation theory: speakers will converge towards the speech of their interlocutor in order to emphasize solidarity, and diverge from their interlocutor's speech in order to increase social distance. This is based on the assumption that convergence will be positively evaluated and divergence negatively evaluated. Trudgill's study of his speech in a sociolinguistic interview and Coupland's study of a travel agency assistant's speech illustrate this theory. But some examples of codeswitching can also be interpreted in this light: Heller's examples of codeswitching between francophone and anglophone employees could be interpreted as convergence, and Myers-Scotton's example of a (marked) switch to English to communicate authority could be interpreted as divergence.

Bell's theory of audience design provides useful additional insights by distinguishing between different types of audience. It is not only the person addressed who will affect someone's speech but also (though to a lesser extent) others who are involved in the interaction. Like Myers-Scotton, Bell argues that style is not always responsive: it may have an initiative function – as when a speaker switches style to redefine a relationship. Bell suggests that on such occasions speakers are addressing their audience as if the audience were someone else. Often speakers are switching towards a 'referee', that is, someone not involved in the interaction but who is nevertheless salient. Speech divergence can be redefined as initiative shifting since the speaker is not simply diverging *away* from the addressee but *towards* another reference group. Finally, as you can see in the following quotation, Bell argues that audience design provides a comprehensive and integrative model of speaker style: other contextual factors that influence people's speech may be re-interpreted in terms of audience.

> … speakers associate classes of topics or settings with classes of persons. They therefore shift style when talking on those topics or in those settings as if they were talking to addressees whom they associate with the topic or setting. Topics such as occupation or education, and settings such as office or school, cause shifts to a style suitable to address an employer or teacher. Similarly, intimate topics or a home setting elicit speech appropriate for intimate addressees – family or friends. The basis of all style shift according to nonpersonal factors lies then in audience-designed shift.
>
> (Bell, 1984, p. 181)

Accommodation theory itself has been considerably developed and refined since its early beginnings. Here I mention one or two developments that seem particularly relevant here. An article by Giles et al. (1991) provides a more systematic review.

The theory now recognizes that speakers do not always accommodate to how their addressee actually speaks. There are obvious limitations – speakers cannot put on any accent (or whatever) at will. But, in addition, speakers sometimes converge towards the variety they expect their addressee to speak, or that is associated with their addressee, rather than to the variety the addressee is actually speaking. (This could explain why Trudgill, in his sociolinguistic interviews, used more nonstandard speech to his male informants than to his female informants.)

People will vary in the extent to which they converge. Difference in status between the speakers is likely to be a factor here (Giles et al. point to evidence that subordinates are more likely to converge towards a superior than vice versa). But there may be several reasons why it is more, or less, in a speaker's interests to converge. In some situations it may be important to maintain aspects of a distinctive identity, but without necessarily implying hostility (for example, a teacher in a classroom may use a standard variety of English because that's what is expected of a teacher rather than simply to express social distance from pupils). Giles et al. term this 'complementarity'.

A related point is that the meanings of accommodation need to be interpreted in context; it is not always the case that convergent speakers intend to decrease social distance, nor that convergence will be positively evaluated. Giles et al. cite several examples of alternative interpretations.

Finally, Giles et al. concede that what is interpreted as accommodation may be an artefact. They give the example of an interviewee who converges towards the high-status language variety used by the interviewer: this may be because of a wish to appear in a certain way (e.g. as competent) rather than simply due to a desire to converge.

Identity-based theories such as the markedness model have different origins, and different emphases, from audience design and accommodation theory but I do not think they are necessarily incompatible. Speakers do adopt certain language varieties in order to lay claim to a certain identity (or set of identities), but this is always in relation to other participants. At a general level, speakers are taking account both of their own identities and those of their interlocutors in 'designing' the way they speak. One common feature of the three theories is that design is seen most frequently as responsive, as when speakers fall into expected patterns of convergence or complementarity. But speakers may also make marked or divergent choices in a bid to redefine a relationship.

Divergent convergence?

Francophone shoppers in Montreal, Canada, were heard to address anglophone shop assistants in fluent English to ask for the services of a francophone assistant. While this is an example of linguistic convergence the act is clearly one of dissociation.

Jamaican schoolteachers, who usually use a standardized form of English in the classroom, sometimes 'converged' in mockery or disparagement of their pupils' creolized forms when the latter were being disruptive, inattentive or lacking in academic effort.

Attempts by an English-speaking tourist to use the language of the countries he was visiting did not always meet with success:

> In sojourns in Latin America and Southeast Asia, the author's use of inelegant but workable host-country language or expressions often was countered with requests to proceed in English, even when the host's competence in it was severely limited. Some people perceived the visitor's initiative as a pejorative reflection on their English ability; still others appeared pleased with the effort, but indicated that they preferred to practise their English.
> (Ellingsworth, 1988, p. 265)

(Adapted from examples cited in Giles et al., 1991, pp. 12, 36 and 75)

8.5   CONCLUSION

This chapter has discussed 'speaking style' in English: it has looked at how speakers draw on different varieties of English, and switch between English and other languages, to communicate aspects of their identity and to negotiate relationships with others. It has also looked at different traditions of research: research that has adopted a quantitative approach, identifying general patterns of variation; and qualitative research, emphasizing the meanings of speakers' language use in different contexts. Such methodological considerations seem important to me, not least because different methods provide different kinds of evidence and allow different judgements to be made about the use of English and other languages (contrast, for instance, the rather different preoccupations of researchers such as Edwards and Sebba).

While most of this chapter has focused on issues to do with language and identity, I also discussed some of the grammatical constraints that operate when speakers switch between English and other languages (though even here social factors turned out to be an important influence on the extent to which English was integrated into another language's grammar).

Finally, I discussed some theories that have addressed the motivations for speakers' variable language use, suggesting that speakers can be seen as relatively creative 'designers' of language.

The research referred to throughout the chapter suggests that such design is not a simple process. Speakers are able to draw on a wide range of linguistic resources, the meanings of which are often subtle and ambiguous. They negotiate identities, relationships, contexts moment by moment. They may have to balance conflicting identities, and their attempts to initiate certain relationships may be contested. Furthermore the project remains unfinished: relationships between individuals change, and social groups realign themselves; the English language also changes, in terms of both its structure and its relationship to other languages. Speaking style reflects these processes but also, necessarily, contributes to them.

Reading A

HARK, HARK THE LARK: MULTIPLE VOICING IN DJ TALK

Nikolas Coupland

In 1985 I published an exploratory paper focusing on the stylistic creativity of a radio disc jockey (DJ), Frank Hennessy (FH), who was at that time a local radio presenter in Cardiff (Coupland, 1985). FH is a broad-accented speaker of the Cardiff English dialect who is well known in the community not only as a radio presenter but also as an entertainer, folksinger/songwriter, social commentator and humorist. His popular image is built around his affiliation to, and promotion of, local Cardiff culture and folklore, in large measure through his dialect. For many, he typifies the nonstandard Cardiff voice, perhaps even the stereotypical Cardiff worldview: a nostalgia for dockland streets and pubs, a systematic ambivalence to 'Welshness', a sharp, wry humour and a reverence for the local beers, in particular 'Brain's Dark Ale'. In general, his show is a celebration of in-group regional solidarity.

Figure 1 is a transcript of a continuous sequence from FH's radio show beginning with him reading out a letter from a listener. FH's speech is interspersed by the playing of a record (the Checkmates's *Proud Mary*) at line 7. The extract ends when another record is cued and played.

Transcription notes

- This is a verbatim transcript: it includes common expressions such as 'um' and 'er' and, like many research transcripts, it is not punctuated.

- The symbols in round brackets above certain words indicate sociolinguistic variables that were investigated. The numbers below show how they were scored. Both conventions are explained below.

- Wide spacing between words gives a rough indication of pauses.

1   dear Frank   would you please give a mention on your birthday spot for

2   (au) our brother (h) whose birthday is on the second of June well that was
    0   0

3   yesterday (C) wasn't it so (ou)(C) it's a (h) happy birthday to (name) and lots of love
             0   1   0   0   0

4   from your sisters (names) and Mum of course   and also (ou) from all
                       0 1 0   1

5   your family   his (h) name is (name) and (h) he lives at Seven (ou) Oaks (ou) Road
                    0   1   1   1

6   Ely in (a:) Cardiff   (h) happy birthday (name) (cues record)   (h) here's the
           3   0   0   1

7   Checkmates   (au) Prou(r)d Mary   yeah (record plays and fades) oh good
                    2   0

8   music there   the Checkmates and (au) Prou(r)d Mary   and the wall of
                                        2   1

9   (au) sound (r) there of Phil Spector   unmistakable of course   they (au) sound
    2   1   2

10 as if they goi(ng) bananas (a:) do(C)n't they   talk (au) about banan(a:)as   we got
               1   4   1   2   4

11 (aː) (r)(aː)   (ng)   (t) (C) (ai)   (r)
    Bananarama coming up next   but it's time to limber up this Sunday
    4 0 3   1   0 0 1   1

12   (aː)   (r)   (C)   (C)
    with the Margaret Morris Movement Special   that's a special day of
         1   0   0   0

13 (ai)   (aː)
    exercise and dance at the National Sports Centre for Wales   it
    2   3

14 (aː)   (au)(t)   (au)   (ou)   (ou)   (ai)
    started about an hour ago at ten o'clock and it goes until five o'clock
    2   2 1   2   1   1   2

15 (aː)   (au)   (aː)   (aː)   (r)
    this afternoon   now the Margaret   Margaret Morris Movement is
    3   2   0   1   1

16   (r)   (C)   (C)
    a unique form of recreative   movement   and it's um   well it's a
         0   0   0

17   (ai)   (t) (C) (ou)
    system of exercise   which achieves physical fitness   but it's also
         2   0 1   (R)

18   (ng)   (t)   (t)   (t)   (t)
    capable of developing creative and aesthetic qualities which make it
              1   0   0   0   0

19   (ng)   (aː)
    exceptional   in physical education and training   are you with me
                                            0   (R)

20   (ai) (ou)(t)   (C)
    ah   'cause I'm totally confused   anyway it's equally suitable for
         2   1 1   0

21 men and women of all ages as well as children even the kids can join

22   (ou)   (ou)   (t)
    in with this   and er the muscular control and coordination make it
                           1   1   0

23   (r)   (r)   (ng)
    an excellent preparation for all sporting and athletic activities   now
         0   1   0

24 (aː)   (ou)
    all sessions today are absolutely free   so if the weather's a little bit
    (R)   1

25 gone against you   and you fancy   well not running round in the
         (r)   (ng)(r)(au)
                        0   1 0 2

26 (r)   (t)   (ng) (t)   (ai) (C)
    rain   but er you fancy doing a bit of exercise it's all on at the
    0   0   1   1   2   1

27 National Sports Centre for Wales   that's at Pontcanna of course
                                         (C)
                                         0

28 (aː)   (r) (ou)   (ou)   (ai)   (au) (ai)
    started an hour ago you can go any time up until about five o'clock
    3   1 1   1   2   2   2

29 (ng)   (ou)   (aː)   (ai)   (aː) (r)(aː)
    this evening   so there we are   as I said   Bananarama   here
    1   1   4   2   0 0 4

30 (aː)   (r)   (ai)
    they are   with a little touch of (cues record) Rough Justice   I'll
    4   (A)   (R)

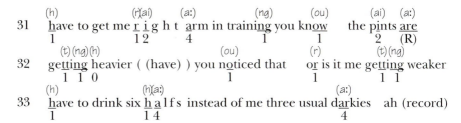

*Figure 1   Transcript of a
Cardiff disc jockey's speech*

The extract conveys something of the in-group framing of the show. Many correspondents are regular contributors and have therefore become, to an extent, radio personalities in their own right. Some open their letters with even more familiar forms of address than the 'dear Frank' instance in the extract – '[h]ello, Franky Boy', 'hi, hi Frank', '[h]ow's things, Our Kid'. The show often carries announcements of local events, such as the 'Margaret Morris Movement Special' introduced at line 12 of the extract. Other instances include a quiz feature asking listeners to supply the original name of Wimbourne Street in 'lovely old Splott' (a long-established working-class Cardiff city district) and the names of six paddle-steamers which operated in the Bristol Channel after World War Two.

Cardiff English

The show can be said to be *constituted dialectally*. Cardiff dialect is not merely an incidental characteristic of FH's own speech; it permeates much of the performance and imbues it with a regional significance. For instance, vernacular Cardiff speech does not regularly distinguish between the quality of the long /ɑː/ sound in words such as *dark* and *park* and the short /a/ in words such as *cat*. Cardiff pronunciation can be represented phonetically as [æː] and [æ] and this vowel quality has become a stereotyped indicator of Cardiff speech. FH's radio show draws on the associations of this pronunciation; it has the informal title *Hark, Hark, the Lark* and is introduced and punctuated by a distinctive jingle – a whimsical, sung fanfare of the words 'Hark, hark the lark in Cardiff Arms Park' with an [æː] vowel quality predominating throughout. FH perpetuates this phonological theme in his own catchphrases, such as 'it's remarkable', 'well there we are' and 'that's half tidy'. Notice how the extract ends with a list of phono-opportunities for [æː] in highly prominent positions during the final three lines of transcript: *arm, halfs* meaning 'halves' or 'half-pints', and *Darkies* (pints of Dark Ale).

Correspondents often make their own contribution to this dialectal theme, sometimes consciously ending their letters with an opportunity for FH to produce a broad Cardiff pronunciation; for example, 'yours through a glass darkly, signed Prince of Darkness' (both of these are again oblique references to dark ale), 'don't forget Derby day', or simply the words *ta* (thank you) or *tarra* (goodbye). This single sound, then, is a highly productive focus for the symbolic expression of shared Cardiff provenance and accompanying attitudes and allegiances.

The sound can be treated as a sociolinguistic variable (aː) in analyses of variation in Cardiff speech: technically, ways of realizing the variable can be represented as positions on a five-point scale running from 0 to 4, with 4 being maximally nonstandard and 0 being standard (the RP realization). There is of course a full repertoire of other sociolinguistic variables available – in this case, sounds that have both more vernacular Cardiff and more standard pronunciations. These include (ai), the pronunciation of the first part of the diphthong in *like, time*, etc., and (au), the pronunciation of the first part of the diphthong in *now, house*, etc.; each of these variables is represented on a three-point scale running from 0 to 2, again with the higher numbers indicating more nonstandard forms. Other variables can be represented as either standard (0) or nonstandard (1):

(ng)   the pronunciation of -ing in words such as runn*ing*, someth*ing*, etc. as either -*ing* or -*in*;

(h)   the presence or absence of /h/ at the beginning of a word;

(C)   whether consonant clusters are simplified (or reduced) in certain positions (e.g. ne*xt d*ay; don'*t t*hey; i*t's*);

(t)   the pronunciation of /t/ between vowels (e.g. be*tt*er, lo*t* of);

(r)   the pronunciation of /ɾ/ before vowels;

(ou)   the pronunciation of the first part of the diphthong in *know, coal*, etc.

In Figure 1, each possible realization of a salient Cardiff English pronunciation feature is underlined. The relevant sociolingustic variable is set out above the line, and the number below the line shows how standard or nonstandard each realization is. (R means that the feature is too reduced phonetically to be scored; A means that the realization is an Americanized version.)

Options for interpretation

What are we to do with arrays of style-representing numbers like those that appear in the extract? In line with much conventional sociolinguistic research, we might want to aggregate the scores for particular pronunciation variables across many such extracts. If we do this, we reach the very unsurprising conclusion that, for all the variables we have listed above, FH's speech is generally very nonstandard. But it is only uniformly nonstandard in the case of one variable (ou). For all others, we get high percentages but percentages that derive from *varying* stylistic performance from instance to instance.

A next step might therefore be to try to isolate the micro-contexts of FH's speech. The context is, from one point of view, unvarying. After all, we have a single speaker who is speaking, ostensibly, to the same audience over the course of the show. But it seems possible and potentially productive to establish categories of context on the basis of topics of talk, or modes of discourse, or in relation to specific communicative activities within the show. We can see, even in this extract, how FH's performance involves him in reading listeners' letters (lines 1–6), making public announcements (presumably based on prepared written sources (the Margaret Morris episode), doing 'record-speak' (e.g. 'here's the Checkmates Proud Mary', lines 6–7) and being funny (e.g. 'I'll have to get me right arm in training you know', lines 30–31).

Some generalizations can be made on this basis. For instance, FH tends to use consistent Cardiff pronunciations when talking about Cardiff people and events. He also does this when he makes joking references to his own incompetence. But he uses more standard pronunciations in connection with structuring and publicizing the show, when 'competence' and 'expertise' become more salient aspects of his identity, as the italicized features in these other examples demonstrate:

we've got for the ne*xt* t*w*o h*ou*rs s*o* stay with me until two o'clock

Frank *H*ennessy *he*re on CBC two two one metres medium wave and
n*i*nety-six VHF in ste*re*o

FH does not use standard forms for all the variables on such occasions: those that
are 'corrected' are generally stigmatized features in social dialect terms (for
example, 'h-dropping'). Specifically Cardiff features such as (aː) are left in their
local forms to continue marking in-group identity.

There are boundary problems inherent in this 'micro-contextual' approach.
Is the link between the two records in the extract ('they sound as if they going
bananas don't they', line 10) humour – and a phono-opportunity for (aː) – or
record-speak? FH's announcement of the dance event is interspersed with
humorous commentary on the announcement itself ('are you with me ah 'cause
I'm totally confused', lines 19–20). It also shows elements of spontaneous ad-
libbing ('now all sessions today are absolutely free so if the weather's a little bit
gone against you and you fancy well not running round in the rain …', lines
24–6). Any text-based typology, assigning utterances to contextual types, is therefore imprecise. Although it allows us to produce some interesting general correla-
tions between stylistic 'levels' and contexts, the approach does not ultimately
appear to do justice to the moment-to-moment creativity of FH's own performance.

This is so for at least three reasons. First, FH is not limited to the alternation
between more and less standard realizations of Cardiff English. Sometimes he
uses features from other dialects. He adopts American features to introduce some
songs, including the 'yeah' in line 7 of the extract and, perhaps surprisingly, the
title of the Bananarama song in line 30. There are other features elsewhere in the
recording; for instance, south-west of England dialect features in connection with
a mention of Dorsetshire, and Cockney features to introduce a song by Joe Brown
and His Bruvvers.

Secondly, a correlational account cannot capture the interplay between style,
content and key. Some of the dialect mimicry is playful, as in the case of American
features parodying slick DJ patter. Again, the 'social meaning' of broad Cardiff
dialect seems different depending on whether the focus of the talk is Frank
himself (in which case it conveys humour through self-deprecation) or cultural
history (in which case it conjures social solidarity and a sense of community).

But thirdly and crucially, there is the theoretical consideration that the
various configurations of 'context' do not exist independently of FH's speech
forms. It is often the case that we can only identify a 'contextual type' *by virtue of*
the stylistic attributes of FH's speech. He is the orchestrator of contexts, and this
removes the empirical basis that justifies correlation.

A theoretical realignment for the study of style

I have referred above to FH's 'performance' in the DJ role. FH is clearly a media
'performer' in the specific sense of seeking to entertain and developing his media
persona(e) with a degree of self-consciousness and overt planning and scripting.
Variation in his speech and in particular his dialect can therefore be said to be not
only styled but *stylized*. But 'performance' is also the appropriate term because of
Frank's stylistic creativity. His styles are not situational reflexes. They are ways of
drawing simultaneously on multiple sets of social meanings.

In this case, more than merely representing a speech community (Cardiff),
dialect opens up a range of potential personal and social identities for FH, and

diverse bases on which he can relate to his audience. Through stylistic choices in dialect, he can project but then momentarily undermine his 'ethnic Cardiff' persona with a pastiche of the slick American DJ ('yeah').

Conversely, he can undermine this 'DJ' projection with a strongly dialectized admission of personal incompetence ('I'll have to get me right arm in training'). He can manufacture the persona of the competent public announcer, then parody this role (and the announced event?) both referentially and through a dialect switch. Cardiff English is not merely 'Frank's voice' but one of many culturally loaded voices that FH, and presumably his audience too, can manipulate for relational and other interactional purposes.

These critical readings of stylistic shifts are far less consistent with the dominant tradition within sociolinguistics than with the work of the Russian theorist Bakhtin. In his paper on 'The problem of speech genres' (written in 1952–3 and reproduced in Emerson and Holquist, 1992), Bakhtin writes of 'such *fictions* as "the listener"' (p. 68) and of how any speaker

> presupposes not only the existence of the language system he [sic] is using, but also the existence of preceding utterances – his own and others' – with which his given utterance enters into one kind of relation or another (builds on them, polemicizes with them or simply presumes that they are already known to the listener)
>
> (Bakhtin, 1992, p. 69).

This idea of 'multiple voicing' arguably has a more direct relevance to the study of *dialect* style than to any other dimension of linguistic variation. Dialects are indeed 'the drive belts from the history of society to the history of language' (Bakhtin, 1992, p. 65), replete with social and cultural echoes, associations and 'dialogic reverberations' (p. 94). Bakhtin writes that 'Our speech ... is filled with others' words, varying degrees of otherness and varying degrees of "our-own-ness", [which] ... carry with them their own evaluative tone, which we assimilate, rework and re-accentuate' (Bakhtin, 1992, p. 89). The 'Hark, Hark' analysis is well summarized as FH borrowing, reworking and re-accentuating dialect styles, creatively and multidimensionally.

Acknowledgement

I am very grateful to Mr Frank Hennessy for his permission to use data from the radio show and for his interest and co-operation.

References

COUPLAND, N. (1985) '"Hark, Hark the Lark": social motivations for phonological style-shifting', *Language and Communications*, vol. 5, no. 3, pp. 153–71.

This reading was specially commissioned for this book.

Reading B

STRATEGIC AMBIGUITY: CODE-SWITCHING IN THE MANAGEMENT OF CONFLICT

Monica Heller

This extract draws on examples from a study of language shift from English to French in a large company in Montreal in Quebec, Canada. A language law passed in Quebec in the 1970s had established French as the language of work. At the time of the study, many anglophone managers in the company were being replaced by young francophone managers. Heller discusses some of the factors that, in this context, cause speakers to codeswitch between English and French.

Heller found two new patterns of language use in the company: anglophones used some French routines when talking to one another; younger francophones tended not to use English routines (though older francophones did). Heller comments:

> Why is this happening? In this company it is the use of French that now legitimates one's presence, whereas until very recently the language of power in private enterprise was English. Francophones thus have an interest in defining themselves as such. To use English is to evoke the conventions of the old regime when the English were in power.

Codeswitching allows anglophones some claim on the rights and obligations associated with French – though not all of them (anglophones do not wish to 'pass' entirely because of 'the continued advantage of being English in the North American business world').

[Code-switching] enables a speaker to do things he or she would otherwise not be able to do: in the case of this company gain access to situations to which the criterion of access is ability to speak French, without actually having to be French. By the same token it is possible to avoid some of the responsibilities of categorical language choice through this kind of code-switching.

This is notably the case with a small group of anglophones who have been recently recruited. Not only did they accept their jobs in the awareness of (and in some ways desirous of) the condition that they work in French, they themselves are not part of the long-established Montreal anglophone community and so have nothing invested in the local ethnolinguistic struggle. They came from other provinces, several are married to francophones, and one was actually of franco-phone origin although he had lost the language. Thus they need to avoid the categorical alignment with one group or the other that categorical language choice would represent. For this reason I call them 'marginals'. For them codeswitching represents a way of maintaining access to both networks without having to take on the responsibilities associated with full membership in one or the other (such as commitment to a career in Quebec or geographical career mobility).

(1) Two marginals use code-switching with each other:

F	Charles	*bonjour Henri*	hello Henri
F	Henry	*bonjour*	hello
F	Charles	*comment ça va?*	how's it going?
F	Henry	*bien toi?*	fine you?
F	Charles	*ça va bien j'ai une question pour toi*	it's going fine I have a question for you
F	Henry	*oui?*	yes?
E	Charles	what are the specs for …	

Another outstanding pattern of code-switching is that which occurs in intergroup interaction at the management level, the frontier of change. Here, such official interactions as department meetings are supposed to occur in French. However, some young newly promoted francophones find themselves presiding over meetings where there are older anglophones, who were originally in line for promotion but who were blocked because they do not speak French, and older francophones who are used to working in English. There are often also other young francophones present. What to do? If the francophones only speak French they will seem hostile to the anglophones, since they will have deliberately erected a language barrier which will prevent anglophones from participating (and everyone knows that the francophones are able to speak English). Yet the francophones like these anglophones, they are friends; furthermore, they consider themselves to be nice people who would never deliberately be nasty to somebody else. Finally, they recognize their need for the expertise and experience that the anglophones have; the anglophones are, after all, generally senior to these young francophones (and this adds the dimension of respect for elders to the picture). If the francophones speak only English, however, their legitimacy is undermined; their rapid promotion was based not only on their technical ability but also on the principle of francophone control of private enterprise. Answer: code-switch, and thereby do neither, permitting the accomplishment of the task at hand (to take care of the order of business), the management of personal relations (maintaining good relationships with anglophones) and the maintenance of the legitimacy of one's status as a francophone manager. Similarly, the anglophones must legitimate their presence through some use of French.

(2) Albert, the young new francophone manager, uses English to talk to Bob, an anglophone who is junior in rank to Albert but his senior in age and experience, and French to open the meeting:

E	Albert	he would have got
E	Bob	he's twenty-one years of age
E	Albert	yeah twenty-one years of age

F		(pause) *bon mais vous pouvez fermer la porte c'est tout ce qu'on va avoir aujourd'hui*	good but you can close the door that's all we're going to have today

(3) Claude, an older francophone used to working in English, reads his report in English, but directs comments on the report in French to Albert:

Claude	*oui uh vacation staff Roland Masse George Kovacs cette seminare la semaine prochaine Roland Masse George Kovacs* again *uh uh temp Denis Blais* he's on the lubrication survey *Leo Charrette uh* working on the expense budget but he's going off for two weeks *hein? il prend deux semaines de vacances ça je l'avais donné ça y a un bout de temps*	eh? he's taking two weeks' vacation that I gave that a while ago

(4) Bob uses French routines or short phrases in otherwise English episodes:

(a)   E   Albert   oh Monday afternoon we have a
                                meeting with Daniel Vincent
       E   Bob   what time is it?
            Albert   uh
       E   Claude   right signs
       F   Albert   *douze heures*   twelve o'clock
       E   signs
       F   Bob   *quelle place?*   what place?
       E   Albert   I think it's my office
(b)   E   Albert   uh it's like passing the buck to
                                somebody but uh (laughs) can you
                                spend some time some time with
                                Pierre (unint) Monday it could be a
                                good thing
       F   Bob   *avec plaisir*   with pleasure

It is noteworthy that Bob can even use code-switching to defuse an argument between Claude and Albert.

(5) Bob uses code-switching to de-escalate an argument between Claude and Albert in which he has been called in to arbitrate:

E   Bob   okay good but I think I'm just not sure if
                        Claude I got the complete message
                        clearly as I understand it Albert will look
                        for from you in the hand-written form
                        the one you'll pass over to him will have
                        breakdowns as opposed to your full sheet
                        going to him
E   Claude   no I don't need to prepare that because I
                        already got it
E   Bob   okay good
E   Claude   I'm only summarizing
F   Bob   mm fine *fini?*   finished
F   Claude   *vendu*   sold
                        (pause)
E   Albert   do you see that? Gaz Naturel? increase in
                        price

In the meeting discussed here there was a fourth person present, a young francophone who had no personal ties with anyone in the group, and who occupied a position in which the use of English was largely unnecessary. He never spoke English during the meeting, there was no reason for him to do so, his position with respect to the French/English boundary being such that his distance from it rendered code-switching meaningless. Aside from this fourth person, code-switching in this situation accomplishes the ambiguity of not choosing frames of reference. Once the participants use code-switching to neutralize the tension between French and English, they can all participate in the meeting. Further, code-switching becomes available as a conversation, management device (Albert uses English to include Bob, Bob uses French to enter the conversation. Claude uses French to gain his boss's ear) and as a device for managing interpersonal relations (Bob uses French to make peace between Claude and Albert).

Source: Heller, 1988, pp. 84–90

Reading C

CODESWITCHING WITH ENGLISH: TYPES OF SWITCHING, TYPES OF COMMUNITIES

Carol Myers-Scotton

This extract draws on Carol Myers-Scotton's research on codeswitching in Kenya and Zimbabwe. Myers-Scotton's model of codeswitching suggests that languages (codes) are 'indexical' of social relationships: they establish a speaker as a certain kind of person in relation to others. More specifically, they index a particular set of rights and obligations that will hold between participants in an interaction. A speaker will, then, select a code that indexes the rights and obligations he/she wishes to be in force between him/herself and others. In this extract, Myers-Scotton identifies different patterns of codeswitching based on the notion of 'markedness'. An 'unmarked' choice means an expected choice, one that is associated with the type of interaction in which it occurs. A 'marked' choice means one that is not expected in that context. It is an attempt to redefine a relationship.

Sequential unmarked choices

This pattern consists of a switch from one unmarked choice to another one when external forces (e.g. a new participant, a new topic) alter the expected balance of rights and obligations and therefore the relative markedness of one code vs. another. ...

Example (1) illustrates sequences of unmarked choices in East Africa, with English as a component.

(1) A school principal who speaks English and Swahili in addition to his first language is in Nairobi on a visit. He wishes to call on a friend working for a large automobile sales and repair establishment. While speaking to the guard at the gate, he uses Swahili as an unmarked choice, but once inside the office, he switches to English as the unmarked choice there.

Guard (Swahili)	*Unapenda nikusaidie namna gani?*	In what way do you want me to help you?
Principal (Swahili)	*Ningependa kumwona Peter Mbaya*	I would like to see Peter Mbaya.
Guard (Swahili)	*Bwana Peter hayuko saa hii. Ingia na uende kwa* office *ya* inquiries *na umngoje. Atarudi.*	Mr Peter isn't here right now. Go inside to the inquiry office and wait for him. He'll return.
Receptionist (English)	Good morning. Can I help you?	
Principal (English)	Good morning. I came to see Mr Mbaya.	
Receptionist (English)	He is out but will soon be here. Have a seat and wait for him.	

Switching as an unmarked choice

When participants are bilingual peers, the unmarked choice may be switching, but with no changes at all in setting, participants, topic, or any other situational feature. That is, for ingroup communication – especially in an informal setting – the pattern of alternating between two varieties may [itself] be unmarked ... When the unmarked state of affairs is simultaneous participation in two rights and obligations balances, each associated with a different social identity, speakers switch between two codes, each one being unmarked in the specific context for one of the identities. The overall pattern of switching is the major social message (i.e. dual identities) in this type of switching, each individual switch point need have no social significance at all ... [Examples 2 and 3 illustrate this type of switching.] Although the transcript does not show it, there are no hesitation phenomena and no change in the stress pattern.

(2) A school principal from Western Kenya is in Nairobi visiting a friend who is an administrator at the Government Printer. Their conversation has been in their shared mother tongue, Lwidakho, when a telephone call interrupts them.

Administrator (English, Lwidakho)	(on telephone)	
	Good afternoon. This is Gabriel.	
	Oh, Elijah. *Mbulili unvele muwale uvira khulishi?*	How are you? I heard you were sick.
	Yes, with Henry. He's been here about an hour.	
Administrator (English)	(to Henry, the principal)	
	When are you returning?	
Principal (English)	The first week of next month – before schools reopen.	
Administrator (Lwidakho, English, Swahili)	(on telephone)	
	Alatsya lisitsa lyukhura mu mweli muluya.	He'll go during the first week of the new month.
	Yes, I'll tell him that.	
	LAKINI, BWANA, SIKU HIZI HUONEKANI. UMEPOTEA WAPI?	But, mister, you aren't seen these days. Where are you lost?

(3) Two University of Zimbabwe students are chatting in their dormitory. Their shared mother tongue, the Karanja dialect of Shona, is the matrix language.

| Student (Shona, English) | *Oramba a-chi-ngo-*deliberat-*a a-chi-ngo-*deliberat-*a kwava kuzoti tava kusvika pai mu-*class *tava kutosvika pa-ma-*classes. (Note: At issue is the status of 'class' as a loan word or a switch.) | She kept on deliberating up to a point when we were about to reach the classrooms. |

Codeswitching as a marked choice

Switching away from the expected, away from the unmarked choice ... is a negotiation to replace the current – and unmarked – rights and obligations set with another one. ...

Marked choices to ingroup varieties among group members typically encode solidarity. Quite another effect typically results from switching to varieties associated with education and/or authority. Such switches often encode more social distance between participants, sometimes out of anger or a desire to lower the addressee's or increase one's own status. Because it is associated with authority (either in former colonial regimes or in present governments or educational systems), English is often the language of such a marked switch, especially in the Third World. Note, however, that the indexical message of a code is context-specific: in some contexts English may encode solidarity, even though it is a second language, such as between highly educated peers. Example (4) illustrates two different marked choices, one to a mother tongue not shared by all (communicating solidarity with the speaker's ethnic group member, but distance from the others) and one to English (communicating authority).

(4) Four young office workers in the same government ministry in Nairobi are chatting. Two are Kikuyu, one is a Kisii, and one is a Kalenjin. Swahili–English switching has been the unmarked choice up to the switch to Kikuyu. The conversation about setting up a group 'emergency fund' has been proceeding when the Kikuyus switch to Kikuyu to make a negative comment about what has just been said, a marked choice communicating solidarity between the two Kikuyus but distancing them from the others. At this point, the Kisii complains in Swahili and English and the Kalenjin makes a switch from Swahili to a sentence entirely in English, a marked choice, to return the discussion to a more business-like plane.

Kikuyu II (Kikuyu)	*Andu amwe nimendaga, kwaria maundu maria matari na ma namo.*	Some people like talking about what they're not sure of.
Kikuyu I (Kikuyu)	*Wira wa muigi wa kigina ni kuiga mbeca. No tigucaria mbeca.*	The work of the treasurer is only to keep money, not to hunt for money.
Kisii (Swahili, English)	*Ubaya wenu ya Kikuyu ni ku-*assume *kila mtu anaelewa Kikuyu.*	The bad thing about Kikuyus is assuming that everyone understands Kikuyu.
Kalenjin (Swahili, English)	*Si mtumie lugha ambayo kila mtu hapa atasikia?* (said with some force): We are supposed to solve this issue.	Shouldn't you use a language which every person here understands?

Codeswitching as an exploratory choice presenting multiple identities

In nonconventionalized exchanges or simply when meeting someone for the first time and when all the relevant social identity factors of the other person or other situational factors are not known, multiple identities sometimes are presented via codeswitching as an exploratory choice. In these circumstances, since no unmarked choice is obvious, speakers may switch in order to settle upon a code which will be mutually acceptable as the unmarked choice of the exchange. Accepting a code as the basis for the conversation, of course, means accepting the balance of rights and obligations indexed by that code. Example (5) illustrates such switching in a community where English is a frequent component of exploratory switching. Note that this type of switching highlights the interactional nature of codeswitching as a negotiation of identities; while any speaker can switch to any code to negotiate a particular relationship, for the negotiation to succeed requires that the addressee reciprocate with this code.

(5) A young man has come into the manager's office in a Nairobi business establishment. The young man begins in English, but finally switches to Swahili, following the manager's lead. Either language would be a possible choice, but each communicating different relationships. The manager's insistence on Swahili denies the young man's negotiation of the higher status associated with English.

Young man (English)	Mr Muchuki has sent me to you about the job you put in the paper.	
Manager (Swahili)	*Ulituma barua ya* application *?*	Did you send a letter of application?
Young man (English)	Yes, I did. But he asked me to come to see you today.	
Manager (Swahili)	*Ikiwa ulituma barua, nenda ungojee majibu. Tutakuita ufike kwa* interview *siku itakapofika.*	If you've written a letter, then go and wait for a response. We will call you for an interview when the letter arrives.
	Leo sina la suma kuliko hayo.	Today I haven't anything else to say.
Young man (Swahili)	*Asante. Nitangoja majibu.*	Thank you. I'll wait for the response.

Codeswitching showing multiple identities in non-conventionalized exchanges is also used as a neutral strategy. Since each code communicates a particular identity in a given situation, when it is unclear which identity offers the speaker the most positive evaluation, the speaker may see codeswitching as a solution.

Source: Myers-Scotton, 1989, pp. 333–9

9 GOOD AND BAD ENGLISH

Donald Mackinnon

9.1 INTRODUCTION

It is sometimes hard to write dispassionately about the English language. Earlier chapters have documented the different forms taken by English, and how these have changed over the centuries. We have also looked at how English has been used, alongside other languages, in different parts of the English-speaking world. A constant theme has been the sets of beliefs and values with which these forms and uses of English have been associated. Researchers have set out to investigate such beliefs and values: Chapter 7, for instance, discussed different methods used to elicit people's views about the qualities of English accents, such as their correctness or attractiveness. But language scholars themselves have been anything but dispassionate in their observations. Chapters 3–5 mentioned the part played, historically, by language scholars in constructing certain 'stories' of English. And Chapter 1 discussed contemporary linguists' judgements about the validity of native and nonnative or standard and nonstandard varieties of the language.

In this chapter, as someone trained in philosophy not linguistics, I provide a more detailed examination of judgements about the quality of English made both by linguists and by nonlinguists; and I discuss some of the arguments that have been put forward in support of such judgements. I shall look mainly at evidence from British English, the variety with which I am most familiar.

9.2 MAKING JUDGEMENTS ABOUT ENGLISH

What judgements, then, can we make about the quality of English? Can we reasonably make any? The answers these questions receive from professional linguists are often very different from answers given by those I shall call, for lack of a better term, ordinary people.

The judgements of ordinary people

Judgements about the quality of English are of course commonplace – in education, in politics, in everyday life, and very conspicuously in the mass media. A recent and quite unremarkable report in a British newspaper had this to say:

> Standards in this year's GCSE English examination have slipped dramatically following the reintroduction of old-fashioned written exam papers. Examiners across the country confirm a real and sudden decline in the quality of English used … The news will rekindle the furious battle between those who argue that the methods of testing are solely to blame and those who claim that there is a real slide in pupils' English – particularly in spelling, grammar and punctuation.
>
> (Hugill and O'Connor, *Observer*, 24 July 1994)

Here it is simply assumed that people's English can be of better or worse quality, that quality can improve or decline, and (I think) that it can be uncontroversially identified and even measured, using such criteria as spelling, grammar and punctuation. The authors of this newspaper article allow that there is some dispute about the *facts* of the case – whether there really have been changes in pupils' spelling, grammar and punctuation, or whether it just looks that way because of changes in GCSE assessment, with less emphasis on pupils' course work and more on a final, formal examination – but they do not even acknowledge the possibility of disagreement about whether any such changes should be thought of as a *decline*.

Activity 9.1   *(Reading A)*

Reading A contains a selection of extracts from news items, feature articles and letters published in *The Times* newspaper during the year July 1993 to June 1994 on the subject of complaints and worries about the English language. Read through the extracts fairly quickly, and for each one keep a brief record of your reactions. I give some of my own reactions from time to time later in this chapter. Whether or not those who write for or to *The Times* count as ordinary people is a moot point. (*The Times*'s own advertisements used to suggest that its readers were 'top people'!) Here, though, I use them as a convenient if highly imperfect sample of ordinary people, or at least of people who are nonlinguists.

The relativism of linguists

But though commonplace, judgements about language are controversial. Many linguists today argue that the kinds of judgement most commonly made about quality in language are radically misguided. Some, indeed, seem to believe that *all* judgements of good or bad in language are ill-founded. The more moderate forms of this position have themselves been quite well represented in *The Times* in recent years, notably in the regular columns on language by Philip Howard. But we can also find a more extreme example while remaining with *The Times* – appropriately enough since the linguist in question, Jean Aitchison, is the Rupert Murdoch Professor of Language and Communication at the University of Oxford.

Activity 9.2   *(Readings B and C)*

Reading B, 'Of dipsticks and the joys of a double negative', by Valerie Grove, is an article from *The Times* about Professor Aitchison and her views, based on an interview with her. Reading C is a short article by Jean Aitchison, 'Why do purists grumble so much?', from the London newspaper the *Evening Standard*. Read these, and make brief notes of your reactions to them before reading on. Again, I shall give my own reactions to some of Aitchison's arguments throughout this chapter.

I do not think that Jean Aitchison is merely saying that linguistics as a discipline is neutral – as, for example, the science of acoustics is neutral in that it does not identify particular sounds or sequences of sounds as beautiful or ugly. She *is* saying this ('Laying down rules is not my job'), but she is saying more. She monitors what her interviewer in Reading B tendentiously calls 'illiterate developments' with a 'benign', not a neutral eye. She positively welcomes variety, and appears to treat almost all varieties and usages as equally acceptable.

It is *almost* all usages, though; even Aitchison is prepared to draw lines somewhere. She disapproves of some of the language used by the authorities and the media during the Gulf War, as she explains in her *Evening Standard* article

(Reading C). And Valerie Grove is probably wrong in thinking that Aitchison 'would merely note such locutions [as *brunette* and *bluestocking*] in her database'. Aitchison might be willing to let 'cliche-ridden journalese' pass, but she disapproves of language she considers sexist – even her own, as she explains in the preface to the fourth edition of her book *Teach Yourself Linguistics*:

> in this edition, I have tried to avoid the sexist linguistic usages found in the earlier versions, which misleadingly implied in places that only males of our species could talk. I have done this partly by using the plural (*people* instead of *he*), partly by using indefinites (*a person, anyone*) followed by a plural pronoun (*if anyone is surprised, they should see how increasingly common this usage is*), and partly by interchanging *he* and *she* in places where a neutral between sexes pronoun is required.
>
> (Aitchison, 1992, p. viii)

In this chapter I want to consider what value judgements we can and cannot reasonably make about language. My discussion is in two parts. First I look at the general issue of judgements of good and bad – the sorts of judgement linguists like Jean Aitchison seem to say we cannot sensibly make, and the sorts many ordinary people not only do make but consider very important. To help me, I make use of H.W. Fowler's classic handbook, *A Dictionary of Modern English Usage*, first published as a guide to speakers and writers in 1926 and still in print (though since 1965 in a version much modified by Sir Ernest Gowers; I use Fowler's original text here). Secondly, I want to look at the exception even linguists often seem prepared to make, the special case of 'political correctness' in language. Here I focus mainly on a single publication, a guide produced by my own employer, the British Open University. These publications are both British, of course.

The 'colonial twang' in New Zealand

The boys of ten or twelve years ago did not have the careless way of pronouncing vowels that they have nowadays. I think it is getting worse and worse every year. If you take a class of thirty at the beginning of the year I do not think you will find more than three or four who will say 'house' correctly. Of course I do not believe in overdoing it, as you find in the case of some people who have been Home, but at the same time the word is 'house' and not 'heouse.' Again a great many, instead of saying 'Oh, no,' say 'Ow, neow.' But you very rarely find a boy dropping his h's.

(A college principal giving evidence to the Cohen Commission on Education in 1912, cited in Gordon and Deverson, 1989, p. 31)

What hope is there for change when we find two of the Principals of the largest secondary schools in New Zealand ... using these expressions: 'taime-table' for 'time-table'; 'Ai' for 'I'; 'may own' for 'my own' ...

(A member of the Cohen Commission deploring the rise of a 'colonial-genteel' pronunciation in reaction to the 'colonial twang', cited in Gordon and Abell, 1990, p. 27)

Kuds are kids

Sir – What is happening to the humble letter "i" in New Zealandese? In many mouths HIM becomes HUM, JIM is JUM and TILL is TULL. I overheard a young girl telling her friend on the phone that she had been to a doctor and had to take six different PULLS a day. After four repetitions, she had to spell it to be understood.

During a recent fashion award feature on television, a number of people gave their views on fashions, clothing, quality, price, etc. One woman, otherwise well spoken, had me puzzled by the phrase "What the KUDS want to buy in boutiques." The third time round the penny dropped. KUDS are KIDS.

(Extract from a letter to the *New Zealand Listener*, cited in Gordon and Deverson, 1989, p. 35)

Turn-off or turn-on?

Few things stick out as sorely as an unattractive accent, and Singaporeans, according to Mr Terry Matkin, a speech trainer with the Singapore Broadcasting Corporation, are remarkably obsessed with speech.

"I've had people calling to say, 'He said it this way, is that correct?'," he says.

"The English would never bother about something like this – they just go and do it. People here, however, are genuinely very interested in the standards of the spoken word."

Certainly most Singaporeans are critical of some presenter or other, and many have shot letters to the media about the garbled grammar and speech of some radio presenters.

Some detest the American accent, finding it "vulgar", as Miss Vanessa Liew, 30, an English teacher puts it.

Some, like Mr Jacob Tan, 28, a freelance writer, hate the nasal Australian drawl because "they sound like yobs". And others, like Mr Isamil Iskandar, 19, a student, resent the posh, round tones of the British Broadcasting Corporation accent because the speaker can sound so "uptight".

(The Straits Times, 22 August 1992)

Janadas Devan writes an open letter to SIM on accents over radio and TV

Chairman

Singapore International Media (SIM)

Dear Sir,

I WISH to inform you that I have ceased listening to 90.5 FM. The last straw was one of your announcers reporting a traffic jam at Care-lang. If you have difficulty, sir, guessing where Care-lang is, you will understand my fury. (Care-lang is what you and I have known all our lives as Kallang.)

This was not an isolated incident. Fifteen minutes before I learnt of the traffic accident at Care lang, I discovered our Ambassador to the United States was Mr S. R. Nay-then (Nathan). And about a month ago, I was told that China's paramount leader was Mr Dank Shopping (Deng Xiaoping).

I also wish to inform you, sir, that I have ceased viewing some of your programmes on Channel 5, which use presenters who look Asian but speak an English that none of my Singaporean friends speak. I can understand perfectly if you need to hire an Asian-American to cover world finance because he happens to be the best in the field.

But the fact that American accents surface now with astonishing frequency on our air-waves can only indicate an aesthetic determination on the part of some of your producers that only such accents are proper, and that the rest of us have accents that are improper. On purely nationalist grounds, I refuse to countenance this belief.

(The Straits Times, 21 October 1994)

Fowler confines his attention largely to British English, not because he is ignorant of other varieties but because he regards them almost as foreign languages. In an earlier book he said firmly that 'Americanisms are foreign words, and should be so treated', that is, treated on a par with words from French or German, with no more intention thereby to insult American English than these other languages (Fowler and Fowler, 1905, p. 11).

Complaints about the quality of English can be found in other English-speaking countries too, as you can see in the boxes above. Here is another example:

> In your article on international brands I have been quoted as saying that Lacoste has a phobia 'against' bad quality. You can have a phobia 'about' something, not against it. I am sure I said 'about' in the interview. You may consider this a minor detail, we don't.

> (Jayant Kochar, President, Sports and Leisure Apparel Limited, New Delhi, *India Today*, 30 September 1994, p. 9)

But in countries other than Britain or the United States there is a complicating factor, especially strong perhaps in countries that have been British colonies (and have remained colonies until more recently than the USA!). In Britain the complaints are made by comparison with Standard British English. But elsewhere complaints and unfavourable judgements are often made by comparison not with a local Standard English but with a variety from outside – usually British or American English. Thus, even a professor at the Indian Institute of Technology, who is using computers to chart the Indianization of English, can refer to aspects of the process as 'deterioration', and to the examples of Indian English he collects as 'mistakes' (McCrum, Cran and MacNeil, 1992, pp. 363–5).

Not all judgements about American or British English see these varieties in a favourable light, as the boxes above show. Chapter 7 reviews different reactions to English accents.

9.3   JUDGEMENTS OF GOOD AND BAD LANGUAGE

Activity 9.3   *(Allow 10–15 minutes)*

Look again at the collection of judgements in Reading A and your own comments on them. Try to recall other judgements that you have heard, or indeed that you yourself would make. Spend a few minutes thinking about what different *kinds* of favourable or unfavourable judgement can be made about examples of English. Draw up a list and compare it with mine below.

If you have any handbooks of English usage – such as Fowler's *Modern English Usage* itself or any of its successors – you might find it helpful, as I did, to look at the kinds of judgement they make.

Comment

Here is the list I came up with.

1   We may judge examples of English to be straightforwardly *correct* or *incorrect*.

2   We may judge the examples to be *beautiful* or *ugly*.

3   We may judge them to be *socially acceptable* or *unacceptable* – the latter in the sense of being characteristic of a social group or category inferior in some way to the one we belong to, or aspire to belong to.

4   We may judge them to be *morally acceptable* or *unacceptable*. As with all moral judgements, we may be judging the speaker's or writer's intentions, or the effects of what they say, or both.

5   We may judge them to be more or less *useful* for some purpose (such as expressing abstract thought, or being easy to sing).

6   We may judge them to be *appropriate* or *inappropriate* for some purpose or context (such as an academic paper, an exam answer, a job interview or a love letter).

7   Finally, we may distance ourselves from any of the above judgements, but consider that other people will make them. Thus we may not ourselves regard a split infinitive as incorrect, a Birmingham accent as ugly or the word 'lady' as offensive, but we may acknowledge that many people do – and perhaps therefore treat these usages as *controversial*, avoiding them ourselves and recommending others to avoid them.

Some of the above judgements can be made about an individual example of language; or about an individual person's or group of people's use of language; or more generally still, about some language variety, or even about English as such.

As you can see, my list of judgements in Activity 9.3 is very rough and ready, with lots of overlapping and criss-crossing of categories, and certainly no claim to being exhaustive. As a result, the actual judgements people make and the arguments they pursue do not always fall neatly into one and only one of my categories. For example, *The Times* columnist in Reading A (extract 4) who objected to the turning of nouns into verbs seems to be saying both that this is incorrect and that the results are ugly, and also to be changing the emphasis from the first to the second in moving from 'to access' to 'to outsource'. One possible counterargument might be this, in the words of the BBC TV series *The Story of English*:

> [An asset] of English is that it has a grammar of great simplicity and flexibility. Nouns and adjectives have highly simplified word-endings. This flexibility extends to the parts of speech themselves. Nouns can become verbs and verbs nouns in a way that is impossible in other languages …
> (McCrum et al., 1992, p. 43)

In responding like this, we would be moving from criticism in terms of incorrectness or ugliness to defence in terms of usefulness, and from criticism of a handful of people to celebration of certain characteristics of the English language itself.

But in the interests of clarity I try here to keep the categories separate, and consider what is involved in each – though I may not always succeed. First, and in some ways most important, is correctness.

Correctness

Fowler unhesitatingly judges usages to be correct or incorrect. To take just one of many examples, he says that the phrase *due to* is 'impossible' in sentences like the following: 'The old trade union movement is a dead horse, largely d. to the incompetency of the leaders' (Fowler, 1926, p. 123).

It is interesting to compare Fowler here with the *Oxford Guide to English Usage* (Weiner, 1983) – a modern counterpart in that both are explicitly based on the experience and resources of the *Oxford English Dictionary* of their day. The *Oxford Guide* is usually more hesitant than Fowler about making definite judgements of correct and incorrect, as we see below when we contrast its treatment of *due to* with Fowler's. It does make some judgements, however; for example: 'The past tense has -*a*-, the past participle -*u*-, in *begin, drink* … It is an error to use *begun, drunk* … for the past tense …' (Weiner, 1983, p. 24).

Chapter 4 discusses the history of some perceptions of correct English.

But how do we – or Fowler, or the compiler of the *Oxford Guide* – know when something in language is correct or incorrect? What, indeed, do we mean by saying it is correct or incorrect? And why should we be concerned about correctness?

Spelling

To explore these questions I shall focus on **spelling**, and begin with a few clear-cut examples. When Susan Elkin writes in *The Times* (see Reading A, extract 9) that spelling mistakes such as *seperate, sentance,* and *sponsered* are commonplace among teachers, we may or may not be sceptical about her facts, but few of us, I imagine, could sincerely claim that we did not consider these to be mistakes, or that we did not know what is meant by calling them 'mistakes'. Nevertheless, let us pursue our questions a little, at the expense of labouring the obvious. What do we mean by saying that *seperate* or *sentance* is a spelling *mistake*?

First, it is clearly not a mistake of the same kind as writing that the earth is flat or that two plus two equals five. It is more like breaking a rule in football or a

convention in table etiquette. The first instances are mistakes concerning facts
about the world, or necessary truths – these facts and truths cannot be changed;
the truths are true everywhere and the mistakes mistaken everywhere; human
beings discover them, but do not make the truths true, or the mistakes mistaken.
By contrast, the second instances are breaches of human-made rules and conventions. These rules and conventions can and do change from time to time and vary
from place to place. And of course all this is true of spelling. Spellings do change,
as you have already seen in Chapter 2. And spellings do vary from place to place.
Indeed one of the mistakes Elkin mentions – using 'licence' as a verb – would be
correct in American English, which has of course become the basis of standard
spelling in many other parts of the English-speaking world.

Secondly, there is – at least for English – no authoritative body to lay down the
correct spelling of words; in this respect it is more like table etiquette than the
rules of football. Of course particular organizations can define correct spellings
and other usages for their own purposes, as with the 'house style' of a publishing
house or the BBC; they may be important influences beyond their own walls, but
they have no wider authority.

Nevertheless dictionaries are often treated as authorities. If we want to know
how a word is spelled, most of us look it up in a dictionary. Again we can illustrate
this from *The Times*. When a columnist on the newspaper, Candida Crewe, set her
readers a spelling test which her father had prepared 20 years before, it provoked
the following letter:

> no doubt thousands [of readers] were, like me, furious at the familiar
> words on which they tripped up ... I scored an undistinguished 15
> correct out of 21 ... Ms Crewe should, however, add a rider if she
> publicises this test anywhere else. Three of these words have alternative
> spellings, at least if my dictionary (Collins, third edition, 1991) is to be
> believed. They are: *impostor* or *imposter*; *obbligato* or *obligato*; and *vermilion*
> or *vermillion*. If I had not spotted these alternatives, I should have scored
> only a shameful 13 out of 21.
>
> (J.P. Griffiths, *The Times*, 24 August 1993)

I could not resist looking up these words in my own dictionary, the *Longman New
Universal Dictionary* (Procter et al., 1982) – like *Collins Dictionary of the English
Language*, a British work. I found that in two of the three cases *Longman* and
Collins were in agreement: *Longman* also recognized *imposter/impostor* and *vermil-
ion/vermillion* as alternative spellings. But in the third case, *Longman* gave only
obbligato; there was no recognition of *obligato* as an alternative. So, which dictionary is correct? Is *obligato* a correct spelling or is it not?

These are naive questions of course. A dictionary – any dictionary – is not
quite the authority that Mr Griffiths seems to treat it as being. It does have
authority of a kind, but that authority is secondary. This is recognized explicitly by
the compilers of recent dictionaries – such as *Collins* and *Longman* – whose work is
based on a large 'corpus' of actual language use which is analysed statistically. Sue
Engineer, a lexicographer with Longman Dictionaries, explains the company's
current (1995) policy as follows:

> ... where two variants are common, we give the most frequent first and
> separate them by a comma, where one is far less frequent than the other
> (e.g. jail and gaol), we separate them by 'also'.

As we are now entirely a producer of ELT [English Language Teaching] dictionaries, we depart from this convention to show a 'world English' spelling, shared by British and American English, before a purely or predominantly British one. So although 'enquire' is three times as frequent as 'inquire' on the written part of the British National Corpus, we give 'inquire' as our main form, and we give 'economise' as a variant spelling of 'economize' although it is the spelling of three out of five BNC entries.

... spellings appearing on corpus have been through house rules and spelling checkers, but the latter don't stop people from the kind of mis spelling that is actually writing down the wrong word, e.g. 'she refused to be phased by this' (instead of fazed) or 'he got his just desserts'. In theory, one of these could become common enough to include as a variant. It would be up to the lexicographer to decide whether the inclusion would be useful to a student, and whether the student should be warned that many people think the spelling is incorrect.

(I am grateful to Sue Engineer for this information.)

So, if enough people within a community use a word with a particular spelling, that spelling stands a good chance of getting into the dictionary (though the Longman lexicographers at least also make a judgement as to which variants would be useful to students of English as a foreign language).

If it is numbers in current practice that determine correct spellings, then Mr Griffiths may have less reason to reproach himself than he imagines. It all depends on just *how many* thousands were 'tripped up' like him. If the numbers are high enough, then their spelling 'mistakes' turn almost automatically into acceptable alternative spellings. So to complain that some 'error' in spelling is becoming common can be self-defeating.

Thirdly, however, current practice is not always uniform, and the process by which spellings change seems more likely to be gradual than sudden. So there will sometimes be an ambiguous state when certain spellings are possibly in transition from being old mistakes to being newly correct. At least one of the 'mistakes' identified by *The Times* writers (see Reading A, extract 8) seem to me to be of this character: the use of the apostrophe with the letter *s* – in contexts unpoliced by teachers, editors or handbooks – to indicate the plural rather than the traditional usage to indicate possession. My local shop sells *potato's, onion's* and *carrot's*. Its window has cards advertising the services of a gardener – *hedge's trimmed, lawn's mowed*, all at reasonable rates –, and offering *kitten's* free to good homes. Not *rate's* or *home's*, though; the new rules emerging for the apostrophe may well turn out to be as complicated and confusing as the old, and in time the teachers, editors and handbooks may have to explain and enforce *them*. An unexpected example of the transition comes in the book *Cox on Cox*, in which the chair of the UK govern-ment's working group on English in the National Curriculum sets out the group's views and his own. The cover and title page display, respectively, the newer and the older attitudes to the apostrophe (see Figure 9.1). Nor are the new rules confined to the United Kingdom: among several examples in India, I spotted a notice at the entrance to a school which read: *Visitors car's must not be parked in the playground*.

It seems likely that dictionaries, though attempting to represent current spelling practice, will lag some way behind the usages we have just been looking at. This is because the texts the dictionaries use in their corpus are, by and large, *published* texts. Unlike shop-window notices, published texts *have* usually been

The use of the apostrophe is here taken to be a matter of *spelling*. Other writers regard it as a matter of *punctuation*. Nothing of any significance is at stake here.

Figure 9.1 *Use of the apostrophe*
(Cox, 1991, front cover and p. i)

policed. As Sue Engineer notes, they have normally been read and 'corrected' by an editor, and have often been made to conform to a publisher's house style. Thus they have already been filtered for idiosyncrasy or breach of traditional rules, even before they get into the dictionary-makers' corpus.

Why, then, *should* we spell correctly? Or at least, why should we regard correct spelling as being of great importance, so that if people like Susan Elkin had their way a substantial part of every child's life would be devoted to learning it? English spelling has not always been uniform, as we know, and in other areas of life we do not automatically admire uniformity. People do not all dress in the same way, or adopt the same hairstyle; they do not all enjoy the same types of music or food, or laugh at the same jokes. Why should uniformity be thought more desirable in spelling?

It is noticeable, I think, that though complaints are very common, reasons are rarely given, or are sketchy in the extreme – a sign, perhaps, of how much the value of uniformity in spelling is taken for granted. Susan Elkin, for example, has only this to offer by way of reasons: 'Accuracy in spelling, like incisiveness of expression, is a route to precision.'

Of course one can imagine spelling so idiosyncratic that it is difficult to understand what is meant. I doubt if that is very common, though. Indeed I

See Chapter 2 for a
discussion of handwriting.

cannot actually recall ever being seriously puzzled or misled by misspellings. Even
the pupil in my schoolteaching days in Glasgow who wrote about 'the chooky
embra' was easily intelligible in context. (The context was 'the queen and the
chooky embra'. If you still can't guess, look at the end of this section.) By contrast,
I am often puzzled and sometimes totally defeated by bad handwriting, including
increasingly my own as I get older. But for some reason handwriting attracts much
less complaint than spelling, and bad handwriting never seems to be taken as a
sign of illiteracy, let alone of 'general incompetence', which as we see below can
be attributed on the basis of bad spelling. I have read countless books over the
years whose acknowledgements include unblushing thanks to a secretary for
deciphering the author's bad handwriting. I have yet to read even one where a
secretary or editor is thanked for correcting the author's bad spelling.

Should idiosyncratic spelling be a reason for anxiety? It is sometimes argued
that *individuals* – even a large minority of individuals – can spell carelessly and still
be understood only because they depend on the more conscientiously spelling
majority. (In the same way, perhaps, individual motorists can break rules without
disrupting traffic too much because the majority obey them.) But will communication not break down badly if this rule-following majority disappears? I doubt it.
In some countries, such as Britain and the USA, little variety in spelling is
tolerated. But this is not so everywhere.

I studied the public spellings of English words in 1994 in a small town near
Bangalore in India (see Figure 9.2). Many of the spellings – in carefully painted
shop signs and notices – do not conform to standard British or American spelling;
they do not correspond to any standard Indian spelling either. But I do not think it
is helpful to characterize these nonstandard spellings simply as errors. When one
shop offers *pluming* services in its main sign, and *plumbing* in the more detailed
description underneath, when two shops in the same chain just a few streets apart
are respectively a *bakery* and a *bakary*, when one can find a *general store* and a *genaral
store* side by side, when even a street trolley calls itself a *tiffen centre* on the front and
a *tiffin center* on the side, surely this state of affairs is better described as a relaxed
acceptance of variety than as a large number of mistakes.

There are also positive arguments *against* treating spelling as a very important
part of life and learning. Elkin has, I think, unwittingly displayed the strongest of
these: correct spelling demands much more labour than it merits, especially for
young children. The time and effort that she suggests devoting to spelling could
surely be much better spent – indeed in most schools I dare say they *are* much
better spent – on matters more interesting and worthwhile than memorizing a set
of complicated but arbitrary conventions.

Another advantage is that a relaxed attitude to spelling frees writers from
unnecessary fears and worries and enables them to concentrate on what to say and
how to express it. This would be of particular benefit to those who argue
vehemently that correctness is important, only to be horribly embarrassed when –
inevitably – they themselves slip up in their writing or proofreading. For those of
us who argue against treating spelling as either rigid or important, the penalties
for making what even we regard as mistakes are much less severe. I myself have
used the word *judgements* several times in this chapter, and in my first draft I typed
one of these – a plural, not a possessive – as *judgement's*. This was a slip, and when
someone drew my attention to it I corrected it at once. But, as you know, I argue in
this very chapter that using the apostrophe to indicate the plural is becoming an
acceptable alternative to using it for possession. So I was not too embarrassed, and
no gleeful fingers were pointed in my direction. Indeed, the colleague who
spotted the mistake wondered if I had put the apostrophe there deliberately, like

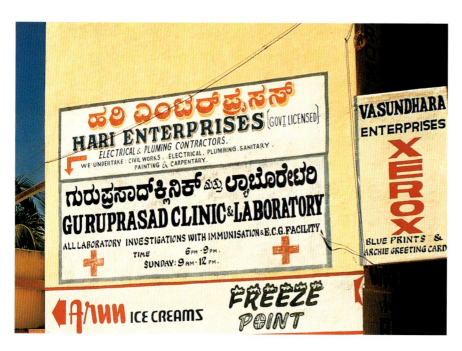

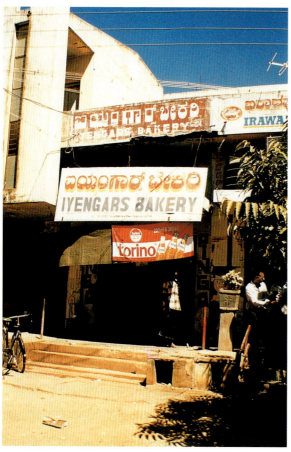

Figure 9.2
Indian shop signs

Aitchison's *hopefully*, as a gesture of defiance! By contrast, Professor Anthony O'Hear, reading the beautifully printed version of his pamphlet *Education and Democracy* (O'Hear, 1991), must have blushed when he reached page 15. Elsewhere in the pamphlet, he pours scorn on a college willing to interview an applicant for a place on an infant teachers' course who had written *eductation* and *aquire*. On page 15, O'Hear's own text offers us *sience*.

Besides, advances in technology may soon transform the notion of spelling in such a way as to bypass all the arguments above. As wordprocessors, with their 'spellcheck' software, become cheaper and more widespread, spelling may become less and less a matter of individual skill or choice. Two consequences seem quite possible. Before long, writers may be judged by their spelling no more than at present they are judged by the shapeliness of the type in a wordprocessed document. And despite the fears of some about a forthcoming anarchy of spelling variations, the wordprocessor may actually lead to a wider standardization of English spelling worldwide than ever before, as computers and software seem to become ever more similar and interchangeable. In a small way, we may have seen the beginnings of this in the vocabulary of computing itself, where already some American spellings have become standard in British English. For example, the spelling of the word *disc* remains as I have just written it in most contexts in British English, but not in relation to computers, where it has become *disk*.

And finally, who or what was the 'chooky embra'? If you have not guessed, it was His Royal Highness Prince Philip, the *Duke of Edinburgh*.

Accent and dialect

Concentrating on spelling, as I have done, has a major drawback, however: it implies concentrating on *written* English. But there are important variations that are solely or primarily characteristic of *spoken* English.

In England, critics of certain stigmatized pronunciations (such as the 'glottal stop' that is becoming prevalent in several accents), or word or sentence forms other than those of Standard English, have usually treated them as though they were simple mistakes – almost as though the speaker was trying to speak Standard English, in Received Pronunciation, but getting it wrong.

Besides, they often seem to have treated the 'mistakes' as being *random* errors. Their opponents, often linguists, have usually responded by pointing out that 'nonstandard' dialects – let alone the standard varieties in use in other countries of the United Kingdom and other parts of the world – have rules and regularities of their own, which are just as systematic as those of Standard English. A recent example can be found in a letter to the *Guardian*:

> I am disheartened to see that in his report of findings on children's use of non-standard English, your Education Editor … is still prepared to use expressions such as 'wrong usage', 'speak properly' and 'pure' … The majority of the population of this country, children and adults, speaks some form of non-standard English. Dialect forms of the kind you cite are evidence of rule-governed grammatical systems which have a long and honourable history – and a doubtless imperishable vitality …
>
> ((Dr) Hilary Hillier, Department of English Studies, University of Nottingham, *Guardian*, 22 April 1995, p. 24)

Of course people *can* make mistakes in grammar or pronunciation when trying to speak Standard English or Received Pronunciation, and one of the ways in which they are likely to do so is by importing features of some nonstandard dialect or

Chapter 7 discusses
changing evaluations of
English accents in different
parts of the world.

accent. But this is not unique to Standard English or Received Pronunciation. Anyone trying to speak in a nonstandard variety can make mistakes in it too, and one of the ways in which they may do so is by importing features of Received Pronunciation or Standard English. There is no reason, then, to accord any special privilege to Received Pronunciation or Standard English as regards judgements of correctness and incorrectness. Is there any reason, though, to accord special privilege to systematic or rule-governed usages?

Activity 9.4   *(Allow about 5 minutes)*

Look again at Gay Doyle's letter from *The Times* (Reading A, extract 10), in which she quotes a student as saying, among other things, 'It don't ma't'er' and 'You only needs two Es'. ('E' is the lowest pass grade in the English A-level exam.)

Assuming that Ms Doyle has quoted her accurately, should we judge the student's English to be correct or incorrect? In particular, does it make a difference if her use of *it don't* and *you needs* is the result of a dialect in which these are regular forms, or a purely personal departure from Standard English?

Comment

I cannot help feeling that it does make a difference – that speaking in a regular, rule-governed, nonstandard dialect is easy to defend as correct, whereas an individual variation from Standard English practice is more difficult to treat as anything but a mistake. But I cannot justify this feeling. If the student is trying to speak Standard English, then she is making a mistake, regardless of whether her *it don't* and *you needs* are regular dialectal forms or an individual idiosyncrasy. And if she is not trying to speak Standard English – regardless of whether or not her use of nonstandard English is deliberate – why should her departures need to stem from some other system of rules? An analogy: if I choose to depart from current local fashion in some of the clothes I wear, why should this be considered more acceptable if my departures stem from a fashion of some other time and place rather than from my own individual choice and preference?

Mistakes and changes in meaning

I wrote above that I am rarely if ever seriously troubled by spelling mistakes. However, I could not make the same claim about usages that are on the boundaries of being mistakes and changes in *meaning*. Take, for example, the two meanings of *disinterested* in current use: 'impartial' and 'uninterested'. Whenever I read the word *disinterested* – knowing that it has alternative meanings – I can usually guess fairly confidently from the context which is intended. But I cannot now use the word myself, with either meaning, as I know that some of my readers would interpret it one way and some the other way. Other words are even more troublesome, for instance *refute*. If I read that John *refuted* Jane's assertions, does the writer mean simply that John *denied* her assertions (the newer meaning), or that he *proved* them to be false (the older one)? It is often impossible to say.

Another example is discussed by Aitchison and Grove in Reading B – what Grove calls 'the common misuse of "may" for "might"'. Aitchison's initial argument is simply from usage: *may* and *might* are being used more and more to mean the same; this sort of thing often happens with words; why should it upset us?

Grove has two criticisms. The first (which she repeats several times) is that saying *may* where traditionally one would have said *might* results in statements that are false. The second is that the conflation of *may* and *might* reduces the distinctions that we can make in language. Aitchison's reply to the second criticism is to deny it, implicitly claiming that we can always find new ways of making such distinctions. Grove's response is to ask why we should go to the trouble of finding new ways, when the already existing *may* and *might* are so useful. Aitchison's answer is that the process of conflating *may* and *might* is now impossible to stop.

This debate is developed quite fully and satisfactorily, but Aitchison apparently did not reply to Grove's first criticism, so let us see what we think of it. One of the two (actually three!) 'idiotic examples' quoted by Grove is this: 'The Queen may have married several suitors before she met Prince Philip.' And let us recall her first criticism of it:

> it pretends that something possibly did happen, when we know for a fact
> it did not. The Queen might have married other men. But she did not.
> We cannot say she may have. It is not true; it is wrong; it is false …

Activity 9.5   *(Allow about 5 minutes)*

How convinced are you by this criticism?

I am not at all convinced. Grove, it seems to me, is simply purporting to interpret the word *may* in its traditional sense although she knows it is intended in a different sense. It is not surprising that doing this can result in false statements. In the newer sense of the words, where *may* and *might* mean the same, the statement she objects to is perfectly true.

What she might have argued instead, as I argued above, is that a transitional stage involves ambiguity and possible misunderstanding. For most readers there is probably little danger in this example; most people probably know that the Queen did not in fact marry anyone else before Prince Philip. But where we are not so well informed, the dangers of confusion are real. (What exactly should we understand by 'Before he became king, George IV may have married a commoner'?)

To sum up, I do believe that a state of ambiguity about the meaning of words is a more serious matter than ambiguity about correct spelling. But this is probably an inevitable consequence of inevitable change in language, and its importance is easy to exaggerate. I doubt if it applies to more than a handful of words at any time. For most words with older and newer meanings existing side by side – such as *flaunt* ('display ostentatiously' and 'flout') – there is probably no real confusion, since their meanings are so remote from one another.

So far we have dealt with correctness. Now for the second kind of judgement on my list.

Beauty and ugliness

Fowler (1926) has no more hesitation about making aesthetic judgements than he has about saying what is incorrect. *Question as to* is an 'ugly & needless but now common formula'; *orotund* is 'at once a monstrosity in its form & a pedantry in its use'; and as for 'elegant variation' (that is, the 'mechanical replacing of a word by a synonym' for no reason other than to avoid repetition), his indignation is worth quoting at length:

> It is the second-rate writers, those intent rather on expressing themselves prettily than on conveying their meaning clearly, & still more those whose notions of style are based on a few misleading rules of thumb, that are chiefly open to the allurements of elegant variation ... first terrorized by a misunderstood taboo, next fascinated by a newly discovered ingenuity, & finally addicted to an incurable vice ... There are few literary faults so widely prevalent, & this book will not have been written in vain if the present article should heal any sufferer of his infirmity.
>
> (Fowler, 1926, pp. 130–1)

And the principle implied here underlies many, probably most, of Fowler's aesthetic judgements throughout *Modern English Usage* – a strong preference for the clear, the plain, the straightforward, the functional over the pretty, the fancy, the decorative, the ornate. He had stated this principle still more explicitly some 20 years earlier in *The King's English,* written jointly with his brother, F.G. Fowler:

> Anyone who wishes to become a good writer should endeavour, before he allows himself to be tempted by the more showy qualities, to be direct, simple, brief, vigorous and lucid.
>
> This general principle may be translated into practical rules in the domain of vocabulary as follows:
>
> Prefer the familiar word to the far-fetched.
> Prefer the concrete word to the abstract.
> Prefer the single word to the circumlocution.
> Prefer the short word to the long.
> Prefer the Saxon word to the Romance.

These rules are given roughly in order of merit; the last is also the least.

(Fowler and Fowler, 1906, p. 11)

Both elegant variation and ornateness are characteristic of *eloquence,* as discussed in Chapter 4, and the Fowlers here are on the side of the Puritans.

Here, the Fowlers are taking sides (taking the fashionable side for the first half of the twentieth century) in an ancient and still lively aesthetic debate, spanning the visual arts and music as well as language, about the desirability of decoration and ornament (see, for example, Brolin, 1985).

Obviously this debate is not going to be settled here. Indeed, I am inclined to treat aesthetic judgements about language as being, in the colloquial sense, 'matters of taste', that is matters in which reasoned argument has a rather limited part to play.

Social judgements

I wonder how you reacted to item 3 in my list of the kinds of judgement we make about language (Activity 9.3, comment) – where I say we judge some usages to be socially unacceptable 'in the sense of being characteristic of a social group or category inferior in some way to the one we belong to, or aspire to belong to'. These judgements need not correspond to any traditional hierarchies, of course, as earlier chapters have shown. The speech of the rich and the powerful may impress the poor and powerless as little as the other way round. Such judgements – especially in the form where those with high social status condemn the speech of those they regard as socially inferior – probably stand out from the others on the list, in that these are the sorts of judgement many people today would not readily admit to making themselves, while suspecting that they sometimes lurk behind the judgements other people make.

Fowler (1926), as we might expect, was less inhibited, referring explicitly and frequently to 'the uneducated', 'the ignorant', 'the illiterate' and so on.

But something similar, if less open, may be happening when people today refer disparagingly to the language of salespeople, management consultants, sports personalities (and commentators), police officers or journalists on popular newspapers. This often seems to be a matter of disapproval of their way of life or disdain towards their pretensions as much as disapproval of their language as such.

An interesting interplay of linguistic and social judgement can be found in extract 10 from *The Times* in Reading A, where in addition to criticizing the spelling and grammar of the girl under discussion, the writer introduces some odd spellings of her own into her quotation from the girl's speech. It is quite a common practice for writers to indicate accents other than Received Pronunciation by nonstandard spellings (even though standard spelling is far from being a written representation of Received Pronunciation). I assume that *ma't'er* is of that character, intended to convey something of the girl's pronunciation, though I can only guess what exactly that was (a glottal stop?). But *a ninfant teacher* goes further. What could possibly be conveyed about the girl's pronunciation by writing this instead of *an infant teacher*? What we have here derives, I would guess, from a literary tradition. In many English novels of the nineteenth and early twentieth centuries the speech of working-class people, uneducated people, or (sometimes) children is often written with misspellings that convey nothing about pronunciation. Somewhere in P.G. Wodehouse, the *ennui* suffered by the aristocratic central characters is spoken of by a servant as *onwee*. Since 'onwee' is probably as close as most English people from any social class ever get to the French pronunciation, I assume that this – in Wodehouse as in *The Times* letter – is put in as a marker of social inferiority, not of pronunciation.

What look like representations of pronunciation or accent cannot always be taken at face value.

Activity 9.6   *(Allow 5–10 minutes)*

Re-read Jean Aitchison's 'Why do purists grumble so much?' (Reading C), paying particular attention to the example of *shot up* and *shooted up* as variant past tenses, in different situations, of *shoot up*. Note down your reactions to this example and compare them with mine.

Comment

My first reaction was that if Aitchison was trying to persuade readers of the *Evening Standard* to accept different variants of language as equally correct, each in its context, then this example was not very tactfully chosen. It is in danger of confirming the prejudices of those who associate bad grammar with crime, moral degeneracy and social breakdown (see Reading A, extract 2).

On reflection, though, I think Aitchison's example makes a very important point – though one that she might perhaps have spelled out a little more explicitly. Any moral, aesthetic, political or social judgements we may make about language users, or about the way of life in which a language variety is used, should surely be offered explicitly as such, and not presented as judgements about their *language*.

Moral judgements

Fowler actually makes very few explicitly moral judgements about language, and those he does make serve to remind us sharply that we live today in a moral world very different from that of an elderly upper-middle-class English gentleman in the 1920s. Some of his judgements may perhaps provoke ironic amusement now rather than serious offence, as when he says that 'to call a woman a female is exactly as impolite as to call a lady a woman ... it is reasonably resented' (Fowler, 1926, p. 175). But another of his judgements will give today's readers a severe jolt:

> *nigger*, applied to others than full or partial negroes, is felt as an insult by the person described, & betrays in the speaker, if not deliberate inso-lence, at least a very arrogant inhumanity.
> (Fowler, 1926, p. 474)

These issues are considered in the penultimate section of this chapter, which looks specifically at discrimination in language. Here, it is enough to say that I think language usage is as much open to moral judgement as any other human activity. Language can be used with virtuous or vicious intentions, and its use can have beneficial or harmful effects. (And virtuous intentions do not guarantee beneficial effects any more than harmful results always stem from vicious inten-tions.)

This is something that I think Aitchison glosses over in her defence of the tabloid or 'popular' press. 'The *Sun's* use of language is impressive and vigorous', she tells us in her interview with Valerie Grove (Reading B), giving what I found a surprising example: '*Gotcha*, from the Falklands War ... was a remarkably good headline for the *Sun's* purposes.' This makes a startling contrast with what she says in her *Evening Standard* article (Reading C) about the language of the Gulf War. There she criticizes the 'manipulation of people's lives by the dishonest use of language' in such words and phrases as *surgical, precision* and *pinpoint accuracy*. The result and perhaps the intention, she argues, was that many people were misled into thinking that it was mainly buildings, not humans, that were harmed by the Allied bombings.

Could it not equally well be said, though, that *surgical, precision* and *pinpoint accuracy* were remarkably good for the purposes of the Allied propagandists in governments, armed forces and the media? If this invites the objection that their purposes were not good purposes, might the same not be said about those of the *Sun*? The *Gotcha!* headline (*Gotcha!* represents a colloquial pronunciation of 'Got you!') was used of the sinking by a British submarine of the Argentinian battleship *General Belgrano*, with the loss of hundreds of lives, mostly of young conscripts. '*Gotcha!*' seems designed to trivialize these deaths and the political and military decisions that led to them. If the headline was indeed remarkably successful in doing so, that is not self-evidently something to be applauded.

Appropriateness

In recent years 'appropriateness' has become extremely important for many linguists, playing almost an equivalent role to that of 'correctness' for Fowler and his generation. You will recall the stress laid on appropriateness by Aitchison in Reading C. The *Oxford Guide* has this to say:

> The emphasis of [our] recommendations is on the degree of acceptabil-ity in standard English of a particular use, rather than on a dogmatic distinction of right and wrong. Much that is sometimes condemned as

'bad English' is better regarded as appropriate in informal contexts but inappropriate in formal ones. The appropriateness of usage to context is indicated by the fairly rough categories 'formal' and 'informal', 'standard', 'regional', and 'non-standard', 'jocular' and so on.

(Weiner, 1983, p. x)

I am not convinced, though, that replacing correctness with appropriateness solves many of the problems associated with correctness. For there is disagreement about what is appropriate for different contexts, just as there is disagreement about what is correct. And over the years opinions change about what is appropriate for particular contexts, exactly as opinions change about what is correct.

So why *should* we consider certain language varieties to be inherently appropriate or inappropriate for certain activities or contexts? Denying that there is a single standard of correctness that applies across all contexts has not taken us very far if we then allow that there is a single standard of correctness that applies within each context. Why should we allow this? *Why* is the expression *over the top* (Reading A, extract 3) inappropriate for historical analysis – or is it for examination answers? *Why* would a more formal word, like *excessive*, be more appropriate?

Controversial usage

Now I want to consider how we sometimes adopt, recommend or avoid certain usages not because of our own judgements about them, but because of the judgements we believe, rightly or wrongly, that other people will make. If we compare Fowler with the *Oxford Guide* we frequently find similar recommendations, and up to a point similar arguments to support them. But whereas Fowler always speaks firmly and unapologetically in his own voice, the *Oxford Guide* often makes its final recommendations by reference to what other people may approve or, more often, disapprove of. This is illustrated by the *Oxford Guide's* treatment of *due to* – which it is interesting to compare with Fowler's, quoted above in the section on correctness. The *Oxford Guide* gives three usages for the phrase, the third of which runs as follows:

> [*due to*] = owing to. A sentence … like *He suffered a few days' absence of mind due to sunstroke* can be equated with *He suffered a few days' absence of mind owing to sunstroke.* In this way *due to* has borrowed from *owing to* the status of independent compound preposition, a use not uncommon even with good writers, e.g. … *Due to an unlikely run of nineteens and zeros, I gained the equivalent of three hundred pounds* (Graham Greene).
> • The use of *due to* as a compound preposition is widely regarded as unacceptable. It can often be avoided by the addition of the verb *to be* and *that,* e.g. *It is due to your provident care that … improvements are being made* (New English Bible).

(Weiner, 1983, p. 104)

Here, the *Oxford Guide* is giving as one of the accepted usages of the phrase exactly the usage condemned as 'impossible' by Fowler. It is worth emphasizing that the difference between them is not just a matter of changes in usage of and opinion about *due to* between the 1920s and the 1980s. On the contrary, Fowler makes it clear that the usage he disapproves of is common in 1926; and the *Oxford Guide* makes it equally plain that the usage it allows is widely disapproved of in 1983. The difference lies in a changed attitude to these agreed facts of usage and disapproval. Fowler simply dismisses those who use *due to* as equivalent to *owing to* as 'the illiterate'. The *Oxford Guide* uses a 'bullet' (•) whenever it wants to warn that a common usage may be unacceptable in some circles. It is hard to imagine Fowler ever feeling the need for such a typographical device, or ever advising readers as to how they may avoid a usage that *he* judges correct on the grounds that other people will disapprove of it. Just as he will condemn certain usages no matter how many people allow them, he will defend others no matter how many voices are raised against them – splitting infinitives, beginning a sentence with a conjunction, ending one with a preposition, using 'firstly' instead of 'first' and so on. (Examples can be found in his book under the headings 'Fetishes' and 'Superstitions'.)

The contrast between Fowler and the *Oxford Guide* is striking, then, but it is not total. Whereas Fowler's appeal to usage is thoroughly elitist, the *Oxford Guide* is basically democratic; but even for the latter, users of English are not all quite equal. The *Oxford Guide* finds it appropriate to mention that the usage of *due to* in question is not uncommon 'even with good writers'.

In discussing correctness in spelling above, I mentioned that some people say they treat spelling as if it were important only because they believe other people regard it as really being important. Paul Coggle, writing in *The Times*, puts it like this:

> Despite the undeniable logic of the spelling-is-unimportant school, it has to be recognised that in our society poor spelling is widely regarded as a sign of illiteracy and that judgements are made about a person's general competence on the basis of their ability to spell correctly. There is no doubt that for large numbers of employers the general presentation of a job application and CV is one of the important criteria used for sifting and prioritising the piles of hopeful applications. A misspelt word can and usually does mean instant rejection. Teachers who do not acknowledge this fact are severely impairing their students' chances of success in the job market. Similarly, companies that allow spelling errors to creep into their promotional literature risk being discredited in the eyes of potential clients.

(Paul Coggle, *The Times*, 10 April 1994)

However, Coggle goes on to confess that he himself can be influenced by misspellings:

> I must confess to being rather shocked recently to read the following evaluation of one of my courses by a second-year undergraduate: 'Greater attention to gramer was helpfull, as I had forgotton what I learned at school.' The message is clear enough, but for me the misspelling somehow invalidated the judgment passed by this individual.

Activity 9.7   *(Allow about 10 minutes)*

Consider what Coggle says above in two parts, following the division shown. First, how convinced are you by his argument that despite what he calls 'the undeniable logic of the spelling-is-unimportant school', teachers, companies and people in general should treat spelling *as if* it were important, because other people use it as a basis for far-reaching judgements? Secondly, how far would you share Coggle's own reactions to his student's spelling? Make a note of your conclusions, which you can then compare with my comments below.

You may remember from Chapter 4 that appeals to literature as a yardstick for good usage have a long history.

Comment

I take the second question first, as it seems much easier to answer. Coggle comes close to acknowledging that his reaction to the misspellings he quotes is not entirely rational. It is surely even more irrational than he recognizes, and provides an amusing warning about the dangers of paying too much attention to spelling at the expense of meaning, even for someone as thoughtful and self-aware as he is. For what is the judgement by the student that is supposedly invalidated by their poor spelling? It is that the student needs and welcomes more help with their English! Even if other judgements by the student might somehow be invalidated by bad spelling, surely the most enthusiastic advocate of correctness should agree that that one is actually supported.

The first question is trickier, for several reasons. In the first place, I do not know how widespread or how strong the tendency actually is to judge people's 'general competence' by their spelling. A reading of *The Times* and other newspapers, especially their correspondence columns, might suggest that it is fervent and all but universal, but such evidence has to be treated with caution. We do not know how representative the writers of newspaper letters and articles are of the population at large, even the British population. Nor do we know how concern with spelling is related to age. If it is indeed true that young people today – even those with academic qualifications – have not been taught to pay much attention to spelling, grammar and so on, then this may have more far-reaching effects than the critics have noticed. If young people's own English is less 'correct' than that of previous generations, perhaps as they come to occupy positions of responsibility and power their judgements of other people will be correspondingly less influenced by *their* English.

9.4   POLITICAL CORRECTNESS

I mentioned above that many linguists who are generally unwilling to make judgements of good and bad about language do allow one major exception: they are prepared to condemn and proscribe language they hold to be sexist, racist or in some other way discriminatory against groups of disadvantaged people – language, in a now hackneyed phrase, that is 'politically incorrect'. And if we once more turn to contributors to *The Times*, we find a striking mirror image of this state of affairs. As we have seen in Reading A, the typical stance of *The Times* contributors is to complain about the way the English language is currently used, and to call for improvement. But with regard to **political correctness** this is reversed. What we find in *The Times* is defence of the language as it is now, and hostility and mockery towards attempts to reform or correct it.

Reactions to political correctness

> In Singapore, according to the English-born sociolinguist Anthea Fraser Gupta, political correctness, as exemplified by 'the deliberate use of non-sexist language' is 'quite unusual'. In fact, 'it is so rare that I, and other colleagues, have had the experience of having our non-sexist original changed into a sexist printed version by editors' (Gupta, 1994, p. 2).

Let us begin, once more, by looking at a few examples from *The Times*, this time examples of reactions to attempts to combat discriminatory language.

The columnist Bernard Levin is predictably colourful and vigorous in his own language on the subject. The title of his column of 31 May 1993 is 'All Joe McCarthy's children now', and his opening sentence reads: 'The cult of political correctness is seeping evilly from American university campuses.' He proceeds in the same vein. The United States is experiencing 'an atrocious form of censorship'; people's reluctance to stand and fight against it is 'odious and craven', 'a shameful cowardice which indelibly stain[s] America's record of tolerance and liberty' (Levin, 1993).

Another example is Peter McKay, writing a fortnight or so before Bernard Levin:

> We've had the jokes about the new nursery rhyme, Baa Baa, er, Afro-Caribbean Sheep, and dismissive books on the subject but Political Correctness (PC), the modern gospel of nondiscriminatory language, is still flourishing ...
>
> The PC doctrine was developed by the modern apostles of feminism, who, in America, choose to call themselves womyn, instead of women, to remove recognition of their oppressors. To most people it is a harmless joke, good for a few laughs on some dim situation comedy. But it is not a joke to those who seek the power to change our thoughts and our lives. Or to their victims ...
>
> (Peter McKay, *The Times*, 17 May 1993)

And numerous other examples could be found, similarly characterized, it seems to me, by hostility relieved only by attempts at humour.

In these articles the authors' judgements are supported with examples (sometimes the same examples) in which political correctness can be interpreted as oppressive, or ridiculous, or both. In none that I have found is there much attempt to understand why reasonable and sensible people might want to take and recommend steps to avoid discriminatory language, or to discover whether such steps might have any beneficial consequences.

A case study: the *Open University Guide*

In this section I want to consider what can be said for and against political correctness in language. I do not consider the particular examples cited in *The Times*; rightly or wrongly, these do give the impression of having been chosen and described to show political correctness at its worst. As I am an Open University lecturer, I take my examples from nearer home – from a booklet on non-discriminatory language produced for its staff by the Open University, which itself caused something of a storm in the British press when it appeared in 1993 – *An Equal Opportunities Guide to Language and Image* (Open University, 1993), hereafter called 'the *OU Guide*'. My purpose is not to criticize or defend this booklet as such, however, but to use it to raise questions of general interest.

Before I begin let me set two limits to this huge task. First, I am interested here specifically in discrimination in or by *language* – specifically the English language – and so I shall be as brief as I can, at the expense of being dogmatic, about discrimination in general. (I have written elsewhere about the general issue, at greater length and I hope less dogmatically: see Open University, 1989.) By 'discrimination' I mean – and I think most people using the word in this context mean – making or acting on *irrelevant* or *improper* distinctions. So the 'sexist' variety of discrimination would involve making irrelevant or improper distinctions on the basis of sex, the 'ageist' variety on the basis of age, and so on. This implies, of course, that not all distinctions made on the basis of sex or age are necessarily discriminatory: in casting a play or a TV soap opera, for example, the sex and age of the actors do seem to be relevant matters and ones quite proper to consider.

Secondly, the *OU Guide* casts its net more widely than obviously discrimatory language usage. It also offers a great deal of general advice about language, particularly about writing 'plain, readable English' – including such hints as using the active rather than the passive form of a verb, using only one main idea in a sentence and cutting out surplus words (for instance, writing 'many' rather than 'a large number of'). All this might seem irrelevant to the avoidance of discrimination, but the *OU Guide*'s argument is that writing that is difficult to read itself discriminates against certain groups, notably 'the very people we [at the Open University] aim to encourage … people who want a second chance to gain educational qualifications' (pp. 4–5). As it happens, I agree with the general argument, while remaining unconvinced by some of the particular suggestions – including some of the examples I quoted. But I do not try to deal with general issues of readability here.

The *OU Guide* begins by setting out its underlying aims:

> to create the conditions whereby people are treated solely on the basis of their merits, abilities and potential, regardless of gender, colour, ethnic or national background, age, socio-economic background, disability, religious or political beliefs, family circumstances, sexual orientation or other irrelevant distinction.

(Open University, 1993, p. 3)

Then it proceeds to offer advice about spoken and written English, first in general terms and then in relation to a number of possible bases of discrimination in turn: age, ethnicity, disability, gender and sexual orientation. Before looking at some of these in detail I would like to pause for a moment and consider the basic question: in what ways can language be discriminatory?

As you may recall, I think that with any moral discussions, not just those about discrimination or language, we must distinguish between judgements about *intentions* and judgements about *effects*. Language usage may be discriminatory, then, in two basic ways: it may reveal discriminatory intentions or attitudes in the speaker or writer (regardless of its effects); or it may have discriminatory effects (regardless of the attitudes of the speaker or writer).

Activity 9.8   *(Allow about 10 minutes)*

Read the following recommendations from the *OU Guide* and decide whether they are based on judgements about the intentions or attitudes expressed by some usage, or on judgements about a usage's possible effects, or both – or other things entirely.

1   Do not say 'non-white' or 'coloured' as this displays white ethnocentrism – deviation from the supposed norm – which can obviously be offensive to black people. (p. 9)

2   'People with disabilities' is a term which is commonly used, but saying 'disabled people' is preferable since it emphasises that people are disabled by a society that doesn't accommodate them, not by their condition itself. (p. 11)

3   … try not to use phrases that equate a physical condition with a shortcoming, like 'blind spot' or 'deaf to entreaties'. (p. 12)

4   'Man' at one time meant only 'person' or 'human being'. Although it technically still has this generic meaning, 'adult male person' tends to be the image the word calls up … using 'man' in its generic sense … can be misleading or confusing in educational texts. (p. 14)

5   The words we use can reflect the different standards applied to women and men. Avoid irrelevant modifiers like 'woman doctor' or 'male nurse' … (p. 14)

Comment

Of these, I find numbers 4 and 5 straightforward. The implicit recommendation in number 4 – to avoid using *man* in its generic sense – is based on a judgement purely about the possible misleading or confusing effects that such usages can have. And number 5 is purely about the attitudes expressed: *woman doctor* and *male nurse* are to be avoided because they reflect the assumption (on the part of the speaker or writer among others) that a doctor can normally be assumed to be male and a nurse female. Number 1 seems to me a little more complicated, because the judgements on which the recommendation is based are about *both* the attitudes expressed (white ethnocentrism) and the possible effects (offence to black people). But no new principle is introduced.

Numbers 2 and 3, however, do not so readily fit into my categories so far. In number 2 the preferred term is preferred because it is thought to emphasize a particular fact about disabled people; it gives more, or more correct, information. It may be, of course, that the authors believe that giving such information is important because of the attitudes it expresses, or the effects it has on readers, though they have not written this in so many words.

In writing number 3 the authors might also believe that the phrases in question are to be avoided because they reveal insensitivity on the part of the writer, or are likely to offend blind or deaf people. But what is actually written makes the judgement seem almost an aesthetic one, a question of good and bad taste.

The *OU Guide* makes rather general claims about the discriminatory properties of certain words and phrases. But individual speakers or writers might well respond that they themselves had no such discriminatory intentions. How reasonable would such a response be?

Activity 9.9   *(Allow about 5 minutes)*

To focus for a moment on the issue of sexist language, suppose that an adult man calls an adult woman a girl, is then told that this reveals a condescending attitude on his part, and defends himself (sincerely) as follows:

> I don't feel condescending at all, either towards women in general or towards this woman. I called her a girl simply because that was common practice around me when I was younger, and old language habits die hard. Quite possibly this linguistic practice began because men in the past did regard women condescendingly. But if I now use the word unthinkingly, that does not necessarily reveal that I share the attitudes of

my male ancestors – any more than my saying the sun 'rises' and 'sets' implies that I have retained the pre-Copernican belief that it is the sun that goes round the earth.

Is this a good defence?

Comment

I do think this argument has some force, and that it draws attention to a distinction worth making; this is between the attitudes of an individual user of language and those of a language-speaking community. An individual may use words of the kind the *OU Guide* disapproves of, but not necessarily have the attitudes it attributes to these usages – even subconsciously. But that does not mean that the *OU Guide* is necessarily wrong in saying that particular usages express particular attitudes. Language is not a private matter, and meanings and connotations may be widely shared without being universal. I do not think, then, that the imaginary speaker has been entirely successful in defending his use of the term *girl*. Even if he really does not have a condescending attitude, he would surely be wise to learn that this is what the word applied to an adult woman normally expresses, and that he is liable to be quite reasonably misunderstood if he uses it.

Deborah Cameron has taken arguments like this a stage further:

> Meaning works by contrast: the words you choose acquire force from an implicit comparison with the ones you could have chosen, but did not. By coining alternatives to traditional usage, therefore, the radicals have effectively *politicised all the terms*. They have made it impossible for anyone to speak or write without appearing to take up a political position, for which they can then be held accountable. Thus if I say, 'Ms X is the chair of Y' I convey one standpoint; if I say 'Miss X is the chairman of Y' I convey another. What I cannot do any more is say either of these things and hope to convey by it only 'a certain woman holds a certain office in a certain organisation'.
>
> (Cameron, 1994, pp. 31–2)

Of course the factual claims on which recommendations about language are based can be controversial. Take for example the claim quoted above that disabled people are disabled by the way society and the environment are arranged, not by their own condition. This seems to me at least an exaggeration, admittedly an exaggeration of a neglected truth – that disabilities are often exacerbated, and made more widely disabling than they need be, by social and environmental arrangements. But there surely *are* bodily conditions that are disabling in themselves, that restrict what people can do in any set of social and environmental arrangements.

This raises some far-reaching issues. One of the things the *OU Guide* wants to do is create *positive images* of categories of people who have often been viewed negatively. But the examples it chooses are all of cases where, in the authors' view, the negative view has been not just negative but *mistaken*. Thus, having listed some of the undesirable attributes often associated with being old (such as dependency, rigidity of thought and the inability to learn new things), the *OU Guide* says firmly: 'Factually, such views are incorrect.' And throughout the booklet there seems to be an assumption that being accurate and presenting positive images go un-problematically together. For example, the checklist on pages 9 and 10 of the *OU*

Guide includes: 'Make sure that cultures and societies are represented *accurately … showing their effectiveness and achievements.*' Or again, page 12 advises: 'Try to avoid *false or negative* stereotypes.' (The emphasis is mine in both cases.) I could not find a single instance in which the *OU Guide* criticizes an image for being inaccurate by being too *favourable* or too *optimistic.* There is no suggestion anywhere that accuracy might require the mention of faults, failures, drawbacks and dangers too.

There is an obvious potential conflict here. There must be times when being accurate, and indeed honest, might create a less positive, less encouraging image than could be created by ignoring or glossing over uncomfortable truths. (Are there really no 'undesirable attributes' *correctly* associated with growing old?) Unless this fact is faced, there seems to be a danger that attempts to avoid discriminatory language might result in the concealment of the harsher truths about human life behind a screen of euphemism.

Activity 9.10   *(Allow 5–10 minutes)*

At the end of its section on disability, the *OU Guide* offers a checklist of terms, in two columns, under the headings 'Don't say' and 'Do say'. One set of phrases in the 'don't say' column is *victim of, crippled by, suffering from* and *afflicted by,* for which the 'do say' alternatives are *person who has, person with.* Another set refers to wheelchairs. The 'don't say' phrases are *wheelchair bound* and *confined to a wheelchair,* and the 'do say' alternatives *wheelchair user* and *uses a wheelchair.*

What, in your opinion, are the advantages *and* the disadvantages of following such recommendations? Which do you think are greater?

Comment

I think the advantages and the disadvantages can be summed up in the words I have just been using: 'positive images' and 'euphemism' respectively. It seems clear to me that there are both gains and losses in a language policy of this kind. Take wheelchairs as an example. The different usages above do seem to express, and quite possibly to encourage, very different attitudes to wheelchairs and the lives that can be led in them. On the one hand the phrase 'confined to a wheelchair' does seem to place emphasis on the restrictions a wheelchair imposes rather than on the possibilities it offers. On the other hand, to say that someone who cannot walk 'uses a wheelchair', employing the same form of words as when saying someone who can walk 'uses a wheelbarrow' or 'uses a lawnmower' does not seem quite right either. To me, at least, this sounds like an uncomfortable euphemism, in danger of refusing to recognize the seriousness of the problems people in wheelchairs face.

But there is another aspect to all this. The *OU Guide* introduces the checklist I have referred to in Activity 9.10 in the following way: 'Groups representing disabled people have tried to establish a vocabulary for dealing with the problem of appropriate language' (p. 12). And this is a theme that recurs throughout. Sometimes the text justifies its recommendations with *arguments,* of the sorts we have been examining. At other times it supports them as well, or instead, by referring to the wishes of the people to whom language usages apply. Indeed, at one point it says so explicitly: 'Use *the* term which different groups use about themselves' (p. 10, my emphasis). This seems both sensible and courteous, but it is not without its problems.

First, does not this policy imply that ethnic groups are more homogeneous than in fact they are (as the *OU Guide* actually acknowledges elsewhere)? Different members of the same group can and often do have different preferences. Some people of Afro-Caribbean descent (the *OU Guide*'s term) living in Britain object to being called *West Indian*; others do not. (Some object to *Afro-Caribbean* too, preferring *African Caribbean*.) Or again, on page 9 the *OU Guide* instructs its readers as follows: '*Black*: Use as "black people", not "blacks".' But this preference does not seem to be universal either; for example, a letter in the *Guardian* (8 June 1993), published round about the same time as the *OU Guide*, began 'We are a group of blacks, Asians and Jews ...'

Secondly, when an argument *and* a group preference are presented, they do not always pull in the same direction. Thus the *OU Guide* puts *the disabled* and *the blind* in a 'Don't say' column, and offers arguments in support (these focus on the disability as people's defining feature). But it puts *the deaf* in a 'Do say' column, and in support of this reports that some people in the deaf community prefer to use the expression *the deaf* as a political term.

Thirdly, do *individuals* have rights over the use of words or phrases about themselves that are not enjoyed by others, even where their preferences conflict with those of others in the relevant category? May individual gay men, for instance, call gay men *homosexual* if they so choose? May women use the generic *he* or *man* if they wish? In both cases, some do. To put the question more pointedly, what right do the authors of such a guide have to tell people how and how not to use language to describe themselves?

9.5   CONCLUSION

I began this chapter by asking what judgements we could reasonably make about the quality of English – if indeed we could reasonably make any. As you will know by now, I do think we can make some – rather more indeed than some linguists would seem to allow. I do not think judgements about the beauty or ugliness of language are always disguises for prejudices of other kinds. And I do not think our moral judgements about language need or should be confined to the condemnation of sexism, racism or other manifestations of what is 'politically incorrect'.

Having said all that, though, I do find myself on the side of the linguists in most of the disputes I have discussed – on the side of Professor Aitchison against the purists who grumble so much. I have little sympathy with those who insist on *correctness* in grammar, spelling and meaning – without recognizing that correctness depends totally on how language is actually used, that usages vary and change, and above all that even genuine mistakes are usually of little or no importance.

Reading A
EXTRACTS FROM *THE TIMES*

1   The BBC is to publish the first comprehensive guide to 'BBC English' in its 67-year history in an attempt to rid programmes of Americanisms, clichés, jargon, inaccuracies and bad taste … It advises [journalists and presenters] to avoid adjectives and to use short words and sentences. Journalese such as brainchild, blaze and row are to be replaced by idea, fire and debate. Expressions such as full-scale, literally and total are banned … The emphasis is more on taste and usage than grammar. Journalists are reminded to refer to 'black and Asian people' rather than just blacks and not to call women 'girls'. … Expressions such as hopes dashed, sighs with relief, only time will tell, spark off, trigger and spell out are pure clichés and should not be used … The guide is at times cavalier with grammar, condoning the use of short sentences beginning with 'and' or 'but' …

(5 July 1993)

2   Simon Jenkin's article … is a travesty of the prime minister's speech … Mr Major said that he was determined 'to get back to self-discipline and respect for the law, consideration for others, accepting responsibility for yourself and your family and not shuffling it off on the state', to restore proper schooling in grammar and spelling, and crime-free streets. What is objectionable about these objectives?

(Letter from Sir Gilbert Longden, October 1993. In fairness, it must be added that Mr Major himself, while regarding grammar and spelling as serious matters, did not associate them quite so closely as Sir Gilbert does with crime-free streets.)

3   It's just not on. The sloppy language of Britain's most articulate 18-year-olds has taken a hammering from one of Britain's biggest A-level examination boards … Take the A-level history student whose analysis of Martin Luther's excommunication by the Catholic church was direct, to say the least. 'Luther came in for a lot of stick,' the candidate wrote. Or the pupil who summed up the radical theology of John Calvin, the 16th century Protestant reformer, with the words: 'Calvin's ideas were over the top.'

It is a worrying trend towards colloquialism that A-level examiners from the London examinations board say is increasing. They also complain of poor spelling, grammar and handwriting …

(26 December 1993)

4   Please stop abusing the adjective 'brilliant', which is now routinely used to congratulate one for the simplest action, such as giving someone a telephone number, or the correct spelling of one's name. Still on the linguistic front, could we stop assuming that any noun can automatically be turned into a verb? 'To access' may be a battle already lost, but I draw the line at 'to impact', heard last week. As for 'to outsource', words fail me.

(1 January 1994)

5   The Queen's English Society said a national survey of 250 companies found that one in three was concerned about recruits' poor spelling. Employers said

only one in seven school-leavers was 'good' at written English and one in three youngsters aged 16 to 18 could not speak English properly. They also complained that some university graduates spoke poorly and struggled with spelling, grammar and punctuation. Common spelling errors included *seperate* for separate, *liason* for liaison, *accomodate* for accommodate and *buisness* for business.

Dr Bernard Lamb of London University, the report's author, said: 'The report shows how completely untrained many school and college-leavers are for real life ...'

(16 February 1994)

6   They struggle to string words together in the right order, do not understand basic grammatical rules and are stumped by straightforward general knowledge questions about the country they are studying. These are not the failings of pupils at an inner-city comprehensive, but glaring weaknesses among undergraduates at one of Britain's most prestigious and ancient institutions: Oxford University. They have been exposed by Richard Sheppard, a fellow in German at Magdalen College, as evidence of an alarming decline in students' grasp of basic grammatical principles that would have been second nature to O-level candidates 10 years ago ...

(20 February 1994)

7   Graduates training to become teachers do not know the basic principles of grammar that they will be expected to teach to primary school pupils, a study reveals. More than half have such a poor grasp of English grammar that they cannot recognise that 'and' is a conjunction, identify 'in' as a preposition or explain the difference between a clause and a phrase. Up to a third struggled with the terms *adverb* or *pronoun* in the grammar test, which was taken by postgraduate teachers training to become primary school teachers and was based on the level of knowledge expected of the average 11-year-old in the government's blueprint for English lessons ...

(13 March 1994)

8   We have become resigned to a general decline in literacy and spelling standards, but it still comes as a shock when one of London's cultural centres is an offender.

The Barbican is displaying a marvellous collection of photographs ... marred by the most illiterate captions you are ever likely to see. They are an object lesson in how not to use the apostrophe, that most abused part of the English language. Many plurals are rendered with the apostrophe (e.g. 'journey's'). When it should be used, it is often omitted (e.g. 'its anybodys race'). Misspellings are rife. Visitors are surely entitled to better ...

(19 March 1994)

9   *Confectionary, off-license, potatos* (sic). You see them every time you go out. Only last week a national broadsheet newspaper (not *The Times*, happily) printed *licenced* (sic) in large letters on its front page. Even in these days of computerised spell-checkers a business letter, circular or pamphlet which gets such as *receive, business* and *practised* right is a rarity. Apostrophes, also part of spelling, are routinely scattered about like errant tadpoles ...

There is no doubt that spelling standards continue to decline and that must be attributable to something which is happening – or more to the point, not happening – in schools …

Two years ago government concern led to a decision that GCSE candidates would be penalised by up to 5 per cent for poor spelling, but marginal tinkering with exam grades and marks, years after the problem should have been avoided, makes not a jot of difference. As a teacher myself, I'm afraid it's going to take something much more radical, and earlier, to stop the rot.

… It needs drumming in didactically and systematically from the very beginning of school alongside learning to read. As a child learns to read words, by whatever method, he should also be helped to master their spelling. Where there is a logic – cat, rat, bat; strap, street, strong – then attention should be focused on it. And where there isn't – home, come, comb; rough, cough, dough – then irregularities have to be noticed and memorised. Spelling games help. Different ways of finding out or checking how to spell something must be taught. There is nothing wrong, moreover, with spelling lists and dictations to reinforce the learning.

It is vital that children should understand from the beginning that spelling really matters. At present too many are allowed to think that it is a minor concern. Awareness of its importance should be inculcated as second nature …

Most subjects require some writing and every teacher should be a teacher of spelling. … Disturbingly, the reason spelling is not emphasised is that far too many teachers are themselves indifferent spellers … Mistakes inside school on blackboards, noticeboards and in comments on children's work – *seperate, sentance, sponsered* (sic) – are commonplace.

Accuracy in spelling, like incisiveness of expression, is a route to precision. For children to be denied the right to develop into confident adults for whom correct spelling is automatic, because too many teachers can't or won't teach it properly, is scandalous.

(Susan Elkin, 18 April 1994)

10 … The real problem lies in the very poor level of entrant to teacher training – the discredited BEd degree for primary school teachers. We are well into the generation of semi-literate teachers. Three years ago, in a comprehensive school in the south, I 'dared' to point out spelling and grammatical errors to a resentful and stupid girl struggling with A-level English literature. 'It don't ma't'er,' came the retort. 'I'm gonna be a ninfant teacher. You only needs two Es.'

(Letter from Gay Doyle, 19 June 1994)

Reading B

OF DIPSTICKS AND THE JOYS OF
A DOUBLE NEGATIVE

Valerie Grove

Oxford's new professor of language and communication on the importance of popular idiom and the vitality of change: 'Words have always changed meaning. I want to keep an enormous variety going.'

In what cliche-ridden journalese do I dare describe Oxford's new Rupert Murdoch Professor of Language and Communication? As a windsurfing vicar's daughter aged 54, brunette and 5ft 2in. Or, as a bluestocking classics graduate of Girton, who was once seduced from teaching Ancient Greek into editing a folk music magazine.

Prof Jean Aitchison would merely note such locutions in her database. Her role is to study the media and to ask, how are we using language? why? and is it changing?

One might have expected the professor to deliver a topical and witty inaugural lecture, 'Language Joyriding'. What is less predictable is her fondness for the joke, particularly the cartoon, as a tool of scholarship. Snoopy, Gary Larson's The Far Side, Dennis the Menace, Augusta in the Evening Standard: she rightly realises the cartoon can reflect trends and popular idioms with stunning succinctness. (I refer readers to a good example from this week's New Yorker. Middle-aged couple on sofa, smoking. One leaps up: 'The kids! Quick. Stash the cigs.')

When the new science of linguistics lured her back to academe as the LSE's (London School of Economics) first lecturer and reader of linguistics, she stayed ten years and wrote five books: 'A cosy little hole,' she says, 'where I stayed until something amazing cropped up which it now has.'

Her branch of linguistics is concrete and applied, quite removed from the obfuscations of Chomsky's abstract theories. Her most recent project was on the language of 11 to 14-year-olds. 'One of the rare words we tested them with was "dipstick". But even 11-year-olds knew it, apparently from [the television series] Only Fools and Horses. One of these kids said: "Dipstick is what my dad calls me".' (Prof Aitchison has identified 120 schoolchildren's words for dumbo, the favourite being wally.)

Though a mistress of classical grammar, she need not agonise about restraining illiterate developments; she monitors them with a benign eye. Linguistics is about how English is, not how it ought to be. The English language, as my colleague Philip Howard observes, is not just a drill-yard for grammarians. 'Laying down rules,' she says, 'is not my job.' She defiantly inserted a 'hopefully' in her first lecture. 'I deliberately use it, in the same sense as hoffentlich, indicating what is generally to be hoped. I consciously began doing that when I saw that Michael Holroyd, whose writing I admire, gets excellent effects from adverbial clauses as links.'

I allow Prof Aitchison her hopefullys. But we part company over the common misuse of 'may' for 'might'. I cited two idiotic examples. 'I may have died if the boat had not rescued me'; 'You think you may have become prime minister if you had gone to a different school?' and 'The Queen may have married several suitors before she met Prince Philip'. That one came from Australia. Yes, said Prof Aitchison, this usage has arrived from the Antipodes. 'May and might are becoming indistinguishable,' she said equably. 'Might is no longer realised to be the past tense of may, and the old subjunctive is going, so there is an overlap, and whenever you get an overlap you get a falling-together. It's perfectly predictable. Why does it upset you?'

'Because it pretends that something possibly did happen, when we know for a fact it did not. The Queen might have married other men. But she did not. We cannot say she may have. It is not true; it is wrong; it is false; it reduces the distinction we can make in language.'

But the professor says: 'What happens is that once things fall together, you are obliged to find different ways to say them. It's like "uninterested" and "disinterested": you have to say bored, and impartial.

'But why go to this trouble, when "might" was so useful?'

'I think "may" and "might" have fallen together to such an extent it is impossible to stop it. Once things start to blur, it's like flaunt and flout in the United States. People avoid them and find alternatives. The modals like may and might are blurred in Britain now. But when I was teaching in Tennessee, people would use a double modal, "might could". "Could you come round tomorrow morning?" "Ah might could." I loved that,' said the professor.

She also robustly welcomes the double negative, quoting: 'We don't know no one what don't want no nine inch nails.' 'In Chaucer and in many languages, the more negatives you have the more negated it is. I have a lovely example from the Appalachians: "I don't know nothing about no cheques or nothing".'

'If you look at animals with rigid systems, they are very disadvantaged. Gould, who writes on evolution, cites the blue-footed booby, which works by rule of thumb: if it's in the nest they feed it, if it falls out they don't. We don't just say something is blue or green, we are allowed to say bluey-green. I came across an interesting case history of someone with obsessive-compulsive disorder who could not bear the fact that words had imprecise meanings.

'Many people,' she said, 'who have hobby-horses like may and might, can get quite unbalanced about it, and miss out on the truly important questions, like the extent to which they are being bamboozled by language, by metaphors carrying them along certain paths without noticing.

'I'd like to stop people worrying about linguistic trivia like whether it should be graffito not graffiti. Much more important is that people should analyse language and know how it is being used.'

As Michael Dobbs said on [the radio programme] Start the Week, the game of politics is a goldmine for students: when the Tories lost the battle over getting people not to call the community charge the poll tax, they lost the debate.

'Lawyers should be worried,' Prof Aitchison says, 'by the metaphors journalists use about the legal profession. They write about "tangled skeins", "webs" and complicated muddles of thread, implying that lawyers are paid huge sums to unravel complications of their own making. Then there is the common metaphor for society being layered like a cake, which suggests a more rigid class system than we actually have. An actor said recently: "We were poor, but we had a piano, so I suppose we were middle-class." Society is more interwoven than layered; it is not to do with economics but with lifestyle.'

The slipperiness of language is apparent everywhere. As T. S. Eliot said, words strain, crack and sometimes break … slip, slide, perish, decay with imprecision, will not stay still.

'I disagree with Evelyn Waugh when he said that words have inalienable meanings, departure from which is "either conscious metaphor or inexcusable vulgarity". Words have always changed their meanings. I want to keep an enormous amount of variety going.'

From the music hall song, reinforced over 150 years by journalism, come useful coinages like jingoism; from trendy shopfronts we find a greengrocer calling itself a 'Fruitique'. Prof Aitchison watches as the prefix mini prospers, while maxi is rapidly eclipsed by mega.

She approves of blendings like brunch ('I'm particularly keen to catch affluenza,' she says. 'The disease of being too rich.') And as for neologisms such as wimp, with its phonetic echoes of simpering and whimpering, it would be extremely hard now to get by without it.

And like The Times stylebook, she has properly decided to allow 'their' in place of 'his-or-her' after a singular pronoun. She cites autochondria 'to describe someone with excessive concern for the health of their car'.

Oxford has welcomed its new professor in her berth at Worcester College. 'I think at first they feared a Sun journalist would be foist upon them. But when people ring me for my opinion of what's in The Sun, I tell them The Sun's use of language is impressive and vigorous.' The Guardian challenged her when she was first appointed, over The Sun's Lady Moon headline: 'How Sarah made a plonker of Sir Bonker' and she replied that, like Gotcha, from the Falklands war, it was a remarkably good headline for The Sun's purposes.

People who fuss about words, she said, usually make fools of themselves. The missionaries in Papua New Guinea managed to get 'blari' (bloody) out of pidgin, but ignored 'bagarap' (bugger up), thinking its etymology obsolete, so it is still used for anything from a mix-up to an air crash.

Which brings the professor to her swear words cartoon, in which two Martian Daleks are confronted by a flight of stairs: 'Well, that's certainly asterisk asterisk asterisked our plan to conquer the Universe.'

Source: Grove, 1993

Reading C
WHY DO PURISTS GRUMBLE SO MUCH?

Jean Aitchison

Jean Aitchison is Rupert Murdoch Professor of Language and Communication at Oxford University.

Humpback whales alter their songs every year, and a songthrush was heard to incorporate the chirp-chirp of a modern phone into its melody. No one has complained. So why do so many people grumble about change in the English language?

Language is not decaying due to neglect. It is just changing, like it always did.

On investigation, pessimism about language has a long tradition: 'Tongues, like governments, have a natural tendency to degeneration' wrote the lexicographer Samuel Johnson (1755). From at least his time, there has been dissatisfaction with current usage, as well as a belief that 'correct' English exists somewhere. In the 18th century, this was usually identified as upper-middle-class speech, artificially supplemented by imitations of various Latin usages, such as avoidance of 'split infinitives', as in 'to loudly complain'.

Language lamenters mostly haven't understood how language works. In language change, new variants grow up alongside existing ones, often as stylistic alternatives. Usually each variant is relevant in a particular situation. You might say 'tara' on leaving a pal in the Midlands, but goodbye to one in London. The past tense of 'shoot up' is 'shot up' in 'The cat shot up the tree', but 'shooted up' of drugs: 'Someone passed me this syringe ... and I shooted up' (The Guardian).

Face-to-face interaction between individuals is necessary for language change, according to recent research. Estuary English speakers get it from their pals, not from the BBC. Media language doesn't affect the language of individuals, apart from popularising the occasional word such as 'bonk'. So where do journalists come in? The media can help combat prejudices against regional accents and stylistic variations by pointing out that variety is the norm and appropriateness the key: the right words and style for the right occasion, and that no one 'style' is correct at all times. But, above all, journalists could discourage moans over trivia. Such complaints divert attention from a far more serious language threat, the manipulation of people's lives by the dishonest use of language. Take the 'surgical' speech in the Gulf War. There was talk of air-strikes with 'pinpoint accuracy', and 'precision' bombing. These phrases misled many people into believing that the war was primarily an attack on buildings, and that humans were mostly unharmed. It may be more important to detect manipulation of this type than to worry about whether the word 'media' is singular or plural.

As AP Herbert once said: 'Worry about words ... For whatever else you may do, you will be using words always.' But, he might have added, it is important to worry about them in the right way.

Source: Aitchison, 1994

REFERENCES

ABDULAZIZ, M.M.H. (1991) 'East Africa (Tanzania and Kenya)' in CHESHIRE, J. (ed.) *English Around the World*, Cambridge, Cambridge University Press.

ABERCROMBIE, D. (1981) 'Extending the Roman alphabet: some orthographic experiments of the past four centuries' in ASHER, R.E. and HENDERSON, E.J.A. (eds) *Towards a History of Phonetics*, Edinburgh, Edinburgh University Press.

AHULU, S. (1994) 'Styles of Standard English', *English Today*, vol. 10, no. 4, pp. 10–17.

AITCHISON, J. (1992) *Teach Yourself Linguistics*, 4th edn, London, Hodder & Stoughton.

AITCHISON, J. (1994) 'Why do purists grumble so much?', *Evening Standard*, 27 April.

AITKEN, A.J. (1984) 'Scots and English in Scotland' in TRUDGILL, P. (ed.) *Language in the British Isles*, Cambridge, Cambridge University Press.

ALEXANDER, G. (1982) 'Politics of the pronoun in the literature of the English Revolution' in CARTER, R. (ed.) *Language and Literature*, London, Allen & Unwin.

ALEXANDER, L. (1990) 'Fads and fashions in ELT', *English Today*, January.

ALLASON-JONES, L. (1989) *Women in Roman Britain*, London, British Museum Publications.

BAILEY, R.W. (1992) *Images of English*, Cambridge, Cambridge University Press.

BAILEY, R.W. and ROBINSON, J.L. (eds) (1973) *Varieties of Present-day English*, New York, Macmillan.

BALL, P., GALLOIS, C. and CALLAN, V. (1989) 'Language attitudes: a perspective from social psychology' in COLLINS, P. and BLAIR, D. (eds) *Australian English: the language of a new society*, Queensland, University of Queensland Press.

BAMGBOSE, A. (1971) 'The English language in Nigeria' in SPENCER, J. (ed.) *The English Language in West Africa*, London, Longman.

BAMGBOSE, A. (1982) 'Standard Nigerian English: Issues of identification' in KACHRU, B.B. (ed.) *The Other Tongue: English across cultures*, Urbana/Chicago, University of Illinois Press.

BARTLETT, R. (1993) *The Making of Europe*, Harmondsworth, Penguin.

BAUGH, A.C. and CABLE, T. (1978) A *History of the English Language*, 3rd edn, London, Routledge & Kegan Paul.

BEAL, J. (1993) 'The grammar of Tyneside and Northumbrian English' in MILROY, J. and MILROY, L. (eds) *Real English: the grammar of English dialects in the British Isles*, London, Longman.

BELL, A. (1984) 'Language style as audience design', *Language in Society*, vol. 13, no. 2, pp. 145–204.

BELL, A. (1991) *The Language of News Media*, Oxford, Blackwell.

BENNETT, J.A.W. and SMITHERS, G.V. (eds) (1968) *Early Middle English Verse and Prose*, Oxford, Oxford University Press.

BICKHAM, G. ([1741] 1941) *The Universal Penman*, New York, Dover.

BLISS, A. (1984) 'English in the south of Ireland' in TRUDGILL, P. (ed.) *Language in the British Isles*, Cambridge, Cambridge University Press.

BRADLEY, D. (1991) '/ae/ and /aː/ in Australian English' in CHESHIRE, J. (ed.) *English around the World: sociolinguistic perspectives*, Cambridge, Cambridge University Press.

BRIDGES, R. (1913) *A Tract on the Present State of English Pronunciation*, Oxford, Oxford University Press.

BROLIN, B.C. (1985) *Flight of Fancy: the banishment and return of ornament*, New York, St Martin's.

BROOKS, C. (1985) *The Language of the American South*, Athens, Ga., University of Georgia Press.

BROWN, A. (1988) 'The staccato effect in the pronunication of English in Malaysia and Singapore' in FOLEY, J. (ed.) *New Englishes: the case of Singapore*, Singapore, Singapore University Press.

BROWN, L. (ed.) (1993) *New Shorter Oxford English Dictionary*, Oxford, Clarendon.

BULLOKAR, W. ([1586] 1977) *Bref Grammar for English*, Delman, N.Y., Scholars' Facsimiles & Reprints.

BURNLEY, D. (1992) *The History of the English Language: a source book*, London, Longman.

CAMERON, D. (1994) '"Words, words, words": the power of language' in DUNANT, S. (ed.) *The War of the Words: the political correctness debate*, London, Virago.

CAMERON, D. and COATES, J. (1988) 'Some problems with the variable sex' in COATES, J. and CAMERON, D. (eds) *Women in their Speech Communities*, London, Longman.

CARVER, E.M. (1992) 'The Mayflower to the Model-T: the development of American English' in MACHAN, T.W. and SCOTT, C.T. (eds) *English in its Social Contexts: essays in historical sociolinguistics*, Oxford, Oxford University Press.

CHAMBERS, J.K. and TRUDGILL, P. (1980) *Dialectology*, Cambridge, Cambridge University Press.

CHENG, C-C. (1992) 'Chinese varieties of English' in KACHRU, B.B. (ed.) *The Other Tongue: English across cultures*, 2nd edn, Urbana/Chicago, University of Illinois Press.

CHESHIRE, J. (1982) *Variation in an English Dialect*, Cambridge, Cambridge University Press.

CHESHIRE, J. (1991) (ed.) *English around the World: sociolinguistic perspectives*, Cambridge, Cambridge University Press.

CHESHIRE, J., EDWARDS, V. and WHITTLE, P. (1993) 'Nonstandard English and dialect levelling' in MILROY, J. and MILROY, L. (eds) *Real English: the grammar of English dialects in the British Isles*, London, Longman.

CHESHIRE, J. and MILROY, J. (1993) 'Syntactic variation in nonstandard dialects: background issues', in MILROY, J. and MILROY, L. (eds) *Real English: the grammar of English dialects in the British Isles*, London, Longman.

CHRISTENSEN, T. (1992) 'Standard English and the EFL classroom', *English Today*, vol. 31, no. 8, 3 July, pp. 11–15.

CHRISTOPHERSEN, P. (1990) Letter to the editor, *English Today*, vol. 23, no. 6, 3 July, pp. 61–2.

CLANCHY, M.T. (1993) *From Memory to Written Record: England 1066–1307*, 2nd edn, Oxford, Blackwell.

CLYNE, M. (1992) 'Pluricentric languages – introduction' in CLYNE, M. (ed.) *Pluricentric Languages: differing norms in different nations*, Berlin/New York, Mouton de Gruyter.

COATES, J. (1986) *Women, Men and Language*, 2nd edn, London, Longman.

COPPETIERS, R. (1987) 'Competence differences between native and near-native speakers', *Language*, vol. 63, pp. 544–73.

COUPLAND, N. (1984) 'Accommodation at work', *International Journal of the Sociology of Language*, vols 4–6, pp. 49–70.

COX, B. (1991) *Cox on Cox: an English curriculum for the 1990s*, London, Hodder & Stoughton.

CRELLIN, V.H. (1989) 'Towards a common cursive script: American influences', *Journal of Educational Administration and History*, vol. 31, no. 1, pp. 1–8.

CROWLEY, T. (1989) *The Politics of Discourse: the standard language question in British cultural debates*, Basingstoke, Macmillan Education.

CRYSTAL, D. (1985) 'Commentary on the English language in a global context' in QUIRK, R. and WIDDOWSON, H.G. (eds) *English in the World: teaching and learning the language and literatures*, Cambridge, Cambridge University Press for the British Council.

CRYSTAL, D. (1987) *Cambridge Encyclopedia of Language*, Cambridge, Cambridge University Press.

CRYSTAL, D. (1988) *The English Language*, Harmondsworth, Penguin.

CRYSTAL, D. (1992) *An Encyclopedic Dictionary of Language and Languages*, Oxford, Blackwell.

CUTFORTH, R. (1955) *René Cutforth Reporting*, London, Arco.

DAWSON, G. and KENNEDY-SKIPTON, L. (1968) *Elizabethan Handwriting*, London, Faber & Faber.

DeCAMP, D. (1958) 'The genesis of the Old English dialects: a new hypothesis', *Language*, vol. 34, pp. 232-44.

DOBSON, S. (1969) *Larn Yersel Geordie*, Newcastle upon Tyne, Frank Graham.

DONALDSON, W. (1986) *Popular Literature in Victorian Scotland*, Aberdeen, Aberdeen University Press.

DOWNING, J. (1964) *The Initial Teaching Alphabet*, London, Cassell.

EARLE, A.M. (1899) *Child Life in Colonial Days*, New York, Macmillan.

ECKERSLEY, C.E. (1937) *An Everyday English Course for Foreign Students*, London, Longman.

EDWARDS, V. (1986) *Language in a Black Community*, Clevedon, Multilingual Matters.

EDWARDS, V. (1993) 'The grammar of southern British English' in MILROY, J. and MILROY, L. (eds) *Real English: the grammar of English dialects in the British Isles*, London, Longman.

ELLINGSWORTH, H.W. (1988) 'A theory of adaptation in intercultural dyads' in KIM, Y.Y. and GUDYKUNST, W.G. (eds) *Theories in Intercultural Communication*, Newbury Park, Calif., Sage.

ELLIS, A.J. (1890) *English Dialects: their sounds and homes*, London, Kegan Paul, French, Trübner & Co.

FAIRBANK, A. (1968) *A Book of Scripts*, Harmondsworth, Penguin.

FERRY, A. (1988) *The Art of Naming*, Chicago, Chicago University Press.

FILPPULA, M. (1991) 'Urban and rural varieties of Hiberno-English' in CHESHIRE, J. (ed.) *English around the World: sociolinguistic perspectives*, Cambridge, Cambridge University Press.

FOWLER, H.W. (1926) *Dictionary of Modern English Usage*, Oxford, Clarendon.

FOWLER, H.W. and FOWLER, F.G. (1906) *The King's English*, Oxford, Clarendon.

GELLING, M. (1984) *Place-names in the Landscape*, London, Dent.

GILES, H. and POWESLAND, R. (1975) *Speech Style and Social Evaluation*, London, Academic Press.

GILES, H., COUPLAND, N. and COUPLAND, J. (1991) 'Accommodation Theory: communication, context and consequence' in GILES, H., COUPLAND, J. and COUPLAND, N. (eds) *Contexts of Accommodation: developments in applied sociolinguistics*, Cambridge, Cambridge University Press.

GIMSON, A.C. (1989,) *An Introduction to the Pronunciation of English,* 4th edn, rev. S. Ramsaran, London, Edward Arnold.

GOODMAN, S. and GRADDOL, D. (eds) (1996) *Redesigning English: new texts, new identities*, London, Routledge/The Open University.

GORDON, E. and ABELL, M. (1990) 'The objectionable colonial dialect: historical and contemporary attitudes to New Zealand speech', in BELL, A. and HOLMES, J. (eds) *New Zealand Ways of Speaking English*, Clevedon, Multilingual Matters.

GORDON, E. and DEVERSON, T. (1989) *Finding a New Zealand Voice: attitudes towards English use in New Zealand*, Auckland, New House.

GÖRLACH, M. (1991) *Introduction to Early Modern English*, Cambridge, Cambridge University Press.

GOUDY, F.W. ([1942] 1963) *The Alphabet and Elements of Lettering*, New York/London, Dover/Constable and Co.

GRADDOL, D., CHESHIRE, J. and SWANN, J. (1994) *Describing language*, 2nd edn, Buckingham, Open University Press.

GRAVES, R. (1966) 'Language levels', *Encounter*, May.

GROVE, V. (1993) 'Of dipsticks and the joys of a double negative', *The Times*, London Features Section, 17 November.

GUMPERZ, J. (1982) *Discourse Strategies*, Cambridge, Cambridge University Press.

GUPTA, A.F. (1994) 'Non-sexist language', *Singapore Association for Applied Linguistics Quarterly*, no. 27, pp. 2–4.

GUY, G. and VONWILLER, J. (1989) 'The high rising tone in Australian English' in COLLINS, P. and BLAIR, D. (eds) *Australian English: the language of a new society*, Queensland, University of Queensland Press.

HARRIS, J. (1991a) 'Conversatism versus substratal transfer in Irish English', in TRUDGILL, P. and CHAMBERS, J.K. (eds) *Dialects of English: studies in grammatical variation*, London, Longman.

HARRIS, J. (1991b) 'Ireland' in CHESHIRE, J. (ed.) *English around the World: sociolinguistic perspectives*, Cambridge, Cambridge University Press.

HARRIS, J. (1993) 'The grammar of Irish English' in MILROY, J. and MILROY, L. (eds) *Real English: the grammar of English dialects in the British Isles*, London, Longman.

HARRIS, R. and TAYLOR, T.J. (1980) *Landmarks in Linguistic Thought: the western tradition from Socrates to Saussure*, London, Routledge.

HARRISON, T. (1987) *Selected Poems*, 2nd edn, Harmondsworth, Penguin.

HAUGEN, E. ([1966] 1972) 'Dialect, language, nation' in PRIDE, J.B. and HOLMES, J. (eds) *Sociolinguistics*, Harmondsworth, Penguin; first published in *American Anthropologist*, vol. 68, pp. 922–35.

HECTOR, L.C. (1966) *The Handwriting of English Documents*, London, Edward Arnold.

HELLER, M. (1988) 'Strategic ambiguity: code-switching in the management of conflict' in HELLER, M. (ed.) *Codeswitching: anthropological and sociolinguistic perspectives*, Berlin, Mouton de Gruyter.

HELLER, M. (1990) 'The politics of codeswitching: processes and consequences of ethnic mobilization', workshop paper presented at 'Impact and Consequences: broader considerations', 22–4 November, Brussels, Network on Codeswitching and Language Contact.

HELLER, M. (1992) 'The politics of codeswitching and language choice', *Journal of Multilingual and Multicultural Development*, vol. 13, nos. 1 & 2, pp. 123–42.

HOGG, R. (1992) 'Introduction' in HOGG, R. (ed.) *Cambridge History of the English Language*, vol. 1, Cambridge, Cambridge University Press.

HOLMES, J. (1992) *An Introduction to Sociolinguistics*, London, Longman.

HORVATH, B. (1985) *Variation in Australian English*, Cambridge, Cambridge University Press.

HUGHES, A. and TRUDGILL, P. (1987) *English Accents and Dialects: an introduction to social and regional varieties of British English*, 2nd edn, London, Edward Arnold.

HUSPEK, M.R. (1986) 'Linguistic variation, context and meaning: a case of -ing/in ' variation in North American workers' speech', *Language in Society*, vol. 15, pp. 154–5.

IHALAINEN, O. (1991) 'Periphrastic *do* in affirmative sentences in the dialect of East Somerset' in TRUDGILL, P. and CHAMBERS, J.K. (eds) *Dialects of English: studies in grammatical variation*, London, Longman.

JIBRIL, M. (1991) 'The sociolinguistics of prepositional usage in Nigerian English' in CHESHIRE, J. (ed.) *English Around the World*, Cambridge, Cambridge University Press.

JOHNSON, S. (1755) *A Dictionary of the English Language*, London, W. Strachan for T.P. Knapton, T & T. Longman et al.

JONES, D. (1907) *Phonetic Transcriptions of English Prose*, Oxford, Clarendon.

JOYCE, P. (1991) *Visions of the People*, Cambridge, Cambridge University Press.

KACHRU, B.B. (1985) 'Standards, codification and sociolinguistic realism: the English language in the outer circle' in QUIRK, R. and WIDDOWSON, H.G. (eds) *English in the World: teaching and learning the language and literatures*, Cambridge, Cambridge University Press for the British Council.

KACHRU, B.B. (1986) *The Alchemy of English: the spread, models and functions of non-native Englishes*, Oxford, Pergamon.

KACHRU, B.B. (1991) 'Liberation linguistics and the Quirk concern', *English Today*, vol. 25, no. 7, 1 January, pp. 3–13.

KACHRU, B. B. (1992) *The Other Tongue: English across cultures*, 2nd edn, Urbana/Chicago, University of Illinois Press.

KALLEN, J. (1991) 'Sociolinguistic variation and methodology: *after* as in Dublin variable' in CHESHIRE, J. (ed.) *English Around the World*, Cambridge, Cambridge University Press.

KANYORO, M.R.A. (1991) 'The politics of the English language in Kenya and Tanzania' in CHESHIRE, J. (ed.) *English Around the World*, Cambridge, Cambridge University Press.

KASTOVSKY, D. (1992) 'Semantics and vocabulary' in HOGG, R. (ed.) *Cambridge History of the English Language*, vol. 1, Cambridge, Cambridge University Press.

KEMP, J.A. (1972) *John Wallis's Grammar of the English Language*, London, Longman.

KNOWLES, G. O. (1978) 'The nature of phonological variables in Scouse' in TRUDGILL, P. (ed.) *Sociolinguistic Patterns in British English*, London, Edward Arnold.

KUMAR, A. (1986) 'Certain aspects of the form and function of Hindi–English code-switching', *Anthropological Linguistics*, summer.

LABOV, W. (1968) 'The reflection of social processes in linguistic structures' in FISHMAN, A. (ed.) *Readings in the Sociology of Language*, The Hague, Mouton.

LABOV, W. (1972) *Sociolinguistic Patterns*, Oxford, Blackwell.

LABOV, W. (1978) 'On the use of the present to explain the past' in BALDI, P. and WERTH, R. (eds) *Readings in Historical Phonology*, Philadelphia, Pennsylvania State University Press.

LABOV, W. (1992) 'The three dialects of English' in ECKERT, P. and LABOV, W. (eds) *New Ways of Analyzing Sound Change*, New York, Academic Press.

LANHAM, L.A. and McDONALD, C.A. (1979) *The Standard in South African English and its Social History*, Heidelberg, Julius Gross.

LASS, R.G. (1987) *The Shape of English: structure and history*, London, Dent.

LASS, R.G. (1992) 'Phonology and morphology' in BLAKE, N. (ed.) *Cambridge History of the English Language*, vol. 2, Cambridge, Cambridge University Press.

Le PAGE, R.B. and TABOURET-KELLER, A. (1985) *Acts of Identity: creole-based approaches to language and ethnicity*, Cambridge, Cambridge University Press.

LETTE, K. (1993) *Foetal Attraction*, London, Picador.

LEVIN, B. (1993) 'All Joe McCarthy's children now', *The Times*, 31 May.

LIGON (1647) *A True and Exact History of the Island of Barbados*, London, Moseley.

LILY, W. ([1542] 1945) *A Shorte Introduction of Grammar*, intro. K.J. Flynn, Delman, N.Y., Scholars' Facsimiles & Reprints.

LOCHHEAD, L. (1989) *Mary Queen of Scots Got Her Head Chopped Off* and *Dracula*, Harmondsworth, Penguin.

LORIMER, W.L. (tr.) (1988) *The New Testament in Scots*, Harmondsworth, Penguin.

LOWTH, R. ([1762] 1968) *A Shorte Introduction to English Grammar: with critical notes*, Menston, Scholar Press; first published London, J. Hughes for A. Miller and R. & J. Dodsley.

MacDONALD, C. (1981) *Variation in the Use of Modal Verbs with Special Reference to Tyneside English*, University of Newcastle, unpublished PhD thesis.

MAYBIN, J. and MERCER, N. (eds) (1996) *Using English: from conversation to canon*, London, Routledge/The Open University.

MAZRUI, A. (1973) 'The English language and origins of African nationalism' in BAILEY, R.W. and ROBINSON J.L. (eds) *Varieties of Present-day English*, New York, Macmillan.

McARTHUR, T. (ed.) (1992) *Oxford Companion to the English Language*, Oxford, Oxford University Press.

McCLURE, J.D. (1988) *Why Scots Matters: the Scots language is a priceless national possession*, Edinburgh, Saltire Society.

McCRUM, R., CRAN, W. and MacNEIL, R. (1992) *The Story of English*, 2nd edn, London, Faber & Faber/BBC Books.

McINTOSH, A. (1969) 'The analysis of written Middle English' in LASS, R. (ed.) *Approaches to English Historical Linguistics*, New York, Holt, Rinehart & Winston.

McNEILL, M. (1971) *Vere Foster 1819–1900: an Irish benefactor*, Newton Abbot, David & Charles.

MEHROTRA, R.R. (1982) 'Indian English: a sociolinguistic profile' in PRIDE, J.B. (ed.) *New Englishes*, Rowley, Mass., Newbury House.

MERCER, N. and SWANN, J. (eds) (1996) *Learning English: development and diversity*, London, Routledge/The Open University.

MILLER, J. (1993) 'The grammar of Scottish English' in MILROY, J. and MILROY, L. (eds) *Real English: the grammar of English dialects in the British Isles*, London, Longman.

MILROY, J. (1992a) 'On the sociolinguistics and history of /h/ dropping in English' in MILROY, J. (ed.) *Linguistic Variation and Change*, Oxford, Blackwell.

MILROY, J. (1992b) 'The study of geographical variation in Middle English' in BLAKE, N. (ed.) *Cambridge History of the English Language*, vol. 2, Cambridge, Cambridge University Press.

MILROY, J. and MILROY, L. (1985) *Authority in Language: investigating language prescription and standardisation*, London, Routledge & Kegan Paul.

MILROY, J. and MILROY, L. (eds) (1993) *Real English: the grammar of English dialects in the British Isles*, London, Longman.

MILROY, L. (1987) *Language and Social Networks*, 2nd edn, Oxford, Blackwell.

MOLLOY, F. (1985) *No Mate for the Magpie*, London, Virago.

MÜHLHÄUSLER, P. and HARRÉ, R. (1990) *Pronouns and People: the linguistic construction of social and personal identity*, Oxford, Blackwell.

MYERS-SCOTTON, C. (1989) 'Codeswitching with English: types of switching, types of communities', *World Englishes*, vol. 8, no. 3, pp. 333–46.

MYERS-SCOTTON, C. (1993a) *Duelling Languages: grammatical structure in codeswitching*, Oxford, Clarendon.

MYERS-SCOTTON, C. (1993b) *Social Motivations for Codeswitching: evidence from Africa*, Oxford, Clarendon.

MYRES, J. (1986) *The English Settlements*, Oxford, Clarendon.

O'HEAR, A. (1991) *Education and Democracy: the posturing of the left establishment/against the educational establishment*, Claridge Blasts no. 2, London, Claridge.

OPEN UNIVERSITY (1981) E263 *Language in Use*, Block 7, *Language, Variation and Diversity*, Milton Keynes, The Open University.

OPEN UNIVERSITY (1989) E208 *Egalitarianism*, Unit 22, *Exploring Educational Issues*, Milton Keynes, The Open University.

OPEN UNIVERSITY (1993) *An Equal Opportunities Guide to Language and Image*, Milton Keynes, The Open University.

ORWELL, G. (1949) *Burmese Days*, Harmondsworth, Penguin in association with Martin Secker & Warburg.

PAGE, R.I. (1987) *Runes*, London, British Museum Publications.

PAKIR, A. (1991) 'The range and depth of English-knowing bilinguals in Singapore', *World Englishes*, vol. 10, no. 2, pp. 167–79.

PALMER, F. (1984) *Grammar,* 2nd edn, Harmondsworth, Penguin.

PANDHARIPANDE, P. (1990) 'Formal and functional constraints in code-mixing' in JACOBSON, R. (ed.) *Codeswitching as a Worldwide Phenomenon*, New York, Peter Lang.

PARKES, M.B. (1982) *The Scriptorium of Wearmouth-Jarrow,* The Jarrow Lecture 1982.

PITMAN, I. (undated) *The Manual of Phonography: an exposition of Sir Isaac Pitman's system of phonography or phonetic shorthand*, London, Pitman & Sons.

PLATT, J. (1991) 'Social and linguistic constraints on variation in the use of two grammatical variables in Singapore English', in CHESHIRE, J. (ed.), *English Around the World,* Cambridge, Cambridge University Press.

PLATT, J., WEBER, H. and HO, M.L. (1984) *The New Englishes,* London, Routledge & Kegan Paul.

POPLACK, S. (1980) 'Sometimes I'll start a sentence in Spanish y termino en espanol: toward a typology of code-switching', *Linguistics,* vol. 18, pp. 581–618.

POPLACK, S., SANKOFF, D. and MILLER, C. (1988) 'The social correlates and linguistic processes of lexical borrowing and assimilation', *Linguistics,* vol. 26, pp. 47–104.

PRESTON, D.R. (1993) 'Folk dialectology' in PRESTON, D.R. (ed.) *American Dialect Research,* Amsterdam, John Benjamins.

PROCTER, P. et al. (eds) (1982) *Longman New Universal Dictionary*, Harlow, Longman.

PROPP, V.I. (1958) *Morphology of the Folktale,* Austin, University of Texas Press.

PUTTENHAM, G. ([1589] 1936) *The Arte of English Poesie,* edited G.D. Willock and A. Walker, Cambridge, Cambridge University Press.

QUIRK, R. (1985) 'The English language in a global context' in QUIRK, R. and WIDDOWSON, H.G. (eds) *English in the World: teaching and learning the language and literatures,* Cambridge, Cambridge University Press for the British Council.

QUIRK, R. ([lecture originally given 1988] 1990) 'Language varieties and standard language', *English Today,* vol. 6, no. 1, January, pp. 3–10.

QUIRK, R. and GREENBAUM, S. (1973) *A University Grammar of English,* London, Longman.

QUIRK, R., GREENBAUM, S., LEECH, G. and SVARTVIK, J. (1972) *A Grammar of Contemporary English,* London, Longman.

QUIRK, R., GREENBAUM, S., LEECH, G. and SVARTVIK, J. (1985) *A Comprehensive Grammar of the English Language,* London, Longman.

RAMSON, W.E. (1988) (ed.) *Australian National Dictionary,* Melbourne, Oxford University Press.

ROBINS, R.H. (1989) *General Linguistics: an introductory survey,* 4th edn, London, Longman.

ROMAINE, S. (1992) 'Creole English' in McARTHUR, T. (ed.) *Oxford Companion to the English Language,* Oxford, Oxford University Press.

SAMUELS, M.L. (1969) 'Some applications of Middle English dialectology' in LASS, R. (ed.) *Approaches to English Historical Linguistics,* New York, Holt, Rinehart & Winston.

SCOTT, W. ([1815] 1986) *Ivanhoe,* Harmondsworth, Penguin.

SEBBA, M. (1993) *London Jamaican: language systems in interaction,* London, Longman.

SEY, K.A. (1973) *Ghanaian English: an exploratory study,* London, Macmillan.

SHAW, G.B. (1962) *Androcles and the Lion* (printed in Shaw's alphabet), Harmondsworth, Penguin.

SHAW, G.B. ([1910] 1972) *Pygmalion* in *The Bodley Head Bernard Shaw: collected plays with their prefaces,* vol. IV, London, Max Reinhardt/The ,Bodley Head.

SHERLEY-PRICE, L. (1968) *Bede, A History of the English Church and People,* Harmondsworth, Penguin.

SIEGEL, J. (1991) 'Variation in Fiji English' in CHESHIRE, J. (ed.) *English Around the World,* Cambridge, Cambridge University Press.

SIMPSON, D. (1986) *The Politics of American English 1776–1850,* Oxford, Oxford University Press.

SIMPSON, J.A. and WEINER, E.S.C. (eds) (1989) *Oxford English Dictionary,* 2nd edn, Oxford, Oxford University Press; 1st edn edited J.A.H. Murray, H. Bradley, W.A. Craigie and C.T. Onions.

STALLYBRASS, P. (1988) 'An inclosure of the best people in the world: nationalism and imperialism in late sixteenth century England' in SAMUEL, R. (ed.) *Patriotism: the making and unmaking of British national identities,* London, Routledge.

STALLYBRASS, P. and WHITE, A. (1986) *The Politics and Poetics of Transgression,* London, Methuen.

TODD, L. (1984) *Modern Englishes: pidgins and creoles,* Oxford/London, Blackwell in association with André Deutsch.

TRIPATHI, P.D. (1992) 'The chosen tongue', *English Today,* vol. 32, no. 8, 4 October, pp. 3–11.

TRUDGILL, P. (1974) *The Social Differentiation of English in Norwich,* Cambridge, Cambridge University Press.

TRUDGILL, P. (1983) 'Acts of conflicting identity: the sociolinguistics of British pop-song pronunciation' in TRUDGILL, P. (ed.) *On Dialect: social and geographical perspectives,* Oxford, Blackwell.

TRUDGILL, P. (1984) *Language in the British Isles,* Cambridge, Cambridge University Press.

TRUDGILL, P. (1986) *Dialects in Contact,* Oxford, Blackwell.

TRUDGILL, P. and CHAMBERS, J.K. (eds) (1991) *Dialects of English: studies in grammatical variation,* London, Longman.

TRUDGILL, P. and HANNAH, J. (1994) *International English,* 3rd edn, London, Edward Arnold.

VERMA, S.K. (1982) 'Swadeshi English: form and function' in PRIDE, J.B. (ed.) *New Englishes,* Rowley, Mass., Newbury House.

WALES, K. (1994) 'Royalese: the rise and fall of "the Queen's English"', *English Today,* vol. 10, no. 3, pp. 3–10.

WALKER, J. ([1791] 1968) *A Critical Pronouncing Dictionary and Expositer of the English Language,* Menston, Scholar Press; first published London, G.G. & J. Robinson, T. Cadell and W. Davies.

WALKERDINE, V. (1985) 'Dreams from an ordinary childhood' in HERON, L. (ed.) *Truth, Dare or Promise: girls growing up in the fifties,* London, Virago.

WALVIN, J. (1993) *Black Ivory: a history of British slavery,* London, Fontana.

WARDHAUGH, R. (1987) *Languages in Competition: dominance, diversity and decline*, Oxford, Blackwell in association with André Deutsch.

WEBSTER, N. ([1789] 1991) 'An essay on the necessity, advantages and practicability of reforming the mode of spelling, and of rendering the orthography of words correspondent to the pronunciation' in CROWLEY, T. (ed.) *Proper English: readings in language, history and cultural identity*, London, Routledge.

WEE KIAT (1992) *Women in Men's Houses*, Singapore, Landmark.

WEINER, E.S.C. (1983) *Oxford Guide to English Usage*, Oxford, Oxford University Press.

WELLS, J. (1982) *Accents of English*, vol. 1 *Introduction*, vol. 2 *The British Isles*, vol. 3 *Beyond the British Isles*, Cambridge, Cambridge University Press.

WHITELOCK, D. (1967) *Sweet's Anglo Saxon Reader*, rev. edn, Oxford, Oxford University Press.

WILKINS ([1668] 1968) *An Essay Towards a Real Character and a Philosophical Language*, Menston, Scholar Press; first published London, Royal Society.

WILLIAMS, G. (1985) *When was Wales?*, Harmondsworth, Penguin.

WINER, L. (1993) *Varieties of English around the World: Trinidad and Tobago*, Amsterdam, John Benjamins.

WOLFRAM, W. (1991) *Dialects and American English*, Englewood Cliffs, N.J., Prentice Hall.

WRIGHTSON, K. (1991) 'Estates, degrees and sorts: changing perceptions of class in Tudor and Stuart England' in CORFIELD, P.J. (ed.) *Language, History and Class*, Oxford, Blackwell.

HISTORICAL TIME-

	External Events	Political Context	Date (AD)	Linguistic Context		Texts
		410 Romans leave Britain	**400**		c.400	The runic inscription from Caistor-by-Norwich
449	Anglo-Saxon invasions		450	Start of Old English period		
			500			
			550			Gildas *Ruin and Conquest of Britain*
597	Augustine (Roman missionary) arrives in Kent		**600**			
625	Rise of Northumbria					
650	Rise of Mercia		650			
					688	*Laws of Wessex*
			700	First Old English texts appear	c.700	Ruthwell Cross
					c.700	Lindisfarne Gospels
					c.700	Franks Casket
735	Bede dies				731	Bede's *Ecclesiastical History* (in Latin)
			750			
					c.750	*Beowulf* composed
787	Viking invasions begin					

-LINE HISTORICAL

External Events	Political Context	Date (AD)	Linguistic Context	Texts
		800		
	849–899 King Alfred	850		
878 Alfred defeats Danes at Ethandun				*Anglo-Saxon Chronicles*
886 Danelaw established		**900**		c.890 Alfred's Preface to the *Pastoral Care*
		950		
	991 Danish king takes English throne – Aethelred exiled	**1000**		OE gloss added to Lindisfarne Gospels by Aldred
		1050		c.1040 *Marvels of the East*
	1066 Norman Conquest
1066 William I			
	1087 William II			1086 *Domesday Book*
	1100 Henry I	**1100**	1100 Notional start of Middle English period	
	1135 Stephen			
	1154 Henry II	1150		
	1171 Invasion of Ireland
1172 Henry II becomes king of Ireland			*The Owl and the Nightingale*
	1189 Richard I
1199 John			

HISTORICAL TIME-

External Events	Political Context	Date (AD)	Linguistic Context	Texts
		1200		Ancrene Wisse York Fragment
	1216 Henry III			1215 *Magna Carta*
		1250		
	1272 Edward I			
	1284 Wales annexed			
Establishing London as commercial capital		**1300**		
	1307 Edward II			
	1314 Robert the Bruce (of Scotland) defeats English at Bannockburn			*Polychronicon* (Latin)
	1327 Edward III			
1337 Start of Hundred Years War				
1348 Black Death (first outbreak)		**1350**		
	1377 Richard II			
	1399 Henry IV	**1400**		1385 Trevisa's *Polychronicon*
	1413 Henry V			
	1422 Henry VI			1421 Lydgate's *Siege of Thebes*
		1450	Growth of Chancery Standard	*Mappula Angliae* Document authorizing Sir John Talbot as chancellor of Ireland
1473 Copernicus born	1461 Edward IV			1473 Caxton prints first English book
	1483 Edward V			
	1483 Richard III			
	1485 Henry VII			1490 Caxton's *Eneydos*
1534 English Reformation (Henry VIII breaks with Roman Church)	1509 Henry VIII	**1500**	Notional start of Early Modern English	1526 Tyndale's English translation of Bible
Expansion of Oxford and Cambridge Universities	1536 First Act of Union between England and Wales			1542 Lily's Grammar
Transition from farm to pasture in England, weaving industry and wealth; poor laws force beggars and tramps to labour				1545 Ascham's *Toxophilus*
1562 Hawkins starts British slave trade	1547 Edward VI	**1550**		1549 Book of Common Prayer
1564 Shakespeare born	1553 Lady Jane Grey			1569 Hart's *Orthographie*
1567 Beginning of Puritanism	1553 Mary I			1586 Bullokar's Grammar
1577 Francis Drake sails round world	1558 Elizabeth I			1589 Puttenham's *Arte*
				1590 Spenser's *Faerie Queen*
1588 English settlement in Gambia				1591– Shakespeare's plays

-LINE HISTORICAL

External Events	Political Context	Date (AD)	Linguistic Context	Texts
1600 East India Company chartered	1603 James I (=James VI of Scotland)	**1600**		1611 Authorized Bible
1607 English settlement at Jamestown				1611– John Donne's metaphysical poetry
1609 12,000 English and Scots protestants settle in Ulster	1625 Charles I			1623 First folio of Shakespeare's complete works
1627 Colonization of Barbados				1647 Ligon's account of Barbados
1632 French Academy established	1649–1660 Commonwealth (= Republic)	**1650**		1651 Hobbe's *Leviathan*
1642–5 English Civil War	1660 Restoration of monarchy			1653 Wallis's Grammar
	1660 Charles II			1665 *Philosophical Transactions*
1660 Royal Society established				1668 Wilkins's *Essay towards a Real Character*
				1674 John Ray's *Collection of Words*
	1685 James II			1676 Fox's *Journal* (Quaker)
	1689 William III Mary II			1687 Newton's *Principia Mathematica*
		1700		
	1702 Anne			
	1707 Act of Union between England and Scotland (Great Britain)			1704 Netwon's *Opticks*
	1714 George I			1712 Swift's Proposal
	1727 George II			
				1741 Bickham's *Universal Penman*
		1750		
	1760 George III			1755 Johnson's Dictionary
				1762 Lowth's Grammar
1775–83 American War of Independence				
1788 Penal colonies established in Australia				1789 Webster's Essay
1789 French Revolution				1791 Walker's Dictionary
	1801 Act of Ireland unites Britain and Ireland (United Kingdom)	**1800**		1802 Wordworth's Ballads
1807 British slave trade ends				
	1820 William IV			
	1837 Victoria			
		1850		
				1858 Proposal for New English Dictionary (OED)
1870 Compulsory elementary schooling	1867 Canada given self-government			
1873 New Shakespeare Society				
1880s 'scramble' for African colonies Revival movements for Irish Gaelic				
	1901 Edward VII	**1900**		1898 *English Dialect Dictionary*
	1901 Australia given self-government			
	1910 George V			
	1921 Irish Free State (Irish Republic) established			1923 'In Praise o' Lancashire'
	1931 British Commonwealth created			
	1936 Edward VIII			
	1936 George VI	**1950**		
	1952 Elizabeth II			
				1988 *Australian National Dictionary*
		2000		

IPA consonant and vowel charts

The charts below provide examples of International Phonetic Alphabet (IPA) consonant and vowel symbols (only some of these are used in the book). They also indicate how the corresponding sounds are articulated.

IPA consonant symbols (not all possible symbols are shown)

Manner of articulation	Bilabial voiceless	Bilabial voiced	Labio-dental voiceless	Labio-dental voiced	Dental or interdental voiceless	Dental or interdental voiced	Alveolar voiceless	Alveolar voiced	Retroflex voiceless	Retroflex voiced	Palato-alveolar voiceless	Palato-alveolar voiced	Palatal voiceless	Palatal voiced	Velar voiceless	Velar voiced	Uvular voiceless	Uvular voiced	Labio-velar voiceless	Labio-velar voiced	Glottal voiceless	Glottal voiced
Nasal		m						n		ɳ				ɲ		ŋ						
Plosive	p	b			t̪	d̪	t	d	ʈ	ɖ			c	ɟ	k	g	q				ʔ	
Fricative	ɸ	β	f	v	θ	ð	s	z	ʂ	ʐ	ʃ	ʒ			x	ɣ	χ	ʁ			h	
Approximant				ʋ				ɹ						j					ʍ	w		
Lateral fricative							ɬ															
Lateral approximant								l														
Trill		ʙ						r										ʀ				
Tap or flap								ɾ		ɽ												

Place of articulation

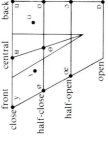

Rounded vowels

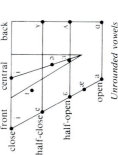

Unrounded vowels

IPA symbols for unrounded and rounded vowels

Consonants are described according to whether they are voiced (i.e. whether the vocal cords in the larynx vibrate during their articulation); their manner of articulation (e.g. 'fricatives' are produced when the stream of air from the lungs is forced through a narrow constriction; and 'plosives' when the air stream is blocked altogether and then released); and their place of articulation. The chart shows, for instance, that the sound [t] is an unvoiced alveolar plosive (it is produced without vocal fold vibration; and the tongue tip forms a closure against the alveolar ridge, temporarily blocking the flow of air); [d] is almost identical except that it is voiced.

Vowels are described according to whether the lips are rounded or unrounded; whether the highest point of the tongue is relatively close (i.e. high in the mouth) or open (i.e. low in the mouth); and whether the highest point of the tongue is towards the front or back of the mouth. Additional symbols allow other dimensions to be represented: for instance, the marker ː indicates a long vowel, which can be described as close, front and unrounded: it is the sound of the vowel in *bead* in many English accents.

ACKNOWLEDGEMENTS

Grateful acknowledgement is made to the following sources for permission to reproduce material in this book:

Text

Pages 29–32: Crystal, D., 1988, *The English Language* pp. 1–7, Penguin Books, 1988, copyright © David Crystal, 1988. Reproduced by permission of Penguin Books Ltd; *page 32:* Courtesy of Conseil Communal Prévention, Saint Herblain; *pages 37–40:* Quirk, R. 1990, 'Language varieties and standard language', *English Today 21*, vol. 16, no. 1, pp. 3–10, Cambridge University Press; *pages 81–91:* Abercrombie, D., 1981, 'Extending the Roman Alphabet' from Asher, R.E. and Henderson, E.J.A. (eds) *Towards a History of Phonetics*, Edinburgh University Press; *pages 133–5:* Crystal, D., 1990, *The English Language*, pp. 152–60, Penguin, London, Copyright © David Crystal, 1988, reproduced by permission of Penguin Books Ltd.; *pages 167–71:* Harris, R. and Taylor, T.J., 1989, *Landmarks in Linguistic Thought: From Socrates to Saussure*, Routledge; *page 197:* Carver, C.M., 1992, 'The Mayflower to the Model-T: The development of American English', in Machan, T.M. and Scott, C.T., 1992, *English in its Social Context*, Oxford University Press Inc.; *pages 213–16:* Ramson, W.S. (ed.) 1988, *The Australian National Dictionary*, Oxford University Press (Australia); *pages 216–19:* Bamgboṣe, A., 1982, 'Standard Nigerian English: Issues of identification' in Kachru, B.B., 1982, *The Other Tongue*, pp. 102–7, © 1982 by the Board of Trustees of the University of Illinois Press. Used with permission of the author and of the University of Illinois Press; *pages 219–21:* McArthur, T. (ed.) 1992, *The Oxford Companion to the English Language*, Oxford University Press, by permission of Oxford University Press; *page 230:* Eckersley, C.E., 1937, *An Everyday English Course for Foreign Students*, Longman Group Limited; *pages 252–3:* Beal, J., 1993, 'The grammar of Tyneside and Northumbrian English' in Milroy, J. and Milroy, L., 1993, *Real English: The Grammar of English Dialects in the British Isles*, Longman Group Limited; *pages 256–8:* Harris, J., 1993, 'The grammar of Irish English', in Milroy, J. and Milroy, L., 1993, *Real English: The Grammar of English Dialects in the British Isles*, Longman Group Limited; *page 261:* Simpson, J.A. and Weiner, E.S.C., 1989, *The Oxford English Dictionary*, Clarendon Press, by permission of Oxford University Press; *page 283:* Harrison, T., 1981, 'Them & [uz]', *Continuous 50 Sonnets from the School of Eloquence*, Rex Collings Limited; *pages 289–92:* Guy, G. and Vonwiller, J., 1989, 'The high rising tone in Australian English' in Collins, P. and Blair, D., 1989, *Australian English: The language of a new society*, University of Queensland Press; *page 315:* Sebba, M., 1993, *London Jamaican: Language Systems in Interaction*, Longman Group Limited; *pages 331–3:* Heller, M. (ed.) 1988, *Codeswitching: Anthropological and sociological perspectives*, Mouton de Gruyter. A Division of Walter de Gruyter & Co.; *pages 334–7:* Myers-Scotton, C., 1989, 'Codeswitching with English: types of switching, types of communities', *World Englishes*, vol. 8, no. 3, pp. 333–46, Basil Blackwell Ltd; *page 338:* Hugill, B. and O'Connor, M., 1994, 'Standards in this year's GCSE …', *Observer*, 24 July 1994; *page 340 (right):* Gordon, E. and Deverson, T., 1989, 'Kuds are Kids', *Finding a New Zealand Voice*, p. 35, New House Publishers Limited; *page 341 (top left):* Long, S., 'Turn-off or turn-on', *The Straits Times*, 22 August 1992, Singapore Press Holdings; *page 341 (top right):* Devan, J., 1994, 'Why must Kallang be Care-lang?', *The Straits Times*, 21 October 1994, © Janadas Devan; *page 341 (bottom):* Kochar, J., 1994, 'In your article …', *India Today*, 30 September 1994, © Jayant Kochar, President, Lacoste Sports and Leisure Apparel Limited; *page 344:* Griffiths, J.P., 1993, 'Alternative spellings', Feature section, *The Times*, 24 August 1993, © J.P. Griffiths; *pages 344–5:* © Sue Engineer, Association Lexicographer, Longman ELT, 19 May 1995; *page 350:* Hillier, H., 1995, 'I am disheartened …', *Guardian*, 22 April 1995, © Dr Hilary Hillier; *page 365 (1):* Frean, A., 1993, 'The BBC is to publish …', *The Times*, 5 July 1993, © Times Newspapers Limited 1993; *page 365 (2):* Longden, Sir G., 1993, 'Simon Jenkin's article …', *The Times*, October 1993, © Sir Gilbert Longden; *page 365 (3):* Hymas, C., 1993, 'A-Level students get a lot of stick', *The Times*, 26 December 1993, © Times Newspapers Limited 1993; *page 365 (4):* 'Resolving problems', *The Times*, 1 January 1994, © Times Newspapers Limited, 1994; *pages 365–6 (5):* 'Employers blame teachers for poor spelling', *The Times*, 16 February 1994, © Times Newspapers Limited, 1994; *page 366 (6):*

Hymas, C., 1994, 'Oxford students fail basic grammar test', *The Sunday Times*, 20 February 1994, © Times Newspapers Limited, 1994; *page 366 (8)*: 'Putting them in their place: The highwayman', *The Times*, 19 March 1994, © Times Newspapers Limited, 1994; *pages 366–7 (9)*: Elkin, S., 1994, 'It's never too early to learn how to spell', *The Times*, 18 April 1994, © Times Newspapers Limited, 1994; *page 367 (10)*: Doyle, G., 'Teachers brought to book', *The Sunday Times Newspaper*, 19 June 1994, © Times Newspapers Limited, 1994; *pages 368–70*: Grove, V., 1993, 'Dipsticks and the joys of a double negative', *The Times*, 17 November 1993, © Times Newspapers Limited 1993; *pages 370–71*: Aitchison, J., 1994, 'Why do purists grumble so much?', *Evening Standard Newspaper*, 27 April 1994, Solo Syndication Limited.

Figures

Figure 1.1: Brown, 1993, *The Oxford English Dictionary (Shorter)*, © Oxford University Press 1973, 1993, by permission of Oxford University Press; *Figure 1.2:* Myers-Scotton, C., 1993, 'Major languages of Kenya', *Social Motivations for Codeswitching*, Clarendon Press by permission of Oxford University Press; *Figure 2.4:* First page of Bede's *Ecclesiastical History of the English People* Cotton ms Tiberius CII folio 5v, by permission of the British Library; *Figure 2.5:* Franks Casket © British Museum; *Figure 2.10:* The opening of St John in the Lindisfarne Gospels Cotton ms Nero DIV folio 211, by permission of the British Library; *Figure 2.11:* ms fr 9198, folio 19 *Scribe at work in the scriptorium* © Cliché Bibliothèque Nationale de France, Paris; *Figure 2.12:* The Lindisfarne Gospels folio 5v, showing the initial 'P' of the word 'Plures' Cotton ms Nero DIV folio 5v, by permission of the British Library; *Figure 2.14:* Bede's Commentary on the Book of Proverbs ms Bodl. 819, folio 16v, the Bodleian Library, University of Oxford; *Figures 2.16 and 2.17:* The Marvels of the East Cotton ms Tiberius BV (part I) folio 81, by permission of the British Library; *Figure 2.18:* Alfred's Preface to his Old English translation of Pope Gregory the Great's *Pastoral Care* ms Hatton 20, folio 2v, the Bodleian Library, University of Oxford; *Figure 2.19:* A page from the epic Old English poem *Beowulf* Cotton ms Vitellius AXV (part II) folio 133, by permission of the British Library; *Figure 2.20:* Domesday Book, Dorset: The Public Record Office, London; *Figure 2.21:* Goudy, F.W., 1942, 'Gothic Minuscule' from Chapter VII 'The development of Gothic', *The Alphabet and Elements of Lettering*, Dover Publications Inc.; *Figure 2.22:* Part of a specimen sheet of an Oxford scribe c. 1340 ms e Mus. 198*, folio 8r, the Bodleian Library, University of Oxford; *Figure 2.23:* Siege of Thebes Royal 18 DII folio 148, by permission of the British Library; *Figure 2.24 (top):* L. a. 241, Letter of Richard Broughton by permission of The Folger Shakespeare Library; *Figure 2.24 (bottom):* L. a. 597, Letter of Lady Lettice Kynnersley, by permission of The Folger Shakespeare Library; *Figure 2.25:* Hofer, P., 1941, *The Universal Penman* engraved by George Bickham, 1743, Dover Publications Inc.; *Figure 2.26:* Earle, A.M., 1899, *Child Life in Colonial Days*, The Macmillan Company 1957, Macmillan Publishing Company Inc.; *Figure 2.32:* Shaw, B., 1962, *Androcles and the Lion*, (Shaw Alphabet edition) 1962, Penguin Books, by permission of the Society of Authors on behalf of the Bernard Shaw Estate; *Figure 4.1:* *The History of Troy*, Le Fevre, Raduz folio 16r, John Rylands University Library of Manchester; *Figure 4.5:* STC 15614, An Introdvction of the Eyght Partes of Latine Speache, folio A5r, by permission of The Folger Shakespeare Library; *Figure 4.7:* An eighteenth-century coffee-house, Mary Evans Picture Library; *Figures 4.9 and 4.10:* Simpson, J.A. and Weiner, E.S.C., 1989, *The Oxford English Dictionary*, Oxford University Press, by permission of Oxford University Press; *Figure 1 (page 173):* Newton, I. (3rd edition, 1726), *Philosophiae Naturalis Principia Mathematica* 8703F8 T. P. 9071036, by permission of the British Library; *Figure 3 (page 175):* Hooke, R., 1665, *Micrographia: Or some physiological descriptions of minute bodies made by magnifying glasses with observations and inquiries thereupon* 435e19 T. P. 8972506, by permission of the British Library; *Figure 4 (page 175):* *Philosophical Transactions* vol. 1 no. 1, reproduced by permission of the Syndics of Cambridge University Library; *Figure 5.7:* Bokamba, E.G., 1991, 'West Africa' in Cheshire, J., 1991, *English around the World: sociolinguistic perspectives*, p. 494, Cambridge University Press; *Figure 7.4:* Wells, J.C., 1986, *Accents of English I: An introduction*, Cambridge University Press; *Figure 7.5:* Wolfram, W., 1991, *Dialects and American English*, p. 77, Prentice Hall; *Figure 7.6:* Coates, J., 1986, *Women, Men and Language: A sociolinguistic account of sex differences in* *language*, p. 59, Longman Group Limited; *Figure 7.8*: Preston, D.R., 1993, *American Dialect Research*, John Benjamins B.V. Publishing Company; *Figure 8.1*: Trudgill, P., 1986, Dialects in Contact, p. 8, Basil Blackwell Ltd; *Figure 8.3*: Poplack, S., 1980, 'Sometimes I'll start a sentence in Spanish, Y termino en Español: towards a typology of code-switching', *Linguistics 18*, p. 586, Mouton de Gruyter. A Division of Walter de Gruyter & Co; *Figure 9.1*: Cox, B., 1991, *Cox on Cox: An English Curriculum for the 1990s*, Hodder & Stoughton, by permission of Hodder Headline PLC; *Figure 9.2*: Photographs by permission of Donald Mackinnon.

Tables

Table 6.1: Cheshire, J. and Milroy, J., 1993, 'Syntactic variation in non-standard dialects: background issues' in Milroy, J. and Milroy, L. (eds) 1993 *Real English: the grammar of English dialects in the British Isles*, Longman Group UK Limited; *Table 6.2*: Beal, J., 1993, based on McDonald, 1981, and Harris, 1993, in Milroy, J. and Milroy, L., 1993, *Real English: the Grammar of English Dialects in the British Isles*, Longman Group Limited; *Table 6.3*: Hughes, A. and Trudgill, P., 1987, *English Accents and Dialects: an introduction to social and regional varieties of British English*, Edward Arnold, © 1979 and 1987 Arthur Hughes and Peter Trudgill, by permission of Hodder Headline PLC; *Table 6.5*: Beal, J., 1993, in Milroy, J. and Milroy, L., 1993, *Real English: the Grammar of English Dialects in the British Isles*, Longman Group Limited; *Tables 7.1 and 7.2*: Graddol, D., Cheshire, J. and Swann. J., 1994, *Describing Language* Second edition, Open University Press; *Table 7.4*: Gimson, A.C., 1970, *An Introduction to the Pronunciation of English*, Edward Arnold, by permission of Hodder Headline PLC; *Table 8.1*: Edwards, V., 1986, *Language in a Black Community*, Multilingual Matters Ltd.

Other illustrations

Page 9: Dobson, S., 1969, *Larn Yersel Geordie*, Butler Publishing, © Rosalind Scott Dobson; *page 13*: Reproduced by kind permission of Punch; *page 16*: Photograph by permission of Magnus John; *page 20*: Aislin © 1977. Reproduced by permission of Terry Mosher (Aislin), *The Gazette*, Montreal; *page 36*: by kind permission of PLANTU; *page 104*: Photograph by permission of Dick Leith; *page 225*: 'Grab a Grin', by Mahase Calpu, reproduced by permission of Trinidad Express Newspapers Limited; *page 302*: Bryan McAllister.

INDEX